750 Best
Appetizers

750 Best Appetizers

From dips & salsas to spreads & shooters

Judith Finlayson & Jordan Wagman

Robert
ROSE

750 Best Appetizers
Text copyright © 2011 Judith Finlayson and Jordan Wagman
Photographs copyright © 2011 Robert Rose Inc.
Cover and text design copyright © 2011 Robert Rose Inc.

Some of the recipes in this book have appeared in other cookbooks.

For complete cataloguing information, see page 556.

Disclaimer
The recipes in this book have been carefully tested by our kitchen and our tasters. To the best of
our knowledge, they are safe and nutritious for ordinary use and users. For those people with food
or other allergies, or who have special food requirements or health issues, please read the suggested
contents of each recipe carefully and determine whether or not they may create a problem for you.
All recipes are used at the risk of the consumer.

We cannot be responsible for any hazards, loss or damage that may occur as a result of any
recipe use.

For those with special needs, allergies, requirements or health problems, in the event of any
doubt, please contact your medical adviser prior to the use of any recipe.

Design and Production: Kevin Cockburn/PageWave Graphics Inc.
Editor: Carol Sherman
Recipe Editor: Jennifer MacKenzie
Copy Editor: Karen Campbell-Sheviak
Indexer: Gillian Watts
Photography: Colin Erricson
Associate Photographer: Matt Johannsson
Food Styling: Kathryn Robertson
Prop Styling: Charlene Erricson

Cover image: Mini Smoked Salmon and Sour Cream Puff Pastry Tartlets (page 166) and
Mini Potato Galette with Caviar and Crème Fraîche (page 176)

We acknowledge the financial support of the Government of Canada through the Book Publishing
Industry Development Program (BPIDP) for our publishing activities.

Published by Robert Rose Inc.
120 Eglinton Avenue East, Suite 800, Toronto, Ontario, Canada M4P 1E2
Tel: (416) 322-6552 Fax: (416) 322-6936
www.robertrose.ca

Printed and bound in Canada

1 2 3 4 5 6 7 8 9 TCP 19 18 17 16 15 14 13 12 11

Contents

Introduction. 6

Dips and Spreads 7

Salsas. 69

Shooters. 97

Wraps and Rolls 127

Savory Tarts, Dumplings and Crêpes 159

Crackers, Crostini, Toasts and Pizza 205

Panini, Sandwiches and Tartines. 255

Fish and Seafood 277

Sticks and Picks 323

Knives and Forks 357

Cheese Please 371

Mostly Veggies and Bar Noshes 399

Poultry and Meat 459

Slow Cooker 483

Desserts. 509

Basics and Condiments 535

Acknowledgments 556

Index. 557

Introduction

Appetizers. What a word! The concept of small bites or plates of food that stimulate the palate evokes a myriad of images from mundane to magnificent. What would the 1950s be without a bag of potato chips and dip (usually dehydrated onion soup mixed with sour cream) or the 1980s without fresh tomato bruschetta? By the time the new millennium arrived, small bites were moving into the realm of fine dining. Few places capture this trend more vividly than the legendary Chicago restaurant Alinea. Patrons dine on a tasting menu (as many as 27 courses) consisting of a series of intricate nibbles created by über-chef Grant Achatz.

Today's tasting menus are a clear sign that appetizers have traveled well beyond the party circuit. In many ways, a series of tidbits that whet your taste buds also defines the way we eat now. No longer just a course served prior to dinner, or cocktail party fare, appetizers are often the meal itself. More and more, as they do at Alinea, people are sitting down to dine on a series of small plates.

It's a peripatetic approach to eating, captured in the concept of "grazing." But, in actual fact, it's been with us for quite some time. Greek mezes, Italian antipasti, Chinese dim sum, Spanish tapas and Scandinavian smorgasbord to name just a few, are all variations on the theme. Perhaps because finger foods pair well with cocktails, beer or a glass of wine, and inviting someone over for a drink invariably includes a little something to eat, small bites have always been linked with the idea of hospitality. When people get together to enjoy one another's company, food and drink are usually part of the package.

Refreshing libations and flavorsome nibblies stimulate conversation and encourage conviviality. They are the web and woof of hospitality, which is the heartbeat of this book. There are more than 750 recipes to choose from because we've tried to make sure you have a selection to suit every possible occasion — from a dress-down backyard barbecue to the most elegant sit-down dinner. We've also considered the need to satisfy a variety of dietary preferences, from strictest vegans to wide-ranging omnivores. And since we know you're probably doing lots of things at once, many recipes can be prepared ahead of time, or if you're so inclined, made in your slow cooker, while you're busy with something else.

Because we do it so often ourselves, we understand that you're likely to have invited people over before you know what you want to serve. That's why we've structured the book to cover a broad range of options. There are 16 chapters built around specific types of dishes (for instance, Dips and Spreads or Salsas) or specific ingredients (such as Fish and Seafood or Cheese Please.) Some recipes are categorized by presentation — for instance, Wraps and Rolls or Sticks and Picks. We've tried to make it easy for you to transform the glimmer of an idea you had for a party into an exciting reality that will be fondly remembered in times to come.

To suit contemporary lifestyles, most recipes fit the bill for easy entertaining — gathering round the kitchen island, sampling a potpourri of textures and flavors. Some are extremely easy to make. Recipes such as Buttered Radishes (page 404), or Salumi (page 131) rely on top quality produce or excellent prepared foods to produce a virtually instantaneous solution to your entertaining needs. Others, such as Eggplant and Date Salsa (page 75) or Mojo de Cilantro (page 11) take a bit more time to prepare, but provide a unique taste experience. Some, such as Oyster and Artichoke Gratin (page 315) or Sweet Pea and Potato Croquettes (page 410), even include a wow factor for those times when you really want to impress.

With so many recipes to choose from, we've provided you with the basis to get any gathering off to a lively start. No matter how easy they are to prepare, a tray of appetizers always seems celebratory and there is nothing like home-cooked food to make people feel welcomed. Use this book to create hors d'oeuvres that will delight your family and friends — then relax and enjoy the party yourself.

— Judith Finlayson & Jordan Wagman

Dips and Spreads

Dips are the most sociable of recipes. They are a great catalyst for getting a party off to a good start because they encourage guests to congregate around, scooping and munching. Like the ultimate party girl, they promote mixing and mingling.

Dips (and their kissing cousins, slightly thicker spreads) play key roles in many cultures and some have traveled internationally. Middle Eastern hummus, Greek tzatziki, Mexican guacamole and French tapenade, to name just a few — are now regularly enjoyed in many different parts of the world.

Most dips are easy to make and can be prepared ahead of time. They are happily coupled with store-bought dippers but if you feel like bumping things up a notch, they are very amenable to more elaborate pairings (see page 31 for suggestions on crudités, page 35 for ideas about bread and page 42 for more thoughts on dippers). Dips cater to a wide variety of tastes and can satisfy many different dietary preferences, from the strictest vegans to wide-ranging omnivores.

Creamy Watercress Dip 9
Green Goddess Dipping Sauce 9
Spinach Tofu Dip 10
Springtime Dill Dip 10
Mojo de Cilantro 11
Cilantro Lime Dip 11
Cucumber Cottage Cheese Dip 12
Lemon Garlic Dip 12
Dill Cucumber Dip 13
Feta Cucumber Dip 13
Tzatziki 14
Roasted Red Pepper Tzatziki 14
Canary Island Red Pepper Mojo 15
Feta and Roasted Red Pepper Dip 15
Easy Roasted Red Pepper Dip 16
Feta and Yogurt Dip 16
Smoky Eggplant Dip with Yogurt 17
Baba Ghanouj 18
Eggplant Caviar 19
Greek-Style Eggplant Dip 19
Black Pepper Goat Cheese Dip 20
Roasted Carrot and Yogurt Dip 20
Beet and Goat Cheese Spread 21
Tahini-Spiked Beet Spread 21
Roasted Tomato and Pumpkin Seed Dip 22
Roasted Tomato Dip 23
Easy Tahini Dip 23
Muhammara 24
Roasted Pepper and Sweet Potato Dip 25
Sweet Potato Spread 26
Guacamole 26
Avocado-Salsa Dip 27

Avocado Cream Cheese Dip 27
Avocado Ancho Chile Dip 28
Cheesy Avocado Dip 28
Anchovy-Spiked Avocado Dip 29
Warm Anchovy Dip 29
Salmorejo 30
Mofongo 31
Pepper-Spiked Plantain Dip 32
Roasted Fennel Dip 33
Creamy Roquefort Dip 33
Egg and Olive Spread 34
Classic Spinach and Water Chestnut Dip 35
Cheesy Spinach Dip 36
Warm Spinach Dip 37
Roasted Potato Dip 37
Greek-Style Garlic-Spiked Potato Dip 38
Blue Cheese Dip 38
Caramelized Red Onion Dip 39
Smoky Baked Onion Dip 40
Roasted Onion Dip 41
Creamy Green Onion Dip 41
Grilled Scallion and Corn Dip 42
Peppery Peanut Dip 43
Thai Peanut Dip 43
Mushroom Tomato Spread 44
Roasted Zucchini Dip 44
Artichoke and Olive Tapenade 45
Green Olive Tapenade 45
Parsley-Laced Tapenade 46
Tuna Tapenade 46
Anchoyade de Croze 47
Lemon-Laced Butterbean Dip 48

continued on next page

Feta-Spiked Edamame Dip. 49
Zucchini Hummus 49
Basil and White Bean Spread 50
Refried Nachos. 50
Hummus from Scratch 51
Easy Hummus 52
Smoked Oyster Hummus 52
Cauliflower and Lentil Hummus
   Spiked with Cumin 53
Down-Home Hummus 54
Roasted Red Pepper Hummus. 55
Oil-Poached Garlic Hummus 56
Walnut Hummus. 57
Black Bean Spread. 57
Hot and Smoky Bean Dip. 58
Chive and Navy Bean Dip. 58
BTs on Lettuce 59

Greek Salad Dip 59
Taramasalata 60
Honey Mustard Dip. 60
Pommery Mustard Dip 61
Roasted Garlic Sour Cream Dip 61
Smoked Salmon Sour Cream Spread. 62
Tuna and Roasted Red Pepper Dip 62
Tuna and Artichoke Scoop 63
Tonnato 64
Dill-Spiked Crab Scoop 65
Ham and Roasted Pepper Spread with
   Hearts of Palm 66
Blueberry and Yogurt Dip 67
Fig Yogurt Dip. 67
Champagne and Raspberry Dip 68
Mango Dip 68

Creamy Watercress Dip

Makes about 1 cup (250 mL)

Make this garden-fresh dip when watercress is in season. Serve with crudités such as cucumber slices, carrot or celery sticks or hearts of romaine.

Tip

Because this dip contains watercress, which will become soggy, we don't recommend storing it for longer than overnight.

6 cups	packed watercress (leaves and tender stems, tough stems discarded)	1.5 L
6	green onions, white with a bit of green, cut into 2-inch (5 cm) lengths	6
4 oz	cream cheese, softened	125 g
2 tbsp	mayonnaise	30 mL
	Salt and freshly ground black pepper	

1. In a food processor fitted with metal blade, pulse watercress and green onions until coarsely chopped. Add cream cheese and mayonnaise and process until smooth, about 30 seconds. Season to taste with salt and pepper and pulse to blend.
2. Transfer to a serving bowl. Cover and refrigerate for at least 1 hour to allow flavors to meld or overnight.

Green Goddess Dipping Sauce

Makes about 1½ cups (375 mL)

This is the perfect summer dip because it makes a fabulous partner for a wide variety of garden vegetables. Crisp hearts of romaine lettuce, small wedges of radicchio, sliced cucumber, radishes or cherry tomatoes all benefit from a brush with this tasty blend. If you're looking for something more substantial, consider cold cooked shrimp or crab claws.

½ cup	mayonnaise	125 mL
½ cup	plain Greek-style (pressed) yogurt (see Tips, page 17)	125 mL
½ cup	Italian flat-leaf parsley leaves	125 mL
¼ cup	snipped chives	60 mL
¼ cup	fresh tarragon leaves	60 mL
4	anchovy fillets	4
2 tbsp	freshly squeezed lemon juice	30 mL
1 tbsp	white wine or Champagne vinegar	15 mL
½ tsp	salt or to taste	2 mL
	Freshly ground black pepper	

1. In a food processor fitted with metal blade, process mayonnaise, yogurt, parsley, chives, tarragon, anchovies, lemon juice, vinegar, salt, and pepper to taste until smooth. Taste and adjust seasoning. (You may want a bit more lemon juice and/or salt.)
2. Transfer to a serving bowl. Cover and refrigerate for at least 1 hour to allow flavors to meld or overnight.

Spinach Tofu Dip

Makes about 2 cups (500 mL)

Light and healthful, all this tasty dip needs is a crisp rice cracker to complete the experience.

Tip

Because this dip contains a significant quantity of spinach, which is likely to become soggy, we don't recommend storing it for longer than overnight.

8 oz	soft or medium tofu, cubed	250 g
6	green onions, white with a bit of green, cut into chunks	6
2	cloves garlic, quartered	2
¼ cup	mayonnaise	60 mL
¼ cup	sour cream	60 mL
1 tbsp	freshly squeezed lemon juice	15 mL
2 tsp	Dijon mustard	10 mL
1 tsp	salt	5 mL
8 cups	loosely packed baby spinach	2 L
	Freshly ground black pepper	

1. In a food processor fitted with metal blade, process tofu, green onions, garlic, mayonnaise, sour cream, lemon juice, Dijon mustard and salt until smooth. Add spinach and pulse until very finely chopped and blended, about 10 times. Season to taste with pepper.

2. Transfer to a serving bowl. Cover and refrigerate for at least 1 hour to allow flavors to meld or overnight.

Springtime Dill Dip

Makes about 1 cup (250 mL)

Don't underestimate this dip because it is so easy to make. It is quite delicious accompanied by simple crudités such as cucumber slices, celery sticks, or blanched asparagus. It you want to bump things up a notch, serve it with Salt-Roasted Potatoes (page 405), an absolutely divine pairing.

½ cup	mayonnaise	125 mL
½ cup	plain Greek-style (pressed) yogurt (see Tips, page 17)	125 mL
½ cup	packed fresh dill fronds	125 mL
4	green onions, white part with a bit of green, cut into 2-inch (5 cm) pieces	4
½ tsp	salt	2 mL
	Freshly ground black pepper	

1. In a food processor fitted with metal blade or mini bowl attachment, process mayonnaise, yogurt, dill, green onions, salt, and pepper to taste until smooth and blended, about 1 minute.

2. Transfer to a serving bowl and serve or cover and refrigerate overnight.

Mojo de Cilantro

Makes about ½ cup (125 mL)

If you've been traveling in the Canary Islands and have enjoyed a cilantro sauce that seems to be ubiquitous there, here's a version you can make at home. It makes a delicious dip for Salt-Roasted Potatoes (page 405), boiled or grilled shrimp, Bruschetta (page 231) or even plain potato chips.

2 cups	packed fresh cilantro leaves	500 mL
1 tbsp	white wine vinegar	15 mL
2	cloves garlic, quartered	2
1	long red or green chile pepper, quartered	1
1 tsp	ground cumin (see Tips, page 25)	5 mL
⅓ cup	extra virgin olive oil	75 mL
	Salt and freshly ground black pepper	

1. In a food processor fitted with metal blade or mini bowl attachment, pulse cilantro, vinegar, garlic, chile pepper and cumin until finely chopped, stopping and scraping down sides of bowl as necessary. With motor running, slowly add oil through feed tube and process just until blended. Season to taste with salt and pepper.

2. Transfer to a small serving bowl and set aside for 30 minutes to allow flavors to meld. Serve at room temperature.

Cilantro Lime Dip

Makes about 1¼ cups (300 mL)

Use this dip to complete a southwestern-themed party. Serve with tortilla chips for dipping or use it as a topping for a Classic Cheese Quesadilla (page 152).

Tip

We prefer to use full-fat or whole milk yogurt in this recipe because it has a deeper flavor profile but if you prefer, use a lower-fat alternative.

½ cup	coarsely chopped fresh cilantro leaves	125 mL
½ cup	plain yogurt (see Tip, left)	125 mL
¼ cup	freshly squeezed lime juice	60 mL
2 tbsp	cream cheese, softened	30 mL
¼ tsp	ground cumin (see Tips, page 25)	1 mL
⅛ tsp	salt	0.5 mL

1. In a bowl, combine cilantro, yogurt, lime juice, cream cheese, cumin and salt until smooth. Serve immediately or cover and refrigerate for up to 3 days.

Cucumber Cottage Cheese Dip

Makes about 1¼ cups (300 mL)

This refreshing dip is light and tasty. It's ideal for guests who are trying to gain control of their waistlines, but others will enjoy it, too. Serve with crudités or crackers.

Tip

Using pressed dry cottage cheese produces a dip that is substantial enough to adhere to veggie dippers.

½ cup	unsalted dry pressed cottage cheese (about 8 oz/250 g) (see Tip, left)	125 mL
1 tbsp	mayonnaise	15 mL
½	English cucumber, peeled, seeded and cut into chunks	½
4	green onions, white part with a bit of green, cut into chunks	4
2 tbsp	fresh dill fronds, optional	30 mL
	Salt and freshly ground black pepper	

1. In a food processor fitted with metal blade, process cottage cheese and mayonnaise until smooth and light. Add cucumber, green onions and dill, if using, and pulse until chopped and blended. Season to taste with salt and pepper.
2. Transfer to a serving bowl or cover and refrigerate for up to 3 days.

Lemon Garlic Dip

Makes about 1½ cups (375 mL)

An all-purpose dip for use on sandwiches or just to add a lemon note to fresh vegetables.

Tip

Convenience products are available everywhere and we encourage their use on one condition — no preservatives. Don't shy away from great-quality frozen products such as puréed garlic.

¾ cup	sour cream	175 mL
⅓ cup	dry pressed cottage cheese (see Tip, above)	75 mL
¼ cup	freshly squeezed lemon juice	60 mL
1 tbsp	minced garlic (see Tip, left)	15 mL
1 tbsp	thinly sliced green onions	15 mL

1. In a bowl, combine sour cream, cottage cheese, lemon juice, garlic and green onions until smooth. Serve immediately or cover and refrigerate for up to 3 days.

Dill Cucumber Dip

Makes about 1½ cups (375 mL)

This is fantastic as a dip with pita bread or fresh cut cucumbers. It's also the ultimate garnish to Homemade Spiced Gravlax (page 288).

Tip

When serving cold dips, particularly those that contain a high proportion of dairy, consider lining a deep platter with crushed ice and use it to surround the bowl. Arranging crudités over the ice will help to keep them nicely chilled as well.

1¼ cups	sour cream (see Tip, below)	300 mL
½ cup	grated English cucumber	125 mL
¼ cup	coarsely chopped fresh dill fronds	60 mL
1 tsp	grated lemon zest	5 mL
1 tsp	white balsamic or apple cider vinegar	5 mL
½ tsp	salt	2 mL
⅛ tsp	freshly ground black pepper	0.5 mL

1. In a bowl, combine sour cream, cucumber, dill, lemon zest, vinegar, salt and pepper. Cover with a tight-fitting lid and refrigerate for 1 day before serving or for up to 3 days. Stir well before serving.

Variation

If you like mint, feel free to replace the dill with mint in this recipe.

Feta Cucumber Dip

Makes about 1½ cups (375 mL)

A refreshing creamy dip that is wonderful with warm breads, Crisp Pita Bread or any of its seasoned variations (page 216).

Tip

We prefer to use full-fat or whole milk yogurt in this recipe because it has a deeper flavor profile but if you prefer, use a lower-fat alternative. The same holds true for sour cream.

¾ cup	plain yogurt (see Tip, left)	175 mL
½ cup	crumbled feta cheese	125 mL
½ cup	grated English cucumber	125 mL
1 tsp	finely chopped fresh thyme leaves	5 mL

1. In a bowl, combine yogurt, feta, cucumber and thyme until smooth. Serve immediately or cover and refrigerate for up to 3 days.

Variation

Combine ¼ cup (60 mL) Feta Cucumber Dip with 2 tbsp (30 mL) red wine vinegar and ½ cup (125 mL) each chopped cucumbers, large chopped tomatoes and kalamata olives for a lovely quick Greek Salad.

Tzatziki

Makes about 2½ cups (625 mL)

This classic Greek condiment is a great dip with warm pita, Crisp Pita Bread (page 216) or crudités. It also makes a great dipping sauce for Chicken Souvlaki (see Variation, page 341).

Tip

Be sure to seed your cucumber. Otherwise your tzatziki is likely to be watery.

2 cups	plain Greek-style (pressed) yogurt (see Tips, page 17)	500 mL
1	cucumber, peeled, seeded and cut into chunks (see Tip, left)	1
½ cup	loosely packed Italian flat-leaf parsley leaves or fresh dill fronds	125 mL
2	cloves garlic, coarsely chopped	2
2 tbsp	extra virgin olive oil	30 mL
2 tbsp	freshly squeezed lemon juice	30 mL
1 tsp	salt	5 mL

1. In a food processor fitted with metal blade, process yogurt, cucumber, parsley, garlic, olive oil, lemon juice and salt until smooth.
2. Transfer to a serving bowl. Cover and refrigerate until chilled or for up to 3 days.

Roasted Red Pepper Tzatziki

Makes about 2 cups (500 mL)

If you enjoy the fresh flavor of tzatziki but are looking for something a little different, try this. It makes a great dip for crudités and pita. For something more substantial, serve with a platter of boiled or grilled shrimp and provide wooden skewers for dipping. It also makes a great accompaniment to Chicken Kabobs (page 341).

2	red bell peppers, roasted and quartered (see Tips, page 24) or store-bought	2
1	field cucumber, seeded and cut into chunks, or ½ English cucumber, cut into chunks	1
6	green onions, white part with a bit of green, cut into chunks	6
½ cup	plain Greek-style (pressed) yogurt (see Tips, page 17)	125 mL
2	cloves garlic, coarsely chopped	2
½ tsp	ground cumin	2 mL
	Salt and freshly ground black pepper	

1. In a food processor fitted with metal blade, process roasted peppers, cucumber, green onions, yogurt, garlic and cumin until smooth. Season to taste with salt and pepper.
2. Transfer to a serving bowl. Cover and refrigerate until thoroughly chilled or for up to 3 days.

Canary Island Red Pepper Mojo

Makes about ⅔ cup (150 mL)

This is a toned-down variation on a classic hot sauce that is served in the Canary Islands. There it often accompanies a traditional dish known as wrinkled potatoes. For a spectacular appetizer, cook up a batch of Salt-Roasted Potatoes (page 405), put them on skewers and use this Mojo as a dipping sauce. Boiled or grilled shrimp make equally delicious dippers.

1	long red chile, chopped (see Tips, page 35)	1
1 tsp	hot paprika	5 mL
1 tsp	ground cumin (see Tips, page 25)	5 mL
2	cloves garlic, chopped	2
2	red bell peppers, roasted and quartered (see Tips, page 24) or store-bought	2
3 tbsp	red wine vinegar	45 mL
½ cup	extra virgin olive oil	125 mL
	Salt	

1. In a food processor fitted with metal blade, pulse chile pepper, paprika, cumin, garlic, roasted peppers and vinegar until chopped and blended, about 5 times. With motor running, add olive oil through feed tube and process until smoothly blended, about 1 minute. Season to taste with salt. Transfer to a bowl and serve.

Feta and Roasted Red Pepper Dip

Makes about 1¾ cups (425 mL)

If you have the ingredients on hand, this tasty dip can be ready to serve in about 5 minutes. Serve it with crudités, crackers or pumpernickel rounds for an elegant appetizer.

Tip

Use creamy feta cheese (about 26% M.F.). The lower-fat versions produce a drier dip. If your results seem dry, add 1 tsp (5 mL) or so of extra virgin olive oil and pulse.

8 oz	feta cheese (see Tip, left)	250 g
2	red bell peppers, roasted and quartered (see Tips, page 24) or store-bought	2
	Hot pepper sauce, optional	

1. In a food processor fitted with metal blade, process feta, roasted peppers, and hot pepper sauce, if using, until smooth, about 30 seconds, stopping and scraping down sides of the bowl as necessary.

2. Transfer to a bowl and serve or cover and refrigerate for up to 3 days. If refrigerated allow to stand at room temperature for 20 minutes before serving.

Easy Roasted Red Pepper Dip

Makes about 1½ cups (375 mL)

Serve this when gorgeous red peppers are abundant in farmers' markets and relatively inexpensive. It's incredibly easy to make and delivers tremendous bang for the effort invested. It's great with thinly sliced baguette, warm pita bread or crudités.

2	red bell peppers, roasted and quartered (see Tips, page 24) or store-bought	2
¼ cup	mayonnaise	60 mL
2 tbsp	Italian flat-leaf parsley leaves	30 mL
1	anchovy fillet	1
1	clove garlic, coarsely chopped	1
2 tsp	extra virgin olive oil	10 mL
2 tsp	white wine vinegar flavored with tarragon	10 mL
2 tbsp	plain Greek-style (pressed) yogurt (see Tips, page 17)	30 mL
	Salt and freshly ground black pepper	

1. In a food processor fitted with metal blade, process roasted peppers, mayonnaise, parsley, anchovy, garlic, olive oil and vinegar until smoothly puréed.

2. Transfer to a serving bowl and stir in yogurt. Season to taste with salt and pepper. Serve immediately or cover and refrigerate for up to 3 days.

Feta and Yogurt Dip

Makes about 1 cup (250 mL)

Vegetarian Friendly

Nothing could be simpler to make than this herb-infused spread. A small bowl of olives makes a nice accompaniment. Serve with Crisp Pita Bread (page 216), warm pita, crackers or crudités.

1 cup	crumbled feta (about 8 oz/250 g)	250 mL
1 cup	plain yogurt, preferably Greek-style (pressed) (see Tips, page 17)	250 mL
½ cup	fresh dill fronds	125 mL
½ cup	snipped chives	125 mL
	Freshly ground black pepper	
	Extra virgin olive oil	

1. In a food processor fitted with metal blade, process feta, yogurt, dill, chives, and pepper to taste until smooth, about 30 seconds. Transfer to a serving bowl and drizzle with olive oil.

Smoky Eggplant Dip with Yogurt

Makes about 2½ cups (625 mL)

This dip is delicious with raw vegetables or on pita triangles or crusty French bread. For the most flavor, use a smoker or grill the eggplant on a charcoal barbecue. If you're using a gas barbecue, place dampened wood chips in a smoke box, following the manufacturer's instructions.

Tips

If you are using a smoker, the eggplant will cook in about 1¼ hours at 200°F (100°C). The skin will not blister as it will on a barbecue.

Make an effort to get Greek-style yogurt, also known as "pressed." It is lusciously thick and adds beautiful depth to this and many other dishes. If you can't find Greek yogurt, you can make your own. *To make Greek-style yogurt:* Line a sieve with a double layer of cheesecloth or paper towels. Add plain yogurt, cover and refrigerate overnight. The watery component will have drained out and you will be left with lovely thick yogurt.

- **Preheat gas or charcoal barbecue to high**

1	medium eggplant (about 1 lb/500 g)	1
⅓ cup	plain full-fat yogurt, preferably Greek-style (pressed) (see Tips, left)	75 mL
6	cherry tomatoes	6
1	green onion, cut into chunks	1
1	clove garlic, coarsely chopped	1
1 tsp	freshly squeezed lemon juice	5 mL
½ tsp	salt	2 mL
	Freshly ground black pepper	
1 tbsp	finely chopped dill fronds	15 mL
	Finely chopped black olives, optional	

1. Prick eggplant in several places with a fork. Place eggplant on preheated grill. Cook, turning several times, until skin is blackened and blistered, about 30 minutes. Set aside until cool enough to handle.

2. Scoop out eggplant flesh and place in a food processor fitted with metal blade. Discard skin and stem. Add yogurt, tomatoes, green onion, garlic, lemon juice, salt, and pepper to taste. Process until smooth.

3. Transfer to a serving bowl and cover and refrigerate for at least 3 hours until thoroughly chilled or for up to 2 days. To serve, garnish with dill, and olives, if using.

Baba Ghanouj

Makes about 2 cups (500 mL)

No mezes platter would be complete without a bowl of this ambrosial eggplant dip. We find some versions a bit overpowering so we have tamed the stronger flavors in this version. Serve with pita triangles or crudités. If you have any leftover, it makes a great spread for sandwiches and a fabulous topping for burgers or meat patties.

Tip

It is usually more convenient to cook eggplant for Baba Ghanouj in the oven. However, if it is the season, you may want to try grilling it on the barbecue. The smoky taste adds great flavor to the dip and is the traditional cooking method in the Middle East, where this dip originates.

- **Preheat oven to 400°F (200°C)**

1	large eggplant (about 1½ lbs/750 g)	1
½ cup	plain yogurt, preferably Greek-style (pressed) (see Tips, page 17)	125 mL
¼ cup	tahini paste	60 mL
¼ cup	freshly squeezed lemon juice	60 mL
¼ cup	Italian flat-leaf parsley leaves	60 mL
2	cloves garlic, coarsely chopped	2
½ tsp	salt	2 mL
	Finely chopped parsley, optional	

1. Prick eggplant in several places with a fork. Place on a baking sheet and bake in preheated oven until blackened and soft, about 1 hour. Alternatively, place on a gas or charcoal grill preheated to high and cook, turning several times, until skin is blackened and blistered and eggplant is very soft, about 40 minutes (see Tip, left). Let cool.

2. Scoop out eggplant flesh and place in a food processor fitted with metal blade. Discard skin and stem. Add yogurt, tahini, lemon juice, parsley, garlic and salt and process until smooth, about 1 minute.

3. Transfer to a serving dish and garnish with additional parsley, if using. Serve at room temperature or cover and refrigerate for up to 2 days.

Eggplant Caviar

Makes about 2½ cups (625 mL)

This spread/dip is very easy to make and delicious. Not only is it a great entertaining dish, it's also wonderful to have on hand for snacking since it is loaded with nutrients. Serve with sliced baguette, warm pita bread or sliced veggies.

1	medium eggplant (about 1 lb/500 g)	1
1 cup	cherry tomatoes	250 mL
½ cup	Italian flat-leaf parsley leaves	125 mL
4	cloves garlic	4
4	green onions, white part only, cut into chunks	4
3 tbsp	freshly squeezed lemon juice	45 mL
2 tbsp	extra virgin olive oil	30 mL
	Salt and freshly ground black pepper	

1. Preheat oven to 400°F (200°C). Prick eggplant in several places with a fork. Place on a baking sheet and bake in preheated oven until blackened and softened, about 45 minutes. Set aside.

2. Scoop out eggplant flesh and place in a food processor fitted with metal blade. Discard skin and stem. Add remaining ingredients. Process until smooth.

3. Transfer to a bowl. Cover and refrigerate for at least 3 hours until thoroughly chilled or for up to 2 days.

Greek-Style Eggplant Dip

Makes about 2 cups (500 mL)

Just a tad tart and loaded with nutrition, this delicious dip is a regular feature of mezes platters in its native Greece. It is incredibly refreshing, perfect for the summer but substantive enough to transition to colder seasons. Great on grilled pita bread or as a dip for crudités (see page 31).

1	medium eggplant (about 1 lb/500 g)	1
½	small red onion, quartered	½
2	cloves garlic, coarsely chopped	2
1 cup	cherry or grape tomatoes	250 mL
¼ cup	packed Italian flat-leaf parsley leaves	60 mL
¼ cup	extra virgin olive oil	60 mL
2 tbsp	red wine vinegar	30 mL
	Salt and freshly ground black pepper	

1. Follow Step 1 above. Scoop out eggplant flesh and discard skin and stem.

2. In a food processor, pulse onion and garlic until puréed. Add eggplant and remaining ingredients. Pulse until blended but still chunky. Season with salt and pepper.

3. Transfer to a bowl. Cover and refrigerate for 2 hours.

Black Pepper Goat Cheese Dip

Makes about 1½ cups (375 mL)

Here's a very spicy, creamy treat for your palate that goes great with Savory Baked Crostini (page 220), Grilled Herbed Crostini (page 220) or Crisp Pita Bread (page 216).

⅔ cup	soft goat cheese (about 7 oz/210 g)	150 mL
½ cup	whole milk	125 mL
¼ cup	finely chopped cherry tomatoes	60 mL
2 tbsp	thinly sliced green onions	30 mL
1 tbsp	minced garlic	15 mL
1 tsp	freshly ground black pepper	5 mL
1 tsp	white balsamic vinegar	5 mL

1. In a bowl, mash together goat cheese and milk until smooth. Fold in tomatoes, green onions, garlic, pepper and vinegar until combined. Serve immediately or cover and refrigerate for up to 3 days.

Roasted Carrot and Yogurt Dip

Makes about 1½ cups (375 mL)

If you're looking for a slightly different but delicious taste sensation, try this Middle-Eastern-inspired dip. It's perfect on Crisp Pita Bread (page 216) but if you want to go the extra mile, try enhancing the regional flavors with Crisp Pita Bread with Dukkah (see Variations, page 216).

- **Preheat oven to 425°F (220°C)**

8	carrots, peeled and cut into chunks	8
2 tbsp	olive oil	30 mL
2	cloves garlic, minced	2
2 tsp	ground cumin (see Tips, page 25)	10 mL
1 tsp	ground coriander	5 mL
1 tbsp	harissa	15 mL
¾ cup	plain Greek-style (pressed) yogurt (see Tips, page 17)	175 mL
	Finely chopped parsley	

1. In a bowl, combine carrots and oil. Transfer to a baking sheet and roast in preheated oven, turning, until soft, about 45 minutes. Let cool.

2. In a food processor, pulse carrots, garlic, cumin, coriander and harissa until coarsely chopped. Add yogurt and pulse until blended. Spoon into a bowl and garnish with parsley. Serve warm.

Beet and Goat Cheese Spread

Makes about 1½ cups (375 mL)

This spread is amazing paired with Lamb and Red Onion Sliders (page 269) Grilled Herbed Crostini (page 220), grilled pita bread or Crisp Pita Bread (page 216).

Tip

To maintain the bright color of the beets, place 2 tbsp (30 mL) vinegar in a bowl. Roll scrubbed beets in the vinegar before roasting.

- **Preheat oven to 400°F (200°C)**

2	medium beets, scrubbed	2
	Olive oil	
1 tsp	fresh dill fronds	5 mL
½ cup	soft goat cheese, at room temperature	125 mL
½ cup	sour cream (see Tip, page 13)	125 mL

1. Place beets on a rimmed baking sheet or in a baking dish. Toss with oil and cover with foil. Roast in preheated oven until tender, about 1 hour. Remove from oven. Let beets cool, then using a piece of paper towel, rub off skins. Coarsely chop. (You should have ¾ cup/175 mL.)
2. In a food processor fitted with metal blade, purée beets and dill until smooth.
3. In a bowl, mash together goat cheese and sour cream until smooth. Stir in beet purée. Serve immediately or cover and refrigerate for up to 3 days.

Tahini-Spiked Beet Spread

Makes about 1½ cups (375 mL)

This Middle-Eastern-inspired spread is delightfully different and extremely nutritious. It's particularly delicious with grilled or toasted whole-grain pita bread, but plain baguette works well, too. It's great for entertaining because you can make it well ahead if you're rationing your time.

- **Preheat oven to 400°F (200°C)**

4	medium beets, scrubbed	4
	Olive oil	
⅓ cup	plain yogurt, preferably Greek-Style	75 mL
¼ cup	tahini	60 mL
¼ cup	fresh dill fronds	60 mL
2 tbsp	freshly squeezed lemon juice	30 mL
2	cloves garlic, coarsely chopped	2
	Salt and freshly ground black pepper	

1. Follow Step 1 above but spoon off 2 tbsp (30 mL) of the cooking juice.
2. In a food processor fitted with metal blade, process beets, remaining ingredients, 1 tsp (5 mL) salt, pepper to taste, and reserved cooking juice until smooth. Transfer to a bowl. Serve at room temperature.

Roasted Tomato and Pumpkin Seed Dip

Makes about 2¼ cups (550 mL)

If you're looking for something a little different, try this Mexican-inspired dip. It is as nutritious as it is tasty. Serve with tostadas or tortilla chips.

Tips

One jalapeño produces a timidly spiced dip. If you like heat, add more to suit your taste.

Roasted tomatoes freeze very well so it's a good idea to make extra to have on hand. Roast tomatoes and let cool to room temperature. Transfer to a freezer bag and store frozen until needed for up to 3 months.

- **Preheat oven to 400°F (200°C)**

10	plum tomatoes, halved lengthwise	10
1 tbsp	olive oil	15 mL
1 tsp	dried oregano	5 mL
½ cup	hulled pumpkin seeds (pepitas)	125 mL
2 cups	cooked drained white beans	500 mL
4	green onions, white part with a bit of green, cut into chunks	4
¼ cup	coarsely chopped cilantro	60 mL
1 to 3	jalapeño peppers, seeded and quartered (see Tips, left)	1 to 3
1 tsp	salt	5 mL
	Freshly ground black pepper	

1. In a bowl, combine halved tomatoes and olive oil. Toss until evenly coated. Place on a baking sheet cut side up and sprinkle evenly with oregano. Roast in preheated oven until soft and just starting to brown around the edges, about 20 minutes. Set aside.

2. Meanwhile, in a skillet over medium heat, toast pumpkin seeds until fragrant and they begin to pop, about 3 minutes. Transfer to a food processor fitted with metal blade.

3. Add beans, green onions, cilantro, jalapeño pepper to taste, salt and reserved tomatoes. Process until smooth. Season to taste with pepper.

4. Transfer to a serving bowl. Serve immediately or cover and refrigerate for up to 2 days. If refrigerated, let stand at room temperature for about 20 minutes before serving to allow the flavors to develop.

Roasted Tomato Dip

Makes about 1½ cups (375 mL)

Vegan Friendly

Roasted tomatoes take on a sweet smoky flavor, try them once and you'll be hooked. Best served beside warm Classic Garlic Bread (page 210), Margherita Pizza Pockets (page 253) or with crudités for dipping.

- **Preheat oven to 450°F (230°C)**

2 cups	cubed ripe tomatoes	500 mL
1 tsp	extra virgin olive oil	5 mL
½ tsp	salt	2 mL
2 tbsp	finely diced onion	30 mL
2 tbsp	chopped fresh basil leaves	30 mL
1 tsp	balsamic vinegar	5 mL
½ tsp	freshly ground black pepper	2 mL

1. On a rimmed baking sheet, combine tomatoes, oil and salt. Roast in preheated oven until soft, about 10 minutes. Turn oven to broil and roast tomatoes until golden brown, about 5 minutes (see Tips, page 22).
2. Transfer tomato mixture to a food processor fitted with metal blade. Add onion, basil, vinegar and pepper and pulse until smooth. Serve immediately or cover and refrigerate for up to 3 days.

Easy Tahini Dip

Makes about 1¾ cups (425 mL)

Vegan Friendly

This recipe can be put together in a jiffy with ingredients you're likely to have on hand, and is exotic and delicious enough to seem like you went to a great deal of trouble. Serve with warm pita bread or any Middle Eastern flatbread, or for something special, Cumin-Dusted Cauliflower (page 429) or Lebanese Meatballs (page 469).

1 cup	packed Italian flat-leaf parsley leaves	250 mL
½ cup	tahini	125 mL
½ cup	freshly squeezed lemon juice	125 mL
¼ cup	cold water	60 mL
2	cloves garlic, coarsely chopped	2
1 tsp	salt	5 mL
¼ tsp	ground cumin (see Tips, page 25)	1 mL
	Freshly ground black pepper	

1. In a food processor fitted with metal blade, process parsley, tahini, lemon juice, water, garlic, salt and cumin until smoothly blended, about 30 seconds. Season to taste with pepper. Transfer to a serving bowl. Serve at room temperature.

Muhummara

Makes about 2 cups (500 mL)

Depending upon your source, this roasted red pepper and walnut dip is Armenian, Turkish or Syrian in origin. Healthful and delicious, it is a welcome addition to any meze platter. Serve with warm pita bread.

Tips

To roast peppers: Preheat broiler. Place pepper(s) on a baking sheet and broil, turning two or three times, until skin on all sides is blackened, about 25 minutes. Transfer to a heatproof bowl. Cover with a plate and let stand until cool. Remove and, using a sharp knife, lift skins off. Discard skins, core and seeds.

Pomegranate molasses is available in well-stocked supermarkets or markets specializing in Middle Eastern foods.

Aleppo chiles are Syrian in origin. They are moderately hot and quite fruity and lend pleasant authenticity to recipes with a Middle Eastern slant. A smaller quantity of cayenne will produce a similar amount of heat.

2	red bell peppers, roasted and quartered (see Tips, left) or store-bought	2
1 cup	walnut halves, toasted	250 mL
1/2 cup	fresh bread crumbs, lightly toasted	125 mL
4	green onions, white part with a bit of green, cut into chunks	4
2	cloves garlic, coarsely chopped	2
2 tbsp	freshly squeezed lemon juice	30 mL
1 tbsp	pomegranate molasses (see Tips, left)	15 mL
2 tsp	ground Aleppo pepper or 1/4 tsp (1 mL) cayenne pepper (see Tips, left)	10 mL
2 tsp	ground cumin (see Tips, page 25)	10 mL
1/2 tsp	salt	2 mL
1/2 cup	extra virgin olive oil	125 mL

1. In a food processor fitted with metal blade, pulse roasted peppers, walnuts, bread crumbs, green onions, garlic, lemon juice, pomegranate molasses, Aleppo pepper, cumin and salt until finely chopped and combined, about 15 times, stopping and scraping down sides of the bowl as necessary.

2. Add olive oil and pulse until desired texture is achieved. Transfer to a serving bowl. Serve immediately or cover and refrigerate for up to 3 days. If refrigerated, before serving, let stand at room temperature for about 20 minutes to allow the flavors to develop.

Roasted Pepper and Sweet Potato Dip

Makes about 3 cups (750 mL)

Roasting vegetables intensifies their flavors and brings out inherent sweetness. This dip is basically a medley of healthful vegetables, roasted and blended, with minimal accents. It's chock full of nutrition and delicious to boot. Serve with tortilla chips, warm pita, rice crackers or even sliced baguette.

Tips

For best flavor, toast and grind cumin yourself. *To toast seeds:* Place seeds in a dry skillet over medium heat and cook, stirring, until fragrant, about 3 minutes. Immediately transfer to a mortar or a spice grinder and grind.

We always use flat-leaf rather than curly parsley because it has more flavor.

- **Preheat oven to 400°F (200°C)**

1	sweet potato (about 8 oz/250 g)	1
1	green bell pepper	1
1	large tomato, halved, cut side brushed with olive oil	1
3	cloves garlic, unpeeled	3
1	jalapeño pepper, optional	1
2 tsp	extra virgin olive oil	10 mL
1 tsp	ground cumin (see Tips, left)	5 mL
	Salt and freshly ground black pepper	
2 tbsp	finely chopped Italian flat-leaf parsley leaves	30 mL

1. On a rimmed baking sheet, roast sweet potato, bell pepper, tomato, garlic, and jalapeño, if using, in preheated oven. Turn bell pepper and jalapeño several times to blacken on all sides and when they are nicely blistered (about 20 minutes for the jalapeño and 30 minutes for the bell pepper), transfer to a bowl, cover with a plate and let sweat. Turn garlic once and when very soft, remove from oven and let cool. When tomato is softened and skin looks very wizened (about 30 minutes) remove from oven and let cool. When sweet potato is soft (about 50 minutes), remove from oven and let cool.

2. When cool enough to handle, peel pepper(s) and cut into chunks. Squeeze garlic out of skins. Remove skin from tomatoes and cut out core. Scoop sweet potato out of skin. Discard skins and core.

3. Transfer pepper(s), garlic, tomato and sweet potato to a food processor fitted with metal blade. Add olive oil, cumin, and salt and pepper to taste. Process until smooth and blended, about 1 minute. Transfer to a serving bowl and garnish with parsley. Serve warm.

Sweet Potato Spread

Makes about 1⅓ cups (325 mL)

This spread is perfect served on warm Yogurt Flatbread (page 217) or Grilled Herbed Crostini (page 220). You can easily store in the freezer for up to 3 months.

Tip

Before serving, drizzle the top with 1 tbsp (15 mL) pure maple syrup.

2 cups	diced sweet potato (unpeeled)	500 mL
3 cups	water	750 mL
¼ cup	unsalted butter, at room temperature, and diced	60 mL
⅛ tsp	ground cinnamon	0.5 mL

1. In a large saucepan over medium heat, bring sweet potato and water to a boil. Reduce heat and boil gently until soft, about 5 minutes. Drain. Using a hand mixer or a stand mixer fitted with paddle attachment, add butter and cinnamon and whip until smooth. Serve immediately or cover and refrigerate for up to 3 days.

Guacamole

Makes 2 cups (500 mL)

Guacamole is a classic for a reason. It is very easy to make, loaded with nutrition and absolutely delicious. Serve this with tostadas, tortilla chips or Carnitas (page 343).

Tips

If fresh tomatoes aren't in season, you may want to substitute cherry or grape tomatoes instead. You'll need 10 for this quantity.

If you are a heat seeker, use a second jalapeño. One makes a pleasantly mild guacamole.

3	small avocados, such as Hass	3
1	tomato, cored and peeled (see Tips, left)	1
4	green onions, white part only, or 1 slice (about ½ inch/1 cm) red onion	4
1 to 2	jalapeño peppers, seeded and cut in half (see Tips, left)	1 to 2
½ cup	fresh cilantro leaves	125 mL
3 tbsp	freshly squeezed lime juice	45 mL
	Salt	

1. In a food processor fitted with metal blade, process avocados, tomato, green onions, jalapeño pepper to taste, cilantro and lime juice until desired texture is achieved. (We like ours a bit chunky.) Season to taste with salt. Transfer to a serving bowl.

Avocado Salsa Dip

Makes about 3 cups (750 mL)

Here's a dip that tastes every bit as good as made-from-scratch guacamole.

Tips

Use mild to hot salsa. The degree of heat in the salsa will determine the spiciness of the dip.

If you like the tartness of lemon, use the maximum amount. For a milder flavor, use less.

Dip keeps covered with plastic wrap and refrigerated for up to 4 hours.

1¼ cups	tomato salsa	300 mL
1 cup	cooked sweet green peas	250 mL
½	red onion, quartered	½
2	cloves garlic, coarsely chopped	2
2 tbsp	pickled jalapeño peppers	30 mL
1 to	freshly squeezed lemon juice	15 to
2 tbsp	(see Tips, left)	30 mL
2	small avocados, cut into chunks	2
	Salt and freshly ground black pepper	
	Finely chopped cilantro or parsley, optional	

1. In a food processor, purée salsa, peas, onion, garlic, jalapeños and lemon juice. Add avocados and pulse until desired texture is achieved. (We like ours a bit chunky.) Season to taste with salt and pepper.
2. Transfer to a serving bowl. Garnish with cilantro, if using. Serve immediately.

Avocado Cream Cheese Dip

Makes about 2½ cups (625 mL)

If you live in northern climates, this is a great dip to make in spring when the first spring onions and parsley start coming into markets.

Tip

Dip keeps covered with plastic wrap and refrigerated for up to 4 hours.

8 oz	softened cream cheese, cut into cubes	250 g
6	green onions, white with a bit of green, cut into chunks	6
½ cup	fresh Italian flat-leaf parsley leaves	125 mL
¼ cup	freshly squeezed lemon juice	60 mL
2 tbsp	sour cream	30 mL
1	clove garlic, coarsely chopped	1
	Salt and freshly ground black pepper	
2	large ripe avocados, cut into chunks	2

1. In a food processor, process cream cheese, onions, parsley, lemon juice, sour cream, garlic and ½ tsp (2 mL) salt until smooth. Add avocados and process until desired texture is achieved.
2. Transfer to a serving bowl. Season with pepper to taste. Serve immediately.

Avocado Ancho Chile Dip

Makes about 1 cup (250 mL)

This dip is a variation on the theme of guacamole and is wonderful with Carnitas (page 343), tacos or tortilla chips.

1	avocado, cut into chunks (about 1 cup/250 mL)	1
¼ cup	mayonnaise	60 mL
1 tbsp	cream cheese	15 mL
1 tsp	rice wine vinegar	5 mL
1 tsp	grainy (Pommery) mustard	5 mL
¼ tsp	salt	1 mL
¼ tsp	ancho chile powder	1 mL
¼ tsp	liquid honey	1 mL

1. In a food processor fitted with metal blade, pulse avocado, mayonnaise, cream cheese, vinegar, mustard, salt, ancho chile and honey until smooth. Transfer to a serving bowl. Serve immediately or cover with plastic wrap, pressing down on surface of dip, and refrigerate for up to 4 hours.

Cheesy Avocado Dip

Makes about 3 cups (750 mL)

If you're looking for an avocado-based dip that differs from guacamole, the addition of feta cheese, parsley and dill turns this relative into a deliciously different treat. Serve it on warm pita bread or, if you don't want to stray too far from the original, with tostadas or tortilla chips.

1 cup	cherry or grape tomatoes	250 mL
4	green onions, white part with a bit of green, cut into chunks	4
¼ cup	fresh Italian flat-leaf parsley leaves	60 mL
¼ cup	fresh dill fronds	60 mL
1	clove garlic	1
2	avocados, cut into chunks	2
4 oz	feta cheese	125 g
1 tbsp	freshly squeezed lemon juice	15 mL
	Salt and freshly ground black pepper	

1. In a food processor fitted with metal blade, pulse tomatoes, green onions, parsley, dill and garlic until chopped, about 10 times. Add avocados, feta and lemon juice and process until smooth, about 30 seconds. Season to taste with salt and pepper.

2. Transfer to a serving bowl. Serve immediately or cover with plastic wrap, pressing down on surface of dip, and refrigerate for up to 4 hours.

Anchovy-Spiked Avocado Dip

Makes about 2 cups (500 mL)

If you're a fan of guacamole, but would enjoy a slightly different flavor profile, try this. Although avocados and anchovies may not seem like an obvious pairing, they complement each other surprisingly well. Serve with tostadas or tortilla chips.

3	small avocados, such as Hass, cut into chunks	3
8	cherry tomatoes	8
6	green onions, white part with a bit of green, cut into chunks	6
4	anchovy fillets	4
¼ cup	sour cream	60 mL
2 tbsp	freshly squeezed lemon juice	30 mL
	Salt and freshly ground black pepper	

1. In a food processor fitted with metal blade, process avocados, tomatoes, green onions, anchovies, sour cream and lemon juice until desired texture is achieved. Season to taste with salt and pepper.
2. Transfer to a serving bowl. Serve immediately or cover with plastic wrap, pressing down on surface of dip, and refrigerate for up to 4 hours.

Warm Anchovy Dip

Makes about 1½ cups (375 mL)

To many the mere mention of an anchovy is a turn off but "melted" with Dijon mustard and served with crudités, this is one of the most special flavors ever. The French serve this dip with freshly cut carrots, button mushrooms, cauliflower or any other seasonal vegetable.

1 cup	roughly chopped anchovy fillets	250 mL
⅓ cup	extra virgin olive oil	75 mL
1 tsp	Dijon mustard	5 mL
1 tsp	minced garlic	5 mL
1 tsp	liquid honey	5 mL
½ tsp	sherry vinegar	2 mL

1. In a stainless steel or other heatproof bowl, combine anchovies, oil, mustard, garlic, honey and vinegar and heat over simmering water in a double boiler, stirring often, until anchovies are dissolved, about 20 minutes. Serve immediately or cover and refrigerate for up to 3 days. If refrigerated, reheat before serving.

Salmorejo

Makes about 3 cups (750 mL)

This creamy tomato dip, which resembles a thick gazpacho, is a specialty of Andalusia, a region of Spain. Serve it with crudités — slices of green bell pepper are particularly tasty — cold boiled shrimp or Salt-Roasted Potatoes (page 405). In Spain, it is traditionally served with chunks of grilled bread so Bruschetta (page 231) would work well, too.

Tip

To peel tomatoes: Bring a large pot of water to a boil. Using a knife, make an X in the bottom (non-stem end) of the tomato. Spear tomato at the stem end with a fork and immerse in boiling water for about 30 seconds. (You want the skin to loosen, but you don't want to cook the tomato.) Place under cold running water, turning to cool. Beginning with the X cut, lift off the skin. Repeat until all tomatoes are peeled.

1 cup	packed cubed (1 inch/2.5 cm) day-old country-style bread (about 2 slices)	250 mL
1½ lbs	ripe tomatoes (3 medium), peeled, cored and cut into chunks (see Tip, left)	750 g
2	cloves garlic, coarsely chopped	2
1 tbsp	sherry vinegar	15 mL
	Salt and freshly ground black pepper	
½ cup	extra virgin olive oil	125 mL
3	thin slices Serrano ham or prosciutto, slivered	3
2	hard-cooked eggs, cooled and thinly sliced (see Tips, page 34)	2

1. In a bowl, combine bread with water to cover. Set aside for 5 minutes. Drain and squeeze liquid out of bread. Set bread aside.

2. In a food processor fitted with metal blade, pulse tomatoes and bread until coarsely chopped, about 10 times. Add garlic, vinegar, and salt and pepper to taste and process until smoothly blended, about 1 minute. With motor running, add olive oil through the feed tube in a steady steam. Taste and adjust seasoning. (It should be on the salty side because the salty flavor will diminish with chilling.)

3. Transfer to a serving bowl. Cover tightly and chill for at least 3 hours to allow flavors to meld or overnight. When you're ready to serve, garnish with slivered ham and sliced eggs.

Mofongo

Make about 2 cups (500 mL)

If you're looking for something a little off the beaten path, try this. Mofongo is a plantain purée that is very popular in the Caribbean. Serve this with crudités or tortilla chips.

Tips

If you prefer, use a food processor to purée the mixture.

Traditionally, when using chile peppers, the veins and seeds are removed. If you're a heat seeker, leave them in.

2	ripe plantains, peeled and cut into ½-inch (1 cm) slices	2
1½ cups	chicken broth	375 mL
6	slices bacon	6
½ cup	minced onion	125 mL
2	cloves garlic, finely chopped	2
½ to 1	jalapeño pepper, seeded and minced	½ to 1
3 tbsp	finely chopped fresh cilantro leaves	45 mL
	Salt and freshly ground black pepper	

1. In a small saucepan over medium heat, combine plantain slices and chicken broth. Bring to a boil. Cover, reduce heat and simmer until plantains are very tender, about 10 minutes. Remove from heat and let cool slightly.

2. Meanwhile, in a skillet, cook bacon until crisp. Drain on paper towel and crumble. Set aside.

3. Add onion to skillet and cook, stirring, until softened, about 2 minutes. Add garlic and jalapeño to taste and cook, stirring, for 1 minute. Remove from heat. Add plantains with liquid and, using a fork or potato masher, mash. Add crumbled bacon and stir well to make sure mixture is well integrated. Season to taste with salt and pepper. Serve warm.

Crudités for Dipping

Crudités are cut-up vegetables used for dipping. Popular choices are broccoli and cauliflower florets, peeled baby carrots, spears of Belgian endive and cherry tomatoes. If you're looking for something a little different, try thin slices of fennel, small radicchio leaves or hearts of romaine, blanched asparagus, radishes, including thin slices of peeled daikon, or even sliced canned hearts of palm (see page 66 for preparation instructions). And don't forget old standbys such as carrot or celery sticks and thinly sliced cucumber or zucchini. Another favorite is blanched Brussels sprouts, which are particularly good with strongly flavored dips, or cooked new potatoes (page 406).

Pepper-Spiked Plantain Dip

Makes about 3 cups (750 mL)

This is a variation on Mofongo (page 31) that is suitable for vegans. Instead of using bacon to add flavor to the pleasantly bland plantains, onion, garlic and peppers are softened in olive oil before puréeing. Cooking the plantains in water flavored with ketchup takes the place of chicken broth. This is great with tortilla chips or warm pita bread.

Tips

Use the chile pepper that suits your taste. Long red or green or jalapeños all work well in this recipe.

Traditionally, when using chile peppers, the veins and seeds are removed. If you're a heat seeker, leave them in.

1½ cups	water	375 mL
3 tbsp	ketchup	45 mL
2	ripe plantains, peeled and cut into ½-inch (1 cm) slices	2
2 tbsp	olive oil	30 mL
1	onion, finely chopped	1
1	green bell pepper, chopped	1
1	chile pepper, seeded and chopped (see Tips, left)	1
4	cloves garlic, chopped	4
1 tsp	dried oregano	5 mL
1 tsp	salt	5 mL
	Freshly ground black pepper	

1. In a saucepan over medium heat, combine water and ketchup. Stir well to combine. Add plantains and bring to a boil. Cover, reduce heat and simmer until plantains are tender, about 10 minutes. Remove from heat and let cool slightly.

2. Meanwhile, in a separate saucepan, heat oil over medium heat. Add onion, bell pepper, chile and garlic and stir well. Reduce heat to low, cover and cook until vegetables are very tender, about 10 minutes. Stir in oregano, salt, and pepper to taste. Remove from heat and let cool slightly.

3. In a food processor fitted with metal blade, process cooked plantains with liquid and pepper mixture until smoothly blended, about 1 minute. Transfer to a serving bowl. Serve warm.

Roasted Fennel Dip

Makes about 1⅔ cups (400 mL)

For those of you yet to experience the succulent flavor of roasted fennel, go out and buy one now. It's delicious! Serve with wedges of raw fennel or with Roasted Potato Wedges (page 404). Parsnip Chips and Taro Root Chips (see Variations, page 213) would be wonderful too.

- **Preheat oven to 450°F (230°C)**

Roasted Fennel Purée

1	fennel bulb, cut into quarters	1
2 tbsp	water	30 mL
1 tbsp	olive oil	15 mL
¼ tsp	salt	1 mL
½ cup	sour cream (see Tip, page 13)	125 mL
1 tbsp	white balsamic vinegar	15 mL
½ tsp	coarsely chopped fresh thyme leaves	2 mL
¼ tsp	grated lemon zest	1 mL

1. *Roasted Fennel Purée:* On a baking sheet, combine fennel bulb, water, olive oil and salt. Roast in preheated oven until fennel is caramelized and soft, about 40 minutes. Transfer to a food processor fitted with metal blade or use an immersion blender in a tall container and purée until smooth.

2. In a bowl, combine 1⅓ cups (325 mL) fennel purée, sour cream, vinegar, thyme and lemon zest. Serve immediately or cover and refrigerate for up to 3 days.

Creamy Roquefort Dip

Makes about 2 cups (500 mL)

Rich and delicious, this dip is also very refreshing when served with crisp leaves of romaine lettuce or radicchio. It's also very good with Salt-Roasted Potatoes (page 405) or spears of Belgian endive.

6 oz	Roquefort cheese	175 g
¾ cup	half-and-half (10%) cream	175 mL
2 tbsp	fresh tarragon leaves (about 30)	30 mL
	Salt and freshly ground black pepper	

1. In a food processor fitted with metal blade, process Roquefort, cream and tarragon until smoothly blended, about 30 seconds. Season to taste with salt and pepper.

2. Transfer to a serving dish. Cover and refrigerate until ready to serve or for up to 3 days.

Egg and Olive Spread

Makes about 1½ cups (375 mL)

It's easy to overlook old-fashioned egg salad as an appetizing hors d'oeuvre because it is such a common filling for sandwiches. But it's a classic for a reason: it tastes good and appeals to a wide variety of people. It's also a great solution for unexpected guests because you can make it from ingredients you're likely to have on hand. Serve this with a plate of pumpernickel rounds or dark rye bread, or use as a topping for Basic Crostini (page 219).

Tips

To hard-cook eggs: Place eggs in a saucepan in a single layer and add cold water to cover by 1 inch (2.5 cm). Cover and bring to a boil over high heat. Remove from heat and let stand for 10 minutes. Using a slotted spoon, transfer to a bowl of ice water. Let cool for 5 minutes. Remove eggshells under cool running water.

Olive paste is available in the deli section of many supermarkets.

4	hard-cooked eggs (see Tips, left) peeled and chopped	4
2 tbsp	mayonnaise	30 mL
6	pimento-stuffed green olives, finely chopped	6
	Salt and freshly ground black pepper	
	Hot or sweet paprika	
	Pumpernickel rounds or dark rye bread	

1. In a bowl, combine eggs, mayonnaise and olives. Mix well. Season to taste with salt and pepper.
2. Using an ice cream scoop, mound into a small serving bowl. Dust lightly with paprika. Accompany with pumpernickel rounds or dark rye bread.

Variations

Egg and Chive Spread: Substitute 1 tbsp (15 mL) finely chopped chives for the olives.

Egg and Roasted Red Pepper Spread: Substitute 2 small roasted red peppers, finely chopped, for the olives.

Egg and Black Olive Crostini: Spread each Basic Crostini (page 219) with 1 tsp (5 mL) black olive paste (see Tips, left) and top with Egg and Roasted Red Pepper Spread.

Classic Spinach and Water Chestnut Dip

Makes about 2 cups (500 mL)

Versions of this dip have been around for decades but it just doesn't go away — probably because it qualifies as comfort food. It's great with traditional crudités, such as celery sticks, warm pita, toast points, sliced baguette, or chunks of sourdough bread.

Tips

For this quantity of spinach leaves, use a 1 lb (500 g) bunch of fresh spinach. Remove the stems and discard.

Use the kind of red or green chile you have easy access to. Long red or Thai bird's eye both work well in this recipe. If you're heat averse, seed and devein the chile before using.

For this quantity of water chestnuts, use about two-thirds of an 8-oz (227 g) can, drained.

2 tbsp	unsalted butter	30 mL
1	leek, white and light green part only, cleaned and thinly sliced	1
2	cloves garlic, chopped	2
10 oz	fresh spinach leaves (see Tips, left)	300 g
2 tsp	grainy Dijon mustard	10 mL
1/4 to 1/2	long red or green chile pepper (see Tips, left)	1/4 to 1/2
4 oz	cream cheese, softened	125 g
1/4 cup	sour cream	60 mL
1/2 cup	sliced water chestnuts (see Tips, left)	125 mL
	Salt and freshly ground black pepper	

1. In a skillet, melt butter over medium heat. Add leek and cook, stirring, until softened, about 5 minutes. Add garlic and cook, stirring, for 1 minute. Add spinach and toss until wilted, about 2 minutes. Remove from heat and stir in mustard and chile pepper to taste.

2. Transfer to food processor fitted with metal blade. Add cream cheese, sour cream and water chestnuts and process until smooth, about 1 minute. Transfer to a serving bowl. Season to taste with salt and pepper.

Breads for Dipping

Simply prepared bread, such as sliced baguette or warm pita bread, or crackers are among the most popular accompaniments for dips because they are easy-to-serve and versatile, blending as they do with a wide variety of textures and flavors. Breadsticks, crostini, either store-bought or homemade (pages 219 and 220), chunks of focaccia (particularly tasty with Warm Anchovy Dip, page 29) and Bruschetta (page 231) are also good choices. If you're looking for something a bit more elaborate, try seasoning pita bread (Crisp Pita Bread, page 216) or make Pita Chips (Variation, page 216) or making your own flatbread such as Yogurt Flatbread (page 217).

Cheesy Spinach Dip

Makes about 4 cups (1 L)

Hot dips loaded with bubbling melted cheese are one of life's guilty pleasures. This version provides the same decadent pleasure but the addition of healthful ingredients like spinach and tomato reduces the guilt factor. Serve with sliced baguette, melba toast or potato chips, store-bought or homemade (page 215).

Tip

If you have an ovenproof serving dish of the appropriate size, by all means use it to bake and serve this recipe.

- **Preheat oven to 400°F (200°C)**
- **Lightly greased baking dish (see Tip, left)**

1 tbsp	oil	15 mL
2	onions, finely chopped	2
4	cloves garlic, minced	4
10 oz	fresh spinach leaves, coarsely chopped	300 g
1	tomato, peeled, seeded and chopped	1
2 cups	shredded Cheddar cheese, divided	500 mL
4 oz	cream cheese, softened	125 g
2 tbsp	sour cream	30 mL
1 tbsp	vegan or regular Worcestershire sauce	15 mL
	Salt and freshly ground black pepper	

1. In a skillet, heat oil over medium heat. Add onions and cook, stirring, until softened, about 3 minutes. Add garlic and spinach and cook, stirring, until spinach is nicely wilted, about 4 minutes.

2. Transfer to a food processor fitted with metal blade. Add tomato, $1\frac{1}{2}$ cups (375 mL) of the Cheddar cheese, cream cheese, sour cream and Worcestershire sauce. Process until smooth. Season to taste with salt and pepper.

3. Transfer to prepared dish. Sprinkle remaining $\frac{1}{2}$ cup (125 mL) of Cheddar evenly over top. Bake in preheated oven until mixture is bubbling and top is lightly browned, about 25 minutes.

Warm Spinach Dip

Makes about 1½ cups (375 mL)

This dip is a wonderful appetizer or snack on a cold winter day. Serve with tortilla chips or as a garnish on Beef and Parmesan Sliders (page 268).

Tip

Instead of ramekins, place the mixture in a 2-cup (500 mL) baking dish and bake in preheated oven until surface is bubbling, about 35 minutes.

- **Preheat oven to 300°F (150°C)**
- **Two 8-oz (250 mL) ramekins (see Tip, left)**

1¼ cups	sour cream (see Tip, page 13)	300 mL
½ cup	coarsely chopped spinach, blanched, thoroughly dried	125 mL
⅓ cup	freshly grated Parmesan cheese	75 mL
¼ cup	shredded Cheddar cheese	60 mL
½ tsp	minced garlic	2 mL
¼ cup	thinly sliced green onions	60 mL

1. In a bowl, combine sour cream, spinach, Parmesan and Cheddar cheeses and garlic and divide equally into two ramekins. Bake in preheated oven until tops are golden brown and beginning to bubble, about 20 minutes. Remove from heat, garnish with green onions and serve immediately.

Roasted Potato Dip

Makes 1⅓ cups (325 mL)

Dollop a touch of this dip on top of Bacon-Studded Cheese and Onion Tart (page 245) or as a dip for Zesty Cheddar Crisps (page 207) or Parmesan Crisps (page 208) for a flavor that will rival any loaded baked potato out there. It is just delicious.

- **Preheat oven to 375°F (190°C)**
- **Food mill or potato ricer**

8 oz	baking potato (about 1 potato)	250 g
½ cup	sour cream (see Tip, page 13)	125 mL
1 tbsp	minced garlic	15 mL
1 tbsp	grainy (Pommery) mustard	15 mL
½ tsp	finely chopped fresh thyme leaves	2 mL

1. In preheated oven, roast potato until fork tender, about 1 hour. Cut potato in half and scoop white flesh from skin, discarding skin. Press potato through a ricer into a bowl. Let cool to room temperature.

2. Add sour cream, garlic, mustard and thyme and mix well to combine. Serve immediately or cover and refrigerate for up to 3 days.

Greek-Style Garlic-Spiked Potato Dip

Makes about 2 cups (500 mL)

This version of the Greek sauce skordalia is made with mashed potatoes rather than bread. It is particularly delicious. Serve with warm pita, Crisp Pita Bread (page 216) or crudités.

Tip

Refrigerating this dip will cause it to congeal and dramatically intensify the flavor of the garlic. It is best served soon after it is made, at room temperature.

1 lb	russet (Idaho) potatoes, boiled in their skins, cooled, peeled and coarsely chopped (about 2)	500 g
4	cloves garlic, coarsely chopped	4
¼ cup	freshly squeezed lemon juice	60 mL
½ cup	coarsely chopped blanched almonds, toasted (see Tips, page 74 and 103)	125 mL
½ cup	extra virgin olive oil	125 mL
	Salt and freshly ground black pepper	
	Finely chopped parsley	

1. In a food processor fitted with metal blade, process garlic until finely chopped, stopping and scraping down sides of the bowl. Add potatoes and pulse to blend, about 10 times. Add lemon juice and almonds and pulse to blend, about 5 times. With motor running, add olive oil through the feed tube and process until mixture is smooth and blended. Season to taste with salt and pepper.
2. Transfer to serving bowl. Garnish with parsley and serve immediately at room temperature.

Blue Cheese Dip

Makes about 1½ cups (375 mL)

When you hear blue cheese dip, two foods come to mind — Classic Buffalo Chicken Wings (page 473) and fresh cut celery sticks. This dip goes perfectly with either or just as well spread on a sliced baguette.

1½ cups	crumbled blue cheese, about 6 oz (175 g)	375 mL
½ cup	milk	125 mL
2 oz	cream cheese, softened	60 g
1 tsp	dried oregano	5 mL

1. In a bowl, combine blue cheese, milk, cream cheese and oregano until smooth. Serve immediately or cover and refrigerate for up to 3 days. If refrigerated, reheat before serving.

Caramelized Red Onion Dip

Makes about 2 cups (500 mL)

Gone are the days when onion dip invariably involved a package of dried soup. Full of sweet red onions, this tasty alternative is very easy to make and the results are more than worth the extra effort. Serve with good-quality packaged potato chips, Homemade Potato Chips (page 215) or, for a more healthful option, spears of Belgian endive.

Tips

If you have a small (approx. 2 quart) slow cooker, it is a very convenient tool for caramelizing onions. For instructions, see Step 1, page 494.

You can caramelize the onions up to 2 days ahead of time and refrigerate until ready to use. Reheat gently before continuing with the recipe.

4	red onions, quartered	4
4	cloves garlic	4
2 tbsp	unsalted butter	30 mL
4 oz	cream cheese, cubed and softened	125 g
½ cup	sour cream	125 mL
2 tbsp	vegan or regular Worcestershire sauce	30 mL
2 tbsp	fresh thyme leaves	30 mL
	Salt and freshly ground black pepper	
	Finely snipped chives	

1. In a food processor fitted with slicing blade, slice red onions and garlic.

2. In a large skillet, melt butter over medium heat. Add red onions and garlic and stir well. Cook, stirring, until onions are browned and caramelized, about 25 minutes (see Tips, left).

3. Replace slicing blade with metal blade. Add caramelized onion mixture, cream cheese, sour cream, Worcestershire sauce, thyme, and salt and pepper to taste. Process until well blended, about 30 seconds. Transfer to a serving dish and garnish with chives.

Smoky Baked Onion Dip

Makes about 2 cups (500 mL)

On those days when you feel like throwing caution to the wind, open a bag of good potato chips and serve up a batch of this luscious dip — one of life's little indulgences. It is also good with melba toast or sliced baguette.

Tips

If you have an ovenproof serving dish of the appropriate size, by all means use it to make this dish.

Smoked paprika has great flavor but it can be overpowering. Add the smaller quantity and taste. If you prefer stronger flavor add the remainder.

- **Preheat oven to 400°F (200°C)**
- **Lightly greased baking dish (see Tips, left)**

1	large Spanish onion (about 12 oz/375 g), finely chopped	1
1 tbsp	olive oil	15 mL
1½ cups	shredded Swiss cheese	375 mL
8 oz	cream cheese, softened	250 g
½ cup	freshly grated Parmesan cheese, divided	125 mL
¼ cup	mayonnaise	60 mL
1 tbsp	vegan or regular Worcestershire sauce	15 mL
½ to 1 tsp	hot smoked paprika (see Tips, left)	2 to 5 mL
	Salt and freshly ground black pepper	

1. In a microwave-safe bowl large enough to accommodate all the ingredients, combine onion and oil. Cover and microwave on High for 2 minutes. Stir well. Add Swiss cheese, cream cheese, ¼ cup (60 mL) of the Parmesan, mayonnaise, Worcestershire sauce, paprika and salt and pepper to taste. Mix well. Transfer to prepared dish. Sprinkle remaining Parmesan evenly over top.

2. Bake in preheated oven until mixture is bubbling and top is lightly browned, about 25 minutes. Serve immediately.

Roasted Onion Dip

Makes about 1½ cups (375 mL)

Serve beside warm Steamed Pork Dumplings (page 202) or Savory Fried Shrimp Wontons (page 203). Or it's great with just potato chips.

Tip

Shallots are wonderful when roasted, too. Use 3 to 4 shallots. Adjust the cooking time slightly and cook for about 45 minutes.

- **Preheat oven to 400°F (200°C)**

2	medium onions	2
½ tsp	minced capers	2 mL
1 tbsp	balsamic vinegar	15 mL
1 tbsp	tomato ketchup	15 mL
¼ tsp	fresh rosemary leaves	1 mL
¼ tsp	freshly ground black pepper	1 mL

1. Place onions on a baking sheet and roast in preheated oven until soft, about 1 hour. Let cool to room temperature, then peel and mince. (You should have 1 cup/250 mL.)

2. In a bowl, combine onions, capers, vinegar, ketchup, rosemary and pepper. Serve immediately or refrigerate for up to 3 days.

Creamy Green Onion Dip

Makes about 1 cup (250 mL)

Why not try this dip over Grilled Pizza with Braised Leeks and Tomato (page 252), flatbread or Crisp Pita Bread (page 216). There's something about the spicy raw flavor with crisp dough or bread.

Tip

Try using this dip as a condiment, topping Mushroom Phyllo Triangles (page 204) with a dollop.

¾ cup	coarsely chopped green onions	175 mL
⅓ cup	mayonnaise	75 mL
1 tsp	red wine vinegar	5 mL
2	cloves garlic	2
½ tsp	salt	2 mL

1. In a food processor fitted with metal blade, pulse green onions, mayonnaise, vinegar, garlic and salt until smooth. Serve immediately or cover and refrigerate for up to 3 days.

Variation

In the springtime, when ramps (also known as wild leeks) become available, they will make a perfect substitute for green onions in this recipe.

Grilled Scallion and Corn Dip

Makes about 1⅔ cups (400 mL)

This dip is an amazing summertime recipe that is perfect on Polenta Crostini (page 229), Parmesan Crisps (page 208), tortilla chips or crudités, such as bell peppers.

Tips

Scallions, also known as green onions, are widely available and perfect raw where a subtle onion-note is needed. When grilled, they become smoky and contrast the sweetness of the corn beautifully.

To grill corn: Preheat barbecue grill to high. Grill ears of corn, husks on, rotating often until dark brown all over, about 20 minutes. Transfer to a plate and let cool for 5 minutes or until cool enough to handle. Remove husk and silks and, using a serrated knife, cut kernels from cob.

Chipotle peppers are smoked jalapeño peppers. They can be found dried (whole or ground) or combined with adobo sauce and canned.

- **Preheat barbecue to medium-high**

3	green onions (scallions) (see Tips, left)	3
½ tsp	olive oil	2 mL
1 cup	grilled corn kernels (see Tips, left)	250 mL
½ cup	rice vinegar	125 mL
¼ cup	water	60 mL
¼ cup	coarsely chopped fresh cilantro leaves	60 mL
2 tbsp	coarsely chopped cherry tomatoes	30 mL
2	cloves garlic	2
½ tsp	salt	2 mL
⅛ tsp	chipotle powder	0.5 mL
⅛ tsp	freshly ground black pepper	0.5 mL

1. In a bowl, combine green onions and oil to coat. Grill, turning often, until golden brown and soft, 4 to 5 minutes. Transfer to a food processor fitted with metal blade. Add corn, vinegar, water, cilantro, tomatoes, garlic, salt, chipotle and black pepper and pulse until smooth. Serve immediately or cover and refrigerate for up to 3 days.

Handmade Dippers

While crudités, plain crackers or sliced baguette are almost always appropriate for dipping, from time to time, it can be fun to try something a little different, which may even involve a bit of work. Deep-fry thin slices of plantain (page 211) or beets (page 213) or use Homemade Potato Chips (page 215). Some dips can also double as spreads, so they may make a tasty topping for crêpe-like breads such as Buckwheat Blinis (page 198), Crêpes Parmentier (page 200) or Indian-Style Roti (page 201). Since dips come from so many cultural traditions and contain so many different combinations of ingredients, it can be fun to let your imagination run wild.

Peppery Peanut Dip

Makes about 1½ cups (375 mL)

Here's a delicious and nutritious dip that is very easy to make. It is a perfect accompaniment to a platter of crudités. For something a little different, try serving fresh strawberries as dippers.

1 cup	peanut butter	250 mL
6	green onions, white part with a bit of green, cut into chunks	6
1	jalapeño pepper, seeded and quartered	1
8	fresh basil leaves (approx.)	8
2 tsp	finely grated lemon zest	10 mL
¼ cup	freshly squeezed lemon juice	60 mL
¼ cup	warm water (approx.)	60 mL
1 tbsp	soy sauce	15 mL

1. In a food processor fitted with metal blade, process peanut butter, green onions, jalapeño pepper, basil, lemon zest and juice, water and soy sauce until smooth and blended. Add more warm water, if necessary, to make a smooth and creamy consistency. Transfer to a serving bowl and garnish with whole basil leaves.

Thai Peanut Dip

Makes about 2 cups (500 mL)

This versatile dip is wonderful with hot crisps, fresh spring rolls or crudités.

Tip

We suggest using the Agave and Ginger-Scented Peanuts (page 455) for this recipe. However, a roasted, unsalted peanut would substitute nicely.

1¾ cups	Agave and Ginger-Scented Peanuts (see page 455)	425 mL
¾ cup	soy sauce	175 mL
¼ cup	hoisin sauce	60 mL
¼ cup	water	60 mL
1 tbsp	rice vinegar	15 mL
1 tsp	coarsely chopped fresh cilantro leaves	5 mL
1 tsp	coarsely chopped green onions	5 mL
½ tsp	hot pepper sauce	2 mL

1. In a food processor fitted with metal blade, pulse nuts, soy sauce, hoisin, water, vinegar, cilantro, green onions and hot pepper sauce until smooth. Serve immediately or cover and refrigerate for up to 3 days.

Roasted Zucchini Dip

Makes about 1¼ cups (300 mL)

It's incredible what happens to zucchini when its roasted. Then you add sour cream and yum! Serve with crudités, such as carrot or celery sticks, or Crispy Zucchini Fingers (page 419) — the contrast of zucchini flavors is amazing.

● **Preheat oven to 350°F (180°C)**

1½ cups	coarsely chopped zucchini	375 mL
¼ cup	extra virgin olive oil	60 mL
¼ tsp	salt	1 mL
¼ tsp	freshly ground black pepper	1 mL
½ cup	sour cream (see Tip, page 13)	125 mL
1 tbsp	freshly squeezed lemon juice	15 mL
1 tsp	minced rinsed capers	5 mL

1. On a rimmed baking sheet, combine zucchini, oil, salt and pepper and mix well to coat. Roast in preheated oven until soft, about 15 minutes.
2. Transfer mixture to a food processor fitted with metal blade and pulse until smooth. Transfer to a bowl and add sour cream, lemon juice and capers and mix well to combine. Serve immediately or cover and refrigerate for up to 3 days.

Mushroom Tomato Spread

Makes about 1½ cups (375 mL)

When served with raw button mushrooms or spread on warm Grilled Herbed Crostini (page 220), this easy spread is very comforting.

Tip

Mushrooms contain a high proportion of water. By adding salt early in the cooking process water will be leached out of the mushrooms and evaporate, leaving them dry and flavorful.

1 tbsp	each olive oil and unsalted butter	15 mL
4 cups	sliced button mushrooms	1 L
2 tbsp	coarsely chopped drained oil-packed sun-dried tomatoes	30 mL
2	thyme sprigs	2
1 tsp	salt	5 mL
¼ cup	soft goat cheese	60 mL
1 tbsp	sherry vinegar	15 mL
1 tsp	thinly sliced green onions	5 mL

1. In a saucepan, heat oil and butter over medium heat. Add mushrooms, tomatoes, thyme and salt and cook, stirring, until all liquid from mushrooms is evaporated, about 10 minutes (see Tip, left). Remove from heat and discard thyme sprigs. Add goat cheese, sherry and onions.
2. Transfer to a food processor fitted with metal blade and pulse until smooth. Transfer to a serving bowl.

Artichoke and Olive Tapenade

Makes about 2 cups (500 mL)

Here's a slightly different spin on tapenade. With the addition of artichokes, it's a bit lighter than the norm. It's delicious served on warm pita or Crisp Pita Bread (page 216).

Tips

We always use flat-leaf rather than curly parsley because it has more flavor.

1	can (14 oz/398 mL) artichoke hearts, drained	1
½ cup	pitted black olives	125 mL
¼ cup	Italian flat-leaf parsley leaves	60 mL
2 tbsp	drained capers	30 mL
2 tbsp	freshly squeezed lemon juice	30 mL
2	anchovy fillets	2
2	cloves garlic	2
¼ cup	extra virgin olive oil	60 mL
	Salt and freshly ground black pepper	
	Paprika, optional	

1. In a food processor fitted with metal blade, pulse artichokes, olives, parsley, capers, lemon juice, anchovies and garlic until finely chopped, about 10 times. Add olive oil and pulse to blend, about 5 times. Season to taste with salt and pepper.

2. Transfer to a serving bowl. Cover and refrigerate for at least 2 hours or for up to 1 day. Dust lightly with paprika, if using, before serving.

Green Olive Tapenade

Makes about 1 cup (250 mL)

Vegan Friendly

If you're looking for something a little different, try this. It is much lighter than the traditional tapenade made with black olives. Served on crackers, crostini (pages 219 and 220) or sliced baguette, it makes a wonderful accompaniment to cocktails in the garden on a warm summer night.

1 cup	pitted drained green olives	250 mL
¼ cup	fresh basil leaves	60 mL
2	cloves garlic, coarsely chopped	2
1 tbsp	drained capers	15 mL
¼ cup	extra virgin olive oil	60 mL
1 tbsp	freshly squeezed lemon juice	15 mL

1. In a food processor fitted with metal blade, pulse olives, basil, garlic and capers until finely chopped. Add olive oil and lemon juice and pulse just until blended.

2. Transfer to a small serving bowl. Cover and refrigerate for at least 2 hours or for up to 3 days.

Parsley-Laced Tapenade

Makes about 1¼ cups (300 mL)

The addition of parsley and a roasted red pepper adds lightness to tapenade, which tends to be heavy. Serve this on sliced baguette or celery sticks or as part of an antipasto table.

Tip

For best results, use olives from the Mediterranean region. Do not use canned black olives, which are completely lacking in taste.

8 oz	pitted drained black olives (see Tip, left)	250 g
2 tbsp	drained capers	30 mL
1 cup	loosely packed Italian flat-leaf parsley leaves	250 mL
2	anchovy fillets	2
1	clove garlic, coarsely chopped	1
1	roasted red bell pepper, seeded and coarsely chopped	1
¼ cup	extra virgin olive oil	60 mL

1. In a food processor fitted with metal blade, pulse olives, capers, parsley, anchovies, garlic and roasted pepper until chopped and combined, about 10 times, stopping and scraping down sides of the bowl as necessary. Add olive oil and pulse until desired texture is achieved.

2. Transfer to a serving bowl. Serve immediately or cover and refrigerate for up to 3 days. If refrigerated, before serving, let stand at room temperature for about 20 minutes to allow the flavors to develop.

Tuna Tapenade

Makes about ¾ cup (175 mL)

Known as Provençal caviar, tapenade is a flavorful mixture of capers, olives and anchovies, among other ingredients. Here, the addition of tuna lightens up the result. Serve this with carrot or celery sticks, sliced cucumber, crackers or Basic Crostini (page 219). It also makes a delicious filling for hard-cooked eggs (see Variations, page 64).

1	can (6 oz/170 g) tuna, preferably Italian, packed in olive oil, drained	1
4	anchovy fillets	4
2 tbsp	drained capers	30 mL
1 tbsp	freshly squeezed lemon juice	15 mL
1	clove garlic, coarsely chopped	1
10	pitted black olives	10
¼ cup	extra virgin olive oil	60 mL

1. In a food processor fitted with metal blade, pulse tuna, anchovies, capers, lemon juice, garlic and olives until ingredients are combined but still chunky, about 10 times. Add olive oil and pulse until blended, about 5 times. Spoon into a bowl, cover tightly and refrigerate for at least 2 hours or for up to 3 days.

Anchoyade de Croze

Makes about 1½ cups (375 mL)

This unusual but delicious spread is named after the French cookbook author Austin de Croze, who invented it. It is traditionally spread on country bread brushed with olive oil and baked, a form of Bruschetta (page 231), but warm crostini or even sliced baguette work well, too.

Tips

Use the chile pepper of your choice. We have also made this using 1½ tbsp (22 mL) drained chopped hot pickled banana peppers, which produces a very nice result.

Orange blossom water is available in specialty stores and Middle Eastern markets. It is very strongly flavored. This quantity produces a nice result, but if you like the taste, add a bit more after the ingredients have been combined and pulse to blend.

4	dried figs	4
1	can (2 oz/60 g) anchovy fillets, drained (about 12)	1
12	blanched almonds (see Tips, page 103)	12
2	cloves garlic	2
1	small red onion, quartered	1
1	roasted red pepper (see Tips, page 24)	1
1	bottled chile pepper (see Tips, left)	1
¼ cup	fresh Italian flat-leaf parsley leaves	60 mL
¼ cup	fresh tarragon leaves	60 mL
2 tbsp	freshly squeezed lemon juice	30 mL
½ tsp	fennel seeds, crushed	2 mL
¼ cup	extra virgin olive oil (approx.)	60 mL
½ tsp	orange blossom water (see Tips, left)	2 mL
	Hot pepper sauce, optional	

1. In a bowl of warm water, soak figs until softened, about 15 minutes. Drain, remove tough stem ends and chop coarsely.

2. In a food processor fitted with metal blade, pulse figs, anchovies, almonds, garlic, red onion, roasted pepper, chile pepper, parsley, tarragon, lemon juice and fennel several times to chop. With motor running, add olive oil through feed tube and process until a smooth paste is formed, about 1 minute. Add orange blossom water, and hot pepper sauce to taste, if using.

3. Transfer to a serving bowl. Cover and refrigerate for at least 2 hours or for up to 3 days.

Lemon-Laced Butterbean Dip

Makes about 1 cup (250 mL)

Delicious and healthful, this Mediterranean-inspired dip is very easy to make. Serve it with Crisp Pita Bread (page 216), sliced baguette or crudités.

Tips

To soak lima beans: Bring dried beans to a boil in 6 cups (1.5 L) water over medium heat. Boil rapidly for 3 minutes. Cover, turn off element and let stand for 1 hour. Drain.

We always use flat-leaf rather than curly parsley because it has more flavor.

1 cup	dried lima beans, soaked (see Tip, left)	250 mL
¼ cup	freshly squeezed lemon juice	60 mL
¼ cup	extra virgin olive oil	60 mL
1 tsp	salt	5 mL
	Freshly ground black pepper	
½ cup	loosely packed Italian flat-leaf parsley leaves	125 mL
4	green onions, white part only, cut into chunks	4

1. In a large pot of water, cook soaked beans until tender, about 30 minutes. Scoop out about 1 cup (250 mL) of the cooking liquid and set aside. Drain beans, rinse under cold running water and pop out of their skins. Discard skins.

2. In a food processor fitted with metal blade, pulse cooked beans, lemon juice, olive oil, salt, and pepper to taste until blended, about 5 times. Gradually add just enough bean cooking water through the feed tube to make a smooth emulsion, pulsing to blend, about 10 times. Add parsley and green onions and pulse until chopped and integrated, about 5 times.

3. Transfer to a serving bowl. Cover and refrigerate for up to 2 days or until ready to use.

Feta-Spiked Edamame Dip

Makes about 2 cups (500 mL)

Healthful and refreshing, this delicious dip is also visually attractive — it's an extremely pretty shade of green. It's great with pita bread, tortilla chips, cucumber slices and celery sticks.

Tip

Because this dip contains arugula, which will become soggy, we don't recommend storing it for longer than overnight.

2 cups	frozen shelled edamame beans, thawed	500 mL
4 cups	packed baby arugula leaves	1 L
2	green onions, white part with a bit of green, cut into chunks	2
½ cup	crumbled feta cheese (about 3 oz/90 g)	125 mL
¼ cup	extra virgin olive oil	60 mL
2 tbsp	freshly squeezed lemon juice	30 mL
	Salt and freshly ground black pepper	

1. In a pot of boiling salted water, boil edamame beans until tender, about 2 minutes. Scoop off 1 cup (250 mL) of the cooking liquid and set aside. Drain beans and transfer to food processor. Add arugula and green onions and pulse until coarsely chopped.
2. Add feta, oil, lemon juice and salt and pepper to taste and process until smooth, about 1 minute. With motor running, add enough cooking liquid to make a smooth purée. Transfer to a serving bowl. Serve immediately.

Zucchini Hummus

Makes 1½ cups (375 mL)

Everyone loves hummus. Here's a version made from that garden favorite, zucchini. It has similar flavor notes to the traditional version, but is different enough to intrigue your taste buds. The addition of toasted sesame seeds adds pleasant texture, as well as flavor. It's great with warm pita bread.

3 cups	cubed zucchini (½ inch/1 cm)	750 mL
½ cup	Italian flat-leaf parsley leaves	125 mL
¼ cup	tahini	60 mL
¼ cup	extra virgin olive oil	60 mL
2 tbsp	freshly squeezed lemon juice	30 mL
2 tsp	ground cumin (see Tips, page 53)	10 mL
1	clove garlic	1
1 tsp	salt	5 mL
Pinch	cayenne pepper	Pinch
1 tbsp	toasted sesame seeds (see Tip, page 124)	15 mL
	Sweet paprika, optional	

1. In a food processor, process zucchini, parsley, tahini, oil, juice, cumin, garlic, salt and cayenne until smooth. Taste and adjust lemon juice and/or salt. Add sesame seeds and pulse to blend. Transfer to bowl and sprinkle with paprika.

Basil and White Bean Spread

Makes about 3 cups (750 mL)

If you don't tell, no one will ever guess how easy it is to make this delicious and sophisticated spread. Serve this with sliced baguette or crackers or use as a topping for crostini (pages 219 and 220). You'll need about 24 crostini.

2 cups	cooked drained white kidney (cannellini) beans (see Tip, page 237)	500 mL
2 cups	packed Italian flat-leaf parsley leaves (see Tips, page 48)	500 mL
2 tbsp	Basil Pesto (page 549) or store-bought	30 mL
4	cloves garlic, coarsely chopped	4
1 tbsp	extra virgin olive oil	15 mL
1 tbsp	freshly squeezed lemon juice	15 mL
	Salt and freshly ground black pepper	

1. In a food processor fitted with metal blade, process beans, parsley, basil pesto, garlic, olive oil and lemon juice until smooth, about 1 minute. Season to taste with salt and pepper. Transfer to a serving bowl. Serve immediately or cover and refrigerate for up to 2 days. If refrigerated, before serving, let stand at room temperature for about 20 minutes to allow the flavors to develop.

Refried Nachos

Makes about 4 cups (1 L)

A favorite of teenagers, nachos are also a great comfort food dish. In this recipe, the degree of spice depends upon the heat of the salsa and whether you add the optional chile. If you are heat averse, use a mild salsa and skip the chile. If you are a heat seeker, use a spicy one and add the chipotle pepper in adobe sauce. Serve with tortilla chips or tostadas.

1	can (14 oz/398 mL) refried beans	1
1 cup	tomato salsa	250 mL
1	jalapeño pepper, seeded and minced, or 1 chipotle pepper in adobo sauce, minced, optional	1
1	can (4½ oz/127 mL) chopped green chiles, drained	1
2 cups	shredded Cheddar or Monterey Jack cheese	500 mL
	Tortilla chips or tostadas	

1. In a saucepan over medium heat, bring beans, salsa, jalapeño and green chiles to a boil. Stir in cheese until melted. Serve with tortilla chips or tostadas for dipping. (You can also do this in the microwave. Place beans, salsa and chiles in a microwave-safe dish. Microwave on High until bubbling, about 4 minutes. Stir in cheese and microwave until melted, about 1½ minutes.)

Hummus from Scratch

Makes about 3 cups (750 mL)

Although it's more work, cooking dried chickpeas rather than using canned chickpeas produces the tastiest hummus. Try this and see if you agree. Warm pita or Crisp Pita Bread (page 216) is a favorite accompaniment, but it's also good with crudités. Hummus also makes a great sauce for grilled kabobs, particularly lamb and a great topping for roasted eggplant (see Variation, below).

Tips

If you're in a hurry, instead of setting the chickpeas aside to soak, cover the pot and bring to a boil. Boil for 3 minutes. Turn off heat and soak for 1 hour. Drain and rinse thoroughly with cold water. Then proceed with cooking as in Step 2.

For added flavor, when cooking the chickpeas (Step 2), add garlic, bay leaves or a bouquet garni made from your favorite herbs tied together in a cheesecloth bag.

1 cup	dried chickpeas (see Tips, left)	250 mL
1/3 cup	tahini	75 mL
1/3 cup	extra virgin olive oil	75 mL
1/4 cup	freshly squeezed lemon juice	60 mL
1/4 cup	Italian flat-leaf parsley leaves	60 mL
2	cloves garlic (approx.)	2
1 tsp	ground cumin (see Tips, page 53)	5 mL
1 tsp	salt (approx.)	5 mL
1/2 tsp	freshly ground black pepper	2 mL
1/4 tsp	cayenne pepper, optional	1 mL
	Sweet paprika, optional	

1. In a large saucepan, combine chickpeas and 3 cups (750 mL) cold water. Set aside to soak for at least 6 hours or overnight. Drain and rinse thoroughly with cold water.

2. Return drained chickpeas to saucepan and add 3 cups (750 mL) cold fresh water. Cover and bring to a boil over medium-high heat. Reduce heat and simmer until chickpeas are tender, about 1 hour. Scoop out about 1 cup (250 mL) of cooking water and set aside. Drain and rinse chickpeas.

3. In a food processor fitted with metal blade, process cooked chickpeas, tahini, olive oil, 1/4 cup (60 mL) of the cooking water and lemon juice until smooth, about 30 seconds, stopping and scraping down sides of the bowl as necessary. If necessary, add additional cooking water and pulse to blend. (You want the mixture to be quite creamy.) Add parsley, garlic, cumin, salt, pepper, and cayenne, if using, and process until smooth, about 15 seconds. Taste and adjust garlic, lemon juice and/or salt to suit your taste. Process again, if necessary. Spoon into a serving bowl and dust with paprika, if using.

Variation

Roasted Eggplant with Hummus: Cut 1 eggplant into 1/2-inch (1 cm) thick slices. Brush with olive oil and bake in a 400°F (200°C) oven for about 25 minutes. Top with hummus.

Easy Hummus

Makes about 1½ cups (375 mL)

Use as both a dip and a spread. Serve with crudités or Pita Chips (see Variations, page 216) or as a condiment on Mini Falafel Sandwiches (page 276).

Tip

We prefer to use no-salt-added chickpeas, which are usually available in organic or natural food sections in large grocery stores or fine food shops.

½ cup	water	125 mL
3	cloves garlic	3
2 cups	canned chickpeas, drained and rinsed (see Tip, left and page 55)	500 mL
¼ tsp	ground cumin (see Tips, page 53)	1 mL
½ tsp	hot pepper sauce	2 mL
1 tbsp	extra virgin olive oil	15 mL
1 tsp	salt	5 mL

1. In a medium saucepan, bring water and garlic to a boil over high heat. Reduce heat and boil gently until water is fully evaporated, about 10 minutes. Add chickpeas and cover and cook until chickpeas are tender to the touch, about 5 minutes. Add cumin, hot pepper sauce, olive oil and salt. Transfer to a food processor and purée until smooth, about 30 seconds, stopping and scraping down sides of the bowl as necessary. If hummus is too thick, add warm water to reach desired consistency.

Smoked Oyster Hummus

Makes about 3 cups (750 mL)

This intriguing spread is a variation on traditional Middle Eastern hummus. It always gets rave reviews. Serve with pita bread, Crisp Pita Bread (page 216) or crudités, such as celery sticks, peeled baby carrots or sliced cucumbers.

Tip

Use a bottled roasted red pepper or roast your own (see Tips, page 24).

2 cups	cooked chickpeas, drained and rinsed (see Tip, above and page 55)	500 mL
¼ cup	freshly squeezed lemon juice	60 mL
¼ cup	extra virgin olive oil	60 mL
1	large roasted red pepper (see Tip, left)	1
4	cloves garlic	4
½ tsp	salt	2 mL
1	can (3 oz/90 g) smoked oysters, drained	1
	Freshly ground black pepper	

1. In a food processor fitted with metal blade, process chickpeas, lemon juice, olive oil, roasted pepper, garlic and salt until smooth, about 30 seconds, stopping and scraping down sides of the bowl as necessary.
2. Add oysters and pulse just to chop and combine, about 5 times. Season to taste with pepper.

Cauliflower and Lentil Hummus Spiked with Cumin

Makes about 4 cups (1 L)

The next time you're having a party, try this deliciously different variation on the theme of hummus. This makes a big batch but can easily be halved. Serve with warm pita bread.

Tips

For this quantity of lentils, use 1 can (14 to 19 oz/ 398 to 540 mL) drained rinsed lentils or cook 1 cup (250 mL) dry lentils.

For best flavor, toast and grind cumin seeds yourself. *To toast seeds:* Place seeds in a dry skillet over medium heat, and cook, stirring, until fragrant, about 3 minutes. Immediately transfer to a mortar or a spice grinder and grind.

Aleppo chiles are Syrian in origin. They are moderately hot and quite fruity and lend pleasant authenticity to recipes with a Middle Eastern slant. A smaller quantity of cayenne will produce a similar amount of heat.

4 cups	cauliflower florets (1 small head), cooked and drained	1 L
2 cups	cooked drained brown or green lentils (see Tips, left)	500 mL
½ cup	extra virgin olive oil (approx.)	125 mL
⅓ cup	tahini	75 mL
¼ cup	freshly squeezed lemon juice	60 mL
6	green onions, white part with a bit of green, cut into chunks	6
½ cup	Italian flat-leaf parsley leaves	125 mL
4	cloves garlic, coarsely chopped	4
1 tbsp	ground cumin (see Tips, left)	15 mL
2 tsp	ground Aleppo pepper or ½ tsp (2 mL) cayenne pepper (see Tips, left)	10 mL
1 tsp	salt	5 mL
	Freshly ground black pepper	

1. In a food processor fitted with metal blade, process cooked cauliflower, lentils, olive oil, tahini and lemon juice until smooth, about 30 seconds, stopping and scraping down sides of the bowl as necessary. If necessary, add 1 to 2 tbsp (15 to 30 mL) of olive oil and pulse to blend. (You want the mixture to be quite creamy.)

2. Add green onions, parsley, garlic, cumin, Aleppo pepper, salt, and black pepper to taste and process until smooth, about 15 seconds. Taste and adjust garlic, lemon juice and/or salt to suit your taste. Process again, if necessary.

3. Transfer to a serving bowl. Serve immediately or refrigerate for up to 1 day. If refrigerated, before serving, let stand at room temperature for about 20 minutes to allow the flavors to develop.

Down-Home Hummus

Makes 3 cups (750 mL)

If you're a fan of hummus but are getting tired of the same old thing, try this variation on the theme. Black-eyed peas, peanuts and peanut butter stand in for chickpeas and tahini. Green bell pepper and sweet onion complete the Southern spin on this tasty and nutritious spread. Serve with crudités or warm pita bread.

Tips

For this quantity of black-eyed peas, use 1 can (14 to 19 oz/ 398 to 540 mL) drained and rinsed or cook 1 cup (250 mL) dried chickpeas.

If you have cooked the peas yourself, scoop out about 1 cup (250 mL) of the cooking water before draining and set aside.

1	green bell pepper, chopped	1
½ cup	roasted peanuts	125 mL
½	sweet onion, such as Vidalia or red onion, quartered	½
2	cloves garlic (approx.)	2
2 cups	cooked drained black-eyed peas (see Tips, left)	500 mL
2 tbsp	peanut butter	30 mL
2 tbsp	warm water or bean cooking water (approx.) (see Tip, left)	30 mL
2 tbsp	freshly squeezed lemon juice	30 mL
2 tbsp	extra virgin olive oil	30 mL
1 tsp	salt	5 mL
½ tsp	freshly ground black pepper	2 mL
¼ tsp	hot pepper sauce	1 mL

1. In a food processor fitted with metal blade, pulse bell pepper, peanuts, onion and garlic until finely chopped, about 10 times. Add peas, peanut butter, water, lemon juice, olive oil, salt, black pepper and hot pepper sauce and process until smooth, about 30 seconds, stopping and scraping down sides of the bowl as necessary. If necessary, add additional warm water and pulse to blend. (You want the mixture to be quite creamy.) Taste and adjust lemon juice, garlic and/or hot sauce to suit your taste. Process again, if necessary.

2. Transfer to a serving bowl. Serve immediately or cover and refrigerate for up to 1 day. If refrigerated, before serving, let stand at room temperature for about 20 minutes to allow the flavors to develop.

Roasted Red Pepper Hummus

Makes about 1¾ cups (425 mL)

This subtle twist on a classic dip is wonderful when spread on wedges of sweet bell pepper.

Tips

For this quality of chickpeas, use 1 can (14 to 19 oz/398 to 540 mL), drained and rinsed or cook 1 cup (250 mL) dried chickpeas.

For best flavor, toast and grind cumin seeds yourself. *To toast seeds:* Place seeds in a dry skillet over medium heat, and cook, stirring, until fragrant, about 3 minutes. Immediately transfer to a mortar or a spice grinder and grind.

- **Preheat oven to 300°F (150°C)**

1	red bell pepper	1
2 tbsp	extra virgin olive oil	30 mL
½ cup	water	125 mL
3	cloves garlic	3
2 cups	cooked chickpeas, drained and rinsed (see Tips, left)	500 mL
½ tsp	hot pepper sauce	2 mL
½ tsp	salt	2 mL
¼ tsp	ground cumin (see Tips, left)	1 mL

1. Rub bell pepper with oil to fully coat. Place in a baking dish and roast in preheated oven until skin is blistered but pepper still maintains its shape, about 45 minutes. Let cool. Over a bowl, using a strainer, peel and remove stem and seeds. Reserve residual liquid.

2. In a medium saucepan, bring water and garlic to a boil over high heat. Reduce heat and boil gently until water is fully evaporated, about 10 minutes. Add chickpeas and cover and cook until chickpeas are tender to the touch, about 5 minutes. Drain chickpeas and transfer to a food processor.

3. Add roasted pepper with reserved liquid, hot pepper sauce, salt and cumin and purée until smooth, about 30 seconds, stopping and scraping down sides of the bowl as necessary. If hummus is too thick, add warm water to reach desired consistency.

Oil-Poached Garlic Hummus

Makes about 1½ cups (375 mL)

Poached garlic in olive oil imparts the most delicate sweet garlic flavor you've ever tasted. Parsnip Chips (see Variations, page 213) would be great with this hummus.

Tips

For best flavor, toast and grind cumin yourself. *To toast seeds:* Place seeds in a dry skillet over medium heat and cook, stirring, until fragrant about 3 minutes. Immediately transfer to a mortar or a spice grinder and grind.

Garlic-flavored oil is wonderful to cook with and is even perfect in vinaigrettes. It should be kept refrigerated for up to 1 week only and then discarded.

2 cups	extra virgin olive oil	500 mL
½ cup	garlic cloves	125 mL
½ cup	water	125 mL
2 cups	cooked chickpeas, rinsed and drained (see Tips, page 55)	500 mL
1 tsp	grated lemon zest	10 mL
1 tbsp	freshly squeezed lemon juice	15 mL
½ tsp	salt	2 mL
¼ tsp	ground cumin (see Tip, left)	1 mL

1. In a medium saucepan over medium heat, bring olive oil and garlic to a simmer. Reduce heat to keep oil hot, but not simmering, and poach until soft, 15 to 20 minutes. Be sure to watch closely and adjust the temperature to avoid burning, which will impart a very bitter flavor. Using a slotted spoon, transfer garlic to a bowl and set aside.

2. In another medium saucepan, bring water to a boil over high heat. Add chickpeas and cover until chickpeas are very soft and hot. Drain and transfer to a food processor. Add poached garlic, lemon zest and juice, salt, cumin and ¼ cup (60 mL) of the reserved olive oil and purée until smooth, about 30 seconds, stopping and scraping down sides of the bowl as necessary. If hummus is too thick, add warm water to reach desired consistency. Serve immediately or refrigerate up to 3 days.

Walnut Hummus

Makes about 1½ cups (375 mL)

If you're looking for something a little different, try this tasty spin on hummus, made with walnuts instead of chickpeas. It is particularly delicious served on a strip of crisp sweet red pepper, but also works well with other crudités, as well as pita bread.

1½ cups	walnut halves	375 mL
2 tbsp	tahini	30 mL
2 tbsp	freshly squeezed lemon juice	30 mL
1 tbsp	extra virgin olive oil	15 mL
1	clove garlic, chopped	1
½ tsp	hot paprika	2 mL
½ tsp	salt	2 mL
	Freshly ground black pepper	

1. In a food processor fitted with metal blade, process walnuts, tahini, lemon juice, olive oil, garlic, paprika and salt until smooth, about 30 seconds, stopping and scraping down sides of the bowl as necessary. Season to taste with pepper and pulse to blend.

2. Transfer to a serving bowl. Serve immediately or cover and refrigerate for up to 1 day. If refrigerated, before serving, let stand at room temperature for about 20 minutes to allow the flavors to develop.

Black Bean Spread

Makes about 1¼ cups (300 mL)

Ole! This spread is an amazing addition to any Mexican-inspired appetizer such as Chicken and Black Bean Quesadillas (page 476) or Ultimate Nachos (page 212).

1½ cups	canned cooked black beans, drained and rinsed	375 mL
1 cup	water	250 mL
½ tsp	salt	2 mL
¼ tsp	ground cumin (see Tip, page 56)	1 mL
1 tbsp	coarsely chopped fresh cilantro leaves	15 mL

1. In a pot over medium heat, bring beans, water, salt and cumin to a boil. Transfer to a blender or use an immersion blender and purée until smooth. Return beans to stove and, over medium-low heat, simmer, stirring constantly, until thick, about 20 minutes. Remove from heat. Add cilantro and mix thoroughly to combine. Serve immediately or cover and refrigerate for up to 3 days.

Hot and Smoky Bean Dip

Makes about 3 cups (750 mL)

Served bubbling hot, this cheesy dip with just a hint of spice and smoke makes a great cold weather treat. Serve with tortilla chips, tostadas or sliced baguette.

Tip

For this quality of black-eyed peas, use 1 can (14 to 19 oz/398 to 540 mL), drained and rinsed or cook 1 cup (250 mL) dried black-eyed peas.

- **Preheat oven to 350°F (180°C)**

2 cups	cooked drained black-eyed peas (see Tip, left)	500 mL
1	roasted red pepper (see Tips, page 24)	1
2	green onions, white part with a bit of green, cut into chunks	2
2 tbsp	drained chopped pickled hot banana peppers	30 mL
1 to 2 tsp	smoked paprika	5 to 10 mL
2 cups	shredded Cheddar cheese	500 mL
¼ cup	mayonnaise	60 mL
¼ cup	sour cream	60 mL

1. In a food processor fitted with metal blade, pulse peas, roasted pepper, green onions, banana peppers and paprika until chopped and blended, about 20 times. Add cheese, mayonnaise and sour cream and process until desired texture is achieved. Transfer to an ovenproof serving dish and bake in preheated oven until hot and bubbling, about 20 minutes.

Chive and Navy Bean Dip

Makes about 1½ cups (375 mL)

Raw chives add a wonderful peppery note to the navy beans. This dip is perfect with crisp tortilla chips or Beet Chips (page 213).

¼ cup	extra virgin olive oil	60 mL
1⅓ cups	cooked white navy beans	325 mL
1¼ cups	coarsely chopped fresh chives	300 mL
¼ cup	raw peanuts	60 mL
1 tsp	salt	5 mL
1 tsp	sherry vinegar	5 mL

1. In a saucepan, heat oil over medium heat. Add beans, chives and peanuts and cook, stirring, until chives are bright green and soft, 3 to 5 minutes. Remove from heat. Add salt and vinegar. Transfer to a food processor fitted with metal blade and pulse until smooth. Transfer to a serving bowl. Serve immediately or cover and refrigerate for up to 3 days.

BTs on Lettuce

Makes about 1½ cups (375 mL)

This dip is meant to capture the lusciousness of a BLT sandwich made with fresh ripe tomatoes.

Tip

Chilled wedges of iceberg lettuce, hearts of romaine or even radicchio make a perfect base for this dip.

4 oz	cream cheese, softened	125 g
¼ cup	buttermilk	60 mL
2 tbsp	mayonnaise	30 mL
1	clove garlic	1
1	large tomato, peeled, seeded and quartered	1
6	slices bacon, cooked and crumbled	6
½ cup	Italian flat-leaf parsley leaves	125 mL
3	green onions, white part with a bit of green, cut into chunks	3
	Lettuce (see Tip, left)	

1. In a food processor fitted with metal blade, purée cream cheese, buttermilk, mayonnaise and garlic. Add tomato, bacon, parsley and green onions and pulse until chopped and blended, about 6 times.
2. Transfer to a serving bowl. Serve immediately with crisp cold lettuce or cover and refrigerate for up to 2 days.

Greek Salad Dip

Makes about 1¾ cups (425 mL)

Vegetarian Friendly

Serve this dip with warm pita bread or Crisp Pita Bread (page 216). If you're looking for a showstopper presentation, hollow out a whole rye bread and fill the cavity with Greek Salad Dip. Tear the rye "flesh" into large two-bite pieces and use that as the dipper...it's yummy!

1 cup	crumbled feta cheese	250 mL
½ cup	heavy or whipping (35%) cream	125 mL
½ cup	grated English cucumber	125 mL
½ cup	finely chopped ripe tomato	125 mL
1 tbsp	grated red onion	15 mL
1 tbsp	minced kalamata olives	15 mL

1. In a bowl, mash together feta and cream until smooth. Fold in cucumber, tomato, red onion and olives. Cover and refrigerate overnight before serving.

Variation

Add ¼ cup (60 mL) Champagne or white wine vinegar to this recipe to create a wonderful vinaigrette suitable for any salad but specifically great on a Greek one.

Taramasalata

Makes about 1 cup (250 mL)

This delicious concoction is a fixture of Greek mezes. Serve with grilled pita bread.

Tips

Tarama (carp roe) is available in stores specializing in Greek provisions.

After soaking and squeezing the bread dry, you should have about $\frac{1}{2}$ cup (125 mL).

$\frac{1}{2}$ cup	tarama, thoroughly rinsed under cold running water and drained (see Tips, left)	125 mL
1	small red onion, quartered	1
2	thick slices day-old white bread, crusts removed, soaked in water and squeezed dry (see Tips, left)	2
$\frac{1}{4}$ cup	freshly squeezed lemon juice	60 mL
$\frac{1}{2}$ cup	extra virgin olive oil	125 mL
	Pita bread	
	Crudités, optional	

1. In a food processor fitted with metal blade, process tarama and red onion for 1 minute. Add bread and process until smooth. Add lemon juice and pulse to blend. With motor running, add oil through feed tube and process until pale pink and very creamy.
2. Transfer to a serving bowl. Cover and refrigerate for at least 2 hours or for up to 2 days. Serve with pita bread or crudités, if desired.

Honey Mustard Dip

Makes about 1$\frac{1}{2}$ cups (375 mL)

Vegetarian Friendly

Serve with Ham and Cheese Crostini (page 222) or Sesame and Parmesan Pizza Sticks (page 254) for dipping. This sweet and spicy dip will also pair with Spice-Rubbed Rack of Lamb (page 467) or Lamb and Red Onion Sliders (page 269).

$\frac{1}{2}$ cup	liquid honey or agave syrup	125 mL
$\frac{1}{2}$ cup	Dijon mustard	125 mL
$\frac{1}{4}$ cup	grainy (Pommery) mustard	60 mL
$\frac{1}{4}$ cup	crème fraîche, sour cream or plain yogurt	60 mL
2 tbsp	apple cider vinegar	30 mL
1 tbsp	chopped thyme leaves	15 mL

1. In a bowl, combine honey, Dijon, Pommery, crème fraîche, vinegar and thyme until smooth. Serve immediately or cover and refrigerate for up to 3 days. Bring the dip to room temperature before serving.

Pommery Mustard Dip

Makes about 1½ cups (375 mL)

Use as a garnish for sliders (pages 265 to 269) or a dip for crudités — but remember, no double dipping!

Tip

Pommery or stone-ground mustard is made from spices, vinegar and whole mustard seeds and is widely used in France. A classic Dijon would work well in its place.

1 cup	crème fraîche	250 mL
¼ cup	grainy (Pommery) mustard (see Tip, left)	60 mL
¼ cup	ricotta cheese	60 mL
1 tbsp	soft goat cheese	15 mL
1 tsp	finely chopped fresh thyme leaves	5 mL
½ tsp	hot pepper flakes	2 mL
½ tsp	Champagne vinegar or white wine vinegar	2 mL
¼ tsp	salt	1 mL
¼ tsp	freshly ground black pepper	1 mL

1. In a bowl, combine crème fraîche, mustard, ricotta, goat cheese, thyme, hot pepper flakes, vinegar, salt and pepper until smooth. Serve immediately or cover and refrigerate for up to 3 days. Bring dip to room temperature before serving.

Roasted Garlic Sour Cream Dip

Makes about 1½ cups (375 mL)

It's amazing how sweet garlic can become when roasted. Serve with Homemade Potato Chips (page 215), Salt-Roasted Potatoes (page 405) or Bacon-Spiked Rösti Cakes (page 407).

Tip

We prefer to use full-fat or whole milk yogurt and sour cream in this recipe because it has a deeper flavor profile but if you prefer, use a lower-fat alternative.

• **Preheat oven to 400°F (200°C)**

2	bulbs garlic	2
2 tbsp	extra virgin olive oil	30 mL
¼ tsp	salt	1 mL
½ cup	plain yogurt (see Tip, left)	125 mL
½ cup	sour cream	125 mL
1 tsp	finely chopped chives	5 mL

1. Cut whole garlic bulbs in half along their "equator" and thoroughly coat with olive oil. Combine the two halves and wrap in foil. Roast in preheated oven until bulbs are soft, about 1 hour. Let cool to room temperature. Squeeze garlic out of skins into a bowl to release caramelized cloves. Sprinkle with salt.

2. In a bowl, combine ½ cup (125 mL) roasted garlic, yogurt, sour cream and chives. Cover and refrigerate overnight to allow flavors to meld or for up to 3 days.

Smoked Salmon Sour Cream Spread

Makes about 1⅓ cups (325 mL)

This smoky spread is has more texture than most and would be perfect on flatbread, sliced baguette, cut into bite-sizes pieces for afternoon tea or even as a variation in Steamed Leek and Smoked Salmon Pinwheels (page 143).

¾ cup	sour cream (see Tip, page 61)	175 mL
½ cup	finely diced smoked salmon	125 mL
1 tbsp	grated lemon zest	15 mL
1 tbsp	finely diced gherkins	15 mL
½ tsp	coarsely chopped fresh dill fronds	2 mL

1. In a bowl, combine sour cream, smoked salmon, lemon zest, gherkins and dill. Serve immediately or cover and refrigerate for up to 3 days.

Tuna and Roasted Red Pepper Dip

Makes about 1 cup (250 mL)

This tasty dip is great with crudités, crackers, crostini or even plain sliced baguette.

Tips

You can use drained bottled roasted peppers or roast and peel them yourself (see Tips, page 24).

Piment d'Espelette is a dried mild chile pepper from the Basque region of France. It adds a nice flavor to this recipe, but if you don't have it, cayenne pepper makes a fine substitute.

1	jar (7 oz/210 g) Italian or Spanish tuna, packed in olive oil, drained	1
⅓ cup	mayonnaise	75 mL
2	red bell peppers, roasted and quartered (see Tips, page 24) or store-bought	2
2 tbsp	drained capers	30 mL
1 tbsp	freshly squeezed lemon juice	15 mL
¼ tsp	piment d'Espelette or ⅛ tsp (0.5 mL) cayenne pepper (see Tips, left)	1 mL

1. In a food processor fitted with metal blade, process tuna, mayonnaise, roasted peppers, capers, lemon juice and piment d'Espelette until smooth, about 15 seconds.
2. Transfer to a serving bowl. Cover and chill for at least 4 hours or overnight.

Tuna and Artichoke Scoop

Makes about 2 cups (500 mL)

Canned tuna and artichokes are great convenience foods. They also taste very good together. Serve this with sliced baguette, crackers or crudités.

Tips

To hard-cook eggs: Place eggs in a saucepan in a single layer and add cold water to cover by 1 inch (2.5 cm). Cover and bring to a boil over high heat. Remove from heat and let stand for 10 minutes. Using a slotted spoon, transfer to a bowl of ice water. Let cool for 5 minutes. Remove eggshells under cool running water.

When serving cold dips, particularly those that contain a high proportion of dairy, consider lining a deep platter with crushed ice and use it to surround the bowl. Arranging crudités over the ice will help to keep them nicely chilled as well.

2	hard-cooked eggs, yolks and whites separated (see Tips, left)	2
⅓ cup	extra virgin olive oil	75 mL
1 tsp	salt	5 mL
½ tsp	freshly ground black pepper	2 mL
1 tbsp	white wine vinegar	15 mL
1	can (14 oz/398 mL) artichoke hearts, drained	1
1	can (6 oz/170 g) tuna, drained	1
1	red bell pepper, roasted and quartered (see Tips, page 24) or store-bought	1
1	clove garlic, coarsely chopped	1
2 tbsp	toasted pine nuts	30 mL
2 tbsp	Italian flat-leaf parsley leaves	30 mL

1. Press cooked egg yolks through a fine sieve into a bowl. Gradually whisk in oil until combined. Whisk in salt, pepper and vinegar until combined. Set aside.

2. In a food processor fitted with metal blade, pulse egg whites, artichokes, tuna, roasted pepper, garlic, pine nuts and parsley until chopped, about 10 times. Add egg yolk mixture and pulse until blended, about 5 times.

3. Transfer to a serving bowl. Cover and refrigerate for at least 3 hours or for up to 2 days.

Tonnato

Makes about 1½ cups (375 mL)

Don't be fooled by the simplicity of this recipe: it is a mouthwatering combination. Amazingly versatile, this ambrosial mixture excels as a dip. Make it the centerpiece of a tasting platter, surrounded by celery sticks and cucumber slices or tender leaves of Belgian endive. It also performs well as a topping for asparagus (see Variations, right) or as sauce for plated appetizers or salade composée, for which the ingredients are arranged on a plate rather than tossed together) (see Variations, right).

Tip

Don't confuse real mayonnaise with "mayonnaise-type" salad dressings, which are similar in appearance. Mayonnaise is a combination of egg yolks, vinegar or lemon juice, olive oil and seasonings. Imitators will contain additional ingredients, such as sugar, flour or milk. Make your own or make sure the label says mayonnaise and check the ingredients.

¾ cup	mayonnaise	175 mL
½ cup	Italian flat-leaf parsley leaves	125 mL
2	green onions, white part only, cut into 2-inch (5 cm) lengths	2
1 tbsp	drained capers, optional	15 mL
1	can (6 oz/170 g) tuna, preferably Spanish or Italian, packed in olive oil, drained	1
	Freshly ground black pepper	
	Crudités (see page 31)	

1. In a food processor fitted with metal blade, process mayonnaise, parsley, green onions, and capers, if using, until smooth. Add tuna and pepper to taste. Pulse until chopped and blended, about 15 times.

2. Transfer to a small bowl and serve surrounded by crudités for dipping. If not using immediately, cover and refrigerate for up to 3 days.

Variations

Tonnato-Stuffed Eggs: (Serves 6 to 8) Hard-cook 4 eggs (see Tips, page 63). Let cool and peel. Cut in half lengthwise. Pop out the yolks and mash with ¼ cup (60 mL) Tonnato. Mound the mixture back into the whites. Dust with 1 tsp (5 mL) paprika, if desired.

If you prefer a plated appetizer, simply cut the peeled cooked eggs in half, arrange them on a platter and spoon the sauce over top.

Asparagus with Tonnato: (Serves 4) Arrange 1 can or jar (16 oz/330 g approx.) white asparagus, drained, on a small platter or serving plate. Top with ¼ cup (60 mL) Tonnato. Use cooked fresh green asparagus in season, if desired. You can also turn this into a salad by spreading a layer of salad greens over a large platter. Arrange the asparagus over the greens and top with Tonnato.

Dill-Spiked Crab Scoop

Makes about 3 cups (750 mL)

Fresh, light and easy to make, this tasty starter is very festive because crab is a luxury item. Serve it with vegetable sticks, leaves of Belgian endive, baguette or crackers. You can also use it to fill avocado halves (see Variation, below).

Tips

If you are using celery hearts, which produce the best results, add any leaves to the work bowl along with the celery.

Our preference is the pasteurized crabmeat, which you can find in cans in the refrigerated section of supermarkets. But regular canned or thawed drained frozen crabmeat works well, too.

½ cup	mayonnaise	125 mL
¼ cup	fresh dill fronds	60 mL
4	green onions, white part with just a hint of green, cut into 3-inch (7.5 cm) chunks	4
1	small shallot, quartered	1
2	stalks celery, cut into 3-inch (7.5 cm) chunks (see Tips, left)	2
2 tbsp	extra virgin olive oil	30 mL
2 tbsp	freshly squeezed lemon juice	30 mL
1 tsp	salt	5 mL
	Freshly ground white pepper	
2 cups	drained cooked crabmeat (about 1 lb/500 g) (see Tips, left)	500 mL

1. In a food processor fitted with metal blade, pulse mayonnaise, dill, green onions, shallot, celery, olive oil, lemon juice, salt, and white pepper to taste until vegetables are chopped and mixture is blended, about 10 times, stopping and scraping down sides of the bowl as necessary. Add crabmeat and pulse until nicely integrated, about 5 times.

2. Transfer to a serving bowl. Cover and refrigerate for at least 2 hours or overnight.

Variation

Crab-Stuffed Avocado: If you have leftovers, use them to stuff avocado halves. It makes a great lunch or a plated appetizer.

Ham and Roasted Pepper Spread with Hearts of Palm

Makes 1½ cups (375 mL)

This spread, which has retro overtones, is updated with the addition of hearts of palm for dipping. This tropical vegetable is widely available in cans and adds an exotic touch to this simple, yet very tasty spread.

Tips

Use bottled roasted peppers or roast them yourself (see Tips, page 24.)

Soaking the hearts of palm in acidulated water (Step 2) removes any tinny taste that may come from the can.

2	red bell peppers, roasted and coarsely chopped (see Tips, left) or store-bought	2
4 oz	Black Forest ham, coarsely chopped	125 g
1	long green or jalapeño pepper, seeded and quartered	1
3 tbsp	mayonnaise	45 mL
3 tbsp	freshly squeezed lemon juice, divided	45 mL
1 tbsp	extra virgin olive oil	15 mL
½ tsp	Worcestershire sauce	2 mL
	Salt and freshly ground black pepper	
2	cans (each 14 oz/398 mL) hearts of palm (see Tips, left)	2

1. In a food processor fitted with metal blade, process roasted peppers, ham, chile pepper, mayonnaise, 1 tbsp (15 mL) of the lemon juice, olive oil, Worcestershire sauce, and salt and pepper to taste until smooth. Transfer to a serving bowl. Cover and refrigerate for at least 3 hours or overnight.

2. One hour before you're ready to serve, drain hearts of palm. Place in a long shallow baking dish and add water to cover. Add remaining 2 tbsp (30 mL) of lemon juice. Cover and refrigerate.

3. When you're ready to serve, drain and cut individual hearts lengthwise into halves or quarters, depending upon their size. Place bowl of spread in the center of a platter and surround with palm slices. To serve, spread ham mixture evenly over sliced hearts of palm.

Variation

Instead of hearts of palm serve this spread with celery sticks, cucumber slices or pita bread.

Blueberry and Yogurt Dip

Makes about 1½ cups (375 mL)

This is perfect with Fruit Skewers (page 330) or fresh peach or apple wedges. Use the leftovers on your breakfast cereal.

Tip

When serving cold dips, particularly those that contain a high proportion of dairy, consider lining a deep platter with crushed ice and use it to surround the bowl. Arranging crudités over the ice will help to keep them nicely chilled as well.

⅔ cup	blueberries	150 mL
½ cup	water	125 mL
2 tbsp	agave syrup	30 mL
1 cup	plain yogurt	250 mL
½ tsp	grated lemon zest	2 mL
¼ tsp	vanilla extract	1 mL

1. In a saucepan, combine blueberries, water and agave and bring to a boil over medium heat. Reduce heat and boil gently until liquid is reduced by one-quarter. Transfer to a blender or use an immersion blender and purée until smooth.

2. Transfer to a bowl and let cool to room temperature. Fold in yogurt, lemon zest and vanilla until smooth. Serve immediately or cover and refrigerate for up to 3 days.

Variation

Try crème fraîche or sour cream in place of yogurt in this recipe. They impart a tasty sour note.

Fig Yogurt Dip

Makes about 1½ cups (375 mL)

This dip is perfect for fresh cut apples, pears or strawberries.

Tip

Fig purée can be found in most gourmet shops and sometimes in large supermarkets.

1 cup	plain yogurt (see Tip, page 61)	250 mL
2 tbsp	fig purée (see Tip, left)	30 mL
1 tbsp	packed brown sugar	15 mL
1 tbsp	pure maple syrup	15 mL
1 tbsp	grated lemon zest	15 mL
1 tbsp	freshly squeezed lemon juice	15 mL

1. In a bowl, combine yogurt, fig purée, brown sugar, maple syrup, lemon zest and juice. Cover and refrigerate for 1 hour before serving or store for up to 3 days.

Champagne and Raspberry Dip

Makes about 1½ cups (375 mL)

Each bite is like a delightful sip of a Kir Royale. Serve this dip next to a bowl of fresh strawberries and a glass of Champagne for an excellent brunch or dessert offering.

½ cup	Champagne or Prosecco	125 mL
1 tbsp	granulated sugar	15 mL
½ cup	golden or red raspberries	125 mL
1 tsp	apricot jam	5 mL
1	fresh basil leaf	1
½ cup	whipped cream	125 mL

1. In a saucepan, bring Champagne and sugar to a boil over medium heat. Reduce heat and boil gently until reduced by three-quarters, about 5 minutes. Remove from heat. Add raspberries, jam and basil leaf. Transfer to a blender or use an immersion blender and purée until smooth. Let cool to room temperature.

2. Fold whipped cream, one-third at a time, into raspberry mixture and serve immediately.

Mango Dip

Makes about 1¾ cups (425 mL)

Close your eyes and take a bite...off to the tropics you go! Enjoy with fresh cut fruit, Sweet Wontons (page 526) or Raspberry Puff Pastry Fingers (page 531).

Tip

The simplest way to peel a mango is with a vegetable peeler. Use a paring knife to cut away the flesh from the pit.

1 cup	chopped mango (see Tip, left)	250 mL
1 cup	water	250 mL
1 tbsp	granulated sugar	15 mL
1 tsp	coarsely chopped fresh mint leaves	5 mL
½ tsp	Champagne vinegar or apple cider vinegar	2 mL
1 cup	whipped cream	250 mL

1. In a saucepan, bring mango, water and sugar to a boil over medium heat. Reduce heat to low and simmer until liquid is reduced by half and mango is very soft, about 8 minutes. Add mint and vinegar. Transfer to a blender or use an immersion blender and purée until smooth. Transfer to a bowl and let cool to room temperature.

2. Fold whipped cream, one-third at a time, into mango purée and refrigerate for at least 1 hour before serving.

Salsas

With a rainbow of textures and flavors, from salty and sweet to spicy and sour, salsas are the ultimate condiment. Made with fresh, seasonal ingredients, they are refreshing and nutritious. Most people know salsas as tomato-based dips for tortilla chips but they are a great deal more. As you'll see, they can contain many different kinds of ingredients, from raw bananas and tropical fruits to cooked beans and corn, and dried fruit. The combinations are endless.

    In this chapter, you'll find many recipes that are very simple to make but mouthwateringly delicious. Use our salsas on their own as a dip, or to liven up another dish such as Carnitas (page 343). Or have some fun and create a first-course salsa bar. Prepare two or three salsa recipes and accompany them with a selection of dippers such as tortilla chips, Green Plantain Chips (page 211), rice crackers, cucumber slices — whatever strikes your fancy as compatible combinations.

Summer Tomato Salsa	70
Fresh Tomato Salsa	70
Green Tomato Salsa	71
Fresh Salsa Verde	71
Tomato Balsamic "Jam"	72
Tomato and Spinach Salsa	72
Bloody Mary Salsa	73
Roasted Onion Salsa	73
Roasted Beet Salsa	74
Eggplant and Date Salsa	75
Warm Eggplant Salsa	76
Roasted Red Pepper Salsa	76
Navy Bean Salsa	77
Kidney Bean Salsa	77
Edamame Salsa	78
Red Radish and Goat Cheese Salsa	78
Asparagus Salsa	79
Green Bean Salsa	80
Roasted Cubanelle Pepper and Black Bean Salsa	80
Portobello Mushroom and Feta Cheese Salsa	81
Warm Mushroom Salsa	82
Roasted Corn Salsa	82
Cucumber and Roasted Corn Salsa	83
Avocado Corn Salsa	83
Avocado Black Bean Salsa	84
Pepper Confetti Salsa	84
Warm Banana Salsa	85
Black Bean and Pineapple Salsa	85
Chipotle Pineapple Salsa	86
Pineapple Banana Salsa	86
Minty Mango Salsa	87
Pineapple Mango Salsa	87
Classic Mango Salsa	88
Mango Water Chestnut Salsa	88
Margarita Mango Salsa	89
Thai-Inspired Green Mango Salsa	89
Apple Salsa	90
Cucumber Watermelon Salsa	90
Apple and Dried Cranberry Salsa	91
Strawberry and Rhubarb Salsa	91
Feta-Spiked Watermelon Salsa with Chile	92
Tropical Fruit Salsa	92
Jicama Salsa	93
Suneeta's Cilantro Mint Chutney	93
Yogurt Mint Chutney	94
Date and Tamarind Chutney	94
Jicama Strawberry Salsa	95
Spicy Nectarine Salsa	95
Shrimp Salsa	96
Warm Salami and Red Pepper Salsa	96

Summer Tomato Salsa

Makes about 1½ cups (375 mL)

Nothing says summer like a beautiful tomato. Warm Grilled Herbed Crostini (page 220), Pita Chips (see Variations, page 216) or tortilla chips would be the usual pairings and all are fantastic.

1¼ cups	diced tomato	300 mL
½ cup	finely diced shallots	125 mL
5 tsp	extra virgin olive oil	25 mL
1 tbsp	chiffonade fresh basil (see Tip, page 76)	15 mL
1 tsp	balsamic vinegar	5 mL
½ tsp	salt	2 mL
⅛ tsp	freshly ground black pepper	0.5 mL

1. In a bowl, combine tomato, shallots, olive oil, basil, vinegar, salt and pepper. Cover and let stand at room temperature for at least 1 hour to allow flavors to meld or for up to 4 hours.

Fresh Tomato Salsa

Makes about 2¼ cups (550 mL)

This is a Mexican fresh salsa, often called pico de gallo. Make it when tomatoes are in season — otherwise the results are likely to be disappointing. It's delicious with tortilla chips. It also makes a great accompaniment to Carnitas (page 343), Corn Cakes (page 199) and Corn Arepas (page 187).

Tip

Using puréed rather than minced garlic ensures it is evenly distributed throughout the salsa, producing just a welcome hint of flavor.

2 cups	diced (¼ inch/0.5 cm) ripe field tomatoes	500 mL
¼ cup	very finely chopped red or green onion	60 mL
¼ cup	very finely chopped fresh cilantro leaves	60 mL
1 to 2	jalapeño peppers or 2 to 4 serrano chiles, seeded and minced	1 to 2
1	clove garlic, puréed (see Tip, left, and page 128)	1
1 tbsp	freshly squeezed lime juice	15 mL
½ to 1 tsp	salt	2 to 5 mL

1. In a bowl, combine tomatoes, green onion, cilantro, chile pepper to taste, garlic, lime juice and salt to taste. Toss to combine. Set aside at room temperature for 15 minutes to meld flavors. Serve within 3 hours of preparation. Left to sit the tomatoes become soggy and the onion and garlic start to dominate.

Green Tomato Salsa

Makes about 1½ cups (375 mL)

This recipe proves that green tomatoes can be as tasty as those pretty red ones. Crunchy tortilla chips, crisp Beet Chips (page 213) or Crisp Pita Bread (page 216) would all pair perfectly with this flavorful salsa.

1¼ cups	diced green tomatoes	300 mL
¼ cup	finely diced onion	60 mL
¼ cup	diced red tomato	60 mL
2 tbsp	freshly squeezed lime juice	30 mL
1 tsp	minced garlic	5 mL
½ tsp	ground cumin (see Tips, page 56)	2 mL
¼ tsp	finely diced seeded jalapeño	1 mL
¼ tsp	salt	1 mL

1. In a bowl, combine green tomatoes, onion, red tomato, lime juice, garlic, cumin, jalapeño and salt. Cover and let stand at room temperature for 1 hour to allow flavors to meld or for up to 4 hours.

Fresh Salsa Verde

Makes about 1 cup (250 mL)

This is a Mexican "raw" salsa made with cooked tomatillos instead of tomatoes. Although you can use drained canned tomatillos, the taste is much brighter when made with those that are fresh. Increasingly, this bitter fruit is being grown throughout North America, so look for it at farmers' markets. Serve with tortilla chips, Carnitas (page 343) or arepas (pages 186 to 187).

2 cups	fresh tomatillos (about 9), husked	500 mL
1 to 2	jalapeño peppers, coarsely chopped	1 to 2
2 tbsp	coarsely chopped red or green onion	30 mL
1	clove garlic, coarsely chopped	1
½ cup	packed fresh cilantro leaves	125 mL
½ tsp	salt	2 mL

1. In a small saucepan over medium heat, combine tomatillos and water to cover. Bring to a boil. Reduce heat and simmer just until tender, about 10 minutes. Drain, let cool slightly and transfer to a food processor fitted with metal blade. Pulse to chop, 2 or 3 times. Add jalapeños to taste, onion, garlic, cilantro and salt and pulse until jalapeños are finely chopped and mixture is well integrated, about 10 times. Set aside at room temperature for 15 minutes to allow flavors to meld. Serve within 3 hours of preparation.

Tomato Balsamic "Jam"

Makes about 1 cup (250 mL)

If you're looking for a twist on the regular tomato salsa, this is definitely it! This is a fantastic accompaniment to crostini (pages 219 and 220) or sliced cucumber or atop halved cherry tomatoes.

2 tbsp	balsamic vinegar	30 mL
1½ cups	diced seeded tomato	375 mL
1 tsp	coarsely chopped fresh oregano leaves	5 mL
¼ tsp	salt	1 mL
	Freshly ground black pepper	

1. In a small saucepan, bring balsamic vinegar to a boil over medium-high heat. Reduce heat and simmer until vinegar is reduced to a syrup consistency, about 3 minutes. Remove from heat and add tomatoes, oregano, salt, and pepper to taste. Let cool to room temperature and serve.

Tomato and Spinach Salsa

Makes about 1½ cups (375 mL)

This tasty salsa can garnish the perfect crisp Savory Baked Crostini (page 220), Homemade Potato Chips (page 215) or even for Black Bean and Feta Shooter (page 113).

Tip

Chiffonade is a French culinary term for slicing into thin ribbons — in this case spinach. Stack spinach leaves into a neat pile and roll into a small cigar shape. With a sharp knife, slice across the cigar to form thin ribbons and delicately fluff the spinach with your hands to separate.

1¼ cups	diced ripe tomato	300 mL
1 cup	chiffonade spinach leaves (see Tip, left)	250 mL
2 tbsp	extra virgin olive oil	30 mL
1 tsp	freshly squeezed lemon juice	5 mL
1	clove garlic, thinly sliced or minced	1
¼ tsp	chopped fresh thyme leaves	1 mL
⅛ tsp	salt	0.5 mL
⅛ tsp	freshly ground black pepper	0.5 mL

1. In a bowl, combine tomato, spinach, olive oil, lemon juice, garlic, thyme, salt and pepper. Serve within 3 hours of preparation.

Bloody Mary Salsa

Makes about 1½ cups (375 mL)

Here's a wonderful alternative to the real deal! For the perfect pairing serve this atop peeled celery stalks or even as a garnish for fresh shucked oysters.

Tip

Celery tends to be very fibrous and "stringy." Using a vegetable peeler, peel the celery, exposing the white, delicate flesh.

1⅔ cups	diced tomato	400 mL
1 tbsp	finely diced seeded jalapeño	15 mL
1 tbsp	finely diced gherkins	15 mL
1 tbsp	vodka	15 mL
1 tsp	vegan or regular Worcestershire sauce	5 mL
1 tsp	finely diced celery (see Tip, left)	5 mL
½ tsp	hot pepper sauce	2 mL
½ tsp	salt	2 mL

1. In a bowl, combine tomato, jalapeño, gherkins, vodka, Worcestershire sauce, celery, hot pepper sauce and salt. Refrigerate and marinate for 1 hour or for up to 4 hours.

Roasted Onion Salsa

Makes about 1¼ cups (300 mL)

It is amazing what happens to an onion when roasted — it becomes as sweet as sugar. This sweetness contrasts wonderfully with One-Bite Corn Dogs (page 353). The salsa is also perfect with salty tortilla chips or Bagel Chips (page 215).

- **Preheat oven to 400°F (200°C)**

2	onions (unpeeled)	2
¼ cup	finely diced red bell pepper	60 mL
1 tbsp	red wine vinegar	15 mL
½ tsp	Dijon mustard	2 mL
¼ tsp	chopped fresh thyme leaves	1 mL
¼ tsp	chopped fresh oregano leaves	1 mL

1. Place onions on a baking sheet and roast in preheated oven until skins are browned and crisp and onions are fork tender, about 1 hour. Transfer to a bowl and let stand until cool enough to handle, preferably overnight, covered and refrigerated. Peel off skins and dice onions, reserving any accumulated juices.

2. In a bowl, combine roasted onions and any reserved liquid, bell pepper, vinegar, Dijon, thyme and oregano. Cover and refrigerate for at least 1 hour to allow flavors to meld or for up to 3 days before serving.

Roasted Beet Salsa

Makes about 1¼ cups (300 mL)

Beets are like candy after roasting. Serve with crisp Beet Chips (page 213) or Taro Root Chips (see Variations, page 213).

Tip

Slivered almonds are very thin and can burn quite quickly if not watched closely. Because of this, we prefer to toast them on the stovetop. *To toast almonds:* In a skillet over medium-high heat add enough almonds just to cover the bottom of the skillet and, stirring constantly, toast until fragrant and golden brown, 2 to 3 minutes.

- **Preheat oven to 200°F (100°C)**

1½ lbs	beets, unpeeled	750 g
	Olive oil	
	Salt	
¼ cup	toasted slivered almonds (see Tip, left)	60 mL
1 tbsp	sherry vinegar	15 mL
1 tbsp	extra virgin olive oil	15 mL
½ tsp	fresh thyme leaves	2 mL

1. Place beets on a rimmed baking sheet or in a baking dish. Toss with oil, sprinkle with 1 tsp (5 mL) salt and cover with foil. Roast in preheated oven until tender, about 2 hours. Remove from oven, spoon off 2 tbsp (30 mL) of the cooking juice and set aside. Discard any excess juice. Let beets cool just until they are cool enough to touch, then using a piece of paper towel, rub off skins and dice.

2. In a bowl, combine 1¼ cups (300 mL) diced beets, almonds, vinegar, olive oil, thyme and ⅛ tsp (0.5 mL) salt. Cover and refrigerate for at least 1 hour to allow flavors to meld or for up to 3 days before serving.

Eggplant and Date Salsa

Makes about 1½ cups (375 mL)

This salsa is a Middle Eastern flavor explosion, just amazing over Hummus from Scratch (page 51) or with warm wedges of pita or Pita Chips (see Variations, page 216).

Tip

We prefer the pungent taste of Greek kalamata olives but almost any black olive would work well here. Just be sure not to use those that come in cans because they have no flavor.

2 tbsp	olive oil	30 mL
2 cups	diced unpeeled eggplant	500 mL
¾ tsp	salt	3 mL
¼ tsp	chopped fresh thyme leaves	1 mL
½ cup	finely diced tomato	125 mL
¼ cup	finely diced dried dates	60 mL
¼ cup	finely diced sweet onion	60 mL
1 tbsp	sweet barbecue sauce	15 mL
1 tsp	minced black olives (see Tip, left)	5 mL
1 tsp	freshly squeezed lemon juice	5 mL
¼ tsp	cracked black peppercorns	1 mL

1. In a large skillet, heat oil over medium heat. Add eggplant, salt and thyme and cook, stirring, until eggplant is soft, about 10 minutes. Transfer to a bowl and let cool to room temperature.

2. Add tomato, dates, onion, barbecue sauce, olives, lemon juice and peppercorns to eggplant mixture and mix well. Cover and let stand at room temperature for at least 1 hour to allow flavors to meld or refrigerate for up to 1 day before serving.

Variation

Dates are quite easy to find in grocery stores but in this recipe could easily be replaced by prunes, dried apricots or dried peaches.

Warm Eggplant Salsa

Makes about 1½ cups (375 mL)

This is a great accompaniment to Hummus from Scratch (page 51), Bagel Chips (page 215) or even crisp Beet Chips (page 213).

Tip

Chiffonade is a French culinary term for slicing into thin ribbons. In this case it is basil. Stack washed and dried leaves of basil into a neat pile and roll into a small cigar shape. With a sharp knife, slice across the cigar to form thin ribbons and delicately fluff the basil with your hands to separate.

2 tbsp	olive oil	30 mL
2 cups	diced unpeeled eggplant	500 mL
¾ tsp	salt	3 mL
½ cup	finely diced roasted red bell pepper (see Tips, page 24)	125 mL
½ cup	finely diced tomato	125 mL
¼ cup	finely diced shallot	60 mL
2 tbsp	sherry vinegar	30 mL
¼ tsp	cracked black peppercorns	1 mL
1	basil leaf, chiffonade (see Tip, left)	1

1. In a large skillet, heat oil over medium heat. Add eggplant and salt and cook, stirring, until eggplant is soft, about 10 minutes. Transfer to a bowl and let cool to room temperature.
2. Add roasted pepper, tomato, shallot, vinegar, peppercorns and basil to eggplant and mix well. Serve immediately or cover and refrigerate for up to 1 day.

Roasted Red Pepper Salsa

Makes about 1¼ cups (300 mL)

Try this incredibly sweet-and-smoky flavored salsa that might just replace tomato salsa. Try it with tortilla chips, wedges of red bell pepper, or for something a little more extravagant, on top of a grilled cheese sandwich.

¾ cup	diced roasted red bell pepper (see Tips, page 24)	175 mL
½ cup	diced tomato	125 mL
¼ cup	finely diced red onion	60 mL
1 tbsp	red wine vinegar	15 mL
1 tbsp	agave syrup	15 mL
1 tsp	minced rinsed capers	5 mL

1. In a bowl, combine roasted pepper, tomato, red onion, vinegar, agave syrup and capers. Serve immediately or cover and let stand at room temperature for up to 4 hours.

Navy Bean Salsa

Makes about 2 cups (500 mL)

This salsa is packed full of flavor, so much so you may just be tempted to eat it all by itself. Serve as an accompaniment to Carnitas (page 343) or Beef and Parmesan Sliders (page 268) or just dip crunchy tortilla chips into the salsa — all would be perfect with this salsa.

Tip

Cook dried beans from scratch or used drained, rinsed canned beans. 1 cup (250 mL) dried beans makes 2 cups (500 mL) cooked.

1¼ cups	cooked drained navy beans (see Tip, left)	300 mL
⅓ cup	finely diced celery	75 mL
¼ cup	finely diced carrot	60 mL
2 tbsp	finely diced red onion	30 mL
2 tbsp	finely diced bell pepper	30 mL
1 tbsp	thinly sliced green onions	15 mL

Vinaigrette

3 tbsp	sherry vinegar	45 mL
2 tbsp	extra virgin olive oil	30 mL
1 tbsp	grainy (Pommery) mustard	15 mL
1 tsp	herbes de Provence	5 mL
½ tsp	salt	2 mL
¼ tsp	freshly cracked peppercorns	1 mL

1. In a bowl, combine beans, celery, carrot, red onion, bell pepper and green onions.
2. *Vinaigrette:* In another bowl, combine vinegar, olive oil, mustard, herbes de Provence, salt and pepper. Whisk well to emulsify. Stir into vegetables and mix well. Serve immediately or cover and refrigerate for up to 1 day.

Kidney Bean Salsa

Makes about 2 cups (500 mL)

Bean salsas are so wonderful they can almost be eaten all on their own, but where's the fun in that? Dip tortilla chips or Bagel Chips (page 215) into the salsa and munch away.

1¼ cups	cooked drained kidney beans	300 mL
⅓ cup	grilled corn kernels (see Tips, page 42)	75 mL
¼ cup	coarsely chopped cherry tomatoes	60 mL
2 tbsp	finely diced sweet onion	30 mL
1 tbsp	thinly sliced green onions	15 mL
	Vinaigrette (see above)	

1. In a large bowl, combine kidney beans, corn, cherry tomatoes, onion and green onions.
2. Stir vinaigrette into vegetables and mix well. Serve immediately or cover and refrigerate for up to 1 day.

Edamame Salsa

Makes about 1 cup (250 mL)

Edamame (also known as soy beans) are delicious and quite good for you, too. Plunge an endive spear or romaine leaf into the salsa to serve the perfect vegan appetizer.

³⁄₄ cup	frozen shelled edamame beans, thawed	175 mL
¼ cup	diced cucumber	60 mL
1 tsp	grated lemon zest	5 mL
1 tbsp	freshly squeezed lemon juice	15 mL
1 tsp	extra virgin olive oil	5 mL
1 tsp	thinly sliced red chile pepper	5 mL
½ tsp	minced garlic	2 mL
¼ tsp	salt	1 mL

1. In a pot of boiling salted water, boil edamame until tender, about 2 minutes. Drain and rinse under cold water until chilled. Drain well and transfer to a bowl.

2. Add cucumber, lemon zest and juice, olive oil, chile pepper, garlic and salt to edamame and mix well. Let stand at room temperature for at least 1 hour to allow flavors to meld or cover and refrigerate o for up to 1 day before serving.

Red Radish and Goat Cheese Salsa

Makes about 1½ cups (375 mL)

The delicate peppery flavor combined with a tart creamy goat cheese is perfect with a wedge of Crispy Potato Galette (page 417), freshly cut Belgian endive spear or crostini (pages 219 and 220).

1 cup	diced red radishes	250 mL
¼ cup	finely diced white onion	60 mL
1 tbsp	soft goat cheese	15 mL
1 tbsp	coarsely chopped fresh basil leaves	15 mL
2 tsp	Champagne vinegar or white wine	10 mL

1. In a bowl, combine red radishes, onion, goat cheese, basil and vinegar. Cover and refrigerate for at least 1 hour to allow flavors to meld or for up to 3 days before serving.

Asparagus Salsa

Makes about 1½ cups (375 mL)

A one-of-a-kind food experience when paired with king oyster mushrooms (see King Oyster Mushroom and Asparagus Salsa Canapé, page 438) but also a superb garnish for Tomato Avocado Shooter (page 112) or on top of crostini (pages 219 and 220).

Tips

When blanching green vegetables, salt is very useful for adding flavor. It is also quite instrumental in bringing the vibrant green color out long before the vegetable is overcooked. For maximum effect, we suggest 1 tbsp (15 mL) salt for every 6 cups (1.5 L) of water.

We recommend using pure sea salt rather than refined table salt. It has a clean, crisp taste and enhanced mineral content, unlike table salt, which has a bitter acrid taste and contains unpleasant additives to prevent caking.

1¼ cups	finely chopped asparagus	300 mL
	Ice water	
⅓ cup	finely diced cherry tomatoes	75 mL
⅓ cup	grilled corn kernels (see Tips, page 42)	75 mL
2 tbsp	finely diced red onion	30 mL
1 tbsp	coarsely chopped dried cranberries	15 mL
1 tbsp	coarsely chopped toasted almonds	15 mL
1 tsp	malt vinegar	5 mL
1 tsp	extra virgin olive oil	5 mL
½ tsp	chopped fresh basil leaves	2 mL
¼ tsp	salt	1 mL
¼ tsp	freshly ground black pepper	1 mL
⅛ tsp	hot pepper flakes	0.5 mL

1. In a pot of boiling salted water, blanch asparagus until vibrant green and al dente, about 2 minutes. Drain and immediately plunge into a bowl of ice water to stop the cooking process. Let stand until well chilled. Drain well.

2. In a bowl, combine asparagus, tomatoes, corn, red onion, cranberries, almonds, vinegar, olive oil, basil, salt, pepper and hot pepper flakes. Let stand at room temperature for at least 1 hour to allow flavors to meld or cover and refrigerate for up to 8 hours before serving.

Green Bean Salsa

Makes about 1²⁄₃ cups (400 mL)

A very fresh salsa that is wonderful in the summer time atop thick slices of plum tomatoes, sliced English cucumbers or hearts of romaine leaves.

Tip

Haricots vert or French beans would work very nicely in this recipe.

1⅓ cups	finely chopped green beans (see Tip, left)	325 mL
	Ice water	
¼ cup	diced tomato	60 mL
1 tsp	thinly sliced or minced garlic	5 mL
1 tsp	Basil Pesto (page 549) or store-bought	5 mL
¼ tsp	salt	1 mL

1. In a pot of boiling salted water, blanch green beans until bright green and al dente, 4 to 5 minutes. Drain and immediately plunge into a bowl of ice water to stop the cooking. Let stand until well chilled. Drain well.

2. In a bowl, combine green beans, tomato, garlic, basil pesto and salt. Serve immediately or cover and refrigerate for up to 8 hours.

Roasted Cubanelle Pepper and Black Bean Salsa

Makes about 2 cups (500 mL)

Cubanelle peppers combined with chipotle powder create a wonderfully smoky salsa that is just delightful with tortilla chips or Green Plantain Chips (page 211).

Tip

Cubanelle peppers are long, narrow sweet peppers with a very mild flavor. These peppers are green to yellow in color when unripe and bright red when fully ripe.

1 cup	diced peeled grilled Cubanelle pepper (see Tip, left)	250 mL
½ cup	cooked drained black beans (see Tip, page 77)	125 mL
¼ cup	finely diced cherry tomatoes	60 mL
3 tbsp	freshly squeezed lime juice	45 mL
2 tbsp	coarsely chopped fresh cilantro leaves	30 mL
⅛ tsp	chipotle powder	0.5 mL
⅛ tsp	ancho chile powder	0.5 mL
Pinch	salt	Pinch

1. In a bowl, combine Cubanelle peppers, black beans, tomatoes, lime juice, cilantro, chipotle powder, ancho powder and salt. Serve immediately or cover and refrigerate for up to 1 day.

Portobello Mushroom and Feta Cheese Salsa

Makes about 2 cups (500 mL)

A very simple and hearty salsa that is quite versatile. Use atop a grilled pizza or Classic Flatbread (page 218) or just plunge Pita Chips (see Variations, page 216) or Bagel Chips (page 215) into the salsa for a real explosion of textures and flavor.

Tip

Chiffonade is a French culinary term for slicing into thin ribbons. In this case it is basil. Stack washed and dried leaves of basil into a neat pile and roll into a small cigar shape. With a sharp knife, slice across the cigar to form thin ribbons and delicately fluff the basil with your hands to separate.

• **Preheat barbecue grill to high**

4	portobello mushrooms	4
2 tbsp	olive oil	30 mL
1 tbsp	balsamic vinegar	15 mL
1/4 cup	feta cheese	60 mL
2 tbsp	thinly sliced green onions, green part only	30 mL
1 tbsp	minced drained oil-packed sun-dried tomato	15 mL
1 tbsp	chiffonade fresh basil leaves (see Tip, left)	15 mL
1 tsp	sherry vinegar	5 mL
1/2 tsp	salt	2 mL

1. Remove stems from mushrooms and peel outside layer off caps. In a shallow dish, combine oil and balsamic vinegar. Add mushroom caps and turn to coat. Place stem side up on preheated grill, close lid and grill until liquid begins to form in the cavity where the stem used to be, 5 to 6 minutes. Flip over and grill until tender, about 3 minutes. Transfer to a bowl and let cool.

2. Dice mushrooms, reserving any accumulated liquid in bowl. Return chopped mushrooms to bowl and add feta cheese, green onions, sun-dried tomato, basil, vinegar and salt and mix well. Serve immediately or cover and refrigerate for up to 3 days.

Warm Mushroom Salsa

Makes about 1½ cups (375 mL)

Here's a simple appetizer created for those sudden pop-in guests — the only problem? They may just "pop in" more often. Pair with Classic Garlic Bread (page 210), Homemade Potato Chips (page 215) or Savory Baked Crostini (page 220).

Tip

Stack washed and dried Brussels sprout leaves into a neat pile and lay flat on a cutting board. With a sharp knife, slice across the leaves to create thin ribbons, also known as chiffonade.

2 tbsp	extra virgin olive oil	30 mL
4 cups	quartered mushrooms	1 L
2	cloves garlic, thinly sliced	2
¾ cup	thinly sliced or chiffonade Brussels sprouts leaves (see Tip, left)	175 mL
1 tsp	chopped fresh thyme leaves	5 mL
½ tsp	salt	2 mL
¼ tsp	freshly ground black pepper	1 mL
1 tbsp	sherry vinegar	15 mL

1. In a large skillet, heat oil over medium heat. Add mushrooms and cook, stirring, until soft, 7 to 8 minutes. Add garlic, Brussels sprouts, thyme, salt and pepper and cook, stirring, until Brussels sprout leaves are tender, about 5 minutes. Remove from heat and add vinegar. Transfer to a bowl and serve immediately or cover and refrigerate for up to 3 days. To reheat, warm on low heat, stirring often until warmed through, 3 to 5 minutes.

Roasted Corn Salsa

Makes about 1⅔ cups (400 mL)

This is one of the sweetest salsas you will ever taste. Refried Nachos (page 50), Pita Chips (see Variations, page 216) or Fresh Corn Cakes (page 449) would all be wonderful accompaniments.

1 cup	grilled corn kernels (see Tips, page 42)	250 mL
½ cup	diced tomato	125 mL
2 tbsp	thinly sliced green onions	30 mL
2 tbsp	finely diced red onion	30 mL
2 tbsp	coarsely chopped fresh cilantro leaves	30 mL
2 tsp	freshly squeezed lemon juice	10 mL
¼ tsp	salt	1 mL

1. In a bowl, combine corn, tomato, green onions, red onion, cilantro, lemon juice and salt. Let stand at room temperature for at least 1 hour to allow flavors to meld or cover and refrigerate for up to 1 day before serving.

Cucumber and Roasted Corn Salsa

Makes about 1½ cups (375 mL)

A refreshing salsa that is so perfectly filled with summer flavors you can serve all on its own on a Chinese soup spoon. Serve with slices of English cucumbers or crunchy Beet Chips (page 213) to add one more textural dimension to this salsa. Either way, it is superb.

1 cup	finely diced peeled seeded English cucumber	250 mL
½ cup	grilled corn kernels (see Tips, page 42)	125 mL
1 tbsp	sliced cherry tomatoes	15 mL
1 tbsp	apple cider vinegar	15 mL
1 tbsp	mayonnaise	15 mL
1 tsp	agave syrup or liquid honey	5 mL
1 tsp	coarsely chopped fresh basil	5 mL
¼ tsp	salt	1 mL
	Freshly ground black pepper	

1. In a bowl, combine cucumber, corn, tomatoes, vinegar, mayonnaise, agave syrup, basil, salt, and pepper to taste. Cover and refrigerate for at least 1 hour to allow flavors to meld or for up to 1 day before serving.

Avocado Corn Salsa

Makes about 4 cups (1 L)

Refreshing and delicious, this savory salsa is perfect with crisp tostadas or tortilla chips. It also makes a great finish for Carnitas (page 343). If you're feeling festive, launch the evening with a round of margaritas.

Tip

If you have cold-pressed avocado oil, by all means substitute it for the olive oil.

1½ cups	cooked corn kernels, cooled	375 mL
1 tsp	extra virgin olive oil (see Tip, left)	5 mL
2	avocados, diced	2
½	red bell pepper, diced	½
½ cup	finely diced red onion	125 mL
½	habanero pepper, seeded and diced	½
¼ cup	freshly squeezed lime juice (about 1 lime)	60 mL
¼ cup	freshly squeezed orange juice (about ½ an orange)	60 mL
2 tbsp	minced fresh oregano leaves	30 mL
	Salt and freshly ground black pepper	

1. In a bowl, combine corn and olive oil. Toss well. Add avocados, bell pepper, red onion, habanero, lime juice, orange juice and oregano. Toss well to combine. Season to taste with salt and black pepper. Refrigerate for about 30 minutes to allow flavors to meld.

Avocado Black Bean Salsa

Makes about 3 cups (750 mL)

In addition to being very tasty, this salsa is highly nutritious. Serve it on tostadas or tortilla chips, or use hearts of romaine lettuce as a dipper.

Tip

To prevent oxidization, don't dice your avocados until you have completed the rest of the chopping. Once diced, add to remaining ingredients and toss immediately.

2	avocados, diced (see Tip, left)	2
1 cup	diced peeled tomatoes	250 mL
1 cup	cooked drained black beans	250 mL
1	poblano pepper, seeded and diced	1
½ cup	finely diced red onion	125 mL
½	jalapeño pepper, seeded and diced	½
¼ cup	freshly squeezed lime juice	60 mL
2 tbsp	freshly squeezed orange juice	30 mL
1 tsp	puréed garlic	5 mL
2 tbsp	finely chopped fresh cilantro leaves	30 mL
	Salt and freshly ground black pepper	

1. In a bowl, combine avocados, tomatoes, beans, poblano pepper, red onion, jalapeño pepper, lime juice, orange juice, garlic and cilantro leaves. Toss well to combine. Season to taste with salt and black pepper. Cover and refrigerate for 30 minutes to allow flavors to meld.

Pepper Confetti Salsa

Makes about 1½ cups (375 mL)

This very colorful salsa will brighten any crisp chip that it adorns. Try it with crostini (pages 219 and 220), sweet Parsnip Chips (see Variations, page 213) or tortilla chips.

½ cup	finely diced tomato	125 mL
⅓ cup	each finely diced red, orange and yellow bell peppers	75 mL
⅓ cup	finely diced peeled English cucumber	75 mL
1 tbsp	finely diced red onion	15 mL
1 tbsp	vodka	15 mL
1 tsp	minced garlic	5 mL
1 tsp	extra virgin olive oil	5 mL
½ tsp	each grated lemon zest and juice	2 mL
¼ tsp	each salt and Herbes de Provence	1 mL
¼ tsp	hot pepper sauce	1 mL
¼ tsp	vegan or regular Worcestershire sauce	1 mL

1. In a large bowl, combine tomato, bell peppers, cucumber, onion, vodka, garlic, oil, lemon zest and juice, salt, herbes, hot sauce and Worcestershire. Serve or cover and let stand for up to 4 hours.

Warm Banana Salsa

Makes about 1 cup (250 mL)

Why not try a dessert appetizer party? This salsa is wonderful as a garnish on Sweet Wontons (page 526) or Chocolate Toasts (page 510) for a creative and fun-filled party.

1/4 tsp	sesame seeds	1 mL
1/4 cup	finely diced dried apricots	60 mL
1 1/4 cups	diced bananas	300 mL
1 tsp	agave syrup	5 mL
1 tsp	freshly squeezed lemon juice	5 mL

1. Preheat a large skillet over medium heat until hot. Add sesame seeds and toast, stirring often, until slightly brown, about 3 minutes. Add apricots and cook, stirring, until warmed through, about 2 minutes. Add bananas, agave syrup and lemon juice. Stir to combine. Transfer to a bowl and serve warm or let cool to room temperature.

Black Bean and Pineapple Salsa

Makes about 2 cups (500 mL)

This Caribbean-inspired salsa pairs perfectly with Green Plantain Chips (page 211) or tortilla chips.

Tip

For best results toast and grind the coriander seeds yourself. *To toast seeds:* Place seeds in a dry skillet over medium heat and cook, stirring, until fragrant, about 3 minutes. Immediately transfer to a mortar or a spice grinder and grind.

1 cup	cooked drained black beans (see Tip, page 77)	250 mL
1/2 cup	finely diced pineapple	75 mL
1/4 cup	finely diced red bell pepper	60 mL
1/4 cup	finely diced lime segments	60 mL
2 tbsp	finely diced red onion	30 mL
2 tbsp	coarsely chopped fresh cilantro leaves	30 mL
1/2 tsp	finely chopped seeded jalapeño pepper	2 mL
3 tbsp	freshly squeezed lime juice	45 mL
2 tbsp	extra virgin olive oil	30 mL
1 tbsp	agave syrup	15 mL
1 tsp	chipotle powder	5 mL
1/2 tsp	salt	2 mL
1/2 tsp	ground coriander (see Tip, left)	2 mL

1. In a bowl, combine black beans, pineapple, bell pepper, lime segments, red onion, cilantro and jalapeño pepper.
2. Add lime juice, olive oil, agave syrup, chipotle powder, salt and coriander and mix well. Serve immediately or cover and refrigerate for up to 1 day.

Chipotle Pineapple Salsa

Makes about 1¼ cups (300 mL)

A sweet and spicy salsa that will not only delight your palate but all of your guests, too. Try this with tortilla chips, Green Plantain Chips (page 211) or crispy Beet Chips (page 213).

1¼ cups	diced pineapple	300 mL
1 tsp	sherry vinegar	5 mL
½ tsp	minced chives	2 mL
½ tsp	coarsely chopped fresh cilantro leaves	2 mL
¼ tsp	chipotle powder	1 mL

1. In a bowl, combine pineapple, vinegar, chives, cilantro and chipotle powder. Cover and refrigerate for at least 1 hour to allow flavors to meld or for up to 1 day before serving.

Pineapple Banana Salsa

Makes about 4 cups (1 L)

Except for the fresh pineapple, you can make this luscious salsa from ingredients you're likely to have on hand. This is delicious on tortilla chips and tostadas or Green Plantain Chips (page 211).

Tips

If you don't have access to a mild chile pepper such as serrano, substitute about half of a jalapeño pepper instead.

Because you're using the zest of the orange, we recommend using organically grown fruit.

3 cups	diced fresh pineapple (about ½ a small one)	750 mL
3	bananas, peeled and very thinly sliced (about ⅛ inch/3 mm)	3
1	mild chile pepper, such as serrano, seeded and minced (see Tips, left)	1
1 tsp	finely grated orange zest (see Tips, left)	5 mL
⅓ cup	freshly squeezed orange juice	75 mL
2 tbsp	finely chopped mint	30 mL
2 tbsp	finely chopped cashews, optional	30 mL

1. In a bowl, combine pineapple, bananas, chile pepper, orange zest and juice, mint, and cashews, if using. Toss well. Set aside for 10 minutes to meld flavors.

2. Transfer to a serving bowl and serve immediately. Because this salsa contains bananas, it doesn't keep well. It is best served within a few hours of being prepared.

Minty Mango Salsa

Makes about 5 cups (1.25 L)

This simple salsa is very easy to make, yet delicious. It is great with tortilla chips. For something a little different, try serving it on hearts of romaine lettuce or Green Plantain Chips (page 211).

2	mangos, diced (about 4 cups/1 L)	2
½ cup	finely diced red onion	125 mL
½	red bell pepper, diced	½
1	jalapeño pepper, seeded and minced	1
¼ cup	freshly squeezed lime juice	60 mL
1 tbsp	minced fresh mint leaves	15 mL

1. In a large bowl, combine mangos, red onion, bell pepper, jalapeño pepper, lime juice and mint. Toss well. Set aside for 10 minutes to meld flavors. Transfer to a serving bowl and serve.

Pineapple Mango Salsa

Makes 8 cups (2 L)

For a simple presentation, serve this fruity salsa with tostadas or tortilla chips. If you're feeling more ambitious, make Green Plantain Chips (page 211). It even makes a nice finish for grilled chicken or shrimp.

Tips

The finer your dice, the smaller your dipper can be. If you are using small tortilla chips, err on the side of a fine dice.

If your fruit is not as sweet as you would like add 1 to 2 tsp (5 to 10 mL) sugar or agave syrup before mixing the salsa.

1	pineapple, cored and diced (see Tips, left)	1
2	mangos, diced	2
1	small red onion, finely diced (about ⅓ cup/75 mL)	1
1	red bell pepper, finely diced	1
1	jalapeño pepper or 2 serrano chiles, seeded and minced	1
1 tbsp	finely chopped fresh cilantro leaves	15 mL
¼ tsp	puréed gingerroot (see Tip, page 88)	1 mL
	Granulated sugar, optional (see Tips, left)	
¼ cup	freshly squeezed lime juice	60 mL

1. In a large bowl, combine pineapple, mangos, red onion, bell pepper, jalapeño pepper, cilantro, ginger, and sugar, if using. Mix well. Add lime juice and toss well. Set aside for 10 minutes to meld flavors. Transfer to a serving bowl and serve.

Classic Mango Salsa

Makes about 1½ cups (375 mL)

Vegan Friendly

This salsa is wonderful and so darn easy to make. It's great with tortilla chips. For something a little different, try it along side Salmon Sliders (page 266).

1¼ cups	diced mango	300 mL
¼ cup	diced tomato	60 mL
1 tbsp	minced chives	15 mL
2 tsp	chiffonade fresh mint leaves	10 mL
1 tsp	light soy sauce	5 mL
1 tsp	sweet chili sauce	5 mL
1 tsp	freshly squeezed lime juice	5 mL

1. In a bowl, combine mango, tomato, chives, mint, soy sauce, chili sauce and lime juice. Cover and refrigerate for at least 1 hour to allow flavors to meld or for up to 8 hours before serving.

Mango Water Chestnut Salsa

Make about 4 cups (1 L)

Vegan Friendly

The addition of water chestnuts puts an Asian spin on this tasty salsa. Continue that direction by serving it on thin slices of daikon radish, crisped in ice water and drained, or plain rice crackers.

Tip

To purée peeled ginger: Use a fine, sharp-toothed grater such as Microplane.

1	mango, diced (about 2 cups/500 mL)	1
1	red bell pepper, finely diced	1
1	can (8 oz/227 mL) sliced water chestnuts, drained, rinsed and slivered	1
½	red onion, minced	½
1	jalapeño pepper, minced	1
¼ cup	freshly squeezed lime juice	60 mL
1 tbsp	freshly puréed gingerroot (see Tip, left)	15 mL

1. In a large bowl, combine mango, bell pepper, water chestnuts, red onion, jalapeño pepper, lime juice and ginger. Toss well. Set aside for 10 minutes to meld flavors. Transfer to a serving bowl and serve.

Margarita Mango Salsa

Makes about 1¾ cups (425 mL)

The addition of tequila to this salsa creates the perfect adults-only salsa. Serve alongside Classic Crab Cakes (page 307) or Panko-Crusted "Fish Sticks" (page 322).

1½ cups	diced mango	375 mL
¼ cup	thinly sliced green onions, green part only	60 mL
1 tbsp	finely diced seeded jalapeño pepper	15 mL
1 tbsp	coarsely chopped fresh cilantro	15 mL
1 tsp	finely diced red bell pepper	5 mL
2 tbsp	freshly squeezed lime juice	30 mL
1 tbsp	tequila	15 mL

1. In a bowl, combine mango, green onions, jalapeño, cilantro, bell pepper, lime juice and tequila. Cover and refrigerate for at least 1 hour to allow flavors to meld or for up to 8 hours before serving.

Thai-Inspired Green Mango Salsa

Makes about 1¾ cups (425 mL)

A wonderful accompaniment to any Thai-inspired meal. Good enough to be served on its own, it can also add that wow factor to Peanut-Crusted Beef Tenderloin Satays (page 351).

Tip

Roasted unsalted peanuts can substitute easily for Agave and Ginger-Scented Peanuts, but if you feel like going that extra distance, these nuts are really perfect with green mangos.

1½ cups	diced green mango	375 mL
¼ cup	Agave and Ginger-Scented Peanuts (page 455) (see Tip, left)	60 mL
¼ cup	diced red onion	60 mL
5 tsp	rice vinegar (see Tips, page 305)	25 mL
1 tsp	finely diced red bell pepper	5 mL
1 tsp	coarsely chopped fresh cilantro	5 mL
¼ tsp	hot pepper flakes	1 mL
¼ tsp	agave syrup	1 mL

1. In a bowl, combine mango, peanuts, red onion, vinegar, bell pepper, cilantro, hot pepper flakes and agave syrup. Cover and refrigerate for at least 1 hour to allow flavors to meld or for up to 1 day before serving.

Apple Salsa

Makes about 1¾ cups (425 mL)

Vegan Friendly

Try this wonderful salsa on top of a slice of Cheddar cheese or for the more adventurous, Apple Cinnamon Phyllo Purses (page 519).

Tip

Gala apples are light red in color with sweet, very mild apple flavor. Any crisp, sweet apple would be a great substitute.

1 cup	finely diced Gala apples (see Tip, left)	250 mL
¾ cup	finely diced Granny Smith apples	175 mL
⅓ cup	dried cranberries	75 mL
1 tbsp	finely diced shallots	15 mL
1 tbsp	Champagne vinegar or apple cider vinegar	15 mL
1 tsp	fig marmalade or other fruit marmalade	5 mL
¼ tsp	salt	1 mL
Pinch	ground cardamom	Pinch

1. In a bowl, combine Gala and Granny Smith apples, cranberries, shallots, vinegar, marmalade, salt and ground cardamom. Cover and refrigerate for at least 1 hour to allow flavors to meld or for up to 8 hours before serving.

Cucumber Watermelon Salsa

Makes 4 cups (1 L)

Vegan Friendly

Try serving this tasty salsa like a small salad alongside grilled vegetables, chicken or lamb. Or pass the rice crackers, tortilla chips or Green Plantain Chips (page 211). Either way, it makes a very refreshing hot weather nibbly.

2 cups	diced seeded cucumber (about 1)	500 mL
2 cups	diced seeded watermelon	500 mL
16	fresh mint leaves (about 2 sprigs), finely chopped	16
1 tbsp	freshly squeezed orange juice	15 mL
1 tbsp	freshly squeezed lime juice	15 mL
2 tsp	light agave syrup (see Tip, page 91)	10 mL
1 tsp	finely minced seeded jalapeño pepper	5 mL
	Salt	

1. In a bowl, combine cucumber, watermelon, mint, orange juice, lime juice, agave syrup and jalapeño. Toss well to combine. Season to taste with salt. Cover and refrigerate for 30 minutes or for up to 4 hours to allow flavors to meld.

Apple and Dried Cranberry Salsa

Makes about 1½ cups (375 mL)

This salsa is almost like eating a piece of apple pie! It is wonderful on seared pork tenderloin medallions or on top of a slice of Cheddar cheese.

1½ cups	finely diced peeled Granny Smith apples	375 mL
¼ cup	coarsely chopped dried cranberries	60 mL
2 tsp	Champagne vinegar or white wine	10 mL
1 tsp	packed brown sugar	5 mL
1 tsp	apricot jam or preserves	5 mL

1. In a bowl, combine apples, cranberries, vinegar, brown sugar and apricot jam. Cover and refrigerate for at least 1 hour to allow flavors to meld or for up to 8 hours before serving.

Strawberry and Rhubarb Salsa

Makes about 1 cup (250 mL)

This salsa is incredible when paired with Deep-Fried Brie (page 388) or crostini (pages 219 and 220).

Tip

Agave syrup is produced from the agave plant and because it contains a high percentage of fructose, it is much sweeter than honey.

1 cup	diced strawberries, divided	250 mL
1 cup	diced rhubarb	250 mL
½ cup	sweet white wine	125 mL
2	cardamom pods	2
½ cup	blueberries	125 mL
1 tbsp	agave syrup (see Tip, left)	15 mL
¼ tsp	finely chopped fresh thyme leaves	1 mL
⅛ tsp	finely chopped fresh mint leaves	0.5 mL
	Ground cardamom	

1. In a medium saucepan, bring ½ cup (125 mL) of the strawberries, rhubarb, white wine and cardamom pods to a boil over medium heat. Reduce heat and simmer, stirring often, until rhubarb is soft, 3 to 5 minutes. Strain mixture through a fine-mesh sieve, reserving liquid. Transfer solids to a bowl, discarding cardamom pods, and let cool. Return reserved cooking liquid to saucepan and bring to a simmer over medium-low heat. Simmer until reduced to a syrup, about 6 minutes. Add to reserved strawberry mixture in bowl.

2. Add remaining strawberries, blueberries, agave syrup, thyme, mint, and ground cardamom to taste and mix well. Serve immediately or cover and refrigerate for up to 2 days.

Feta-Spiked Watermelon Salsa with Chile

Makes about 4 cups (1 L)

You may think this is an unusual combination of ingredients, but watermelon, feta and chile are wildly compatible. Serve this with rice crackers or tortilla chips and expect to wow your guests.

4 cups	diced seeded watermelon	1 L
¼ cup	crumbled feta cheese	60 mL
2 tbsp	plain yogurt	30 mL
2 tbsp	finely chopped fresh cilantro leaves	30 mL
½ tsp	mild chile powder such as ancho, New Mexico or Aleppo	2 mL
2 tbsp	toasted pumpkin seeds (pepitas)	30 mL
	Salt	

1. In a bowl, combine watermelon, feta, yogurt, cilantro, chile powder and toasted pumpkin seeds. Toss well to combine. Season to taste with salt. Cover and refrigerate for 30 minutes or for up to 4 hours to allow flavors to meld.

Tropical Fruit Salsa

Makes about 1¼ cups (300 mL)

Close your eyes and picture the sunshine and the ocean as you taste a real taste of the tropics atop a Green Plantain Chip (page 211).

Tip

To remove vanilla seeds from pod: Using a sharp knife, slice pod lengthwise and using the back of the knife, gently scrape the pod to release the seeds.

½ cup	finely diced pineapple	125 mL
⅓ cup	finely diced kiwifruit	75 mL
¼ cup	finely diced mango	60 mL
¼ cup	grapefruit segments	60 mL
1 tsp	finely diced red bell pepper	5 mL
½ tsp	minced chives	2 mL
½ tsp	chopped fresh cilantro leaves	2 mL
¼ tsp	vanilla seeds (see Tip, left)	1 mL

1. In a bowl, combine pineapple, kiwi, mango, grapefruit, bell pepper, chives, cilantro and vanilla seeds. Cover and refrigerate for at least 1 hour to allow flavors to meld or for up to 1 day before serving.

Jicama Salsa

Makes about 1½ cups (375 mL)

Jicama is a crunchy refreshing vegetable, a cross between an apple and potato. The combination of jicama with citrus creates a tropical island experience that can be served with something as simple as a slice of cheese or more extravagantly atop Brown Sugar-Scented Peach Sabayon (page 527).

1½ cups	diced peeled jicama	375 mL
1 tsp	grated orange zest	5 mL
⅓ cup	freshly squeezed orange juice	75 mL
¼ cup	orange segments	60 mL
1 tsp	minced chives	5 mL
1 tsp	finely chopped fresh basil leaves	5 mL
1 tsp	finely chopped fresh mint leaves	5 mL
½ tsp	agave syrup	2 mL
⅛ tsp	salt	0.5 mL
⅛ tsp	freshly ground black pepper	0.5 mL

1. In a bowl, combine jicama, orange zest and juice, orange segments, chives, basil, mint, agave syrup, salt and pepper. Refrigerate and marinate for at least 1 hour or for up to 3 days before serving.

Suneeta's Cilantro Mint Chutney

Makes 1 cup (250 mL)

This recipe is adapted from one that appeared in Easy Indian Cooking *by Suneeta Vaswani. It makes a very fresh-tasting salsa that is delicious on Green Plantain Chips (page 211) or tortilla chips. It also makes a wonderful dipping sauce for cold boiled shrimp or samosas (pages 192 to 196).*

4 cups	loosely packed cilantro leaves	1 L
1	long red chile pepper	1
½ cup	fresh mint leaves	125 mL
¼ cup	freshly squeezed lime juice	60 mL
2 tbsp	minced gingerroot	30 mL
1 tsp	minced garlic	5 mL
1 tsp	ground cumin	5 mL
2 tsp	granulated sugar	10 mL
½ tsp	salt	2 mL

1. In food processor fitted with a metal blade, process cilantro, chile pepper, mint, lime juice, ginger, garlic, cumin, sugar and salt until smoothly puréed, stopping and scraping down the sides of the bowl as necessary.

Yogurt Mint Chutney

Makes 1 cup (250 mL)

Thanks to Suneeta Vaswani for allowing us to use this recipe, which appeared in her book Easy Indian Cooking. *It is simple to make and very delicious. It makes a great dipping sauce for samosas (pages 192 to 196.)*

1 cup	plain yogurt, divided	250 mL
8	mint leaves	8
½ to 1	long green or red chile pepper	½ to 1
2 tbsp	fresh cilantro leaves	30 mL
¼ tsp	salt or to taste	1 mL

1. In a blender, blend ¼ cup (60 mL) of the yogurt, mint, chile pepper, cilantro and salt into a smooth paste. Transfer to a bowl. Stir into remaining yogurt.

2. Cover and refrigerate until chilled before serving. (Chutney can be stored in an airtight container in the refrigerator for up to 1 week. Do not freeze.)

Date and Tamarind Chutney

Makes about 1½ cups (375 mL)

This Indian-inspired treat is lusciously delicious. It's amazing served with slightly sweet crackers, such as fruit and nut crisps or British-type oat biscuits. If you want to keep the experience geographically contained, serve it on Indian-Style Roti (page 201).

Tip

Some brands of tamarind purée contain pieces of pits. If you notice pits in yours, strain through a fine sieve after soaking.

1 cup	hot water	250 mL
1 tsp	Demerara or other raw cane sugar	5 mL
2 oz	unsalted Thai tamarind purée, broken into pieces (about 2 tbsp/30 mL) (see Tip, left)	60 g
8 oz	pitted soft dates such as medjool (about 1 cup/250 mL)	250 g
1	long red chile pepper, seeded and coarsely chopped	1
½ tsp	ground cumin (see Tips, page 56)	2 mL

1. In a small bowl, combine hot water and sugar. Stir well until sugar is dissolved. Add tamarind and set aside for 30 minutes.

2. In food processor fitted with metal blade, process dates, chile pepper, cumin and tamarind mixture until smooth and creamy, about 1 minute. Add water, if necessary, and pulse to create a smooth texture. Serve immediately or cover and refrigerate in an airtight container for up to 1 week.

Jicama Strawberry Salsa

Makes about 1½ cups (375 mL)

If you've never had a jicama you're missing out. The crunchy refreshing fruit pairs beautifully with the sweetness of strawberries and is perfect on top of apple and pear slices, crunchy Green Plantain Chips (page 211) or Sweet Wontons (page 526).

1½ cups	diced peeled jicama	375 mL
1 cup	diced strawberries	250 mL
¼ cup	Bing cherries, cut in half	60 mL
1 tbsp	extra virgin olive oil	15 mL
1 tbsp	balsamic vinegar	15 mL
1 tsp	agave syrup	5 mL
1 tsp	finely chopped fresh basil leaves	5 mL
⅛ tsp	salt	0.5 mL
Pinch	chipotle powder	Pinch

1. In a bowl, combine jicama, strawberries, cherries, olive oil, balsamic vinegar, agave syrup, basil, salt and chipotle powder. Cover and refrigerate for at least 1 hour to allow flavors to meld or for up to 8 hours before serving.

Spicy Nectarine Salsa

Makes about 1½ cups (375 mL)

Here's an awesome and unique way to use this sweet stone fruit. Serve with crostini (pages 219 and 220) for a delightful summertime appetizer or serve on top of peach slices — either way it's a salsa not to be missed.

1¼ cups	diced nectarines	300 mL
3 tbsp	freshly squeezed lime juice	45 mL
1 tbsp	finely diced red onion	15 mL
1 tsp	chopped fresh cilantro leaves	5 mL
½ tsp	thinly sliced green onion	2 mL
¼ tsp	Asian chili sauce, such as sambal oelek	1 mL

1. In a bowl, combine nectarines, lime juice, red onion, cilantro, green onion and chili sauce. Cover and refrigerate for at least 1 hour to allow flavors to meld or for up to 8 hours before serving.

Shrimp Salsa

Makes about 2 cups (500 mL)

If you're looking for a salsa that is a bit more substantial than one made exclusively with vegetables or fruit, try this. It is great with tortilla chips, Green Plantain Chips (page 211) or even sliced cucumber. For a special treat, try using it with Corn Arepas (page 187).

8 oz	cooked salad shrimp (about 1½ cups/375 mL)	250 g
1 tbsp	extra virgin olive oil	15 mL
1	clove garlic, puréed	1
1	avocado, diced	1
2	tomatoes, peeled and diced (about 1 cup/250 mL)	2
¼ cup	finely diced red onion	60 mL
1	jalapeño pepper, seeded and minced	1
¼ cup	freshly squeezed lime juice	60 mL
1 tsp	salt	5 mL
	Freshly ground black pepper	

1. In a bowl, combine shrimp, olive oil and garlic. Toss well. Add avocado, tomatoes, red onion, jalapeño, lime juice, salt, and black pepper to taste. Mix well. Cover and refrigerate for 1 hour.

Warm Salami and Red Pepper Salsa

Makes about 1 cup (250 mL)

This is absolutely incredible with crostini (pages 219 and 220) or Classic Flatbread (page 218).

Tip

There are numerous types of salami, such as Genoa or saucisson, and all vary in texture, heat and even the type of meat used. For this recipe we suggest using a mild beef salami that has a smooth texture.

1 cup	diced salami (see Tip, left)	250 mL
⅓ cup	diced red bell pepper	75 mL
1 tbsp	agave syrup	15 mL
1 tbsp	apple cider vinegar	15 mL
1 tbsp	thinly sliced green onion, green part only	15 mL
1 tsp	thinly sliced long red chile pepper	5 mL

1. In a medium saucepan over high heat, sauté salami until warmed through, about 5 minutes. Remove from heat and add bell pepper, agave syrup, vinegar, green onion and chile pepper and stir well to combine. Transfer to a bowl and serve immediately or cover and refrigerate for up to 3 days. Serve warm or bring to room temperature before serving.

Shooters

Shooters are robustly flavored soup-like drinks that are powerful mouthfuls of flavor. Usually presented in small portions (about 2 oz/60 mL) each, they get any gathering off to a lively start. In hot weather, served in elegant glassware, well-chilled shooters are beautiful to look at and very refreshing. In winter, make them warm and hearty and pour them into demi-tasse cups, like a shot of espresso. Passed on a tray, they make a great addition to a garden party. If you're serving a sit-down dinner, think about offering each guest a shooter as an amuse bouche to launch the meal with panache. Some of the more substantial shooters could also be served in larger portions as a soup course for a sit-down dinner.

Indian-Spiced Tomato Cooler 98
Cumin Mint Cooler 98
Sangrita 99
Melon-Spiked Mexican Rice Milk 100
Green Gazpacho 101
Tomato Gazpacho 102
Almond Gazpacho with Green Grapes 103
Tipsy Tomato Shooter. 104
Cucumber Avocado Shooter 105
Watermelon Cooler. 105
Summer Borscht 106
Spicy Carrot Cooler 107
Cold Cantaloupe Shooter 108
Cold Pineapple Cilantro Shooter 108
Thandai 109
Mango Lassi. 110
Banana Lassi 110
Strawberry Rhubarb Shooter 111

Rum-Spiked Watermelon Shooter 112
Tomato Avocado Shooter. 112
Black Bean and Feta Shooter. 113
Potato and Smoked Bacon Purée 114
Sweet Onion Shooter. 115
Beet and Goat Cheese Shooter 116
Savory Almond Shooter 116
Sweet Corn Shooter. 117
Mushroom Shooter. 118
Hawaiian Shiitake Shooter 119
Acorn Squash Sage Shooter 119
Carrot Ginger Shooter 120
Spring Scallion and Tomato Shooter. 121
Broccoli Pesto Shooter. 122
Red Pepper Chive Shooter. 123
Thai Coconut Shooter 124
Shrimp Bisque 125
Clam Tomato Chowder. 126

Indian-Spiced Tomato Cooler

Makes 12 servings

Deeply flavorful, this makes a very refreshing hot-weather shooter. It's good on it's own, but you can increase the quantity, add a shot of vodka and some ice and call it an Indian-inspired Bloody Mary. Roasting the tomatoes intensifies their flavor and the cumin adds a hint of earthiness.

- Preheat oven to 425°F (220°C)
- Twelve 2-oz (60 mL) shooter glasses

4	medium tomatoes	4
½ cup	water	125 mL
½ tsp	ground cumin (see Tips, page 114)	2 mL
¼ to ½	long red chile pepper	¼ to ½
	Salt and freshly ground black pepper	

1. Cut tomatoes in half and place on a rimmed baking sheet. Roast in preheated oven until they look wizened, about 45 minutes. Let cool. Remove skins and transfer to a blender. Add water, cumin and chile pepper to taste. Purée until smooth. Season generously with salt and black pepper. Cover and refrigerate until thoroughly chilled, at least 2 hours or for up to 3 days. Serve chilled.

Cumin Mint Cooler

Makes 16 servings

Spicy, tart and intriguingly flavored, this is a traditional cooler in India, where they understand heat. This version is adapted from Suneeta Vaswani's excellent book The Complete Book of Indian Cooking.

Tips

One chile produces a very spicy result, which is refreshing on a hot day.

You can also make this in a food processor fitted with the metal blade.

- Sixteen 2-oz (60 mL) shooter glasses

2 tsp	cumin seeds	10 mL
1 cup	mint leaves	250 mL
¼ cup	fresh cilantro leaves	60 mL
¼ cup	unsalted Thai tamarind purée, broken into pieces (see Tip, page 94)	60 mL
½ to 1	long green chile pepper, seeded and coarsely chopped (see Tips, left)	½ to 1
1 tbsp	coarsely chopped gingerroot	15 mL

1. In a dry skillet over medium heat, toast cumin until fragrant, stirring constantly, about 3 minutes. Transfer to a mortar or a spice grinder and grind.

2. In a blender (see Tips, left), combine mint, cilantro, tamarind, chile pepper, ginger and reserved cumin. Add 1 cup (250 mL) cold water and blend until very smooth. Transfer to a large pitcher. Add 3 cups (750 mL) cold water. Cover and refrigerate until thoroughly chilled, for at least 3 hours or for up to 3 days.

Sangrita

Makes 12 servings

Make this Mexican-inspired spicy tomato-citrus juice during the dog days of summer, when tomatoes are abundant and in season. It's delicious as a non-alcoholic refreshment but if you want to bump up the experience, add a dash of vodka, or as they often do in Mexico, a splash of tequila.

Tips

If you're serving this over ice, use larger glasses.

Use a whole jalapeño only if you are a true heat seeker. It produces a very spicy result.

- **Twelve 4-oz (125 mL) glasses (see Tips, left)**

3 lbs	plum (Roma) tomatoes (15 to 20), cut into chunks	1.5 kg
½ to 1	jalapeño pepper (see Tips, left)	½ to 1
½ cup	loosely packed cilantro (leaves and stems)	125 mL
1 cup	freshly squeezed orange juice	250 mL
⅓ cup	freshly squeezed lime juice	75 mL
⅓ cup	freshly squeezed lemon juice	75 mL
2 tsp	salt or to taste	10 mL
	Agave syrup, optional	

1. Place a large sieve over a large measuring cup or bowl with a pouring spout and line with two layers of dampened cheesecloth.

2. In a blender, working in batches, purée tomatoes, jalapeño to taste, cilantro, orange juice, lime juice and lemon juice. Pour into sieve. When most of the liquid has passed through, collect the corners of the cheesecloth and twist to form a tight ball. Using your hands, squeeze out remaining liquid. Discard solids. Season with salt.

3. Cover and refrigerate until thoroughly chilled, for at least 3 hours. If it is not sweet enough for you, add agave syrup, to taste. Serve very cold, over ice, if desired.

Melon-Spiked Mexican Rice Milk

Makes 12 servings

This is a Mexican-inspired version of horchata, a cold drink that is Spanish in origin. Served over ice, it is, not surprisingly, very refreshing on a hot day. The addition of cantaloupe to this traditional drink is an idea that came from a recipe by Diana Kennedy, the doyenne of Mexican cooking.

Tips

You can turn this into a cocktail by offering 4-oz (125 mL) servings with the addition of a shot of white rum.

When buying Demerara sugar, check the label to make sure you are getting pure raw cane sugar. Some brands are just refined sugar in disguise. If you prefer, used piloncillo, unrefined Mexican sugar, which is sold in cones in Latin markets. Use half of a 4-oz (125 g) cone in this recipe.

- **12 glasses**

½ cup	long-grain rice, preferably brown	125 mL
4 cups	water	1 L
1	piece (about 4 inches/10 cm) cinnamon stick, broken into pieces	1
¼ cup	Demerara or other raw cane sugar (see Tips, left)	60 mL
1	small cantaloupe (about 1½ lbs/750 g)	1
¼ cup	freshly squeezed lime juice (approx.)	60 mL
	Agave syrup, optional	
	Ice cubes	

1. In a large saucepan, combine rice and water. Cover and set aside for 4 hours. Add cinnamon stick and sugar and bring to a boil. Reduce heat and simmer until rice is very tender, about 45 minutes. Set aside and let cool. Remove cinnamon stick and discard.

2. Cut cantaloupe into quarters and trim off peel, leaving seeds intact. Add to rice mixture.

3. Transfer to a blender or food processor fitted with metal blade, in batches, or use an immersion blender, and purée.

4. Place a strainer over a large measuring cup or bowl with a pouring spout and line with two layers of dampened cheesecloth. Add rice mixture in batches and stir gently to help the liquid pass through. When the last batch has been strained, collect the corners of the cheesecloth and twist them to form a tight ball. Squeeze to extract as much of the remaining liquid as possible. Discard solids and stir lime juice into liquid. Cover and refrigerate until thoroughly chilled, for at least 3 hours.

5. When you're ready to serve, taste mixture and add more lime juice, if desired. If the drink is not sweet enough, stir in agave syrup to suit your taste. (Be careful; it is much more concentrated in sweetness than sugar.) Serve over ice.

Green Gazpacho

Makes 16 servings

If you have a craving for a refreshing shot of gazpacho before tomatoes have reached their most luscious peak but cucumbers and arugula are abundant, try this. The fresh chile adds a pleasant bit of heat, but if you're heat averse, the soup is fine without it.

Tip

When cold, we love to serve shooters in clear glassware because most are intensely colored and look very pretty. When hot, they require a heatproof vessel and work well in espresso or demi-tasse cups. But if you don't have appropriate glassware, feel free to serve cold shooters in cups — your guests won't complain.

- **Sixteen 2-oz (60 mL) shooter glasses (see Tip, left)**

1	slice (about ½ inch/1 cm) day-old country bread, crust removed	1
1	green bell pepper, quartered	1
6	green onions, white with a bit of green, cut into 2-inch (5 cm) chunks	6
1	long red chile pepper, optional	1
1	clove garlic	1
2 cups	packed trimmed arugula (about 1 bunch)	500 mL
½	English cucumber or 1 field cucumber, seeded, peeled and cut into chunks	½
3	large ripe tomatoes, peeled and quartered	3
2 tbsp	red wine vinegar	30 mL
1 tsp	salt	5 mL
½ cup	extra virgin olive oil	125 mL
	Freshly ground black pepper	

1. In a bowl, soak bread in 1 cup (250 mL) water. Squeeze dry and set aside.

2. In a food processor fitted with metal blade, pulse bell pepper, green onions, chile pepper, if using, and garlic until chopped, about 15 times, stopping and scraping down sides of the bowl once or twice. Add arugula, cucumber, tomatoes, vinegar and salt and pulse until coarsely chopped, about 10 times. Add reserved bread and pulse to blend, about 5 times. With motor running, add olive oil through the feed tube. Season to taste with black pepper.

3. Transfer to a pitcher, cover and refrigerate until thoroughly chilled, for at least 3 hours or overnight.

Tomato Gazpacho

Makes 16 servings

When you mention gazpacho, a version of this recipe — built around fresh tomatoes, cucumber, olive oil and vinegar — is usually what comes to mind. However, in Spain, its country of origin, gazpacho refers to a soupy salad, thickened with bread, which can be made from a wide variety of ingredients ranging from lettuce to almonds. We love to make this when fresh tomatoes and cucumbers are in season. As with most cold soups, we recommend that you keep extra chilling in the refrigerator for a perfect snack on a hot day.

Tip

Extra virgin olive oil is called for here because of its more complex flavors, which will enhance the soup. Also, since the oil is not heated it will maintain all of its flavor and healthful properties.

- **Sixteen 2-oz (60 mL) shooter glasses**

1	slice (about $1/2$ inch/1 cm) day-old country bread, crust removed	1
1	red bell pepper, quartered	1
$1/2$	small red onion	$1/2$
1 to 2	jalapeño peppers, seeded and quartered	1 to 2
1 to 2	cloves garlic	1 to 2
3	large ripe tomatoes, peeled, cored and quartered	3
1	cucumber, peeled and cut into chunks (1 inch/2.5 cm)	1
2 tbsp	sherry or red wine vinegar	30 mL
1 tsp	salt	5 mL
$1/2$ cup	extra virgin olive oil (see Tip, left)	125 mL
	Freshly ground black pepper	

1. Soak bread in $1/2$ cup (125 mL) water. Squeeze dry and set aside.

2. In a food processor fitted with metal blade, pulse bell pepper, red onion, jalapeño and garlic to taste until chopped, about 15 times, stopping and scraping down sides of the bowl once or twice. Add tomatoes, cucumber, vinegar and salt and pulse until coarsely chopped, about 10 times. Add reserved bread and pulse to blend, about 5 times. With motor running, add olive oil through feed tube. Season with black pepper to taste.

3. Transfer to a pitcher, cover and refrigerate until thoroughly chilled, for at least 3 hours or for up to 3 days.

Almond Gazpacho with Green Grapes

Makes 8 servings

Serve this soup very cold for a refreshing treat on a hot summer's day. This makes a small quantity, but small servings are appropriate and the recipe can easily be doubled. It's a great way to use up leftover baguette.

Tips

For the best flavor, buy almonds with the skin on and blanch them yourself. *To blanch almonds:* Drop almonds in a pot of rapidly boiling water and boil until the skins start to pucker. Transfer to a colander and rinse well under cold running water. Using your hands, pop the almonds out of their skins. Place on paper towels and let dry for at least 10 minutes, changing the paper towels, if necessary.

Although it may seem like a lot of work, it is important to press the liquid out of the solids until they are virtually dry. Otherwise your gazpacho will lack the rich almond flavor that makes this soup so delicious.

- **Eight 2-oz (60 mL) shooter glasses**

1	piece (about 3 inches/7.5 cm) stale baguette, crust removed	1
1 cup	blanched almonds (see Tips, left)	250 mL
1	clove garlic	1
2 tbsp	best-quality sherry vinegar (approx.)	30 mL
2 cups	ice water, divided	500 mL
2 tbsp	extra virgin olive oil (see Tip, page 102) plus additional for drizzling	30 mL
	Salt and freshly ground white pepper	
4	seedless green grapes, halved	4

1. Soak bread in ½ cup (125 mL) water and squeeze dry and set aside.

2. In a food processor fitted with metal blade, process almonds until quite fine, about 20 seconds, stopping and scraping down sides of the bowl once or twice. Add garlic, vinegar, reserved bread and ½ cup (125 mL) of the ice water and process until smooth, about 10 seconds. Add olive oil, remaining 1½ cups (375 mL) of water, and salt and white pepper to taste and process until blended.

3. Place a fine sieve over a large measuring cup or bowl with a pouring spout and strain soup. Using a wooden spoon, press against solids to extract as much liquid as possible (see Tips, left).

4. Cover and refrigerate until thoroughly chilled, for at least 3 hours or for up to 3 days. Before serving, taste and adjust seasoning. You may need to add a bit more vinegar as well as salt and pepper. To serve, pour into glasses and garnish each with half a grape. Drizzle with olive oil.

Tipsy Tomato Shooter

Makes 16 servings

Served in shot-type glasses, this simple gin-spiked tomato soup looks quite elegant. A garnish of minced jalapeño pepper adds a zesty finish, but if you don't like heat, dill works well, too.

Tip

For best results, use Italian San Marzano tomatoes when making this soup. They are reputedly the best tomatoes in the world and are very flavorful. If you're using domestic tomatoes, you may want to add 1 tsp (5 mL) or so tomato paste and a pinch of sugar before simmering the soup.

- **Sixteen 2-oz (60 mL) shooter glasses**

2 tbsp	butter	30 mL
1	onion, chopped	1
1	carrot, peeled and chopped	1
2	cloves garlic, chopped	2
½ tsp	salt	2 mL
½ tsp	freshly ground pepper, preferably white	2 mL
1	can (14 oz/398 mL) tomatoes with juice (see Tip, left)	1
2 cups	chicken or vegetable broth	500 mL
½ cup	half-and-half (10%) cream	125 mL
¼ cup	gin	60 mL
	Finely chopped dill or minced jalapeño pepper	

1. In a large saucepan, melt butter over medium heat. Add onion and carrot and cook, stirring, until softened, about 5 minutes. Add garlic, salt, and pepper and cook, stirring, for 1 minute. Add tomatoes with juice and broth and bring to a boil. Cover, reduce heat to low and simmer until flavors meld, about 25 minutes.

2. Transfer to a blender or food processor, in batches, or use an immersion blender, and purée. Transfer to a pitcher, cover and refrigerate until thoroughly chilled, for at least 3 hours or for up to 3 days. When you're ready to serve, stir in cream and gin. Taste and adjust seasoning. Pour into glasses and garnish with dill.

Cucumber Avocado Shooter

Makes 16 servings

This soup is so easy to make, yet surprisingly delicious. Serve this at summer parties, when the heat is sweltering — it is remarkably refreshing.

Tip

Use the quantity of jalapeño that suits your taste. If you prefer just a bit of heat, use half of one. If you like the taste of chile, use a whole one.

- **Sixteen 2-oz (60 mL) shooter glasses**

1	English cucumber, seeded and cut into 3-inch (7.5 cm) chunks	1
2	avocados	2
1 cup	plain yogurt, preferably Greek-style	250 mL
¼ cup	coarsely snipped chives	60 mL
½ to 1	jalapeño pepper, halved and seeded	½ to 1
2 tbsp	freshly squeezed lime juice	30 mL
2 tbsp	fresh cilantro leaves	30 mL
	Salt and freshly ground white pepper	

1. In a food processor fitted with metal blade, purée cucumber, avocados, yogurt, 1 cup (250 mL) cold water, chives, jalapeño to taste, lime juice, cilantro, salt and white pepper to taste until smooth. Transfer to a pitcher, cover and refrigerate until chilled, for at least 3 hours.

Watermelon Cooler

Makes 6 servings

On a hot day, few things are more refreshing than a cold slice of watermelon. With that in mind, add some citrus, a hint of ginger and some mint for garnish and you have the perfect summer drink. If you're looking for something particularly festive, blend it with an equal quantity of cold prosecco (see Variation, right).

- **Six 4-oz (125 mL) glasses**

4 cups	cubed (1 inch/2.5 cm) seeded watermelon	1 L
2 tbsp	agave syrup	30 mL
½ tsp	finely grated lime zest	1 mL
2 tbsp	freshly squeezed lime juice	30 mL
1 tsp	minced gingerroot	5 mL
	Fresh mint leaves	

1. In a blender, purée watermelon, agave syrup, lime zest and juice and ginger until smooth and liquidy. Transfer to a pitcher, cover and refrigerate until thoroughly chilled, about 3 hours. Serve cold, garnished with mint.

Variation

Watermelon Prosecco Cooler: Combine Watermelon Cooler with an equal quantity of chilled prosecco.

Summer Borscht

Makes 16 servings

This soup is worth serving based on its luscious color alone but it's delicious and refreshing to boot. Served in clear crystal shooter glasses, it makes a very elegant presentation and will get any garden party off to a great start.

Tip

When cold, we love to serve shooters in clear glassware because most are intensely colored and look very pretty. When hot, they require a heatproof vessel and work well in espresso or demi-tasse cups. But if you don't have appropriate glassware, feel free to serve cold shooters in cups — your guests won't complain.

- **Sixteen 2-oz (60 mL) shooter glasses**

1 tbsp	butter or olive oil	15 mL
1	shallot, sliced	1
2	cloves garlic, chopped	2
2	whole cloves	2
2	whole allspice	2
	Salt and freshly ground black pepper	
2	medium beets, peeled and quartered (8 oz/250 g)	2
2 cups	chicken or vegetable broth	500 mL
1 tbsp	liquid honey, optional	15 mL
1 cup	plain yogurt, preferably Greek-style (pressed) (see Tips, page 107), or soy yogurt	250 mL
¼ cup	minced seeded cucumber	60 mL
¼ cup	minced red onion	60 mL
1 tbsp	finely chopped fresh dill fronds	15 mL

1. In a saucepan, melt butter over medium heat. Add shallot and garlic and cook, stirring, until softened, about 3 minutes. Add cloves, allspice, and salt and pepper to taste and cook, stirring, for 1 minute. Add beets and broth and bring to a boil. Cover, reduce heat to low and simmer until beets are tender, about 20 minutes. Remove and discard cloves and allspice. Stir in honey, if using.

2. Using an immersion blender, purée until smooth. Or, place a strainer over a large measuring cup or bowl with a pouring spout and strain soup. Transfer solids and 1 cup (250 mL) of the liquid to a food processor fitted with metal blade. Purée until smooth. Return solids to liquid and stir well. Cover and refrigerate until thoroughly chilled, for at least 3 hours or for up to 3 days. When you're ready to serve, whisk in yogurt. Taste and adjust seasoning.

3. In a small bowl, combine cucumber, red onion and dill. Stir to combine. To serve, ladle soup into glasses and garnish with cucumber mixture.

Spicy Carrot Cooler

Makes 16 servings

Carrots, seasoned with warm spices such as cumin and cayenne and finished with yogurt, make a surprisingly refreshing summer cooler.

Tips

If you like heat, add more cayenne — as much as ⅛ tsp (0.5 mL).

Make an effort to get Greek-style yogurt, also known as "pressed." It is lusciously thick and adds beautiful depth to this and many other dishes. Greek yogurt is available in well-stocked supermarkets and specialty stores. If you can't find it, you can make your own. *To make Greek-style yogurt:* Line a sieve with a double layer of cheesecloth or paper towels. Add plain yogurt, cover and refrigerate overnight. The watery component will have drained out and you will be left with lovely thick yogurt.

- **Sixteen 2-oz (60 mL) shooter glasses**

1 tbsp	butter	15 mL
1	small onion, chopped	1
3	carrots, chopped	3
1	clove garlic, minced	1
1 tsp	ground cumin (see Tips, page 114)	5 mL
1 tsp	sweet paprika	5 mL
½ tsp	granulated sugar	2 mL
½ tsp	salt	2 mL
Pinch	cayenne (see Tips, left)	Pinch
2 tsp	red wine vinegar	10 mL
2 cups	chicken or vegetable broth	500 mL
⅓ cup	plain full-fat yogurt, preferably Greek-style (see Tips, left)	75 mL
	Finely chopped dill or parsley	

1. In a large saucepan, melt butter over medium heat. Add onion and carrots and cook, stirring, until softened, about 7 minutes. Add garlic, cumin, paprika, sugar, salt and cayenne and cook, stirring, for 1 minute. Stir in vinegar. Add broth and bring to a boil. Reduce heat and simmer until carrots are very tender, about 20 minutes. Let cool slightly (so yogurt doesn't curdle when added). Stir in yogurt.

2. Transfer to a blender or food processor fitted with metal blade, in batches if necessary, or use an immersion blender, and purée until smooth. Cover and refrigerate until thoroughly chilled, for at least 3 hours. Taste and adjust seasoning. Pour into glasses and garnish with dill.

Cold Cantaloupe Shooter

Makes 16 servings

For an eye-popping presentation, serve in a Chinese soup spoon with a trio of finely diced cantaloupe, honeydew and watermelon.

- **Sixteen 2-oz (60 mL) shooter glasses**

4 cups	chopped cantaloupe	1 L
1 cup	guava nectar or pineapple juice	250 mL
¼ cup	orange segments	60 mL
1 tbsp	granulated sugar	15 mL
½ tsp	salt	2 mL
½ tsp	ground cardamom	2 mL

1. In a blender, purée cantaloupe, guava nectar, orange segments, sugar, salt and cardamom until smooth. Place a fine-mesh strainer over a large bowl and strain soup, discarding solids. Cover and refrigerate until thoroughly chilled or overnight before serving.

Cold Pineapple Cilantro Shooter

Makes 12 servings

This is incredible served on a warm summer day — it's so refreshing. Try freezing the soup in ice cube trays covered with plastic wrap, just before frozen, stick a Popsicle stick in the middle of each cube!

Tip

More often than not, foods seasoned warm will require additional seasoning if served cold. In this instance the shooter may require a little more agave, vanilla or cilantro.

- **Twelve 2-oz (60 mL) shooter glasses**

3 cups	water	750 mL
2 cups	chopped pineapple	500 mL
1 tsp	agave syrup	5 mL
⅛ tsp	vanilla extract	0.5 mL
¼ cup	coarsely chopped fresh cilantro leaves	60 mL

1. In a saucepan over medium heat, bring water, pineapple, agave syrup and vanilla to a boil. Reduce heat and boil gently until liquid is reduced by one-quarter, 10 to 12 minutes. Add cilantro. Transfer to a blender, or use an immersion blender, and purée until smooth. Transfer to a pitcher, cover and refrigerate until thoroughly chilled or overnight. Check seasoning (see Tip, left) before serving.

Thandai

Makes 12 servings

Thandai is a gently spiced sweet milk-based drink from Northern India. On a hot day it is very refreshing and quite delicious. It is often made using only almonds but here additional cashews enhance the complexity.

Tip

When cold, we love to serve shooters in clear glassware because most are intensely colored and look very pretty. When hot, they require a heatproof vessel and work well in espresso or demi-tasse cups. But if you don't have appropriate glassware, feel free to serve cold shooters in cups — your guests won't complain.

- **Twelve 2-oz (60 mL) shooter glasses**

2 tsp	cumin seeds (see Tips, page 114)	10 mL
15	blanched almonds (see Tips, page 103)	15
6	unsalted roasted cashews	6
8	cardamom pods (black or green), crushed	8
1	piece (about 2 inches/5 cm) cinnamon stick	1
¼ cup	liquid honey	60 mL
¾ cup	boiling water	175 mL
2 cups	milk	500 mL

1. In a dry skillet over medium heat, toast cumin seeds, stirring constantly, until fragrant, about 3 minutes. Transfer to a mortar or a spice grinder and grind very coarsely.

2. Transfer cumin to a heatproof bowl or cup with a volume of at least 2 cups (500 mL). Add almonds, cashews, cardamom pods and cinnamon stick. In a measuring cup, combine honey and boiling water. Stir well to combine. Pour over nut mixture and set aside until slightly cooled, about 5 minutes.

3. Transfer to a blender, or use an immersion blender, and purée until smooth. Line a fine sieve with two layers of cheesecloth and place over a bowl or pitcher. Add nut mixture and strain, using a wooden spoon to press out liquid, extracting as much of the liquid as possible. Collect the corners of the cheesecloth and twist them to form a tight ball. Using your hands, squeeze out remaining liquid. Discard solids. Stir in milk. Cover and refrigerate until thoroughly chilled, for at least 3 hours or for up to 3 days.

Mango Lassi

Makes about 4 cups (1 L)

Lassi is an Indian drink that is often used to mitigate spicy meals. In India, it is usually part of the breakfast buffet at large hotels. It is flavorful and refreshing and makes an interesting starter for a summer meal.

- **Sixteen 2-oz (60 mL) servings**

2 cups	finely chopped very ripe fresh mango (about 1 large)	500 mL
¾ cup	plain full-fat yogurt, preferably goat's milk (see Tip, below)	175 mL
½ cup	buttermilk (see Tip, below)	125 mL
½ cup	ice cubes	125 mL

1. In a blender, purée mango, yogurt and buttermilk until smooth. Pour half of mixture into a large pitcher. Add ice cubes to liquid remaining in the blender and blend until ice is chopped and mixture is frothy. Add to pitcher and stir well. Cover and refrigerate until thoroughly chilled, for at least 1 hour or for up to 3 days.

Banana Lassi

Makes 16 servings

Lassi is a perfect beverage for a garden party on a hot summer day. Refrigerate leftovers and enjoy them for breakfast.

Tip

Using buttermilk instead of regular milk helps to create a more "Indian flavor," although plain milk will do. Goat milk yogurt, which is slightly more acidic than that made from cow's milk, will also help to create a more authentic taste.

- **Sixteen 2-oz (60 mL) shooter glasses**

3	ripe bananas, cut into chunks	3
1 cup	plain full-fat yogurt, preferably goat's milk (see Tip, left)	250 mL
1 cup	buttermilk (see Tip, left)	250 mL
1 cup	ice cubes	250 mL

1. In a blender, purée bananas, yogurt and buttermilk until smooth. Pour half of mixture into a large pitcher. Add ice cubes to liquid remaining in the blender and blend until ice is chopped and mixture is frothy. Add to pitcher and stir well. Cover and refrigerate until thoroughly chilled, for at least 1 hour or for up to 3 days.

Strawberry Rhubarb Shooter

Makes 18 servings

This shooter is a savory alternative to the usual strawberry and rhubarb combination. A garnish of finely diced strawberries and lavender or thyme leaves would make this particularly elegant.

Tips

A Riesling or Sauternes white wine works very well in this recipe but don't be afraid to use your favorite white wine — it is after all, all about what you like.

In spring and summer lavender grows in many herb gardens everywhere, but in the absence of fresh lavender, dried lavender would substitute nicely but should be added with the strawberries and white wine.

- **18 espresso or demi-tasse cups**

1 tbsp	unsalted butter	15 mL
1 tbsp	packed brown sugar	15 mL
1¼ cups	diced rhubarb	300 mL
¼ cup	diced onion	60 mL
¾ cup	thinly sliced strawberries	175 mL
¼ cup	sweet white wine (see Tips, left)	60 mL
½ cup	hot water	125 mL
¼ tsp	coarsely chopped fresh lavender flowers (see Tips, left)	1 mL
¼ cup	heavy or whipping (35%) cream	60 mL

1. In a saucepan, melt butter and brown sugar over medium heat until bubbles start forming and mixture starts to caramelize, 2 to 3 minutes. Add rhubarb and onion and cook, stirring, until rhubarb is soft, 5 to 6 minutes. Add strawberries and white wine and bring to a boil. Reduce heat and boil until liquid is reduced by half, about 5 minutes. Add hot water and lavender. Transfer to a blender, or use an immersion blender, and purée until smooth. Place a fine-mesh strainer over a large bowl and strain soup, discarding solids. Stir in cream. Serve immediately or refrigerate for up to 3 days. If refrigerated, reheat before serving.

Rum-Spiked Watermelon Shooter

Makes 8 servings

This makes a wonderful aperitif to serve on a hot summer day.

Tip

When cold, we love to serve shooters in clear glassware because most are intensely colored and look very pretty.

- **8 shooter glasses**

4 cups	coarsely chopped seedless watermelon	1 L
1 tbsp	coconut-flavored rum	15 mL
1 tsp	liquid honey	5 mL
½ tsp	salt	2 mL

1. In a food processor fitted with a metal blade or using an immersion blender in a tall measuring cup, purée watermelon until smooth. With the back of a large spoon, press the watermelon through a fine-mesh strainer over a bowl extracting all of the watermelon juice and discarding any pulp. Add rum, honey and salt and stir well to combine. Serve immediately or refrigerate for up to 3 days.

Tomato Avocado Shooter

Makes 15 servings

A unique way to enjoy avocado. Garnish with a chiffonade of basil and crumbled goat cheese.

Tip

You can use an immersion blender instead of a blender.

- **Fifteen 2-oz (60 mL) shooter glasses**

1 tbsp	olive oil	15 mL
2 cups	diced tomatoes	500 mL
¾ cup	diced onion	175 mL
1 tsp	minced garlic	5 mL
2 cups	chicken or vegetable broth	500 mL
1	large avocado, cut into chunks	1
1 tbsp	coarsely chopped fresh basil leaves	15 mL
1 tbsp	white balsamic vinegar	15 mL
½ tsp	salt	2 mL
2 tbsp	heavy or whipping (35%) cream	30 mL

1. In a saucepan, heat oil over medium heat. Add tomato, onion and garlic and cook, stirring, until tomatoes are broken down, about 5 minutes. Add broth and bring to a boil. Reduce heat and simmer for 5 minutes. Add avocado, basil, vinegar and salt. Remove from heat and add cream. Transfer to a blender and purée until smooth. Serve immediately.

Black Bean and Feta Shooter

Makes 16 servings

Feta cheese adds an incredible tangy salty flavor to this shooter. It's the perfect complement to black beans. Garnish with diced avocado, which adds a lovely textural and temperature contrast.

Tip

You can make a ground cumin spice mixture and use it here if you like. It's a combination of equal parts cumin seeds, coriander seeds, hot pepper flakes and mustard seeds. Spice blends can be conveniently stored in pepper mills and ground when needed or in a mortar and grind with a pestle, which provides the freshest flavor. If storing in a pepper mill, be sure to label it to keep track of ingredients.

- **Sixteen 2-oz (60 mL) shooter glasses**

1 tbsp	unsalted butter	15 mL
¾ cup	diced onion	175 mL
1 tsp	minced garlic	5 mL
1 cup	diced tomatoes	250 mL
1⅔ cups	cooked drained black beans (see Tip, page 77)	400 mL
3 cups	chicken or vegetable broth	750 mL
1 tsp	salt	5 mL
½ tsp	ground cumin (see Tip, left)	2 mL
½ cup	coarsely chopped fresh cilantro leaves	125 mL
½ cup	crumbled feta cheese	125 mL

1. In a saucepan, melt butter over medium heat. Add onion and garlic and cook, stirring, until onion is translucent, about 5 minutes. Add tomatoes and black beans and cook, stirring, until tomatoes are broken down, about 5 minutes. Add chicken broth, salt and cumin and bring to a boil. Reduce heat and boil until liquid is reduced by one-quarter, about 10 minutes. Stir in cilantro and feta cheese. Serve immediately or transfer to a bowl, cover and refrigerate for up to 3 days.

Potato and Smoked Bacon Purée

Makes 16 servings

This soup is packed with smoky flavor. It's like eating Southern barbecue. This shooter is very classy served in a Chinese soup spoon garnished with fresh thyme leaves and a touch of whipped cream.

Tips

Because leeks can be gritty, it is customary to slice and rinse them before using. *To clean leeks:* Fill a sink full of lukewarm water. Split the leeks in half lengthwise and submerge in the water, swishing them around to remove all traces of dirt. Transfer to a colander and rinse thoroughly under cold water.

For the best flavor, toast and grind whole cumin seeds rather than buying ground cumin. *To toast cumin seeds:* Simply stir seeds in a dry skillet over medium heat until fragrant, about 3 minutes. Immediately transfer to a spice grinder or mortar and grind.

- **Sixteen 2-oz (60 mL) shooter glasses**

¼ cup	finely diced double smoked bacon	60 mL
2 cups	cubed russet (Idaho) potatoes	500 mL
1½ cups	thinly sliced leeks, white and light green parts only (see Tips, left)	375 mL
1 cup	thinly sliced red onion	250 mL
2	thyme sprigs	2
1 tsp	ground cumin (see Tips, left)	5 mL
¼ tsp	chipotle powder	1 mL
2 cups	chicken or vegetable broth	500 mL
1 cup	water	250 mL
¼ cup	heavy or whipping (35%) cream	60 mL
1 tsp	fresh thyme leaves, optional	5 mL
¼ tsp	salt	1 mL
	Freshly ground black pepper	

1. In a large saucepan over medium heat, cook bacon until cooked through, about 8 minutes. (Do not cook until too crispy or it will be too chewy.) Add potatoes, leeks, red onion, thyme, cumin and chipotle powder and cook, stirring, until onions are soft, 10 to 12 minutes.

2. Add chicken broth and water and bring to a boil. Cover pot, reduce heat to low and simmer until potatoes are almost breaking down, about 20 minutes. Discard thyme sprigs. Transfer to a blender or food processor fitted with metal blade, in batches if necessary, or use an immersion blender, and pulse just until broken down (be sure not to over blend as soup can become gluey). Let cool for about 15 minutes. Before serving, stir in cream, thyme, if using, salt, and pepper to taste. Serve immediately or refrigerate for up to 3 days. Reheat before serving.

Sweet Onion Shooter

Makes 16 servings

Vegetarian Friendly

Try this shooter either warm or cold. Garnish shooter with crème fraîche or, for a wonderful textural contrast, crispy fried shallots or onions or Shoestring Onion Rings (page 422).

Tip

Herbes de Provence is a robust mixture of dried herbs such as thyme, fennel and lavender, among others. You can buy it prepackaged, often in pretty little pottery crocks and it is worth having because it is a very flavorful addition to certain recipes.

- **16 espresso or demi-tasse cups**

2 tbsp	unsalted butter	30 mL
4 cups	thinly sliced onions	1 L
¾ cup	thinly sliced parsnip	175 mL
1 cup	dry white wine	250 mL
2 cups	chicken or vegetable broth	500 mL
½ tsp	salt	2 mL
¼ tsp	freshly ground black pepper	1 mL
¼ tsp	herbes de Provence (see Tip, left)	1 mL

1. In a large saucepan, melt butter over medium heat. Add onions and parsnip and cook, stirring, until onions begin to caramelize, about 15 minutes. Add wine and bring to a boil. Reduce heat and boil until liquid is reduced by half, about 3 minutes. Add chicken broth, salt, pepper and herbes de Provence and bring to a simmer. Simmer until reduced by one-quarter, 10 to 12 minutes. Transfer to a blender or food processor fitted with metal blade, in batches, if necessary, or use an immersion blender, and purée until smooth. Serve immediately or refrigerate for up to 3 days. If refrigerated, reheat before serving.

Beet and Goat Cheese Shooter

Makes 8 servings

The combination of beet and goat cheese is typically found in salad form but boy is it delicious as a shooter. Garnish with sour cream or crème fraîche and toasted almonds.

- **8 espresso or demi-tasse cups**

1 tbsp	olive oil	15 mL
2 cups	cubed peeled beets	500 mL
2/3 cup	diced red onion	150 mL
2	thyme sprigs	2
2 cups	chicken or vegetable broth	500 mL
1/4 cup	milk, warmed	60 mL
2 oz	soft goat cheese	60 g
1/2 tsp	sherry vinegar	2 mL

1. In a saucepan, heat oil over medium heat. Add beets, onion and thyme and cook, stirring, until onion is translucent, about 10 minutes. Add broth and bring to a boil. Reduce heat and simmer until beets are soft, 10 to 12 minutes. Transfer to a blender and purée until smooth. Transfer to a bowl and add milk, cheese and vinegar and whisk until goat cheese melts into soup.

Savory Almond Shooter

Makes 12 servings

Adapted from the traditional Spanish Christmas soup, this almond shooter can be served as a savory or dessert appetizer. For a savory offering, a garnish of chopped cilantro leaves would be perfect, and for a dessert shooter, add a sprinkle of dark or light brown sugar.

Tip

If refrigerating, reheat before serving.

- **12 espresso or demi-tasse cups**

1 tbsp	unsalted butter	15 mL
2/3 cup	diced onion	150 mL
1 tbsp	minced garlic	15 mL
1 tsp	whole coriander seeds	5 mL
3/4 cup	whole almonds	175 mL
2 cups	chicken broth	500 mL
1/4 cup	thinly sliced green onions	60 mL

1. In a saucepan, melt butter over medium heat. Add onion, garlic and coriander and cook, stirring, until onion is translucent, about 5 minutes. Add almonds and cook, stirring, until toasted, about 10 minutes. Add broth and bring to a boil. Reduce heat and simmer, about 5 minutes. Add green onions. Transfer to a blender and purée until smooth. Place a mesh strainer over a bowl and strain soup, discarding solids. Serve or refrigerate for up to 3 days (see Tip, left).

Sweet Corn Shooter

Makes 16 servings

This shooter is as good as eating corn straight from the cob. In the height of corn season this may be the only soup you choose to make, it's that good! Garnish with a drizzle of brown butter (see Tips, below) for a lovely nutty accent.

Tips

To make brown butter: Warm 2 tbsp (30 mL) unsalted butter over medium heat and melt, stirring often, until butter turns light brown in color and gives off a nutty aroma, about 3 minutes.

Corn cobs have so much flavor even after kernels have been removed. For an intensely corn-flavored shooter, we recommend adding them to the saucepan to extract all of that wonderful corn flavor. When removing them, be sure to scrape any liquid that has made its way into the cavities of the cob — no flavor should be left behind.

- **16 espresso or demi-tasse cups**

1 tbsp	unsalted butter	15 mL
1 tsp	olive oil	5 mL
3 cups	fresh corn kernels, cobs reserved	750 mL
1/2 cup	diced celery	125 mL
2	cloves garlic	2
1 tsp	salt	5 mL
1/2 tsp	ground cumin seeds (see Tips, page 114)	2 mL
4 cups	chicken or vegetable broth	1 L
3	thyme sprigs	3
1/4 cup	fresh cilantro leaves	60 mL

1. In a large saucepan, heat butter and oil over medium-high heat. Sauté corn kernels, cobs, celery, garlic, salt and cumin until corn kernels are soft, about 5 minutes. Add chicken broth and thyme and bring to a boil. Reduce heat and simmer until celery is soft and broth is flavorful, about 10 minutes. Discard cobs and thyme sprigs. Add cilantro. Transfer to a blender or food processor fitted with metal blade, in batches, if necessary, or use an immersion blender, and purée until smooth. Serve immediately or refrigerate for up to 3 days. If refrigerated, reheat before serving.

Mushroom Shooter

Makes 16 servings

The absolute best way to enjoy a button mushroom. There's something very comforting and cozy about Mushroom Shooters served on a cold evening. Garnish with truffle oil or sour cream.

Tip

Although we suggest using white button mushrooms for this recipe, cremini, chanterelle or portobello mushrooms would all be wonderful, but definitely more expensive.

- **16 espresso or demi-tasse cups**

1 tbsp	unsalted butter	15 mL
1 tbsp	olive oil	15 mL
4 cups	sliced button mushrooms (see Tip, left)	1 L
¾ cup	diced onion	175 mL
2 tbsp	minced garlic	30 mL
3	thyme sprigs	3
3 cups	chicken or vegetable broth	750 mL
½ tsp	salt	2 mL
½ tsp	freshly ground black pepper	2 mL
2 tbsp	heavy or whipping (35%) cream	30 mL
1 tbsp	sherry vinegar	15 mL

1. In a saucepan, heat butter and oil over medium heat. Add mushrooms, onion, garlic and thyme and cook, stirring, until mushrooms are soft, about 8 minutes. Add broth, salt and pepper and bring to a boil. Reduce heat and simmer until liquid is reduced by one-quarter, about 10 minutes. Transfer to a blender, or use an immersion blender, and purée until smooth. Transfer to a bowl and whisk in cream and vinegar. Serve immediately or cover and refrigerate for up to 3 days. If refrigerated, reheat before serving.

Hawaiian Shiitake Shooter

Makes 8 servings

This very powerful shooter is packed full of flavor and is best served aerated (see Tip, below).

Tip

To aerate shooters, just before serving, using an immersion blender close to surface of hot soup, blend to form lots of bubbles. Spoon foam from top into shooter glasses and repeat until all vessels are full.

- **8 espresso or demi-tasse cups**

1 tbsp	unsalted butter	15 mL
1½ cups	chopped shiitake mushroom caps	375 mL
1½ cups	chicken or vegetable broth	375 mL
½ cup	whole milk	125 mL
1 tbsp	each hoisin sauce and soy sauce	15 mL
1 tbsp	packed brown sugar	15 mL

1. In a saucepan, melt butter over medium heat. Add mushrooms and cook, stirring, until caramelized, 4 to 5 minutes. Add broth, milk, hoisin sauce, soy sauce and brown sugar and bring to a boil. Transfer to a blender, in batches if necessary, or use an immersion blender, and purée until smooth. Serve immediately or refrigerate for up to 3 days. Reheat before serving.

Acorn Squash Sage Shooter

Makes 16 servings

Squash paired with sage will warm your insides on a cold fall or winter's day. Garnish with melted butter or Pesto Oil (page 122).

Tip

Serve shooter immediately or transfer to a bowl, cover and refrigerate for up to 3 days. If refrigerating, add the sage leaves and reheat just before serving.

- **16 espresso or demi-tasse cups**

1 tbsp	olive oil	15 mL
1 tsp	unsalted butter	5 mL
3 cups	diced acorn squash	750 mL
2	cloves garlic	2
	Salt and freshly ground black pepper	
4 cups	chicken or vegetable broth	1 L
1 tbsp	pure maple syrup	15 mL
1 tbsp	coarsely chopped fresh sage leaves	15 mL

1. In a saucepan, heat oil and butter over medium heat. Add squash, garlic and 1 tsp (5 mL) salt and cook, stirring, until squash is caramelized, 10 to 15 minutes. Add broth and bring to a simmer. Reduce heat and boil gently until squash is falling apart, 15 to 20 minutes. Add syrup, sage and ½ tsp (2 mL) pepper. Transfer to blender and purée until smooth. Serve immediately.

Carrot Ginger Shooter

Makes 16 servings

Super simple to prepare, this Asian-inspired shooter can be served hot or cold. If serving warm, garnish with crushed Agave and Ginger-Scented Peanuts (page 455) or use finely chopped roasted peanuts. If serving cold, garnish with a dollop of sour cream.

Tips

When cold, we love to serve shooters in clear glassware because most are intensely colored and look very pretty. When hot, they require a heatproof vessel and work well in espresso or demi-tasse cups. But if you don't have appropriate glassware, feel free to serve cold shooters in cups — your guests won't complain.

To easily grate ginger: Store your ginger in the freezer and grate frozen. Don't bother peeling the ginger as the peel will not affect the flavor or texture.

- **Sixteen 2-oz (60 mL) shooter glasses (see Tips, left)**

1 tbsp	unsalted butter	15 mL
2 cups	coarsely chopped peeled carrots	500 mL
¼ cup	finely diced dried apricots	60 mL
1 tbsp	finely grated gingerroot (see Tips, left)	15 mL
3 cups	chicken or vegetable broth	750 mL
1 tsp	salt	5 mL
1 tsp	agave syrup	5 mL
1 tsp	coarsely chopped fresh cilantro leaves	5 mL
½ tsp	freshly ground black pepper	2 mL
⅔ cup	heavy or whipping (35%) cream	150 mL

1. In a saucepan, melt butter over medium heat. Add carrots and cook, stirring, until caramelized, 8 to 10 minutes. Stir in apricots and ginger. Add chicken broth and salt and bring to a boil. Reduce and simmer until liquid is reduced by one-quarter, about 15 minutes. Add agave syrup, cilantro and pepper. Transfer to a blender, or use an immersion blender, and purée mixture until smooth. Stir in cream. Serve immediately or transfer to a bowl, cover and refrigerate for up to 3 days. If refrigerated, reheat before serving.

Spring Scallion and Tomato Shooter

Makes 16 servings

If you live in northern climates, this is a great shooter to make in spring when the first spring scallions and ramps (also known as wild leeks) start coming into markets. The ease of preparation and refreshing flavors will remind you of how delicious springtime can be.

Tip

Chipotle powder is made from finely grated smoked jalapeños and adds a wonderful smoky and spicy flavor to your foods. It can be found in the dry herb and spice sections of most large supermarkets. Smoked paprika or ancho chile powder would also substitute nicely here.

- **16 espresso or demi-tasse cups**

1 tbsp	olive oil	15 mL
1 tsp	unsalted butter	5 mL
2 cups	diced tomatoes	500 mL
1 cup	coarsely chopped green onions or ramps	250 mL
1/4 cup	diced onion	60 mL
2	cloves garlic	2
1/4 tsp	chipotle chile powder (see Tip, left)	1 mL
3 cups	chicken or vegetable broth	750 mL
1/2 tsp	salt	2 mL

1. In a medium saucepan, heat oil and butter over medium-high heat. Sauté tomatoes, green onions, onion, garlic and chipotle powder until onion is soft and tomatoes are breaking down, 5 to 6 minutes. Add broth and salt and bring to a boil. Reduce heat and simmer until liquid is reduced by one-quarter, about 10 minutes. Transfer to a blender or food processor fitted with metal blade, in batches if necessary, or use an immersion blender, and purée until smooth. Serve immediately or refrigerate for up to 3 days. If refrigerated, reheat before serving.

Broccoli Pesto Shooter

Makes 16 servings

A vibrant green soup that has flavors just as bright. Basil Pesto is easy to make but great quality pestos are also available in your local food shops, too, so now there's no excuse not to make this shooter.

Tip

When cold, we love to serve shooters in clear glassware because most are intensely colored and look very pretty. When hot, they require a heatproof vessel and work well in espresso or demi-tasse cups. But if you don't have appropriate glassware, feel free to serve cold shooters in cups — your guests won't complain.

- **16 espresso or demi-tasse cups**

1	bunch broccoli	1
1 tbsp	olive oil	15 mL
1/2 tsp	unsalted butter	2 mL
1/4 cup	diced onion	60 mL
2	cloves garlic	2
1/4 tsp	salt	1 mL
1/4 tsp	freshly ground black pepper	1 mL
3 1/2 cups	chicken or vegetable broth	875 mL
1 1/2 tbsp	Basil Pesto (page 549) or store-bought	22 mL

1. Cut stems from broccoli heads. Coarsely chop heads and measure 2 1/2 cups (625 mL) florets. Trim thick peel off stems and coarsely chop stems, then measure 1 1/2 cups (375 mL). Reserve any remaining broccoli for another use.

2. In a medium saucepan, heat oil and butter over medium heat. Add broccoli stems, onion, garlic, salt and pepper and cook, stirring, until onion is soft, about 5 minutes. Add chicken broth and bring to a boil. Add broccoli florets and reduce heat and boil gently until soft, 8 to 10 minutes. Remove from heat and add pesto. Transfer to a blender or food processor fitted with metal blade, in batches if necessary, or use an immersion blender, and purée until smooth. Serve immediately or refrigerate for up to 3 days. If refrigerated, reheat before serving.

Variation

Pesto Oil: Combine 2 tbsp (30 mL) extra virgin olive oil and 1 tbsp (15 mL) pesto and garnish shooter with a little drizzle of this flavored oil.

Red Pepper Chive Shooter

Makes 16 servings

Chives add a subtle peppery note to a sweet pepper — the contrast is absolutely perfect. If you prefer, garnish with 1/2 tsp (2 mL) crème fraîche.

Tip

To roast peppers: Preheat broiler. Place pepper(s) on a baking sheet and broil, turning two or three times, until skin on all sides is blackened, about 25 minutes. Transfer to a heatproof bowl. Cover with a plate and let stand until cool. Remove and, using a sharp knife, lift skins off. Discard skins, core and seeds.

- **16 espresso or demi-tasse cups**

1 tbsp	olive oil	15 mL
3 cups	diced red bell peppers	750 mL
1 cup	coarsely chopped roasted red bell peppers (see Tip, left)	250 mL
1/2 cup	diced peeled carrots	125 mL
1 tbsp	thinly sliced garlic	15 mL
1/2 cup	dry white wine	125 mL
3 cups	chicken or vegetable broth	750 mL
1/4 cup	coarsely chopped fresh chives	60 mL
	Crème fraîche, optional	

1. In a saucepan, heat oil over medium-low heat. Add diced peppers, roasted peppers, carrots and garlic and cook, stirring, until diced peppers are soft, about 20 minutes. Add wine and bring to a boil. Boil until liquid is reduced by half, about 5 minutes. Add broth and bring to a boil. Reduce heat and simmer until peppers are breaking apart, about 10 minutes. Add chives. Transfer to a blender or food processor fitted with metal blade, in batches if necessary, or use an immersion blender, and purée until smooth. Serve immediately or refrigerate for up to 3 days. If refrigerated, reheat before serving. Garnish with crème fraîche, if using.

Thai Coconut Shooter

Makes 12 servings

This is a very simple recipe packed full of Thai flavor. Your guests may be fooled into thinking that you slaved all day but we know the truth. A garnish of toasted sesame seeds and toasted sesame oil gives this already explosive shooter even more taste.

Tip

To toast sesame seeds: Place seeds in a dry skillet and cook, stirring, over medium heat until fragrant and turning golden, about 4 minutes.

- **12 espresso or demi-tasse cups**

1 tsp	toasted sesame oil	5 mL
1¼ cups	chopped tomatoes	300 mL
2	cloves garlic	2
2 tsp	Thai green curry paste	10 mL
1 tsp	puréed gingerroot	5 mL
1½ cups	unsweetened coconut milk	375 mL
¾ cup	water	175 mL
½ cup	heavy or whipping (35%) cream	125 mL
1 tbsp	soy sauce	15 mL
½ tsp	rice vinegar	2 mL
	Toasted sesame seeds (see Tip, left)	

1. In a saucepan, heat oil over medium-low heat. Add tomato, garlic, curry paste and ginger and cook, stirring, until tomatoes are breaking apart, 6 to 8 minutes. Add coconut milk and water and bring to a boil. Transfer to a blender or food processor fitted with metal blade, in batches if necessary, or use an immersion blender, and purée until smooth. Place a fine-mesh strainer over a large bowl and strain soup, discarding solids. Add cream, soy sauce and vinegar. Garnish with sesame seeds and serve immediately or refrigerate for up to 3 days. If refrigerated, reheat before serving.

Shrimp Bisque

Makes 8 servings

It's truly amazing what you can do with leftover shrimp shells! So many people would discard them but never again after you taste this recipe!

Tip

When cold, we love to serve shooters in clear glassware because most are intensely colored and look very pretty. When hot, they require a heatproof vessel and work well in espresso or demi-tasse cups. But if you don't have appropriate glassware, feel free to serve cold shooters in cups — your guests won't complain.

* **8 espresso or demi-tasse cups (see Tip, left)**

1 tbsp	olive oil	15 mL
2 cups	shrimp shells	500 mL
1¼ cups	diced onions	300 mL
¾ cup	diced celery	175 mL
¾ cup	dry white wine	175 mL
2 cups	chicken broth	500 mL
1 cup	coarsely chopped tomato	250 mL
¼ tsp	salt	1 mL
¼ tsp	freshly ground black pepper	1 mL
½ cup	heavy or whipping (35%) cream	125 mL

1. In a saucepan, heat oil over medium heat. Add shrimp shells, onions and celery and cook, stirring, until onions are soft and translucent, about 4 minutes. Add wine and bring to a boil. Reduce heat and boil gently until liquid is reduced by half, about 5 minutes. Add broth, tomato, salt and pepper and bring to a boil. Boil until liquid is reduced by half, 15 to 20 minutes. Place a fine-mesh strainer over a large bowl and strain soup, discarding solids. Return to saucepan and bring to a boil over medium-high heat. Reduce heat and boil gently until liquid is reduced by one-quarter, about 5 minutes. Remove from heat and stir in cream. Serve immediately.

Clam Tomato Chowder

Makes 8 servings

This Manhattan clam chowder is very tasty. Serve in an espresso cup with espresso spoon and garnish with crushed soda crackers or crostini (pages 219 and 220).

Tips

Clams and mussels tend to be quite sandy. By soaking in water and cleaning the surface of the bivalves with a regular scouring pad you will remove most, if not all, of the sand and dirt.

To grill corn: Preheat barbecue grill to high. Grill ears of corn, husks on, rotating often until dark brown all over, about 20 minutes. Transfer to a plate and let cool for 5 minutes or until cool enough to handle. Remove husk and silks and, using a serrated knife, cut kernels from cob.

- **8 espresso or demi-tasse cups**

1 tbsp	olive oil	15 mL
1 lb	little neck clams, scrubbed (see Tips, left)	500 g
1 cup	clam juice	250 mL
½ cup	tomato purée or crushed tomatoes	125 mL
½ cup	tomato juice	125 mL
¼ cup	diced peeled sweet potato	60 mL
1 tbsp	thinly sliced or minced garlic	15 mL
½ cup	grilled corn kernels (see Tips, left)	125 mL
½ cup	diced green beans	125 mL
2	thyme sprigs	2
1 tsp	small capers, drained	5 mL
½ tsp	finely chopped fresh dill fronds	2 mL

1. In a saucepan, heat oil over medium heat. Add clams and cook, covered, until clams are beginning to open and releasing liquid, 3 to 4 minutes. Using a slotted spoon, transfer clams in shells to a bowl, leaving behind residual liquid in pan. Add clam juice, tomato purée, tomato juice, sweet potato and garlic to pan. Reduce heat to medium-low, cover and simmer until potatoes are al dente, about 6 minutes. Add corn, green beans and thyme and continue to simmer, covered, until beans are vibrant green, about 2 minutes. Remove from heat and keep covered. Discard any clams that do not open.

2. Remove clams from shells. Discard shells. Stir clams with any accumulated liquid into chowder. Stir in capers and dill. Serve immediately.

Wraps and Rolls

For most North Americans of a certain age, eating Chinese egg rolls dipped in sticky plum sauce evokes fond memories of being a kid. But Chinese cuisine is far from alone in celebrating the pleasures of the perfect roll. From Vietnamese salad rolls and nori-wrapped sushi to Mexican tacos, virtually every culture has its signature wraps and rolls. Served hot or cold, the endless combinations of fillings encased in a wide variety of meats, vegetables or dough make for a kaleidoscope of culinary experiences.

Since many of the recipes in this chapter, such as Salumi (page 131), are extremely simple and easy to make, you can use them to experiment with new textures, techniques and flavors. On the other hand, feel free to make them just because they are delicious entirely on their own terms. Or make them just because they are yummy and fun, like Pigs in a Blanket (page 148).

Prosciutto-Wrapped Asparagus 128
Roasted Fingerling Wraps. 128
Enoki Wraps. 129
Warm Prosciutto-Wrapped Dates 130
Prosciutto-Wrapped Caramelized Cantaloupe . . . 130
Salumi 131
Genoa Salami Rolls 132
Smoked Turkey and Asparagus Rolls 132
Salmon Asparagus Wraps 133
Beef Tenderloin Salad Rolls. 134
Prosciutto and Smoked Mozzarella
    Eggplant Rolls. 135
Tomato-Stuffed Bacon Rolls. 136
Middle Eastern Salad Rolls 136
Barbecue Rib Steak with Onion Sprouts
    and Truffle Vinaigrette 137
Vegetarian Vietnamese Fresh Rolls 138
Eggplant, Tomato and Basil Rolls 139
Pear and Brie Cheese "Rolls" 140
Crispy Vegetarian Spring Rolls 141
Fresh Shrimp Rolls 142
Steamed Leek and Smoked Salmon Pinwheels . . 143

Spinach and Feta Roll-Ups. 144
Anchovy-Spiked Roasted Pepper and
    Feta Roll-Ups 145
Dill-Spiked Mushroom and Cheese Roll-Ups 146
Walnut-Laced Gorgonzola and Leek Roll-Ups . . . 147
Pigs in a Blanket. 148
Pepper-Wrapped Chorizo. 149
Chicken and Broccoli Crystal Fold 150
Chicken Pinwheels with Couscous 151
Chicken Dogs and Pickled Onions 152
Classic Cheese Quesadilla 152
Classic Tuna Sushi 153
Beef Sushi 154
Deconstructed Caesar Salad 155
Cabbage and Duck Confit Rolls 155
Maple-Glazed Bacon and Tomato
    Lettuce Wraps 156
Smoked Salmon and Pickled Onion
    Lettuce Wraps 156
Baby Bok Choy and Tofu Bundles
    with Peanut Sauce 157
Mini Braised Pork Tacos 158

Prosciutto-Wrapped Asparagus

Makes 6 pieces

The combination of salt-cured ham and delicate slightly crunchy asparagus is a match made in heaven. This is very easy to make and the recipe can be increased to meet your needs (see Tip, below). Serve at room temperature.

Tip

Make as few or as many of these as you need. Basically, you'll need 1 thin slice of prosciutto for 2 thin asparagus spears.

- **Preheat barbecue grill to high or broiler**

12	thin asparagus spears, well trimmed (see Tip, left)	12
	Extra virgin olive oil	
	Freshly ground black pepper	
	Freshly grated Parmesan	
6	slices prosciutto, cut in half	6

1. Brush asparagus liberally with olive oil. Place on preheated grill or under broiler and cook, turning once, until tender, about 4 minutes. Transfer to a work surface. Season with pepper to taste and sprinkle liberally with Parmesan. Wrap each spear tightly with prosciutto, leaving the tip exposed. Serve warm.

Roasted Fingerling Wraps

Makes 24 pieces

Easy-to-make and delicious, these are perfect nibblies for a cocktail party.

Tip

To purée garlic: Use a fine sharp-toothed grater such as those made by Microplane.

3	cloves garlic, puréed	3
2 tbsp	extra virgin olive oil	30 mL
12	fingerling potatoes, cut in half lengthwise	12
	Freshly ground black pepper	
12	slices prosciutto, cut in half lengthwise	12

1. In a small bowl, combine garlic and olive oil. Stir well. Cover and set aside for 30 minutes to allow flavors to meld. Strain through a fine sieve, discarding garlic.

2. Meanwhile, preheat oven to 400°F (200°C). In a bowl, combine potatoes and garlic-infused oil. Toss well. Place potatoes on a rimmed baking sheet, cut side down, and roast in preheated oven until tender and browned, about 30 minutes. Set aside until cool enough to handle. Season to taste with black pepper.

3. Wrap each potato half in a slice of prosciutto and spear with a toothpick. Serve warm or at room temperature.

Enoki Wraps

Makes 12 appetizers

Enoki mushrooms, which look like a cluster of small flower buds, have a mild taste and pleasantly crunchy texture. They are reputed to have many healthful properties. Here they are combined with salty prosciutto brushed with persillade, for a tasty treat.

Tips

To purée garlic: Use a fine sharp-toothed grater such as those made by Microplane.

When separating the mushrooms, trim the common bottom and discard, leaving just enough of the base to maintain the desired clusters.

• **Preheat barbecue grill to high or broiler**

Persillade

¼ cup	finely chopped Italian flat-leaf parsley	60 mL
2 tsp	freshly squeezed lemon juice	10 mL
1	clove garlic, puréed (see Tips, left)	1
12	slices prosciutto	12
6 oz	enoki mushrooms, separated into 12 bunches (see Tips, left)	175 g
	Freshly ground black pepper	

1. *Persillade:* In a small bowl, combine parsley, lemon juice and garlic. Stir well and set aside.

2. On a clean work surface, spread 1 slice prosciutto. Brush lightly with persillade and season to taste with pepper. Fold to make an even strip about 1½ inches (4 cm) wide. Wrap tightly around stems of 1 mushroom cluster, holding mushrooms together like a bouquet. Repeat until all mushrooms and prosciutto are used up. Place on preheated grill or under broiler and cook, turning once, just until prosciutto starts to brown, about 4 minutes. Serve warm.

Warm Prosciutto-Wrapped Dates

Makes 12 pieces

Nothing could be easier to make than these delicious little tidbits. They are on the rich side, so assume that two are the maximum any guest will be able to consume. You can easily adjust the quantity to suit your needs.

- **Preheat oven to 400°F (200°C)**

12	thin slices prosciutto	12
12	soft pitted dates	12
1/4 cup	Gorgonzola cheese, optional	60 mL

1. Use 1 slice prosciutto per date. Place date on prosciutto. Stuff center with about 1 tsp (5 mL) Gorgonzola, if using. Fold sides over and roll up to form a packet.
2. Place on a baking sheet. Bake in preheated oven, turning once, until dates are sizzling and prosciutto starts to brown, about 10 minutes.

> **Variation**
>
> **Prosciutto-Wrapped Figs:** Substitute 6 fresh figs, cut in half, for the dates. If using Gorgonzola, place on top of cut side of fig before wrapping.

Prosciutto-Wrapped Caramelized Cantaloupe

Makes 16 pieces

Salty prosciutto is just perfect when paired with the sweetness of cantaloupe. Honeydew or even seedless watermelon would also work wonderfully.

- **Preheat broiler**

16	cubes (1 1/2 inches/4 cm square) cantaloupe	16
4 oz	sliced prosciutto (about 8 slices), cut in half lengthwise	125 g
1 tsp	granulated sugar	5 mL

1. Place prosciutto on a work surface pointing north to south. Place one cube of cantaloupe on end closest to you. Roll up prosciutto around the melon. Place on a baking sheet with one side of melon facing up. Repeat with remaining prosciutto and melon. Dust exposed melon with sugar and broil until sugar is caramelized and golden brown, about 2 minutes. Serve immediately.

Salumi

Salumi is a term used to describe cured meats usually made from pork. In addition to salami, it includes delicacies such as prosciutto, speck, pancetta, mortadella, guanciale and sopressata. Bresaola (air-dried beef) has always been part of the Italian salumi basket but in recent years artisans such as Armandino Batali in Seattle have pushed the envelope on ingredients, creating tasty treats such as Lamb Prosciutto, a trend that is likely to continue.

Although good salumi is expensive, it can be a lifesaver when you're entertaining because it is a virtually instantaneous appetizer. Unless you're cooking for vegetarians, a salumi platter is almost always appropriate. Arrange thin slices of prosciutto and various kinds of salami, cubes of mortadella and small bowls of good olives on a pretty serving plate with an ample supply of crusty bread. If you're so inclined, add your own homemade touches. Wrap prosciutto around thin slices of ripe cantaloupe or fresh figs. Add ramekins of *Caper-Studded Caponata* (page 498), *Celery Root Rémoulade* (page 432), *Baked Ricotta* (page 383) or *Baked Goat Cheese* (page 383). In Italy, *Sweet-and-Sour Cipollini* (page 425) are also a traditional antipasti accompaniment.

In this chapter we've also included numerous recipes for salumi rolls that are a bit more complicated. Salty prosciutto (or its less common relative, speck) is a perfect complement for many vegetables and fruits. Try it with cooked asparagus (*Proscuitto-Wrapped Asparagus*, page 128), enoki mushrooms (*Enoki Wraps*, page 129), fingerling potatoes (*Roasted Fingerling Wraps*, page 128), or dates (*Warm Proscuitto-Wrapped Dates*, page 130). When combined with other ingredients, salumi offers a no-fuss way to create synergy among flavors, producing results that are much more than the sum of their parts.

If you feel like getting a little fancier, try making some simple salumi rolls.

- Wrap thinly sliced salami, prosciutto or speck around bread sticks.
- Cut thinly sliced prosciutto into strips and wrap around chunks of fresh pineapple.
- Spread thinly sliced salami with *Pimento Cheese* (page 379) or *Arugula-Spiked Goat Cheese* (page 374). Roll up and spear with a toothpick, if necessary.
- Brush sliced mortadella with grainy Dijon mustard mixed with an equal quantity of mayonnaise. Lay a thin piece of Italian fontina cheese on top, roll up and secure with a toothpick.

Genoa Salami Rolls

Makes 6 rolls

This sophisticated appetizer is made with simple ingredients. Try dipping these rolls into Caramelized Red Onion Dip (page 39) for an extraordinary combination.

Tip

After hard-cooking the eggs, let cool. Remove whites and use for another purpose.

2	hard-cooked egg yolks (see Tip, left and page 63)	2
1 tbsp	mayonnaise	15 mL
1 tsp	finely chopped Italian flat-leaf parley leaves	5 mL
6	slices Genoa salami	6
6	cornichon pickles, cut in half lengthwise	6
1 tbsp	diced seeded tomato	15 mL

1. In a bowl, whisk together egg yolks, mayonnaise and parsley until smooth. Transfer to a small sandwich bag, remove the air and close. With scissors, cut a small hole in one corner of the bag. Set aside.

2. To assemble, place salami on a work surface and pipe yolk mixture down the center. Garnish with pickles and tomato and roll to enclose. Pierce salami with a toothpick and place on a serving platter. Make these the same day as serving. Pickles tend to overpower everything else if made too far in advance.

Smoked Turkey and Asparagus Rolls

Makes 10 rolls

With so many people avoiding bread, this wrap is a great option for lunch or afternoon tea appetizers. For a more refined look slice the rolls on the bias and serve on a platter.

10	asparagus spears, trimmed	10
10	smoked turkey slices	10
3 tbsp	barbecue sauce	45 mL
¼ cup	julienned red bell pepper	60 mL

1. In a pot of boiling salted water, blanch asparagus until vibrant green and al dente, about 2 minutes. Drain and immediately plunge into a bowl of ice water to stop the cooking process. Let stand until well chilled. Drain well.

2. On a clean work surface, brush top side of 1 turkey slice with about 1 tsp (5 mL) barbecue sauce. Lay 1 asparagus spear on top, leaving the tip exposed. Add bell pepper and wrap turkey tightly. Repeat until all ingredients are used up. Serve immediately or refrigerate for up to 4 hours.

Salmon Asparagus Wraps

Makes 12 spears

Make these delicious treats when asparagus is in season, abundant and inexpensive. You can increase or decrease the quantity to suit your needs. These are just suggested ratios for seasonings and salmon.

Tips

Orange flower water is available in stores specializing in products from the French province of Provence, or Middle Eastern markets. It is intensely flavored. If you don't have it, substitute an equal quantity of orange extract or 2 tsp (10 mL) finely grated orange zest.

Any fresh chile pepper will work in this recipe. Use a quantity that suits your taste.

You will likely have to cut each piece of salmon in half crosswise, depending upon how it is sliced. You want to be able to wrap the asparagus so most of the stalk is covered and the salmon overlaps nicely to form a reasonable seal.

● **Preheat barbecue grill to high or broiler**

12	asparagus spears, trimmed	12
	Extra virgin olive oil	
1/4 cup	mayonnaise	60 mL
1 tsp	orange flower water (see Tips, left)	5 mL
	Finely minced chile pepper (see Tips, left), optional	
4 oz	thinly sliced smoked salmon (approx.) (see Tips, left)	125 g
	Freshly ground black pepper	

1. Brush asparagus liberally with olive oil and place on preheated grill or under broiler and cook, turning once, until tender, about 4 minutes.

2. In a small bowl, combine mayonnaise, orange flower water, and chile pepper, if using. Stir well and set aside.

3. On a clean work surface, brush top side of 1 salmon slice liberally with mayonnaise mixture. Season liberally with black pepper. Lay 1 asparagus spear on top, leaving the tip exposed and wrap tightly. Repeat until all salmon and asparagus is used up. Serve immediately or cover and refrigerate until ready to serve for up to 4 hours.

Beef Tenderloin Salad Rolls

Makes 10 rolls

The delicate texture of beef tenderloin pairs wonderfully with mixed baby greens. When available the peppery flavor of arugula or lemon-scented sorrel leaves would both add tremendous flavor.

Tips

A beef tenderloin is also called filet or filet mignon.

When meat is removed from heat, it continues to cook for a period of time, allowing the juices to be more evenly distributed as it cools.

4 oz	beef tenderloin (see Tips, left)	125 g
¼ tsp	freshly ground black pepper	1 mL
1 tsp	olive oil	5 mL
¼ cup	sherry vinegar	60 mL
1 tbsp	minced roasted red bell pepper (see Tip, page 123) or store-bought	15 mL
1 tbsp	extra virgin olive oil	15 mL
1 tsp	Dijon mustard	5 mL
Pinch	salt	Pinch
1 cup	mixed baby salad greens	250 mL

1. Evenly coat tenderloin with black pepper. In a skillet, heat oil over medium heat. Sear beef, turning often, until caramelized on all sides, 2 to 3 minutes per side. Let meat stand for at least 10 minutes or for up to 20 minutes (see Tips, left). Cut across the grain into 10 thin slices and set aside.

2. In a bowl, whisk together vinegar, roasted pepper, extra virgin olive oil, mustard and salt.

3. Bundle the salad leaves, ends together, to form 10 bouquets of baby greens. Wrap 1 slice of beef around ends of each bouquet and place rolls on a serving platter standing up with the leaves of greens at the top. Drizzle each with vinaigrette and serve immediately.

Prosciutto and Smoked Mozzarella Eggplant Rolls

Makes about 16 rolls

Melted cheese with a slightly smoky flavor, prosciutto and eggplant make a glorious combination. These rolls are much easier to make than they appear, so go ahead and wow your guests. The recipe can be doubled or tripled to suit your needs.

Tips

Cut prosciutto and cheese slightly smaller than eggplant slices.

Smoked mozzarella has a delicious smoky flavor. It is available in the deli section of many supermarkets.

1	eggplant (about 1 lb/500 g)	1
1 tbsp	salt	15 mL
2 tbsp	extra virgin olive oil	30 mL
16	thin slices prosciutto, pancetta or speck (see Tips, left)	16
16	thin slices smoked mozzarella (about 4 oz/125 g) (see Tips, left)	16

1. With a sharp knife, cut off round bottom of eggplant to make a flat end. Stand eggplant upright and cut vertically into thin slices, about $\frac{1}{4}$ inch (0.5 cm) thick, discarding first and last slices with top layer of skin. Sprinkle with salt and let stand until water is extracted from eggplant, removing most of its bitterness, about 45 minutes. Rinse under cold running water and pat dry with paper towel.

2. Preheat broiler. Brush eggplant on one side with olive oil. Place on broiling pan and broil until turning golden, about 3 minutes. Remove from oven, turn over and brush other side with oil. Place under broiler and broil until turning golden, about 3 minutes.

3. Lay a piece of prosciutto and a piece of mozzarella over each eggplant slice. Roll up, jelly-roll fashion, and place on broiling pan seam side down. Place under preheated broiler and broil until cheese is melted, about 3 minutes. Serve warm.

Variation

Goat Cheese and Sun-Dried Tomato Eggplant Rolls: In a bowl, combine 4 oz (125 g) soft fresh goat cheese, 3 tbsp (45 mL) minced reconstituted sun-dried tomatoes, 8 fresh basil leaves, cut in a thin chiffonade, and 1 clove garlic, finely minced. Mix well. Spread over prebroiled eggplant slices, leaving a thin border around the edges. Roll up and broil as per above.

Tomato-Stuffed Bacon Rolls

Makes 12 rolls

This is a one bite BLT explosion and is perfect for breakfast or lunch appetizer.

Tip

Because vacuum-packed, grocery store bacon varies in moisture content, we've offered a time range in the method to reflect that.

- **Preheat oven to 350°F (180°C)**
- **Mini muffin tins, lightly greased**

6	bacon slices	6
12	cherry tomatoes	12
¼ cup	thinly sliced iceberg lettuce	60 mL
2 tbsp	Lemon Horseradish Aïoli (page 537)	30 mL
⅛ tsp	freshly ground black pepper	0.5 mL

1. Cut bacon strips in half crosswise. Place in muffin tin, overlapping ends by ¼ inch (0.5 cm) to form a tube. Press bacon toward outside to open center of tube. Bake until rolls are firm and bacon starts to crisp at edges, 15 to 20 minutes. Remove rolls and let cool.

2. With a sharp knife, remove one-quarter of each tomato from top. In a bowl, combine lettuce, 1 tbsp (15 mL) aïoli and pepper and toss well to coat.

3. Divide tomatoes equally among bacon rolls, cut-side up. Garnish with lettuce mixture.

Middle Eastern Salad Rolls

Makes 12 salad rolls

Influenced by a salad often served in Israel for breakfast, lunch or dinner, this wrap is full of fresh Middle Eastern flavor and is quite healthy, too.

Tip

You can use store-bought hummus here, if desired.

6	iceberg lettuce leaves, cut in half	6
½ cup	Easy Hummus (page 52)	125 mL
½ cup	grated carrot	125 mL
½ cup	coarsely chopped kalamata olives	125 mL
½ cup	diced English cucumber	125 mL
½ cup	coarsely chopped tomato	125 mL
¼ cup	Italian flat-leaf parsley leaves	60 mL
1 tbsp	hot pepper sauce	15 mL
1 tbsp	freshly squeezed lemon juice	15 mL

1. Place lettuce on a work surface with natural curve facing up to create a bowl shape. Spoon 4 tsp (20 mL) hummus down center. Divide carrot, olives, cucumber and tomato equally on top. Top with equal amounts of parsley, pepper sauce and lemon juice. Roll up lettuce to enclose and place seam side down.

Barbecue Rib Steak with Onion Sprouts and Truffle Vinaigrette

Makes about 15 appetizers

The flavor of truffles is quite something — earthy and very pungent — and when combined with a very flavorful rib steak, this appetizer may just become that five-star addition to your appetizer menu. We should all experience truffles at least once in our life.

Tip

We recommend using pure sea salt rather than refined table salt. It has a clean, crisp taste and enhanced mineral content, unlike table salt, which has a bitter acrid taste and contains unpleasant additives to prevent caking.

2 tbsp	extra virgin olive oil	30 mL
1 tbsp	minced garlic	15 mL
1 tbsp	finely chopped fresh thyme	15 mL
1 tsp	freshly ground black pepper	5 mL
2 lbs	boneless beef rib steak, about 1½ inches (4 cm) thick	1 kg
½ tsp	salt	2 mL
2 cups	onion or alfalfa sprouts	500 mL
2 tbsp	Truffle Vinaigrette (page 542)	30 mL

1. In a small bowl, combine oil, garlic, thyme and pepper. Place steak in a shallow dish and rub thoroughly with marinade. Cover and refrigerate for at least 1 hour or preferably overnight.

2. Preheat greased barbecue grill to high. Remove steak from marinade, discarding marinade. Place on preheated grill, close lid and grill until steak is caramelized on bottom, about 10 minutes. Flip and grill until caramelized, 7 to 10 minutes. Transfer to a cutting board, tent with foil and let stand for at least 10 minutes or for up to 20 minutes before slicing.

3. Cut beef across the grain into 15 thin slices and place on a work surface pointing north to south. Season with salt. Divide sprouts equally into small bouquets and place on steak at the end closest to you. Wrap slice around the sprouts and roll to enclose. Place rolls on a serving platter standing up with tops of sprouts at the top. Drizzle each with truffle vinaigrette and serve immediately.

Vegetarian Vietnamese Fresh Rolls

Makes 8 rolls

This is almost a two-for-one recipe — the fresh rolls are wonderful all on their own but the leftover marinade creates the perfect dipping sauce.

Tips

To julienne asparagus, cut into thin slices lengthwise and slice those slices into thin strips.

For a wonderful dipping sauce, in a small ramekin, combine the remaining dressing with ¼ cup (60 mL) soy sauce and 1 tbsp (15 mL) coarsely chopped Agave and Ginger-Scented Peanuts (page 455).

Dressing

2 tbsp	soy sauce	30 mL
2 tbsp	sweet Asian chili sauce	30 mL
½ tsp	toasted sesame oil	2 mL
½ tsp	rice vinegar (see Tips, page 305)	2 mL
½ tsp	minced garlic	2 mL
½ tsp	finely chopped pickled ginger	2 mL
¼ tsp	minced gingerroot	1 mL
2 cups	shredded baby bok choy	500 mL
¾ cup	julienned blanched asparagus (see Tips, left)	175 mL
¾ cup	julienned peeled carrots	175 mL
½ cup	julienned English cucumber	125 mL
¼ cup	julienned mango	60 mL
¼ cup	finely chopped toasted peanuts	60 mL
8	10-inch (25 cm) rice paper wrappers	8
3 cups	hot water	750 mL
	Dipping sauce, optional (see Tips, left)	

1. *Dressing:* In a bowl, combine soy sauce, chili sauce, oil, vinegar, garlic, pickled ginger and minced ginger.

2. In another bowl, combine bok choy, asparagus, carrots, cucumber, mango and peanuts. Add 2 tbsp (30 mL) dressing and toss well. Divide into 8 equal portions.

3. Working with one rice paper at a time, submerse in hot water until pliable, about 30 seconds. Place on a work surface. Spread one-portion of the vegetable mixture in a strip across the lettuce leaf about one-third away from the edge closest to you, leaving about 1 inch (2.5 cm) on either side. Fold the edge closest to you over the filling and pull gently toward you to encase the filling. Fold the sides toward the middle, then continue to roll up tightly. Place rolls under a damp cloth to stay moist because the wrappers tend to dry out quickly. Serve rolls immediately with dipping sauce, if using, or refrigerate for up to 1 hour. Serve whole or for a small hors d'oeuvre, cut in half on the diagonal and place on a serving platter.

Eggplant, Tomato and Basil Rolls

Makes 16 rolls

This perfect Italian food appetizer is like eating eggplant Parmesan. If you are so inclined, serve this with Oven-Roasted Cherry Tomato Sauce (page 546) or Basil Pesto (page 549) as the dipping sauces or if you're feeling adventurous, serve both.

Tip

For best results, buy good quality Parmesan and grate it yourself. If you must use already-grated cheese, buy it from an Italian market or deli or a good cheese shop and ask to make sure it doesn't contain any "filler."

1	medium eggplant	1
½ tsp	salt	2 mL
2 tbsp	olive oil (approx.)	30 mL
2 tbsp	balsamic vinegar	30 mL
16	fresh basil leaves	16
1	medium tomato	1
⅓ cup	freshly grated Parmesan cheese (see Tip, left)	75 mL
	Dipping sauce, optional	

1. Cut eggplant crosswise into 16 slices, each about ⅛ inch (3 mm) thick. Trim the edges of each slice creating 3-inch (7.5 cm) squares. Discard trimmings. Place eggplant on a baking sheet and sprinkle with salt. Let stand until water is extracted from eggplant, removing most of its bitterness, about 45 minutes. Rinse eggplant under cold water and pat dry with paper towel.

2. In a skillet, heat oil over medium heat. Add eggplant, in batches, as necessary, and fry until golden brown, 3 to 4 minutes. Turn and fry for 1 minute. Add more oil between batches if necessary. Transfer eggplant to a bowl. Toss with balsamic vinegar. Let cool to room temperature.

3. Cut tomato crosswise into 8 slices, each about ⅛ inch (3 mm) thick. Cut each slice in half so you have 16 half-moon shape slices. Place eggplant flat on a work surface. Place 1 tomato slice, 1 basil leaf and about 1 tsp (5 mL) of the cheese on side closest to you. Roll into a cigar shape and place seam side down on a platter. Serve immediately, with dipping sauce, if desired.

Pear and Brie Cheese "Rolls"

Makes 12 rolls

Here's a simple yet elegant way to pair the classic flavor combination of pear and Brie cheese.

Tips

When you cut the pear, choose the 12 slices from the center that are most uniform in size to use for these rolls.

Fig marmalade can be found in most specialty food shops and some large supermarkets.

2 cups	water	500 mL
1 tsp	pure maple syrup	5 mL
1	firm ripe pear	1
	Ice water	
1 tbsp	fig marmalade, warmed (see Tips, left)	15 mL
2½ oz	Brie cheese, cut into 12 cubes	75 g
12	fresh chervil leaves, optional	12

1. In a saucepan over medium heat, bring water and maple syrup to a simmer. Meanwhile, cut pear in half lengthwise and scoop out core and stem. Place cut side down and cut lengthwise into 12 paper-thin slices. Reserve any extra pear for another use. Add pears to saucepan and simmer until soft and pliable, about 2 minutes. Using a slotted spoon, transfer pears to a bowl of ice water to stop the cooking process and let stand until chilled. Drain and pat dry with paper towel.

2. Place pear slices on a work surface pointing north to south and spread ¼ tsp (1 mL) fig marmalade over surface of each. Place one cube Brie at end closest to you and roll pear around cheese. Place seam side down on a serving platter. Garnish with a chervil leaf, if using, and serve immediately.

Crispy Vegetarian Spring Rolls

Makes about 25 rolls

Here's one appetizer that takes us back to our childhood, but there are two glaring differences; first, these are made by you and not on a production line and second, there's no gooey plum sauce to dip. Serve this very classic Chinese appetizer with Basic Sweet-and-Sour Sauce (page 547).

Tip

Spring roll wrappers are usually found frozen and are widely available in Asian markets and some grocery stores. There are wrappers available for vegans, too. Look for Spring Home TYJ Spring Roll Pastry. They are sensational and remain crisp whether baked or fried.

- **Candy/deep-fry thermometer**

4 cups	thinly sliced Savoy cabbage	1 L
1 cup	julienned red bell pepper	250 mL
1 cup	julienned yellow bell pepper	250 mL
½ cup	julienned peeled carrots	125 mL
1 cup	thinly sliced shiitake mushrooms	250 mL
5 tsp	rice vinegar	25 mL
1 tbsp	puréed gingerroot	15 mL
2 tsp	toasted sesame oil	10 mL
¼ cup	soy sauce	60 mL
25	spring roll wrappers (see Tip, left)	25
2 tbsp	cornstarch	30 mL
	Oil	

1. In a large bowl, combine cabbage, red and yellow bell peppers, carrots, mushrooms, vinegar, ginger, sesame oil and soy sauce. Cover and refrigerate to marinate overnight. Strain well, discarding liquid.

2. Place spring roll wrapper flat on a work surface. Spoon about 5 tsp (25 mL) of vegetable mixture on the side closest to you. Evenly spread vegetable mixture in a straight line across the wrapper, leaving about 1-inch (2.5 cm) border on each side of wrapper. Fold sides of wrapper over filling then starting at the edge closest to you, roll up to form a spring roll. Roll in cornstarch to absorb any residual liquid from the stuffing.

3. In a large saucepan or Dutch oven, heat 3 inches (7.5 cm) of oil over medium-high heat to 350°F (180°C). (You can also use a deep fryer; follow the manufacturer's instructions.) Fry spring rolls until golden brown and crispy, 3 to 5 minutes. Transfer to paper towels to drain excess oil and serve immediately.

Fresh Shrimp Rolls

Makes 16 rolls

This is a very refreshing roll that is so delicious and light it can be served at any time of day. For a special treat, cooked crab or lobster would be an extravagant substitute for shrimp. If you prefer to make this without shrimp for your guests, replace the shrimp with avocado and enjoy.

Dipping sauce

1/4 cup	finely chopped roasted peanuts	60 mL
2 tbsp	soy sauce	30 mL
2 tbsp	sweet Asian chili sauce	30 mL
2 tbsp	fresh squeezed lime juice	30 mL
1/2 tsp	toasted sesame oil	2 mL
1/2 tsp	minced garlic	2 mL
1/2 tsp	finely chopped pickled ginger	2 mL

Rolls

16	colossal black tiger shrimp, cooked, peeled and chilled (see Shrimp Guide, page 299)	16
16	10-inch (25 cm) rice paper wrappers	16
4 cups	hot water	1 L
8	butter or Bibb lettuce leaves, cut in half	8
2 cups	julienned mango	500 mL
1/2 cup	julienned English cucumber	125 mL
1/4 cup	chopped fresh cilantro leaves	60 mL

1. *Dipping Sauce:* In a bowl, combine peanuts, soy sauce, chili sauce, lime juice, oil, garlic and ginger. Cover and refrigerate for at least 30 minutes before serving or for up to 1 week.

2. *Rolls:* Cut shrimp in half lengthwise. Working with one rice paper wrapper at a time, submerse in hot water until pliable, about 30 seconds. Place on a work surface. Place half a lettuce leaf in middle of wrapper. Divide mango, cucumber and cilantro into 16 equal portions. Spread vegetables in a strip across the lettuce leaf about one-third away from the edge closest to you, leaving about 1 inch (2.5 cm) on either side. Place 2 pieces of shrimp on top of vegetables, fold edge closest to you over filling and pull gently toward you to encase filling. Fold sides toward middle, then continue to roll up tightly. Place rolls under a damp cloth to stay moist because wrappers tend to dry out quickly. When finished rolling serve rolls immediately or refrigerate with the damp cloth up to 1 hour. Serve with dipping sauce.

Steamed Leek and Smoked Salmon Pinwheels

Makes about 20 pieces

Leeks and smoked salmon combine to form this sophisticated brunch or lunch appetizer. How about adding a crunch by placing the pinwheels on Pita Chips (see Variations, page 216) or Beet Chips (page 213).

Tip

Cut the leek lengthwise, but not all the way through the leek. Cut just to the middle, which, when separated, yields five, almost equal size layers. The hearts of the leek can be reserved for another use.

* **Steamer basket**

10	thyme sprigs	10
1	leek, white part only, layers separated (see Tip, left)	1
1 tbsp	sour cream	15 mL
1 tbsp	coarsely chopped fresh dill	15 mL
½ tsp	freshly squeezed lemon juice	2 mL
5 oz	smoked salmon (about 10 slices)	150 g

1. Arrange thyme over the bottom of a steamer basket set in a pot of simmering water. Place leeks on top of thyme. Cover and steam until soft, 10 to 12 minutes. Let leeks cool to room temperature. Discard thyme.

2. In a bowl, combine sour cream, dill and lemon juice.

3. To assemble, place one layer of leek on a work surface with the edges of the natural curve facing up. Place 2 slices of smoked salmon over top to cover entire leek. Drizzle about ¾ tsp (3 mL) of sour cream mixture in the middle of smoked salmon. Starting from side closest to you, begin rolling leek and smoked salmon, creating a log. With a very sharp knife, slice crosswise into quarters. Place on a platter, smoked salmon side face up, to resemble a pinwheel. Repeat with remaining leek and salmon. Serve immediately.

Spinach and Feta Roll-Ups

Makes 12 pieces

If you like the flavors in spanakopita but are looking for a slightly different presentation, try this. Phyllo pastry is rolled up, jelly-roll fashion, producing quick-bite pinwheels.

Tips

Fresh spinach can be gritty, so be sure to wash it well, preferably by immersing it in a basin of lukewarm water. After it has been washed, be sure to leave the water on the leaves. This is the cooking liquid.

Your phyllo sheets should be about 16- by 12-inches (40 by 30 cm). You can work with rectangles that approximate this size, but if the configuration or size of your phyllo sheet is dramatically different, roll it out to something that roughly conforms.

When working with the thawed phyllo (Step 3), be sure to keep it covered with a damp clean tea towel. Until you brush it with melted butter, it will quickly dry out when exposed to air.

- **Preheat oven to 400°F (200°C)**
- **Baking sheet, lined with parchment paper**

Filling

10 oz	fresh spinach leaves (see Tips, left)	300 g
6	green onions, white part with a bit of green, finely chopped	6
1	clove garlic, minced	1
3 tbsp	finely chopped Italian flat-leaf parsley	45 mL
1 tbsp	finely chopped dill	15 mL
4 oz	crumbled feta cheese	125 g
1	egg, beaten	1
	Salt and freshly ground black pepper	
3	sheets thawed phyllo pastry (see Tips, left)	3
1/4 cup	melted unsalted butter	60 mL

1. *Filling:* In a saucepan, place wet spinach leaves. Cover tightly and cook over medium heat until spinach is wilted, about 4 minutes. Transfer to a colander and drain off liquid. Chop spinach finely.

2. In a bowl, combine chopped spinach, green onions, garlic, parsley, dill and feta. Mix well. Add egg and mix well. Season to taste with salt and black pepper. Set aside.

3. On a work surface, cut phyllo sheets in half crosswise to form 6 sheets. Working quickly, brush each sheet with melted butter, stacking them on top of each other. When all 6 sheets are in place, arrange with one long end closest to you. Spread spinach filling evenly over the top, leaving about a 1-inch (2.5 cm) border on long end farthest away from you. Beginning with the long end closest to you, roll up jelly-roll fashion to form a log. Using a sharp knife, score into 12 slices across the log, approximately 1 inch (2.5 cm) apart.

4. Brush top with melted butter. Place on prepared baking sheet and bake in preheated oven until light golden, about 20 minutes. Let cool on baking sheet for 5 minutes. Slice along scored marks and serve warm.

Anchovy-Spiked Roasted Pepper and Feta Roll-Ups

Makes 12 pieces

The flavors in this yummy roll are unusual and zesty. It is perfect with a glass of robust red wine.

Tip

To roast peppers: Preheat broiler. Place pepper(s) on a baking sheet and broil, turning two or three times, until skin on all sides is blackened, about 25 minutes. Transfer to a heatproof bowl. Cover with a plate and let stand until cool. Remove and, using a sharp knife, lift skins off. Discard skins, core and seeds.

- **Preheat oven to 400°F (200°C)**
- **Baking sheet, lined with parchment paper**

Filling

4 oz	feta cheese	125 g
1	red bell pepper, roasted (see Tip, left) or store-bought	1
1 tbsp	chopped pickled hot banana pepper, optional	15 mL
2	anchovies, coarsely chopped	2
1/4 cup	Italian flat-leaf parsley leaves	60 mL
3	sheets thawed phyllo pastry (see Tips, page 144)	3
1/4 cup	melted butter	60 mL

1. *Filling:* In a food processor fitted with metal blade, process feta, roasted pepper, banana pepper, if using, anchovies and parsley until smooth, stopping and scraping down sides of the bowl as necessary, about 1 minute. Set aside.

2. On a work surface, cut phyllo sheets in half crosswise to form 6 sheets. Working quickly, brush each sheet with melted butter, stacking them on top of each other. When all 6 sheets are in place, arrange with one long end closest to you. Spread feta filling evenly over the top, leaving about a 1-inch (2.5 cm) border on long end farthest away from you. Beginning with the long end closest to you, roll up jelly-roll fashion to form a log. Using a sharp knife, score into 12 slices across the log, approximately 1 inch (2.5 cm) apart.

3. Brush top with melted butter. Place on prepared sheet and bake in preheated oven until light golden, about 20 minutes. Let cool on baking sheet for 5 minutes. Slice along scored marks and serve warm.

Dill-Spiked Mushroom and Cheese Rolls-Ups

Makes 12 pieces

Mushrooms and creamy cheese punctuated with a hit of bitter dill make a perfect pairing for rich crispy phyllo pastry.

Tip

Your phyllo sheets should be about 16- by 12-inches (40 by 30 cm). You can work with rectangles that approximate this size, but if the configuration or size of your phyllo sheet is dramatically different, roll it out to something that roughly conforms.

- **Preheat oven to 400°F (200°C)**
- **Baking sheet, lined with parchment paper**

Filling

2 tbsp	unsalted butter	30 mL
4 oz	sliced mushrooms	125 g
2 tbsp	chopped shallot	30 mL
3 oz	cream cheese, softened	90 g
2 tbsp	freshly grated Parmesan cheese	30 mL
2 tbsp	chopped fresh dill fronds	30 mL
	Salt and freshly ground black pepper	
3	sheets thawed phyllo pastry (see Tip, left and page 144)	3
¼ cup	melted unsalted butter	60 mL

1. *Filling:* In a skillet, melt butter over medium-high heat. Sauté mushrooms and shallot until mushrooms begin to lose their liquid, about 6 minutes. Transfer to a food processor fitted with metal blade. Add cream cheese, Parmesan, dill, and salt and black pepper to taste. Process until smooth, stopping and scraping down sides of the bowl as necessary, about 1 minute. Set aside.

2. On a work surface, cut phyllo sheets in half crosswise to form 6 sheets. Working quickly, brush each sheet with melted butter, stacking them on top of each other. When all 6 sheets are in place, arrange with one long end closest to you. Spread feta filling evenly over the top, leaving about a 1-inch (2.5 cm) border on long end farthest away from you. Beginning with the long end closest to you, roll up jelly-roll fashion to form a log. Using a sharp knife, score into 12 slices across the log, approximately 1 inch (2.5 cm) apart. Brush top with melted butter. Place on prepared sheet and bake in preheated oven until light golden, about 20 minutes. Let cool on baking sheet for 5 minutes. Slice along scored marks and serve warm.

Walnut-Laced Gorgonzola and Leek Rolls-Ups

Makes 12 pieces

The combination of Gorgonzola and leeks with a smattering of walnuts is heavenly but not for the faint of heart. The assertive flavors pair beautifully with a glass of robust red wine.

Tip

Because leeks can be gritty, it is customary to slice and rinse them before using. *To clean leeks:* Fill a sink full of lukewarm water. Split the leeks in half lengthwise and submerge in the water, swishing them around to remove all traces of dirt. Transfer to a colander and rinse thoroughly under cold water.

- **Preheat oven to 400°F (200°C)**
- **Baking sheet, lined with parchment paper**

Filling

1½ tbsp	unsalted butter	22 mL
2	leeks, white part only, thinly sliced	2
½ cup	cubed (1 inch/2.5 cm) Gorgonzola (about 2½ oz/75 g)	125 mL
2 tbsp	heavy or whipping (35%) cream	30 mL
2 tbsp	freshly grated Parmesan cheese	30 mL
¼ cup	chopped walnuts	60 mL
	Salt and freshly ground black pepper	
3	sheets thawed phyllo pastry (see Tips, page 144)	3
¼ cup	melted unsalted butter	60 mL

1. *Filling:* In a skillet, melt butter over medium-high heat. Sauté leeks until softened, about 5 minutes. Transfer to a food processor fitted with metal blade. Add Gorgonzola, cream, Parmesan and walnuts and process until smooth, stopping and scraping down sides of the bowl as necessary, about 1 minute. Season to taste with salt and black pepper. Set aside.

2. On a work surface, cut phyllo sheets in half crosswise to form 6 sheets. Working quickly, brush each sheet with melted butter, stacking them on top of each other. When all 6 sheets are in place, arrange with one long end closest to you. Spread filling evenly over the top, leaving about a 1-inch (2.5 cm) border on long end farthest away from you. Beginning with the long end closest to you, roll up jelly-roll fashion to form a log. Using a sharp knife, score into 12 slices across the log, approximately 1 inch (2.5 cm) apart.

3. Brush top with melted butter. Place on prepared sheet and bake in preheated oven until light golden, about 20 minutes. Let cool on baking sheet for 5 minutes. Slice along scored marks and serve warm.

Pigs in a Blanket

Makes 12 sausage rolls

Sausage rolls are an American tradition, made plain or fancy as you prefer. All you need is a sheet of thawed puff pastry and sausage. Add condiments to suit your taste. Here we offer three versions: one made with frankfurters seasoned with spicy mustard, another more traditional sausage-based version and a third option, made with uncooked Italian sausage meat. All are delicious.

Tips

If using sausage, the length of your sausage will influence the length of the pastry strip or the number of sausages you will need. If you are using short sausages (about 4 inches/10 cm), you will need 2 sausages per strip when cut to the specified size.

When rolling pastry, the shorter side should approximate the length of your frankfurter. Cut crosswise into 4 equal strips each about 10 by 4 inches (25 by 10 cm).

- **Baking sheet, lined with parchment paper**
- **Preheat oven to 425°F (220°C)**

8 oz	puff pastry, thawed, preferably all-butter	250 g
12 oz	good-quality frankfurters (about 4)	375 g
¼ cup	Dijon mustard	60 mL
1	red bell pepper, roasted	1
½ tsp	hot Asian chile sauce, such as sambal oelek	2 mL
1	egg, beaten with 1 tbsp (15 mL) water	1

1. On a lightly floured surface, roll pastry into a rectangle approximately 16 by 10 inches (40 by 25 cm). Trim ends off frankfurters and center on pastry.

2. In a mini food processor, process mustard, roasted pepper and chile sauce until puréed and smooth. Brush frankfurters liberally with mustard mixture.

3. Fold 1 long side of the pastry over to cover frankfurter. Brush both long edges of pastry with egg wash, fold over and press to seal. Trim excess pastry from ends.

4. Cut each roll crosswise into 1-inch (2.5 cm) pieces. Place seam side down on prepared baking sheet, about 2 inches (5 cm) apart. Brush surface of pastry liberally with egg wash. Repeat until all pastry and frankfurters are used up. Bake in preheated oven until puffed and golden, about 20 minutes.

Variations

Classic Sausage Rolls: Substitute pork breakfast sausage or bratwurst for the frankfurters. Poach in equal parts white wine and water for about 10 minutes. Drain and let cool. Brush sausages with the roasted pepper mixture or Dijon mustard.

Italian Sausage Rolls: Substitute 8 oz (250 g) hot or sweet Italian sausage, removed from casings, for the frankfurters. Omit mustard mixture. In a food processor, pulse half small red onion and 2 cloves garlic until chopped. Add 1 egg, ¼ cup (60 mL) bread crumbs and sausage and pulse to blend. Complete Step 1. Spoon one-quarter of the sausage mixture lengthwise down the center of each pastry strip. Complete Step 3, cover and refrigerate (1 to 2 hours), then complete Step 4.

Pepper-Wrapped Chorizo

Makes 24 tapas

This recipe is a spin on a classic Spanish tapas dish in which chorizo is simmered in red wine. Although delicious, this is a substantial starter, particularly if served with chunks of country bread, so plan accordingly.

Tip

To roast peppers: Preheat broiler. Place pepper(s) on a baking sheet and broil, turning two or three times, until skin on all sides is blackened, about 25 minutes. Transfer to a heatproof bowl. Cover with a plate and let stand until cool. Remove and, using a sharp knife, lift skins off. Discard skins and prepare according to recipe directions.

3	red bell peppers, roasted (see Tip, left) or store-bought	3
1 lb	fresh chorizo sausage	500 g
1 tbsp	olive oil	15 mL
1	onion, finely chopped	1
2	cloves garlic, minced	2
2	bay leaves	2
1 tsp	cracked black peppercorns	5 mL
1	rosemary sprig, optional	1
1 cup	dry red wine	250 mL
2 tbsp	finely chopped Italian flat-leaf parsley	30 mL
	Country-style bread, optional	

1. Prick sausage all over with a fork. In a skillet just large enough to hold the sliced sausage in a single layer, heat oil over medium-high heat. Add chorizo, cover and cook, turning several times, until lightly browned and chorizo has rendered some of its fat. Set aside until cool enough to handle. Cut into rounds about 1 inch (2.5 cm) thick. (You should have 24.) Drain off all but 1 tbsp (15 mL) fat from pan.

2. Return skillet to medium heat. Add onion and garlic and cook, stirring, until onion is softened, about 3 minutes. Add bay leaves, peppercorns, and rosemary, if using, and cook, stirring, for 1 minute. Add wine and bring to a boil. Add chorizo rounds in a single layer. Cover and cook, turning chorizo as necessary to ensure all sides have been in contact with the wine, until cooked through, about 20 minutes. Using a slotted spoon, transfer chorizo to a bowl. Add parsley and toss well. Set wine mixture aside.

3. Cut each red pepper on the vertical into 8 strips. Wrap a strip of pepper around the casing of a chorizo round and secure with a toothpick. Repeat until all chorizo and peppers are used up. Transfer to a small platter and cover with wine mixture. Serve warm or at room temperature, with chunks of warm country bread, if desired.

Variation

Substitute pork sausage or Italian sausage for the chorizo.

Chicken and Broccoli Crystal Fold

Makes 12 crystal folds

This healthy fresh roll is perfect for a lunch or midday hors d'oeuvres party.

Tips

Sweet Asian chili sauce is a mixture of chiles, sugar, vinegar and other spices and can be found in Asian markets or in the Asian section of some large supermarkets.

To grate peeled ginger: Use a fine, sharp-toothed grater such as Microplane.

2 tsp	toasted sesame oil	10 mL
1 cup	finely chopped boneless skinless chicken thighs (about 8 oz/250 g)	250 mL
¼ cup	thinly sliced onion	60 mL
¾ cup	coarsely chopped broccoli florets	175 mL
¼ cup	finely diced tomato	60 mL
2 tbsp	coarsely chopped roasted peanuts	30 mL
1 tbsp	coarsely chopped fresh cilantro leaves	15 mL
1 tbsp	soy sauce	15 mL
1 tsp	thinly sliced green onion	5 mL
1 tsp	sweet Asian chili sauce (see Tips, left)	5 mL
½ tsp	puréed gingerroot (see Tips, left)	2 mL
6	leaves iceberg lettuce, cut in half	6

1. In a skillet, heat oil over medium heat. Add chicken and onion and cook, stirring, until onion is translucent, about 3 minutes. Add broccoli and cook, stirring, until vibrant green, 3 to 5 minutes.

2. In a bowl, combine tomato, peanuts, cilantro, soy sauce, green onion, chili sauce and ginger. Fold into chicken mixture and combine. Spoon about 2 tbsp (30 mL) of the mixture into each lettuce leaf, wrap lettuce around filling and serve immediately.

Chicken Pinwheels with Couscous

Makes about 16 pieces

Simple, yet somewhat exotic thanks to Mediterranean ingredients such as couscous, almonds, dates and a hint of saffron, these tasty tidbits will delight your guests. They are somewhat substantial, so work best as cocktail party fare.

Tips

If you prefer, use chicken cutlets, which have already been pounded. They cost more but are very convenient.

Use whole wheat rather than regular couscous. It is more nutritious and just as easy to prepare.

We like the heat in hot paprika, but if you're heat averse, use sweet paprika, instead.

- Preheat oven to 325°F (160°C)
- Baking sheet, lined with parchment paper

½ cup	chicken broth or water	125 mL
Pinch	saffron threads, crumbled	Pinch
¼ cup	couscous (see Tips, left)	60 mL
¼ cup	finely chopped blanched almonds	60 mL
¼ cup	finely chopped soft dates	60 mL
2 tbsp	finely chopped dried cherries	30 mL
½ tsp	ground cinnamon	2 mL
	Salt and freshly ground black pepper	
12 oz	boneless skinless chicken breast	375 g
2 tbsp	olive oil	30 mL
½ tsp	hot paprika (see Tips, left)	2 mL

1. In a saucepan over medium-high heat, bring broth to a boil. Add saffron and stir until infused. Add couscous in a steady stream, stirring constantly. Cover, remove from heat and let stand for 15 minutes. Fluff with a fork and use your hands to break up any clumps. Add almonds, dates, cherries and cinnamon and stir well. Season to taste with salt and black pepper.

2. Meanwhile, place chicken on a cutting board between two pieces of plastic wrap, each about twice the size of the chicken breast. Using a meat mallet or the flat side of a cleaver, pound the chicken to about ¼-inch (0.5 cm) thickness. You should have two pieces, each about 6 inches (15 cm) wide when pounded. Remove plastic and cut each lengthwise to form 4 strips in total, each about 3 inches (7.5 cm) wide.

3. Brush top side of each strip with oil. Spread one-quarter of filling over each, then roll up lengthwise. Place on prepared baking sheet, seam side down. Brush tops and sides of rolls with olive oil and dust tops evenly with paprika. Bake in preheated oven until chicken is no longer pink inside, about 25 minutes.

4. Let cool slightly. If necessary, trim ends so you have a neat finish and cut into ½-inch (1 cm) slices. Spear with toothpicks (from seam side to top) and serve warm or at room temperature.

Chicken Dogs and Pickled Onions

Makes 32 pieces

A take on traditional Pigs in a Blanket (page 148), this recipe will work with any sausage or hot dog because it's the onions that make the recipe. The contrast of the buttery pastry and the acidic onions is wonderful.

Tip

It is important to drain pickled onions thoroughly to avoid a soggy pastry.

• **Preheat oven to 325°F (160°C)**

8 oz	puff pastry, thawed	250 g
8	chicken wieners, cut into quarters	8
1/4 cup	drained Pickled Onions (page 551)	60 mL
1	egg, beaten with 1 tbsp (15 mL) water	1

1. On a lightly floured surface, roll pastry into a 10-inch (25 cm) square. Using a pizza cutter or knife, cut 32 rectangles about 3 by 1 inch (7.5 by 2.5 cm). Place 1 piece of wiener lengthwise on each rectangle, parallel with the long sides of the pastry. Spoon about 1/2 tsp (2 mL) of the pickled onion on top of wiener and roll up pastry to enclose. Place seam side down on a baking sheet. Brush surface of pastry with egg wash. Bake in preheated oven until golden brown, 15 to 20 minutes.

Classic Cheese Quesadilla

Makes 12 or 24 wedges

This quintessential Mexican food can be served morning, noon or night. Serve a wedge to garnish Tomato Gazpacho (page 102) or Tomato Avocado Shooter (page 112) or plunge into Avocado and Ancho Chile Dip (page 28). Either way you are about to make an excellent appetizer guests will love.

6	6-inch (15 cm) whole wheat or corn tortillas	6
1/2 cup	shredded Cheddar cheese	125 mL
1/2 cup	shredded Gruyère cheese	125 mL
1/2 cup	diced red onion	125 mL
1/4 tsp	each salt and freshly ground pepper	1 mL
2 tsp	unsalted butter, divided	10 mL

1. Place 3 of the tortillas on a work surface. Spread equal amounts of Cheddar cheese, Gruyère cheese and onion over each. Season with salt and pepper. Cover with remaining 3 tortillas.

2. In a large skillet, melt 1 tsp (5 mL) of the butter over medium heat. Add 1 quesadilla at a time, and fry, turning once, until crisp on both sides and cheese is melted, 2 to 3 minutes per side. Transfer to a cutting board and cut each quesadilla into 4 or 8 wedges. Add more butter to pan and adjust heat as necessary between quesadillas. Serve immediately.

Classic Tuna Sushi

Makes 12 pieces

This sushi is a Japanese appetizer on most catering menus everywhere, but here's a secret; it's so much better and cheaper when you make it yourself. Sushi grade tuna is widely available and your local fishmonger can help you get it in advance of making this appetizer. Great fish makes all the difference in the world.

Tips

Running your fingers under warm water will prevent the very sticky rice from sticking to your fingers.

When making the rice, it is important to resist the temptation to remove the cover and sneak a peek. It's imperative you keep the steam and heat inside the pan so do all you can not to open it.

- **Bamboo sushi mat**

2 tbsp	rice vinegar (see Tips, page 154)	30 mL
2 tbsp	granulated sugar	30 mL
1 tsp	salt	5 mL
½ cup	sushi rice (see Tips, page 293)	125 mL
2	nori sheets	2
1 tbsp	Wasabi Aïoli (page 537), divided	15 mL
2 oz	yellowfin tuna, cut into thin strips	60 g
¼ cup	julienned cucumber, divided	60 mL
½ tsp	toasted sesame seeds	2 mL

1. In a saucepan over medium heat, combine vinegar, sugar and salt and bring to a simmer. Transfer to a bowl.

2. In a fine-mesh strainer, rinse rice thoroughly under cold water until water runs clear, about 5 minutes. Transfer to a saucepan. Add 1 cup (250 mL) water and bring to a boil over medium heat. Cover, reduce heat to low and simmer for 5 minutes. Remove from heat and let steam, covered, for 15 to 20 minutes. Transfer rice to a bowl and season with vinegar mixture, folding gently to combine.

3. Place 1 nori sheet, shiny side down, on sushi mat and spoon half of rice into middle of sheet. With moistened fingers (see Tips, left), press rice to evenly cover nori sheet. Spread about 1½ tsp (7 mL) of Wasabi Aïoli in a thin strip about 1 inch (2.5 cm) from edge of nori sheet closest to you. Place half of tuna and half of cucumber along the length of aïoli. Garnish with sesame seeds over entire surface of rice.

4. From bottom of sushi mat, fold nori over ingredients to encase them, gently press mat to seal. With one hand, grab top of the mat and pull away from your body while other hand keeps the mat firm against nori. Continue to roll away from you until roll is formed. Place roll seam side down and drape bamboo mat over roll. Gently press to form roll into a square shape and set aside. Repeat with second sheet and remaining ingredients. Using a very sharp knife, slice roll in half and each half into thirds, yielding 6 pieces per roll. Place sushi pieces, spiral side facing up, on a platter and serve.

Beef Sushi

Makes 12 pieces

This variation of the classic sushi roll will satisfy the carnivores in the family.

Tips

There is a difference between rice vinegar and seasoned rice vinegar. Both are usually made from fermented rice or rice wine, but rice vinegar does not contain any additional sugar or sodium. Our preference is Japanese rice vinegar which is very mild flavored and almost colorless.

Running your fingers under warm water will prevent the very sticky rice from sticking to your fingers.

2 tbsp	rice vinegar (see Tips, left)	30 mL
2 tbsp	granulated sugar	30 mL
1 tsp	salt	5 mL
1/2 cup	sushi rice	125 mL
2	nori sheets	2
1 tbsp	Sriracha sauce	15 mL
2 oz	Asian-Seared Beef Tenderloin (page 468), cut into thin strips, divided	60 g
1/4 cup	strips roasted red pepper (see Tip, page 149)	60 mL
1/2 tsp	toasted sesame seeds	2 mL

1. In a saucepan over medium heat, combine vinegar, sugar and salt and bring to a simmer. Transfer to a bowl.

2. In a fine-mesh strainer, rinse rice thoroughly under cold water until water runs clear, about 5 minutes. Transfer to a saucepan. Add 1 cup (250 mL) water and bring to a boil over medium heat. Cover, reduce heat to low and simmer for 5 minutes. Remove from heat and let steam, covered, for 15 to 20 minutes. Transfer rice to a bowl and season with vinegar mixture, folding gently to combine.

3. Place 1 nori sheet, shiny side down, on sushi mat and spoon half rice into the middle of sheet. With moistened fingers (see Tips, left), press rice to evenly cover nori sheet. Spread about 1 1/2 tsp (7 mL) of the Sriracha in a thin strip about 1 inch (2.5 cm) from edge of the nori sheet closest to you. Place half of the beef and half of roasted red pepper along the length of Sriracha and garnish with sesame seeds over entire surface of rice.

4. From bottom of sushi mat, fold nori over ingredients to encase them, gently press mat to seal. With one hand, grab top of mat and pull away from your body while other hand keeps the mat firm against nori. Continue to roll away from you until roll is formed. Place roll seam side down and drape bamboo mat over roll. Gently press to form roll into a square shape and set aside. Repeat with second sheet and remaining ingredients. Using a very sharp knife, slice roll in half and each half into thirds, yielding 6 pieces per roll. Place the sushi pieces, beef side facing up, on a platter and serve.

Deconstructed Caesar Salad

Makes 12 pieces

These familiar flavors are bundled in romaine leaves and are ready to be devoured. A Tomato Balsamic "Jam" (page 72) garnish adds some beautiful color and sweet flavor.

Tip

Although lemon segments will work in this dish, we prefer making "supremes" which are much more delicate. Separate citrus fruit into wedges and remove skin, pith and membrane.

12	romaine heart leaves	12
12	oil-packed anchovy fillets, drained	12
2	roughly chopped hard-cooked eggs	2
1/4 cup	thinly sliced red onion	60 mL
1/4 cup	coarsely chopped lemon segments	60 mL
1 tsp	thinly sliced garlic	5 mL
2 tbsp	freshly grated Parmesan cheese	30 mL
1 tbsp	capers, rinsed	15 mL
2 tbsp	sherry vinegar	30 mL
1 tbsp	extra virgin olive oil	15 mL

1. Place lettuce on a work surface with natural curve facing up. Divide anchovies, eggs, onion, lemon segments, garlic, cheese and capers among leaves. Drizzle with vinegar and oil. Place on a platter and serve.

Cabbage and Duck Confit Rolls

Makes 10 rolls

If you haven't tried duck confit, this French classic is so easy and well worth the modest effort. Present this with the butter lettuce leaves open and place on a platter to allow the beautiful colors to shine through.

Tip

Very good-quality duck confit can be found vacuum packed in gourmet food shops and some grocery stores.

1 tsp	unsalted butter	5 mL
1 cup	packed sliced red cabbage	250 mL
1/2 tsp	salt	2 mL
1 cup	chicken broth or duck stock	250 mL
1/2 cup	shredded duck confit (see Tip, left)	125 mL
1 tsp	red wine vinegar	5 mL
10	leaves butter lettuce	10
3 tbsp	hoisin sauce	45 mL
1/4 cup	coarsely chopped chives	60 mL

1. In a saucepan, melt butter over medium heat. Add cabbage and salt and cook, stirring, until wilted, about 2 minutes. Add broth, duck and vinegar and bring to a boil. Reduce heat and simmer, stirring often, until liquid is reduced by three-quarters, about 6 minutes.

2. Place lettuce on a surface with natural curve facing up. Spoon 1 tsp (5 mL) of hoisin in middle. Divide duck mixture on top and wrap lettuce around filling and place seam side down. Garnish with chives.

Maple-Glazed Bacon and Tomato Lettuce Wraps

Makes 6 wraps

BLT lovers watch out! You have met your match. Serve this as a brunch, lunch or dinner appetizer alongside a little extra Creamy Green Onion Dip (page 41). It's delicious. Present this with the butter lettuce leaves open and place on a white platter to allow the colors to shine through.

3	iceberg lettuce leaves, cut in half	3
12	slices Maple-Glazed Bacon (page 480)	12
½ cup	julienned seeded tomato	125 mL
2 tbsp	Creamy Green Onion Dip (page 41)	30 mL

1. Place lettuce on a work surface with natural curve facing up to create a bowl shape. Place 2 pieces of bacon and tomato in middle. Drizzle about 1 tsp (5 mL) dip over top. Wrap lettuce around filling and place seam side down to hold together on a serving platter. Serve immediately.

Smoked Salmon and Pickled Onion Lettuce Wraps

Makes 6 wraps

Pickled onions accent the smoky flavor of salmon very well in this simple but delicious lettuce wrap.

6	large Boston lettuce leaves	6
8 oz	sliced smoked salmon (about 16 slices)	250 g
½ cup	drained Pickled Onions (page 551)	125 mL
¼ cup	coarsely chopped fresh chives	60 mL
1 tbsp	finely grated lemon zest	15 mL

1. Place lettuce on a work surface with the natural curve facing up to create a bowl shape. Place 2 slices of the smoked salmon over top to cover entire lettuce leaf, overlapping as necessary. Garnish with 4 tsp (20 mL) onions, 2 tsp (10 mL) chives and ½ tsp (2 mL) lemon zest. Repeat with remaining lettuce leaves. Wrap lettuce around filling and serve immediately.

Baby Bok Choy and Tofu Bundles with Peanut Sauce

Makes 10 bundles

For a more refined look, serve this one-biter with a garnish of Edamame Salsa (page 78) on a Chinese soup spoon.

10	cubes (1 inch/2.5 cm) firm tofu	10
1 tbsp	soy sauce	15 mL
1 tbsp	packed brown sugar	15 mL
1 tsp	toasted sesame oil	5 mL
2 tbsp	finely diced red bell pepper	30 mL
2 tbsp	finely diced red onion	30 mL
4 cups	water	1 L
1 tsp	salt	5 mL
10	leaves baby bok choy	10
	Peanut Sauce (page 554)	

1. In a bowl, combine tofu, soy sauce and brown sugar. Cover and let marinate for a minimum of 1 hour or for up to 2 hours.

2. In a skillet, heat oil over medium heat. Add tofu and cook, stirring, until golden brown and fragrant, 3 to 4 minutes. Add bell pepper and onion and transfer to a bowl. Save residual cooking liquid.

3. In a saucepan, bring water and salt to a boil. Blanch bok choy until soft, about 2 minutes. Remove from heat and dry on a tea towel.

4. To assemble, place one cube tofu on thick end of leaf. Wrap leaf around tofu tucking the excess leaf underneath to seal and place on a serving platter. Drizzle bundles with any liquid that has accumulated in the bowl (at most 1/4 tsp/1 mL per bundle) and serve immediately with Peanut Sauce for dipping.

Mini Braised Pork Tacos

Makes 16 tacos

Don't be intimidated, it's just braised pork. We've made this so darn easy to make but don't divulge the secret to your guests. Let them think you slaved all day long. A garnish of Avocado Black Bean Salsa (page 84) would be perfect, but for the more daring person, give Chipotle Pineapple Salsa (page 86) a try to add some tropical flair.

Tip

For best flavor, toast and grind cumin yourself. *To toast seeds:* Place seeds in a dry skillet over medium heat and cook, stirring, until fragrant, about 3 minutes. Immediately transfer to a mortar or a spice grinder and grind.

- **Preheat oven to 265°F (130°C)**
- **Ovenproof saucepan with lid**

1½ lbs	boneless pork shoulder or blade (butt)	750 g
½ tsp	salt	2 mL
1 tbsp	olive oil	15 mL
2 cups	chicken broth	500 mL
1	orange, cut in half	1
½ tsp	ground cumin (see Tip, left)	2 mL
2 tbsp	sour cream	30 mL
2 tbsp	coarsely chopped fresh cilantro leaves	30 mL
¼ tsp	ancho chile powder	1 mL
8	6-inch (15 cm) corn or flour tortillas, cut in half and warmed	8
1 cup	packed thinly sliced iceberg lettuce	250 mL
32	cubes (½ inch/1 cm) tomatoes	32

1. Season pork shoulder with salt. In saucepan, heat oil over medium-high heat. Sear pork shoulder, turning often, until all sides are golden brown, about 3 minutes. Flip and continue to sear all sides until caramelized, 7 minutes more. Add chicken broth. Squeeze in orange to release all juice and add orange to pan. Add cumin and bring to a simmer. Cover and transfer saucepan to preheated oven. Braise for 2 hours. Flip over, cover and continue to braise until meat is falling apart, about 1 hour. Remove pork shoulder from the cooking liquid, reserving cooking liquid, and transfer pork to a cutting board. Let cool. Finely chop shoulder, discarding excess fat, and transfer to a bowl. Add ¼ cup (60 mL) of cooking liquid and toss to combine. Stir in sour cream, cilantro and chile powder.

2. Place tortillas on a work surface. To assemble, divide pork mixture equally among tortillas. Garnish with shredded lettuce and 2 pieces of tomato. Fold in half and serve immediately.

Savory Tarts, Dumplings and Crêpes

There is something incredibly comforting about a savory filling encased in pastry or a warm flatbread finished with an aromatic topping. Possibly because we usually think of pastry as being sweet, savory pastries seem to hold a special place in our hearts.

Many cultures include savory pastries in their culinary repertoires, from steamed Asian dumplings and Indian samosas to Mediterranean phyllo and the Jewish knish. Pastry-based appetizers make perfect party food because no matter how easy they are to make, they always have a celebratory air. Your guests will inevitably believe you've gone the extra mile just to make them happy.

Crab Tartlets 160
Salsa-Spiked Cheese Tartlets 161
Spinach and Artichoke Tartlets 162
Prosciutto-Spiked Spinach and Ricotta Tartlets . . 163
Tartlet Pastry. 164
Potato Pastry 165
Mini Smoked Salmon and Sour Cream
    Puff Pastry Tartlets 166
Mini Caramelized Onion Puff Pastry Tartlets 167
Mini Tomato and Olive Tapenade
    Puff Pastry Tartlets 168
Berry-Glazed Fig Tart 169
Goat Cheese and Carmelized Onion
    Vol-au-Vent. 170
Creamy Mushroom Vol-au-Vent 171
Anchovy-Spiked Leek and Tomato Galettes 172
Butternut Galette with Basil Drizzle 173
Tomato Mozzarella Galettes 174
Herb-Spiked Ricotta Galettes 175
Mini Potato Galettes with Caviar
    and Crème Fraîche. 176
Phyllo Bundles 176
Ham and Cheese Phyllo Bundles 177
Walnut-Spiked Blue Cheese Bundles 177
Spinach and Pine Nut Bundles 178
Paprika-Spiked Mushroom Bundles 179
Oregano and Cheese Bundles 180
Pancetta and Potato Bundles. 181

Crust for Empanaditas 182
Corn and Cheese
    Empanaditas 183
Salsa and Chicken Empanaditas 183
Roasted Pepper and Cheese Empanaditas 184
Ground Beef and Chile-Laced Empanaditas. 185
Cheese Arepas. 186
Corn Arepas. 187
Knish Pastry 188
Beef Knishes 189
Potato Knishes. 189
Cheese Knishes 190
Mushroom Knishes. 190
Kasha Knishes 191
Samosa Pastry. 192
Meat Samosas 193
Shrimp Samosas 194
Chicken Samosas 195
Vegetable Samosas 196
Socca de Nice 197
Buckwheat Blinis 198
Corn Cakes 199
Crêpes Parmentier 200
Indian-Style Roti. 201
Steamed Pork Dumplings. 202
Savory Fried Shrimp Wontons 203
Mushroom Phyllo Triangles with
    Grilled Scallion and Corn Dip 204

Crab Tartlets

Makes about 30 tartlets

Serve these little tarts when you want to make an impression. They look and taste extremely elegant, yet are not at all difficult to make.

Tip

Our preference is the pasteurized crabmeat, which you can find in cans in the refrigerated section of supermarkets. But regular canned or thawed drained frozen crabmeat works well, too.

* **Preheat oven to 375°F (190°C)**

30	prebaked Tartlet Pastry (page 164) or Potato Pastry (page 165) shells	30
1 tbsp	oil	15 mL
2	shallots, minced	2
Pinch	cayenne pepper	Pinch
4 oz	drained cooked crabmeat (about 2/3 cup/150 mL) (see Tip, left)	125 g
2 tbsp	freshly grated Parmesan cheese	30 mL
1 tbsp	finely chopped fresh tarragon or Italian flat-leaf parsley leaves	15 mL
1 tsp	freshly squeezed lemon juice	5 mL
3	egg yolks	3
1½ cups	half-and-half (10%) cream	375 mL
	Salt and freshly ground black pepper	

1. In a skillet, heat oil over medium heat. Add shallots and cook, stirring, until softened, about 3 minutes. Stir in cayenne. Remove from heat and add crabmeat, Parmesan, tarragon and lemon juice. Stir well and set aside.

2. In a bowl, whisk egg yolks, cream, and salt and pepper to taste until smoothly blended. Place a sieve over a measuring cup large enough to accommodate the mixture or bowl with a pouring spout and strain.

3. Fill each pastry shell about half full with crab mixture and pour egg mixture over top until almost full. Bake in preheated oven until custard is set, about 15 minutes. Let cool slightly in pan on a wire rack, about 5 minutes. Serve warm.

Variation

Pancetta-Spiked Pea Tartlets: Substitute 2 tbsp (30 mL) diced pancetta and ½ cup (125 mL) sweet green peas, thawed if frozen, for the crabmeat. Omit cayenne, Parmesan and lemon juice. Soften pancetta with the shallots and continue with Step 3.

Salsa-Spiked Cheese Tartlets

Makes 36 tartlets

One advantage to these tasty nibblies is that they can be made from ingredients you're likely to have on hand, which makes them perfect for unexpected guests.

Tips

If you prefer, substitute 2 tsp (10 mL) Mexican-style chile powder, which is a mixture of spices and chiles, for the oregano and ancho chile powder.

If you have leftover Fresh Tomato Salsa (page 70), you can refrigerate it and use it to make these little tarts. It is a great use for fresh salsa that has lost some of its vibrancy.

The degree of spiciness in your salsa will determine the heat level of your tarts.

36	prebaked Tartlet Pastry (page 164) or Potato Pastry (page 165) shells	36
¾ cup	heavy or whipping (35%) cream	175 mL
3	egg yolks	3
1 tsp	ancho chile powder (see Tips, left)	5 mL
1 tsp	dried oregano	5 mL
½ tsp	salt	2 mL
	Freshly ground black pepper	
½ cup	tomato salsa (see Tips, left)	125 mL
1 cup	shredded Monterey Jack cheese	250 mL
	Finely chopped cilantro, optional	

1. In a bowl or measuring cup, preferably with a pouring spout, whisk cream and egg yolks. Whisk in chile powder, oregano, salt, and pepper to taste. Add salsa and mix well. Set aside.

2. Place about 2 tsp (10 mL) of the shredded cheese in each pastry shell. Pour in salsa mixture. Bake in preheated oven until cheese is melted and top is nicely browned, about 10 minutes. Let cool slightly on a wire rack, about 5 minutes. Garnish with cilantro, if using. Serve warm.

> ### Variation
>
> **Salsa-Verde Spiked Cheese Tarts:** Substitute an equal quantity of salsa verde (or Fresh Salsa Verde, page 71) for the tomato salsa.

Spinach and Artichoke Tartlets

Makes 36 tartlets

*Spinach, artichoke
and creamy cheese is
a classic combination,
probably because
these ingredients
work so well together.
Combined in
pop-in-your mouth
tartlets, they are a
savory treat.*

Tip

Fresh spinach can be gritty,
so be sure to wash it well,
preferably by immersing in
a basin of lukewarm water.

36	pre-baked Tartlet Pastry (page 164) or Potato Pastry (page 165) shells	36
1 tbsp	oil	15 mL
2 tbsp	chopped shallot (1 small)	30 mL
1	clove garlic, coarsely chopped	1
4 cups	packed coarsely torn fresh spinach leaves (about 8 oz/250 g) (see Tip, left)	1 L
½ cup	coarsely chopped artichoke hearts (3 to 4 whole, thawed if frozen)	125 mL
4 oz	cream cheese, cubed and softened	125 g
½ cup	shredded mozzarella cheese	125 mL
2 tbsp	freshly grated Parmesan cheese	30 mL
¼ tsp	freshly grated nutmeg	1 mL
	Salt and freshly ground black pepper	

1. In a skillet, heat oil over medium heat. Add shallot and cook, stirring, until softened, about 3 minutes. Add garlic and spinach and cook, stirring, until spinach is nicely wilted, about 2 minutes. Let cool slightly.

2. Transfer to a food processor fitted with metal blade. Pulse until finely chopped, about 6 times. Add artichokes, cream cheese, mozzarella, Parmesan, nutmeg, and salt and pepper to taste and pulse until combined. Spoon into pastry shells (about 1 tbsp/ 15 mL per shell). Bake in preheated oven until hot and bubbling, about 20 minutes. Let cool slightly in pan on a wire rack, about 5 minutes. Serve warm.

Variation

Spinach and Hearts of Palm Tarts: Substitute an equal quantity of chopped hearts of palm for the artichokes. Unless you live in an area where they are grown, expect to purchase hearts of palm in a can. Refrigerate any extras and use them in salads as you would use cold asparagus.

Prosciutto-Spiked Spinach and Ricotta Tartlets

Makes about 36 tartlets

With the addition of flavorful prosciutto, these creamy little bites pack a savory punch.

Tips

Fresh spinach can be gritty, so be sure to wash it well, preferably by immersing it in a basin of lukewarm water. After it has been washed, be sure to leave the water on the leaves. This is the cooking liquid.

Ricotta cheese usually has a moisture content of between 72 and 80%, which means it is quite watery and will make your crust soggy. You can drain it yourself. Place a double layer of cheesecloth in a strainer, place the strainer over a mixing bowl and add ricotta. Cover with plastic wrap and place a plate over the plastic to press the cheese down. Refrigerate for about 8 hours. Discard liquid that has accumulated in the bowl. Or look for ricotta that has been predrained. The package will state that it has a moisture content of about 65%.

- **Preheat oven to 375°F (190°C)**

36	prebaked Tartlet Pastry (page 164) or Potato Pastry (page 165) shells	36
1 lb	fresh spinach, stems removed (see Tips, left)	500 g
2 tbsp	unsalted butter	30 mL
1	small onion, finely chopped (about ½ cup/125 mL)	1
½ cup	finely chopped prosciutto (about 3 oz/90 g)	125 mL
	Salt and freshly ground black pepper	
1	egg	1
½ cup	freshly grated Parmesan cheese	125 mL
½ cup	heavy or whipping (35%) cream	125 mL
½ tsp	freshly grated nutmeg	2 mL
1 cup	drained ricotta (see Tips, left)	250 mL

1. In a saucepan, place wet spinach leaves. Cover tightly and cook over medium heat until spinach is wilted, about 4 minutes. Transfer to a colander and drain well. When cool enough to handle, using your hands, squeeze out excess liquid. Chop finely and set aside.

2. In a skillet, melt butter over medium heat. Add onion and cook, stirring, until softened, about 3 minutes. Add prosciutto and cook, stirring, for 1 minute. Stir in chopped spinach and remove from heat. Season to taste with salt and pepper. Set aside.

3. In a bowl, whisk egg, Parmesan, cream and nutmeg. Add ricotta and spinach mixture and stir well. Spoon about 1 heaping tbsp (20 mL) into each muffin cup. Bake in preheated oven until filling is set and just beginning to brown, about 15 minutes. Transfer to a wire rack and let cool slightly before serving.

Tartlet Pastry

Makes enough for 30 to 36 tartlets

This is a good basic pastry recipe that works well with any of the tartlets.

Tip

Shells can be baked up to 4 hours ahead and held at room temperature.

- **36 nonstick mini muffin cups**
- **2½-inch (6 cm) round cutter**

1½ cups	all-purpose flour	375 mL
½ tsp	salt	2 mL
½ cup	cold unsalted butter, cubed	125 mL
1	egg yolk	1
4 tbsp	ice water (approx.)	60 mL

1. In food processor fitted with metal blade, pulse flour and salt until blended, about 5 times. Add butter and pulse until mixture resembles large-flake oatmeal, about 8 times. In a small bowl, beat egg yolk and 2 tbsp (30 mL) of the ice water. Add to mixture and pulse just until incorporated, about 6 times.

2. Pinch the mixture between your thumb and fingers. If it doesn't hold together, add 1 tbsp (15 mL) water and pulse 3 times. Pinch again. If it still doesn't hold together, repeat with remaining water. Process just until a ball is about to form. Transfer to a lightly floured work surface and knead lightly. Divide dough into 2 batches, wrap tightly in plastic and refrigerate for at least 1 hour or for up to 2 days.

3. *To bake shells:* Preheat oven to 375°F (190°C). Working with one batch of dough at a time, on a lightly floured surface, roll from the center out into a large circle about $\frac{1}{16}$ inch (2 mm) thick. Using round cutter, cut into 30 to 36 small circles (depending on the recipe) and press into mini muffin cups. Repeat with remaining dough. Prick holes in the bottom of dough and bake in preheated oven until lightly browned, about 10 minutes. Let cool in pans on a wire rack.

Potato Pastry

Makes enough for 36 tartlets

If you're timid about making pastry, this version, which is sturdier than most, is a bit easier to work with than most conventional recipes.

Tip

Shells can be baked up to 4 hours ahead and held at room temperature.

- **36 nonstick mini muffin cups**
- **2½-inch (6 cm) round cutter**

½ cup	cooled mashed potato (about half a small 6 oz/175 g potato)	125 mL
1¼ cups	all-purpose flour (approx.)	300 mL
1 tbsp	fresh thyme leaves or 1 tsp (5 mL) dried	15 mL
½ tsp	salt	2 mL
4 tbsp	cold unsalted butter, cubed	60 mL
1	egg yolk, beaten	1
1 tsp	ice water (approx.)	5 mL

1. In food processor fitted with metal blade, pulse flour, thyme and salt to blend. Add butter and pulse until mixture resembles large-flake oatmeal, about 8 times. Add mashed potato and egg yolk and pulse to blend about 10 times. Sprinkle ice water over top and pulse just to blend, 2 to 3 times.

2. Pinch a bit of dough between your fingers. It should look like it will come together with a light kneading. If not, add a bit more (about ½ tsp/2 mL) ice water and pulse to blend. Transfer dough to a clean surface and knead until it holds together. Divide dough into 2 batches, wrap tightly in plastic and refrigerate for at least 1 hour or for up to 2 days.

3. *To bake shells:* Preheat oven to 375°F (190°C). Working with one batch of dough at a time, on a lightly floured surface, roll from the center out into a large circle about ¹⁄₁₆ inch (2 mm) thick. Using round cutter, cut into 30 to 36 small circles (depending on the recipe) and press into mini muffin cups. Repeat with remaining dough. Prick holes in the bottom of dough and bake in preheated oven until lightly browned, about 10 minutes. Let cool in pans on a wire rack.

Mini Smoked Salmon and Sour Cream Puff Pastry Tartlets

Makes 16 tartlets

It's incredible how these simple ingredients create a very sophisticated appetizer. To impress your guests even more, try a garnish of salmon roe or tobiko (flying fish roe).

Tips

This tartlet is meant to be eaten at room temperature so feel free to make the shells a day in advance and assemble just before serving. Store baked shells in a cookie tin at room temperature.

If you don't feel like making your own preserved lemon, use bottled ones, which are available in markets specializing in Middle Eastern foods or well-stocked supermarkets.

- **Preheat oven to 400°F (200°C)**
- **2-inch (5 cm) round cutter or drinking glass**
- **2 baking sheets, one lined with parchment paper**

8 oz	puff pastry, thawed	250 g
12	thin slices smoked salmon, each about 3 by 2 inches (7.5 by 5 cm)	12
5 tsp	sour cream	25 mL
1 tbsp	finely chopped Preserved Lemons (page 554) (see Tips, left)	15 mL
½ tsp	fresh thyme leaves	2 mL

1. On a lightly floured surface, roll out puff pastry to a 10-inch (25 cm) square. Using round cutter, cut 16 circles from pastry. Place on prepared baking sheet, at least 1 inch (2.5 cm) apart. With the tines of a fork, prick the pastry all over. Place another sheet of parchment paper on top of pastry, then place second baking sheet on top to weigh pastry down. Bake in preheated oven until pastry is golden brown, about 20 minutes. Remove top baking sheet and parchment paper. Let tartlet shells cool on pan on a wire rack.

2. Drape a slice of smoked salmon over top of each tartlet shell. Spoon sour cream and preserved lemon in the middle of smoked salmon, dividing equally. Garnish each tartlet with 3 or 4 thyme leaves and serve immediately.

Mini Caramelized Onion Puff Pastry Tartlets

Makes 16 tartlets

Caramelizing onions is the simple process of extracting and browning the natural sugars of the onions. It makes a versatile ingredient that can be used as a condiment on a grilled pizza or Bacon-Spiked Chopped Liver Spread (page 475) or here as the star of the show. Sitting on top of flaky pastry, these onions create a sweet, very simple recipe that is perfect any time of day.

Tip

These tartlets are perfect at room temperature, too, and the pastry stays nice and crisp.

- **Preheat oven to 400°F (200°C)**
- **2-inch (5 cm) round cutter or drinking glass**
- **Baking sheet, lined with parchment paper**

8 oz	puff pastry, thawed	250 g
½ cup	Caramelized Onions (page 552)	125 mL
32	very thin lengthwise slices garlic (about 3 cloves)	32

1. On a lightly floured surface, roll out puff pastry to a 10-inch (25 cm) square. Using round cutter, cut 16 circles from pastry. Place on prepared baking sheet, at least 1 inch (2.5 cm) apart. With the tines of a fork, prick the pastry all over.

2. Divide caramelized onions equally among pastry circles and spread to cover. Garnish each with 2 garlic slices overlapping in the middle of the tartlet. Bake in preheated oven until pastry is golden brown around edges, about 20 minutes. Serve immediately or let cool on pan on a wire rack.

Mini Tomato and Olive Tapenade Puff Pastry Tartlets

Makes 16 tartlets

This appetizer, influenced by the Provence region in France, has a wonderful contrast of flavors and textures. You can easily substitute roughly chopped black olives of your choice for the tapenade.

Tip

We recommend using pure sea salt rather than refined table salt. It has a clean, crisp taste and enhanced mineral content, unlike table salt, which has a bitter acrid taste and contains unpleasant additives to prevent caking.

- Preheat oven to 400°F (200°C)
- 2-inch (5 cm) round cutter or drinking glass
- Baking sheet, lined with parchment paper

8 oz	puff pastry, thawed	250 g
3	plum (Roma) tomatoes	3
1 tbsp	extra virgin olive oil	15 mL
1 tbsp	fresh thyme leaves	15 mL
¼ tsp	salt	1 mL
¼ tsp	freshly ground black pepper	1 mL
⅓ cup	Parsley-Laced Tapenade (page 46) or store-bought	75 mL

1. On a lightly floured surface, roll out puff pastry to a 10-inch (25 cm) square. Using cutter, cut 16 circles from pastry. Place on prepared baking sheet, at least 1 inch (2.5 cm) apart. With the tines of a fork, prick the pastry all over.

2. Cut tomatoes crosswise into 16 equal slices. Place one tomato slice on each pastry circle. Drizzle evenly with olive oil and sprinkle with thyme, salt and pepper. Bake in preheated oven until tomato is soft and tartlet is golden brown around edges, about 20 minutes. Garnish with tapenade and serve immediately.

Berry-Glazed Fig Tart

Makes 8 servings

This traditional French classic is so easy to make. If you have 45 minutes, you have time to create this sensational treat.

Tips

A beaten egg has many uses, from "fastening" pieces of puff pastry to one another to battering of fish for "fish and chips" to providing a golden brown finish to pies.

Agave syrup is produced from the agave plant and because it contains a high percentage of fructose, it is much sweeter than honey.

- **Preheat oven to 300°F (150°C)**

Glaze

¾ cup	blueberries	175 mL
¼ cup	water	60 mL
1 tbsp	agave syrup (see Tips, left)	15 mL
1 tbsp	raspberry jam or preserve	15 mL
8 oz	puff pastry	250 g
1	egg, beaten	1
1 cup	sliced peeled apples	250 mL
1 cup	halved fresh figs	250 mL
1 tbsp	packed brown sugar	15 mL
1 tsp	grated lemon zest	5 mL

1. *Glaze:* In a saucepan, combine blueberries, water, agave syrup and raspberry jam. Bring to a boil over medium heat. Reduce heat and boil gently until liquid is reduced by three-quarters, about 6 minutes. Set aside and let cool to room temperature.

2. On a lightly floured surface, roll out puff pastry to a 10-inch (25 cm) square. Trim a ½ inch (1 cm) strip from all four sides. Place pastry square on prepared baking sheet. Brush beaten egg along edges of the square. Place four strips back on the square on top of the egg to create a raised border (the egg will "glue" the strips into place). Set aside.

3. In a bowl, combine apples, figs, brown sugar and lemon zest. Set aside.

4. To assemble the tart, pour blueberry glaze onto puff pastry and spread evenly within pastry border. Place apple and fig mixture over glaze and spread out evenly. Bake in preheated oven until pastry is golden brown and bottom is crisp, about 30 minutes. Let cool on pan or on a wire rack to room temperature before serving.

Goat Cheese and Caramelized Onion Vol-au-Vent

Makes 18

There's a bit of fussy work in making these because you need to separate the puff pastry after it has been cooked, but if you're looking for something with a Wow factor, look no further. People will be very impressed that you made your own vol-au-vent and will thoroughly enjoy these tasty pop-in-your mouth treats.

Tip

Walnuts contain a high amount of healthy omega-3 fats and because of this become rancid quite quickly. Purchase yours from a purveyor with high turnover and taste before you buy.

- 1½-inch (4 cm) round cutter
- Baking sheet, lined with parchment paper

Vol-au-Vent

8 oz	puff pastry, thawed	250 g

Filling

1	onion	1
1 tbsp	oil	15 mL
2 tbsp	finely chopped walnuts (see Tip, left)	30 mL
½ tsp	finely chopped fresh rosemary	2 mL
1 tbsp	balsamic vinegar	15 mL
	Salt and freshly ground back pepper	
2 oz	soft goat cheese, crumbled	60 g

1. On a lightly floured surface, roll puff pastry to a 10-inch (25 cm) square, about ⅛ inch (3 mm) thick. Using cutter, cut 36 circles. Brush tops with water, then stack half of the circles on top of the other half, wet sides together. Place on prepared baking sheet, cover with plastic wrap and refrigerate for 30 minutes.

2. *Filling:* Slice onion in half lengthwise. Place flat side down on cutting board and slice very thinly lengthwise.

3. In a skillet, heat oil over medium heat. Add onion and cook, stirring, until it begins to brown, about 6 minutes. Add walnuts and rosemary and cook, stirring, for 1 minute. Add vinegar and cook, stirring, until it evaporates, about 1 minute. Season to taste with salt and pepper. Remove from heat and stir in goat cheese. Let cool.

4. When you're ready to serve, preheat oven to 400°F (200°C). Remove plastic and bake vol-au-vent until golden, about 12 minutes. Transfer to a wire rack and let cool for 2 minutes.

5. Using a small sharp knife, cut through the joint to separate tops from bottoms of vol-au-vent. Spoon onion mixture into bottoms, dividing equally. Replace tops, place on a platter and serve warm.

Creamy Mushroom Vol-au-Vent

Makes 18

Crisp light puff pastry filled with creamy mushrooms is a marriage made in heaven. And homemade vol-au-vent will have your guests thinking you're a culinary genius when, in fact, they are very easy to make.

Tip

Italian flat-leaf parsley is preferred because it has much more flavor than the curly leaf variety.

- **1½-inch (4 cm) round cutter**
- **Baking sheet, lined with parchment paper**

Vol-au-Vent

8 oz	puff pastry, thawed	250 g

Filling

1	clove garlic, minced	1
1 tbsp	finely chopped flat-leaf parsley leaves	15 mL
1 tbsp	fresh thyme leaves	15 mL
1 tbsp	freshly squeezed lemon juice	15 mL
⅛ tsp	hot paprika	0.5 mL
2 tbsp	oil	30 mL
6 oz	white mushrooms, finely chopped	175 g
2 tsp	all-purpose flour	10 mL
3 tbsp	heavy or whipping (35%) cream	45 mL
	Salt and freshly ground black pepper	

1. On a lightly floured surface, roll puff pastry to a 10-inch (25 cm) square, about ⅛ inch (3 mm) thick. Using cutter, cut 36 circles. Brush tops with water, then stack half the circles on top of the other half, wet sides together. Place on prepared baking sheet, cover with plastic wrap and refrigerate for 30 minutes.

2. *Filling:* Meanwhile, in a bowl, combine garlic, parsley, thyme, lemon juice and paprika. Mix well and set aside.

3. In a skillet, heat oil over medium-high heat. Sauté mushrooms until liquid is evaporated, about 7 minutes. Sprinkle flour evenly over mushrooms and stir well. Add parsley mixture and cream and sauté until sauce is thickened. (This will happen almost immediately.) Season to taste with salt and pepper.

4. When you're ready to serve, preheat oven to 400°F (200°C). Remove plastic and bake vol-au-vent until golden, about 12 minutes. Transfer to a wire rack and let cool for 2 minutes.

5. Using a small sharp knife, cut through the joint to separate tops from bottoms. Spoon mushroom mixture into bottoms, dividing equally. Replace tops, place on a platter and serve warm.

Anchovy-Spiked Leek and Tomato Galettes

Makes 16 mini galettes

Sweet mild-tasting leeks combined with tomatoes and a hint of pungent anchovies makes a great combination. A finish of soft, peppery cheese is the pièce de résistance.

Tips

Italian flat-leaf parsley is preferred because it has much more flavor than the curly leaf variety.

Egg wash has many different uses. Here it enhances the browning of the crust.

- **Preheat oven to 375°F (190°C)**

8 oz	puff pastry, thawed	250 g
1 tbsp	olive oil	15 mL
2	leeks, white and light green parts only, cleaned and thinly sliced (see Tips, page 173)	2
2 cups	cherry tomatoes	500 mL
2 tbsp	finely chopped Italian flat-leaf parsley leaves	30 mL
2	anchovy fillets, minced	2
1	clove garlic, minced	1
1	egg yolk, beaten with 1 tsp (5 mL) water	1
4 oz	pepper-flavored soft fresh cheese, such as Boursin	125 g

1. Prepare Pastry for Galettes (page 175). Meanwhile, in a bowl, combine oil, leeks and tomatoes. Toss until well coated. Spread out on baking sheet. Roast in preheated oven, stirring occasionally, until leeks begin to brown and tomatoes have collapsed, about 30 minutes. Transfer to a bowl. Add parsley, anchovies and garlic and toss well. Set aside until cool.

2. When you're ready to bake pastry, preheat oven to 400°F (200°C). Place another baking sheet on top of parchment to weigh the pastry down. Bake in preheated oven for 5 minutes. Transfer sheet to a rack and let cool slightly. Brush with egg wash.

3. Divide leek mixture equally among galettes. Spoon about 1 tsp (5 mL) of the cheese over top of each pastry. Bake in preheated oven until pastry is golden and cheese is beginning to brown and melt, about 20 minutes. Let cool on pan on a wire rack for 5 minutes. Serve warm.

Butternut Galette with Basil Drizzle

Makes 32 mini galettes

These tasty morsels are a bit of work, but they are worth it. They are deliciously different.

Tips

You'll need 1 small butternut or acorn squash for this quantity.

Because leeks can be gritty, it is customary to slice and rinse them before using. *To clean leeks:* Fill a sink full of lukewarm water. Split the leeks in half lengthwise and submerge in the water, swishing them around to remove all traces of dirt. Transfer to a colander and rinse thoroughly under cold water.

If you like a bit of heat leave the veins and seeds in the chile pepper before mincing.

1 lb	puff pastry, thawed	500 g
1 tbsp	unsalted butter or oil	15 mL
3 cups	cubed (½ inch/1 cm) peeled butternut squash (see Tips, left)	750 mL
1	leek, white and light green parts only, cleaned and thinly sliced (see Tips, left)	1
½ tsp	dried oregano	2 mL
½ cup	chicken or vegetable broth or water	125 mL
1	long red chile pepper, seeded and minced	1
	Salt and freshly ground black pepper	
1 cup	grated Asiago cheese	250 mL

Basil Drizzle

¼ cup	finely chopped fresh basil leaves	60 mL
1	clove garlic, minced	1
¼ cup	heavy or whipping (35%) cream	60 mL
1 tbsp	freshly squeezed lemon juice	15 mL

1. Prepare Pastry for Galettes (page 175). Meanwhile, in a skillet, melt butter over medium heat. Add squash and leek and cook, stirring, until softened, about 5 minutes. Add oregano and cook, stirring, for 1 minute. Stir in broth, cover and reduce heat to low. Simmer until squash is very tender, about 10 minutes. Remove from heat. Using a fork, mash squash. Stir in chile pepper and season to taste with salt and pepper. Set aside.

2. When you're ready to bake pastry, preheat oven to 400°F (200°C). Place another baking sheet on top of parchment to weigh the pastry down. Bake in preheated oven for 5 minutes. Transfer sheet to a rack and let cool slightly.

3. Spoon about 1 heaping tbsp (20 mL) of squash mixture in center of each round. Sprinkle squash evenly with Asiago cheese. Return to preheated oven and bake until edges are golden and cheese is melted, about 20 minutes. Let cool on baking sheets on rack for 5 minutes.

4. *Basil Drizzle:* Meanwhile, in a bowl, combine basil, garlic, cream and lemon juice. Mix well. When galettes have cooled slightly, drizzle mixture over top of each tart. Transfer to a platter and serve warm.

Tomato Mozzarella Galettes

Makes 16 mini galettes

Serve these Mediterranean-inspired pastries when you like the idea of zesty flavor but are also longing for comfort food. The tomatoes, oregano and olives deliver zest and the creamy melted cheese and warm pastry are sublimely comforting.

Tip

Olive paste is available in the deli section of many supermarkets. If you can't find it, you can make your own (see page 233).

- **Preheat oven to 400°F (200°C)**
- **2 rimmed baking sheets, one lined with parchment paper**

8 oz	puff pastry, thawed	250 g
3 cups	halved cherry or grape tomatoes	750 mL
1 tbsp	extra virgin olive oil	15 mL
1 tsp	dried oregano	5 mL
	Salt	
¼ cup	olive paste (approx.) (see Tip, left)	60 mL
1 cup	finely diced fresh mozzarella	250 mL
	Chopped fresh basil, optional	

1. Prepare Pastry for Galettes (page 175).

2. Meanwhile, in a bowl, combine tomatoes and oil. Toss well. Transfer to unlined baking sheet cut-side up. Sprinkle with oregano and roast in preheated oven until softened and wizened, about 20 minutes. Remove from oven, sprinkle to taste with salt and let cool.

3. When you're ready to bake, place another baking sheet on top of parchment to weigh the pastry down. Bake in preheated oven for 5 minutes. Transfer baking sheet to a rack and let cool slightly.

4. Spread each round with olive paste, dividing equally and leaving a border of about ¼ inch (0.5 cm). Spoon tomato halves in center on each round and diced mozzarella on top of tomatoes. Return to preheated oven and bake until edges of pastry are puffed and golden and cheese is melted and browning, about 15 minutes. Transfer to a platter and sprinkle with basil, if using. Serve warm.

Herb-Spiked Ricotta Galettes

Makes 16 mini galettes

Creamy ricotta with a hint of sharp Parmesan and mild herbs is a glorious combination. These warm pastries are melt-in-your-mouth delicious.

Tips

You can prepare the pastry and the ricotta filling up to 1 day ahead and refrigerate separately until you're ready to bake.

We prefer to use full-fat or whole milk ricotta cheese in this recipe because it has a deeper flavor profile but if you prefer, use a lower-fat alternative.

• **Preheat oven to 400°F (200°C)**

8 oz	puff pastry, thawed	250 g
1 cup	whole milk ricotta cheese (see Tips, left)	250 mL
½ cup	freshly grated Parmesan cheese	125 mL
1	egg, beaten	1
2 tbsp	finely snipped chives	30 mL
1 tbsp	fresh thyme leaves	15 mL
Pinch	freshly grated nutmeg	Pinch
	Extra virgin olive oil	
	Salt and freshly ground black pepper	

1. Prepare Pastry for Galettes (see below and Tip, left).

2. In a bowl, combine ricotta, Parmesan, egg, chives, thyme and nutmeg. Mix well. When you're ready to bake, place another baking sheet on top of parchment to weigh the pastry down. Bake in preheated oven for 5 minutes. Transfer baking sheet to a rack and let cool slightly.

3. Spoon cheese mixture in center of each round, dividing equally. Bake in preheated oven until edges of pastry are puffed and cheese is set and slightly browned, about 20 minutes. Transfer to a platter, drizzle lightly with olive oil and season to taste with salt and pepper. Serve warm.

Preparing Pastry for Galettes

On a lightly floured surface, roll out each 8 oz (250 g) of pastry into a 12-inch (30 cm) square about ⅛ inch (3 mm) thick. Using a 3-inch (7.5 cm) round cutter, cut into 16 circles. (You will need to re-roll pastry scraps once or twice to get the required number.) Place on a baking sheet, lined with parchment paper, at least 1 inch (2.5 cm) apart and cover with another sheet of parchment. Refrigerate for at least 30 minutes, until chilled, or cover entire sheet with plastic wrap and refrigerate for up to 1 day.

Mini Potato Galettes with Caviar and Crème Fraîche

Makes 14 galettes

This is a variation on a traditional potato galette. Caviar does not have to be a very expensive ingredient. Sure, you could spend a fortune on beluga or sevruga caviar but salmon roe or tobiko (flying fish roe) are inexpensive good-quality substitutes.

3 tbsp	olive oil	45 mL
1	russet (Idaho) potato (about 8 oz/250 g), coarsely shredded	1
¼ tsp	salt	1 mL
2 tbsp	crème fraîche	30 mL
1¾ tsp	salmon roe or tobiko	8 mL

1. In a large skillet, heat oil over medium heat. Spoon about 1 tbsp (15 mL) of the potatoes into oil for each galette and fry until crisp and golden brown, about 5 minutes per side. Transfer to a plate, lined with paper towels to drain. Season with salt.

2. To assemble, spoon crème fraîche in middle of potato galettes, dividing evenly and garnish with caviar.

Phyllo Bundles

Makes 24 bundles

Cut phyllo pastry into squares, stack in layers and twist to close to create traditional bundles. Placing the bundles in mini muffin cups to bake ensures that they have shape and are nicely uniform.

Tip

If you have a pastry board it is probably large enough to accommodate the phyllo sheets comfortably.

- **24 nonstick mini-muffin cups**

6	sheets phyllo pastry, thawed	6
⅓ cup	unsalted butter, melted	75 mL

1. Place phyllo on work surface or a dry tea towel and cover with a damp tea towel.

2. On a large cutting board, working quickly, stack 3 sheets at a time. Cut phyllo into 12 equal squares, each about 4 inches (10 cm). Cover with damp towel as completed.

3. When all squares are cut, place 8 phyllo squares on the board at a time and brush with butter. Place a second phyllo square on top of the first at a 45° angle and brush with butter. You should now have something resembling an 8-point star. Place a third square on top of the other 2, in the original position and brush with butter.

4. Repeat with remaining phyllo and butter. Fill squares with desired filling, place in muffin cups, twist to close and brush with butter. Bake according to recipe directions.

Ham and Cheese Phyllo Bundles

Makes 24 bundles

Ham and cheese are a classic pairing. The addition of roasted red pepper puts a slightly new spin on the combo. The tasty result is rich and comforting.

Tip

Use a store-bought roasted pepper or roast, peel, seed and mince one yourself (see Tip, page 184).

- **Preheat oven to 350°F (180°C)**
- **24 nonstick mini-muffin cups**

1	recipe Phyllo Bundles (page 176)	1
2 tbsp	mayonnaise	30 mL
1 tsp	Dijon mustard	5 mL
Pinch	cayenne pepper	Pinch
2 cups	shredded Swiss cheese	500 mL
4 oz	ham, diced	125 g
1	red bell pepper, roasted and minced	1
	Freshly ground black pepper	

1. In a bowl, combine mayonnaise, mustard and cayenne Stir in remaining ingredients. Season with pepper.
2. Place about 1½ tbsp (22 mL) of filling in the center of each phyllo square. Fold sides up, then twist to close.
3. Place bundles in mini-muffin cups and brush tops with melted butter. Repeat until all phyllo squares are filled. Bake in preheated oven until pastry is light golden and cheese is melted, 15 to 20 minutes. Serve warm.

Walnut-Spiked Blue Cheese Bundles

Makes 24 bundles

Vegetarian Friendly

This combination is delicious any time of the year, but the cranberries seem particularly appropriate for the holiday season.

1	recipe Phyllo Bundles (page 176)	1
4 oz	cream cheese, softened	125 g
4 oz	blue cheese, crumbled	125 g
¼ cup	finely chopped dried cranberries	60 mL
¼ cup	finely chopped walnuts	60 mL
2 tsp	finely grated orange zest	10 mL

1. In a bowl, combine cream cheese and blue cheese. Using a wooden spoon, mix well until blended. Add cranberries, walnuts and orange zest and mix well.
2. Place about 2 tsp (10 mL) of the filling in the center of each phyllo square. Fold sides of phyllo up around filling, then twist tops to close.
3. Follow Step 3 above.

Spinach and Pine Nut Bundles

Makes 24 bundles

If you're looking for a phyllo filling that is based on spinach but doesn't contain cheese, try this. The pine nuts add flavor and crunch and the sumac, a spice used in Middle Eastern cooking, adds pleasant tanginess.

Tips

In place of the bunch of spinach, use one 10 oz (300 g) bag spinach leaves, trimmed, or frozen spinach. Thaw and drain it well before chopping.

To toast pine nuts: Place nuts on a rimmed baking sheet and roast in a 350°F (180°C) oven for about 8 minutes, shaking the pan once or twice, until nicely browned. You can also toast them in a skillet over medium heat, stirring often, until nicely browned, about 5 minutes.

Ground sumac is available in the spice sections of well-stocked supermarkets.

This recipe can be prepared ahead of time. Place bundles in muffin cups, cover and refrigerate for up to 2 hours or freeze in plastic wrap for up to 2 weeks. Add about 10 minutes to baking time.

- **Preheat oven to 350°F (180°C)**
- **24 nonstick mini-muffin cups**

1	recipe Phyllo Bundles (page 176)	1
1 tbsp	olive oil	15 mL
1	onion, finely chopped	1
2	cloves garlic, minced	2
1 lb	fresh spinach, stems removed	500 g
½ cup	finely chopped Italian flat-leaf parsley leaves	125 mL
½ cup	pine nuts, toasted and chopped (see Tips, left)	125 mL
1 tbsp	freshly squeezed lemon juice or 1 tsp (5 mL) finely grated lemon zest	15 mL
1 tsp	ground sumac (see Tips, left)	5 mL
	Salt and freshly ground black pepper	

1. Prepare bundles. In a skillet, heat oil over medium heat. Add onion and cook, stirring, until softened, about 3 minutes. Add garlic and cook, stirring, for 1 minute. Add spinach, in batches if necessary, and toss until wilted. Transfer to a colander and drain well. Chop spinach coarsely and transfer to a bowl.

2. Add parsley, pine nuts, lemon juice and sumac and mix well. Season to taste with salt and pepper.

3. Place a generous tbsp (20 mL) of the filling in center of each phyllo square. Fold sides of phyllo up around filling, then twist tops to close.

4. Place in mini-muffin cups and brush tops with melted butter. Bake in preheated oven until pastry is light golden and filling is hot, 15 to 20 minutes. Serve warm.

Paprika-Spiked Mushroom Bundles

Makes 24 bundles

This mushroom filling is creamy yet a tiny bit pungent. It's a take on Hungarian paprikash sauce, which marries well with rich crispy phyllo, like a savory strudel.

Tips

Use your food processor to make easy work of dicing the mushrooms. Remove stems and place caps, in batches, around work bowl fitted with metal blade. Be careful not to overpack. Pulse until desired result is achieved, being careful not to overprocess.

This recipe can be prepared ahead of time. Place bundles in muffin cups, cover and refrigerate for up to 2 hours or freeze in plastic wrap for up to 2 weeks. Add about 10 minutes to the baking time.

- **Preheat oven to 350°F (180°C)**
- **24 nonstick mini-muffin cups**

1	recipe Phyllo Bundles (page 176)	1
2 tbsp	unsalted butter	30 mL
1	shallot, minced	1
10 oz	mushrooms, diced (see Tips, left)	300 g
2 tsp	freshly squeezed lemon juice	10 mL
1 tbsp	sweet paprika	15 mL
	Salt and freshly ground black pepper	
½ cup	sour cream	125 mL
¼ cup	finely chopped Italian flat-leaf parsley leaves	60 mL

1. Prepare bundles. In a skillet, melt butter over medium-high heat. Sauté shallots and mushrooms until liquid is evaporated, about 6 minutes. Remove from heat. Add lemon juice, paprika and salt and pepper to taste and stir well. Stir in sour cream and parsley.

2. Place about 1 tbsp (15 mL) of the filling in the center of each phyllo square. Fold sides of phyllo up around filling, then twist tops to close.

3. Place in mini-muffin cups and brush tops with melted butter. Bake in preheated oven until pastry is light golden and filling is hot, 15 to 20 minutes. Serve warm.

Oregano and Cheese Bundles

Makes 24 bundles

This combination of fresh oregano and salty halloumi cheese is beautifully balanced between creamy and tart. The optional sumac, the powder ground from a bitter red berry, adds a barely perceptible hint of tanginess.

Tips

Halloumi is very salty so there is no added salt in this recipe. If you feel it is necessary, add to the filling to taste.

This recipe can be prepared ahead of time. Place bundles in muffin cups, cover and refrigerate for up to 2 hours or freeze in plastic wrap for up to 2 weeks. Add about 10 minutes to the baking time.

Be sure to purchase your sumac from a Middle Eastern market or a reputable purveyor. In some parts of the world sumac berries are poisonous.

- **Preheat oven to 350°F (180°C)**
- **24 nonstick mini-muffin cups**

1	recipe Phyllo Bundles (page 176)	1
8 oz	halloumi cheese, shredded (about 2 cups/500 mL)	250 g
2 cups	fresh oregano leaves, finely chopped	500 mL
½ cup	finely chopped Italian flat-leaf parsley leaves	125 mL
3 tbsp	extra virgin olive oil	45 mL
1 tsp	ground sumac, optional	5 mL
	Freshly ground black pepper	

1. Prepare bundles. In a bowl, combine cheese, oregano, parsley, olive oil, and sumac, if using. Toss well. Season to taste with pepper.

2. Place a generous tbsp (20 mL) of filling in the center of each phyllo square. Fold sides of phyllo up around filling, then twist tops to close.

3. Place in mini-muffin cups and brush tops with melted butter. Bake in preheated oven until pastry is light golden and cheese is melted, 15 to 20 minutes. Serve warm.

Pancetta and Potato Bundles

Makes 12 bundles

This combination of garlic-mashed potatoes seasoned with green onion, Parmesan cheese and a bit of olive oil, then wrapped in salty pancetta and baked, is delicious.

Tip

If your pancetta is sliced exceptionally thin, it may tear into strips when you try to work with it. No problem. Just overlap the strips in the tins until you've covered the bottom and sides, then fold them over each other on top.

- **Preheat oven to 425°F (220°C)**
- **12-cup nonstick mini-muffin tin**

2	medium potatoes (about 12 oz/375 g total), peeled	2
6	cloves garlic	6
2	green onions, white part with a bit of green, finely minced	2
2 tbsp	freshly grated Parmesan cheese	30 mL
1 tbsp	extra virgin olive oil	15 mL
	Salt and freshly ground black pepper	
4 oz	thinly sliced pancetta (see Tip, left)	125 g

1. In a pot of salted water, cook potatoes and garlic until potatoes are tender. Drain and put through a ricer (or mash smoothly) into a bowl. Add green onions, Parmesan, olive oil, and salt and pepper to taste and mix well. Set aside.

2. Line muffin cups with pancetta, making sure bottom and sides of cups are thoroughly covered and that pancetta spills over the top. Spoon about 1 tbsp (15 mL) of potato mixture into each cup. Fold pancetta over to cover top.

3. Bake in preheated oven until pancetta is nicely sizzling, about 15 minutes. Let cool slightly, lift bundles out of tins and place on a small platter. Serve warm.

Crust for Empanaditas

Makes enough for 18 empanaditas

Empanaditas are bite-size empanadas, Mexican-inspired filled turnovers. It is conventional to fry them, but they are equally delicious baked in the oven, a more appropriate method for those who are health conscious.

Tip

Egg wash has many uses, from "fastening" pieces of puff pastry to one another to providing a golden brown finish to pies. Its uses are virtually endless. Here the addition of milk intensifies the browning capacity of the crust.

- **Preheat oven to 375°F (190°C)**
- **4-inch (10 cm) round cutter**
- **Baking sheet, lined with parchment paper**

1½ cups	all-purpose flour	375 mL
½ tsp	salt	2 mL
½ cup	cold unsalted butter, cubed	125 mL
1	egg yolk	1
4 tbsp	ice water, divided (approx.)	60 mL
	Filling (see pages 183 to 185)	

Egg Wash

1	egg yolk	1
2 tbsp	milk	30 mL

1. In food processor fitted with metal blade, pulse flour and salt until blended, about 5 times. Add butter and pulse until mixture resembles large-flake oatmeal, about 8 times. In a small bowl, beat egg yolk and 2 tbsp (30 mL) of the ice water. Add to mixture and pulse just until incorporated, about 6 times.

2. Pinch mixture between your thumb and fingers. If it doesn't hold together, add 1 tbsp (15 mL) water and pulse 3 times. Pinch again. If it still doesn't hold together, repeat with remaining water. Process just until a ball forms. Transfer to a lightly floured work surface and knead lightly.

3. On a lightly floured surface, roll out dough to $\frac{1}{16}$-inch (2 mm) thickness. Using round cutter, cut out 18 circles. (If necessary, knead trimmings and re-roll.)

4. Lightly brush edges of rounds with water, then place about 1 tbsp (15 mL) of the filling in the center. Fold in half and use the tines of a fork to press the edges together to seal.

5. *Egg Wash:* In a small bowl, beat egg yolk and milk until blended. Brush empanaditas with egg wash on all sides. Place at least 1 inch (2.5 cm) apart on prepared sheet and bake in preheated oven until nicely browned, about 30 minutes.

Corn and Cheese Empanaditas

Makes 18 empanaditas

This traditional filling is a Mexican version of comfort food. Accompany with a bowl of Fresh Tomato Salsa (page 70) or Fresh Salsa Verde (page 71) and expect them to quickly disappear.

Tip

If you prefer, substitute a blended chile powder for the ancho or New Mexico one.

1 cup	mashed cooked potatoes	250 mL
½ cup	cooked corn kernels	125 mL
4	green onions, white part with a bit of green, finely chopped	4
2 oz	feta cheese or queso fresco, crumbled	60 g
2	red or green chiles, seeded and minced	2
1 tsp	dried oregano	5 mL
1 tsp	ancho or New Mexico chile powder	5 mL
	Salt and freshly ground black pepper	
1	recipe Crust for Empanaditas (page 182)	1

1. In a bowl, combine potatoes, corn, green onions, feta, chiles, oregano, chile powder, and salt and pepper to taste. Mix well. Let cool slightly, if necessary. If not using immediately, cover and refrigerate until ready to use, for up to 2 days. Use to fill Crust for Empanaditas and bake as directed in Step 5, page 182.

Salsa and Chicken Empanaditas

Makes 18 empanaditas

This combination of chicken, chiles and cheese, with a hint of sour cream is ambrosial. Pass additional salsa verde for dipping.

Tip

Use prepared salsa verde or make your own (page 71).

1 cup	diced cooked chicken breast	250 mL
½ cup	salsa verde (see Tip, left)	125 mL
¼ cup	soft goat cheese or queso fresco, crumbled	60 mL
¼ cup	sour cream	60 mL
3	green onions, white part with a bit of green, finely chopped	3
	Salt and freshly ground black pepper	
1	recipe Crust for Empanaditas (page 182)	1

1. In a bowl, combine chicken, salsa, cheese, sour cream, green onions, and salt and pepper to taste. Use to fill Crust for Empanaditas (Step 4, page 182) and bake as directed in Step 5, page 182.

Roasted Pepper and Cheese Empanaditas

Makes 18 empanaditas

This filling was inspired by one made by Chicago chef Rick Bayless. It is lusciously delicious.

Tip

To roast peppers: Preheat broiler. Place pepper(s) on a baking sheet and broil, turning two or three times, until skin on all sides is blackened, about 25 minutes. Transfer to a heatproof bowl. Cover with a plate and let stand until cool. Remove and, using a sharp knife, lift skins off. Discard skins and prepare according to recipe directions.

2	red bell peppers, roasted and diced (see Tip, left, or store-bought)	2
1 tbsp	oil	15 mL
1	onion, finely chopped	1
2	cloves garlic, minced	2
1 tsp	dried oregano	5 mL
1 tsp	ancho or New Mexico chile powder	5 mL
1/8 tsp	cayenne pepper	0.5 mL
	Salt and freshly ground black pepper	
1/2 cup	heavy or whipping (35%) cream	125 mL
1 cup	shredded Monterey Jack cheese	250 mL
1	recipe Crust for Empanaditas (page 182)	1

1. In a skillet, heat oil over medium heat. Add onion and cook, stirring, until softened, about 3 minutes. Add garlic, oregano, chile powder, cayenne, and salt and pepper to taste and cook, stirring, for 1 minute. Add roasted peppers and cream and stir well. Simmer, stirring, until liquid is evaporated, about 2 minutes. Remove from heat and stir in cheese. Use to fill Crust for Empanaditas and bake as directed in Step 5, page 182.

Ground Beef and Chile-Laced Empanaditas

Makes 36 empanaditas

This zesty ground beef filling accented with olives is inspired by the Cuban dish known as picadillo. It makes a big batch, perfect for a party, so when using, be sure to double the quantity of crust. Fresh Tomato Salsa (page 70) is great for dipping.

Tip

An easy way to cook the potatoes for this recipe is to microwave them. Place scrubbed potato in a microwave-safe dish. Add cold water to a depth of about ½ inch (1 cm), cover and microwave on High for 3 to 6 minutes or until potato is tender. Leave the lid on and let cool for at least 5 minutes before running under cold water and removing the skins.

2	dried ancho chile peppers	2
1 cup	boiling water	250 mL
1	can (14 oz/398 mL) tomatoes, drained	1
1 tbsp	oil	15 mL
1	onion, finely chopped	1
8 oz	lean ground beef	250 g
4	cloves garlic, minced	4
1 tsp	dried oregano	5 mL
1 tsp	ground cumin	5 mL
½ tsp	ground cinnamon	2 mL
1	potato, cooked, peeled and shredded (about 1 cup (250 mL) (see Tip, left)	1
	Salt and freshly ground black pepper	
¼ cup	chopped green olives (about 10 pitted)	60 mL
2	recipes Crust for Empanaditas (page 182)	2

1. In a bowl, soak chiles in boiling water for 30 minutes, weighing down with a cup to ensure they remain submerged. Drain, discarding soaking liquid and stems. Transfer to a blender. Add tomatoes and purée. Set aside.

2. Meanwhile, in a skillet, heat oil over medium heat. Add onion and ground beef and cook, breaking up beef with a spoon, until meat begins to brown, about 5 minutes. Add garlic, oregano, cumin and cinnamon and cook, stirring, for 1 minute. Add potato and reserved chile mixture and cook, stirring, until heated through. Season to taste with salt and pepper. Remove from heat and stir in olives. Use to fill 2 recipes of Crust for Empanaditas and bake as directed in Step 5, page 182.

Cheese Arepas

Makes about 18

Arepas are a South American (mainly Colombian or Venezuelan) fast food. Making them the traditional way, from scratch with white corn grits can be tricky, but if you have access to arepa flour, which is a form of precooked cornmeal, they are a snap. They are great if you're looking for something that's tasty and a bit different and are particularly delicious topped with a dollop of a complementary salsa such as Fresh Tomato Salsa (page 70), Avocado Corn Salsa (page 83), Avocado Black Bean Salsa (page 84) or Fresh Salsa Verde (page 71).

Tip

Arepa flour is available in well-stocked supermarkets or stores specializing in Latin American products.

1 cup	arepa flour (see Tip, left)	250 mL
1 cup	shredded mozzarella or Monterey Jack cheese	250 mL
½ tsp	salt	2 mL
½ to 1	jalapeño pepper, seeded and minced (see Tips, page 187)	½ to 1
1 cup	warm milk	250 mL
1	egg yolk, beaten	1
¼ cup	oil, divided (approx.)	60 mL

1. In a bowl, combine arepa flour, cheese, salt and jalapeño to taste. Stir well. Add milk and egg yolk and mix until incorporated. Using your hands, knead lightly to form a soft dough.

2. Working with about 2 tbsp (30 mL) of dough at a time, shape into a ball, then flatten into a round, about 2 inches (5 cm) in diameter. Repeat until all dough is used up. You should have about 18 rounds.

3. In a large skillet, heat 2 tbsp (30 mL) of the oil over medium heat. Add arepas, in batches, being careful not to overcrowd the pan, and cook until nicely browned on one side, about 2 minutes. Flip, press down with the back of a spatula and cook until browned on other side, about 2 minutes. Transfer to a serving plate and keep warm. Repeat until all arepas are cooked, adding more oil as necessary between batches. Serve warm.

Corn Arepas

Makes about 18

Make these tasty treats when fresh corn is in season. They are delicious on their own and superb topped with a fresh salsa, such as Shrimp Salsa (page 96), Avocado Corn Salsa (page 83), Avocado Black Bean Salsa (page 84), Fresh Tomato Salsa (page 70) or Fresh Salsa Verde (page 71).

Tips

Arepa flour is available in well-stocked supermarkets or stores specializing in Latin American products.

Use a whole jalapeño for a spicier arepa. If you are true heat seeker, leave the veins and seeds in before chopping the pepper.

1 tbsp	unsalted butter	15 mL
1	shallot, finely chopped	1
1/2 to 1	jalapeño pepper, seeded and minced, optional (see Tips, left)	1/2 to 1
1 cup	corn kernels, thawed if frozen (1 cob)	250 mL
2 tbsp	heavy or whipping (35%) cream	30 mL
1 tbsp	finely chopped fresh oregano leaves	15 mL
1/2 tsp	salt, or to taste	2 mL
	Freshly ground black pepper	
1 cup	arepa flour (see Tips, left)	250 mL
1 cup	water	250 mL
1/4 cup	oil, divided	60 mL

1. In a small skillet, melt butter over medium heat. Add shallot and jalapeño to taste, if using, and cook, stirring, until shallot is softened, about 3 minutes. Stir in corn and cream. Bring to boil, reduce heat to low, cover and simmer until corn is tender, about 4 minutes. Add oregano, salt, and pepper to taste, and stir well. Transfer to a bowl.

2. Stir in arepa flour. Add water and mix until incorporated. Using your hands, knead to form a soft dough.

3. Working with about 2 tbsp (30 mL) of dough at a time, shape into a ball, then flatten into a round about 2 inches (5 cm) in diameter. Repeat until all dough is used up. You should have about 18 rounds.

4. In a large skillet, heat 2 tbsp (30 mL) of the oil over medium heat. Add arepas, in batches, being careful not to overcrowd the pan, and cook until nicely browned on one side, about 2 minutes. Flip, press down with the back of a spatula and cook until browned on the other side, about 2 minutes. Transfer to a serving plate and keep warm. Repeat until all arepas are cooked, adding more oil as necessary between batches. Serve warm.

Knish Pastry

Makes enough for about 36 knishes

Knishes, also known as piroshki, are Jewish comfort food. These small pastries filled with savory fillings are distinguished by a luscious crust. Here we have used a combination of butter, cream cheese and sour cream to produce an especially rich and dense pastry. Choose the filling(s) you like best.

Tip

Egg wash has many uses, from "fastening" pieces of puff pastry to one another to battering of fish for "fish and chips" to providing a golden brown finish to pies. Its uses are virtually endless. Here the addition of milk intensifies the browning capacity of the crust.

- **2 rimmed baking sheets, lined with parchment paper**
- **3-inch (7.5 cm) round cutter**

½ cup	unsalted butter, softened	125 mL
4 oz	cream cheese, softened	125 g
¼ cup	sour cream	60 mL
1¾ cups	all-purpose flour	425 mL
½ tsp	salt	2 mL
	Filling (see pages 189 to 191)	
1	egg, beaten with 1 tbsp (15 mL) water	1

1. In a food processor fitted with metal blade, process butter, cream cheese and sour cream until smooth and creamy, stopping and scraping down the sides of the bowl as necessary. Add flour and salt and pulse to blend, about 10 times. Using your hands, form into a ball. Wrap tightly in plastic and refrigerate for 2 hours or up to overnight.

2. Preheat oven to 400°F (200°C). Divide dough into 4 equal batches and, using your hands, pat each into a flat disk. Lay a piece of plastic wrap about 14 by 12 inches (35 by 30 cm) on your work surface and dust lightly with flour. Place one disk on plastic and dust top lightly with flour. Place another piece of plastic over the disk. Using a rolling pin, roll into a rectangle about ⅛ inch (3 mm) thick. Using the cutter, cut out 9 rounds. (If you can't get enough, don't worry, you can reroll the scraps.) Place a heaping tsp (7 mL) of the filling called for in the recipe down the middle of each round.

3. Lightly moisten bottom edge of dough with egg wash and fold dough over filling to form half moons. Press edges together to seal. (Use the tines of a fork if you like.) Place at least 1 inch (2.5 cm) apart on baking sheet. Repeat with remaining dough, filling and egg wash.

4. Brush tops with egg wash and make a small slash in the middle of the top to allow steam to escape. Bake until top is golden, about 12 minutes. Flip over (the bottoms will likely be nicely browned) and continue baking until tops (now the underside) are deeply golden, about 6 minutes. Serve warm.

Beef Knishes

Makes about 36 knishes

If you fancy a meat-based nibbly these tasty knishes fit the bill, although they are certainly not traditionally Jewish because there is dairy in the crust. Lean ground beef is flavored with caramelized onions, robust garlic and a hint of dill. They are lovely with a glass of robust red wine.

1 tbsp	oil	15 mL
2	onions, finely chopped	2
4	cloves garlic, minced	4
8 oz	lean ground beef	250 g
1 cup	shredded peeled cooked potatoes	250 mL
2 tbsp	finely chopped fresh dill fronds	30 mL
$\frac{1}{2}$ tsp	salt	2 mL
$\frac{1}{2}$ tsp	Worcestershire sauce	2 mL
	Freshly ground black pepper	
1	recipe Knish Pastry (page 188)	1

1. In a skillet, heat oil over medium heat. Add onions and stir well. Cover, reduce heat to low and cook for 20 minutes. Uncover. Increase heat to medium-high and sauté until onions begin to turn golden, about 5 minutes.

2. Add garlic and beef and sauté, breaking up beef with a spoon, until meat browns and is no longer pink, about 5 minutes. Add potatoes, dill, salt and Worcestershire and stir well. Season to taste with pepper. Let cool. Use to fill knishes and bake as directed.

Potato Knishes

Makes about 36 knishes

Vegetarian Friendly

The combination of potatoes, onions and cheese in a rich delicious crust makes these the ultimate comfort food.

2 tbsp	oil	30 mL
2	onions, finely chopped	2
2 cups	shredded peeled cooked potatoes	500 mL
1 cup	shredded Cheddar cheese	250 mL
3 tbsp	finely chopped fresh dill fronds	45 mL
1 tbsp	sour cream	15 mL
1	egg, beaten	1
	Salt and freshly ground black pepper	
1	recipe Knish Pastry (page 188)	1

1. Follow Step 1 above. Stir in potatoes. Remove from heat and stir in cheese, dill, sour cream and egg. Season to taste with salt and pepper. Let cool. Use to fill knishes and bake as directed.

Cheese Knishes

Makes 36 knishes

The combination of caramelized onions, cream cheese and sour cream, spiked with dill is mouthwatering. These knishes will melt in your mouth.

1 tbsp	oil	15 mL
2	onions, finely chopped	2
4 oz	cream cheese, cubed	125 g
2 tbsp	sour cream	30 mL
2 tbsp	finely chopped fresh dill fronds	30 mL
1	egg, beaten	1
	Salt and freshly ground black pepper	
1	recipe Knish Pastry (page 188)	1

1. In a skillet, heat oil over medium heat. Add onions and stir well. Cover, reduce heat to low and cook for 20 minutes. Uncover. Increase heat to medium-high and sauté until onions begin to brown, about 10 minutes. Remove from heat. Stir in cream cheese, sour cream and dill, until cheese is melted. Add egg and stir well. Season to taste with salt and pepper. Let cool. Use to fill knishes and bake as directed.

Mushroom Knishes

Makes 36 knishes

The earthy flavor of mushrooms is a perfect match for pungent onions and dill. Here a hint of garlic and some sour cream round out the flavor profile. Baked in a rich knish pastry, the combination is divine.

2 tbsp	unsalted butter	30 mL
1	onion, finely chopped	1
2	cloves garlic, finely chopped	2
8 oz	sliced mushrooms	250 g
2 tbsp	finely chopped fresh dill fronds	30 mL
2 tbsp	sour cream	30 mL
2 tbsp	dry bread crumbs, such as panko	30 mL
	Salt and freshly ground black pepper	
1	recipe Knish Pastry (page 188)	1

1. In a skillet, melt butter over medium heat. Add onion and garlic and cook, stirring, for 2 minutes. Increase heat to medium-high. Add mushrooms and cook, stirring, until liquid is evaporated, about 8 minutes.

2. Transfer to food processor fitted with metal blade. Add dill, sour cream and bread crumbs and process until chopped and blended. Season to taste with salt and pepper. Let cool. Use to fill knishes and bake as directed.

Kasha Knishes

Makes 36 knishes

Vegetarian Friendly

Knishes made from kasha (toasted buckwheat groats) are traditional. The earthy flavor of kasha marries well with mushrooms and aromatics such as celery and onions. These make a delicious and healthful treat.

Tip

Kasha is toasted buckwheat groats. Buckwheat, which bears no relation to wheat, is actually a highly nutritious seed that is classified as a grain. It is gluten-free and contains a compound, d-chiro-inositol, which may be useful in managing diabetes.

1	egg	1
½ tsp	salt	2 mL
¼ tsp	cayenne pepper	1 mL
⅓ cup	kasha or buckwheat groats (see Tip, left)	75 mL
2 tbsp	olive oil, divided	30 mL
2 tbsp	unsalted butter, divided	30 mL
4 oz	mushrooms, chopped	125 g
2 tbsp	freshly squeezed lemon juice	30 mL
1	onion, finely chopped	1
1	stalk celery, diced	1
2	cloves garlic, minced	2
1 tsp	sweet paprika	5 mL
1 cup	chicken or vegetable broth	250 mL
1	recipe Knish Pastry (page 188)	1

1. In a bowl, beat egg, salt and cayenne until egg is frothy. Add kasha and stir to coat. Heat a skillet over medium heat for 30 seconds. Add kasha mixture, stirring, until egg sets and grains separate, about 3 minutes. Transfer to a bowl and wipe skillet clean.

2. In same skillet, heat 1 tbsp (15 mL) each of the oil and butter over medium-high heat. Sauté mushrooms until liquid is evaporated and they begin to brown, about 6 minutes. Sprinkle with lemon juice and using a slotted spoon, transfer to a bowl and set aside.

3. Add remaining 1 tbsp (15 mL) of oil and butter to pan. Add onion, celery, garlic and paprika and sauté until celery is softened, about 5 minutes. Add cooled kasha mixture and reserved mushrooms and toss well. Add broth and bring to a boil. Reduce heat to low, cover and simmer for 5 minutes. Remove from heat and set aside until kasha is tender and liquid is absorbed, about 10 minutes. Let cool. Use to fill knishes and bake as directed.

Samosa Pastry

Makes enough for 24 samosas

Samosas are small savory pastries stuffed with a variety of fillings. Traditionally they are deep-fried, but we prefer to bake them for a healthier result. They are great topped with a dab of chutney or served with a dipping sauce. Try Suneeta's Cilantro Mint Chutney (page 93) or Yogurt Mint Chutney (page 94) as an accompaniment.

Tip

If you prefer, you can deep-fry the samosas, which is a more traditional method. Heat vegetable oil in a deep skillet (to a depth of about 2 inches/5 cm) or a deep fryer, following manufacturer's instructions, to 375°F (180°C). Add samosas in batches and fry, turning once, if using a skillet, until golden brown and crisp, about 5 minutes. Drain on paper towel. Serve with chutneys.

- **Baking sheets, lined with parchment paper**

2 cups	all-purpose flour	500 mL
½ tsp	salt	2 mL
½ cup	cold unsalted butter, cubed	125 mL
½ cup	whipping (heavy) (35%) or half-and half (10%) cream (approx.)	125 mL
2 tbsp	cornstarch	30 mL
2 tbsp	cold water	30 mL
	Fillings (pages 193 to 196)	
1	egg	1
1 tbsp	cream or milk	15 mL

1. In a bowl, combine flour and salt. Add butter and, using a pastry blender or your fingers, cut in butter until mixture resembles coarse crumbs. Drizzle cream evenly over mixture and mix lightly with a fork. Pinch a small quantity of dough between your thumb and fingers. If it doesn't hold together, add more cream, 1 tbsp (15 mL) at a time, until it does. Knead until smooth. Wrap in plastic and refrigerate for 20 minutes.

2. Divide dough into 4 batches. On a lightly floured surface, roll out each batch, one at a time, very thinly into a large circle. Place a small plate (5 inches/12.5 cm in diameter) on top of circle and, using a sharp knife, cut out rounds of dough (you should get 3 rounds per large circle). Cut circles in half. Repeat until all dough is rolled out, yielding 24 half circles. If necessary, reroll scraps.

3. When you're ready to fill the samosas, combine cornstarch and water and mix well. Set aside.

4. Working with one half circle at a time, moisten half of the straight edge with cornstarch solution. Fold in half, matching the dry straight edge with the wet one and keeping rounded edge open to form a cone. Pinch straight edge to seal. Holding the cone upright, fill with about 2 tbsp (30 mL) of filling. Moisten the inside edge of one side of the rounded top with cornstarch solution, pinch edges together and fold over the cone. Press firmly to seal. Repeat until dough and filling are used up. Place on a tray, wrap in plastic and refrigerate the prepared samosas for up to 8 hours.

5. When you're ready to serve the samosas, preheat oven to 400°F (200°C). Make the egg wash by beating egg and cream in a small bowl. Place samosas on prepared baking sheet and brush tops with egg wash. Bake until top is just turning golden, about 10 minutes. Flip samosas over and brush other side with egg wash. Bake until nicely golden, about 10 minutes. Serve hot.

Meat Samosas

Makes 24 samosas

In India, ground meat (usually lamb or goat) cooked with mixed spices is known as keema. It is ubiquitous and so easy to make, it qualifies as Indian cooking 101. Here we've suggested ground beef, which is more common in this part of the world, as a base and used the simple mixture as a filling for samosas.

Tip

Whether you use cayenne depends upon how much you like heat and the kind of curry powder you use. If your curry powder is mild, you will probably want the additional heat provided by the cayenne. If it is hot, you may want to give it a pass.

1 tbsp	oil	15 mL
1 tbsp	unsalted butter	15 mL
1	onion, finely chopped	1
1 lb	lean ground beef or lamb	500 g
1 tbsp	minced gingerroot	15 mL
2	cloves garlic, minced	2
1 tbsp	curry powder	15 mL
1 tsp	salt	5 mL
1/4 tsp	cayenne, optional (see Tip, left)	1 mL
2 tbsp	finely chopped cilantro leaves	30 mL
1	recipe Samosa Pastry (page 192)	1

1. In a skillet, heat oil and butter over medium-high heat until butter is melted and slightly bubbling. Add onion and beef and cook, breaking up beef with a spoon, until onion is softened and beef is beginning to brown and no longer pink inside, about 5 minutes. Add ginger, garlic, curry powder, salt, and cayenne, if using, and cook, stirring, for 1 minute. Remove from heat and stir in cilantro. Let cool. Use to fill Samosa Pastry and bake as directed in Step 5, above.

Shrimp Samosas

Makes 24 samosas

*Pleasantly spicy,
yet relatively light,
these shrimp-stuffed
samosas are a special
treat. They are
particularly delicious
accompanied by
Suneeta's Cilantro
Mint Chutney
(page 93).*

Tip

An easy way to cook the potatoes for this recipe is to microwave them. Place scrubbed potato in a microwave-safe dish. Add cold water to a depth of about ½ inch (1 cm), cover and microwave on High for 3 to 6 minutes or until potato is tender. Leave the lid on and let cool for at least 5 minutes before running under cold water and removing the skins.

1	small potato, boiled in its skin, cooled, peeled and shredded (see Tip, left)	1
1 tbsp	unsalted butter	15 mL
1 tbsp	oil	15 mL
1	onion, finely chopped	1
1	clove garlic, minced	1
2 tsp	minced gingerroot	10 mL
2 tsp	curry powder	10 mL
1	long red or green chile pepper, seeded and minced	1
10 oz	shrimp, peeled, deveined and chopped	300 g
2 tbsp	finely chopped fresh cilantro	30 mL
1 tbsp	freshly squeezed lemon juice	15 mL
	Salt and freshly ground black pepper	
1	recipe Samosa Pastry (page 192)	1

1. In a skillet, heat butter and oil over medium heat. Add onion and cook, stirring, until softened, about 3 minutes. Add garlic, ginger, curry powder and chile and cook, stirring, for 1 minute. Add shrimp and potato and cook, stirring, just until shrimp turn pink and mixture is well integrated. (Do not overcook; shrimp will become rubbery.) Remove from heat. Stir in cilantro and lemon juice. Season to taste with salt and pepper. Let cool. Use to fill Samosa Pastry and bake as directed in Step 5, page 193.

Chicken Samosas

Makes 24 samosas

Samosas filled with potatoes, peas and chicken are classic. Serve with Yogurt Mint Chutney (page 94) as a dipping sauce.

Tip

An easy way to cook the potato for this recipe is to microwave it. Place scrubbed potato in a microwave-safe dish. Add cold water to a depth of about ½ inch (1 cm), cover and microwave on High for 3 to 6 minutes or until potato is tender. Leave the lid on and let cool for at least 5 minutes before running under cold water and removing the skin.

1 tbsp	oil	15 mL
1 tbsp	unsalted butter	15 mL
½ cup	finely chopped shallots	125 mL
8 oz	ground chicken	250 g
2	cloves garlic, minced	2
2 tsp	finely chopped gingerroot	10 mL
2 tsp	curry powder	10 mL
½ to 1	long red or green chile, seeded and minced	½ to 1
1	potato (about 8 oz/250 g) boiled in its skin, cooled, peeled and shredded (see Tip, left)	1
¾ cup	cooked green peas	175 mL
	Salt and freshly ground black pepper	
1 tbsp	freshly squeezed lemon juice	15 mL
1	recipe Samosa Pastry (page 192)	1

1. In a skillet, heat oil and butter over medium heat. Add shallots and cook, stirring, until softened, about 3 minutes. Add chicken and cook, breaking up with a spoon, until lightly browned and no longer pink, about 5 minutes. Add garlic, ginger, curry powder, and chile to taste and cook, stirring, for 1 minute. Add potato and mix well. Stir in peas. Season to taste with salt and pepper. Remove from heat and stir in lemon juice. Let cool. Use to fill Samosa Pastry and bake as directed in Step 5, page 193.

Vegetable Samosas

Makes 24 samosas

The combination of cauliflower, potato and green peas zestily seasoned is classic Indian. Serve these samosas accompanied by a wet chutney such as Yogurt Mint Chutney (page 94), which is used as a dipping sauce.

Tip

An easy way to cook the potato for this recipe is to microwave it. Place scrubbed potato in a microwave-safe dish. Add cold water to a depth of about 1/2 inch (1 cm), cover and microwave on High for 3 to 6 minutes or until potato is tender. Leave the lid on and let cool for at least 5 minutes before running under cold water and removing the skin.

1 tbsp	unsalted butter	15 mL
1 tbsp	vegetable oil	15 mL
1	onion, finely chopped	1
1 tbsp	ground coriander	15 mL
1 tbsp	ground cumin	15 mL
1 tbsp	minced gingerroot	15 mL
1	long red or green chile pepper, seeded and minced	1
1 tsp	salt (approx.)	5 mL
1	potato (about 8 oz/250 g), cooked in its skin, cooled peeled and shredded (see Tip, left)	1
4 cups	cooked cauliflower florets (1 small), chopped	1 L
3/4 cup	cooked green peas	175 mL
1 tbsp	finely chopped fresh cilantro leaves	15 mL
	Freshly ground black pepper	
1	recipe Samosa Pastry (page 192)	1

1. In a large skillet, heat butter and oil over medium heat. Add onion and cook, stirring, until it begins to brown, about 10 minutes. Add coriander, cumin, ginger, chile and salt and cook, stirring, for 1 minute. Add potato and cauliflower and cook, breaking up cauliflower with a spoon, until mixture is well integrated. Add peas and cilantro and stir well. Season to taste with salt and black pepper. Let cool. Use to fill Samosa Pastry and bake as directed in Step 5, page 193.

Socca de Nice

Makes 12 pancakes

This Provencal specialty is a kind of street food, eaten warm with a glass of wine. Often referred to as chickpea crêpes, they are surprisingly delicious for something that is so easy to make.

Tips

You can cook more than one pancake at a time, depending upon the size of your skillet. Just be sure to make the individual pancakes the size called for and leave lots of room between them in the pan — otherwise they won't get crispy enough. Also, be sure to use all the olive oil, adding it to the pan in batches. It is an important component of the flavor.

Be sure to use good sea salt such as fleur de sel to finish the socca. Table salt has an unpleasant acrid taste that would diminish the result.

- **Preheat broiler**
- **Rimmed baking sheet, lined with parchment paper**

1½ cups	chickpea flour	375 mL
1 tsp	salt	5 mL
½ tsp	herbes de Provence, optional	2 mL
1½ cups	cold water	375 mL
¼ cup	extra virgin olive oil, divided	60 mL
	Sea salt and cracked black peppercorns	

1. In a bowl, whisk chickpea flour, salt, and herbes de Provence, if using. Whisk in water and 1 tbsp (15 mL) of the olive oil. Cover and refrigerate for 1 hour.

2. In a nonstick skillet, heat 1 tbsp (15 mL) of oil over medium heat. Add ¼ cup (60 mL) of the batter per pancake and cook until bottom is browned and top is bubbling (see Tips, left). Transfer to prepared baking sheet, uncooked side up. Repeat, adding more oil between batches, until all batter is used up.

3. Broil until tops are browned, about 4 minutes. Sprinkle liberally with sea salt and pepper. Serve warm.

Buckwheat Blinis

Makes about 36 blini

Blinis have luxurious overtones because they are traditionally served with the best caviar. While you can certainly top these with a dollop of beluga (if you're lucky enough to have some), they are also delicious with thin slices of smoked salmon, a squirt of fresh lemon juice, a spoonful of crème fraîche, liberal amounts of freshly ground black pepper and a sprinkling of finely snipped chives. If you're feeling the need for caviar, try substituting salmon caviar for the smoked salmon. The red bubbles look particularly pretty.

Tip

Blinis are best served immediately after cooking, but you can make them up to 1 day ahead. Cover and refrigerate cooked blini. Brush with extra virgin olive oil or melted butter and heat in 325°F (160°C) oven for about 10 minutes.

• **Preheat oven to 200°F (100°C)**

2 tsp	granulated sugar	10 mL
1 cup	warm whole milk (about 100°F/38°C)	250 mL
1 tsp	active dry yeast	5 mL
½ cup	all-purpose flour	125 mL
½ cup	buckwheat flour	125 mL
½ tsp	salt	2 mL
1	egg, beaten	1
2 tbsp	melted unsalted butter	30 mL
	Oil	

1. In a bowl, combine sugar and warm milk. Stir to dissolve sugar. Sprinkle yeast evenly over top and set aside until frothy, about 10 minutes.

2. In another bowl, combine all-purpose and buckwheat flours and salt. Stir well. Add yeast mixture and mix well. Add egg and butter and mix well. Cover with plastic wrap and set aside in a warm, draft-free place until mixture rises slightly and top is quite bubbly, about 1 hour.

3. Brush nonstick skillet lightly with oil and place over medium heat. Spoon 1 tbsp (15 mL) of batter per blini and cook until bubbles form on the top and underside is brown, about 30 seconds. Flip and cook until golden on the bottom, about 30 seconds. Transfer to a baking sheet as completed and keep warm in preheated oven. Grease skillet and adjust heat between batches, as necessary. Serve warm, with your favorite topping.

Corn Cakes

Makes about 24

These little cakes, which resemble corn-studded blinis, are delicious on their own and quite divine topped with a dollop of salsa. Try Fresh Tomato Salsa (page 70), Fresh Salsa Verde (page 71) or even Two-Tomato Coulis (page 544).

Tip

Use the second jalapeño for a spicier corn cake. If you are a true heat seeker, leave the veins and seeds in before chopping the pepper.

- **Preheat oven to 200°F (100°C)**

2 cups	corn kernels, preferably fresh, thawed if frozen	500 mL
½ cup	packed Italian flat-leaf parsley or cilantro leaves	125 mL
1	shallot, chopped	1
2	cloves garlic, chopped	2
1 to 2	jalapeño peppers, seeded and coarsely chopped (see Tip, left)	1 to 2
1 tsp	salt	5 mL
½ tsp	freshly ground black pepper	2 mL
¼ cup	all-purpose flour	60 mL
3	eggs	3
2 tbsp	unsalted butter, divided	30 mL
2 tbsp	olive oil, divided	30 mL
	Salt, optional	

1. In a food processor fitted with metal blade, pulse corn, parsley, shallot, garlic, jalapeño pepper to taste, salt and black pepper until finely chopped, about 15 times. Add flour and pulse 2 or 3 times to blend. Add eggs and process until smoothly blended, about 30 seconds.

2. In a large skillet, heat 1 tbsp (15 mL) each of the butter and oil over medium heat. Working in batches of about 6 cakes, drop 1 tbsp (15 mL) of batter per cake into pan. Cook until bottoms are brown, about 1 minute. Flip and cook until nicely browned on bottom, about 1 minute. Transfer to a baking sheet. Sprinkle with salt, if using, and keep warm in preheated oven. Repeat until all batter is used up, adding more butter and oil and adjusting heat between batches, as necessary.

Crêpes Parmentier

Makes about 24 mini crêpes

These potato pancakes, which are French in origin, work well like blinis, as an appetizer base. They are delicious topped with smoked salmon and sour cream, Potted Salmon (page 289), Instant Pâté (page 471) with a dab of Jalapeño-Spiked Onion Marmalade (page 545). Or how about tender-crisp asparagus spears, finished with a spot of Foolproof Hollandaise (page 539).

Tips

An easy way to cook the potatoes for this recipe is to microwave them. Place scrubbed potato in a microwave-safe dish. Add cold water to a depth of about ½ inch (1 cm), cover and microwave on High for 3 to 6 minutes or until potatoes are tender. Leave the lid on and let cool for at least 5 minutes before running under cold water and removing the skins.

If you have time, cook the potatoes ahead and refrigerate until you're ready to peel. They will be easier to shred.

- **Preheat oven to 200°F (100°C)**

8 oz	potatoes, boiled in their skins, cooled and peeled (see Tips, left)	250 g
2 tbsp	all-purpose flour	30 mL
1 tsp	baking powder	5 mL
½ tsp	salt	2 mL
	Freshly ground black pepper	
4	eggs	4
¼ cup	half-and-half (10%) cream	60 mL
2 tbsp	heavy or whipping (35%) cream	30 mL
2 tbsp	unsalted butter, divided	30 mL
2 tbsp	olive oil, divided	30 mL
	Salt	

1. In food processor fitted with shredding blade, shred potatoes. Transfer to a bowl and set aside.

2. Replace shredding blade with metal blade, add flour, baking powder, salt, and pepper to taste and pulse to blend. Add eggs and half-and-half and heavy creams and process until smoothly blended, about 30 seconds. Add potatoes and pulse to blend, about 5 times.

3. In a large skillet, preferably nonstick, heat half of the butter and half of the oil over medium heat. Working in batches, drop 1 tbsp (15 mL) of batter per crêpe into pan. Cook until top looks set and bottom is browned, about 2 minutes. Flip and cook on the second side until bottom is browned, about 1 minute. Sprinkle with salt. Transfer to a warm plate and keep warm in preheated oven. Repeat until all batter is used up, adding more butter and oil and adjusting heat between batches, as necessary.

Indian-Style Roti

Makes about 24

Vegan Friendly

Unlike Caribbean roti, which are filled, in India roti are simply a flatbread. Here the dough is made with potatoes and flour seasoned with fresh chiles and curry powder. The results are remarkably tasty. Serve them plain with just a sprinkling of fine sea salt or top with a dollop of your favorite chutney. For something special serve a fresh chutney such as Suneeta's Cilantro Mint Chutney (page 93) or Date and Tamarind Chutney (page 94).

Tips

For best results, use floury potatoes, which are usually oblong in shape and do not contain as much water as waxy varieties. The most common are russet (Idaho) potatoes.

Be sure to use good sea salt such as fleur de sel to finish the roti. Table salt has an unpleasant acrid taste that would diminish the result.

1½ lbs	russet (Idaho) potatoes (about 1 extra large), boiled in their skins until fork-tender, cooled, peeled and shredded (see Tips, page 200)	750 g
2	fresh green chile peppers, seeded and diced	2
4	green onions, white part only, finely chopped	4
¼ cup	finely chopped fresh cilantro leaves	60 mL
1 tsp	salt	5 mL
1 tsp	curry powder	5 mL
1 cup	all-purpose flour	250 mL
¼ cup	oil, divided (approx.)	60 mL
	Sea salt (see Tips, left)	
	Chutney, optional	

1. In a bowl, combine potatoes, chiles, green onions, cilantro, salt and curry powder. Mix well. Gradually add flour, mixing until a soft dough forms and using your hands to knead when the dough becomes too stiff to stir.

2. Pinch off a piece of dough about the size of a walnut and, on a lightly floured surface, roll out dough to a 3-inch (7.5 cm) circle. Repeat until all the dough is used up.

3. In a large heavy skillet, heat 1 tbsp (15 mL) of the oil. Add roti, in batches and cook, turning once, until lightly browned on both sides and slightly puffed, about 2 minutes per side. Place on a warm platter as completed and sprinkle tops lightly with salt. Pass with a bowl of chutney, if using.

Steamed Pork Dumplings

Makes 30 dumplings

These are just as wonderful as the dumplings at your favorite dim sum restaurant.

- **Bamboo or metal steamer basket**

1 lb	ground pork	500 g
¼ cup	coarsely chopped green onions	60 mL
2 tsp	minced fresh gingerroot	10 mL
2 tsp	soy sauce	10 mL
1 tsp	toasted sesame oil	5 mL
30	wonton skins, each about 3 inches (7.5 cm) square or round	30

1. Bring 4 cups (1 L) water to a boil. In a bowl, combine pork, green onions, ginger, soy sauce and sesame oil and mix gently. Set aside.

2. Working with one wonton skin at a time, place on a work surface and spoon 1½ tsp (7 mL) of the pork mixture in the center. Brush two adjoining edges with water. Fold opposite edges over filling to form a triangle.

3. Place a bamboo or metal steamer over a pot of boiling water. Add wontons, in batches as necessary, cover and steam until pork is firm and no longer pink inside, 7 to 10 minutes. Serve immediately.

Variation

Substitute 1 lb (500 g) peeled and deveined coarsely pulsed shrimp for the ground pork and continue recipe as written.

Savory Fried Shrimp Wontons

Makes 10 wontons

For a special treat, serve these wontons with a trio of sauces — Basic Sweet-and-Sour Sauce (page 547), Almost Classic Shrimp Cocktail Sauce (see Variation, page 367). Of course, soy sauce works well, too.

- **Candy/deep-fry thermometer**

	Oil	
1 lb	shrimp, peeled and deveined	500 g
2	green onions	2
1 tsp	puréed gingerroot	5 mL
1 tsp	soy sauce	5 mL
20	wonton skins, each 3 inches (7.5 cm) square or round	20
2 tbsp	water	30 mL

1. In a large, deep saucepan, heat about 4 inches (10 cm) of oil over medium heat until thermometer registers 375°F (190°C).

2. In a food processor fitted with a metal blade, pulse shrimp, green onions, ginger and soy sauce until smooth. Transfer to a bowl, cover and refrigerate for 1 hour.

3. Spread 10 wontons out on work surface and spoon shrimp mixture in the center, dividing equally. Brush water around the shrimp to coat wonton and cover with second wonton, pressing to seal. This should resemble a ravioli.

4. Fry wontons, a few at a time, turning once, until golden brown and crispy, 2 to 3 minutes. Drain on a plate lined with paper towel or tea towel to absorb excess oil. Adjust heat as necessary between batches. Serve hot.

Variation

Divide this shrimp mixture into sixths and make shrimp spring rolls. Follow the same procedure as Crispy Vegetarian Spring Rolls (page 141).

Mushroom Phyllo Triangles with Grilled Scallion and Corn Dip

Makes 8 triangles

Shiitakes add a very meaty texture to these light, flaky pillows of mushrooms. They're so delicious and easy to make and can be served hot or at room temperature.

Tips

If shiitake mushrooms are not to your liking, virtually any mushroom will work for this recipe.

There is a difference between rice vinegar and seasoned rice vinegar. Both are usually made from fermented rice or rice wine, but rice vinegar does not contain any additional sugar or sodium. Our preference is Japanese rice vinegar which is very mild flavored and almost colorless.

- Preheat oven to 400°F (200°C)
- Baking sheet, lined with parchment paper

2 tbsp	unsalted butter, divided	30 mL
3 cups	coarsely chopped shiitake mushroom caps (see Tips, left)	750 mL
1 tbsp	rice vinegar (see Tips, left)	15 mL
1/4 tsp	salt	1 mL
1 tbsp	finely diced white onion	15 mL
1 tbsp	freshly grated Parmesan cheese, preferably Parmigiano-Reggiano	15 mL
1 tsp	coarsely chopped fresh basil leaves	5 mL
1 tsp	finely diced red bell pepper	5 mL
1/4 tsp	coarsely chopped fresh thyme leaves	1 mL
3	sheets phyllo pastry, thawed	3
1/2 cup	Grilled Scallion and Corn Dip (page 42)	125 mL

1. In a saucepan, melt 1 tbsp (15 mL) of the butter over medium-high heat. Sauté mushrooms until soft, about 5 minutes. Add vinegar and salt. Transfer to a bowl and let cool to room temperature. Add onion, cheese, basil, bell pepper and thyme to mushroom mixture.

2. In a small saucepan or in microwave, melt remaining butter over low heat. Place one phyllo sheet on a work surface and brush lightly with melted butter. Stack remaining two sheets on top, buttering each. Cut phyllo crosswise into 2-inch (5 cm) wide strips. Spoon mushroom mixture onto the end of each closest to you, dividing equally. Working with one strip at a time, fold one bottom corner of phyllo over filling to opposite edge, making a triangle shape. Repeat, flipping triangle over and folding up length of strip to encase filling. Repeat with remaining strips to make 8 bundles. Place on a baking sheet. Bake in a preheated oven until golden brown, about 15 minutes. Serve hot or at room temperature, accompanied by dipping sauce.

Crackers, Crostini, Toasts and Pizza

Crisp bread sticks or crackers, crunchy vegetable or flatbread crisps — although store-bought versions are widely available, there is no substitute for the goodness of homemade. Warm cheesy crackers or crisps are a perfect match for a glass of wine. Make your own crostini, bruschetta or pizza dough and you've created a fabulous canvas upon which you can lay an endless array of ingredients. The potential combinations are endless and your guests will keep coming back for more.

Parmesan Crackers 206
Zesty Cheddar Crisps. 207
Parmesan Crisps 208
Salsa-Spiked Cheese Crisps 208
Cheese Straws. 209
Classic Garlic Bread 210
Not-Your-Average Garlic Bread. 210
Green Plantain Chips 211
Ultimate Nachos. 212
Spicy Kale Chips 212
Beet Chips 213
Indian-Spiced Sweet Potato Chips 214
Easy Potato Crisps. 214
Homemade Potato Chips. 215
Bagel Chips 215
Crisp Pita Bread 216
Yogurt Flatbread. 217
Classic Flatbread 218
Basic Crostini 219
Savory Baked Crostini 220
Grilled Herbed Crostini 220
Super Simple Crostini. 221
Ham and Cheese Crostini. 222
Egg and Anchovy Crostini. 222
Cucumber Crostini 223
Caramelized Onion Crostini 223
Goat Cheese and Sun-Dried Tomato Crostini 224
Olive-Spiked Ricotta Crostini 224
Anchovy Crostini. 225
Cheesy Anchovy Crostini 225
Roasted Tomato Crostini 226
Roasted Leek Crostini 226
Mushroom, Spinach and Feta Crostini 227
Super Simple Polenta Crostini 228
Polenta Crostini 229
Spinach Polenta Crostini. 230

Mushroom Polenta Crostini. 230
Bruschetta 231
Tomato-Mozzarella Bruschetta 232
Tomato–Ricotta Salata Bruschetta 232
Arugula-Ricotta Bruschetta. 233
Broccoli Raab Bruschetta. 234
Grilled Vegetable Bruschetta. 235
Chickpea Bruschetta 236
Arugula-Spiked Tuna Bruschetta 236
White Bean Bruschetta. 237
Roasted Red Pepper and White Bean
    Bruschetta 238
Fondue Toasts 238
Chipotle Cheese Toasts 239
Ham and Cheese Toasts 239
Shrimp Toasts 240
Hot Curried Shrimp Toasts 240
Hot and Creamy Crab Toasts 241
Easy Pizza Dough. 242
Pissaladière 243
Spanish-Style Pizza 244
Bacon-Studded Cheese and Onion Tart 245
Pancetta-Spiked Ricotta Pizza 246
Anchoyade on Pita 247
Potato Pizza 248
Easy Artichoke and Mushroom Pizza 249
Easy Chorizo Pizza. 249
Greek-Style Pizza 250
Not-Your-Average Tomato Pizza 250
Grilled Pizza with Swiss Chard and
    Mozzarella 251
Grilled Pizza with Braised Leeks and Tomato 252
Pizza with Grape Jelly and Brie. 253
Margherita Pizza Pockets 253
Sesame and Parmesan Pizza Sticks. 254

Parmesan Crackers

Makes about 4½ dozen

These bite-size crackers are very easy to make and are great nibblers with pre-dinner drinks. Serve them while still warm from the oven. They are very tasty cooled, as well.

Tips

For best results, buy good quality Parmesan and grate it yourself. If you must use already-grated cheese, buy it from an Italian market or deli or a good cheese shop and ask to make sure it doesn't contain any "filler."

Store cooled baked crisps in an airtight container for up to 3 days.

- **Preheat oven to 325°F (160°C)**
- **1-inch (2.5 cm) round glass or cookie cutter**
- **Baking sheet, lined with parchment paper**

1¼ cups	all-purpose flour	300 mL
½ tsp	salt	2 mL
⅛ tsp	cayenne pepper	0.5 mL
¼ cup	cold unsalted butter, cubed	60 mL
1	egg, lightly beaten	1
½ cup	freshly grated Parmesan cheese	125 mL

1. In a food processor fitted with metal blade, pulse flour, salt and cayenne to blend, about 4 times. Sprinkle butter over top of mixture and pulse until butter is the size of large-flake oatmeal. Add egg and Parmesan and pulse until dough begins to form a ball, about 8 times. If dough does not come together, add a bit of cold water, pulsing to incorporate. Remove from work bowl and knead lightly.

2. Dust work surface lightly with flour and roll out dough to about ⅛-inch (3 mm) thickness. Using glass or a cookie cutter, cut into rounds. Place on baking sheets, at least 2 inches (5 cm) apart.

3. Bake in preheated oven, switching and rotating baking sheets halfway through, until nicely browned and fragrant, 22 to 25 minutes. Let cool on baking sheets for 5 minutes, then transfer to a serving plate. Serve warm or at room temperature.

Zesty Cheddar Crisps

Makes about 3 dozen

These are great to nibble on pre-dinner with a glass of red wine. Mix up a batch during the holiday season and keep the dough in the refrigerator. Slice, bake and serve fresh from the oven when guests arrive.

Tip

Hot smoked paprika will lend a smoky, almost bacon-like flavor to these crisps, as well as heat. The flavor will be more intense and complex than that achieved with cayenne alone.

- **Baking sheet, lined with parchment paper**

⅔ cup	all-purpose flour	150 mL
1 tsp	baking powder	5 mL
1 tsp	hot smoked paprika or ¼ tsp (1 mL) cayenne pepper (see Tip, left)	5 mL
½ tsp	salt	2 mL
2 cups	shredded sharp (aged) Cheddar cheese	500 mL
¼ cup	unsalted butter, cubed	60 mL
¼ cup	finely chopped pecans or walnuts	60 mL

1. In a food processor fitted with metal blade, pulse flour, baking powder, paprika and salt until blended, about 4 times. Add shredded cheese and butter and pulse until mixture resembles coarse crumbs, about 20 times. Turn out on a lightly floured board and knead until dough comes together. Shape into a roll about 1 inch (2.5 cm) in diameter. Spread nuts on a cutting board and roll dough in them until well coated. Wrap in plastic wrap and refrigerate until thoroughly chilled, for at least 3 hours or for up to 1 week.

2. When you're ready to bake, preheat oven to 400°F (200°C). Cut dough into slices about ¼ inch (0.5 cm) thick. Arrange on prepared baking sheet, at least 2 inches (5 cm) apart. Bake in preheated oven for 6 minutes. Remove from oven. Using a spatula, turn crisps over and bake until lightly browned, about 6 minutes more. Let cool in pan on rack for 2 minutes. Serve warm.

Parmesan Crisps

Makes 12 crisps

This is a great recipe to have on hand for those times when unexpected guests drop by. Just grate some good Parmesan and 10 minutes later, you'll have tasty nibblies on hand.

- **Preheat oven to 425°F (220°C)**
- **Baking sheet, lined with parchment paper**

1 cup	freshly grated Parmesan cheese	250 mL
	Freshly ground black pepper	

1. Drop heaping tablespoons (20 mL) of cheese at least 2 inches (5 cm) apart on prepared baking sheet. Using a spatula or the back of a spoon, flatten into thin disks.

2. Bake in preheated oven until cheese is melted and golden, 7 to 10 minutes. Season to taste with pepper. Let cool on pan on a wire rack and lift off parchment. Serve immediately or store in an airtight container for up to 3 days.

Salsa-Spiked Cheese Crisps

Makes 16 crisps

These tasty tidbits are great for entertaining. Not only are they easy to make, but they also can be assembled ahead of time then popped in the oven just before your guests arrive. Present them with a warm cheesy pastry and a refreshing drink at the same time.

Tip

You can use prepared salsa or your own homemade Fresh Tomato Salsa or Fresh Salsa Verde (pages 70 and 71).

- **Preheat oven to 400°F (200°C)**
- **2½-inch (6 cm) round cutter**
- **Baking sheet, lined with parchment paper**

8 oz	puff pastry, thawed	250 g
½ cup	tomato salsa or salsa verde (see Tip, left)	125 mL
1 tsp	dried oregano	5 mL
1 cup	finely shredded Monterey Jack cheese	250 mL

1. On a lightly floured work surface, roll out pastry to a 10-inch (25 cm) square. Using cutter, cut into rounds and place 2 inches (5 cm) apart on prepared baking sheet. Prick with a fork then bake in preheated oven just until top is beginning to crisp, about 12 minutes. Remove from oven. Flip rounds over and flatten using a spatula or the back of a large spoon.

2. Meanwhile, in a bowl, combine salsa and oregano. Stir well. Add cheese and stir well. Spoon about 1 tbsp (15 mL) of mixture onto the center of each round. Return to oven and bake until cheese is melted and bubbling, about 10 minutes. Serve warm.

Cheese Straws

Makes about 4 dozen

These tasty straws are a perfect pairing for a pre-dinner glass of wine. This recipe deviates slightly from the norm with the addition of fresh bread crumbs. To turn this into an easy salumi-based appetizer (page 131), wrap the cooled straws in thin slices of prosciutto or salami.

Tips

If your bread is fresh, it will benefit from being dried out a bit in the oven before processing. Place on a baking sheet in a preheated 325°F (160°C) oven, turning once, for 10 minutes.

Italian-style, whole wheat and sourdough bread all work well in this recipe. Just be sure not to use dense, heavily sweetened bread, which will not produce an appetizing result. For the required quantity of bread crumbs, use a sandwich-size or Italian-style loaf. Depending upon the dimensions of the bread you may need to increase the number of slices.

- **Preheat oven to 400°F (200°C)**
- **Baking sheets, lined with parchment paper**

3	slices day-old bread, about 1 inch (2.5 cm) thick, crusts removed, and broken into chunks (see Tips, left)	3
2 cups	shredded Cheddar cheese, preferably aged	500 mL
3 tbsp	unsalted butter, softened	45 mL
1 tbsp	chopped fresh dill fronds	15 mL
¾ cup	all-purpose flour	175 mL
¼ cup	milk or buttermilk	60 mL
½ tsp	salt	2 mL
½ tsp	hot or sweet smoked or plain paprika (see Tips, left)	2 mL

1. In a food processor fitted with metal blade, process bread until fine crumbs. Measure 1½ cups (375 mL) and set aside.

2. In same work bowl fitted with metal blade, process cheese, butter and dill until integrated, scraping down sides of the bowl as required. Add bread crumbs, flour, milk, salt and smoked paprika and process until blended and dough comes together when pinched between your fingers. Transfer to a lightly floured surface and knead lightly.

3. On a lightly floured surface, roll out dough to a rectangle about 6 inches (15 cm) wide and ¼ inch (0.5 cm) thick. Cut into strips, each 6 inches (15 cm) long by ½ inch (1 cm) wide. Cut each strip in half crosswise, then fold in half lengthwise. Roll between your hands to make a cylinder, then transfer to work surface and roll until straw is about 4 inches (10 cm) long. Repeat until all dough has been rolled. Place about 2 inches (5 cm) apart on prepared baking sheets. Bake in preheated oven, switching and rotating baking sheets halfway through, until lightly browned, about 15 minutes.

Classic Garlic Bread

Makes about 20 pieces

For the garlic lovers across the globe, enjoy this classic appetizer. A creative way to present this garlic bread is to serve alongside a selection of toppings. The trio of Basil Pesto (page 549), Truffle Vinaigrette (page 542) and Oven-Roasted Cherry Tomato Sauce (page 546) would hit the spot.

- **Preheat oven to 350°F (180°C)**

¾ cup	unsalted butter, softened	175 mL
2 tbsp	minced garlic	30 mL
1 tbsp	minced chives	15 mL
⅛ tsp	salt	0.5 mL
⅛ tsp	freshly ground black pepper	0.5 mL
1	baguette, about 24 inches (60 cm) long	1

1. In a bowl, combine butter, garlic, chives, salt and pepper. Mix well.
2. Slice baguette lengthwise without fully cutting the bread in half. Spread butter mixture evenly over cut surfaces. Close baguette and wrap loosely in foil. Bake in preheated oven to warm through, about 20 minutes. Cut into 20 slices and serve immediately.

Not-Your-Average Garlic Bread

Makes about 20 pieces

Pressed cottage cheese adds a wonderful creaminess to the very familiar flavor of garlic bread. Serve a slice beside a warm Tomato Avocado Shooter (page 112) or Broccoli Pesto Shooter (page 122) for a comfort food appetizer. Cream cheese or goat cheese can substitute for cottage cheese quite easily.

- **Preheat oven to 350°F (180°C)**

1 cup	dry pressed cottage cheese	250 mL
½ cup	unsalted butter, softened	125 mL
¼ cup	finely grated Parmesan cheese	60 mL
1 tbsp	minced garlic	15 mL
⅛ tsp	salt	0.5 mL
⅛ tsp	freshly ground black pepper	0.5 mL
1	baguette, about 24 inches (60 cm) long	1

1. In a bowl, combine cottage cheese, butter, Parmesan, garlic, salt and pepper. Mix well.
2. Slice baguette lengthwise without fully cutting bread in half. Spread cottage cheese mixture evenly over cut surfaces. Close baguette and wrap in loosely in foil. Bake in preheated oven to warm through, about 20 minutes. Cut into 20 slices and serve immediately.

Green Plantain Chips

Makes about 36 chips

These little tidbits are very versatile. They can be eaten on their own, perhaps sprinkled with a cilantro-lime mixture (see Variation, below) and in that case are best served while still warm. They also make a great accompaniment to many salsas, particularly those made with fruit, such as Minty Mango Salsa (page 87) or Tropical Fruit Salsa (page 92), or a cilantro-based salsa, such as Suneeta's Cilantro Mint Chutney (page 93).

Tip

Green plantains are not easily peeled, unlike their banana relatives. To peel, make a lengthwise slit through the skin with a paring knife, being careful not to cut into the plantain, then lift off the peel.

- **Candy/deep-fry thermometer**

2 cups	oil	500 mL
2	green plantains, peeled and very thinly sliced (see Tip, left)	2
	Salt	

1. In a deep skillet or Dutch oven, heat oil over medium-high heat to 325°F (160°C). (You can also use a deep fryer; follow the manufacturer's instructions.) Fry plantain slices, in batches to avoid crowding, just until they are beginning to turn golden, about 1½ minutes. Using a slotted spoon, remove from oil and transfer to a cutting board. Cover with plastic and pound to about ¼-inch (0.5 cm) thickness.

2. Increase heat of oil to 375°F (190°C). Fry pounded slices, in batches, turning if necessary, until golden, 2 to 3 minutes. Transfer to a paper towel–lined platter and sprinkle with salt.

Variation

Cilantro-Topped Tostanes: Do not sprinkle chips with salt. In a small bowl, combine ¼ cup (60 mL) finely chopped cilantro leaves, 1 tbsp (15 mL) freshly squeezed lime juice and 1 tsp (5 mL) salt. If you like a bit of heat, add minced jalapeño pepper, to taste. Stir well. Sprinkle over warm chips and serve immediately.

Ultimate Nachos

Makes 20 nachos

The classiest way to serve a nacho — from Super Bowl to a dinner party!

Tip

This is a great recipe to prepare ahead of time. Prepare your ingredients the day before and assemble and bake just as your guests arrive. It's not only the Boy Scouts who benefit from being prepared.

- **Preheat oven to 350°F (180°C)**
- **Baking sheet, lined with parchment paper**

20	large corn chips	20
1/4 cup	sliced dill pickles	60 mL
1 tbsp	finely diced tomato	15 mL
1	thin slice prosciutto (about 1 oz/30 g), cut into thin strips	1
1/2 cup	shredded pepper Jack cheese	125 mL
1 tbsp	thinly sliced green onions	15 mL

1. Place chips on prepared baking sheet. Equally distribute pickles, tomato and prosciutto on top. Sprinkle with cheese.

2. Bake in preheated oven until cheese is melted and toppings are heated through, 6 to 8 minutes. Transfer to a platter, garnish with green onions and serve immediately.

Spicy Kale Chips

Makes about 10 servings

Vegan Friendly

Finally a chip with little guilt! Kale chips are so easy to make and can be made with so many different flavorings — be creative. They're a lot like Homemade Potato Chips (page 215) — you can't just stop at one, so be sure to make a lot.

- **Preheat oven to 300°F (150°C)**
- **Baking sheet, lined with parchment paper**

1	bunch kale (about 8 oz/250 g)	1
2 tbsp	olive oil	30 mL
1/2 tsp	salt	2 mL
1/4 tsp	chipotle powder	1 mL
1/4 tsp	granulated sugar	1 mL

1. Remove tough stems from kale and discard. Tear leaves into bite-size pieces (you should have about 2 cups/ 500 mL). In a bowl, combine oil, salt, chipotle powder and sugar. Toss kale pieces in mixture to coat. Spread kale on prepared baking sheet, ensuring the pieces aren't overlapping as this will prevent the chips from crisping (use more baking sheets or bake in batches if necessary). Bake in preheated oven until crisp, about 15 minutes. Let cool to room temperature before serving.

Beet Chips

Makes 25 to 30 chips

Be sure to wear gloves for this recipe or your hands will be purple for your dinner party. Top a chip with Roasted Corn Salsa (page 82) or Roasted Beet Salsa (page 74). The yellow corn contrasts beautifully with the purple chip.

Tips

If you're using a deep fryer, follow the manufacturer's instructions.

Although frying tastes great, a healthier option is to bake these chips. Preheat oven to 375°F (190°C). Toss sliced beets with 1 tbsp (15 mL) olive oil and spread chips out on a parchment paper–lined baking sheet. Bake in a preheated oven until golden brown and crisp, turning every 15 minutes, about 50 minutes. Transfer to a bowl. Combine with almond mixture and toss lightly to coat. Let cool until crisp.

Chips keep in an airtight container for up to 1 day.

- **Candy/deep-fry thermometer**

	Oil	
1 tsp	finely ground toasted almonds	5 mL
1/4 tsp	salt	1 mL
1/8 tsp	ground cinnamon	0.5 mL
1	large beet, peeled	1

1. Fill a deep-fryer, deep heavy pot or deep skillet with 3 inches (7.5 cm) of oil and heat over medium-high heat to 375°F (190°C) (see Tips, left).

2. In a large bowl, combine almonds, salt and cinnamon and mix well to combine. Set aside.

3. Using a mandoline, a food processor fitted with a slicer blade or a very sharp knife, thinly slice beet into 25 to 30 slices. (They should resemble the thickness of potato chips.) Using tongs, gently place 6 chips at a time into the hot oil and deep-fry, turning once, until golden brown and crispy, 2 to 3 minutes. Using a slotted spoon, remove from oil and add to almond mixture, tossing to coat lightly. Let cool on paper towel to absorb excess oil. As chips cool they will become crispy. Serve immediately.

Variations

Taro Root Chips: Taro chips become crisper than any potato chip could ever claim to be. They are wonderful with Tropical Fruit Salsa (page 92) or any fruit salsa. Substitute 1 cup (250 mL) thinly sliced peeled taro root for the beet and 1/8 tsp (0.5 mL) ground dill seed for the cinnamon and almonds.

Parsnip Chips: Parsnips create spectacular sweet and savory crisps. Place a dollop of Mushroom Tomato Spread (page 44) on one end of the chip and enjoy these hearty appetizers. Substitute 2 large peeled parsnips, thinly sliced for the beet and omit the almonds and cinnamon. If you really want to gild the lily, season with 1 tbsp (15 mL) confectioner's (icing) sugar. Or melt 2 oz (60 g) semisweet chocolate and dip cooled parsnip chips about one-quarter of the way into chocolate. Let cool on a parchment paper–lined baking sheet until chocolate is set.

Indian-Spiced Sweet Potato Chips

Makes 6 servings

If you are fortunate enough to visit Vij's, a fabulous nouveau-Indian restaurant in Vancouver that doesn't take reservations, while you wait for your table, you will likely be served sweet potato or cassava fries, seasoned with Indian spices. That's the inspiration for these tasty tidbits.

- • **Candy/deep-fry thermometer**

1 lb	sweet potatoes (about 2), peeled	500 g
1 tsp	ground cumin (see Tips, page 267)	5 mL
1 tsp	ground coriander	5 mL
1 tsp	fine sea salt	5 mL
¼ tsp	hot paprika	1 mL
2 cups	oil, such as peanut or corn (approx.)	500 mL

1. In a food processor fitted with slicing blade, slice potatoes. Transfer to a large bowl. Cover with cold salted water and soak for 10 minutes. Drain in a colander and rinse thoroughly under cold running water. Place in a salad spinner and dry thoroughly.

2. In a small bowl, combine cumin, coriander, salt and paprika. Stir well and set aside.

3. In a deep skillet, Dutch oven or deep-fryer, heat oil over medium-high heat to 325°F (160°C.) Add sweet potato slices, in batches, and fry, stirring frequently to keep them separated and turning once, until they start to curl up and are brown around the edges, about 3 minutes per batch. Using a slotted spoon, transfer to a paper towel–lined plate. Sprinkle with spice mix and serve immediately. Repeat with remaining potatoes.

Easy Potato Crisps

Makes about 20 crisps

These thin slices of roast potatoes make a great base for many spreads. They are particularly good with Smoked Salmon Spread (page 296) or Dill-Spiked Smoked Trout Spread (page 297).

- • **Preheat oven to 400°F (200°C)**

2	potatoes, peeled or unpeeled, thinly sliced (⅛ inch/3 mm)	2
2 tbsp	extra virgin olive oil	30 mL

1. In a bowl, combine potatoes and olive oil. Toss until potatoes are well coated. Place on baking sheet in a single layer and roast in preheated oven, turning once, until potatoes are crisp and browned, about 20 minutes.

Homemade Potato Chips

Makes 6 servings

These chips are delicious with dips such as Caramelized Red Onion Dip (page 39), topped with a dollop of horseradish-infused sour cream or crème fraîche or Lemon Horseradish Aïoli (page 537).

Tip

Cook the chips long enough to ensure they are crisp. They can be browned but still a bit soft in the middle. Turning helps to ensure they cook evenly.

- **Candy/deep-fry thermometer**

1½ lbs	potatoes, peeled (about 2 medium)	750 g
2 cups	oil, such as peanut or corn (approx.)	500 mL
	Fine sea salt	

1. In a food processor fitted with slicing blade, slice potatoes. Transfer to a large bowl. Cover with cold salted water and soak for 10 minutes. Drain in a colander and rinse thoroughly under cold running water. Place in a salad spinner and dry thoroughly.

2. In a deep skillet, Dutch oven or deep-fryer, heat oil over medium-high heat to 350°F (180°C.) Add potato slices, in batches, and fry, stirring frequently to keep them separated and turning once to ensure they brown evenly, until golden, about 5 minutes per batch (see Tip, left). Using a slotted spoon, transfer to a paper towel–lined plate. Sprinkle to taste with salt. Repeat with remaining potatoes.

Bagel Chips

Makes about 16 chips

This crisp versatile chip is delicious all on its own and even better topped with chopped liver, Caramelized Onions (page 552) or Braised Leeks (page 548).

Tip

Your bakery will often have a slicer and would be more than happy to slice your day-old bagels, however a good serrated knife would do the trick.

- **Preheat oven to 350°F (180°C)**
- **Baking sheet, lined with parchment paper**

2	bagels (your favorite variety)	2
1	clove garlic, cut in half	1
2 tbsp	olive oil	30 mL
½ tsp	salt	2 mL

1. Thinly slice each bagel into 8 thin slices. Place on prepared baking sheet. Rub garlic on both sides of bagel slices.

2. In a bowl, combine oil and salt, mixing to dissolve salt. Liberally brush both sides of bagel slices with mixture. Place on prepared baking sheet and bake in preheated oven until golden brown and crisp, about 12 minutes. Serve immediately or store in an airtight container for up to 1 week.

Crisp Pita Bread

Makes 32 crisps

Vegan Friendly

Crisp pita bread, seasoned or unseasoned, makes a nice accompaniment for many spreads and dips. Serve it plain, or choose seasonings that complement what you are serving. Greek-style pita, which doesn't have a pocket, produces a nicely crisp bread. If you're looking for a "chip"–type dipper, use pita with a pocket and separate the tops from bottoms before baking.

- **Preheat oven to 400°F (200°C)**

| 8 | Greek-style pita breads (no pockets) | 8 |
| | Extra virgin olive oil | |

1. Brush pita on both sides with olive oil. Place on baking sheets top side down and bake in preheated oven for 5 minutes.
2. Flip over and bake until pita is crisping and turning golden, for 5 minutes more. Let cool slightly and cut each pita into quarters.

Variations

Grilled Pita Bread: If you prefer a slightly smoky flavor, follow above instructions but grill pita on a hot barbecue, adjusting timing if necessary.

Mediterranean-Spiced Crisp Pita Bread: Follow instructions for Crisp or Grilled Pita Bread, completing Step 1. Remove sheets from oven. After turning pitas, sprinkle each with about 1/2 tsp (2 mL) dried Italian seasoning. Complete Step 2.

Middle Eastern Spiced Crisp Pita Bread: In a small dry skillet, combine 1 tbsp (15 mL) cumin seeds and 1 tsp (5 mL) coriander seeds. Place over medium heat and toast, stirring, until fragrant, about 3 minutes. Transfer to a mortar or spice grinder and grind. Set aside. Follow instructions for Crisp or Grilled Pita Bread, completing Step 1. Remove sheets from oven. After turning pitas, sprinkle each with about 1/2 tsp (2 mL) of the spice mix. Complete Step 2.

Crisp Pita Bread with Dukkah: Follow instructions for Crisp or Grilled Pita Bread, completing Step 1. Remove sheets from oven. After turning pitas, sprinkle each with about 1/2 tsp (2 mL) Dukkah. Complete Step 2. Dukkah, a Middle Eastern condiment is available in specialty markets or you can make you own (page 555).

Pita Chips: Substitute 4 pita with pockets for Greek-style pita bread. Separate layers of pitas horizontally before beginning the recipe. Proceed as for Crisp or Grilled Pita Bread, adding any of the seasonings above, if desired.

Yogurt Flatbread

Makes about 2½ dozen

Warm from the oven, these little flatbreads are yummy on their own, but if you're so inclined, use them as a dipper (try Yogurt Mint Chutney, page 94) or top with a dollop of chutney (Suneeta's Cilantro Mint Chutney, page 93 or Date and Tamarind Chutney, page 94). They also make a good base for spreads such as Smoked Salmon Spread (page 296) or Dill-Spiked Smoked Trout Spread (page 297.)

Tips

You can purchase za'atar in specialty spice shops or make your own. *To make za'atar:* In a small bowl, combine 2 tbsp (30 mL) fresh thyme leaves, 1 tbsp (15 mL) toasted sesame seeds and 1 tsp (5 mL) each ground sumac and coarse sea salt.

To toast sesame seeds: Place seeds in a dry skillet over medium heat and cook, stirring, just until they begin to brown. Immediately transfer to a bowl; once they start to brown they burn quickly.

- **Preheat oven to 350°F (180°C)**
- **2½-inch (6 cm) round cutter**
- **Baking sheets, lined with parchment paper**

2 cups	all-purpose flour	500 mL
1 tsp	baking powder	5 mL
½ tsp	salt	2 mL
1 cup	plain yogurt	250 mL
2 tbsp	extra virgin olive oil	30 mL
	Course sea salt	

1. In a bowl, combine flour, baking powder and salt. Add yogurt and, using a wooden spoon, mix as well as you can. Then use your hands to knead until a soft dough forms. Cover and let rest at room temperature for 1 hour.

2. Divide dough into quarters. Working with one piece at a time, on a lightly floured board, roll out dough to a ⅛-inch (3 mm) thickness. Using cutter, cut into rounds and place on prepared sheets. Repeat until all the dough has been cut into circles, re-rolling scraps.

3. Bake in preheated oven until nicely puffed, about 15 minutes. Remove from oven and preheat broiler. Place flatbreads under broiler until lightly browned. Brush with olive oil and sprinkle with salt. Serve warm.

Variations

Za'atar-Spiked Flatbread: After the flatbreads have been brushed with olive oil, sprinkle with za'atar (see Tips, left). Then finish with salt to taste.

Herb-Spiked Flatbread: In a small bowl, combine 1 tbsp (15 mL) minced fresh thyme leaves and 1 tsp (5 mL) finely grated lemon zest. After the flatbreads have been brushed with olive oil, sprinkle with the mixture, then finish with salt to taste.

Classic Flatbread

Makes about 2½ dozen

This super simple bread is a cross between a crispy flatbread and chewy focaccia and is scrumptious all on its own or with numerous dips, salsa or even vinaigrettes. Plunge a warm piece of this bread into Black Pepper Goat Cheese Dip (page 20), Roasted Corn Salsa (page 82) or Roasted Red Pepper Vinaigrette (page 541).

Tip

Chipotle powder is made from finely grated smoked jalapeños and adds a wonderful smoky and spicy flavor to your foods. It can be found in the dry herb and spice sections of most large supermarkets. Smoked paprika or ancho chile powder would also substitute nicely here.

2¼ cups	warm water (about 100°F/38°C), divided	550 mL
½ tsp	granulated sugar	2 mL
1 tsp	active dry yeast	5 mL
3 cups	unbleached all-purpose flour	750 mL
½ tsp	salt	2 mL
3 tbsp	olive oil, divided	45 mL
1 tbsp	fresh thyme leaves	15 mL
½ tsp	chipotle chile powder or cayenne pepper, optional	2 mL

1. In a bowl, combine ¼ cup (60 mL) warm water and sugar. Sprinkle yeast evenly over top and set aside until frothy, about 10 minutes.

2. In another bowl, combine flour, salt, remaining water and activated yeast mixture. With your hand or using a wooden spoon, mix together until a very sticky dough forms and resembles a very thick pancake batter. (This is very loose dough, do not worry.) Cover bowl with a tea towel or plastic wrap and let rise at room temperature until dough has quadrupled in size.

3. Meanwhile, preheat oven to 300°F (150°C).

4. Spread 1½ tbsp (22 mL) of the olive oil in middle of a rimmed baking sheet. Place dough over oil. Pour remaining oil on top of dough and, using your finger tips, begin to press dough toward the edges of pan and stretch into a rectangle about 18 by 12 inches (45 by 30 cm). Garnish surface with thyme and chipotle powder.

5. Bake in preheated oven until light brown and firm, about 30 minutes. Increase oven temperature to 400°F (200°C) and continue to bake until corners are crisp and golden brown, about 10 minutes. Let cool on pan. Cut into manageable (25 to 30) pieces and serve immediately.

Crostini

Crostini means different things to different people. In French cooking, they are often fried cubes of seasoned bread that are used as a garnish. Here, we are defining Basic Crostini (below) as sliced baguette that is brushed with olive oil, perhaps seasoned with garlic, toasted, and used as a base for canapés. We have also made a Savory Baked Crostini (page 220) that has a hint of spice and fresh herbs, as well as a Grilled Herbed Crostini (page 220) that is particularly delicious with cheese. All these basic crostini can use used as a base for a wide variety of dips and spreads such as Beet and Goat Cheese Spread (page 21),

Black Pepper Goat Cheese Dip (page 20) and Sweet Potato Spread (page 26). We have also made crostini from polenta (page 229).

The term crostini is often used interchangeably with bruschetta (page 231). We have differentiated the two by using larger pieces of country-style bread for bruschetta and grilling rather than toasting it. Although the toppings for bruschetta are often chunky, which means they don't lend themselves well to the smaller-sized crostini, if the texture of the toppings is suitable, the bases can be used interchangeably.

Basic Crostini

Makes 8 crostini

Vegan Friendly

This basic recipe for crostini can be doubled, tripled or quadrupled to suit your entertaining needs. Crostini can be made ahead. After cooling, store in an airtight container for up to 3 days.

• **Preheat broiler**

| 8 | slices baguette (each ¼ inch/0.5 cm thick) Olive oil (see Tip, page 222) | 8 |

1. Brush baguette slices lightly with olive oil on both sides. Place under preheated broiler and toast until golden, turning once, about 2 minutes per side.

Savory Baked Crostini

Makes 24 crostini

There are very few foods that have as many uses as a baked crostini. Like the other basic crostini this makes a great base for any of the Super Simple Crostini (page 221) as well as for many dips and spreads.

Tip

Cooled baked crostini can be stored in an airtight container at room temperature for up to 1 week.

- **Preheat oven to 475°F (240°C)**

24	slices baguette (each about $\frac{1}{2}$ inch/ 1 cm thick)	24
2 tbsp	extra virgin olive oil	30 mL
$\frac{1}{2}$ tsp	cayenne pepper	2 mL
$\frac{1}{4}$ tsp	salt	1 mL
1 tbsp	thinly sliced fresh chives	15 mL

1. In a bowl, combine bread, oil, cayenne, salt and chives and toss well to coat. Place on a baking sheet and bake in a preheated oven until crisp and golden brown, about 6 minutes. Let cool to the touch before serving.

Grilled Herbed Crostini

Makes 24 crostini

Truly the best canvas for cheese...any cheese. It also makes a great base for any of our Super Simple Crostini combinations (see page 221).

Tip

You can marinate the bread in the oil mixture ahead of time for up to 1 hour, covered with plastic wrap, but it's best to grill it just before serving.

- **Preheat barbecue grill to high**

24	slices baguette (each about $\frac{1}{2}$ inch/1 cm thick)	24
2 tbsp	extra virgin olive oil	30 mL
1 tbsp	unsalted butter, melted	15 mL
$\frac{1}{2}$ tsp	freshly ground black pepper	2 mL
$\frac{1}{4}$ tsp	salt	1 mL
1 tbsp	finely chopped fresh thyme leaves	15 mL

1. In a bowl, combine bread, olive oil, butter, pepper and salt and toss well to coat. Grill until golden brown, about 1 minute per side. Remove from heat and toss with fresh thyme. Serve immediately.

Super Simple Crostini

Parmesan Crostini: (Vegetarian Friendly) Using a Parmesan cheese shaver, cut very thin slices of good Parmesan cheese. Arrange over cooled crostini. Drizzle with your best extra virgin olive oil and season to taste with freshly ground black pepper.

Quince-Topped Cheese Crostini: (Vegetarian Friendly) This is a classic Spanish tapas dish. Place thin slices of Manchego cheese on cooled crostini and top with a small cube of quince paste. Look for both ingredients in a well-stocked cheese shop or deli.

Roasted Garlic and Goat Cheese Crostini: (Vegetarian Friendly) Spread roasted garlic (pages 228 and 484) over crostini and top with soft goat cheese.

Smoked Salmon Crostini: Spread cooled crostini with softened cream cheese. Top with a slice of smoked salmon, thinly sliced red onion and capers. Drizzle with a bit of freshly squeezed lemon juice. Season to taste with freshly ground black pepper. Top with a sprig of dill, if desired.

Smoked Trout Crostini: Spoon out enough sour cream or crème fraîche to meet your needs (about 2 tsp/10 mL per thin slice of trout). Stir in drained prepared horseradish to taste (about $1/2$ tsp/2 mL per slice). Place a piece of smoked trout on cooled crostini and drizzle lightly with freshly squeezed lemon juice. Top with a dollop of the horseradish cream and garnish with a small sprig of dill, if desired. If you prefer, substitute smoked salmon for the trout.

Kimchi-Spiked Beef Crostini: Place paper-thin slices of grilled beef tenderloin on cooled crostini. Top with kimchi or sauerkraut. Sprinkle with finely minced fresh chile pepper. Season to taste with freshly ground black pepper.

Beef Crostini with Wasabi Mayo: In a small bowl, combine $1/4$ cup (60 mL) prepared mayonnaise and 1 tsp (5 mL) each rice vinegar and wasabi paste. Mix well. Cut paper-thin slices of grilled marinated flank steak on the diagonal. Place on crostini and top with a dollop of the seasoned mayo. Season to taste with freshly ground black pepper and salt.

Chopped Liver Crostini with Onion Marmalade: Spread Bacon-Spiked Chopped Liver Spread (page 475) or Instant Pâté (page 471) over cooled crostini and top with a dollop of Jalapeño-Spiked Onion Marmalade (page 545).

Ham and Cheese Crostini

Makes 16 crostini

This combination is universal and deliciously old-fashioned. It is particularly good with a glass of robust red wine.

Tip

Seasoning crostini lightly with garlic is common. If you prefer a hint of garlic on your crostini, an easy way to achieve this is to brush them with Garlic-Infused Olive Oil (see page 231).

- **Preheat broiler**

1½ cups	shredded Gruyère cheese	375 mL
3 tbsp	unsalted butter, softened	45 mL
1 tbsp	Dijon mustard	15 mL
½ tsp	hot paprika, optional	2 mL
4	slices Black Forest ham, cut to fit crostini	4
16	Basic Crostini (page 219)	16
	Finely chopped parsley, optional	

1. In a food processor, process cheese, butter, mustard and paprika, if using, until smooth.
2. Place a piece of ham on each crostini. Top with cheese mixture, dividing equally. Place on a baking sheet and broil until cheese begins to brown. Sprinkle with parsley, if using.

Egg and Anchovy Crostini

Makes 6 crostini

Rich, delicious and different, these crostini are perfect for unexpected guests because they can be made from ingredients you're likely to have on hand.

Tip

Use the smallest skillet available and cook the eggs over very low heat, stirring constantly to ensure they don't dry out.

2	eggs	2
1 tbsp	heavy or whipping (35%) cream	15 mL
1 tbsp	unsalted butter	15 mL
2	anchovy fillets, finely minced	2
1	clove garlic, finely minced	1
	Salt and freshly ground black pepper	
6	Basic Crostini (page 219)	6
2 tbsp	finely chopped flat-leaf parsley leaves	30 mL
6	pimento-stuffed green olives, sliced	6

1. In a small bowl, beat eggs and cream. Set aside.
2. In a small skillet, melt butter over medium heat. Add anchovies and garlic and cook, stirring, until anchovies are dissolved, about 1 minute. Reduce heat to low and add egg mixture. Cook, stirring constantly, until eggs are scrambled. Remove from heat and season to taste with salt and pepper. Spoon mixture over crostini. Sprinkle with parsley and garnish with olive.

Cucumber Crostini

Makes 12 crostini

If you're a party sandwiches kind of person (and there are lots of us) but feel the need for an update, try these simply satisfying nibblies. Their lineage is Victorian England, by way of Italy, with a touch of Greece thrown in. Delightful on a sunny summer afternoon, with a glass of cold white wine.

2 tbsp	mayonnaise	30 mL
2 tbsp	crumbled feta cheese	30 mL
2 tbsp	minced green onion, white part only	30 mL
½ tsp	finely grated lemon zest, optional	2 mL
12	Basic Crostini (page 219)	12
12	¼-inch (0.5 cm) thick slices cucumber	12
	Salt and freshly ground black pepper	
	Finely chopped watercress	

1. In a small bowl, using a wooden spoon, beat mayonnaise and feta until smooth and creamy. Add green onion and lemon zest, if using, and mix well.

2. Spread mayo mixture evenly over crostini and top with a cucumber slice. Season to taste with salt (bearing in mind the feta is quite salty) and pepper. Garnish liberally with watercress. Place on a platter and serve immediately or cover and refrigerate for up to 2 hours.

Caramelized Onion Crostini

Makes 32 generous crostini

How can you go wrong with caramelized onions and melted cheese? One friend calls this French onion soup to go. This makes a big batch — but the recipe can be halved.

Tip

You can caramelize the onions up to 2 days ahead and refrigerate until ready to use. Reheat gently before completing the recipe.

3 tbsp	unsalted butter	45 mL
6	onions, thinly sliced on the vertical	6
1 tbsp	granulated sugar	15 mL
1 tbsp	fresh thyme leaves	15 mL
	Salt and freshly ground black pepper	
1 tsp	balsamic vinegar	5 mL
32	Basic Crostini (page 219)	32
8 oz	Swiss or Gruyère cheese, shredded	250 g

1. In a large skillet, melt butter over medium heat. Add onions and cook, stirring, until softened. Stir in sugar and cook, stirring, until onions are browned, about 25 minutes. Stir in thyme, salt and pepper to taste, and vinegar. Remove from heat.

2. Preheat broiler. Spread crostini liberally with onion mixture and sprinkle with cheese. Place under broiler until cheese is melted and browned. Serve immediately.

Goat Cheese and Sun-Dried Tomato Crostini

Makes 16 crostini

Simple, elegant and delicious, these crostini get any meal off to an excellent start.

Tip

If you don't have a mini bowl for your food processor or a mini chopper, mince the sun-dried tomatoes and chives by hand then mash in a bowl with the cheese and oil until well blended.

- Preheat broiler
- Mini-bowl attachment for food processor or mini chopper

4 oz	soft goat cheese	125 g
2	sun-dried tomatoes in olive oil, drained	2
¼ cup	snipped chives	60 mL
1½ tbsp	extra virgin olive oil	22 mL
16	Basic Crostini (page 219)	16

1. In mini bowl of food processor fitted with metal blade, process cheese, sun-dried tomatoes, chives and oil until smooth, about 30 seconds.

2. Spread each crostini liberally with goat cheese mixture. Place on a baking sheet and broil until browned and melted, 2 to 3 minutes. Transfer to a platter and serve hot.

Olive-Spiked Ricotta Crostini

Makes about 18 crostini

Spread this comforting mélange over cooled crostini and serve at room temperature. Or if you prefer a warm crostini, place it under a preheated broiler until the edges begin to brown.

Tip

You can buy prepared olive paste at well-stocked supermarkets and specialty stores or make your own (page 233).

1 cup	extra smooth fresh ricotta	250 mL
2 tbsp	extra virgin olive oil	30 mL
2 tbsp	finely chopped flat-leaf parsley leaves	30 mL
1 tbsp	minced oil-packed sun-dried tomatoes	15 mL
1 tbsp	minced drained capers	15 mL
2 tsp	minced red chile pepper	10 mL
1 tsp	finely grated lemon zest	5 mL
	Salt and freshly ground black pepper	
¼ cup	black olive paste (see Tip, left)	60 mL
18	Basic Crostini (page 219)	18

1. In a bowl, combine ricotta, olive oil, parsley, sun-dried tomatoes, capers, chile pepper and lemon zest. Season to taste with salt and black pepper. Stir well. Cover and refrigerate for up to 3 days. Spread crostini with olive paste and top with ricotta mixture.

Anchovy Crostini

Makes 16 crostini

Here's an appetizer you can make with ingredients you are likely to have on hand — perfect for unexpected guests. It's tasty but pungent, so spread sparingly on the crostini. It's delicious with a glass of robust red wine.

- **Mini-bowl attachment for food processor or mini chopper**

8	anchovy fillets	8
¼ cup	Italian flat-leaf parsley leaves	60 mL
2	cloves garlic, coarsely chopped	2
2 tbsp	extra virgin olive oil	30 mL
16	Basic Crostini (page 219)	16

1. In mini bowl of a food processor fitted with metal blade, pulse anchovies, parsley and garlic to chop, about 8 times, stopping and scraping down sides of the bowl as necessary. Add olive oil and pulse to blend, about 6 times. Spread about ½ tsp (2 mL) of anchovy mixture on each crostini.

Cheesy Anchovy Crostini

Makes 8 crostini

This is a particularly delicious and easy-to-make hot canapé. The pungent anchovies are a perfect complement to the strong taste of smoked mozzarella. Increase the quantity to suit your needs.

Tip

Anchovy paste is available in the refrigerated section of most supermarkets. It is a handy way to add bite to many dishes. As a rule of thumb, substitute about 1 tsp (5 mL) anchovy paste for each anchovy called for in the recipe.

- **Preheat broiler**

8	Basic Crostini (page 219)	8
8 tsp	anchovy paste (see Tip, left)	40 mL
4 oz	smoked mozzarella cheese, thinly sliced and cut to fit crostini	125 g

1. Spread each crostini with 1 tsp (5 mL) anchovy paste. Top with sliced mozzarella. Place on a baking sheet and broil until cheese is melted, about 2 minutes. Transfer to a platter and serve hot.

Variation

Cheesy Anchovy Toasts: If you don't have a baguette to make crostini, you can make this dish using toast triangles. Just toast sliced white bread, remove the crusts, then cut each slice into 8 triangles.

Roasted Tomato Crostini

Makes 12 crostini

Overloaded and delicious, these crostini definitely require napkins because they are likely to drip.

Tips

Buy your anchovies in a jar, rather than a tin. You can keep it in the fridge and use small quantities as needed.

Substitute black olive tapenade for the olive paste.

Omit ricotta. Spread olive paste directly on crostini. Top with a thin slice of fresh mozzarella. Complete the recipe.

- **Preheat oven to 325°F (160°C)**

6	plum (Roma) tomatoes, halved crosswise	6
½ tsp	dried oregano	2 mL
3 tbsp	extra virgin olive oil, divided	45 mL
3	anchovy fillets, minced (see Tips, left)	3
½ tsp	salt	2 mL
1 tbsp	freshly squeezed lemon juice	15 mL
½ cup	extra-smooth ricotta cheese	125 mL
2 tbsp	black olive paste (see Tips, left)	30 mL
12	crostini (pages 219 and 220)	12

1. Place tomatoes cut side up on a baking sheet. Sprinkle with oregano and drizzle with 1 tbsp (15 mL) of oil. Roast in preheated oven until tomatoes are beginning to collapse, about 20 minutes. Let cool slightly.

2. Meanwhile, in a small bowl, combine anchovies and salt. Mix well, mashing them together to break down anchovies. Stir in lemon juice. Whisk in remaining 2 tbsp (30 mL) of olive oil. Set aside.

3. In another small bowl, mix together ricotta and olive paste. Spread each crostini with ricotta mixture. Place a roasted tomato in center and drizzle with anchovy mixture.

Roasted Leek Crostini

Makes 8 crostini

Simple and classic in tone, these toasts are delicious and easy to make. Double or triple the recipe to suit your needs.

Tip

Leeks can be prepared ahead of time and refrigerated for up to 2 days before using. To clean, see Tips, page 173.

- **Preheat oven to 425°F (220°C)**

2	large leeks, white with just a hint of green, cleaned and thinly sliced	2
2 tbsp	olive oil	30 mL
8	crostini (pages 219 and 220)	8
1 tbsp	minced drained capers	15 mL
¼ cup	soft herb-flavored cheese, such as Boursin (approx.)	60 mL

1. In a baking dish, toss leeks with oil. Roast in preheated oven, stirring 2 or 3 times, until leeks are nicely browned, about 30 minutes. Set aside.

2. Preheat broiler. Spoon leeks over crostini. Sprinkle capers evenly over top and finish with a layer of cheese. Place on a baking sheet and broil until cheese begins to brown and melt, 2 to 3 minutes. Transfer to a platter and serve warm.

Mushroom, Spinach and Feta Crostini

Makes 12 crostini

Although this version is very far from the classic crostini it is very delicious.

Tip

Chiffonade is a French culinary term for slicing into thin ribbons — in this case spinach. Stack spinach leaves into a neat pile and roll into a small cigar shape. With a sharp knife, slice across the cigar to form thin ribbons and delicately fluff the spinach with your hands to separate.

- **Preheat oven to 400°F (200°C)**

2 tbsp	olive oil	30 mL
1 tbsp	finely diced bacon	15 mL
4 cups	quartered white mushrooms	1 L
2	cloves garlic, thinly sliced	2
1 tsp	coarsely chopped fresh thyme leaves	5 mL
½ tsp	salt	2 mL
¼ tsp	freshly ground black pepper	1 mL
1 cup	chiffonade spinach (see Tip, left)	250 mL
1 tbsp	sherry vinegar	15 mL
2 tbsp	unsalted butter, softened	30 mL
12	slices baguette, sliced on long bias	12
2 tbsp	crumbled feta cheese	30 mL

1. In a large skillet, heat oil over medium heat. Cook bacon until fat begins to render from bacon, about 2 minutes. Add mushrooms and cook, stirring, until soft, 7 to 8 minutes. Add garlic, thyme, salt and pepper and cook, stirring, until garlic is soft, about 2 minutes. Remove from heat and add spinach and vinegar, stirring until spinach is wilted.

2. Evenly spread butter on one side of baguette slices. Place on a baking sheet and bake in a preheated oven until butter is melted and bread is crisp, 5 to 6 minutes. Spread mushroom mixture and sprinkle feta over top and serve.

Variation

Arugula would add a peppery note to this appetizer and could easily replace spinach in this recipe.

Polenta Crostini

Crostini made from polenta are a nice change from those made from bread. And they are gluten-free, to boot. They can be topped with almost anything you would use to top bread-based crostini, bearing in mind that polenta has a more assertive flavor than white bread. In general terms, you are probably safe with anything that is Italian in flavoring. If you use stone-ground cornmeal to make your polenta, you'll be providing your guests with a nutritious whole-grain nibble.

When cutting polenta crostini, use your imagination. Round or fluted cookie cutters make particularly pretty crostini, but simple rectangles, squares or triangles work well, too. You can even cut animal shapes if you're serving crostini at a children's party.

Super Simple Polenta Crostini

Fontina Cheese Polenta Crostini: (Vegetarian Friendly) Top cut crostini with thinly sliced fontina cheese to taste. Bake in 350°F (180°C) oven until cheese is nicely melted, about 3 minutes.

Roasted Garlic Polenta Crostini: (Vegetarian Friendly) Spread cooled polenta crostini with roasted garlic. *To roast garlic:* Separate head into cloves but do not peel. Place in a small ovenproof container and toss with a bit of olive oil (about 2 tsp/10 mL) per head. Roast in 425°F (220°C) oven until softened, about 30 minutes. To serve, squeeze roasted garlic out of skins and spread over crostini. If desired, add a small dollop of Roasted Red Pepper Coulis (page 543). If you prefer, make roasted garlic in your slow cooker (page 484).

Creamy Gorgonzola with Walnut Polenta Crostini: (Vegetarian Friendly) In a small bowl, combine equal parts Gorgonzola and mascarpone cheese. Mix well. (Some cheese mongers sell a version of this already mixed; if you have access to it, by all means use it.) Spread on cooled polenta crostini to taste. Sprinkle finely chopped walnuts on top.

Tapenade-Topped Polenta Crostini: Spread cooled polenta crostini with your favorite prepared tapenade or any of the following: Tuna Tapenade (page 46), Parsley-Laced Tapenade (page 46) or Artichoke and Olive Tapenade (page 45).

Polenta Crostini

Makes enough for about 36 average-size crostini

If you are looking for something a little different with a bit of Wow! factor, try making your own polenta crostini. It's not hard to do and made with whole-grain stone-ground cornmeal they are a very healthy option to boot.

Tips

If you prefer, substitute vegetable or chicken stock for the water.

Oven-Cooked Polenta: For a low-maintenance method of cooking polenta, use an ovenproof saucepan and after Step 1, cover saucepan and transfer to 350°F (180°C) oven (or if you don't have an ovenproof saucepan, transfer mixture to lightly greased 8-cup/2 L baking dish and cover with foil). Bake until cornmeal is tender and creamy, about 40 minutes.

- **Ovenproof saucepan**
- **13- by 9-inch (33 by 23 cm) baking dish or pan or jelly roll pan, lined with plastic wrap**

4½ cups	water (see Tips, left)	1.125 L
¼ tsp	salt	1 mL
1 cup	stone-ground cornmeal	250 mL
	Oil	

1. In a saucepan over medium heat, bring water and salt to a boil. Gradually stir in cornmeal in a steady stream. Cook, stirring constantly, until smooth and blended and mixture bubbles like lava, about 5 minutes.

2. Reduce heat to low (placing a heat diffuser under the pot if your stove doesn't have a true simmer). Continue cooking, stirring frequently, while mixture bubbles and thickens, until grains are tender and creamy, about 30 minutes, depending upon how finely it was ground.

3. Transfer to prepared dish or pan. Spread warm polenta evenly over the plastic. Cover completely with another piece of plastic and using the palm of your hand, flatten to level. (Don't worry if the edges are a bit uneven or if the polenta doesn't completely cover the bottom of the pan. You can trim it when you make the crostini.) Refrigerate, covered, for at least 6 hours, until chilled and set, or for up to 2 days.

4. When you're ready to serve, preheat oven to 350°F (180°C).

5. Remove plastic and place polenta sheet on a large cutting board. Cut into desired shapes, using a sharp knife or cookie cutters. Brush top side of the shapes with olive oil. Place on a parchment paper–lined baking sheet and bake in preheated oven for 10 minutes. Flip over, brush second side with olive oil and bake until edges begin to crisp, about 10 minutes. Let cool completely on pan on a wire rack before adding toppings.

Spinach Polenta Crostini

Makes about 18 crostini

The addition of fresh mozzarella takes spinach uptown in this simple but elegant topping.

Tips

If you don't have whole nutmeg, use pre-ground nutmeg sparingly.

If you're using bagged spinach, which has been stemmed, you'll need a 10 oz (300 g) bag.

1 tbsp	unsalted butter	15 mL
1	clove garlic, minced	1
	Freshly grated nutmeg (see Tips, left)	
1 lb	fresh spinach, stems discarded, finely chopped (see Tips, left)	500 g
	Salt and freshly ground black pepper	
4 oz	drained fresh mozzarella, shredded	125 g
18	Polenta Crostini (page 229)	18

1. In a skillet, melt butter over medium heat. Add garlic and nutmeg to taste and cook, stirring, for 1 minute. Add spinach and cook, stirring, until wilted, 1 minute.

2. Drain off liquid and season spinach with salt and pepper. Stir in mozzarella. Spoon over crostini.

Mushroom Polenta Crostini

Makes about 18 crostini

Creamy browned mushrooms seasoned with shallots, garlic and tarragon and finished with a good hit of sharp Asiago cheese is a great comfort food and wonderful cold weather treat.

1 tbsp	unsalted butter	15 mL
8 oz	cremini mushrooms, trimmed and sliced	250 g
2	shallots, minced	2
2	cloves garlic, minced	2
2 tbsp	dry sherry	30 mL
2 tbsp	heavy or whipping (35%) cream	30 mL
2 tsp	finely chopped fresh tarragon	10 mL
1/2 cup	grated Asiago cheese	125 mL
	Salt and freshly ground black pepper	
18	Polenta Crostini (page 229)	18

1. In a skillet, melt butter over medium-high heat. Sauté mushrooms until browned, about 7 minutes. Add shallots and garlic and sauté until softened, about 2 minutes. Add sherry and sauté for 1 minute. Add cream and tarragon and bring to a boil. Reduce heat and simmer for 2 minutes to meld flavors.

2. Remove from heat and stir in Asiago until melted. Season with salt and pepper. Spoon over crostini.

Bruschetta

Makes various amounts

Bruschetta is a thick slice of country-style bread that is grilled and flavored with garlic. It provides the foundation upon which an endless array of toppings can be served. Because it can be a bit messy — all part of the fun — we recommend saving it for more casual meals. Just make sure you pass napkins.

• **Preheat broiler or barbecue to high**

> Country-style bread
>
> Garlic-Infused Olive Oil (see below)
>
> Dried oregano or Italian seasoning, optional
>
> Salt and freshly ground black pepper, optional

1. Cut bread into thick (about 1 inch/2.5 cm) slices. Place bread on a baking sheet or directly on the grill. Broil or grill until golden brown on one side, then turn and brown the second side.

2. Remove from heat and brush on one side with Garlic-Infused Olive Oil. Before adding topping, cut bread into manageable pieces. Sprinkle with dried oregano, salt and pepper, as desired depending upon the topping. Add toppings while warm.

Garlic-Infused Olive Oil

To make garlic-infused olive oil, combine 1/4 cup (60 mL) olive oil and 1 tbsp (15 mL) puréed or finely minced garlic (see below). Cover and let steep at room temperature for several hours. Strain through a fine sieve or funnel lined with a paper coffee filter. Discard garlic. Be sure to use the oil immediately as infused oils are a favored medium for bacteria growth.

Puréed garlic is preferable to minced garlic when making an infused oil because it integrates more fully into the oil. To purée garlic, use a fine, sharp-toothed grater, such as those made by Microplane.

Tomato-Mozzarella Bruschetta

Makes 8 bruschetta

This is a classic topping for bruschetta. Make it when tomatoes are in season and at their most luscious. It's filling, so it's enough for 8 people, unless the meal is light.

2 cups	diced peeled tomatoes	500 mL
⅓ cup	diced fresh mozzarella (bocconcini)	75 mL
4	fresh basil leaves, cut into fine chiffonade (see Tip, page 81)	4
	Salt and freshly ground black pepper	
4	large slices warm Bruschetta (page 231), cut in half	4
	Olive Paste (page 233), optional	
	Extra virgin olive oil, optional	

1. In a bowl, combine tomatoes, mozzarella and basil. Toss to combine. Season to taste with salt and pepper.

2. Spread bruschetta with olive paste, if using. Spoon tomato mixture liberally over bread. Drizzle with olive oil, if using. Serve immediately.

Tomato–Ricotta Salata Bruschetta

Makes 8 bruschetta

Ricotta salata is a dense, salty sheep's milk cheese, which bears no resemblance to the ricotta most North Americans know. It adds pleasant bite to field-fresh tomatoes.

2 cups	diced peeled tomatoes	500 mL
2 tbsp	grated ricotta salata	30 mL
2 tbsp	minced green onion, white part only	30 mL
2 tbsp	finely chopped Italian flat-leaf parsley	30 mL
	Sea salt and freshly ground black pepper	
	Olive Paste (page 233), optional	
4	slices warm Bruschetta (page 231), cut in half	4
	Extra virgin olive oil, optional	

1. In a bowl, combine tomatoes, ricotta salata, green onion and parsley. Toss to combine. Season to taste with salt and pepper.

2. Spread bruschetta with olive paste, if using. Spoon tomato mixture liberally over bread. Drizzle with olive oil, if using. Serve immediately.

Arugula-Ricotta Bruschetta

Makes 16 bruschetta

This is a lovely combination of flavors and wonderful to make when fresh arugula is plentiful in farmers' markets. It has a pleasantly mild flavor. If you feel the need to bump it up, add the olive paste or tapenade.

Tip

For best results, buy good quality Parmesan and grate it yourself. If you must use already-grated cheese, buy it from an Italian market or deli or a good cheese shop and ask to make sure it doesn't contain any "filler."

1 cup	fresh ricotta cheese	250 mL
2 tbsp	freshly grated Parmesan cheese	30 mL
1 tbsp	finely snipped chives	15 mL
2 tsp	white wine or champagne vinegar	10 mL
½ tsp	salt	2 mL
2 tbsp	extra virgin olive oil	30 mL
2 cups	baby or wild arugula, coarsely chopped	500 mL
8	slices warm Bruschetta (page 231), cut in half	8
	Olive Paste (see below) or black olive tapenade, optional	
	Freshly ground black pepper	

1. In a bowl, combine ricotta, Parmesan and chives. Mix well. Set aside.

2. In a separate bowl, combine vinegar and salt. Stir until salt is dissolved. Whisk in olive oil. Add arugula and toss until well coated with mixture.

3. Spread bruschetta with olive paste, if using, then spread with ricotta mixture. Top with arugula mixture. Season to taste with pepper. Serve immediately.

Olive Paste

If you feel your topping needs a little flavor boost, spread warm bruschetta with olive paste before adding the topping. You can buy prepared olive paste or make your own. For ¼ cup (60 mL) of olive paste, combine ¼ cup (60 mL) pitted black olives and 2 tbsp (30 mL) extra virgin olive oil in a mini bowl of a food processor or mini chopper. Process until chopped and blended. Cover and refrigerate for up to 5 days.

Broccoli Raab Bruschetta

Makes 8 bruschetta

Call it what you will — rapini or broccoli raab — this green vegetable has no identity problems when it comes to flavor. Assertively pungent, it may take a bit of getting used to. But once you've succumbed to its charms, you'll be a convert forever. Here it is paired with equally self-confident garlic, chile pepper and lemon juice, and just a hint of anchovy. Extra virgin olive oil mellows the result and a generous smattering of Asiago cheese completes the symphony.

Tips

The stems of broccoli raab can be a bit fibrous, so for best results peel before using.

The anchovy adds depth to the flavor rather than taste, but isn't essential.

1 lb	broccoli raab (rapini) (1 bunch), trimmed (see Tips, left)	500 g
¼ cup	extra virgin olive oil, divided	60 mL
6	cloves garlic, thinly sliced and slivered	6
1	anchovy fillet, minced, optional	1
½ to 1	long red chile pepper, minced	½ to 1
1 tbsp	freshly squeezed lemon juice	15 mL
	Salt and freshly ground black pepper	
4	slices warm Bruschetta (page 231), cut in half	4
¼ cup	grated Asiago cheese	60 mL

1. In a large pot of boiling salted water, blanch broccoli raab just until tender, about 3 minutes. Drain well and chop coarsely. Set aside.

2. In a skillet, heat 1 tbsp (15 mL) of the olive oil over medium heat. Add garlic and anchovy and cook, stirring, just until garlic begins to brown and anchovy is dissolved, about 3 minutes. Add broccoli raab and cook, stirring, until nicely tender and mixture is well integrated, about 2 minutes. Add chile pepper to taste and toss well. Remove from heat.

3. Stir in lemon juice and remaining 3 tbsp (45 mL) of olive oil. Season to taste with salt and black pepper. Spoon mixture over warm bruschetta. Sprinkle Asiago evenly over top. Serve warm or at room temperature.

Grilled Vegetable Bruschetta

Makes about 18 bruschetta

This is a great bruschetta to make in late summer when gardens are overflowing with eggplant, zucchini and peppers. Add some freshly picked herbs and a bit of garlic and you have a very tasty treat.

Tips

To cut eggplant and zucchini for grilling: Cut lengthwise in half and cut each half lengthwise in half. Do the same for the eggplant, making one additional cut to each quarter.

To purée garlic: Use a fine sharp-toothed grater, such as those made by Microplane.

If the peppers are not charred but the zucchini and eggplant look done, remove vegetables from the oven and set zucchini and eggplant aside to cool. Preheat broiler. Leave peppers on baking sheet and broil, turning once or twice, until charred.

● **Preheat oven to 400°F (200°C)**

1	eggplant, trimmed and cut lengthwise into 8 wedges (see Tips, left), peeled if desired	1
2	zucchini, trimmed and cut lengthwise into 4 wedges, peeled if desired	2
⅓ cup	extra virgin olive oil, divided	75 mL
2	red bell peppers	2
1 tbsp	fresh thyme leaves	15 mL
1 tbsp	finely chopped Italian flat-leaf parsley leaves	15 mL
1 tsp	puréed garlic (see Tips, left)	5 mL
	Salt and freshly ground black pepper	
9	slices warm Bruschetta (page 231), cut in half	9

1. Place eggplant and zucchini on a rimmed baking sheet. Pour ¼ cup (60 mL) of the oil evenly over the vegetables. Turn to coat on all sides. Place peppers on baking sheet. Roast in preheated oven, turning several times, until peppers are charred (see Tips, left) and vegetables are browning, about 25 minutes.

2. Transfer peppers to a bowl, cover with a plate and set aside. Let remaining vegetables cool, then dice and transfer to a bowl. When peppers are cool, peel, seed and cut into thin strips and add to bowl.

3. Add thyme, parsley, garlic and remaining olive oil to vegetables. Season to taste with salt and pepper. Toss to combine. Spoon over bruschetta.

Chickpea Bruschetta

Makes 16 bruschetta

If you are fond of chickpeas, here is a delicious way to enjoy them. Nicely creamy with hints of lemon, onion, red pepper and garlic, this makes a perfect topping for bruschetta.

Tip

For this quantity of chickpeas, use 1 can (14 to 19 oz/398 to 540 mL) chickpeas, drained and rinsed, or cook 1 cup (250 mL) dried chickpeas.

1 tbsp	olive oil	15 mL
½	red onion, finely chopped	½
½	red bell pepper, finely chopped	½
4	cloves garlic, finely chopped	4
2 cups	cooked drained chickpeas (see Tip, left)	500 mL
2 tbsp	finely chopped parsley	30 mL
3 tbsp	extra virgin olive oil	45 mL
2 tbsp	freshly squeezed lemon juice	30 mL
	Salt and freshly ground black pepper	
8	slices warm Bruschetta (page 231), cut in half	8

1. In a skillet, heat oil over medium heat. Add red onion, bell pepper and garlic and cook, stirring, until softened, about 3 minutes. Add chickpeas and cook, stirring, until heated through. Remove from heat. Using a potato masher, mash chickpeas. (You want them to maintain quite a bit of texture, but also to create a puréed base to hold the mixture together.) Stir in parsley, extra virgin olive oil and lemon juice. Season to taste with salt and pepper.

2. Spoon mixture over warm bruschetta. Serve warm or at room temperature.

Arugula-Spiked Tuna Bruschetta

Makes 20 bruschetta

If you're looking for something delicious but slightly off the beaten track, try this.

1	recipe White Bean Bruschetta topping (page 237)	1
1 cup	finely chopped baby or wild arugula	250 mL
1	jar (7 oz/200 g) oil-packed tuna, drained and chopped	1
10	slices warm Bruschetta (page 231), cut in half	10

1. In a bowl, combine arugula and tuna. Mix well.

2. Spread bruschetta with white bean mixture, then top with arugula mixture.

White Bean Bruschetta

Makes 16 bruschetta

This is a tasty and nutritious topping for bruschetta that has infinite variations (see below). Use it on its own or as the base for slightly more elaborate bruschetta such as Arugula-Spiked Tuna Bruschetta (page 236) or Roasted Red Pepper and White Bean Bruschetta (page 238).

Tip

For this quantity of beans, use 1 can (14 to 19 oz/398 to 540 mL) beans, drained and rinsed, or cook 1 cup (250 mL) dried beans.

2 cups	cooked drained cannellini beans (see Tip, left)	500 mL
½ cup	Italian flat-leaf parsley leaves	125 mL
2 tbsp	extra virgin olive oil	30 mL
1 tbsp	freshly squeezed lemon juice	15 mL
1	clove garlic	1
	Salt and freshly ground black pepper	
	Olive Paste (page 233) or black olive tapenade, optional	
8	slices warm Bruschetta (page 231), cut in half	8

1. In a food processor fitted with metal blade, process parsley, olive oil, lemon juice and garlic until finely chopped and blended. Add beans and pulse until desired consistency is achieved, about 10 times. (You want the beans to maintain some texture.) Season to taste with salt and pepper.

2. Spread bruschetta with olive paste, if using, then spoon bean mixture evenly over top.

Variations

Tomato-Spiked White Bean Bruschetta: Add 2 drained reconstituted sun-dried tomatoes along with the parsley.

White Bean Bruschetta with Sage and Roasted Garlic: Substitute 1 head of roasted garlic (pages 228 or 484) for the garlic and 20 fresh sage leaves for the parsley.

White Bean Bruschetta with Toasted Walnuts: Toast ½ cup (125 mL) walnut halves in 350°F (180°C) oven until fragrant, about 10 minutes. Let cool and chop coarsely. Sprinkle over finished bruschetta.

Salami-Topped White Bean Bruschetta: Sprinkle ½ cup (125 mL) finely chopped salami over finished bruschetta.

Roasted Red Pepper and White Bean Bruschetta

Makes 20 bruschetta

Make this for a special treat when peppers are abundant in farmers' markets.

1	recipe White Bean Bruschetta topping (page 237)	1
2	red bell peppers, roasted and cut into strips (see Tip, page 184) or store-bought	2
2 tbsp	extra virgin olive oil	30 mL
4	anchovy fillets, finely chopped	4
10	slices warm Bruschetta (page 231), cut in half	10

1. In a small bowl, combine roasted peppers, olive oil and anchovies. Toss well.

2. Spread bruschetta with white bean mixture, then top with red pepper mixture.

Fondue Toasts

Makes 16 toasts

Vegetarian Friendly

Fondue is an ultimate comfort food. There is something very homey and relaxing about melted cheese. Here we've spooned it over toast points and run it under the broiler to make entertaining-friendly finger food.

• **Preheat broiler**

1 cup	shredded Gruyère cheese	250 mL
1 tbsp	cornstarch	15 mL
½ cup	dry white wine	125 mL
	Freshly grated nutmeg	
	Freshly ground white or black pepper	
16	toast points (see Tips, page 240)	16

1. In a bowl, combine cheese and cornstarch. Mix well to ensure cheese is well coated.

2. In a saucepan, bring wine to a boil over medium heat. Reduce heat to low. Add cheese mixture and cook, stirring, until mixture is melted and thick, about 2 minutes. Remove from heat and season to taste with nutmeg and pepper.

3. Place toast points on a rimmed baking sheet. Spoon cheese mixture evenly. Broil just until cheese begins to brown, about 2 minutes. Serve immediately.

Chipotle Cheese Toasts

Makes about 24 toasts

Creamy yet nicely spicy, these simple toasts have a lovely combination of textures and flavors. This also makes a nice topping for crostini.

- **Preheat oven to 400°F (200°C)**

1	egg, separated	1
2	green onions, white part only with a bit of green, cut into 2-inch (5 cm) chunks	2
½	chipotle pepper in adobo sauce, drained	½
1 cup	shredded Monterey Jack cheese	250 mL
16	toast points (page 240) or Basic Crostini (page 219)	16
	Freshly ground black pepper	

1. In a food processor fitted with metal blade, process egg yolk, onions and chipotle until chopped. Scrape down sides of bowl. Add cheese and process until smooth.

2. In a bowl, beat egg white until foamy. Add to cheese mixture and pulse to blend, about 5 times.

3. Spread cheese mixture over toast points. Place on rimmed baking sheet and bake until puffed and lightly browned, about 5 minutes. Season to taste with pepper.

Ham and Cheese Toasts

Makes 24 toasts

These charming little bites have a deliciously retro feel. They are very tasty and easy to make.

Tip

If you prefer, use a food processor to mix and chop the cheese, ham and olives.

- **Preheat broiler**

¾ cup	shredded Swiss cheese	175 mL
3 oz	smoked ham, diced	90 g
½ cup	finely chopped pimento-stuffed olives	125 mL
Dash	hot pepper sauce, optional	Dash
2 tbsp	mayonnaise	30 mL
1 tsp	Dijon mustard	5 mL
24	toast points (see Tips, page 240)	24

1. In a bowl, combine cheese, ham, olives and hot pepper sauce, if using (see Tip, left). Mix well.

2. In a small bowl, combine mayonnaise and mustard.

3. Spread mayonnaise mixture evenly over toast points. Spoon cheese mixture evenly on top. Place on rimmed baking sheet and broil until cheese is melted and top is lightly browned, about 3 minutes. Serve warm.

Shrimp Toasts

Makes about 24 toasts

Here's a variation on the theme of Shrimp Toast, a classic party dish from the Old South.

Tips

The amount of salt you add will depend upon how much salt was used when the shrimp were cooked.

To make toast points: Remove the crusts from 3 slices of white bread. Toast. Cut each piece of bread in half on the diagonal, then cut each diagonal in half twice so you have 8 triangles per slice of bread.

- **Preheat oven to 400°F (200°C)**

8 oz	cooked peeled deveined shrimp	250 g
1 tbsp	unsalted butter, softened	15 mL
1 tbsp	sweet sherry	15 mL
1 tbsp	minced red onion	15 mL
1 tsp	prepared horseradish	5 mL
Dash	hot pepper sauce	Dash
	Salt (see Tips, left)	
1	egg white, beaten until frothy	1
24	toast points (see Tips, left)	24

1. In a food processor fitted with metal blade, process shrimp, butter, sherry, onion, horseradish, pepper sauce and salt to taste until smooth. Add egg white and pulse to blend. Spread shrimp mixture over toast points (about 1 tbsp/15 mL per point). Place on a baking sheet and bake in preheated oven until lightly browned, about 10 minutes.

Hot Curried Shrimp Toasts

Makes 16 toasts

It's hard to believe these lusciously flavored toasts are so easy to make.

Tip

If your chutney is a bit chunky, chop it finely before using.

8 oz	cooked salad shrimp, chopped	250 g
1 tbsp	freshly squeezed lemon juice	15 mL
1 tbsp	unsalted butter	15 mL
2 tbsp	minced red onion	30 mL
1 tsp	curry powder	5 mL
2 tbsp	mango or tomato chutney (see Tip, left)	30 mL
	Salt and freshly ground black pepper	
16	toast points (see Tips, above)	16
	Finely chopped parsley or cilantro	

1. In a bowl, combine shrimp and lemon juice. Set aside.
2. In a skillet, melt butter over medium heat. Add onion and cook, stirring, until softened. Stir in curry. Add chutney and cook, stirring, for 1 minute. Add shrimp. Season to taste with salt and pepper. Spoon shrimp mixture over points. Garnish with parsley.

Hot and Creamy Crab Toasts

Makes 24 toasts

Here's another combination that may evoke childhood memories of creamy, cheesy seafood dishes. Warm and comforting, these savory toasts are a perfect start to a cool-weather get-together.

Tip

To make toast points: Remove the crusts from 3 slices of white bread. Toast. Cut each piece of bread in half on the diagonal, then cut each diagonal in half twice so you have 8 triangles per slice of bread.

● **Preheat broiler**

1 tbsp	unsalted butter	15 mL
1 tbsp	all-purpose flour	15 mL
½ cup	warm milk	125 mL
½ cup	shredded Gruyère cheese	125 mL
Pinch	freshly grated nutmeg	Pinch
	Salt and freshly ground black pepper	
1 cup	chopped drained cooked crabmeat	250 mL
24	toast points (see Tip, left)	24
¼ cup	freshly grated Parmesan cheese	60 mL
2 tbsp	finely chopped parsley	30 mL

1. In a saucepan, melt butter over medium heat. Sprinkle in flour and cook, stirring, until frothy, about 1 minute. Gradually whisk in milk and cook, stirring, until mixture is thickened, about 2 minutes. Add cheese and stir until melted. Remove from heat. Add nutmeg and salt and pepper to taste. Stir in crab.

2. Spread crab mixture evenly over toasts. Sprinkle with Parmesan. Place on a baking sheet and broil until Parmesan is melted and mixture is sizzling, about 2 minutes. Transfer to a platter and sprinkle with parsley. Serve warm.

Easy Pizza Dough

Makes 1 pizza crust

This slightly crispy crust is an adaptation of the recipe for pizza dough found in 200 Fast & Easy Artisan Breads by Judith Fertig.

2 cups	unbleached all-purpose flour	500 mL
1 tsp	instant or bread machine yeast	5 mL
1½ tsp	salt	7 mL
¾ cup	lukewarm water (about 100°F/38°C)	175 mL

1. In a bowl, combine flour, yeast and salt. Mix well with a wooden spoon. Add water and stir until just moistened. Beat with wooden spoon, scraping the bottom and sides of the bowl until it forms a lumpy sticky mass, about 40 strokes. If you can't get all the flour mixture incorporated, remove dough from bowl and shape into a disk. Sprinkle remaining flour mixture over disk and knead several times to combine before returning to bowl.

2. Cover the bowl with plastic wrap and let rise at room temperature (72°F/22°C) in a draft-free place for 2 hours. (Dough will have a sponge-like appearance.) Use that day or place the dough, covered with plastic wrap in the refrigerator for up to 9 days before baking.

Pissaladière

Makes 25 pieces

This classic French "pizza" is lusciously delicious when somewhat overloaded with the onion, tomato and anchovy topping. Just make sure to pass a napkin with each succulent slice.

Tips

We like the warm fresh crust, but if you prefer, make this with a prepared pizza crust. You can even use a large rectangular Middle Eastern-style flatbread as a base.

If you have food processor, use it to slice the onions. You'll get nice even slices, which look attractive.

If tomatoes aren't in season, and cherry or grape tomatoes are more flavorful than those available in markets, use them instead. You'll need about 25. Cut in half and arrange over the onions, top side up.

- **Preheat oven to 375°F (190°C)**
- **Baking sheet, lined with parchment paper**

Crust

1	recipe Easy Pizza Dough (page 242) (see Tips, left)	1

Topping

2 tbsp	olive oil	30 mL
3	onions, thinly sliced (see Tips, left)	3
4	cloves garlic, minced	4
1 tsp	dried thyme	5 mL
	Salt and freshly ground black pepper	
12	anchovy fillets, drained (one 2 oz/60 g can)	12
3	tomatoes, peeled and thinly sliced	3
25	pitted black olives	25
	Extra virgin olive oil	
2 tbsp	finely minced parsley	30 mL

1. *Topping:* In a skillet, heat oil over low heat. Add onions and garlic and stir well. Cover and cook, stirring 2 or 3 times, until onions are very soft and just about to turn golden, about 10 minutes. Stir in thyme. Season to taste with salt and pepper. Set aside.

2. Cut anchovy fillets in half lengthwise and set aside.

3. On a floured surface, shape dough into a rectangle about 13 by 9 inches (33 by 23 cm) and place on prepared baking sheet. Spread onion mixture evenly over dough, leaving a border of about $\frac{1}{2}$ inch (1 cm). Arrange tomatoes over onions. Sprinkle anchovies evenly over top. Arrange olives equally spaced in 5 rows in each direction across rectangle (so they are in the center of slices-to-be). Drizzle with extra virgin olive oil. Place on bottom rack of preheated oven and bake until edges are browned and crisp, about 35 minutes. Transfer to a cutting board and sprinkle parsley evenly over top. Let cool slightly.

4. When pizza is cool enough to handle, cut rectangle lengthwise into 5 strips, then crosswise into 5 strips to make 25 rectangles with an olive in the center of each. Serve warm or at room temperature.

Spanish-Style Pizza

Makes 25 pieces

This sweet pepper and tomato pizza, made without cheese, is another example of a traditional pizza that isn't Italian in origin. Known as cocas, these Spanish pizzas, which are traditionally served on a crisp thin crust, come in sweet as well as savory versions.

Tip

We recommend using pure sea salt rather than refined table salt. It has a clean, crisp taste and enhanced mineral content, unlike table salt, which has a bitter acrid taste and contains unpleasant additives to prevent caking.

- **Preheat oven to 375°F (190°C)**
- **Baking sheet, lined with parchment paper**

Crust

1	recipe Easy Pizza Dough (page 242)	1

Topping

2	red bell peppers, thinly sliced	2
2	green bell peppers, thinly sliced	2
3 cups	cherry or grape tomatoes, halved	750 mL
½	Spanish or sweet onion, such as Vidalia, thinly sliced on the vertical	½
3	cloves garlic, slivered	3
2	anchovy fillets, minced, optional	2
3 tbsp	extra virgin olive oil (approx.)	45 mL
	Salt and freshly ground black pepper (see Tip, left)	
1 tbsp	finely chopped fresh oregano leaves	15 mL

1. *Topping:* In a large bowl, combine red and green bell peppers, tomatoes, onion, garlic, anchovies, if using, and olive oil. Toss well.

2. Shape pizza dough into a rectangle about 13 by 9 inches (33 by 23 cm) and place on prepared baking sheet. Spread pepper mixture evenly over dough, leaving a border of about ½ inch (1 cm). Place on bottom rack of preheated oven and bake until edges are browned and crisp and vegetables are soft and beginning to char, about 35 minutes. Transfer to a cutting board. Drizzle lightly with extra virgin olive oil and season to taste with a sprinkling of salt and pepper. Sprinkle oregano evenly over top. Let cool slightly.

3. When pizza is cool enough to handle, cut rectangle lengthwise into 5 strips, then crosswise into 5 strips to make 25 rectangles. Serve warm or at room temperature.

Bacon-Studded Cheese and Onion Tart

Makes about 36 pieces

This is a variation on the Alsatian dish flamiche, which is basically a mixture of leek, eggs and cream on a bread pastry. It is rich and delicious. It is great comfort food for a wintery night.

Tip

Since this is a dish best served in winter, we recommend using cherry or grape tomatoes, which usually have more flavor than regular tomatoes during that season. However, if you are making this when luscious vine-ripened tomatoes are available, by all means substitute thin slices for the smaller tomatoes. You will need about 2 tomatoes.

- **Preheat oven to 375°F (190°C)**
- **Rimmed baking sheet, lined with parchment paper**

1	recipe Easy Pizza Dough (page 242)	1

Topping

8 oz	sliced bacon (about 8 slices)	250 g
3	onions, thinly sliced	3
2	cloves garlic, minced	2
¾ cup	heavy or whipping (35%) cream	175 mL
1	egg, beaten	1
8 oz	Cheddar cheese, shredded	250 g
18	cherry or grape tomatoes, halved (see Tip, left)	18
	Finely chopped parsley	
	Freshly ground black pepper	

1. *Topping:* In a large skillet over medium heat, cook bacon, turning once, just until it is starting to crisp. Drain on paper towel. When cool enough to handle, chop coarsely and set aside.

2. Drain off all but 2 tbsp (30 mL) fat from pan. Add onions and garlic and cook, stirring, until they begin to turn golden, about 10 minutes. Stir in cream. Set aside to let cool slightly. When onion mixture is cool enough to ensure egg won't curdle, stir in egg. Add cheese and stir well.

3. Shape dough into a rectangle about 13 by 9 inches (33 by 23 cm) and place on prepared baking sheet. Spread cheese mixture evenly over pastry and arrange tomato halves cut side up on top. Sprinkle bacon evenly over top.

4. Place on bottom rack of preheated oven and bake until top is golden and edges are browned and crisp, about 35 minutes. Sprinkle liberally with parsley and season to taste with pepper. Cut rectangle lengthwise into 6 strips then crosswise into 6 strips to make 36 rectangles. Let cool slightly and serve.

Pancetta-Spiked Ricotta Pizza

Makes about 36 pieces

Here's a relatively light but flavorful pizza that will satisfy those who are looking for something a bit different.

Tips

If you prefer, make this with a prepared pizza crust. You can even use a large rectangular Middle Eastern flatbread as a base.

Ricotta cheese usually has a moisture content of between 72 to 80%, which makes it quite watery, and will make your crust soggy. You can drain it yourself. Place a double layer of cheesecloth in a strainer, place the strainer over a mixing bowl and add ricotta. Cover with plastic and place a plate over the plastic to press the cheese down. Refrigerate for about 8 hours. Discard liquid that has accumulated in the bowl. Or you can look for ricotta that has been pre-drained. The package will state that it has a moisture content of about 65%.

Use pancetta that has been sliced and cut into thin strips.

Speck is, like pancetta, cured pork. It can be Italian or German in origin.

- **Preheat oven to 375°F (190°C)**
- **Baking sheet, lined with parchment paper**

1	recipe Easy Pizza Dough (page 242) (see Tips, left)	1

Topping

1 cup	drained ricotta cheese (see Tips, left)	250 mL
¼ cup	freshly grated Parmesan cheese	60 mL
1 tsp	dried oregano, crumbled, divided	5 mL
½ tsp	finely grated lemon zest	2 mL
¼ tsp	salt	1 mL
15	cherry tomatoes, halved	15
½ cup	finely chopped pancetta or speck (see Tips, left)	125 mL
2 tbsp	finely chopped Italian flat-leaf parsley	30 mL
	Freshly ground black pepper	
	Extra virgin olive oil	

1. In a small bowl, combine ricotta, Parmesan, ½ tsp (2 mL) of the oregano, lemon zest and salt. Mix well.

2. Shape dough into a rectangle about 13 by 9 inches (33 by 23 cm) and place on prepared baking sheet. Spread ricotta mixture evenly over dough. Arrange tomatoes cut side up evenly over top and sprinkle with remaining oregano. Scatter pancetta evenly over top and sprinkle with parsley. Season to taste with pepper and drizzle with olive oil.

3. Place on bottom rack of preheated oven and bake until edges are browned and crisp, about 35 minutes. Let cool slightly on rack. Cut rectangle lengthwise into 6 strips then crosswise into 6 strips to make 36 rectangles and serve.

Anchoyade on Pita

Makes about 24 pieces

This appetizer is very easy to make yet delicious. Use the size of pita bread you're likely to have on hand and cut into pieces that suit your need.

Tips

For convenience, make the topping ahead of time. Cover and refrigerate until you're ready to use, for up to 2 days.

If you like heat, don't seed the chile and leave the veins in before chopping.

- **Baking sheet, lightly greased**

3 tbsp	olive oil, divided	45 mL
1	onion, sliced	1
4	cloves garlic, coarsely chopped	4
1	fresh chile pepper, seeded and chopped, optional (see Tips, left)	1
12	anchovy fillets, drained (one 2 oz/60 g can)	12
	Cracked black peppercorns	
2 cups	cherry tomatoes, halved	500 mL
6	fresh basil leaves	6
6	small (4½ inch/11 cm) pita breads	6

1. In a skillet, heat 2 tbsp (30 mL) of the oil over medium heat. Add onion and cook, stirring, until softened, about 3 minutes. Add garlic, chile pepper, if using, anchovies and peppercorns and cook, stirring, for 1 minute. Add tomatoes, bring to a boil and cook, stirring, until tomatoes have collapsed and anchovies have disintegrated, about 5 minutes. Transfer to food processor fitted with metal blade. Add basil and process until smooth, about 30 seconds.

2. Meanwhile, preheat oven to 400°F (200°C). Brush both sides of pita with remaining tbsp (15 mL) of oil and place on prepared baking sheet, concave side up. Spread anchoyade evenly over top. Bake in preheated oven until pita begins to crisp and top is fragrant, about 15 minutes. Cut each pita into 4 to 6 wedges.

Potato Pizza

Makes about 12 pieces

The flavor combinations here — mild potatoes with rosemary, onion and smoked mozzarella — are fabulous. They are not the norm on pizza, but the results are very tasty.

Tips

For best results use a mandoline or the thin slicing blade on a food processor to produce even thin slices of potato and onion.

Peel the potato, if you wish, but we like the visual effect of the brown skin on the white background.

We've made this on a large piece (about 12 by 6 inches /30 by 15 cm) prepared Middle Eastern-type flatbread and it was delicious.

- **Preheat oven to 425°F (220°C)**

1	potato (about 8 oz/250 g)	1
1	small red onion, thinly sliced	1
2 tbsp	extra virgin olive oil	30 mL
2	cloves garlic, minced	2
1 tsp	chopped fresh rosemary	5 mL
½ tsp	salt	2 mL
½ tsp	freshly ground black pepper	2 mL
1	herbed flatbread (see Tips, left) or ½ recipe Easy Pizza Dough (page 242)	1
4 oz	smoked mozzarella cheese, shredded	125 g
2 tbsp	freshly grated Parmesan cheese	30 mL

1. Pierce potato all over with a fork. Microwave on High until slightly tender, about 2 minutes . Let cool for 2 minutes. Cut into thin slices (see Tips, left). Transfer to a large bowl. Add red onion, olive oil, garlic, rosemary, salt and pepper. Toss well.

2. If using pizza dough, roll out on a floured surface to a rectangle about 11 by 8 inches (28 by 20 cm). Place flatbread or dough on a baking sheet. Arrange potato mixture evenly over top. Sprinkle mozzarella evenly over potatoes.

3. Bake in preheated oven until potatoes are tender and pizza is crisp, 20 to 25 minutes. Sprinkle Parmesan evenly over top and bake until melted and lightly browned, about 2 minutes more. Cut into small rectangles and serve immediately.

Variation

Instead of herbed flatbread, you could also use naan, spreading the topping over 2 or 3 smaller ones, if necessary, or even pita breads. Use your imagination. The cooking time will stay the same.

Easy Artichoke and Mushroom Pizza

Makes about 12 pieces

This recipe uses prepared flatbread such as lightly seasoned focaccia as a base. It is quick, easy and delicious. Cut into thin wedges if your flatbread is round, or squares if it is rectangular.

Tip

This was tested using a rosemary and onion focaccia, which was particularly delicious.

- **Preheat oven to 400°F (200°C)**

1	large flatbread (about 12 oz/375 g) (see Tip, left)	1
8 oz	fontina cheese, shredded	250 g
1	jar (6 oz/175 mL) marinated artichoke hearts, drained and chopped	1
4 oz	mushrooms, thinly sliced	125 g
	Olive oil	
	Freshly ground black pepper	

1. Place flatbread on a baking sheet. Sprinkle fontina evenly over flatbread, follow with a layer of artichokes and finish with mushrooms. Drizzle olive oil evenly over top.

2. Bake in preheated oven until cheese is melted and crust is browning, about 10 minutes. Season to taste with pepper. Cut into small rectangles. Serve warm.

Easy Chorizo Pizza

Makes about 12 pieces

Spicy chorizo, sweet roasted red pepper and sharp Asiago cheese make a delicious combination and ready-made flatbread provides a no-fuss base.

Tip

If using round flatbread it should be about 12 inches (30 cm) in diameter. If rectangular, about 16 by 7 inches (40 by 18 cm).

- **Preheat oven to 400°F (200°C)**

1	large flatbread (about 12 oz/375 g)	1
4 oz	Asiago cheese, shredded	125 g
8 oz	cured (dry) chorizo sausage, diced	250 g
1	red bell pepper, roasted (see Tip, page 184), thinly sliced	1
	Freshly ground black pepper	
	Finely chopped parsley	

1. Place flatbread on a baking sheet. Sprinkle Asiago evenly over flatbread. Arrange chorizo and roasted pepper slices evenly over cheese.

2. Bake in preheated oven until cheese is melted and crust is browning, about 10 minutes. Season to taste with pepper and garnish with parsley. Cut into small rectangles. Serve warm.

Greek-Style Pizza

Makes about 12 pieces

Halloumi is a mild-tasting sheep's milk cheese that is deliciously salty yet creamy. This recipe is so simple to make, yet delicious.

Tip

For testing, we used a prepared oval flatbread that was about 16 by 7 inches. (40 by 18 cm).

- **Preheat oven to 400°F (200°C)**

1	large Middle Eastern-style flatbread (about 12 oz/375 g) (see Tip, left)	1
8 oz	halloumi cheese, shredded	250 g
2 tsp	dried oregano	10 mL
3 tbsp	lightly toasted sesame seeds (see Tips, page 254)	45 mL
	Extra virgin olive oil	

1. Place flatbread on a baking sheet. Sprinkle cheese evenly over top. Sprinkle oregano evenly over cheese and sprinkle sesame seeds evenly over all. Drizzle with olive oil.
2. Bake in preheated oven until cheese is melted and hot, about 15 minutes. Cut into small rectangles.

Not-Your-Average Tomato Pizza

Makes about 12 pieces

The addition of za'atar, a Middle Eastern spice blend, and fresh chile, transforms what might have been a straightforward tomato pizza into a taste sensation.

- **Preheat oven to 400°F (200°C)**

1	large Middle Eastern-style flatbread (about 12 oz/375 g)	1
2 cups	diced cherry tomatoes	500 mL
1	small red onion, thinly sliced on the vertical	1
1	long red chile pepper, minced	1
1 tbsp	za'atar (see Tips, page 217)	15 mL
	Salt	
2 tbsp	extra virgin olive oil	30 mL
	Finely chopped parsley	

1. Place flatbread on a baking sheet. In a bowl, combine tomatoes, red onion, chile, za'atar, and salt to taste. Add olive oil and toss until ingredients are evenly coated. Spread evenly over flatbread.
2. Bake in preheated oven until hot and crust begins to brown, about 10 minutes. Remove from oven and garnish with parsley. Cut into small rectangles. Serve warm.

Grilled Pizza with Swiss Chard and Mozzarella

Makes 15 pieces

Pizzas made without the classic tomato sauce base are widely known as "blonde pizzas." This blonde pizza encompasses the bright flavor of fresh basil leaves and Swiss chard with a creamy accent of mozzarella. Feel free to use this recipe as a base and substitute kale, spinach or watercress in place of Swiss chard — they're all perfect here. These are just lovely served for a barbecue party in spring or summer.

Tip

As the Basil Pesto sets, the solids separate from the oil. This oil is vibrant green and very flavorful and makes a wonderful garnish on top of the pizza after it's cooked.

• **Preheat barbecue grill to high**

1	recipe Easy Pizza Dough (page 242)	1
2 cups	diced drained fresh mozzarella (bocconcini)	500 mL
1/4 cup	extra virgin olive oil, divided	60 mL
1 tsp	coarsely chopped fresh basil	5 mL
1/4 tsp	salt	1 mL
1/4 tsp	freshly ground black pepper	1 mL
1 tbsp	Basil Pesto (page 549) or store-bought	15 mL
2 cups	coarsely chopped Swiss chard	500 mL
1/2 cup	coarsely chopped green onions	125 mL

1. In a bowl, combine cheese, 2 tbsp (30 mL) of the olive oil, basil, salt and pepper and toss well to coat. Set aside.

2. Place dough on a work surface. Rub 2 tbsp (30 mL) of oil on dough. With your fingers or using a rolling pin, stretch or roll out dough to 1/4-inch (0.5 cm) thickness (the shape doesn't matter in this instance; in fact, oblong shapes are welcome). Place crust on preheated grill, close lid and grill pizza crust until bottom is crisp and golden brown, about 4 minutes. Flip over and evenly coat cooked side of crust with pesto. Arrange Swiss chard and cheese mixture evenly over top. Cover and grill until cheese is melted and bottom is golden brown, about 5 minutes. Transfer to a cutting board and garnish with green onions. Cut into 15 equal portions. Serve immediately.

Grilled Pizza with Braised Leeks and Tomato

Makes 15 pieces

Braised leeks contribute sweetness to this pizza. In the spring months, baby or wild leeks can be found in certain regions and kick up the sweetness to a whole different level.

Tip

For best results, buy good quality Parmesan and grate it yourself. If you must use already-grated cheese, buy it from an Italian market or deli or a good cheese shop and ask to make sure it doesn't contain any "filler."

● **Preheat barbecue grill to high**

1	recipe Easy Pizza Dough (page 242)	1
2 tbsp	extra virgin olive oil	30 mL
$\frac{1}{4}$ tsp	salt	1 mL
$\frac{1}{4}$ tsp	freshly ground black pepper	1 mL
$\frac{1}{2}$ cup	finely grated Parmesan cheese	125 mL
1 cup	finely diced seeded tomatoes	250 mL
$1\frac{1}{2}$ cups	Braised Leeks (page 548)	375 mL
$\frac{1}{4}$ cup	coarsely chopped fresh basil	60 mL

1. Place dough on a work surface. Rub oil on dough. With your fingers or using a rolling pin, stretch or roll out dough to $\frac{1}{4}$-inch (0.5 cm) thickness (the shape doesn't matter in this instance; in fact, oblong shapes are welcome). Grill pizza until bottom is crisp and golden brown, about 4 minutes. Flip over and season with salt and pepper. Evenly coat cooked side of crust with cheese, tomatoes and leeks. Cover and grill until bottom is golden brown, about 5 minutes. Transfer to a cutting board and garnish with basil. Cut into 15 equal portions. Serve immediately.

Pizza with Grape Jelly and Brie

Makes 15 pieces

This pizza is influenced by cheese platters that serve sweet marmalade or jam alongside. Here, we've paired a warm creamy Brie cheese with Concord grape jelly. If you have an hour to spare, try to make the super simple jelly yourself. Otherwise, store-bought jelly would work just fine.

- Preheat barbecue grill to high

1	recipe Easy Pizza Dough (page 242)	1
2 tbsp	extra virgin olive oil	30 mL
2 tbsp	Concord Grape Jelly (page 274) or store-bought	30 mL
1/4 cup	thinly sliced red onion	60 mL
3 oz	Brie cheese, diced	90 g
1/4 cup	coarsely chopped fresh basil	60 mL

1. Place dough on a work surface. Rub oil on dough. With your fingers or using a rolling pin, stretch or roll out dough to 1/4-inch (0.5 cm) thickness. Grill pizza until bottom is crisp and golden brown, about 4 minutes. Flip over and evenly coat cooked side of crust with grape jelly, red onion and Brie. Cover and grill until bottom is golden brown, about 5 minutes. Transfer to a cutting board and cut into 15 equal portions. Garnish with basil.

Margherita Pizza Pockets

Makes 8 pockets

Why buy frozen pizza pockets when these are so easy to make?

Tip

Be creative with your ingredients. Use this recipe as a base and feel free to use your favorite vegetables. Limit the amount of stuffing to about 1 1/2 to 2 tbsp (22 to 30 mL) or you risk the pockets exploding open.

- Baking sheet, lined with parchment paper

1	recipe Easy Pizza Dough (page 242)	1
1/2 cup	shredded mozzarella cheese	125 mL
3 tbsp	Oven-Roasted Cherry Tomato Sauce (page 546)	45 mL
1 tbsp	chiffonade fresh basil leaves	15 mL

1. Place dough on a lightly floured work surface. Cut into 8 equal pieces. Roll each piece into balls and, using your fingers, press and stretch dough into 3-inch (7.5 cm) disks.

2. Place cheese, sauce and basil in center of each, dividing equally. Fold dough over to enclose and pinch to seal. Place on prepared baking sheet, about 2 inches (5 cm) apart. Bake until golden brown, about 10 minutes. Serve immediately.

Sesame and Parmesan Pizza Sticks

Makes about 20 sticks

This recipe is like eating a basket of the tastiest pizza crust ever!

Tips

Consider serving this with Oven-Roasted Cherry Tomato Sauce (page 546) — what a perfect pairing.

To toast sesame seeds: Place seeds in a dry skillet and cook, stirring, over medium heat until fragrant and turning golden, about 4 minutes.

- **Preheat oven 475°F (240°C)**
- **Baking sheet, lined with parchment paper**

1	recipe Easy Pizza Dough (page 242)	1
1 tbsp	unsalted butter, melted	15 mL
1 tbsp	toasted sesame seeds (see Tips, left)	15 mL
1 tbsp	freshly grated Parmesan cheese	15 mL
¼ tsp	salt	1 mL
⅛ tsp	freshly ground black pepper	0.5 mL

1. Place dough on a lightly floured work surface. Using a floured rolling pin, roll out dough to a large rectangle about 12 by 8 inches (30 by 20 cm) and ⅛ inch (3 mm) thick. Brush melted butter over entire surface of dough. Evenly coat with sesame seeds, cheese, salt and pepper. Starting with one long side, fold dough in half to enclose ingredients. Using a rolling pin, roll dough a few times to seal. Cut dough crosswise into ¾-inch (2 cm) wide strips, about 1 inch (2.5 cm) long. Twist dough to form sticks (they should resemble candy canes). Place sticks about ½ inch (1 cm) apart on prepared baking sheet. Bake in a preheated oven until golden brown, about 10 minutes. Serve immediately.

Panini, Sandwiches and Tartines

Sandwiches are the ultimate convenience dish. Not only do they make a great meal any time of the day, but it also doesn't take much imagination to see how these perennial favorites can migrate to the appetizer course. Even at their most stylish, sandwiches bring out the kid in us. They are very easy to make, can be fancy or plain, and just about everyone enjoys eating them in their virtually endless configurations, from elegant open-faced tartines to hearty sliders.

In this chapter we offer a wide selection from Avocado Party Sandwiches (page 270) and mini burgers (Beef and Parmesan Sliders, page 268) to filled and sliced baguettes such as Mini Muffulettas (page 256) or Pan Bagna (page 257). Given the popularity of panini presses, it's a snap to prepare warm "compressed" sandwiches such as Cheese Toasts with Pickled Onions (page 261), which look professionally made. Cut into quarters or eighths, these meal-size sandwiches make popular finger food.

Mini Muffulettas 256
Pan Bagna 257
Open-Faced Shrimp and Cucumber
    Sandwiches 258
Egg and Watercress Rounds 259
Marinated Mushroom Squares 259
Elena Ruz Cubano 260
Cheese Toasts with Pickled Onions 261
Uptown Ham and Cheese 262
The Ultimate Mozzarella en Carozza 263
Grilled Halloumi on Pita 264
Chicken Sliders with Brie 265
Salmon Sliders 266
Turkey Sliders with Chipotle Mayo 267
Beef and Parmesan Sliders 268
Lamb and Red Onion Sliders 269

Avocado-Topped Squares 270
Avocado Party Sandwiches 270
Grilled Goat Cheese Baguettes 271
Warm Croissant, Brie and Caramelized
    Onion Sandwiches 271
Mini Grilled Cheese with Havarti, Fresh Basil
    and Tomato 272
French-Style Grilled Cheese 272
Seared Tuna on Brioche 273
Roast Turkey Pinwheel "Logs" 273
Pine Nut Butter and Jelly Fingers 274
Smoked Salmon and Avocado
    Tea Sandwiches 275
Apple and Goat Cheese "Sandwiches" 275
Mini Falafel Sandwiches 276

Mini Muffulettas

Makes about 32 pieces

Muffulettas are a famous New Orleans sandwich of cold cuts topped with an olive salad. Here they become a variation on the theme of Pan Bagna (page 257), a filled and sliced baguette. One advantage for the busy host is that you can (and should) make these the night before you intend to serve them so the flavor-infused olive oil will soak into the bread. They are easy to make and very yummy.

Tips

If you prefer, use 3 mini baguettes.

Use good-quality olives such as kalamata. Under no circumstances should you use black olives that come out of a can. They have no taste.

If you like heat, spicy salami adds a nice touch.

Olive Salad

1¼ cups	pimento-stuffed green olives, finely chopped	300 mL
¾ cup	pitted black olives, finely chopped (see Tips, left)	175 mL
¼ cup	extra virgin olive oil	60 mL
2 tbsp	finely chopped Italian flat-leaf parsley	30 mL
1 tbsp	drained capers, minced	15 mL
1	clove garlic, minced	1
	Freshly ground black pepper	
1	good-quality baguette (see Tips, left)	1
3 oz	thinly sliced good-quality salami (see Tips, left)	90 g
3 oz	thinly sliced smoked ham	90 g
3 oz	thinly sliced provolone cheese	90 g

1. *Olive Salad:* In a bowl, combine green and black olives, olive oil, parsley, capers and garlic. Mix well and season to taste with pepper.

2. Cut baguette crosswise into 3 equal pieces, then cut each piece in half horizontally. Layer bottom half of each baguette with salami, ham and provolone, folding over to fit, as necessary. Spoon olive salad evenly over top. Wrap tightly in plastic wrap and refrigerate, top side down so the dressing can soak into the bread, for at least 2 hours or up to overnight. To serve, cut into slices about ¾ inch (2 cm) wide.

Pan Bagna

Makes about 32 pieces

Usually, this Provençal-style sandwich is a favorite picnic staple but here it earns its chops as an easy make-ahead tidbit for a tasting platter or canapé tray.

Tip

Spanish or Italian tuna, packed in olive oil, is more moist and flavorful than paler versions packed in water.

1	can (6 oz/170 g) tuna, preferably Spanish or Italian, packed in olive oil, drained (see Tip, left)	1
2 tbsp	each finely chopped red or green onion, celery, parsley, roasted red pepper and pitted black olives (use all or some of the above, depending upon what you have on hand)	30 mL
2 tbsp	mayonnaise	30 mL
1 tbsp	freshly squeezed lemon juice	15 mL
1 tbsp	extra virgin olive oil	15 mL
2 tsp	finely chopped hot banana pepper	10 mL
1 tsp	minced drained capers	5 mL
½ tsp	salt	2 mL
	Freshly ground black pepper	
1	good-quality baguette, hero loaf or 4 crusty rolls, split lengthwise	1

1. In a bowl, combine tuna, vegetables, mayonnaise, lemon juice, olive oil, hot pepper, capers, salt, and black pepper to taste. Mix well.

2. Spread mixture evenly over bottom half of baguette. Cover with the top portion and cut in half. Press down firmly on each piece, then wrap tightly in plastic wrap. Place in a pan and cover with a heavy weight. (A foil-wrapped brick is ideal.) Refrigerate for at least 4 hours or up to overnight. Cut into slices about ¾ inch (2 cm) wide.

Variation

The World's Best Tuna Sandwich: Spread the filling over your favorite bread and serve immediately.

Open-Faced Shrimp and Cucumber Sandwiches

Makes about 16

These sandwiches are a traditional favorite in Scandinavia. Serving them on small rounds of bread rather than hefty slices pretties them up enough to make appetizers. If you're looking to vary the flavor profile, try the vinegar flavored mayo (see Variation, below), instead of the usual lemon-dill.

Tips

You can peel the cucumber or leave the skin on to suit your taste. For best results, use a mandoline or the slicing blade of a food processor to slice the cucumber paper-thin.

This presentation is more elegant on crustless rounds of bread, but if you prefer use sliced baguette.

- 2-inch (5 cm) round cutter

¼ cup	mayonnaise	60 mL
2 tbsp	finely chopped fresh dill fronds	30 mL
½ tsp	finely grated lemon zest	1 mL
8 oz	cooked salad shrimp	250 g
8	slices white or light rye sandwich bread (approx.)	8
2 tbsp	unsalted butter, softened	30 mL
1	small English cucumber, thinly sliced (see Tips, left)	1
	Salt and coarsely ground black pepper	
	Fresh dill fronds	

1. In a bowl, combine mayonnaise, dill and lemon zest. Mix well. Add shrimp and toss until coated.

2. To make bread rounds, place bread on a cutting board, and using cutter, cut 16 rounds. (Depending upon the size of your bread, you'll get about 2 rounds per slice.) Spread butter lightly over bread. Layer cucumber slices on top, dividing equally, then spoon shrimp mixture over cucumber. Season to taste with salt and pepper. Garnish each round with a dill frond.

Variation

For a different flavor, omit dill and lemon zest in Step 1 and add 2 tbsp (30 mL) finely chopped parsley and 2 tsp (10 mL) best-quality sherry vinegar (Pedro Ximenez is fabulous!) to the mayonnaise. Toss with shrimp and complete the recipe.

Egg and Watercress Rounds

Makes about 12

These sweet little rounds have a delightfully Victorian sensibility, but the flavors are compelling enough to appeal to contemporary tastes.

Tip

Depending upon bread, you'll get about 2 rounds per slice.

- **2-inch (5 cm) round cutter**

4	hard-cooked eggs, peeled and chopped	4
¼ cup	finely chopped watercress leaves	60 mL
4	green onions, white part with a bit of green, minced	4
2 tbsp	mayonnaise (see Tips, page 536)	30 mL
2 tbsp	crème fraîche or sour cream	30 mL
	Salt and freshly ground black pepper	
6	slices white sandwich bread	6
2 tbsp	unsalted butter, softened	30 mL
	Small sprigs of watercress	

1. In a bowl, combine eggs, watercress, onions, mayonnaise and crème fraîche. Season with salt and pepper.

2. Place bread on a cutting board, and using cutter, cut 16 rounds. Spread butter lightly over bread, then spoon egg mixture over top, dividing equally. Garnish each round with a watercress sprig.

Marinated Mushroom Squares

Makes 8 pieces

A wonderful addition to any antipasti offering.

- **Preheat oven to 500°F (260°)**

2	slices challah (egg bread)	2
2 tsp	cream cheese, softened	10 mL
1 cup	Marinated Mushrooms (page 548), drained	250 mL
½ cup	freshly grated Parmesan cheese	125 mL
1 tbsp	thinly sliced green onion	15 mL
1 tbsp	finely diced seeded tomato	15 mL

1. Cut crusts from bread. Spread cream cheese evenly over one side. Slice into four equal squares. Spoon mushrooms on top of each quarter, dividing equally, and sprinkle with Parmesan. Place on a baking sheet and bake in a preheated oven until bread is crisp and cheese is melted, about 5 minutes. Garnish with green onion and tomatoes.

Elena Ruz Cubano

Makes about 16 pieces

This deliciously retro variation on a Cuban sandwich is adapted from a Floridian version popularized by Cuban-American Elena Ruz. You may be inclined to pass on the strawberry jam. Don't. It works surprisingly well with the other ingredients.

Tip

If you're not using a panini press, you can use a grill pan. A heavy cast-iron skillet smaller than the grill pan makes a perfect weight. Hamburger presses, or bricks wrapped in foil work well, too.

- **Panini press or grill pan with weight (see Tip, left)**
- **Preheat panini press or grill pan to high**

1	baguette, about 16 inches (40 cm) long	1
6 oz	cream cheese, softened	175 g
¼ cup	strawberry jam, preferably seedless	60 mL
8 oz	thinly sliced smoked turkey	250 g
	Sliced pickled hot banana peppers	
	Freshly ground black pepper	
	Extra virgin olive oil	

1. Cut baguette in half crosswise, then cut each in half lengthwise. Spread cut side of top halves of split baguette with cream cheese and bottoms with jam. Arrange turkey evenly over bottoms. Place hot peppers over turkey, season with pepper to taste and close with tops. Brush outsides all over lightly with olive oil.

2. Place sandwich on preheated panini press, close top and cook until nicely browned, about 4 minutes. Or place in grill pan and press down with weight until bottom is nicely browned. Turn and repeat. Transfer to a cutting board and cut into slices about 1 inch (2.5 cm) wide. Serve warm.

Variation

Traditional Cubano: Substitute 4 oz (125 g) each thinly sliced ham and Swiss cheese for the turkey, mayonnaise to taste for the cream cheese and thinly sliced dill pickle for the hot peppers. Omit the strawberry jam.

Cheese Toasts with Pickled Onions

Makes 16 pieces

If you are having a get-together with a casual theme — like a hoedown or even a Super Bowl party — this variation on a grilled cheese sandwich can't be beat. Hot paprika adds zing and the "pickled" onions seem far more exotic than they actually are.

Tips

If you're not using a panini press, you can use a grill pan or a large skillet. Another heavy cast-iron skillet smaller than the one you are cooking in makes a perfect weight. Hamburger presses, or bricks wrapped in foil work well, too.

If you don't have hot paprika, substitute ¾ tsp (3 mL) sweet paprika mixed with ¼ tsp (1 mL) cayenne pepper.

We prefer to use good whole-grain bread when making these toasts because it is more nutritious, but you can use white bread if you prefer. Removing the crusts is a matter of preference.

- Panini press or grill pan with weight (see Tips, left)
- Preheat panini press or grill pan to high

¼ cup	red wine vinegar	60 mL
1 tbsp	granulated sugar	15 mL
1	sweet onion, such as Vidalia, thinly sliced	1
	Freshly ground black pepper	
3 cups	shredded Cheddar cheese	750 mL
1 tsp	hot paprika (see Tips, left)	5 mL
8	thin slices bread (see Tips, left)	8
2 tbsp	unsalted butter, softened, divided	30 mL

1. In a saucepan, combine vinegar and sugar. Cook over medium heat until sugar is dissolved. Add onion and stir well, tossing to ensure all slices are coated with vinegar mixture. Simmer for 1 minute. Remove from heat and set aside until flavors are infused, about 15 minutes. Season to taste with pepper.

2. In a bowl, combine cheese and paprika. Toss well to ensure paprika is evenly distributed.

3. Arrange 4 slices of the bread on a work surface. Divide cheese mixture evenly among them. Top with pickled onion and remaining bread. Butter outsides of bread.

4. If using panini press, place in preheated press, close top and cook until nicely browned and cheese is melted, about 4 minutes. If using a skillet, add sandwiches, in batches as necessary, and cook, turning once, until cheese is melted and bread is golden, about 4 minutes. Repeat with remaining sandwiches. Cut each sandwich into 4 triangles. Serve hot.

Variation

Substitute fontina cheese for the Cheddar and ¼ cup (60 mL) diced prosciutto for the paprika.

Uptown Ham and Cheese

Makes 36

Using prepared puff pastry with simple ingredients is a great idea because it's an easy way of taking something basic and turning it into a special occasion dish. Here we've encased chili sauce, sliced onions, ham and shredded cheese in puff pastry to make elegant melt-in-your mouth one-bite sandwiches.

Tips

Some packages of puff pastry are slightly smaller or larger than 1 lb (500 g) but any will be fine for this recipe. The pastry will just be slightly thinner or thicker.

The best way to slice the onion is to use a mandoline or the thin slicing blade of a food processor.

- **Preheat oven to 375°F (190°C)**
- **Baking sheet, lined with parchment paper**

1 lb	puff pastry, thawed (see Tips, left)	500 g
¾ cup	tomato-based chili sauce	175 mL
8 oz	thinly sliced smoked ham	250 g
1	sweet onion, such as Vidalia, very thinly sliced (see Tips, left)	1
8 oz	Swiss cheese, shredded	250 g
1	egg, beaten with 1 tbsp (15 mL) water	1

1. If necessary, cut puff pastry in half. On a lightly floured work surface, roll out each piece of puff pastry to a 12-inch (30 cm) square. Place one sheet on prepared baking sheet. Spread chili sauce evenly over pastry, leaving a ½-inch (1 cm) border all around.

2. Arrange ham, onion and cheese in layers over chili sauce. Brush border with some of the egg wash and place second sheet of pastry over top. Fold edges to seal and crimp with a fork, if desired. Brush top with egg wash.

3. Bake in preheated oven until golden, about 40 minutes. Transfer to a cutting board and let cool slightly. Cut into 36 squares. Serve warm.

The Ultimate Mozzarella en Carozza

Makes 16

This Italian classic is something along the lines of cheese-stuffed French toast. Some suggest it should be made with only the finest mozzarella di bufala but adding some roasted red pepper strips provides just enough of an enhancement to make sliced mozzarella from the supermarket just fine.

Tip

You want the mozzarella to cover the entire surface of the bread minus a ¼-inch (0.5 cm) border to allow for melting, so you may need more than 1 slice, depending on the size of your slices and the bread.

- **Preheat oven to 160°F (71°C)**

⅓ cup	thinly sliced roasted red bell pepper strips (see Tip, page 184) or store-bought	75 mL
8	slices white bread, crusts removed and white part squared off	8
4	slices (¼ inch/0.5 cm) mozzarella cheese (approx.) (see Tip, left)	4
2	eggs, beaten	2
¼ cup	half-and-half (10%) cream	60 mL
½ tsp	hot paprika	2 mL
2 tbsp	olive oil, divided	30 mL

1. Place 4 slices of the bread on a clean work surface. Place cheese slices on bread in a single layer to cover the surface of each slice (see Tip, left). Divide red pepper strips evenly among the slices. Top with remaining bread.

2. In a shallow dish large enough to accommodate the bread, beat eggs, cream and hot paprika. One at a time, dip sandwiches in egg solution, turning to cover both sides.

3. In a large skillet, heat 1 tbsp (15 mL) of the oil over medium heat. Add one or two of the sandwiches and cook, turning once, until cheese begins to melt and bread turns golden, about 5 minutes per batch. Transfer to preheated oven until remaining sandwiches are cooked. Repeat with remaining oil and sandwiches.

4. Cut sandwiches in half on the diagonal and then on the other diagonal to make 4 triangles per sandwich. If you want small servings, cut each triangle in half. Serve immediately.

Grilled Halloumi on Pita

Makes 24 pieces

These yummy pitas combine roasted red peppers and melted halloumi cheese with a pleasant hit of za'atar, a Middle Eastern spice mix. The results seem quite exotic but are very easy to achieve.

Tip

You can find ready-made za'atar in spice shops or specialty stores or you can easily make your own. *To make za'atar:* Simply toast ¼ cup (60 mL) sesame seeds in a dry skillet over medium heat, stirring constantly, until lightly browned. Transfer to a mortar. Add 1 tbsp (15 mL) dried thyme, 1 tsp (5 mL) dried sumac powder and 1 tsp (5 mL) coarse sea salt. Pound with a pestle until mixture is blended and seeds are coarsely ground. Use immediately or transfer to an airtight jar and store for up to 6 months.

- **Preheat oven to 400°F (200°C)**
- **Rimmed baking sheet, lined with parchment paper**

3	red bell peppers, roasted and thinly sliced (see Tip, page 184) or store-bought	3
3	6-inch (15 cm) pita pockets	3
3 tbsp	extra virgin olive oil (approx.)	45 mL
8 oz	halloumi cheese, thinly sliced (¼ inch/0.5 cm)	250 g
1 tbsp	za'atar (approx.) (see Tip, left)	15 mL
	Finely chopped Italian flat-leaf parsley leaves	
	Fine sea salt or fleur de sel, optional	

1. Using the tip of a sharp knife, make an opening in the top of 1 pita pocket and, using your hands, gently separate to create a cavern, leaving sides intact. Repeat with remaining pitas.

2. Place pitas on a clean work surface. Brush insides (tops and bottoms) liberally with olive oil. Arrange sliced halloumi on bottom and sprinkle evenly with za'atar. Add roasted peppers. Place filled pitas on prepared baking sheet, cover with foil and bake in preheated oven until cheese is nicely melted, about 20 minutes.

3. Remove from oven and preheat broiler. Place under broiler until tops are lightly browned. Remove from oven, brush with olive oil and sprinkle liberally with za'atar, parsley and sea salt, if using. Cut each pita into 8 wedges. Serve warm.

Chicken Sliders with Brie

Makes about 16 sliders

These are great cocktail party fare and easy to make, too. You can even use leftover chicken or make them from a prepared rotisserie chicken.

Tip

Slider buns are available at well-stocked supermarkets. Some (ideal for this recipe) are miniature hamburger buns, while others resemble small sliced pitas (which will work with this recipe, but produce a heavier result). Slider buns are also extremely inconsistent in terms of size. Readily available offerings range from 2 to 3 inches (5 to 7.5 cm), which changes the number of sliders you'll produce.

2 tbsp	mayonnaise	30 mL
2 tbsp	sun-dried tomato pesto	30 mL
1 tsp	Dijon mustard	5 mL
2 cups	diced ($\frac{1}{4}$ inch/0.5 cm) cooked chicken	500 mL
	Salt and freshly ground black pepper	
16	slider buns, split (approx.) (see Tip, left)	16
8 oz	Brie cheese, thinly sliced to fit buns	250 g
	Baby lettuce leaves, optional	
	Sliced tomato, optional	

1. In a bowl, combine mayonnaise, pesto and mustard. Mix well. Add chicken and toss to combine. Season to taste with salt and pepper.
2. Spread cut side of bottom halves of buns with equal portions of chicken mixture. Lay cheese slices across top halves. Place tops on a baking sheet and broil until cheese is just beginning to melt and run over the side of the bun, about 2 minutes. Garnish bottoms with lettuce and tomatoes, if desired. Place tops on bottoms and serve.

Salmon Sliders

Makes about 8 sliders

What could be better than warm salmon cakes topped with a dollop of tartar sauce? We think the addition of cute little slider buns and the ability to enjoy them while partying.

Tip

Slider buns are available at well-stocked supermarkets. Some (ideal for this recipe) are miniature hamburger buns, while others resemble small sliced pitas (which will work with this recipe, but produce a heavier result). Slider buns are also extremely inconsistent in terms of size. Readily available offerings range from 2 to 3 inches (5 to 7.5 cm), which changes the number of sliders you'll produce.

Easy Tartar Sauce

½ cup	mayonnaise	125 mL
2 tbsp	sweet green pickle relish	30 mL
1	can (7½ oz/213 g) salmon, drained	1
¼ cup	finely chopped red or green onion	60 mL
¼ cup	finely chopped red bell pepper	60 mL
1	egg, beaten	1
½ cup	fine dry bread crumbs, divided	125 mL
1 tsp	dried Italian seasoning	5 mL
	Salt and freshly ground black pepper	
2 tbsp	oil	30 mL
8	slider buns (approx.) (see Tip, left)	8

1. *Easy Tartar Sauce:* In a bowl, combine mayonnaise and relish. Cover and refrigerate.

2. In a bowl, combine salmon, onion, bell pepper, egg, ¼ cup (60 mL) of the bread crumbs, Italian seasoning, and salt and pepper to taste. Mix well. Form mixture into 8 patties, about ½ inch (1 cm) thick. Spread remaining bread crumbs on a plate. Dip each patty into crumbs, covering both sides. Discard any excess crumbs.

3. In a nonstick skillet, heat oil over medium heat. Add patties, in batches, and cook, turning once, until hot and golden, about 2 minutes per side.

4. Serve on warm buns slathered with Easy Tartar Sauce.

> **Variation**
>
> Substitute The Perfect Barbecue Coleslaw (page 550) or Roasted Red Pepper Coulis (page 543) for Easy Tartar Sauce.

Turkey Sliders with Chipotle Mayo

Makes about 12 sliders

Spicy chipotle mayo on miniature turkey burgers make a delicious combination.

Tips

Use bottled mayonnaise or make your own (page 538.)

For best flavor, toast and grind cumin yourself. *To toast cumin:* Place seeds in a dry skillet over medium heat and cook, stirring, until fragrant, about 3 minutes. Immediately transfer to a mortar or a spice grinder and grind.

Top these sliders with any combination of sliced tomatoes, sliced Spanish or red onion, lettuce or sliced avocado.

- **Preheat greased barbecue grill or broiler**

Chipotle Mayo

½ cup	mayonnaise (see Tips, left)	125 mL
1	chipotle pepper in adobo sauce, finely chopped	1
1 tsp	ground cumin seeds, toasted and ground (see Tips, left)	5 mL
1 lb	ground turkey	500 g
1	small onion, minced	1
½ cup	dry bread crumbs	125 mL
1 tbsp	barbecue sauce	15 mL
1	egg, beaten	1
1 tsp	ground cumin	5 mL
½ tsp	salt	2 mL
	Freshly ground black pepper	
	Toppings (see Tips, left)	
12	slider buns (approx.) (see Tip, page 266)	12

1. *Chipotle Mayo:* In a bowl, combine mayonnaise, chipotle pepper and cumin. Stir until blended. Cover and refrigerate for 30 minutes to allow flavors to blend.

2. In a bowl, combine turkey, onion, bread crumbs, barbecue sauce, egg, cumin, salt, and pepper to taste. Mix well. Shape into 12 patties, about ½ inch (1 cm) thick. Grill or place on a baking sheet and broil, turning once, until no longer pink inside, about 10 minutes.

3. Serve sliders on warm buns slathered with Chipotle Mayo and garnish as desired.

Variations

Chicken Sliders with Chipotle Mayo: Substitute ground chicken for the turkey.

Turkey Sliders with Guacamole: Substitute Guacamole (page 26) for the Chipotle Mayo.

Beef and Parmesan Sliders

Makes about 12 sliders

Sure you've had a hamburger, but you haven't had a hamburger like this before!

Tips

Although egg bread provides a wonderful texture, virtually any bread, even dry bread, will work for this recipe.

Slider buns are available at well-stocked supermarkets. Some (ideal for this recipe) are miniature hamburger buns, while others resemble small sliced pitas (which will work with this recipe, but produce a heavier result). Slider buns are also extremely inconsistent in terms of size. Readily available offerings range from 2 to 3 inches (5 to 7.5 cm), which changes the number of sliders you'll produce.

- **Preheat barbecue grill to medium-high**

2	slices egg bread (see Tips, left), crusts removed	2
1/4 cup	milk	60 mL
1 1/4 lbs	lean ground beef	625 g
1/4 cup	freshly grated Parmesan cheese	60 mL
1/4 cup	barbecue sauce	60 mL
1 tbsp	minced garlic	15 mL
1/2 tsp	salt	2 mL
1 tbsp	olive oil	15 mL
12	slider buns (approx.), cut in half (see Tips, left)	12
1 1/2 cups	packed The Perfect Barbecue Coleslaw (page 550)	375 mL

1. In a bowl, combine bread and milk, and, using your hands, crumble the bread into milk creating something resembling a bread purée. Add ground beef, Parmesan cheese, barbecue sauce, garlic and salt and mix just to combine. Shape into twelve 1/2-inch (1 cm) thick patties and place on a plate. Cover and refrigerate for 10 minutes to firm patties.

2. Drizzle olive oil over both sides of patties. Place on preheated barbecue and grill until bottom is browned, about 3 minutes. Flip over and grill until no longer pink inside, 3 to 4 minutes. Transfer to a clean plate and let rest for 5 minutes.

3. Place patties on bottoms of buns and top with coleslaw. Place on a serving platter and lean the tops of the buns on the side of burgers and serve.

Lamb and Red Onion Sliders

Makes about 12 sliders

Ground lamb has a wonderfully rich flavor that is complemented by the sweetness of red onion. It always a good idea to leave the garnishing to your guests and serve with a trio of condiments like Honey Mustard Dip (page 60), Roasted Tomato Dip (page 23) and Roasted Beet Salsa (page 74).

Tip

Although egg bread provides a wonderful texture, virtually any bread, even dry bread, will work for this recipe.

- **Preheat oven to 500°F (260°C)**
- **Large ovenproof skillet**

2	sliced egg bread (see Tip, left), crusts removed	2
¼ cup	milk	60 mL
1¼ lbs	ground lamb	625 g
1 tbsp	Dijon mustard	15 mL
1 tbsp	chopped fresh basil leaves	15 mL
1 tbsp	olive oil	15 mL
2 cups	thinly sliced red onions	500 mL
12	slider buns (approx.), cut in half (see Tips, page 268)	12

1. In a bowl, combine bread and milk and, using your hands, crumble the bread into milk, creating something resembling a bread purée. Add lamb, mustard and basil and mix just to combine. Shape into twelve ½-inch (1 cm) thick patties and place on a plate. Cover and refrigerate for 10 minutes to firm patties.

2. In a large ovenproof skillet, heat oil over medium heat. Cook patties until bottoms are browned, about 4 minutes. Remove patties from skillet. Spread onions over bottom of skillet. Return patties to the skillet, cooked side up, on top of the onions.

3. Transfer skillet to preheated oven and bake until firm to the touch and no longer pink inside, 5 to 7 minutes. Place patties and onions in buns. Serve immediately.

Avocado-Topped Squares

Makes 16 tea sandwiches

This wonderful canapé is perfect for lunch or afternoon tea and the best part — it can be made in a jiffy!

Tip

Dry pressed cottage cheese has a unique texture that can be dry to some people's taste. If you prefer or can't find it, cream cheese or even a creamy goat cheese would be a suitable substitute.

- **Preheat oven to 400°F (200°C)**

½ cup	dry pressed cottage cheese	125 mL
1 tsp	minced garlic	5 mL
¼ tsp	herbes de Provence	1 mL
Pinch	cayenne pepper	Pinch
4	slices challah (egg bread)	4
1	avocado, thinly sliced (about 16 slices)	1
1 tbsp	freshly squeezed lemon juice	15 mL

1. In a bowl, combine cottage cheese, garlic, herbes de Provence and cayenne. Mix well.

2. Cut crusts from breads slices. Evenly spread cheese mixture over each slice of bread. Cut each slice into four squares. Place on a baking sheet and bake in preheated oven until bread is crisp, 8 to 10 minutes.

3. In a bowl, combine avocado and lemon juice. Place one slice of avocado on top of each hot sandwich.

Avocado Party Sandwiches

Makes 10 sandwiches

For whatever reason, these ingredients create a magical sandwich. The ingredients are so simple and widely available that they are perfect for those pop-in guests — morning, noon or night. Why not try a lovely sweet dip with it, too, like Fig Yogurt Dip (page 67) — the combination is out of this world.

- **Preheat oven to 350°F (180°C)**
- **Baking sheet, lined with parchment paper**

1	loaf (about 10 by 4 inches/25 by 10 cm) semolina bread	1
1 tbsp	unsalted butter, softened	15 mL
1 lb	thinly sliced medium Cheddar cheese	500 g
1	avocado, thinly sliced	1
¼ cup	thinly sliced onion	60 mL
Pinch	each salt and freshly ground pepper	Pinch

1. Slice loaf in half horizontally through the center. Butter outside of each slice. Place, buttered side down, on prepared baking sheet. Lay cheese on top of one slice, then avocado and onion. Season with salt and pepper. Cover with second slice and bake until cheese is melted and bread is toasted, 10 to 12 minutes. Let cool and slice into 1-inch (2.5 cm) fingers.

Grilled Goat Cheese Baguettes

Makes about 32 pieces

This recipe is simplicity itself. Just split a baguette lengthwise, fill with fresh goat cheese spiked with herbs, grill and slice. This idea works well with other fillings, too. Try Homemade Herb Cheese (page 373) or Chile Cheese (page 380) for something a little different.

• **Preheat barbecue grill to high**

4 oz	soft goat cheese	125 g
2 tbsp	finely chopped Italian flat-leaf parsley leaves	30 mL
1 tbsp	finely chopped fresh rosemary	15 mL
1	baguette, cut in half lengthwise	1
	Freshly ground black pepper	
	Extra virgin olive oil	

1. In a bowl, combine goat cheese, parsley and rosemary. Mix well.
2. Spread cheese mixture evenly over cut side of bottom of baguette. Season to taste with pepper. Top with remaining bread and brush outside all over lightly with olive oil.
3. Grill, turning once, until exterior is light golden, about 2 minutes per side. Transfer to a cutting board and cut into slices about ¾ inch (2 cm) wide. Serve warm.

Warm Croissant, Brie and Caramelized Onion Sandwiches

Makes 6 pieces

A decadent buttery sweet delight of a sandwich that can take the place of any grilled cheese for lunch, dinner and especially late in the evening.

Tip

Many good-quality ingredients are available but in the absence of a freshly baked croissant from your local patisserie or bakery, good frozen options are usually available in larger supermarkets.

• **Preheat oven to 350°F (180°C)**

2	croissants	2
3 oz	Brie cheese, thinly sliced	90 g
¼ cup	Caramelized Onions (page 552)	60 mL
½ tsp	fresh thyme leaves	2 mL

1. Cut croissants in half horizontally. Place equal amounts of Brie cheese, caramelized onions and fresh thyme on bottom half of croissant, dividing equally. Top with remaining croissant and place on a baking sheet.
2. Bake in preheated oven until cheese is melted and surface of croissant is golden brown and crispy, about 10 minutes. Transfer to a cutting board and cut each croissant crosswise into thirds and serve.

Mini Grilled Cheese with Havarti, Fresh Basil and Tomato

Makes 8 sandwiches

Grilled cheese tends to bring out the child in us but the fresh basil brings a little sophistication to the party. The perfect lunch or late night appetizer, this mini grilled cheese will be a hit with the adults and kids too.

16	slices (½ inch/1 cm) baguette	16
4 oz	thinly sliced Havarti cheese	125 g
8	fresh basil leaves	8
8	cherry tomatoes, thinly sliced	8
1 tbsp	unsalted butter	15 mL

1. Place 8 slices of bread on a work surface. Top with cheese, basil and tomatoes, dividing equally. Cover with remaining bread, forming 8 mini sandwiches.

2. In a skillet, melt butter over medium heat. Cook sandwiches, turning once, until golden brown and cheese is melted, about 2 minutes per side. Serve immediately.

French-Style Grilled Cheese

Makes 4 pieces

This sandwich is a cross between a savory French toast and grilled cheese. This recipe could be easily doubled or tripled.

Tip

The sandwich will puff and be quite soufflé-like because of all the custard absorbed by the bread.

2	slices challah (egg bread)	2
2 oz	thinly sliced Cheddar cheese	60 g
4	plum (Roma) tomato slices	4
¼ cup	milk	60 mL
1	egg, beaten	1
¼ tsp	chipotle powder	1 mL
Pinch	each salt and freshly ground pepper	Pinch
1 tbsp	unsalted butter	15 mL

1. Place one slice of bread on a work surface. Evenly arrange cheese on top to cover entire surface then top with tomato slices, overlapping as necessary. Cover with second bread slice and set aside.

2. In a shallow dish, whisk together milk, egg, chipotle powder, salt and pepper. Add sandwich, turning often, until all egg mixture has been absorbed by the bread.

3. In a skillet, melt butter over medium heat. Cook sandwich, turning once, until golden brown and cheese is melted, about 3 minutes per side. Let cool for 5 minutes. Remove crust and cut into 4 quarters.

Seared Tuna on Brioche

Makes 10 sandwiches

This is one of those rare sandwiches that, like your favorite piece of clothing, goes with everything. You can serve this to your friends as an appetizer at a summer brunch, lunch or dinner party or even to guests at a black-tie event. Be sure to have napkins close by, as this one can get a little messy.

1 tsp	unsalted butter or duck fat	5 mL
6 oz	tuna	175 g
1 tbsp	toasted sesame seeds	15 mL
⅛ tsp	salt	0.5 mL
10	2-inch (5 cm) brioche buns or mini bagels, split	10
⅔ cup	Classic Coleslaw (page 419)	150 mL
1 tsp	thinly sliced green onions	5 mL

1. In a skillet, melt butter over medium-high heat. Coat tuna with sesame seeds and add to pan. Sear, turning once, for 15 to 20 seconds per side. Transfer to a plate and refrigerate until chilled and firm, about 1 hour. Cut into 10 thin slices and set aside.

2. Place bottom halves of the brioche buns on a work surface. Place one slice of tuna on each and top with coleslaw, dividing equally. Garnish with green onions and top with remaining bun. Secure with a toothpick.

Roast Turkey Pinwheel "Logs"

Makes 24 pinwheels

These pinwheel sandwiches are unique and quite elegant.

Tip

This recipe would be exceptional with smoked turkey, roast beef or even pastrami in place of the roasted turkey.

4	slices whole wheat bread, 10 by 4 inches (25 by 10 cm), crust removed	4
6 oz	thinly sliced deli-roasted turkey	175 g
4 tsp	Dijon mustard	20 mL
12	gherkins, sliced in half lengthwise	12

1. Place a sheet of plastic wrap on a work surface. Working with one bread slice at a time, set on top of plastic. Arrange turkey slices on top. Spread mustard in a strip across long side of bread closest to you and arrange 6 gherkin halves on top of mustard. Starting with long edge closest to you, tightly roll up bread and filling jelly-roll style, without squeezing too hard. Wrap tightly in plastic wrap. Repeat with remaining bread. Refrigerate for 30 minutes to 1 hour to firm.

2. Using a sharp knife (not serrated), trim off ends of rolls, then cut each crosswise into 6 equal slices.

Pine Nut Butter and Jelly Fingers

Makes 15 to 20 fingers

The child in all of us loves PB & J. A delightful warm offering for a brunch or lunch appetizer party or even consider it for your next tea party or card game — and oh yeah, kids will love them, too.

Tip

Since they don't make giant size panini presses, the best way to weigh down a large loaf is to cover with a second baking sheet and, here comes the secret...wrap three bricks in tin foil and place on top of the second baking sheet or use a heavy, cast-iron skillet to weigh it down.

Pine Nut Butter

1 cup	toasted pine nuts	250 mL
2 tbsp	hot water	30 mL
1 tbsp	freshly squeezed lemon juice	15 mL
1 tbsp	agave syrup	15 mL

Concord Grape Jelly

2 cups	concord grapes or other flavorful grapes	500 mL
1/2 cup	Cardamom-Scented Simple Syrup (page 528)	125 mL
1 tsp	water	5 mL
1/2 tsp	cornstarch	2 mL
1	Calabrese loaf, about 12 by 4 inches (30 by 10 cm)	1
1 tbsp	unsalted butter	15 mL

1. *Pine Nut Butter:* In a food processor fitted with metal blade, purée pine nuts, water, lemon juice and agave syrup until smooth. Set aside.

2. *Concord Grape Jelly:* In a saucepan over medium heat, bring grapes and syrup to a simmer. (Grapes will release a lot of water.) Reduce heat and boil gently until liquid is reduced by half, about 20 minutes. Remove from heat. Place a strainer over a bowl and using a spoon, press the solids through, removing the seeds.

3. In a small bowl, combine water and cornstarch, stirring well to prevent lumps. Add to grape mixture. Stir well to combine and let cool to room temperature.

4. Preheat oven to 400°F (200°C).

5. Cut bread in half horizontally. Place cut sides up on a work surface. Evenly spread pine nut butter on one side of bread and jelly on the other side. Close sandwich, brush all over outside with butter and wrap in foil. Place sandwich on a baking sheet. Place a weighted baking sheet (see Tip, left) on top of the wrapped sandwich. Bake in preheated oven until bread is crisp and pine nut butter is melted, about 15 minutes. Remove from foil, transfer to a cutting board and cut crosswise into 1-inch (2.5 cm) wide slices and serve immediately.

Smoked Salmon and Avocado Tea Sandwiches

Makes 8 tea sandwiches

Here, the lovely natural fat of avocado helps to cut the very rich smoked salmon.

Tip

The easiest way to slice an avocado is to cut it lengthwise around the pit. Twist the halves to expose two halves. Hit the pit with the heel of a knife and twist to remove. Slice avocado and peel off skin and use avocado as desired.

4	slices challah (egg bread)	4
4 oz	thinly sliced smoked salmon (about 8 slices)	125 g
1	avocado, thinly sliced (see Tip, left)	1
2 tbsp	crème fraîche or sour cream	30 mL
Pinch	salt	Pinch
Pinch	freshly ground black pepper	Pinch

1. Place bread slices on a work surface and remove crusts. Arrange salmon and avocado on top of 2 slices, dividing equally. Spread crème fraîche evenly over the other slices. Season with salt and pepper. Press slices together and cut into 4 squares and serve.

Apple and Goat Cheese "Sandwiches"

Makes 10 sandwiches

A creative way to serve the most basic of appetizers — apple and cheese.

Tip

Many creamy goat cheeses are sold in long tubes, which makes it easy to slice. Keep very cold before slicing but bring to room temperature before using.

2	Granny Smith or other tart apples	2
1 tbsp	freshly squeezed lemon juice	15 mL
10	½-inch (1 cm) thick goat cheese rounds, at room temperature (see Tip, left)	10
1 tsp	freshly ground black pepper	5 mL
10	fresh basil leaves	10

1. Using a very sharp knife and stem facing up, slice apples into 5 slices from each of two sides of the core, yielding 20 round slices. In a bowl, gently toss apples with lemon juice to coat and set aside.

2. Place half of the apple slices on a work surface and place a round of goat cheese in the middle of each. Garnish with pepper and one basil leaf. Cover with another slice of apple and gently press together. Repeat until all ingredients are used and serve immediately.

Mini Falafel Sandwiches

Makes 36 sandwiches

These crispy Middle Eastern balls are just wonderful for a lunch or dinner appetizer party. Although we have created the perfect sandwich, these balls are just lovely all on their own too or dipped into Easy Hummus (page 52) or any of the hummus recipes.

Tip

Mini pita bread, about 3 inches (7.5 cm) in diameter, can be found in select stores. Regular size pita can work here too by slicing into quarters for pie-like shapes.

- **Candy/deep-fry thermometer**

2½ cups	cooked drained chickpeas	625 mL
¾ cup	coarsely chopped fresh cilantro leaves	175 mL
3	cloves garlic	3
1 tsp	salt	5 mL
¾ tsp	ground cumin (see Tips, page 267)	3 mL
½ tsp	hot pepper sauce	2 mL
1 cup	all-purpose flour, divided	250 mL
6 cups	vegetable oil	1.5 L
¾ cup	Easy Hummus (page 52) or store-bought	175 mL
36	3-inch (7.5 cm) pita bread, tops opened to form pocket, cut in half (see Tip, left)	36
½ cup	shredded carrot	125 mL
½ cup	diced cucumber	125 mL

1. In a food processor fitted with metal blade, pulse chickpeas, cilantro, garlic, salt, cumin and hot pepper sauce until smooth, 2 to 3 minutes, scraping down sides of the bowl as necessary. Transfer to a bowl and fold in about 2½ tbsp (37 mL) of flour. Cover and refrigerate for 15 minutes, until chilled, or for up to 1 hour.

2. When you're ready to cook, place oil in a deep saucepan or Dutch oven and heat over medium heat until temperature reaches 350°F (180°C). (You can also use a deep fryer; follow the manufacturer's instructions.) Form chickpea mixture into about 36 balls, about 2 tsp (10 mL) each and lightly dredge in remaining flour. Add falafels to hot oil in batches and fry until balls rise to the surface and are golden brown, about 4 minutes. Remove from oil and drain on paper towels.

3. Add a dollop of hummus on the inside of each pita bread half. Place 1 falafel ball inside. Garnish sandwich with equal amounts of carrots and cucumber and serve immediately.

Fish and Seafood

Because it's quick cooking or in some cases doesn't need to be cooked at all, fish and seafood can offer fast yet sophisticated solutions for appetizers. Many excellent fish products, such as smoked salmon or trout, can be transformed into appetizers, virtually instantaneously — just add sliced baguette and condiments of your choice. Because they tend to be a bit costly, appetizers made from fish and seafood have a celebratory air. But they are also extremely nutritious, often providing valuable and hard-to-get nutrients such as omega-3 fats.

Potted Tuna 278
Tuna Poke 278
Spicy Tuna-Stuffed Eggs 279
Chile-Spiked Tuna Tartare 280
Lemon and Soy-Scented Tuna Slices 280
Spicy Soy–Marinated Tuna 281
Tuna Tartare with Toasted Pine Nuts 281
Poppy Seed–Crusted Yellowfin Tuna 282
Classic Ceviche 283
Mango-Spiked Salmon Ceviche 283
Sliced Scallop "Ceviche" 284
Crab Louis 284
Classic Salmon Tartare 285
Smoked Salmon and Avocado Tartare 285
Asian-Inspired Salmon Tartare 286
Candied Salmon 286
Vodka-Spiked Gravlax with
    Honey Mustard Sauce 287
Homemade Spiced Gravlax with
    Crostini and Capers 288
Potted Salmon 289
Cucumber with Smoked Salmon 290
Martini-Marinated Salmon 290
Honey Mustard-Glazed Salmon with Avocado . . . 291
Mini Salmon en Croûte 292
Classic Salmon Nigiri Sushi 293
Smoked Salmon and Grits Cakes 294
Pacific Salmon Cakes 295
Fresh Salmon Nuggets 296
Smoked Salmon Spread 296
Smoked Salmon Mousse 297
Dill-Spiked Smoked Trout Spread 297
Shrimp in Piri-Piri Butter 298

Spicy Sizzling Shrimp 299
Peppery Shrimp 300
Coconut Shrimp with Cilantro-Lime
    Dipping Sauce 301
Shrimp Tempura 302
Grilled Shrimp with Aïoli 303
Potted Shrimp 304
Twisted Butterfly Shrimp 304
Sushi Rice–Stuffed Shrimp 305
Old-South Shrimp Paste 306
Baked Crab Dip 306
Classic Crab Cakes 307
Crab and Sweet Potato Canapé 308
Sautéed Scallops with Scallion-Spiked
    Mashed Potatoes 309
Pan-Seared Scallops with Spicy Mango Purée . . . 310
Fried Calamari 311
Spicy Seared Calamari 312
Marinated Calamari Antipasti 312
Broiled Oysters with Seasoned Bread Crumbs . . . 313
Baltimore Oysters 314
Oyster and Artichoke Gratin 315
Butter-Crusted Oysters 316
Oysters on the Half Shell with Avocado
    Mignonette 316
Sushi Pizza 317
Sweet Scallop Appetizer 318
Butter-Crusted Black Cod 319
Mussels on the Half Shell 319
Roasted Fingerling Potatoes with Caviar
    and Crème Fraîche 320
Lobster Salad Mille Feuille 321
Panko-Crusted "Fish Sticks" 322

Potted Tuna

Makes about ¾ cup (175 mL)

Here's a take on the classic English technique of "potting," in which ingredients are blended with butter and packed into crockery to be served like pâté. Serve simply on sliced baguette or crostini (pages 219 and 220).

Tip

Tuna packed in olive oil, which is usually Italian or Spanish in origin, is far more flavorful than domestic versions.

¼ cup	unsalted butter, softened	60 mL
2 tsp	finely grated lemon zest	10 mL
3 tbsp	freshly squeezed lemon juice	45 mL
1 tbsp	packed fresh oregano leaves	15 mL
1	clove garlic, quartered	1
½	long red chile pepper, coarsely chopped	½
½ tsp	cracked black peppercorns	2 mL
1	can (6 oz/175 g approx.) tuna, packed in olive oil, drained (see Tip, left)	1

1. In a food processor fitted with metal blade, process butter, lemon zest and juice, oregano, garlic, chile pepper and pepper until smooth, about 20 seconds, stopping and scraping down sides of the bowl as necessary. Add tuna and pulse to just blend.

2. Transfer to a serving bowl. Cover and refrigerate to chill thoroughly for at least 2 hours or up to 2 days.

Tuna Poke

Makes about 1 cup (250 mL)

Poke (pronounced po-kay) is traditionally raw seafood but has evolved to include anything from slightly cooked fish to fried pieces of octopus.

Tip

The vinegar in this recipe will begin to cook the fish as soon as the ingredients are introduced. Serve immediately and do not refrigerate. To prepare for a dinner party, leave the vinaigrette separate from the fish mixture and combine before serving.

Vinaigrette

1 tbsp	soy sauce	15 mL
2 tsp	packed brown sugar	10 mL
½ tsp	rice vinegar (see Tips, page 305)	2 mL
¼ tsp	thinly sliced red chile pepper	1 mL
1 cup	cubed (1 inch/2.5 cm) yellowfin tuna	250 mL
1 tbsp	toasted macadamia nuts, chopped	15 mL
1 tbsp	thinly sliced green onions, green parts	15 mL
1 tbsp	finely chopped toasted nori	15 mL
1 tsp	minced shallots	5 mL

1. *Vinaigrette:* In a bowl, combine soy sauce, sugar, vinegar and chile, stirring until sugar is dissolved. Cover and refrigerate for up to 3 days.

2. In a separate bowl, combine tuna, nuts, onions, nori and shallots. Gently fold in vinaigrette until coated. Serve with Green Plantain Chips (page 211).

Spicy Tuna-Stuffed Eggs

Makes 12

This variation on devilled eggs is one you're likely to see on tapas menus in Spain. The hot smoked paprika is a Spanish touch and adds a distinguishing flavor element.

Tips

Smoked paprika has a very intense flavor. Start with the smaller quantity, then if you feel you want more, increase to ½ tsp (2 mL).

Tuna packed in olive oil, which is usually Italian or Spanish in origin, is far more flavorful than domestic versions. Often sold in a jar.

6	eggs	6
Filling		
3 tbsp	mayonnaise	45 mL
1 tbsp	Dijon mustard	15 mL
¼ to ½ tsp	hot smoked paprika (see Tips, left)	1 to 2 mL
¼ tsp	salt	1 mL
	Freshly ground black pepper	
½ cup	canned tuna, preferably packed in olive oil, finely chopped (see Tips, left)	125 mL
3	green onions, white part with a bit of green, finely chopped	3
2 tsp	minced drained capers	10 mL
	Hot pepper sauce, optional	
	Sweet paprika	

1. In a saucepan, combine eggs and cold water liberally to cover. Bring to a boil over high heat. Cover, remove from element and let stand for 12 minutes. Drain well. Transfer to a bowl of ice water and let stand for 5 minutes. Carefully peel the eggs (see Tips, page 447) and rinse under cold running water.

2. *Filling:* Cut eggs in half lengthwise and carefully scoop out the yolks, leaving the whites intact. In a bowl, combine egg yolks, mayonnaise, mustard, paprika to taste, salt, and pepper to taste. Mix well. Add tuna, green onions and capers and mix well. Season to taste with hot pepper sauce, if using.

3. Spoon filling into whites. Dust lightly with sweet paprika. Cover and refrigerate until ready to serve.

Chile-Spiked Tuna Tartare

Makes about 1 cup (250 mL)

Rich and luscious, all this tuna needs is a simple cracker for a base. If you're looking for a more stylish presentation, serve it alone on Chinese-style porcelain spoons.

Tip

If you don't have a mild chile pepper, use $1/4$ to $1/2$ of a jalapeño pepper, to suit your taste.

2 tbsp	finely diced shallot (about 1 large)	30 mL
1 tbsp	finely snipped chives	15 mL
1 tbsp	mayonnaise	15 mL
1 tbsp	freshly squeezed lemon juice	15 mL
1 tbsp	extra virgin olive oil	15 mL
1	mild chile pepper, such as serrano, finely minced (see Tip, left)	1
2 tsp	minced drained capers	10 mL
8 oz	ahi tuna fillet, cut into $1/4$-inch (0.5 cm) dice (see Tip, page 281)	250 g
	Salt and freshly ground black pepper	

1. In a bowl, combine shallot, chives, mayonnaise, lemon juice, olive oil, chile pepper and capers. Mix well. Add tuna and toss to coat. Season to taste with salt and pepper. Cover and refrigerate for 30 minutes to allow flavors to meld.

Lemon and Soy-Scented Tuna Slices

Makes 10 slices

Sushi-grade tuna is like the Kobe beef of the sea. Enjoy these slices atop Grilled Herbed Crostini (page 220) or Savory Baked Crostini (page 220).

1 tsp	unsalted butter or duck fat	5 mL
6 oz	yellowfin tuna	175 g
1	lemon, cut into 10 slices	1
1 tsp	soy sauce	5 mL
1 tsp	minced green onions	5 mL
$1/2$ tsp	toasted sesame seeds	2 mL
$1/4$ tsp	toasted sesame oil	1 mL

1. In a skillet, melt butter over medium-high heat. Sear tuna on all sides for 15 to 20 seconds per side. Remove from heat and slice into 10 thin slices. Set aside.

2. Arrange lemon slices on an oval platter, overlapping slightly and following the curve of the platter. Place tuna slices on top of lemon and sprinkle with soy sauce, green onions, sesame seeds and oil. Serve immediately.

Spicy Soy–Marinated Tuna

Makes 16 servings

Serve this marinated tuna on porcelain spoons for an appetizer that is extremely elegant, yet simplicity itself. Plain rice crackers also work for a simple presentation.

Tip

If you're not cooking tuna, it is particularly important to use the highest quality you can buy, which is often called sushi-grade or sashimi-grade. Be sure to purchase from a reputable purveyor.

- **16 Chinese-style porcelain spoons, optional**

¼ cup	soy sauce	60 mL
3 tbsp	freshly squeezed orange juice	45 mL
2 tbsp	freshly squeezed lime juice	30 mL
1 tsp	sesame oil	5 mL
½ tsp	puréed garlic	2 mL
½ tsp	puréed gingerroot	2 mL
½ tsp	hot Asian chile sauce, such as sambal oelek	2 mL
1 lb	ahi tuna fillet, cut into ½-inch (1 cm) squares (see Tip, left)	500 g

1. In a bowl, combine soy sauce, orange juice, lime juice, sesame oil, garlic, ginger and chile sauce. Stir well. Add tuna and gently toss until well coated. Cover and refrigerate for 30 minutes.

2. When you're ready to serve, spoon tuna onto porcelain spoons, if using, or transfer to a serving bowl. Serve immediately.

Tuna Tartare with Toasted Pine Nuts

Makes about 2 cups (500 mL)

A very classic restaurant-style appetizer. This is perfect served with warm Classic Flatbread (page 218).

Tip

The pine nuts add a textural contrast to the raw fish.

1 lb	ahi tuna fillet, cut into ¼-inch (0.5 cm) dice (about 2 cups/500 mL) (see Tip, above)	500 g
1 tbsp	diced tomato	15 mL
1 tbsp	diced red onion	15 mL
1 tbsp	Dijon mustard	15 mL
1 tbsp	extra virgin olive oil	15 mL
2 tsp	toasted pine nuts, coarsely chopped	10 mL
1 tsp	finely grated lemon zest	5 mL
¾ tsp	finely chopped fresh basil	3 mL
½ tsp	salt	2 mL

1. In a large bowl, gently combine tuna, tomato, red onion, mustard, olive oil, pine nuts, lemon zest, basil and salt.

Poppy Seed–Crusted Yellowfin Tuna

Makes 25 hors d'oeuvres

Poppy seeds create a very crisp texture around the tuna.

Tip

We recommend using pure sea salt rather than refined table salt. It has a clean, crisp taste and enhanced mineral content, unlike table salt, which has a bitter acrid taste and contains unpleasant additives to prevent caking.

- **Preheat oven to 350°F (180°C)**
- **Ovenproof skillet**

¼ cup	poppy seeds	60 mL
1 tsp	salt	5 mL
1 tsp	freshly ground black pepper	5 mL
1 lb	yellowfin tuna loin	500 g
1 tbsp	olive oil	15 mL
2	thyme sprigs	2
1 cup	whole shallots	250 mL
1 tsp	minced garlic	5 mL
¼ cup	white wine	60 mL

1. In a bowl, combine poppy seeds, salt and pepper and press into tuna loin to thoroughly coat.

2. In an ovenproof skillet, heat oil over medium-high heat. Add thyme and heat until no longer bubbling around thyme. Remove thyme and discard, leaving as much oil in pan as possible. Add tuna and sear quickly, turning, for about 30 seconds per side (the tuna will be crisp on the outside but should remain raw inside). Transfer tuna to a cutting board and, using a very sharp knife, cut into 25 equal slices and set aside.

3. Add shallots and garlic to pan and sauté for 10 seconds just to evenly coat shallots. Add wine. Transfer skillet to preheated oven and bake until shallots are soft, 10 to 12 minutes. Transfer shallots to a cutting board and finely chop. Place each tuna slice flat on a platter and garnish with chopped shallots. Serve immediately.

Classic Ceviche

Makes about 5 cups (1.25 L) • Enough for about 20 people

This version of ceviche, made from fish rather than seafood, is easy to make. The fish "cooks" in the lime juice in about the time it takes you to prepare the other ingredients. This is a colorful dish and makes a very pretty presentation served in a clear glass or crystal bowl. Serve it on porcelain spoons or, as they often do in Mexico, where it originates, with tostadas or tortilla chips.

1 lb	skinless fish fillets, cubed (1/2 inch/1 cm)	500 g
1 cup	freshly squeezed lime juice	250 mL
2	tomatoes, peeled, seeded and diced	2
2 tbsp	extra virgin olive oil	30 mL
2	jalapeño peppers, seeded and diced	2
1	small red onion, quartered vertically and sliced paper thin	1
1	avocado, diced	1
1/4 cup	finely chopped fresh cilantro leaves	60 mL
1 tsp	salt	5 mL

1. In a serving bowl, combine fish and lime juice. Cover and refrigerate until opaque, about 1 hour.
2. Add tomatoes, olive oil, jalapeños, red onion, avocado, cilantro and salt. Toss well. Serve cold.

Mango-Spiked Salmon Ceviche

Makes about 3 cups (750 mL)

Because it is made from a cold water fish, this is not a traditional ceviche but it is delicious nonetheless. Serve it on tostadas, tortilla chips, plain crackers or even crisp lettuce leaves such as hearts of romaine. If you're offering larger servings, think about spooning it into chilled martini glasses and passing forks or small spoons.

8 oz	skinless salmon fillet, cut into 1/4-inch (0.5 cm) dice	250 g
1/4 cup	freshly squeezed lime juice (approx.)	60 mL
1 cup	diced mango (1 small)	250 mL
1 cup	diced avocado	250 mL
2	green onions, white part with a bit of green, thinly sliced	2
1	jalapeño pepper, seeded and diced	1
2 tbsp	minced fresh cilantro leaves	30 mL
1 tbsp	extra virgin olive oil	15 mL
	Salt and freshly ground black pepper	

1. In a serving bowl, combine salmon and lime juice. Cover and refrigerate until opaque, about 15 minutes.
2. Add mango, avocado, onions, jalapeño, cilantro and oil. Season with salt and pepper. Toss well. Serve cold.

Sliced Scallop "Ceviche"

Makes 12 hors d'oeuvres

This recipe really takes ceviche to another level. A quick marinate in lime juice begins the cooking process but once placed under the broiler the sugar takes over and quickly caramelizes, adding a sweet accent. Garnish with peppery chives and toasted sesame seeds to complete this sophisticated yet simple appetizer.

3	large dry scallops, each about 2 oz (60 g)	3
2 tbsp	freshly squeezed lime juice	30 mL
1/2 tsp	brown sugar	2 mL
1/2 tsp	soy sauce	2 mL
1/4 tsp	toasted sesame oil	1 mL
1 tsp	diced fresh chives	5 mL
1/2 tsp	toasted sesame seeds	2 mL

1. With a sharp knife, slice each scallop into 4 rounds and transfer to a bowl. Add lime juice, brown sugar, soy sauce and sesame oil and marinate for 15 minutes. Remove scallops from marinade. Place scallops in a ovenproof skillet.

2. Preheat broiler and broil scallops until lightly caramelized, about 2 minutes. Garnish with chives and sesame seeds. Serve immediately.

Crab Louis

Makes about 1 1/3 cups (325 mL)

Louis sauce is basically a mixture of mayonnaise, chili sauce and other seasonings. Most often used to make Crab Louis, it is also delicious served over cold cooked shrimp or lobster. Crab Louis is delicious as a spread served with thin slices of cucumber, spears of Belgian endive, crackers or thinly sliced baguette. It also makes a spectacular salad served over a bed of lettuce greens and garnished with hard-cooked eggs.

Louis Sauce

3/4 cup	mayonnaise	175 mL
1/4 cup	tomato-based chili sauce	60 mL
2 tbsp	freshly squeezed lemon juice	30 mL
2 tbsp	finely diced green bell pepper	30 mL
1 tbsp	finely chopped red or green onion	15 mL
1 tbsp	finely chopped parsley	15 mL
1/4 tsp	Worcestershire sauce	1 mL
	Finely minced red chile pepper, optional	
2 cups	drained cooked crabmeat	500 mL
	Freshly ground black pepper	

1. *Louis Sauce:* In a bowl, combine mayonnaise, chili, lemon juice, pepper, onion, parsley, Worcestershire sauce, and chile to taste, if using. Mix well.

2. Add crab and toss to combine. Season to taste with pepper.

Classic Salmon Tartare

Makes about 1¼ cups (300 mL)

Rich and delicious, this simple treatment for salmon is hard to beat. Serve on porcelain spoons, dark rye or pumpernickel rounds or cucumber slices. Easy Potato Crisps (page 214) or even Homemade Potato Chips (page 215) also make great companions.

8 oz	skinless salmon fillet, cut into ¼-inch (0.5 cm) dice	250 g
2 tbsp	freshly squeezed lemon juice	30 mL
1	shallot, minced	1
1 tbsp	minced drained capers	15 mL
1 tbsp	extra virgin olive oil	15 mL
2 tsp	finely chopped dill fronds	10 mL
	Salt and freshly ground black pepper	

1. In a bowl, combine salmon, lemon juice, shallot, capers, olive oil, dill, and salt and pepper to taste. Cover and refrigerate for 30 minutes or up to 8 hours.

Smoked Salmon and Avocado Tartare

Makes about 1½ cups (375 mL)

Here's a dish that makes entertaining easy. Serve this on porcelain Chinese-style soup spoons or spoon into a chilled glass serving bowl and surround with thinly sliced rye bread or pumpernickel rounds.

Tip

Be sure to cut the salmon and avocado into small pieces. Otherwise the tartare will be difficult to eat.

3 tbsp	freshly squeezed lime juice	45 mL
2 tsp	soy sauce	10 mL
2 tsp	sesame oil	10 mL
½ tsp	hot Asian chile sauce, such as sambal oelek or Sriracha	2 mL
1 cup	finely diced (about ¼ inch/0.5 cm) avocado (about 2 small) (see Tip, left)	250 mL
3 oz	smoked salmon, finely chopped	90 g
	Salt and freshly ground black pepper	
	Finely snipped chives	

1. In a bowl, combine lime juice, soy sauce, sesame oil and chile sauce. Mix well. Add avocado and smoked salmon and toss well. Season to taste with salt and pepper. Garnish with chives to taste. Serve immediately.

Asian-Inspired Salmon Tartare

Makes about 1¼ cups (300 mL)

Tartare is a very simple yet refined preparation for very fresh fish. Here salmon is prepared with wonderful Asian flair. Serve with Green Plantain Chips (page 211).

Tip

Pickled ginger is available in Asian markets and in the Asian section of larger supermarkets. It ranges in color from white to yellow and pink.

8 oz	skinless salmon fillet, cut into ¼-inch (0.5 cm) dice	250 g
2 tbsp	Wasabi Aïoli (page 537)	30 mL
1 tbsp	toasted sesame seeds	15 mL
1 tbsp	coarsely chopped cilantro, stems removed	15 mL
1 tbsp	soy sauce	15 mL
1 tsp	toasted sesame oil	5 mL
1 tsp	sweet Asian chili sauce	5 mL
1 tsp	finely chopped pickled ginger	5 mL
1 tsp	finely chopped green onion	5 mL

1. In a bowl, gently combine salmon, aïoli, sesame seeds, cilantro, soy sauce, sesame oil, chili sauce, ginger and green onion. Serve immediately or cover and refrigerate for 30 minutes or for up to 8 hours.

Candied Salmon

Makes 5 servings

Why not throw an Asian-inspired appetizer party and serve this with a selection of Classic Tuna Sushi (page 153), Sushi Pizza (page 317) or Classic Salmon Nigiri Sushi (page 293).

- **Preheat oven to 475°F (240°C)**

5	pieces skin-on salmon belly, each 3 oz (90 g) (see Tips, page 293)	5
1 tbsp	each pure maple syrup and brown sugar	15 mL
1 tbsp	soy sauce	15 mL
1 tbsp	coarsely chopped green onions	15 mL
1 tsp	each grated lemon zest and juice	5 mL
1 tsp	minced garlic	5 mL
1 tbsp	unsalted butter	15 mL

1. In a bowl, combine salmon, maple syrup, brown sugar, soy sauce, green onions, lemon zest and juice and garlic. Cover and marinate at room temperature for 20 minutes or in the refrigerator for up to 1 hour.

2. In medium ovenproof skillet, melt butter over high heat. Sear salmon flesh side down for 1 minute. Transfer skillet to preheated oven and bake until flesh is caramelized, 3 to 4 minutes. Serve immediately on a small plate.

Vodka-Spiked Gravlax with Honey Mustard Sauce

Makes about 2 lbs (1 kg)

Gravlax is a delicious treat but it is usually quite pricey. It's very easy to make so why not make your own at a fraction of the price? Gravlax is best served simply on dark rye bread or pumpernickel rounds, preferably topped with a dollop of Honey Mustard Sauce.

Tip

Cut a piece of plastic wrap large enough to fit completely around the salmon, encasing it in a tight seamless envelope.

- **Baking dish, lined with a large piece of plastic wrap**

2 tbsp	pure maple syrup	30 mL
2 tbsp	vodka	30 mL
2	large salmon fillets, skin on, bones removed (each about 1 lb/500 g) (see Tip, page 288)	2
2 tbsp	granulated sugar	30 mL
2 tbsp	coarse sea salt	30 mL
1 tbsp	coarsely ground black peppercorns	15 mL

Honey Mustard Sauce

1/4 cup	Dijon mustard	60 mL
1/4 cup	fresh dill fronds	60 mL
2 tbsp	each liquid honey and pure maple syrup	30 mL
1 tbsp	white wine vinegar	15 mL
1/4 cup	olive oil	60 mL

1. In a bowl, mix together maple syrup and vodka. Brush both sides of 1 piece of salmon liberally with half the mixture and place skin side down in prepared dish.

2. In a separate bowl, combine sugar, salt and pepper. Spread half evenly over top of fillet in dish.

3. Brush remaining fillet liberally on both sides with vodka mixture. Place on top of other fillet, skin side up and sprinkle with remaining salt mixture. Fold up ends of plastic and fold plastic over top to make a tight waterproof envelope. Refrigerate for 36 to 48 hours, turning every 12 hours.

4. *Honey Mustard Sauce:* In a food processor fitted with metal blade, pulse mustard, dill, honey, maple syrup and vinegar until blended and dill is chopped. With motor running, gradually add olive oil through the feed tube until mixture is emulsified. Cover and refrigerate until ready to use. Stir well before serving.

5. When you're ready to serve, scrape off spices and wipe salmon dry with a paper towel. Using a very sharp knife, remove skin. Slice very thinly and serve with sauce.

Homemade Spiced Gravlax with Crostini and Capers

Makes about 12 servings

This very simple, elegant appetizer can be made ahead, sliced and frozen, and ready for unexpected guests.

Tip

Pin bones are long bones that run down the middle of the salmon fillet. We suggest removing the bones before marinating to avoid having to blemish the gorgeous gravlax after the fact. To identify the bones run your fingers down the middle of the fillet against the grain and, once found remove using food safe needle nose pliers or a pin bone remover (tweezers designed for the removal of pin bones) grab and pull gently to remove.

- **Baking sheet, lined with plastic wrap**

¼ cup	granulated sugar	60 mL
2 tbsp	salt	30 mL
1 tbsp	grated lemon zest	15 mL
2 tbsp	freshly squeezed lemon juice	30 mL
½ tsp	whole coriander seeds	2 mL
¼ tsp	freshly ground black pepper	1 mL
8 oz	salmon fillet, skin on, bones removed (see Tip, left)	250 g
12	crostini (pages 219 and 220)	12
1 tbsp	drained capers	15 mL

1. In a bowl, combine sugar, salt, lemon zest and juice, coriander seeds and pepper. Rub half the spice mixture all over salmon fillet. Spread remaining half of spice mixture over bottom of prepared baking sheet. Place salmon flesh-side up on top. Wrap salmon in plastic wrap and refrigerate for 36 to 48 hours, turning every 12 hours.

2. Remove salmon from plastic and discard spices and any accumulated liquid. Rinse salmon under cold water to remove any excess spices and pat dry thoroughly with paper towel. Using a sharp knife, remove skin. Cut salmon across the grain into 12 equal slices.

3. Place a slice of gravlax on top of crostini, folding as necessary, and garnish with capers. Serve immediately.

Feta-Spiked Edamame Dip (page 49) and
Roasted Pepper and Sweet Potato Dip (page 25)

Champagne and Raspberry Dip (page 68)

Pepper Confetti Salsa (page 84) and
Parsnip Chips (Variations, page 213)

Watermelon Cooler (page 105) and
Thai Coconut Shooter (page 124)

Prosciutto-Wrapped Caramelized Cantaloupe (page 130)
and Walnut-Laced Gorgonzola and Leek Rolls (page 147)

Vegetarian Vietnamese Fresh Rolls (page 138)

Mini Smoked Salmon and Sour Cream Puff Pastry Tartlets (page 166)
and Mini Potato Galettes with Caviar and Crème Fraîche(page 176)

Shrimp Samosas (page 194) and
Suneeta's Cilantro Mint Chutney (page 93)

Goat Cheese and Sun-Dried Tomato Crostini (page 224)

Grilled Vegetable Bruschetta (page 235) and
Bacon-Studded Cheese and Onion Tart (page 245)

Mini Falafel Sandwiches (page 276)

Mango-Spiked Salmon Ceviche (page 283)

Twisted Butterfly Shrimp (page 304)
with Cocktail Sauce (page 547)

Pancetta-Wrapped Scallops (page 337)

Coconut-Crusted Chicken Satays (page 343)
and Pineapple Mango Salsa (page 87)

Potato Tortilla with Peppers (page 365)

Walnut-Dusted Cheese Balls (page 372)

Strawberry-Topped Brie (page 390)

Zucchini Fritters (page 418) and Fresh Corn Cakes (page 449)

Smoked Chicken–Stuffed Yellow Pepper (page 479)

Sliced Steak with Horseradish and Roquefort Cheese (page 482)

Oh-So-Retro Swedish Meatballs (page 503)

Quick Chocolate Mousse (page 515) and
Homemade Marshmallows (page 529)

Raspberry Puff Pastry Fingers (page 531)
and Blended Iced Coffee Shooter (page 534)

Potted Salmon

Makes about 1 cup (250 mL)

This combination of poached and smoked salmon bound together by clarified butter and lightly seasoned is elegant and very tasty. It's also a blessing to the busy cook because it can be made ahead of time. Serve simply with sliced baguette, dark rye bread, crostini (pages 219 and 220) toast points or crackers.

Tips

You'll need ½ cup (125 mL) butter to make this amount of clarified butter. *To make clarified butter:* Place butter in a small saucepan and melt over low heat until milk solids accumulate on the bottom of the pan and the pure butterfat has risen to the top. Carefully pour off clear butterfat and discard remaining water and milk solids.

Don't overprocess once you add the salmon. You want it to retain a bit of its texture.

Court Bouillon

1	onion, chopped	1
2	stalks celery, chopped	2
4	parsley sprigs	4
½ cup	white wine or lemon juice	125 mL
8	peppercorns	8
8	whole coriander seeds	8
1	bay leaf	1
	Salt	
8 oz	piece salmon fillet, skin on	250 g
⅓ cup	clarified unsalted butter, divided (see Tips, left)	75 mL
½	red onion, quartered	½
½	long red chile pepper, quartered	½
1 tsp	finely grated lemon zest	5 mL
4 oz	thinly sliced smoked salmon	125 g
2 tbsp	freshly squeezed lemon juice	30 mL
⅛ tsp	freshly ground white pepper	0.5 mL

1. *Court Bouillon:* In a large saucepan, combine 6 cups (1.5 L) water, onion, celery, parsley, wine, peppercorns, coriander, bay leaf and ½ tsp (2 mL) salt. Bring to a boil over medium-high heat. Reduce heat and simmer for 30 minutes. Remove from heat.

2. Add salmon and cover. Set aside for 20 minutes until salmon is cooked through. Lift out salmon and let cool. Discard liquid and solids. When salmon is cool enough to handle, peel off skin and cut into quarters.

3. In a food processor fitted with metal blade, combine red onion, chile pepper and lemon zest. Pulse to chop about 10 times, stopping and scraping down sides of the bowl as necessary. Add smoked salmon, lemon juice, ¼ cup (60 mL) of the clarified butter, white pepper and reserved poached salmon. Pulse until chopped and blended, about 10 times. Season to taste with salt.

4. Transfer to a ramekin and pour remaining clarified butter over top. Cover and refrigerate for 2 hours or for up to 2 days. When serving, let stand at room temperature for 20 minutes to allow flavors to bloom.

Cucumber with Smoked Salmon

Makes about 12 hors d'oeuvres

This is a refreshing appetizer for brunch or lunch on a beautiful spring or summer day. These can be served on the versatile Chinese soup spoons, a slice of cucumber (¼ inch/0.5 cm thick) or even in a small 2-oz (60 g) ramekin.

2 cups	diced peeled English cucumber	500 mL
	Salt and freshly ground black pepper	
½ cup	corn kernels	125 mL
½ cup	finely chopped peeled celery	125 mL
¼ cup	full-fat plain yogurt	60 mL
2 tbsp	white wine vinegar	30 mL
1 tsp	finely chopped dill fronds	5 mL
6	smoked salmon slices, cut in half	6
1 tbsp	finely diced chives	15 mL

1. In a bowl, combine cucumber and 1 tsp (5 mL) salt. Set aside for 30 minutes or for up to 1 hour to soften the cucumber. Drain off liquid. Add corn, celery, yogurt, vinegar, dill and ½ tsp (2 mL) pepper, stirring well to coat evenly. Cover and refrigerate overnight.

2. Place equal amount of cucumber salad on each soup spoon or vessels mentioned in intro and garnish with salmon, folding as necessary to fit, and chives.

Martini-Marinated Salmon

Makes about ¾ cup (175 mL)

If you're looking for a smoked salmon spread that is a bit different and packs some punch try this. It's perfect with sliced baguette or thinly sliced dark rye bread.

Tip

Salmon can be covered and refrigerated for up to 3 days.

4 oz	thinly sliced smoked salmon	125 g
¼ cup	vodka	60 mL
1 tsp	dry vermouth	5 mL
1 tsp	cracked black peppercorns	5 mL
3 oz	cream cheese, softened and cubed	90 g
¼ cup	mayonnaise	60 mL
2 tbsp	finely snipped chives	30 mL
1 tsp	finely grated lemon zest	5 mL

1. Place salmon in a small shallow dish. In a small bowl, combine vodka, vermouth and pepper. Pour over salmon, lifting salmon to ensure the "martini" touches all salmon surfaces. Cover and refrigerate overnight.

2. Drain, discarding liquid. Transfer salmon to food processor. Add cream cheese, mayonnaise, chives and zest. Process until smooth. Serve immediately.

Honey Mustard-Glazed Salmon with Avocado

Makes 12 servings

Honey complements the salmon and avocado wonderfully, helping to cut the natural fat in both. Enjoy this plated appetizer for brunch or lunch.

Tip

To toast sesame seeds: Place seeds in a dry skillet and cook, stirring, over medium heat until fragrant and turning golden, about 4 minutes.

Honey Mustard Glaze

3 tbsp	Dijon mustard	45 mL
1 tbsp	liquid honey	15 mL
½ tsp	freshly ground black pepper	2 mL
½ tsp	toasted sesame seeds (see Tip, left)	2 mL
½ tsp	mustard seeds	2 mL
1	avocado, sliced	1
1 tbsp	freshly squeezed lemon juice	15 mL
1 tbsp	unsalted butter	15 mL
1 tbsp	olive oil	15 mL
1½ lbs	skin-on salmon fillet, cut into 12 pieces	750 g

1. *Honey Mustard Glaze:* In a bowl, combine mustard, honey, pepper, sesame seeds and mustard seeds. Mix well.

2. In another bowl, combine avocado and lemon juice, tossing gently to evenly coat. Set aside.

3. In a nonstick skillet, heat butter and oil over high heat. Sear salmon skin side down until crisp, 3 to 4 minutes. Flip and quickly sear other side for about 30 seconds. Transfer to a plate and let rest for 5 minutes.

4. Place salmon skin side up in middle of a small, preferably a demi-tasse, plate. Brush salmon skin with glaze and garnish with avocado slices. Serve this one- or two-bite appetizer with chopsticks, warm or at room temperature.

Mini Salmon en Croûte

Makes 10 servings

This is a stunning introduction to a plated appetizer meal and rustic enough to be passed around in a more casual setting. The puff pastry lends itself to being eaten as your guests stand around and mingle, and we bet we know what they'll be talking about — your fabulous cooking!

Tips

King oyster mushrooms, the largest of the oyster mushroom family, are perfect for this recipe because they are dryer than your average white button mushroom thus won't leach too much water and make your pastry too soggy. In the absence of the "king," look for regular oyster mushrooms, more expensive chanterelle mushrooms or even honeycomb-looking morel mushrooms.

This dish can be assembled ahead of time and refrigerated for up to 1 day. Brush with egg just before baking and bake as directed.

- **Preheat oven to 275°F (140°C)**
- **Baking sheet, lined with parchment paper**

2 tbsp	olive oil	30 mL
1½ cups	sliced king oyster mushrooms (see Tips, left)	375 mL
2 tbsp	minced drained capers	30 mL
8 oz	puff pastry, thawed	250 g
1¼ lbs	skinless salmon fillet, cut into 10 pieces	625 g
1 tbsp	grated lemon zest	15 mL
Pinch	salt	Pinch
Pinch	freshly ground black pepper	Pinch
1	egg, beaten	1

1. In a skillet, heat oil over high heat. Sauté mushrooms until soft, 3 to 4 minutes. Add capers and remove from heat. Let cool to the touch then coarsely chop.

2. On a lightly floured surface, roll pastry into a 10-inch (25 cm) square and cut into 10 equal squares. Place one piece of salmon in the center of each square and sprinkle with lemon zest. Divide mushroom mixture equally on top of each. Season with salt and pepper.

3. Brush edges with beaten egg, fold pastry over salmon and wrap edges under the package to keep top smooth. Place on prepared baking sheet. Brush tops with beaten egg. Bake in preheated oven until surface is golden brown, about 20 minutes. Serve immediately.

Classic Salmon Nigiri Sushi

Makes 8 nigiri

What was once a delicacy has become mainstream. With sushi restaurants popping up all over the place, many of us spend outrageous dollars for what can easily be made at home. We've made it so darn easy but remember, the quality of fish is everything. Enjoy this appetizer for lunch, dinner or even late in the evening, as a snack.

Tips

Salmon belly is available at your local fish shop. Salmon fillet will work for this recipe but the high-fat content in the belly combined with the sweet marinade makes for a sensational flavor combination.

Sushi rice is made from short-grain Japanese rice and is usually seasoned with rice wine vinegar, salt and sugar. It is widely available in Asian markets and larger supermarkets. We prefer Kokuho Rose Sushi Rice but whatever is available will do the trick, too.

1 cup	sushi rice (see Tips, left)	250 mL
1½ cups	water	375 mL
1 tbsp	rice wine vinegar	15 mL
¼ tsp	salt	1 mL
¼ tsp	granulated sugar	1 mL
3 oz	skinless salmon belly (see Tips, left)	90 g
1 tbsp	thinly sliced green onions	15 mL

1. In a fine-mesh sieve, rinse rice thoroughly under cold water until water runs clear, about 5 minutes. Transfer to a saucepan. Add water and bring to a boil over medium heat. Cover, reduce heat to low and simmer for 5 minutes. Remove from heat and let stand for 15 to 20 minutes. Resist the temptation to remove the cover to sneak a peek — it is important to keep the steam and heat inside the pan.

2. In a bowl, combine vinegar, salt and sugar, mixing well to dissolve. Gently transfer rice to a large bowl and fold in vinegar mixture. Be sure to fold gently so as not to break apart the grains. Set aside.

3. Using a sharp knife, cut salmon across the grain into 8 thin slices. Spoon about 1 tbsp (15 mL) of rice into your moistened hands and roll into a ball. Wrap one slice of salmon over rice and place on a serving plate. Press nigiri onto the platter gently to flatten and garnish with green onions. Repeat with remaining rice and salmon. Serve immediately.

Smoked Salmon and Grits Cakes

Makes about 64 squares

These savory squares are very easy to make and deliciously different. They are great finished with a small dollop of sour cream and a sprinkling of chives, as the recipe calls for. If you're looking for another flavor sensation, try topping each square with Roasted Red Pepper Coulis (page 543).

Tips

If you don't want to stir your grits frequently, use a nonstick saucepan. An occasional stir will be fine so long as the heat is low.

If you can't find stone-ground grits, use coarse stone-ground cornmeal. Do not use the finely ground grits that come in boxes.

- **8-inch (20 cm) square pan, lightly greased**

1½ cups	chicken or vegetable broth	375 mL
½ tsp	salt or to taste	2 mL
½ cup	white or yellow stone-ground corn grits (see Tips, left)	125 mL
¼ cup	heavy or whipping (35%) cream	60 mL
2 tbsp	unsalted butter	30 mL
1	egg, beaten	1
1 tsp	finely grated lemon zest	5 mL
2 tbsp	freshly squeezed lemon juice	30 mL
½ tsp	hot paprika	2 mL
4 oz	smoked salmon, diced	125 g
	Sour cream	
	Finely snipped chives	

1. In a saucepan over medium heat, bring broth and salt to a rapid boil. Add grits in a steady stream and cook, stirring frequently, until smoothly integrated. Stir in cream. Cover, reduce heat to low and simmer gently, stirring occasionally, until grits are soft and creamy, about 40 minutes. Remove from heat.

2. Add butter and egg and stir well with a wooden spoon. Add lemon zest and juice and paprika and stir well. Stir in smoked salmon. Spread evenly in prepared pan and let cool.

3. Cut into 1-inch (2.5 cm) squares and using an inverted spatula remove from pan. Serve at room temperature topped with a small dollop of sour cream and garnished with chives.

Pacific Salmon Cakes

Makes about 12 cakes

This is not your mom's salmon cakes usually made with salmon from a can. Here we use fresh cooked salmon, which creates a lovely brunch or lunch appetizer. Served these cakes with your favorite side salad or simply plunged into a basic Cocktail Sauce (page 547) or a spicy Lemon Horseradish Aïoli (page 537).

Tip

Crispy salmon skin is an underrated garnish and easy to make. Heat a nonstick skillet over medium heat and warm 1 tsp (5 mL) olive oil. Add salmon skin and sear until crisp on bottom, 8 to 10 minutes. Turn and cook other side until crisp, about 5 minutes. Let cool to the touch. Cut into thin strips and use to garnish salmon cakes.

- **Preheat oven to 375°F (190°C)**

1 lb	skinless Pacific salmon fillet	500 g
1 tsp	olive oil	5 mL
$\frac{1}{3}$ cup	finely diced onion	75 mL
2 tbsp	corn kernels	30 mL
1 tbsp	thinly sliced green onions	15 mL
$\frac{1}{4}$ tsp	salt	1 mL
$\frac{1}{8}$ tsp	freshly ground black pepper	0.5 mL
2 tbsp	fine cornmeal	30 mL
1 tbsp	butter (approx.)	15 mL

1. Evenly coat salmon fillet with oil and bake in preheated oven until firm, 20 to 25 minutes. Let cool to the touch and flake salmon.

2. In a bowl, combine salmon, onion, corn, green onions and salt and pepper. Form mixture into 12 equal bite-size cakes, each about $1\frac{1}{2}$ inches (4 cm) thick. Lightly coat both top and bottom in cornmeal. Place on a plate, cover and refrigerate for at least 1 hour or for up to 12 hours.

3. In a nonstick skillet, melt butter over medium heat and fry cakes until golden brown, 2 to 3 minutes per side, adding more butter if necessary. Transfer to a serving platter and serve immediately.

Fresh Salmon Nuggets

Makes 10 nuggets

An appetizer
sophisticated enough
for your guests
and mild enough
for the discerning
palate of children.
This is lovely when
paired with Caper
Lemon Rémoulade
(page 539).

Crust

1 cup	panko bread crumbs	250 mL
2 tbsp	freshly grated Parmesan cheese	30 mL
½ tsp	salt	2 mL
½ tsp	freshly ground black pepper	2 mL
¼ tsp	herbes de Provence	1 mL
6 oz	skinless salmon fillet, cut into 10 cubes	175 g
1 tbsp	olive oil	15 mL

1. *Crust:* In a bowl, combine bread crumbs, cheese, salt, pepper and herbes de Provence. Mix well. Dip salmon pieces, one by one, into crumb mixture, pressing to coat all sides.

2. In a large skillet, heat olive oil over medium heat. Sear salmon until golden brown, about 2 minutes. Flip and sear for 1 minute more. Serve immediately.

Smoked Salmon Spread

Makes about 1½ cups (375 mL)

Serve this with thin
slices of dark rye
bread, pumpernickel
rounds or plain
baguette. It's great
as a stuffing for
cherry tomatoes (see
Variation, page 297,
substituting salmon
spread for the trout)
or as a topping for
Easy Potato Crisps
(page 214).

Tip

Don't overprocess after
adding the salmon. You
want it to be chopped,
not puréed.

½ cup	sour cream	125 mL
3 oz	cream cheese, softened and cubed	90 g
½	small red onion, halved	½
2 tbsp	drained capers	30 mL
2 tbsp	freshly squeezed lemon juice	30 mL
½ tsp	salt	2 mL
4 oz	smoked salmon	125 g
¼ cup	fresh dill fronds	60 mL
	Freshly ground black pepper	

1. In a food processor fitted with metal blade, process sour cream, cream cheese, red onion, capers, lemon juice and salt until smooth, about 30 seconds, stopping and scraping down sides of the bowl as necessary. Add smoked salmon, dill, and pepper to taste. Pulse until chopped and blended, about 10 times (see Tip, left). Serve immediately or cover and refrigerate for up to 3 days.

Smoked Salmon Mousse

Makes about 2 cups (500 mL)

Serve this on thinly sliced baguette, plain biscuits or cocktail-size slices of dark rye bread. Or, make up a batch of Crêpes Parmentier (page 200).

Tip

You may need more cream if using wild salmon, which is likely to have a heavier texture than the farmed variety.

8 oz	smoked salmon	250 g
1/2 to 3/4 cup	heavy or whipping (35%) cream	125 to 175 mL
1 tbsp	freshly squeezed lemon juice	15 mL
2 tbsp	red lumpfish roe	30 mL
	Freshly ground black pepper	

1. In a food processor fitted with metal blade, process smoked salmon, cream and lemon juice until smooth, about 30 seconds. Fold in lumpfish roe. Season liberally with pepper. Spoon into a serving bowl. Serve immediately or cover and refrigerate for up to 2 hours.

Dill-Spiked Smoked Trout Spread

Makes about 2½ cups (625 mL)

Save this for special occasions because smoked trout is a bit pricey. On the other hand, it is so easy to make you could serve it any day of the week. It is great on thin wheat crackers (fairly bland so the taste doesn't interfere with the exquisite flavor of the trout) or, if you're feeling celebratory, on Easy Potato Crisps (page 214) or even on Homemade Potato Chips (page 215).

1 lb	smoked trout fillets, skin and bones removed	500 g
4	green onions, white part with just a bit of green, cut into 3-inch (7.5 cm) lengths	4
1	stalk celery, cut into chunks	1
1/4 cup	fresh dill fronds	60 mL
1/4 cup	mayonnaise	60 mL
2 tbsp	extra virgin olive oil	30 mL
1 tbsp	freshly squeezed lemon juice	15 mL
1 tbsp	Dijon mustard	15 mL

1. In a food processor fitted with metal blade, pulse trout, green onions, celery and dill until finely chopped. Add mayonnaise, olive oil, lemon juice and mustard and process until smooth. Transfer to a serving bowl and refrigerate for at least 3 hours or for up to 2 days.

Variation

Trout Stuffed Tomatoes: Cut the tops of cherry tomatoes and using a small spoon, remove some of the pulp. Spoon about 1 tsp (5 mL) of the trout mixture into each tomato.

Shrimp in Piri-Piri Butter

Makes about 25 shrimp

Nothing could be easier to make than these simple yet delicious shrimp. Serve them on a platter as part of an antipasti table, or provide chunks of country-style bread and napkins. Guests can spoon the shrimp and luscious sauce over the bread and enjoy it like an ad hoc bruschetta. Double or triple the quantity to meet your needs.

Tips

Piri-piri sauce is a hot pepper sauce made from an African chile pepper, which has a unique and intriguing flavor. It can be found in Portuguese markets or specialty stores. If you can't find it substitute another hot pepper sauce, being aware that it might not have the same complexity. If substituting, add in increments and adjust the quantity in case the heat level is higher.

Use a baking dish that is large enough to accommodate the shrimp in a single layer but small enough to ensure they are surrounded by a maximum amount of butter sauce.

● **Preheat oven to 375°F (190°C)**

1 lb	jumbo shrimp, tails left on, peeled, deveined and patted dry	500 g
2 tbsp	kosher salt	30 mL
2 cups	boiling water	500 mL
	Ice cubes	
½ cup	melted unsalted butter	125 mL
2 tsp	puréed garlic (see Tips, page 334)	10 mL
3 tbsp	piri-piri sauce (see Tips, left)	45 mL
2 tbsp	freshly squeezed lemon juice	30 mL
2 tbsp	finely chopped parsley	30 mL
	Salt and freshly ground black pepper	

1. In a bowl, dissolve salt in boiling water. Add ice cubes until room temperature is achieved. Add shrimp and set aside for 15 minutes. Drain and rinse thoroughly under cold running water. Pat dry with paper towels.

2. In a bowl, combine melted butter, garlic and piri-piri sauce. Add shrimp and toss until well coated. Transfer to a baking dish (see Tips, left) pouring any remaining butter mixture evenly over the shrimp.

3. Bake in preheated oven until shrimp are pink and curled, about 10 minutes. Drizzle with lemon juice and sprinkle with parsley. Season to taste with salt and pepper. Serve hot.

Spicy Sizzling Shrimp

Makes about 25 shrimp

These shrimp, Spanish in inspiration, are, basically, poached in olive oil and seasoned with garlic, hot pepper and sherry vinegar. The results are succulent. Serve them on a platter and allow people to spear them with forks, wooden skewers or toothpicks.

Tip

We recommend using pure sea salt rather than refined table salt. It has a clean, crisp taste and enhanced mineral content, unlike table salt, which has a bitter acrid taste and contains unpleasant additives to prevent caking.

- **10-inch (25 cm) skillet**

1 lb	jumbo shrimp, peeled, deveined and patted dry	500 g
2 tbsp	kosher salt	30 mL
2 cups	boiling water	500 mL
	Ice cubes	
1/2 cup	extra virgin olive oil	125 mL
4	cloves garlic, thinly sliced	4
2 tsp	hot pepper flakes	10 mL
1 tbsp	sherry vinegar	15 mL
	Flaky sea salt, such as Maldon	
	Country-style bread	

1. In a bowl, dissolve salt in boiling water. Add ice cubes until room temperature is achieved. Add shrimp and set aside for 15 minutes. Drain and rinse thoroughly under cold running water. Pat dry with paper towels.

2. In a skillet, heat oil and garlic over low heat until the oil begins to shimmer and garlic is fragrant, about 4 minutes. Stir in hot pepper flakes. Add shrimp and cook, stirring and coating shrimp with the warm oil, until firm and pink, about 4 minutes. Using a slotted spoon, transfer shrimp and garlic to a warm platter. Drizzle with vinegar and add cooking oil to taste. Sprinkle with sea salt. Serve with chunks of country bread.

Shrimp Guide

Description of shrimp by size is based on the number of shrimp in a pound (500 g). Although standards have changed over the years and shrimp producers tend to exaggerate the actual size of their shrimp, in general terms, a pound (500 g) of shrimp classified as extra colossal would contain between 5 to 10 shrimp. If buying a pound (500 g) of extra jumbo, you should expect 16 to 20 shrimp. Jumbo range between 21 to 25, extra large 26 to 30 and large are 31 to 35 shrimp per pound (500 g).

Peppery Shrimp

Makes about 25

These qualify as messy finger food but they are a great icebreaker if people are meeting for the first time. They are most succulent if you eat the shells but if you're squeamish, you can suck off the flavorful topping and peel the shrimp before eating.

Tips

You want the legs and head removed from the shrimp. You'll likely need to devein them yourself, leaving the shells on.

Piment d'Espelette is a dried mild chile pepper from the Basque region of France. It adds a nice flavor to this recipe.

- **Candy/deep-fry thermometer**

1 lb	jumbo shrimp, deveined (see Tips, left)	500 g
1 tbsp	kosher salt	15 mL
2 cups	boiling water	500 mL
	Ice cubes	
1 tbsp	Roasted Pepper and Salt (page 552) (approx.)	15 mL
1 tbsp	piment d'Espelette (see Tips, left)	15 mL
1 tsp	hot smoked paprika	5 mL
½ cup	cornstarch	125 mL
	Oil	

1. In a bowl, dissolve salt in boiling water. Add ice cubes until room temperature is achieved. Add shrimp and set aside for 15 minutes. Drain and rinse thoroughly under cold running water. Pat dry with paper towels.

2. Meanwhile, in a small bowl, combine Roasted Pepper and Salt, piment d'Espelette and smoked paprika. Set aside.

3. In a plastic bag, toss dry shrimp with cornstarch until evenly coated.

4. In a deep heavy-bottomed skillet, add oil to a depth of at least 2 inches (5 cm). Heat on medium-high heat to 350°F (180°C). (You can also use a deep fryer; follow the manufacturer's instructions.) Add shrimp to hot oil in batches and cook until golden, about 2 minutes. Using a slotted spoon, transfer to a paper towel–lined plate to drain.

5. Transfer shrimp to a serving platter and sprinkle liberally with salt mixture. Serve immediately.

Coconut Shrimp with Cilantro-Lime Dipping Sauce

Makes about 25

These crispy shrimp represent a decadent combination of flavors and texture. Always popular, they are likely to quickly disappear.

Tips

Count on serving two to three shrimp per person. The number of people you serve will depend upon the size of your shrimp. We like to use jumbo shrimp, which weigh in at about 25 per pound (500 g). If you're using extra large, (about 30 shrimp per pound/ 500 g), increase the quantity of coconut and add an extra egg white, just to be sure you'll have enough coating for all the shrimp.

For best results, brine shrimp before cooking. Dissolve 2 tbsp (30 mL) kosher salt in 1 cup (250 mL) boiling water. Add ice cubes until cool to the touch. Add shrimp. Add water, if necessary, to cover and let brine at room temperature for 15 minutes. Drain and rinse thoroughly under cold running water. Pat dry.

- **Candy/deep-fry thermometer**

1 lb	jumbo shrimp, peeled, deveined and patted dry, preferably brined (see Tips, left)	500 g

Cilantro-Lime Dipping Sauce

1/3 cup	freshly squeezed lime juice	75 mL
2 tbsp	soy sauce	30 mL
2 tbsp	fish sauce	30 mL
2	cloves garlic, minced	2
1	long red chile, seeded and minced	1
1 tbsp	granulated sugar	15 mL
2 tbsp	finely chopped cilantro leaves	30 mL
1/2 cup	cornstarch	125 mL
1/2 tsp	salt	2 mL
2	eggs whites	2
2 cups	shredded unsweetened coconut (approx.)	500 mL
	Oil	

1. *Cilantro-Lime Dipping Sauce:* In a small bowl, combine lime juice, soy sauce, fish sauce, garlic, chile, sugar and cilantro. Mix well and set aside.

2. In a bowl, combine cornstarch and salt. Mix well. In another bowl, beat egg whites until frothy.

3. Dredge shrimp in cornstarch mixture, dip in egg whites, then press into coconut, turning to coat well. Set aside on a platter or baking sheet as completed.

4. In a deep heavy-bottomed skillet, add oil to a depth of at least 2 inches (5 cm). Heat on medium-high heat to 350°F (180°C). (You can also use a deep fryer; follow the manufacturer's instructions.) Add shrimp to hot oil in batches and cook until golden, about 2 minutes. Using a slotted spoon, transfer to a paper towel–lined plate to drain. To serve, dip cooked shrimp in dipping sauce.

Shrimp Tempura

Makes about 25

In Japan and finer Japanese restaurants throughout the world, tempura batter is made from a very fine flour that contains eggs. Good results can be achieved using cake flour, which is softer than all-purpose flour, very cold soda water and fresh eggs. A bit of cornstarch serves to lighten the batter.

Tips

For best results, brine shrimp before cooking. *To brine shrimp:* Dissolve 2 tbsp (30 mL) kosher salt in 1 cup (250 mL) boiling water. Add ice cubes until cool to the touch. Add shrimp. Add water, if necessary, to cover and set aside at room temperature for 15 minutes. Drain and rinse thoroughly under cold running water. Pat dry.

If you don't feel like making your own seasoned salt, use smoked sea salt or a good seasoned salt with a sea salt base that is suggested for seafood.

- **Candy/deep-fry thermometer**

1 lb	jumbo shrimp, peeled with tails left on, if desired, preferably brined (see Tips, left and page 301)	500 g
	Oil	
1	egg	1
1 cup	cake flour	250 mL
5 tbsp	cornstarch, divided (approx.)	75 mL
1¼ cups	ice cold soda water or sparkling mineral water	300 mL
	Green Tea Salt or Roasted Pepper and Salt (page 552), optional (see Tips, left)	

1. In a Dutch oven or wok, add oil to a depth of about 2 inches (5 cm). Heat over medium-high heat until temperature reaches 350°F (180°C).

2. Meanwhile, in a bowl, beat egg. Add flour and 2 tbsp (30 mL) of the cornstarch and mix until combined (it will be very lumpy). Add soda water and mix just until blended.

3. Spread remaining 3 tbsp (45 mL) of cornstarch on a plate or place in a resealable bag and dredge shrimp in it. Holding shrimp by the tail end, dip in batter. Add shrimp to hot oil in batches (about 6 at a time) and fry until crisp and golden, turning once, about 1 minute per side.

4. Transfer to a paper towel–lined plate to drain and sprinkle with Green Tea Salt, if using (see Tips, left).

Variation

Calamari Tempura: Substitute calamari rounds (about ½ inch/ 1 cm thick) for the shrimp. Separate with a fork when adding to the batter to ensure all sides are coated.

Grilled Shrimp with Aïoli

Makes about 50 shrimp

This is a great starter for a summer barbecue. Just be careful. People will eat so many they may not have room for the main course.

Tips

Brining the shrimp firms them up and makes them succulent on the barbecue.

Although plain vegetable oil does the job, you can add a whisper of flavor to the shrimp by brushing them with chili oil or a herb-infused oil such as lemon, garlic or oregano.

2 lbs	jumbo shrimp, shells on	1 kg
Brine		
¼ cup	kosher salt or 2 tbsp (30 mL) table salt	60 mL
2	dried red chile peppers	2
2	cloves garlic, crushed	2
2 tsp	granulated sugar	10 mL
1 cup	boiling water	250 mL
4 cups	cold water (approx.)	1 L
2 tbsp	rice vinegar (see Tips, page 305)	30 mL
	Ice cubes	
¼ cup	oil (see Tips, left)	60 mL
	Aïoli (pages 536 and 537)	

1. Using a knife, slit the shrimp shells along the back, removing the vein but leaving the shells intact. Set aside.

2. *Brine:* In a large heatproof nonreactive bowl, combine salt, chiles, garlic, sugar and boiling water. Stir until salt and sugar are dissolved. Add cold water and vinegar and stir well. Add enough ice cubes to chill the mixture thoroughly.

3. Place shrimp in brining solution, adding additional cold water to cover if necessary. Cover bowl and refrigerate for 30 minutes to 1 hour.

4. Preheat barbecue. Remove shrimp from brine. Discard brine. Rinse shrimp under cold running water and pat dry with paper towel. Brush liberally with oil. Place on preheated grill and cook, turning once, until shrimp are pink and firm, about 2 minutes per side. Serve hot, in their shells, accompanied by aïoli.

Variations

Grilled Shrimp with Sauce Vierge: Substitute Sauce Vierge (page 544) for the Aïoli.

Grilled Shrimp with Two-Tomato Coulis: Substitute Two-Tomato Coulis (page 544) for the Aïoli.

Potted Shrimp

Makes about 1 cup (250 mL)

Potted shrimp is a traditional English dish. This version is nicely flavored with thyme, garlic and mace, the orange covering of the nutmeg shell. Serve on plain crackers or sliced baguette.

Tip

Be sure to chill this dish thoroughly before serving. The butter needs to harden in order to hold it together.

8 oz	peeled deveined shrimp	250 g
1 tbsp	fresh thyme leaves	15 mL
1	clove garlic, chopped	1
	Salt and freshly ground white pepper	
1/8 tsp	ground mace or freshly grated nutmeg	0.5 mL
1/4 cup	clarified butter (see Tips, left, and page 289)	60 mL
1 tbsp	freshly squeezed lemon juice	15 mL

1. In a food processor fitted with metal blade, process shrimp, thyme, garlic, 1/2 tsp (2 mL) salt, 1/4 tsp (1 mL) white pepper and mace until shrimp are finely chopped and mixture is blended, about 15 seconds.

2. In a saucepan over medium heat, bring clarified butter to a simmer. Add shrimp mixture, return to a simmer and cook, stirring, until shrimp are pink and opaque, about 5 minutes. Remove from heat and stir in lemon juice. Transfer to a serving dish, cover and refrigerate until butter solidifies, overnight or for up to 3 days.

Twisted Butterfly Shrimp

Makes 8 to 10 shrimp

Twisting two halves of shrimp creates an interesting presentation. Although an important aspect of cooking is creating food that tastes wonderful, it is important that it looks great, too. Serve with the exquisite Truffle Vinaigrette (page 542) or the classic Cocktail Sauce (page 547).

● **Preheat greased barbecue to high**

8 to 10	extra colossal shrimp, deveined and peeled to the tail	8 to 10
1 tbsp	minced lemon zest	15 mL
1 tbsp	minced garlic	15 mL
1 tsp	brown sugar	5 mL
1/4 tsp	freshly ground white pepper	1 mL

1. Using a sharp knife, cut shrimp in half lengthwise to tail, leaving tail intact. Transfer to a bowl. Add zest, garlic, sugar and pepper and marinate for 1 hour.

2. Remove shrimp from marinade. Holding shrimp at the tail, twist the two halves together to intertwine them and pierce with a toothpick to keep intact. Grill shrimp, turning often, until shrimp are pink and opaque, 2 to 3 minutes. Serve immediately.

Sushi Rice–Stuffed Shrimp

Makes 6 shrimp

This is a fun and creative appetizer that will be a great conversation starter among your guests. Here the rice is stuffed into the cavity of poached shrimp creating a very filling two-biter. Serve alongside Wasabi Aïoli (page 537) or Basic Sweet-and-Sour Sauce (page 547).

Tips

There is a difference between rice vinegar and seasoned rice vinegar. Both are usually made from fermented rice or rice wine, but rice vinegar does not contain any additional sugar or sodium. Our preference is Japanese rice vinegar which is very mild flavored and almost colorless.

Sweet Asian chili sauce is a mixture of chiles, sugar, vinegar and other spices and can be found in Asian markets or in the Asian section of some large supermarkets.

To make pepper curls: Thinly slice sweet red peppers into 2-inch (5 cm) strips and soak in ice water for 1 hour. They will be firm and curly and make a wonderful crispy fresh garnish.

½ cup	sushi rice (see Tips, page 293)	125 mL
1 cup	water	250 mL
1 tsp	rice vinegar (see Tips, left)	5 mL
½ tsp	salt	2 mL
6	colossal shrimp, peeled and deveined	6
3 cups	water	750 mL
1 tbsp	coarsely chopped fresh gingerroot	15 mL
1 tbsp	soy sauce	15 mL
1 tbsp	sweet Asian chili sauce (see Tips, left)	15 mL
1	clove garlic	1
1 tsp	wasabi paste	5 mL
6	red pepper curls or slices (see Tips, left)	6

1. In a fine-mesh strainer, rinse rice thoroughly under cold water until water runs clear, about 5 minutes. Transfer to a saucepan. Add 1 cup (250 mL) water and bring to a boil over medium heat. Cover, reduce heat to low and simmer for 5 minutes. Remove from heat and let steam for 15 to 20 minutes. Resist the temptation to remove the cover to sneak a peek — it is important to keep the steam and heat inside the pan. Add vinegar and salt and mix gently to combine.

2. On a cutting board and using a sharp knife, cut a small incision into underside of shrimp. This will create a pocket for the rice. Set aside.

3. In a saucepan, bring 3 cups (750 mL) water, ginger, soy sauce, chili sauce and garlic to a boil and simmer for 5 minutes to infuse poaching liquid. Add shrimp and cook until firm and opaque, 1 to 2 minutes. Let cool to room temperature.

4. With your finger, spread a pinch of wasabi paste into cavity of shrimp, then fill with about 1 tbsp (15 mL) seasoned sushi rice. Garnish with 1 red pepper curl or slice. Repeat with remaining shrimp and ingredients. Serve immediately.

Old-South Shrimp Paste

Makes about 1½ cups (375 mL)

Shrimp paste is something of an institution in the Old South, where every cook has his or her own recipe. Serve this on crackers (sesame crackers are traditional), toast points or even celery sticks. If you're so inclined you can even use this as a filling for party sandwiches.

Tip

You want the shrimp to be finely chopped but not puréed; it's important to maintain some texture.

6	green onions, white with a bit of green, cut into 2-inch (5 cm) chunks	6
½	green bell pepper, quartered	½
⅓ cup	unsalted butter, cubed	75 mL
1 tbsp	each lemon juice and dry sherry	15 mL
8 oz	cooked salad shrimp	250 g
	Hot pepper sauce	
	Salt and freshly ground black pepper	

1. In a food processor fitted with metal blade, pulse onions and pepper until chopped, stopping and scraping down sides of the bowl. Add butter, lemon juice and sherry and pulse to blend. Add shrimp and pulse until chopped and blended. Season to taste with hot pepper sauce, salt and pepper, pulsing once or twice to blend. Transfer to a serving dish, cover and refrigerate for at least 2 hours until thoroughly chilled.

Baked Crab Dip

Makes about 2 cups (500 mL)

Warm cheesy dips are always a hit, particularly in the cold dark days of winter. Because the flavors in this dip are vaguely Tex-Mex, we like to serve it with tostadas or tortilla chips. Sliced baguette works well, too.

- **Preheat oven to 400°F (200°C)**

1 cup	cooked drained crabmeat (see Tips, page 307)	250 mL
1 cup	shredded Monterey Jack cheese	250 mL
2	green onions, white part with a bit of green, minced	2
½ to 1	jalapeño pepper, minced	½ to 1
3 tbsp	each full-fat sour cream and mayonnaise	45 mL
2 tbsp	freshly squeezed lemon juice	30 mL
1 tbsp	finely chopped cilantro leaves	15 mL
	Salt and freshly ground pepper	

1. In a bowl, combine crab, cheese, onions, jalapeño to taste, sour cream, mayonnaise, lemon juice and cilantro. Season with salt and pepper. Transfer to a small ovenproof dish. Bake in preheated oven until bubbling and lightly browned, about 30 minutes.

Classic Crab Cakes

Makes about 20 cakes

A lovely classic recipe, which will never go out of style.

Tips

Whenever dicing fish and seafood, it is a good idea to fill a large bowl with ice and place a smaller bowl on top of the ice. Use the top bowl to store the diced fish, keeping in cold, while you continue with the recipe and mix ingredients.

These cakes are very good with Caper Lemon Rémoulade (page 539).

Our preference is for pasteurized crabmeat, which you can find in cans in the refrigerated section of supermarkets. But regular canned or thawed drained frozen crab meat works well, too.

- **Baking sheet, lined with parchment paper**

1 lb	pasteurized lump crabmeat (about 2 cups/500 mL)	500 g
1/3 cup	finely diced red bell pepper	75 mL
1/3 cup	finely diced red onion	75 mL
2 tbsp	Dijon mustard	30 mL
1 tbsp	finely grated lemon zest	15 mL
1 tbsp	Worcestershire sauce	15 mL
1 tbsp	coarsely chopped fresh cilantro leaves	15 mL
1 tsp	hot pepper sauce	5 mL
1/4 tsp	salt	1 mL
	Freshly ground black pepper	
3 tbsp	vegetable oil, divided	45 mL
1 1/2 cups	panko bread crumbs	375 mL

1. In a large bowl, combine crab, bell pepper, red onion, mustard, lemon zest, Worcestershire sauce, cilantro, hot pepper sauce, salt, and pepper to taste. Fold until all ingredients are evenly distributed. Break up crab as little as possible; you are looking for large chunks of crab in the final cakes.

2. Spoon 2 tbsp (30 mL) tightly packed crab mixture on prepared baking sheet until all crab is used. Form crab into cakes, about 1 1/2 inches (4 cm) thick. Cover and refrigerate overnight. This will really help to keep them together while cooking.

3. In a large nonstick skillet, heat 1 1/2 tbsp (22 mL) of the oil over medium heat. Place bread crumbs on a plate and coat tops and bottoms of crab cakes. In batches as necessary, fry, turning once, until golden brown and heated through, about 3 minutes per side. Transfer to a platter and repeat until all cakes are cooked, adding more oil and adjusting heat as necessary between batches.

Crab and Sweet Potato Canapé

Makes 12 canapés

The twice-cooked sweet potatoes create a crunchy exterior and fluffy interior, when combined with the sweetness of crab this appetizer is simply amazing!

Tips

Crabmeat is available fresh, frozen and pasteurized (heated to high temperatures to kill bacteria). We suggest using the pasteurized crabmeat for convenience; it's good quality, great tasting and the crabmeat is ready for you to use.

Toasting sesame seeds are quite easy and only takes minutes. *To toast sesame seeds:* In a large skillet over medium-high heat, toast sesame seeds, stirring often, until fragrant and golden brown, 3 to 4 minutes.

- **Candy/deep-fry thermometer**

12	slices (1/8 inch/3 mm thick) skin-on sweet potato	12
	Ice water	
	Oil	
1/2 cup	rice flour or all-purpose flour	125 mL
1	egg, beaten with 1 tbsp (15 mL) water	1
3/4 cup	panko bread crumbs	175 mL
1/8 tsp	salt	0.5 mL
1/2 cup	shredded pasteurized crabmeat (see Tips, left)	125 mL
1 tbsp	toasted sesame seeds	15 mL
1 tbsp	finely chopped green onion	15 mL
1 tbsp	soy sauce	15 mL
1 tsp	coarsely chopped fresh cilantro	5 mL
1/2 tsp	puréed gingerroot	2 mL
1/2 tsp	packed brown sugar	2 mL
1/4 tsp	hot pepper sauce	1 mL

1. Blanch sweet potato slices in boiling water until slightly pliable and fragrant, 1 to 2 minutes. Transfer to ice water to stop the cooking process and drain on paper towels.

2. In a deep saucepan or Dutch oven , place oil to a depth of about 3 inches (7.5 cm). Heat over medium heat until temperature reaches 350°F (180°C). (You can also use a deep fryer; follow the manufacturer's instructions.) Coat blanched sweet potato in flour, egg and bread crumbs. Fry in batches in oil until golden brown, 2 to 3 minutes. Transfer to paper towels to absorb excess oil. Season with salt.

3. In a bowl, combine crab, sesame seeds, green onion, soy sauce, cilantro, ginger, brown sugar and hot pepper sauce. Divide into 12 equal portions and place on top of fried sweet potato. Serve immediately.

Sautéed Scallops with Scallion-Spiked Mashed Potato

Makes about 16 servings (see Tip, below)

This combination of tender sautéed scallops and creamy mashed potato is the epitome of comfort food. Sprinkled with green specks of parsley and served on white porcelain spoons, it is also extremely elegant.

Tip

Bay scallops are tiny and work best in this recipe because three or four will fit on a single spoon and one can be eaten in a single bite. You can use the much larger sea scallops, but you will need to cut them into quarters or even eighths, depending on their size, before sautéing. The number of servings you will get depends upon the size of your scallops and the quantity of mashed potato, which is impossible to predict completely accurately.

- **16 porcelain spoons**

¼ cup	heavy or whipping (35%) cream	60 mL
2	green onions, white part with a bit of green, finely chopped	2
1	potato, peeled, boiled and put through a ricer (see Tip, page 366)	1
	Salt and freshly ground black pepper	
8 oz	bay scallops (see Tip, left)	250 g
½ cup	all-purpose flour	125 mL
1 tbsp	olive oil	15 mL
1 tbsp	butter	15 mL
2	cloves garlic, minced	2
½ cup	finely chopped Italian flat-leaf parsley	125 mL
1 tbsp	freshly squeezed lemon juice	15 mL

1. In a small saucepan, combine cream and green onions. Bring to a boil over medium heat, watching closely to ensure mixture doesn't boil over. Remove from heat and let stand for 5 minutes to meld flavors. In a bowl, combine warm potato and cream mixture. Mix well and season to taste with salt and pepper. Set aside and keep warm.

2. On a plate or in a plastic bag, dredge scallops in flour. In a large skillet, heat oil and butter over medium-high heat. Add garlic and stir well. Add scallops in a single layer and cook, without stirring, until bottoms are seared, about 1 minute. Stir and cook until all sides are lightly browned. Add parsley and stir well. Add lemon juice and stir well. Season to taste with salt and pepper. Remove from heat.

3. Divide mashed potato equally among porcelain spoons. Top with scallops, dividing equally. (The number of scallops you use will depend upon their size.) Repeat until all scallops and potatoes are used. Serve immediately.

Pan-Seared Scallops with Spicy Mango Purée

Makes about 16 servings

Here's a nibbly that can be quickly assembled yet has a special occasion air because good scallops are a bit pricey. The fresh mango topping is very easy to make, but adds to the sense of celebration. Larger sea scallops cut in half are a good size for this recipe.

Tips

Don't worry if your mango is a bit green. The purée is equally good whether sweet or slightly tart.

Most scallops are injected with a chemical solution which plumps them up. Dry scallops come au naturel.

To remove the tough muscle from scallop: Find the small piece of flesh that can be found on the edge of the scallop, often a slightly different color than the main section. Using a sharp paring knife, carefully remove it from the main section before preparing your recipe.

Spicy Mango Purée

1	mango (see Tips, left)	1
1 tbsp	freshly squeezed lime juice	15 mL
1 tbsp	coarsely chopped fresh cilantro leaves	15 mL
1	jalapeño pepper, seeded and coarsely chopped	1
1½ lbs	large dry scallops (about 8), patted dry (see Tips, left)	750 g
1 tsp	ancho chile powder	5 mL
1 tbsp	oil	15 mL
1 tbsp	unsalted butter	15 mL
	Salt	

1. *Spicy Mango Purée:* In mini bowl of a food processor fitted with metal blade, purée mango, lime juice, cilantro and jalapeño until smooth. Set aside.

2. On a plate, spread chile powder. Dip scallops in powder on cut side only.

3. In a large skillet, heat oil and butter over medium-high heat. Add scallops, powdered side down, and cook until bottoms brown, about 1 minute per side.

4. Transfer to a serving platter. Sprinkle liberally with salt and place a dollop of mango purée on each scallop. Spear with toothpicks, if desired. Serve immediately.

Variation

Substitute Sauce Vierge (page 544) for the Spicy Mango Purée.

Fried Calamari

Makes 6 to 8 servings

There is something special about calamari, perhaps because we order them so often in restaurants. But excellent calamari is now widely available and they are very easy to prepare at home.

Tips

Test the temperature of your oil by adding 1 calamari ring. If it sizzles when it hits the oil, it is hot enough.

Serve with Chile-Spiked Aïoli (page 536) or Roasted Red Pepper Coulis (page 543).

Often when buying whole calamari there is some cartilage remaining inside, to remove reach your fingers into the cavity and pull out the clear pliable cartilage and discard.

- **Candy/deep-fry thermometer**

	Oil	
1 cup	milk	250 mL
1 lb	calamari, cleaned and cut into rounds	500 g
1/2 cup	all-purpose flour	125 mL
1/4 tsp	cayenne pepper	1 mL
	Sea salt, such as Maldon or fleur de sel	

1. In a large deep skillet, add oil to a depth of about 1/2 inch (1 cm). Heat over medium-high heat to about 350°F (180°C). (You can also cook the calamari in a deep fryer; follow the manufacturer's instructions.)

2. Meanwhile, place milk in a bowl. Add sliced calamari and toss to coat well. Transfer to a strainer and drain.

3. In resealable bag, combine flour and cayenne. Close top and shake well to blend. Add drained calamari. Close top and toss until well coated with flour mixture.

4. Add calamari, in batches, to oil and fry until golden, about 1 minute. Using a slotted spoon, transfer to paper towels. Using your fingers as a grinder, sprinkle with salt.

Variation

Rice-Crusted Calamari: Rice flour creates a crunchy coating. Serve alongside a creamy Caper Lemon Rémoulade (page 539) or Roasted Cherry Tomato Vinaigrette (page 541). Follow Steps 1 and 2 above. Follow Step 3 but replace flour and cayenne with 1/2 cup (125 mL) rice flour and 2 tbsp (30 mL) all-purpose flour. Continue with Step 4 above. Makes 6 to 8 servings.

Spicy Seared Calamari

Makes 6 servings

Breathtakingly easy and mouthwateringly delicious. What more could you want? Provide people with forks or, if you're feeling particularly informal, use your fingers and offer an abundance of napkins.

Tip

When making this recipe it is important not to crowd the pan. To be tender, the calamari needs to be seared quickly so it doesn't release liquid. The safest strategy is to do this in two batches in a large (at least 12 inch/30 cm) skillet.

2 tbsp	olive oil, divided (see Tip, left)	30 mL
1	clove garlic, minced	1
1 lb	calamari (no tentacles), cleaned and thinly sliced (1/4-inch/0.5 cm rings), rinsed and patted dry	500 g
1 tsp	hot pepper flakes	5 mL
	Salt and freshly ground black pepper	
2 tbsp	finely chopped Italian flat-leaf parsley leaves	30 mL
	Lemon wedges	

1. In a skillet, heat oil over medium-high heat. Add garlic and stir well. Add calamari in one layer without crowding and sprinkle with hot pepper flakes. Cook, stirring, until just opaque, about 1 minute.

2. Transfer to a warm platter. Season to taste with salt and pepper. Repeat until all the calamari is used up. Transfer to a small platter as complete. Sprinkle with parsley and serve immediately, accompanied by lemon wedges for squeezing.

Marinated Calamari Antipasti

Makes 1 3/4 cups (425 mL)

Marinated calamari is perfect when served on top of crispy crostini (pages 219 and 220).

Tip

A fishmonger may clean and cut your calamari for you or, depending on the fish market, they may already have some cleaned and sliced on display. If choosing whole calamari to prepare, buy ones no larger than 6 to 8 inches (15 to 20 cm) in length.

1 tbsp	olive oil	15 mL
8 oz	calamari, cleaned and cut into rounds (see Tip, left)	250 g
1/2 cup	cherry tomatoes, cut in half	125 mL
1/4 cup	thinly sliced onions	60 mL
1/4 cup	pitted halved kalamata olives	60 mL
1 tbsp	freshly squeezed lemon juice	15 mL
1 tsp	coarsely chopped fresh basil leaves	5 mL
1 tsp	fresh thyme leaves	5 mL

1. In a large skillet, heat oil over high heat. Add calamari, tomatoes, onions and olives and sauté until calamari is soft and opaque, about 3 minutes. Remove from heat and add lemon juice, basil and thyme. Toss well. Serve immediately.

Broiled Oysters with Seasoned Bread Crumbs

Makes 12

Fresh seasoned bread crumbs drizzled with melted butter make a perfect topping for oysters on the half shell. Run them under the broiler to crisp the topping and serve with a squeeze of lemon and a glass of Champagne for a perfect celebratory dish. This recipe can easily be doubled or tripled to suit your needs.

Tip

To shuck an oyster: Hold oyster in a tea towel to protect your hand, flat side facing up, and fit an oyster knife into the hinge at the most narrow part and push to release. Twist the knife and run over the top of the shell to separate. Run the blade under the oyster to separate from muscle, reserve liquid (liquor), and use immediately.

- **Preheat broiler**

Seasoned Bread Crumbs

2	slices (about ¾ inch/2 cm), dry white bread, torn into pieces	2
1	shallot, coarsely chopped	1
1	clove garlic, coarsely chopped	1
1 tbsp	coarsely chopped Italian flat-leaf parsley leaves	15 mL
12	oysters on the half shell with juices (see Tip, left)	12
2 tbsp	melted unsalted butter	30 mL
	Freshly ground black pepper	
	Lemon wedges	

1. *Seasoned Bread Crumbs:* In a food processor fitted with metal blade, process bread to make fine crumbs. Add shallot, garlic and parsley and process until very finely chopped and well integrated.

2. Place oysters on a baking sheet and sprinkle each one with about 1 tbsp (15 mL) of the crumb mixture. Drizzle with melted butter. Place under preheated broiler until crumbs are golden, about 3 minutes. Remove from oven and season to taste with pepper. Serve with lemon wedges.

Baltimore Oysters

Makes 6 servings

The combination of crisp bacon bits and oysters in a rich cream base is traditionally associated with the city of Baltimore, although it may be a variation on the 19th century New Orleans dish la médiatrice, in which the mixture is served in crispy rolls (see Variation, below). For ease of presentation, we like to serve this on porcelain spoons, but toast points are more traditional.

Tip

To shuck an oyster: Hold oyster in a tea towel to protect your hand, flat side facing up, and fit an oyster knife into the hinge at the most narrow part and push to release. Twist the knife and run over the top of the shell to separate. Run the blade under the oyster to separate from muscle, reserve liquid (liquor), and use immediately.

4	slices bacon	4
2 cups	shucked oysters (12) with liquor, drained, liquid reserved	500 mL
2 tbsp	all-purpose flour	30 mL
¼ cup	heavy or whipping (35%) cream	60 mL
2 tsp	horseradish	10 mL
	Salt and freshly ground black pepper	
	Porcelain spoons or toast points	

1. In a skillet, sauté bacon over medium-high heat until crisp. Transfer to a paper towel–lined plate to drain. When cool, crumble. Set aside.

2. Drain off all but 1 tbsp (15 mL) fat from pan. Add drained oysters and sauté until edges begin to curl, about 2 minutes. Using a slotted spoon, transfer to a plate. Add flour to pan and cook, stirring, for 1 minute. Add oyster liquor and cream and cook, stirring, until thickened (mixture will be very thick), about 2 minutes. Remove from heat and stir in horseradish. Return oysters to pan. Season to taste with salt and pepper.

3. Place 1 oyster plus sauce on each spoon (or toast point). Sprinkle crumbled bacon over top. Serve immediately.

Variation

Oyster Rolls: This is a more substantial plated appetizer. Allow 1 roll and 3 oysters for each person. Cut the top off a small roll and scoop out the center. Brush inside and out with melted butter. Place in a preheated oven (400°F/200°C) until crisp and lightly browned, about 10 minutes. Spoon oysters with sauce into rolls, sprinkle with crumbled bacon and replace tops. Serve plated.

Oyster and Artichoke Gratin

Makes 6 servings

This recipe was inspired by one that appears in Ralph Brennan's New Orleans Seafood Cookbook. *It is a great special occasion starter.*

Tips

You can shuck oysters yourself or for convenience, buy shucked oysters with liquor from your fishmonger.

To shuck an oyster: Hold oyster in a tea towel to protect your hand, flat side facing up, and fit an oyster knife into the hinge at the most narrow part and push to release. Twist the knife and run over the top of the shell to separate. Run the blade under the oyster to separate from muscle, reserve liquid (liquor), and use immediately.

- **Preheat broiler**
- **6 small (about ½ cup/125 mL) ramekins**

1	can (14 oz/398 mL) artichoke hearts, drained	1
½ cup	freshly grated Parmesan cheese	125 mL
1 tbsp	fresh Italian flat-leaf parsley leaves	15 mL
1	clove garlic	1
⅛ tsp	cayenne pepper	0.5 mL
2 tbsp	extra virgin olive oil	30 mL
½ cup	dry bread crumbs, such as panko	125 mL
2 tbsp	unsalted butter	30 mL
24	shucked oysters, drained, liquor reserved (see Tips, left)	24
	Freshly ground black or white pepper	
	Olive oil for drizzling	

1. In a food processor with metal blade, pulse artichokes, Parmesan, parsley, garlic, cayenne and olive oil until artichokes are finely chopped and mixture is blended, about 10 times. Add bread crumbs and pulse twice. Scrape down sides of the bowl and pulse twice. Set aside.

2. In a large skillet, melt butter over medium-high heat. Add oysters in one layer and cook just until the edges curl, about 1 minute. (Do not overcook.) Remove from heat.

3. Using a slotted spoon, transfer 4 oysters to each ramekin. Add about 3 tbsp (45 mL) oyster liquor to each ramekin and spread about 2 tbsp (30 mL) artichoke mixture over top. Season to taste with pepper. Drizzle liberally with butter mixture from pan, and a bit of olive oil. Broil until tops brown and oysters are bubbling, about 5 minutes. Serve immediately.

Butter-Crusted Oysters

Makes 12 oysters

A classic French technique that is used in some of the top French restaurants.

• **Preheat broiler**

½ cup	chopped fresh thyme	125 mL
½ cup	diced whole wheat bread	125 mL
¾ cup	unsalted butter, cut into cubes	175 mL
¼ cup	chopped Italian flat-leaf parsley leaves	60 mL
Pinch	salt	Pinch
12	Malpeque or other medium-size oysters, shucked, in the shell (see Tips, page 315)	12

1. In a food processor fitted with a metal blade, pulse thyme, bread, butter, parsley and salt until smooth. Transfer to a bowl.
2. Spread butter mixture over entire surface of each oyster. Place oysters on a rimmed baking sheet and broil until crust is golden brown and oyster is slightly firm, about 2 minutes. Serve immediately.

Oysters on the Half Shell with Avocado Mignonette

Makes 12 oysters

If you're confident with your shucking skills, it is fun and interactive to shuck oysters in front of your guests but they can also be shucked a few hours ahead of time and refrigerated until ready to serve. You can also try serving a selection of toppings along side the oysters like freshly grated horseradish, different vinegars or even Cocktail Sauce (page 547) or Preserved Lemons (page 554).

¼ cup	Champagne vinegar or white wine vinegar	60 mL
2 tbsp	finely diced avocado	30 mL
1 tbsp	finely diced shallots	15 mL
1 tsp	grated lemon zest	5 mL
½ tsp	grated fresh horseradish or prepared horseradish	2 mL
¼ tsp	hot pepper sauce	1 mL
12	Malpeque or other medium-size oysters, shucked, in the shell (see Tips, page 315)	12

1. In a bowl, combine vinegar, avocado, shallots, lemon zest, horseradish and hot pepper sauce. Mix well. Divide avocado mixture equally over shucked oysters and serve immediately.

Sushi Pizza

Makes 4 servings

This is not your typical pizza, but a Japanese twist on an Italian classic. Enjoy!

Tips

We suggest two pieces per person but feel free to use your judgment here.

Don't confuse hot Asian chile sauces with tomato-based chili sauce, which is sweet and often substituted for ketchup. The Asian versions are made from ground chiles and are very spicy. They are a great way to instantly add heat and flavor to a dish.

- **Candy/deep-fry thermometer**

½ cup	sushi rice (see Tips, page 293)	125 mL
1 cup	water	250 mL
½ tsp	salt	2 mL
	Oil	
¼ cup	all-purpose flour	60 mL
2 tbsp	mayonnaise	30 mL
1 tsp	hot Asian chile sauce, such as sambal oelek or Sriracha (see Tips, left)	5 mL
4 tsp	flying fish roe (tobiko)	20 mL
2 tsp	finely sliced green onions	10 mL

1. In a fine-mesh strainer, rinse rice thoroughly under cold water until water runs clear, about 5 minutes. Transfer to a saucepan. Add water and bring to a boil over medium heat. Cover, reduce heat to low and simmer for 5 minutes. Remove from heat and let steam for another 15 to 20 minutes. Resist the temptation to remove the cover to sneak a peek — it is important to keep the steam and heat inside the pan. Transfer rice to a bowl, add salt and mix gently to combine.

2. Divide rice in two. With moistened hands, form into two cakes, each about 1 inch (2.5 cm) thick. Place on a plate, cover and refrigerate until firm, about 1 hour.

3. In deep heavy-bottomed skillet, add oil to a depth of at least 2 inches (5 cm). Heat to 350°F (180°C). (You can also use a deep fryer; follow the manufacturer's instructions.) Dredge cakes in flour, dusting off excess. Transfer to oil one at a time to fry until crisp and golden brown, 4 to 5 minutes. Transfer to a paper towel–lined plate to drain.

4. In a bowl, combine mayonnaise and hot sauce. Mix well. Spoon over surface of each crisp cake, dividing equally. Evenly spread fish roe and green onions over top. Cut cake into quarters and serve immediately.

Sweet Scallop Appetizer

Makes about 1¼ cups (300 mL)

*This is wonderful
with a small side
salad or on a warm
slice of crostini
(pages 219 and 220)
or even a simple
cracker (see Tips,
below).*

Tips

When choosing crackers to
accompany appetizers, look
for high-quality versions
that don't have strong
flavors or too much salt.

*To remove the tough
muscle from scallop:* Find
the small piece of flesh
that can be found on the
edge of the scallop, often a
slightly different color than
the main section. Using a
sharp paring knife, carefully
remove it from the main
section before preparing
your recipe.

12 oz	scallops, muscle removed, cut into 1-inch (2.5 cm) cubes (see Tips, left)	375 g
¼ cup	thinly sliced onions	60 mL
3 tbsp	olive oil, divided	45 mL
1 tsp	brown sugar	5 mL
1 tsp	grated lemon zest	5 mL
½ tsp	coarsely chopped fresh thyme leaves	2 mL
¼ tsp	hot pepper flakes	1 mL
½ tsp	toasted sesame seeds	2 mL
¼ tsp	thinly sliced green onions	1 mL
¼ tsp	salt	1 mL

1. In a bowl, combine scallops, onions, 2 tbsp (30 mL) of the olive oil, brown sugar, lemon zest, thyme and hot pepper flakes. Cover and marinate at room temperature for at least 20 minutes or refrigerate for up to 1 hour.

2. In a large skillet, heat remaining 1 tbsp (15 mL) of olive oil over medium-high heat. Sauté scallop mixture until medium rare or until slightly firm to the touch, about 1½ minutes. Transfer to a serving bowl and add sesame seeds, green onions and salt.

Butter-Crusted Black Cod

Makes 16 servings

Black cod is a very buttery fish and combined with the crisp crust it's a five-star appetizer.

Tip

We always use flat-leaf rather than curly parsley because it has more flavor.

- **Preheat oven to 400°F (200°C)**

½ cup	fresh thyme, stems removed	125 mL
½ cup	diced whole wheat bread	125 mL
½ cup	unsalted butter, cut into cubes	125 mL
¼ cup	chopped Italian flat-leaf parsley leaves	60 mL
¼ cup	mascarpone cheese	60 mL
Pinch	salt	Pinch
2 lbs	skin-on black cod fillets, cut into 16 pieces	1 kg
½ cup	sweet white wine	125 mL
1 cup	diced tomatoes	250 mL

1. In a food processor fitted with a metal blade, pulse thyme, bread, butter, parsley, mascarpone and salt until smooth. Transfer to a bowl.

2. Spread butter mixture over flesh side of each piece of cod, fully encasing top with butter. Pour wine into ovenproof baking dish. Place fish butter side up into pan. Bake in preheated oven until crust is golden brown, about 12 minutes. Garnish with tomatoes.

Mussels on the Half Shell

Makes 25 to 30 mussels

Inspired by two of our favorite appetizers — fresh oysters on the half shell and steamed mussels. These are quite refreshing and go perfectly with a barbecue party or clambake or even as an elegant addition to a more sophisticated menu.

1 tbsp	olive oil	15 mL
¼ cup	diced onions	60 mL
1½ lbs	mussels, scrubbed and debearded	750 g
¼ cup	white wine	60 mL
¼ cup	Grape Mignonette (page 545)	60 mL

1. In a large skillet, heat oil over medium heat. Add onions and cook, stirring, until translucent, 3 to 4 minutes. Add mussels and cook, stirring, until they begin to open, 1 to 2 minutes. Add wine and continue to cook until mussels are fully open, about 1 minute. Remove from heat. Remove mussels from shell and separate two shells. Discard any mussels that do not open.

2. Place one mussel on top of one shell and garnish equally with mignonette. Serve immediately.

Roasted Fingerling Potatoes with Caviar and Crème Fraîche

Makes about 15 appetizers

Fingerling potatoes create the perfect base for a potato appetizer. Often no larger than a finger (hence the name), these one or two-biters can be covered with many ingredients. Here they are accented by creamy crème fraîche and salty caviar.

Tip

If you prefer, use flying fish roe, also known as tobiko, in this recipe. It is found in sushi restaurants around the globe and is a cheaper alternative to sevruga or beluga caviar.

- **Preheat oven to 450°F (230°C)**

4 cups	water	1 L
1 lb	fingerling potatoes	500 g
1¼ tsp	salt, divided	6 mL
1 tbsp	olive oil	15 mL
¼ tsp	freshly ground black pepper	1 mL
¼ cup	crème fraîche or sour cream (see Tips, page 321)	60 mL
2 tsp	caviar (see Tip, left)	10 mL

1. In a large ovenproof saucepan, bring water, potatoes and 1 tsp (5 mL) of the salt to a boil over high heat. Reduce heat and simmer until potatoes are fork tender, 10 to 12 minutes. Drain and dry potatoes thoroughly on a paper towel.

2. Toss in olive oil, remaining salt, and pepper. Bake in preheated oven until potatoes are crisp, about 10 minutes. Let cool to the touch.

3. Cut a slit down middle of potato ensuring not to cut through fully. Garnish with crème fraîche and caviar and serve immediately.

Lobster Salad Mille Feuille

Makes 16

A luxurious delight for your senses. Cooking lobster and removing the meat can be a little time consuming so we suggest serving this decadent appetizer for those special occasions. It really is something to be celebrated.

Tips

Crème fraîche is available in well-stocked supermarkets. If you can't find it, you can make your own. *To make crème fraîche:* In a saucepan, heat 1 cup (250 mL) heavy or whipping (35%) cream over low heat until bubbles form around the edges. Transfer to a glass or ceramic bowl. Stir in 2 tbsp (30 mL) sour cream or buttermilk. Cover and let stand at room temperature for 12 hours, or until very thick. Stir well. Cover and refrigerate until you're ready to use.

Toasting sesame seeds are quite easy and only takes minutes. *To toast sesame seeds:* In a large skillet over medium-high heat, toast sesame seeds, stirring often, until fragrant and golden brown, 3 to 4 minutes.

- **Preheat oven to 325°F (160°C)**
- **Baking sheet, lined with parchment paper**

8 oz	puff pastry, thawed	250 g
2 cups	coarsely chopped cooked lobster meat	500 mL
¼ cup	coarsely chopped mango	60 mL
¼ cup	finely chopped green onions	60 mL
¼ cup	crème fraîche (see Tips, left)	60 mL
2 tsp	toasted sesame seeds (see Tips, left)	10 mL

1. On a lightly floured surface, roll out pastry to a 10-inch (25 cm) square. Using a pizza cutter or knife, cut into 32 equal squares. Place on prepared baking sheet, at least 1 inch (2.5 cm) apart. With the tines of a fork, prick the pastry all over. Bake in preheated oven until pastry is golden brown and flaky, about 15 minutes. Let cool.

2. In a bowl, combine lobster, mango, green onions, crème fraîche and sesame seeds. Mix well. Lay half the squares on a flat surface and divide lobster salad equally in the middle of each one. Place remaining squares on top and press gently to form sandwiches. Serve immediately or keep separate and refrigerate salad for up to 1 day and cooled pastry squares in an airtight container for up to 3 days.

Panko-Crusted "Fish Sticks"

Makes 10 fish sticks

Those fish sticks in the frozen food section of the supermarket have given this wonderful classic a bad name. Served with Caper Lemon Rémoulade (page 539) or for a spicy kick Wasabi Aïoli (page 537), you've created a fabulous finger food.

Tip

Panko bread crumbs are used to coat fried foods in Japan. Typically coarser than the bread crumbs used in North America, they tend to achieve a better crust than their counterparts. Cornflake crumbs make an excellent substitute.

- **Preheat oven to 300°F (150°C)**

1 cup	panko bread crumbs (see Tip, left)	250 mL
⅓ cup	freshly grated Parmesan cheese	75 mL
1	egg white	1
1 tsp	water	5 mL
8 oz	skinless sole or striped bass	250 g
2 tbsp	extra virgin olive oil	30 mL
½ cup	Caper Lemon Rèmoulade (page 539)	125 mL

1. In a bowl, combine bread crumbs and Parmesan cheese. Set aside.

2. In another bowl, whisk together egg white and water to fully incorporate. Set aside.

3. Cut fish fillet into 10 "fingers" and toss one finger at a time in egg mixture to fully coat each piece. Drain off majority of egg wash and coat in bread crumb mixture. Repeat until all fingers are fully coated. Discard excess egg and crumbs.

4. In a nonstick skillet, heat oil over medium heat. In batches as necessary, fry fish fingers, turning once, until golden brown and fish flakes easily with a fork, about 2 minutes per side. Serve immediately or let cool to room temperature before serving. Serve with Caper Lemon Rèmoulade.

Sticks and Picks

There is something romantic about eating food on a stick — like camping out, braving the wild. Even food served on cocktail toothpicks has quixotic appeal. It's reminiscent of those sophisticated cocktail parties we see in old movies, where men wore dinner jackets and the butler mixed drinks in a silver shaker.

Here we've tried to capture the gamut, from dishes that would fit right in around a campfire such as Buffalo Chicken Wings (page 346) and One-Bite Corn Dogs (page 353) to more elegant fare such as Japanese-Style Fried Chicken served with Avocado Topping (page 339) and Peanut-Crusted Beef Tenderloin Satay (page 351).

Chile-Fried Tofu 324
Indian-Spiced Tofu with Cucumber Raita 325
Grilled Vegetable Skewers 326
Tomato and Cheese Skewers 327
Red Pepper and Onion Skewers 327
Caramel-Glazed Sweet Potato Skewers 328
Portobello Mushroom Skewers with
   Black Pepper Goat Cheese Dip 329
Caramelized Pineapple Satays 330
Fruit Skewers 330
Eggplant Parmesan Brochettes 331
Fried Banana and Cheese 332
Shrimp Satays 333
Indian-Spiced Shrimp Kabobs 334
Chile-Spiked Shrimp Kabobs 335
Sesame-Dusted Beer-Battered Shrimp
   with Roasted Pepper 336
Pancetta-Wrapped Scallops 337
Beer-Battered Clams 338
Japanese-Style Fried Chicken 339

Chicken Yakitori 340
Chicken Kabobs with Tahini Sauce 341
Traditional Chicken Satays 342
Coconut-Crusted Chicken Satays 343
Carnitas 343
Cilantro Chicken Kabobs 344
Almost-Indian Chicken Kabobs 345
Buffalo Chicken Wings 346
Chicken and Sun-Dried Tomato Croquettes 347
Indonesian Pork Satays 348
Minced Pork and Pineapple Skewers 349
Korean-Style Beef Kabobs 350
Peanut-Crusted Beef Tenderloin Satays 351
Sugarcane with Marinated Beef 352
One-Bite Corn Dogs 353
Meatballs in Lemon Sauce 354
Bacon-Wrapped Sausage Rolls 355
Oregano-Spiked Pork Meatballs 356

Chile-Fried Tofu

Makes 6 to 8 servings

These tasty bites are perfect for vegans, but so delicious others will thoroughly enjoy them, too.

Tips

After draining the tofu, wrap in several layers of paper towel and squeeze lightly to extract excess moisture before cutting into cubes. Otherwise, the flour will not to adhere to the surfaces.

If you're worried about gluten sensitivities, substitute corn flour for the all-purpose.

Use hot or sweet smoked paprika to suit your taste.

Sauce

2 tbsp	water	30 mL
1 tbsp	soy sauce	15 mL
1 tbsp	freshly squeezed lime juice	15 mL
1	package (1 lb/500 g) firm tofu, drained and cubed (½ inch/1 cm) (see Tips, left)	1
¼ cup	all-purpose flour (see Tips, left)	60 mL
2 tsp	smoked paprika (see Tips, left)	10 mL
3 tbsp	oil (approx.)	45 mL
6	green onions, white with a bit of green, thinly sliced	6
4	cloves garlic, thinly sliced	4
1	long red chile pepper, minced	1
	Roasted Pepper and Salt (page 552)	

1. *Sauce:* In a small bowl, combine water, soy sauce and lime juice. Set aside.

2. On a large plate, combine flour and paprika. Mix well. Dredge tofu in mixture, coating well. Discard any excess.

3. In a large skillet, heat 2 tbsp (30 mL) of the oil over medium-high heat. Add dredged tofu in batches and fry, turning often, until all sides are golden, about 5 minutes per batch, adding more oil as necessary. Transfer to a plate and set aside.

4. Reduce heat to medium. Add 1 tbsp (15 mL) of oil to pan, if necessary. Add green onions, garlic and chile pepper and cook, stirring, until garlic begins to brown, about 4 minutes. Add reserved sauce mixture and stir well. Add fried tofu and toss to coat. Transfer to a serving platter. Sprinkle to taste with Roasted Pepper and Salt. Pass with toothpicks or small skewers.

Indian-Spiced Tofu with Cucumber Raita

Makes 6 to 8 servings

These tofu cubes are easy to make and very tasty. The raita makes a great dipping sauce.

Tips

You'll get the best flavor if you toast and grind cumin seeds yourself. *To toast cumin seeds:* Place seeds in a dry skillet over medium heat. Cook, stirring, until fragrant, about 3 minutes. Transfer to a mortar or spice grinder and grind.

If you're worried about gluten sensitivities, substitute corn flour for the all-purpose.

Use hot or sweet paprika to suit your taste.

Cucumber Raita

1 cup	plain yogurt	250 mL
½	English cucumber, grated	½
2 tbsp	finely chopped cilantro leaves	30 mL
½ tsp	ground cumin (see Tips, left)	2 mL
	Salt and freshly ground black pepper	
1	package (1 lb/500 g) firm tofu, drained and cubed (1 inch/2.5 cm) (see Tips, page 324)	1
¼ cup	all-purpose flour (see Tips, left)	60 mL
1 tbsp	curry powder	15 mL
1 tsp	sweet or hot paprika	5 mL
3 tbsp	oil (approx.)	45 mL
2	cloves garlic, minced	2
¼ cup	freshly squeezed lemon juice	60 mL

1. *Cucumber Raita:* In a serving bowl, combine yogurt, cucumber, cilantro and cumin. Mix well. Season to taste with salt and pepper. Cover and refrigerate for at least 30 minutes to allow flavors to meld.

2. On a large plate, combine flour, curry powder and paprika. Mix well. Dredge tofu in mixture, coating well. Discard any excess.

3. In a large skillet, heat 2 tbsp (30 mL) of the oil over medium-high heat. Add dredged tofu in batches and fry, turning often, until all sides are golden, about 5 minutes per batch, adding more oil as necessary. Transfer to a plate and set aside.

4. Reduce heat to medium. Add 1 tbsp (15 mL) of oil to pan. Add garlic and cook, stirring, for 1 minute. Add lemon juice and stir well. Add tofu and toss gently to coat. Transfer to a serving dish. Serve with toothpicks and raita for dipping.

Grilled Vegetable Skewers

Makes 12 skewers

The perfect summer barbecue appetizer. Serve with a Basic Barbecue Sauce (page 553) or a fresh Basil Pesto (page 549). Consider this recipe as a base and use other vegetables in season or based on availability.

Tip

For a foolproof way to prevent burning even when skewers have been soaked, place a sheet of foil toward the bottom of a barbecue grill (side closest to you) and place the skewers on the grill with the exposed wood resting on the foil.

- **Preheat barbecue grill to high (see Tip, left)**
- **12 soaked wooden skewers (page 332)**

12	$\frac{1}{2}$-inch (1 cm) cubes zucchini	12
12	$\frac{1}{2}$-inch (1 cm) squares red bell pepper	12
12	$\frac{1}{2}$-inch (1 cm) cubes eggplant	12
1 tbsp	balsamic vinegar	15 mL
1 tbsp	extra virgin olive oil	15 mL
$\frac{1}{4}$ tsp	salt	1 mL
$\frac{1}{8}$ tsp	freshly ground black pepper	0.5 mL
$\frac{1}{2}$ tsp	chopped fresh basil leaves	2 mL

1. Thread 1 zucchini cube on each wooden skewer, followed by red pepper and eggplant, ensuring point is not exposed.

2. In a shallow dish, combine vinegar, oil, salt and pepper. Place skewers in dish, turning to coat in marinade. Cover and marinate at room temperature for 1 hour.

3. Remove vegetables from marinade. Reserve marinade. Grill vegetables until caramelized, about $1\frac{1}{2}$ minutes. Turn and grill on remaining three sides. Add basil to the leftover marinade and place grilled vegetable skewers back into marinade and turn to coat. Serve immediately.

Tomato and Cheese Skewers

Make 12 skewers

A one-bite tomato mozzarella salad is a perfect brunch appetizer, especially in months when tomatoes are at their sweetest. This recipe can easily be doubled or tripled.

Tip

The size of skewer doesn't matter here, a 3-inch (7.5 cm) or 6-inch (15 cm) skewer would both work beautifully.

- **12 wooden skewers (see Tip, left)**

6	mini fresh mozzarella (bocconcini) balls, cut in half	6
6	cherry tomatoes, cut in half	6
1 tbsp	Basil Pesto (page 549) or store-bought	15 mL
1 tbsp	extra virgin olive oil	15 mL
	Salt and freshly ground black pepper	

1. In a bowl, combine mozzarella, tomatoes, pesto, oil, ¼ tsp (1 mL) salt and pinch of pepper. Toss well to coat. Place one half of the tomato with one half of the mozzarella, cut sides together and pierce with skewer keeping them together. This should resemble a lollipop. Serve immediately or refrigerate for up to 24 hours. (Not any longer or the tomatoes will break down and become soft.)

Red Pepper and Onion Skewers

Makes 16 skewers

A wonderful appetizer for vegans that will be loved by carnivores, too. This is a perfect appetizer for a spring or summer barbecue party and even better when paired with Grilled Scallion and Corn Dip (page 42).

- **16 soaked wooden skewers (page 332)**

1	red bell pepper, roasted (see Tip, page 184)	1
8	green onions	8
3 tbsp	Roasted Red Pepper Vinaigrette (page 541)	45 mL

1. Trim stem off green onions, leaving them intact. In a large pot of boiling water, poach until bulbs are soft, about 5 minutes. Drain and cut in half lengthwise.

2. Cut roasted pepper lengthwise into 16 equal slices. In a bowl, combine roasted pepper slices, green onions and Roasted Red Pepper Vinaigrette and toss well to coat.

3. Place one slice of pepper smooth side down on a flat surface. Place onion on top. Roll two together into a pinwheel. Pierce skewer through onion and pepper. This will resemble a lollipop. Serve immediately.

Caramel-Glazed Sweet Potato Skewers

Makes 12 skewers

The caramel glaze creates a wonderful coating for an already sweet vegetable, creating an appetizer that is almost candy-like. A perfect festive appetizer to serve around Thanksgiving or Christmas time.

Tip

To toast hazelnuts: Spread nuts on a baking sheet and bake in a 250°F (120°C) oven, stirring often, until fragrant and golden brown, 12 to 15 minutes. Let cool to the touch. Rub nuts in small batches between two tea towels to remove skins.

- **12 wooden skewers**
- **Candy/deep fry thermometer**

2 tbsp	cornstarch	30 mL
½ tsp	salt	2 mL
	Oil	
½ cup	granulated sugar	125 mL
2 tbsp	water	30 mL
1 lb	sweet potatoes, peeled and cut into 12 sticks, each 3 inches (7.5 cm) long and ¾ inch (2 cm) wide	500 g
1 tbsp	ground toasted hazelnuts (see Tip, left)	15 mL

1. In a large bowl, combine cornstarch and salt. Mix well. Set aside.

2. When you're ready to cook, place 6 inches (15 cm) oil in a large saucepan or Dutch oven and heat over medium heat until temperature reaches 350°F (180°C). (You can also use a deep fryer; follow the manufacturer's instructions.)

3. In a saucepan, combine sugar and water. Heat over medium heat, stirring gently, just until sugar is dissolved, then bring to a boil, without stirring. Boil gently (reducing heat if necessary), without stirring, until syrup turns a caramel color. Set aside.

4. Meanwhile, lightly dredge sweet potato sticks in cornstarch mixture. Immediately drop in preheated oil and fry, in batches, until golden brown, 3 to 5 minutes. Remove from oil and drain on paper towels. Skewer sweet potato sticks vertically, leaving 3 to 4 inches (7.5 to 10 cm) of skewer exposed and place on a platter. Drizzle caramel sauce over sweet potatoes and garnish with toasted hazelnuts. Serve immediately.

Portobello Mushroom Skewers with Black Pepper Goat Cheese Dip

Makes 8 brochettes

There is something delectable about the combination of mushrooms and goat cheese.

- **8 wooden skewers**

2	portobello mushrooms, each cut into 8 chunks	2
1/3 cup	olive oil, divided	75 mL
2 tbsp	balsamic vinegar	30 mL
Pinch	salt	Pinch
Pinch	freshly ground black pepper	Pinch
1/2 cup	Black Pepper Goat Cheese Dip (page 20)	125 mL

1. In a shallow bowl, combine mushrooms, 3 tbsp (45 mL) of the olive oil and vinegar. Marinate mushrooms at room temperature until most of the marinade is absorbed, about 20 minutes.

2. In a skillet, heat remaining oil over medium heat. Remove mushrooms from marinade, reserving marinade. Fry mushrooms bottom side down until golden brown, about 3 minutes. Flip mushrooms and continue to fry until soft, about 2 minutes. Skewer two pieces of mushroom on each skewer and place on a platter. Season with salt and pepper and remaining marinade. Serve immediately with Black Pepper Goat Cheese Dip.

Caramelized Pineapple Satays

Makes 6 skewers

There is something amazing about warm pineapple but when served with something sweet — watch out, the troops will come running.

- **6 soaked wooden skewers (page 332)**

6	1½-inch (4 cm) cubes pineapple	6
1 tbsp	packed brown sugar	15 mL
1 tbsp	unsalted butter	15 mL
1	cardamom pod, crushed	1

1. Place pineapple cubes on a flat surface and pierce skewers, ensuring point is not exposed. Lightly coat the top with brown sugar.
2. In a skillet, combine butter and cardamom pod and melt over medium heat. Add skewers, brown sugar side down, and cook until caramelized, about 2 minutes. Transfer to a serving platter and discard cardamom pod.

Fruit Skewers

Makes 12 brochettes

We love this combination of fruit but please feel free to substitute based on preference and availability.

Tips

There is always a price to be paid for beautifully cut fruit; in this case that price is leftover fruit. For a fresh start to your day or mid-afternoon snack, coarsely chop scraps of apples, watermelon and peeled kiwifruit and season with liquid honey and vanilla for a salad. Serve immediately or refrigerate for up to 3 days.

- **12 wooden skewers**

1 tbsp	agave syrup or liquid honey	15 mL
1 tsp	fresh squeezed lemon juice	5 mL
½ tsp	finely chopped mint leaves	2 mL
¼ tsp	vanilla extract or vanilla seeds	1 mL
12	1½-inch (4 cm) cubes apple	12
12	1½-inch (4 cm) cubes watermelon	12
12	1½-inch (4 cm) cubes peeled kiwifruit	12

1. In a bowl, combine agave syrup, lemon juice, mint and vanilla. Mix well. Set aside.
2. Thread 1 cube of apple, watermelon and kiwi onto each skewer, ensuring point is not exposed, and place on a platter. Lightly drizzle fruit with agave mixture and serve immediately.

Eggplant Parmesan Brochettes

Makes 5 brochettes

Here's an unique way to serve a very classic Italian dish.

Tips

Usually the size of the skewer will not make a difference to the success of a recipe. This holds true here, although you must ensure the skewer will fit into the skillet. If they are too long, you can cut them to the desired length using kitchen shears or scissors.

For best results, buy good quality Parmesan and grate it yourself. If you must use already-grated cheese, buy it from an Italian market or deli or a good cheese shop and ask to make sure it doesn't contain any "filler."

- **Preheat oven to 350°F (180°C)**
- **5 soaked wooden skewers (see Tips, left, and page 332)**

10	1½-inch (4 cm) cubes peeled eggplant	10
¼ cup	all-purpose flour	60 mL
⅛ tsp	salt	0.5 mL
⅛ tsp	freshly ground black pepper	0.5 mL
1	egg, beaten	1
¼ cup	panko bread crumbs	60 mL
2 tbsp	olive oil	30 mL
2 tsp	Oven-Roasted Cherry Tomato Sauce (page 546) or store-bought	10 mL
2 tbsp	freshly grated Parmesan cheese	30 mL

1. Thread 2 cubes of eggplant on each skewer, ensuring point is not exposed.

2. In a shallow bowl, combine flour, salt and pepper. Mix well. Place egg and bread crumbs in separate shallow bowls. Dip eggplant in flour, turning to lightly coat and tap to remove excess. Dip in egg and then in bread crumbs, turning until fully coated, pressing to coat. Discard excess flour, egg and crumbs.

3. In a large skillet, heat oil over medium heat. Fry eggplant skewers until bottoms are golden brown, about 2 minutes. Turn and continue to fry until all sides are golden brown, about 1½ minutes per side. Transfer to a baking sheet and bake in preheated oven until eggplant is tender, 5 to 7 minutes. Remove from oven and coat surface of eggplant with tomato sauce, dividing evenly, and sprinkle with cheese. Return to oven and bake until cheese is melted, about 3 minutes. Serve immediately.

Fried Banana and Cheese

Makes 12 appetizers

There is no doubt that the combination of banana and cheese has you a little caught off guard but they are a match made in heaven. Paired with Grilled Scallion and Corn Dip (page 42) you have a Mexican-inspired appetizer fit for any guest — child or adult.

Tip

Dipping the banana and cheese into flour, egg and coconut and then egg and bread crumbs creates a wonderfully thick and crisp coating.

- **Twelve 3-inch (7.5 cm) soaked wooden skewers (see below)**

1	large banana, cut into 12 thick slices (about ½ inch/1 cm)	1
6 oz	Havarti cheese, cut into 12 cubes	175 g
	Oil	
½ cup	all-purpose flour	125 mL
2	eggs, beaten	2
½ cup	unsweetened desiccated coconut	125 mL
½ cup	panko bread crumbs	125 mL
½ tsp	salt	2 mL

1. Thread 1 slice of banana and 1 cube of cheese on each skewer, ensuring point is not exposed.

2. When you're ready to cook, place about 3 inches (7.5 cm) oil in a large saucepan or Dutch oven and heat over medium heat until temperature reaches 350°F (180°C).

3. Place flour, eggs, coconut and bread crumbs in separate shallow bowls. Dip skewers in flour, turning to evenly coat shaking off excess. Dip in egg, then coconut, egg again and then in bread crumbs. Discard any excess flour, egg, coconut and crumbs.

4. Fry skewers, in batches, until golden brown and crispy, about 3 minutes. Remove from oil and drain on paper towels. Season with salt and serve immediately.

Soaking Wooden Skewers

Unless they have been soaked, wooden skewers will burn when heated. Before using, soak skewers in cold water to cover until you're ready to use them — for at least 30 minutes or for up to 8 hours.

Shrimp Satays

Makes 24 skewers

These spicy shrimp are fabulous for a summer party. They are great on their own, or for an added touch pass a small bowl of Peanut Sauce (page 554.)

Tip

For best results, brine the shrimp before marinating. *To brine shrimp:* Dissolve 2 tbsp (30 mL) kosher salt in 1 cup (250 mL) boiling water in a large bowl. Add 2 cups (500 mL) ice cubes. Stir well. Add enough cold water to ensure shrimp will be covered. Add shrimp and refrigerate for at least 15 minutes or up to 1 hour. Drain and rinse under cold running water and proceed with recipe.

- **24 soaked wooden skewers (page 332)**

1 lb	large shrimp (about 24), peeled and deveined, preferably brined (see Tip, left)	500 g
3	cilantro sprigs, leaves and stems	3
2	cloves garlic	2
2	Thai chile peppers	2
2 tsp	grated lime zest	10 mL
¼ cup	freshly squeezed lime juice	60 mL
1 tbsp	fish sauce	15 mL
1 tbsp	brown sugar	15 mL
	Oil	

1. In mini-bowl attachment of a food processor or in a mini chopper, purée cilantro, garlic, chile peppers, lime zest and juice, fish sauce and brown sugar. (If you prefer, you can mince the garlic, cilantro and chile peppers and combine with the remaining ingredients in a mixing bowl.) Transfer to a bowl.

2. Add shrimp and toss until well coated with mixture. Cover and refrigerate for 30 minutes or for up to 1 hour.

3. Preheat barbecue or broiler. Thread 1 shrimp per skewer, end to end. Brush liberally with oil and place on preheated barbecue or under broiler. Grill, turning once, about 1 minute per side.

Indian-Spiced Shrimp Kabobs

Makes 12 kabobs

These Indian flavors are remarkably refreshing. Call this curry on a stick. Peeling the shrimp makes for a casual eating experience.

Tips

To grate peeled ginger: Use a fine, sharp-toothed grater such as Microplane.

To purée garlic: Use a fine, sharp-toothed grater, such as those made by Microplane, or put the garlic through a garlic press.

For best flavor, toast and grind cumin and coriander yourself. *To toast seeds:* Place seeds in a dry skillet over medium heat and cook, stirring, until fragrant, about 3 minutes. Immediately transfer to a mortar or a spice grinder and grind.

- **12 soaked wooden skewers (page 332)**

1 lb	large shrimp (about 24), shells on, deveined, preferably brined, rinsed and patted dry (see Tip, page 333)	500 g
¼ cup	plain Greek-style (pressed) yogurt (see Tips, page 341)	60 mL
1 tsp	puréed gingerroot (see Tips, left)	5 mL
1 tsp	puréed garlic (see Tips, left)	5 mL
½ tsp	ground cumin seeds (see Tips, left)	2 mL
½ tsp	ground coriander seeds	2 mL
¼ tsp	cayenne pepper	1 mL
	Freshly ground black pepper	
12	cherry tomatoes	12
1 tbsp	olive oil	15 mL
	Sea salt or Chile Salt (page 552)	
	Lime wedges	

1. In a bowl, combine yogurt, ginger, garlic, cumin, coriander, cayenne, and pepper to taste. Stir well. Add shrimp and toss to ensure all are coated evenly. Cover and refrigerate for 1 hour.

2. When you're ready to cook, preheat barbecue or broiler. Toss tomatoes in olive oil. Thread 1 shrimp lengthwise on a soaked wooden skewer, followed by a tomato and another shrimp. Repeat with remaining skewers, tomatoes and shrimp.

3. Place kabobs on preheated grill and grill, turning once, until shrimp are pink and opaque, about 5 minutes. Sprinkle sea salt evenly over kabobs and finish with a squeeze of lime. Serve immediately.

Chile-Spiked Shrimp Kabobs

Makes 12 kabobs

This simple Mediterranean marinade is enhanced with the addition of mild chile powder. Finished with a sprinkling of parsley or dill, these kabobs are very pretty.

Tips

Piment d'Espelette is a dried mild chile pepper from the Basque region of France. It adds a nice flavor to this recipe.

Ancho is a dried chile, Mexican in origin. It is sweet and mild.

- **12 soaked wooden skewers (page 332)**

1 lb	large shrimp (about 24) peeled, deveined and preferably brined (see Tip, page 333), rinsed and patted dry	500 mL
1/4 cup + 1 tbsp	olive oil	75 mL
1/4 cup	freshly squeezed lemon juice	60 mL
2	cloves garlic, minced	2
2 tsp	mild chile powder, such as piment d'Espelette, Aleppo or ancho (see Tips, left)	10 mL
4	green onions, white part with a bit of green, cut into 2-inch (5 cm) lengths	4
	Finely chopped parsley or dill	
	Salt and freshly ground black pepper	

1. In a shallow dish, combine 1/4 cup (60 mL) of the olive oil, lemon juice, garlic and chile powder. Add shrimp and toss to ensure all are coated evenly. Cover and refrigerate for 1 hour.

2. When you're ready to cook, preheat barbecue or broiler. In a bowl, combine green onions and 1 tbsp (15 mL) of olive oil. Thread 1 shrimp lengthwise on a wooden skewer, followed by a piece of onion and another shrimp. Repeat with remaining skewers, onion and shrimp.

3. Place kabobs on preheated grill or under broiler and cook, turning once until shrimp are pink and opaque, about 5 minutes. Remove from grill and sprinkle liberally with parsley, salt and pepper. Serve immediately.

Sesame-Dusted Beer-Battered Shrimp with Roasted Pepper

Makes about 36 large shrimp

Shrimp fried in batter are a classic. Here, we've added beer to the batter, which adds depth and a pleasant hint of bitterness, and dusted the cooked shrimp with sesame seeds and a seasoned salt. Serve them as is or add a small bowl of shrimp cocktail sauce for dipping (see Tips, below).

Tips

One of the tastiest and easiest sauces for shrimp cocktail is simply a blend of ketchup and horseradish. Just combine 1 cup (250 mL) ketchup with 2 tbsp (30 mL) prepared horseradish and stir well. If you prefer a zestier sauce, try making a double batch of the one used in Almost Classic Shrimp Cocktail (page 367).

The number of shrimp you can cook per batch depends upon the size of your shrimp and the diameter of the cooking vessel. When testing this recipe, we used large shrimp (about 24 per lb/ 500 g) and a Dutch oven that is 10½ inches (26 cm) in diameter.

- • **Candy/deep-fry thermometer**

1 cup	all-purpose flour	250 mL
1 tsp	salt	5 mL
1 tsp	hot paprika	5 mL
1 tsp	baking powder	5 mL
1	egg	1
1 cup	beer	250 mL
2 cups	vegetable oil, such as peanut or corn (approx.)	500 mL
1½ lbs	shrimp, peeled and deveined, preferably brined (see Tip, page 333)	750 g
2 tbsp	sesame seeds	30 mL
	Roasted Pepper and Salt (page 552)	

1. In a food processor fitted with metal blade, pulse flour, salt, paprika and baking powder to combine, 2 or 3 times. Add egg and beer and process until smooth, about 30 seconds. Cover and refrigerate for 2 hours.

2. When you're ready to cook, place oil in a large saucepan or Dutch oven and heat over medium heat until temperature reaches 375°F (190°C). (You can also use a deep fryer; follow the manufacturer's instructions.) Pat shrimp dry with paper towel, dip in batter until well coated and drop in hot oil. Repeat until all shrimp are used up, cooking in batches that allow adequate space between the shrimp. (This will depend on the size of both your shrimp and the cooking vessel.)

3. When shrimp are golden (about 2 minutes) remove from oil and drain on paper towels. Discard any excess batter. Immediately sprinkle fried shrimp with sesame seeds and Roasted Pepper and Salt. Spear with toothpicks and serve.

Pancetta-Wrapped Scallops

Makes various amounts

The secret to making these is to ensure that you have enough pancetta to moisten and flavor the scallops but not so much that you overwhelm their rich but delicate flavor. The pancetta is quite salty, so after the scallops are cooked add a good dash of lemon juice to balance the salt. It also complements the flavor of the scallops. A generous sprinkling of chives completes the dish.

Tips

Short 3-inch (7.5 cm) wooden skewers would work well here.

You want the scallops to be as close to bite-size as possible.

Depending upon your source, sliced pancetta varies in thickness. If your pancetta is very thinly sliced (as it should be) you'll need about half a slice for each scallop (or shrimp).

- **Preheat barbecue**
- **Soaked wooden skewers (see Tips, left, and page 332)**

> Sea scallops, halved, if necessary (see Tips, left)
> Thinly sliced pancetta, about $\frac{1}{2}$ slice per bite-size scallop
> Freshly squeezed lemon juice
> Finely chopped chives

1. Wrap scallops in pancetta (see Tips, left) and spear crosswise with skewers (so white top of scallop is facing up). Grill, turning once, until pancetta begins to crisp and scallop is just firm and opaque, about 5 minutes.

2. Remove from grill. Drizzle with lemon juice and sprinkle with chives. Serve immediately.

Variations

Pancetta-Wrapped Shrimp: Substitute peeled, deveined extra-large or jumbo shrimp for the scallops. Brine before cooking, if possible (page 333.)

If you prefer, place the wrapped scallops (or shrimp) on a parchment-lined baking sheet and bake in a 425°F (220°C) oven until pancetta begins to crisp and scallops are cooked through, about 5 minutes.

Beer-Battered Clams

Makes 24

These light and succulent nuggets of flavor are a great splurge. People will grab them up as they come out of the pan. The cornmeal adds pleasant crunch, but the clams will be delicious with or without it.

Tips

Corn flour is finely ground cornmeal. It is not cornstarch, which is the isolated starch of corn, used for thickening or to soften baking batters. Here corn flour is used to add flavor and lightness to the batter. It is available in well-stocked supermarkets and natural foods stores. If you can't find it, substitute ¼ cup (60 mL) each all-purpose four and cornstarch for the quantity called for here.

You can also use drained canned clams. You'll need about 3 cans (each 4 oz/133 g).

- **Candy/deep fry thermometer**

Batter

½ cup	each all-purpose flour and corn flour	125 mL
1 tbsp	finely ground cornmeal, optional	15 mL
1 tbsp	baking powder	15 mL
1 tsp	salt	5 mL
1 cup	flat beer	250 mL

Ponzo-Style Dipping Sauce, optional

¼ cup	soy sauce	60 mL
2 tbsp	freshly squeezed lime juice	30 mL
1 tbsp	mirin	15 mL
½ tsp	Asian chile sauce, such as sambal oelek	2 mL
	Oil	
2 tbsp	cornstarch	30 mL
24	shucked clams, patted dry (see Tips, left)	24

1. In a bowl, combine all-purpose flour, corn flour, cornmeal, if using, baking power and salt. Stir to combine. Whisk in beer. Cover and refrigerate for 1 hour.
2. *Ponzo-Style Dipping Sauce, if using:* In a small serving bowl, combine soy sauce, lime juice, mirin and sambal oelek. Stir well and set aside.
3. In a Dutch oven or wok, add oil to a depth of 2 inches (5 cm). Heat over medium-high until 350°F (180°C).
4. Spread cornstarch on a plate and dredge clams in it. Dip in batter, covering completely. Add battered clams to hot oil, in batches, and fry, turning once, until crisp and golden, about 1 minute per side. Transfer to paper towels. Spear with toothpicks and serve with sauce.

Variations

Beer-Battered Oysters: Substitute an equal quantity of shucked or drained canned oysters for the clams.

Halibut Balls: Cut 1 lb (500 g) skinless halibut fillets into 1-inch (2.5 cm) square pieces. Dust with cornstarch and dip in batter as per clams. Fry until fish flakes easily when pierced with a sharp knife, about 2 minutes per side.

Japanese-Style Fried Chicken

Makes about 4 dozen pieces

Here's a deliciously different treatment for chicken that is Japanese in origin. It's marinated in a light Asian-flavored marinade, fried in batter, topped with a lightly spiced creamy avocado sauce and, if you're so inclined, wrapped in a small lettuce leaf to add pleasing texture. This is an elegant and very tasty starter.

Tip

For this recipe, you'll need lettuce leaves that have a bit of body and crunch, and are big enough to wrap around the chicken. For instance, you can use pieces of romaine lettuce, after removing the center rib or even leafy lettuce torn into pieces. The leaves in a mesclun mix are too small.

1 lb	skinless boneless chicken (thighs or breasts), cut into 1-inch (2.5 cm) cubes	500 g
2 tbsp	soy sauce	30 mL
1 tbsp	sake or vodka	15 mL
1 tsp	each puréed garlic and gingerroot	5 mL

Avocado Topping

1	small avocado, cut into chunks	1
1 tbsp	freshly squeezed lemon juice	15 mL
2 tbsp	softened cream cheese	30 mL
2 tbsp	mayonnaise	30 mL
1/2	long red or green chile pepper, seeded and minced	1/2
	Salt and freshly ground black pepper	
1/3 cup	each cornstarch and all-purpose flour	75 mL
2 cups	oil, such as peanut or corn (approx.)	500 mL
	Large baby lettuce leaves, optional	

1. In a bowl, combine soy sauce, sake, garlic and ginger. Add chicken and toss until well coated. Cover and set aside to marinate at room temperature for 30 minutes, stirring once or twice to ensure chicken is evenly coated.

2. *Avocado Topping:* Meanwhile, in a bowl, combine avocado and lemon juice. Using a fork, mash until combined. Add cream cheese, mayonnaise and chile and continue mashing until nicely blended and desired texture is achieved. Season to taste with salt and pepper. Cover and set aside.

3. On a large plate or in a resealable bag, combine cornstarch and flour. Mix well. Add drained chicken pieces and toss until well coated with mixture.

4. In a wok or large deep skillet, heat oil over medium-high heat. Add chicken, in batches, and fry, stirring frequently and turning once to ensure they brown evenly, until golden and chicken is no longer pink for breasts or juices run clear for thighs, about 3 minutes per batch.

5. Place a dollop of topping on each chicken piece, wrap in a lettuce leaf, if using, and spear with a toothpick.

Chicken Yakitori

Makes about 20 skewers

Yakitori is chicken and vegetable kabobs, Japanese-style. It often includes parts of the chicken such as hearts, but here we have limited ourselves to white or dark meat and green onions. It's simple and delicious. Making yakitori is fun because it cooks very quickly so it can be prepared almost on demand as guests stand around the barbecue. Traditionally, yakitori is served with cold beer.

- **20 soaked wooden skewers (page 332)**

2 lbs	boneless chicken (thighs or breasts), cut into 1-inch (2.5 cm) cubes	1 kg
10	green onions, white part with a bit of green, cut into 1-inch (2.5 cm) pieces	10
½ cup	each soy sauce and mirin	125 mL
¼ cup	sake	60 mL
1 tbsp	granulated sugar	15 mL
1 tbsp	oil	15 mL

1. Alternate chicken and onion pieces on soaked skewers, 2 each per skewer. Place in a long shallow dish large enough to accommodate skewers in a single layer.

2. In a measuring cup, combine soy sauce, mirin, sake and sugar. Pour off ¼ cup (60 mL) of mixture and stir in oil. Set aside as basting sauce.

3. Pour remainder of soy mixture over skewers, evenly coating. If possible, turn to ensure all sides are well coated. Cover and set aside at room temperature for 30 minutes, spooning mixture over skewers several times.

4. Preheat barbecue. Place skewers on hot grill. Grill, turning and basting with reserved sauce, until chicken is no longer pink inside for breasts and juices run clear for thighs, about 7 minutes. Serve immediately.

Kabobs and Satay made from Chicken or Meat

Although kabobs are usually skewered chunks of meat, when served as appetizers, it is preferable to make them like Asian satay — thin strips of marinated chicken or meat woven onto small wooden skewers. Prepared in this manner, they cook more quickly and can be consumed without a knife in one or two bites.

For use on skewers, meat should be cut thinly. To ease cutting, place the meat in the freezer for 15 minutes to firm it up. Cut the meat with the grain (lengthwise) into thin strips (about ½ inch/1 cm) then cut the strips into pieces that are about 1½ inches (4 cm) long.

Thread the strips onto soaked wooden skewers (1 or 2 pieces per skewer, as per recipe) in a S-pattern, ensuring that the strip begins and ends on the same side of the skewer.

Chicken Kabobs with Tahini Sauce

Makes about 24 kabobs

These tasty kabobs are simple, yet delicious. The Tahini Sauce provides a slightly exotic finish and is particularly easy to make. If you prefer a more traditional approach, serve Chicken Souvlaki (see Variation, below).

Tips

Make an effort to get Greek-style yogurt, also known as "pressed." It is lusciously thick and adds beautiful depth to this and many other dishes. Greek yogurt is available in well-stocked supermarkets and specialty stores. If you can't find it, you can make your own. *To make Greek-style yogurt:* Line a sieve with a double layer of cheesecloth or paper towels. Add plain yogurt, cover and refrigerate overnight. The watery component will have drained out and you will be left with lovely thick yogurt.

If you prefer a more lemony flavor, add 1 tsp (5 mL) finely grated lemon zest to the marinade.

To purée garlic: Use a fine, sharp-toothed grater, such as those made by Microplane, or put the garlic through a garlic press.

- **24 soaked wooden skewers (page 332)**

¼ cup	olive oil	60 mL
3 tbsp	freshly squeezed lemon juice	45 mL
2 tsp	puréed garlic (1 to 2 cloves)	10 mL
1 tsp	dried oregano	5 mL
½ tsp	freshly ground black pepper	2 mL
½ tsp	hot pepper flakes	2 mL
1 lb	skinless boneless chicken, cut for skewers (page 340)	500 g

Tahini Sauce

¼ cup	tahini	60 mL
¼ cup	plain Greek-style (pressed) yogurt	60 mL
3 tbsp	freshly squeezed lemon juice (see Tips, left)	45 mL
1 tsp	puréed garlic (see Tips, left)	5 mL
	Fine sea salt	

1. In a bowl large enough to accommodate the chicken, combine oil, lemon juice, garlic, oregano, pepper and hot pepper flakes. Add chicken and toss to coat. Cover and set aside at room temperature for 30 minutes or in the refrigerator for up to 4 hours.

2. *Tahini Sauce:* Meanwhile, in a small bowl, combine tahini, yogurt, lemon juice and garlic. Stir well. Refrigerate until ready to serve.

3. Preheat barbecue or broiler. Thread chicken on skewers (page 340). Place on preheated barbecue or under broiler and grill, turning once, until no longer pink inside for breasts and juices run clear for thighs, about 3 minutes. Remove from heat and sprinkle with salt to taste. Pass the Tahini Sauce for dipping.

Variation

Chicken Souvlaki: Substitute Tzatziki (page 14) or Roasted Red Pepper Tzatziki (page 14) for the Tahini Sauce.

Traditional Chicken Satays

Makes about 24 skewers

This treatment for satay is traditionally Thai. Easy to make and delicious, it's not surprising that it has become a fashionable North American party food. Serve with Peanut Sauce (page 554).

Tips

If you don't have fresh limes, substitute lemon zest and juice in the chicken marinade.

Don't confuse hot Asian chile sauces with tomato-based chili sauce, which is sweet and often substituted for ketchup. The Asian versions are made from ground chiles and are very spicy. They are a great way to instantly add heat and flavor to a dish.

To purée garlic: Use a fine sharp-toothed grater such as those made by Microplane.

- **24 wooden skewers, soaked (page 332)**

¼ cup	soy sauce	60 mL
½ tsp	grated lime zest	2 mL
2 tbsp	freshly squeezed lime juice	30 mL
1 tbsp	fish sauce	15 mL
1 tbsp	oil	15 mL
1 tsp	granulated sugar	5 mL
1 tsp	hot Asian chile sauce (see Tips, left)	5 mL
1 tsp	each puréed gingerroot and puréed garlic	5 mL
2 lbs	skinless boneless chicken, cut for skewers (page 340)	1 kg
	Peanut Sauce (page 554)	

1. In a bowl large enough to accommodate the chicken, combine soy sauce, lime zest and juice, fish sauce, oil, sugar, chile sauce, ginger and garlic. Add chicken and toss to coat. Cover and set aside to marinate at room temperature for 30 minutes or in the refrigerator for up to 4 hours.

2. When you're ready to cook, preheat grill to medium-high or preheat broiler. Remove chicken from marinade. Discard marinade. Pat dry with paper towel and thread onto skewers. Place on preheated barbecue or under broiler and grill, turning once, until no longer pink inside for breasts and juices run clear for thighs, about 3 minutes. Serve immediately accompanied by Peanut Sauce.

Variation

Coconut-Spiked Chicken Satay: In a bowl, combine ½ cup (125 mL) unsweetened coconut milk, 2 cloves minced garlic, 1 tbsp (15 mL) minced gingerroot, 1 tsp (5 mL) each fish sauce, brown sugar and coriander, ½ tsp (2 mL) each ground cumin and turmeric. Add 1 lb (500 g) boneless skinless chicken breasts, cut for skewers (page 340) and toss until well coated. Cover and set aside to marinate at room temperature for 30 minutes or in the refrigerator for up to 4 hours. When you're ready to cook, follow Step 2 above and thread onto 12 skewers. Serve with Peanut Sauce, if desired.

Coconut-Crusted Chicken Satays

Makes 12 skewers

It's tropical time. Serve this with a Pineapple Mango Salsa (page 87) and it's off to the tropics you go!

Tip

Not all chicken breasts are sold complete with tenderloin. If you happen to purchase a breast with its tenderloin, gently remove it and skewer the tenderloin lengthwise and follow the recipe as written.

- **12 soaked wooden skewers (page 332)**

½ cup	unsweetened desiccated coconut	125 mL
1 tsp	granulated sugar	5 mL
½ tsp	salt	2 mL
2	boneless skinless chicken breasts, cut into 1-inch (2.5 cm) slices (see Tip, left)	2
1 tbsp	olive oil	15 mL
1 tbsp	finely chopped chives	15 mL

1. In a bowl, combine coconut, sugar and salt. Mix well.

2. Thread chicken onto skewers (page 340). Press chicken into coconut mixture, turning to coat. Discard any excess coconut mixture.

3. In a large skillet, heat oil over medium-high heat. Sear satays until bottom is golden brown, about 3 minutes. Flip and continue to sear until chicken is no longer pink inside, about 2 minutes. Transfer to a platter and garnish with chives.

Carnitas

Makes about 36 carnitas

Until you taste them, you won't believe how tasty these bits of deeply browned pork are. To serve, place on a small platter and allow your guests to spear with a toothpick or small skewer. Serve with a salsa such as Fresh Tomato Salsa (page 70), Fresh Salsa Verde (page 71) or Guacamole (page 26).

- **Large frying pan with lid**

| 3 lbs | boneless pork shoulder or blade (butt), cut into 1-inch (2.5 cm) cubes | 1.5 kg |
| 1 tsp | slightly coarse sea salt or kosher salt | 5 mL |

1. Place pork in skillet. Add water just to cover and sprinkle with salt. Cover and bring to a boil over medium heat. Reduce heat and simmer until meat is fork-tender, about 1 hour.

2. Remove lid, stir well, and continue cooking, stirring occasionally, until water is evaporated and meat is nicely browned, about 30 minutes. Transfer to a warmed platter. Sprinkle with sea salt. Serve warm.

Cilantro Chicken Kabobs

Makes about 24 kabobs

These tasty kabobs are Asian in spirit and pack a rich cilantro flavor.

Tips

Eight sprigs of cilantro yields about 100 cilantro leaves.

Don't confuse hot Asian chile sauces with tomato-based chili sauce, which is sweet and often substituted for ketchup. The Asian versions are made from ground chiles and are very spicy. They are a great way to instantly add heat and flavor to a dish.

There is a difference between rice vinegar and seasoned rice vinegar. Both are usually made from fermented rice or rice wine, but rice vinegar does not contain any additional sugar or sodium. Our preference is Japanese rice vinegar which is very mild flavored and almost colorless.

- **24 soaked wooden skewers (page 350)**

10	cilantro sprigs, leaves and stems	10
¼ cup	soy sauce	60 mL
1 tbsp	olive oil	15 mL
1 tbsp	rice vinegar (see Tips, left)	15 mL
2 tsp	cracked black peppercorns	10 mL
2 tsp	oyster sauce	10 mL
6	cloves garlic	6
¼ tsp	cayenne pepper	1 mL
2 lbs	skinless boneless chicken, cut for skewers (page 340)	1 kg

Dipping Sauce

1 cup	water	250 mL
½ cup	granulated sugar	125 mL
8	cilantro sprigs, leaves only (see Tips, left)	8
2	cloves garlic	2
3 tbsp	freshly squeezed lime juice	45 mL
1 tbsp	hot Asian chile sauce	15 mL
1 tbsp	fish sauce	15 mL
½ cup	peanuts, optional	125 mL

1. In a food processor, process cilantro, soy sauce, olive oil, vinegar, peppercorns, oyster sauce, garlic and cayenne until smooth.

2. In a bowl large enough to accommodate the chicken, combine chicken and marinade. Set aside to marinate at room temperature for 30 minutes or refrigerate for up to 4 hours.

3. *Dipping Sauce:* Meanwhile, in a saucepan, combine water and sugar. Bring to a boil over medium heat and cook until syrupy, about 10 minutes. Let cool. In a food processor, combine cilantro, garlic, lime juice, chili sauce, fish sauce, and peanuts, if using. Add cooled syrup and process until smooth.

4. When you're ready to cook, preheat barbecue or broiler. Follow Step 4 (page 345).Serve immediately accompanied by Dipping Sauce.

Almost-Indian Chicken Kabobs

Makes about 12 skewers

With a yogurt-based marinade and some Indian spices, these kabobs take a vaguely south Asian spin, while retaining their independence. They are tasty and unusual.

Tip

We prefer to use full-fat or whole milk yogurt in this recipe because it has a deeper flavor profile but if you prefer, use a lower-fat alternative.

- **12 soaked wooden skewers (approx.) (page 350)**

1 lb	skinless boneless chicken breasts	500 g
2 tbsp	freshly squeezed lemon juice	30 mL
1 tsp	hot paprika	5 mL
1	onion, quartered	1
1	piece (2 inches/5 cm) gingerroot, peeled and quartered	1
1 cup	coarsely chopped cilantro, leaves and stems	250 mL
2 tsp	ground cumin	10 mL
1 tsp	ground coriander	5 mL
¼ tsp	ground cinnamon	2 mL
½ cup	plain yogurt, preferably full-fat (see Tip, left)	125 mL
	Salt and freshly ground black pepper	

1. Place chicken in a shallow dish and rub lemon juice all over. Sprinkle surfaces evenly with hot paprika. Set aside.

2. Meanwhile, in a food processor fitted with metal blade, pulse onion, ginger, cilantro, cumin, coriander and cinnamon to chop and blend, stopping and scraping down sides of bowl as necessary, about 10 times. Add yogurt and pulse to blend, about 5 times. Season to taste with salt and pepper. Set aside.

3. Cut chicken for skewers (page 340). Return to dish. Add marinade and toss until well coated. Cover and set aside to marinate at room temperature for 30 minutes or in the refrigerator for up to 4 hours.

4. When you're ready to cook, preheat barbecue to medium-high or preheat broiler. Remove chicken from marinade. Discard marinade. Thread chicken onto skewers (page 340). Place on preheated barbecue or under broiler and grill, turning once, until chicken is no longer pink inside, about 3 minutes. Serve immediately.

Buffalo Chicken Wings

Makes about 12

What would an appetizer book be without this American classic? Because they are quite substantial, serve these at a party where a meal won't follow. Traditionally, Buffalo wings are deep-fried. Grilled or broiled, they are mouthwatering, with less fat than usual. Double or triple the recipe to suit your needs.

Tips

These wings are moderately spicy; if you prefer a five-alarm version, add more hot pepper sauce.

Spreading wings out as much as possible maximizes the area of skin that is exposed to the heat, producing a browner, crispier result. Stretch the wings out and skewer them lengthwise from the wing tip on soaked bamboo skewers (page 350).

- **Preheat barbecue or broiler**
- **12 soaked wooden skewers (page 350)**

1 tbsp	paprika	15 mL
1 tsp	puréed garlic	5 mL
½ tsp	cayenne pepper	2 mL
½ tsp	hot pepper sauce, or to taste	2 mL
	Freshly ground black pepper	
¼ cup	melted unsalted butter	60 mL
3 lbs	chicken wings, patted dry, about 12 wings	1.5 kg
	Coarsely ground sea salt, optional	

Blue Cheese Sauce

½ cup	mayonnaise	125 mL
2 tsp	freshly squeezed lemon juice	10 mL
1 tsp	puréed garlic (see Tips, page 342)	5 mL
½ tsp	Worcestershire sauce	2 mL
¼ cup	crumbled blue cheese, about 2 oz (60 g)	60 mL
	Freshly ground black pepper	
	Celery sticks	

1. In a bowl large enough to accommodate the wings, combine paprika, garlic, cayenne, hot pepper sauce and black pepper to taste. Stir well. Gradually stir in melted butter until combined. Add chicken wings and toss until they are well coated.

2. Skewer wings (see Tips, left) and place on barbecue or under broiler. Grill, turning once, until crisp and juices run clear when chicken is pierced, about 20 minutes. Transfer to a warm platter and sprinkle lightly with salt, if using.

3. *Blue Cheese Sauce:* Meanwhile, in a food processor, process mayonnaise, lemon juice, garlic, Worcestershire sauce and blue cheese until smooth. Season with pepper to taste. Transfer to a small serving bowl.

4. Serve wings with Blue Cheese Sauce and celery sticks for dipping.

Chicken and Sun-Dried Tomato Croquettes

Makes 12 croquettes

Sun-dried tomato contributes a wonderful sweetness to the chicken croquettes and is further enhanced when dipped into Oven-Roasted Cherry Tomato Sauce (page 546) or decadent Truffle Vinaigrette (page 542).

Tip

Although egg bread provides a wonderful texture, virtually any bread will work, even dry bread, for this recipe.

- **12 soaked wooden skewers (page 350)**
- **Candy/deep fry thermometer**

1	slice challah (egg bread), crust removed (see Tip, left)	1
2 tbsp	milk	30 mL
10 oz	boneless skinless chicken thighs	300 g
2 tbsp	thinly sliced green onion	30 mL
2 tbsp	finely chopped sun-dried tomato	30 mL
1/2 tsp	salt	2 mL
1/4 tsp	freshly ground black pepper	1 mL
1 cup	cornflake crumbs	250 mL
	Oil	

1. In a bowl, combine bread and milk and, using your hands, crumble bread into milk, creating something resembling a bread purée. Set aside.

2. In a food processor fitted with metal blade, pulse chicken, green onion and sun-dried tomato until smooth. Add to bread and milk mixture. Season with salt and pepper and fold well to combine all ingredients. Cover and refrigerate for at least 1 hour until chilled or for up to 3 hours.

3. When you're ready to cook, place 3 inches (7.5 cm) oil in a large saucepan or Dutch oven and heat over medium heat until temperature reaches 350°F (180°C). (You can also use a deep fryer; follow the manufacturer's instructions.)

4. Wrap about 1 tbsp (15 mL) of chicken mixture around top of wooden skewer so it looks like a lollipop. Roll chicken skewer into cornflake crumbs to cover.

5. Add chicken skewers to hot oil in batches and fry until golden brown and chicken is no longer pink inside, 3 to 4 minutes. Remove from oil and drain on paper towels.

Indonesian Pork Satays

Makes about 12 skewers

This version of satay is particularly pleasing because it's entirely self-contained and doesn't require a dipping sauce. The peanut butter and hot pepper flakes in the marinade do the trick.

Tips

Kecap manis is an Indonesian sauce made from soy. It is available in Asian grocery stores. If you don't have it, substitute 3 tbsp (45 mL) soy sauce and 1 tbsp (15 mL) brown sugar for this quantity.

Pork tenderloin is much narrower at one end, which means it is difficult to make even cuts along the length. Prior to cutting the meat with the grain, we recommend you cut it in half crosswise and cut each half lengthwise separately.

For best flavor, toast and grind the cumin and coriander seeds yourself. *To toast seeds:* Place seeds in a dry skillet over medium heat and cook, stirring, until fragrant, about 3 minutes. Immediately transfer to a mortar or a spice grinder and grind.

- **12 soaked wooden skewers (page 350)**

¼ cup	kecap manis (see Tips, left)	60 mL
2 tbsp	peanut butter	30 mL
2 tbsp	freshly squeezed lime juice	30 mL
2	cloves garlic, minced	2
1 tsp	ground coriander (see Tips, left)	5 mL
1 tsp	ground cumin (see Tips, left)	5 mL
½ tsp	ground turmeric	2 mL
½ tsp	hot pepper flakes	2 mL
1 lb	pork tenderloin, cut for satay (see Tips, left, and page 340)	500 g

1. In a small bowl, combine ketchup manis, peanut butter, lime juice, garlic, coriander, cumin, turmeric and hot pepper flakes. Mix well. Add sliced pork and toss well to ensure all pieces are evenly covered with marinade. Cover and set aside at room temperature for 1 hour.

2. Preheat barbecue or broiler. Thread 2 pieces of meat onto each skewer (page 340). Grill, turning frequently, until exterior begins to crisp and just a hint of pink remains inside, about 8 minutes (depending upon how hot your heat source is). Transfer to a serving platter and let cool until cool enough to handle, 1 to 2 minutes. Serve warm.

Minced Pork and Pineapple Skewers

Makes about 10 skewers

These ingredients will remind you of a holiday ham with pineapple glaze, and hey...what could be bad about that?

Tips

Agitating meat often raises the temperature. It is important to lower it as soon as possible. Unless you're refrigerating it, fill a bowl half way with ice and set another bowl containing the pulsed meat on top.

You'll get the best flavor if you toast and grind cumin seeds yourself. *To toast cumin seeds:* Place seeds in a dry skillet over medium heat. Cook, stirring, until fragrant, about 3 minutes. Transfer to a mortar or spice grinder and grind.

- **10 sugarcane (see Tips, page 352) or wooden skewers (page 350)**
- **Candy/deep fry thermometer**

8 oz	pork tenderloin	250 g
4 oz	pork belly or back fat	125 g
1 tbsp	dried cranberries	15 mL
½ tsp	ground cumin (see Tips, left)	2 mL
¼ tsp	salt	1 mL
10	1-inch (2.5 cm) cubes pineapple	10
1 cup	unsweetened desiccated coconut	250 mL
2	eggs, beaten	2
	Oil	

1. In a food processor fitted with metal blade, pulse pork, pork belly, cranberries, cumin and salt until smooth. Transfer to bowl, cover and refrigerate for 10 minutes (see Tips, left).

2. Spoon about 1 tbsp (15 mL) of pork mixture into your hand and flatten. Place one cube of pineapple in the center and fold the meat around the pineapple. Roll into a ball and place on a plate. Repeat with remaining pork mixture and pineapple. Cover and refrigerate for 1 hour. (This will make the meat easier to work with.)

3. When you're ready to cook, place oil in a large saucepan or Dutch oven to a depth of about 3 inches (7.5 cm) and heat over medium heat until temperature reaches 375°F (190°C). (You can also use a deep fryer; follow the manufacturer's instructions.)

4. To crust, place coconut in a shallow dish and eggs in another one. Evenly dip balls in coconut, turning to evenly coat, then into egg and back into coconut. Discard any excess coconut and egg.

5. Add pork balls to hot oil in batches and fry until balls are floating and golden brown, 5 to 6 minutes. Remove from oil and drain on paper towels. Place balls on a plate and pierce sugarcane or skewers into the top and serve immediately.

Korean-Style Beef Kabobs

Makes about 24 kabobs

The ingredients in this marinade are Korean, although the presentation is not traditional. These kabobs are very easy to make and appeal to a wide variety of tastes.

Tips

If you have sucanat in your cupboard, use it for this recipe. The deep molasses flavor enhances those in the marinade.

This may seem like a small amount of marinade for the quantity of meat, but you don't want liquid dripping from the meat. Just make sure to turn the meat while marinating to ensure even coating.

- **24 soaked wooden skewers (approx.) (see below)**

¼ cup	soy sauce	60 mL
2 tbsp	freshly squeezed lime juice	30 mL
2 tbsp	sesame oil	30 mL
1 tbsp	brown sugar, preferably raw cane (see Tips, left)	15 mL
2	cloves garlic	2
1	piece (1 inch/2.5 cm) peeled gingerroot	1
¼ tsp	hot pepper flakes	1 mL
1	whole flank steak (about 2 lbs/1 kg), cut for kabobs (page 340)	1
	Fleur de sel, optional	

1. In a blender, purée soy sauce, lime juice, sesame oil, brown sugar, garlic, ginger and hot pepper flakes until smooth.

2. Place meat strips in a shallow dish just large enough to accommodate them. Add marinade and toss well to coat. Cover and set aside at room temperature, turning once or twice, for 30 minutes or for up to 4 hours in the refrigerator.

3. Preheat barbecue or broiler. Thread meat onto soaked skewers (page 340). Place kabobs on hot grill or under hot broiler and grill, turning once or twice, until desired degree of doneness, about 3 minutes for medium-rare. Sprinkle lightly with fleur de sel, if using.

Soaking Wooden Skewers

Unless they have been soaked, wooden skewers will burn when heated. Before using, soak skewers in cold water to cover until you're ready to use them — for at least 30 minutes or for up to 8 hours.

Peanut-Crusted Beef Tenderloin Satays

Makes 15 satays

A very classic Vietnamese appetizer that is wonderful served alongside Asian-inspired dipping sauces like Basic Sweet-and-Sour Sauce (page 547) or Thai Peanut Dip (page 43).

- **15 wooden skewers**

½ cup	unsalted roasted peanuts	125 mL
1 tsp	packed brown sugar	5 mL
1 tsp	salt	5 mL
10 oz	piece center-cut beef tenderloin	300 g
1 tbsp	unsalted butter	15 mL
1 tbsp	olive oil	15 mL

1. In a food processor fitted with metal blade, pulse peanuts, brown sugar and salt until mixture resembles fine beach sand. Transfer to a shallow bowl.

2. Place tenderloin in peanut mixture and turn and press to coat all over. Discard any excess peanut mixture.

3. In a skillet, heat butter and oil over medium-high heat. Sear beef until bottom is golden brown and caramelized, about 3 minutes. Turn and repeat until all sides are nicely seared, about 15 minutes total. Transfer to a cutting board and let stand for 10 minutes.

4. Using a very sharp knife, slice tenderloin across the grain into 15 thin slices. Roll slices into cigar shapes and skewer meat by weaving the skewer lengthwise in and out of the meat until firmly attached to the skewers. Garnish with any ground peanuts that may have fallen off during the cooking process and serve immediately.

Sugarcane with Marinated Beef

Makes 10 skewers

This meat is so tender it will practically melt in your mouth. Serving the beef around sugarcane skewers is a nice touch, but wooden skewers would work as well.

Tips

Sugarcane can be found in Jamaican specialty shops and some large supermarkets. To prepare, wash sugarcane thoroughly under cold water, and using a sharp knife, cut the stalk at a joint crosswise. Split the stalk lengthwise into quarters and sharpen one edge creating 4 skewers. For this recipe, you would need one stalk with 3 joints, making 12 skewers.

The cooking of the marinated beef is unique because the meat is not turned. This is done for two reasons. First, to achieve the ideal caramelization the beef should be under the broiler for the full 2 minutes and can be served with that side visible. Second, if you flip the beef and cook for another 2 minutes there's a good chance the meat will be overdone.

- **Preheat broiler**
- **10 sugarcane (see Tips, left) or soaked wooden skewers (page 350)**

1 tbsp	soy sauce	15 mL
1 tbsp	freshly squeezed grapefruit or lime juice	15 mL
½ tsp	hot Asian chile sauce, such as sambal oelek	2 mL
½ tsp	agave syrup	2 mL
½ tsp	brown sugar	2 mL
¼ tsp	toasted sesame oil	1 mL
5 oz	piece beef tenderloin	150 g
1 tbsp	thinly sliced green onions	15 mL

1. In a large bowl, combine soy sauce, grapefruit juice, hot sauce, agave syrup, brown sugar and sesame oil. Mix well. Set aside.

2. Cut tenderloin across the grain into 10 slices. Using the side of a knife or a mallet, pound each slice to flatten paper thin, about $\frac{1}{8}$ inch (3 mm). Add to marinade and toss to coat. Marinate for 10 minutes.

3. Remove beef from marinade and discard marinade. Place slices on a flat surface and roll beef around the top of the sugarcane. Place on a rimmed baking sheet and broil until surface begins to brown, about 2 minutes (see Tips, left). Transfer to a platter and garnish with green onions and serve immediately.

One-Bite Corn Dogs

Makes 12 dogs

Here's one bite that will transport you back to your days at the carnival. For the perfect pairing serve this with Honey Mustard Dip (page 60).

Tip

For a truly delicious "dog," buy fresh wieners from a butcher rather than the packaged supermarket kind.

- **12 soaked wooden skewers (page 350)**
- **Candy/deep fry thermometer**

3	wieners, cut into quarters	3
	Oil	
¾ cup	fine cornmeal	175 mL
2	eggs	2
3 tbsp	sour cream	45 mL
1 tsp	finely chopped chives	5 mL
⅛ tsp	salt	0.5 mL
⅛ tsp	freshly ground black pepper	0.5 mL

1. Thread 1 piece of wiener on each skewer vertically ensuring point of the skewer is not exposed.

2. When you're ready to cook, place 6 inches (15 cm) oil in a large saucepan or Dutch oven and heat over medium heat until temperature reaches 325°F (160°C). (You can also use a deep fryer; follow the manufacturer's instructions.)

3. Place cornmeal in a shallow bowl. In another bowl, whisk together eggs, sour cream, chives, salt and pepper until well blended. One at a time, dip wieners into the egg mixture, turning to evenly coat, then into cornmeal. Repeat dipping into both egg mixture and cornmeal. Repeat until all wieners have been coated. Discard any excess egg and cornmeal.

4. Drop, in batches, in preheated oil until golden brown, about 5 minutes. Remove from oil and drain on paper towels. Serve immediately.

Meatballs in Lemon Sauce

Makes about 60 meatballs

Here's a deliciously different, Italian-inspired, approach to cocktail meatballs.

Tip

For best results, buy good quality Parmesan and grate it yourself. If you must use already-grated cheese, buy it from an Italian market or deli or a good cheese shop and ask to make sure it doesn't contain any "filler."

- **Large skillet with lid**

1	onion, quartered	1
20	sage leaves	20
1 tsp	salt	5 mL
	Freshly ground black pepper	
4	slices stale baguette, soaked in ¼ cup (60 mL) water and squeezed dry	4
¼ cup	freshly grated Parmesan cheese (see Tip, left)	60 mL
2 lbs	extra lean ground beef	1 kg
2	eggs	2
½ cup	dry bread crumbs	125 mL
2 tbsp	olive oil	30 mL
2 tbsp	butter	30 mL

Lemon Sauce

1 tsp	freshly grated lemon zest	5 mL
1 cup	dry white wine	250 mL
3 tbsp	freshly squeezed lemon juice	45 mL
	Salt and freshly ground black pepper	

1. In a food processor fitted with metal blade, pulse onion, sage, salt, and pepper to taste, until onion is finely chopped. Add bread and Parmesan. Pulse to blend. Add ground beef and eggs and process until blended, about 1 minute. Shape into meatballs, each about ¾ inch (2 cm) in diameter. Spread bread crumbs on plate and dredge meatballs in them.

2. In a large skillet, heat oil and butter over medium-high heat. Add meatballs, in batches, and brown, turning frequently, about 4 minutes per batch. Return all meatballs to skillet. Cover, reduce heat to medium-low and cook until no longer pink inside, about 15 minutes. Transfer to a deep platter or bowl and keep warm.

3. *Lemon Sauce:* Return pan to element and increase heat to medium-high. Stir in lemon zest. Add wine, bring to a boil and cook, stirring and scraping up brown bits from bottom of pan, for 2 minutes. Stir in lemon juice. Season with additional salt and pepper to taste. Pour sauce over meatballs. Serve warm, accompanied by cocktail toothpicks.

Bacon-Wrapped Sausage Rolls

Makes 24 rolls

Richly decadent, these make perfect companions for a glass of robust red wine.

Tip

The sliced bacon should be on the long side. You will want to cut it in half crosswise and that length should fit or nearly fit around the sausage rolls.

- **Preheat oven to 375°F (190°C)**
- **Baking sheet, lined with parchment paper**

1	onion, quartered	1
2	stalks celery, cut into chunks	2
20	sage leaves	20
	Freshly ground black pepper	
1 lb	good-quality pork sausage meat	500 g
½ cup	dry bread crumbs	125 mL
1	egg, beaten	1
4	slices bacon (see Tip, left)	4

1. In food processor fitted with metal blade, pulse onion, celery, sage, and pepper to taste, until onion is finely chopped, about 15 times. Add pork, bread crumbs and egg and pulse until blended, about 15 times.

2. Cut each slice of bacon lengthwise into 3 ribbons, each about ¼ inch (0.5 cm) wide. Then cut each ribbon in half crosswise. You should have 24 strips.

3. Shape sausage mixture into 24 spheres, about 1 inch (2.5 cm) wide in the middle. Wrap a piece of bacon around the middle of each sphere. (Ideally it will meet on the underside, but if it doesn't, don't worry. It will hold together when cooked.) Place on prepared baking sheet seam side down and cover with foil. Bake in preheated oven for 15 minutes. Remove foil and bake, uncovered, until bacon is golden and rolls are browned and caramelized, about 25 minutes. Let cool slightly then spear with a toothpick. Serve warm.

Oregano-Spiked Pork Meatballs

Makes about 35 meatballs

Flavorful nibblies with a hint of heartiness such as these are perfect for chilly nights.

1	onion, quartered	1
2 tbsp	fresh oregano leaves	30 mL
2 tsp	finely grated lemon zest	10 mL
2 tbsp	oil (approx.)	30 mL
1/4 cup	freshly squeezed lemon juice	60 mL
1 lb	ground pork	500 g
1	egg	1
1 tbsp	sour cream	15 mL
1 tsp	salt	5 mL
	Freshly ground black pepper	
1 cup	dry bread crumbs, such as panko	250 mL
4	cloves garlic, minced	4
1 1/2 cups	dry red wine	375 mL
1	can (28 oz/796 mL) diced tomatoes, drained	1

1. In a food processor fitted with metal blade, pulse onion, oregano and lemon zest until finely chopped, about 8 times, stopping and scraping down sides of bowl as necessary.

2. In a large skillet, heat oil over medium heat. Add onion mixture and cook, stirring, until softened, about 3 minutes. Add lemon juice and cook until syrupy, about 2 minutes. Remove from heat.

3. Add onion mixture to food processor fitted with metal blade. Add pork, egg, sour cream, salt, and pepper to taste, and pulse until blended. Shape into meatballs, each about 3/4 inch (2 cm) in diameter. Roll in bread crumbs. Return pan to medium-high heat, adding more oil, if necessary. Add meatballs, in batches, and brown well. Remove from pan as completed and set aside.

4. Add garlic to pan and cook, stirring, until softened. Add wine, bring to a boil and boil for 2 minutes. Add tomatoes and stir well. Return meatballs to pan. Bring to a boil, cover, reduce heat and simmer until meatballs are cooked through and flavors meld, about 15 minutes. Serve warm, accompanied by cocktail toothpicks.

Knives and Forks

Although it's common to link appetizers with finger foods, not all starters are meant to be eaten by hand. There are occasions, such as elegant dinners, where it is appropriate to enjoy the first course sitting down and eating with a fork. Moreover, many classic appetizers such as shrimp cocktail, Spanish tortilla or old-fashioned quiche, demand a utensil, even if you're enjoying them while standing up. Here are some of our favorite "fork friendly" appetizers.

Asparagus with Hollandaise 358
Puff Pastry Tomato Tart. 358
Mushroom Asparagus Pie 359
Apple Bacon Tart 360
Grilled Portobello Stack with Goat Cheese
    and Roasted Peppers. 361
Poached Artichokes 362
Oven-Roasted Artichokes. 363

Egg and Sweet Pepper Fried Rice 364
Potato Tortilla with Peppers 365
Chorizo Tortilla 366
Mexican-Style Shrimp Cocktail 367
Shrimp-Stuffed Avocado 368
Seared Pickerel with Eggplant and Peppers 369
Fresh Salmon Macaroni and Cheese Gratin 370

Asparagus with Hollandaise

Makes 4 servings

When asparagus is in season it is a pleasure to eat it as often as possible. Topped with rich luscious Hollandaise Sauce, it is a classic presentation — rich, decadent and delicious.

1 lb	asparagus (about 20 stalks), trimmed and peeled	500 g
½ cup	Foolproof Hollandaise (page 539)	125 mL
	Freshly ground black pepper	

1. In a pot of rapidly boiling salted water, blanch asparagus until tender-crisp, about 3 minutes, depending on the thickness of the stems. Drain and transfer to a serving dish. Top with Hollandaise and season to taste with pepper. Serve immediately.

Puff Pastry Tomato Tart

Makes 8 appetizers

Baked tomatoes become so sweet, almost like candy. You'll love them on this plated appetizer. Serve with your favorite side salad.

Tip

This tart makes a wonderful wrapper. Place a ¼ cup (60 mL) of baby green salad onto the middle of a slice and fold around greens for a healthy, lunchtime appetizer.

- **Preheat oven to 400°F (200°C)**
- **10-inch (25 cm) metal pie plate, greased**

8 oz	puff pastry, thawed	250 g
1 lb	plum (Roma) tomatoes	500 g
½ tsp	herbes de Provence	2 mL
½ tsp	olive oil	2 mL
¼ tsp	salt	1 mL
¼ tsp	freshly ground black pepper	1 mL

1. On a lightly floured surface, roll out puff pastry and fit into prepared pie plate.
2. Cut tomatoes crosswise to yield about 20 thin slices. Layer tomatoes around pastry, starting from the outside edge and working in a spiral to the center, overlapping about one-quarter of each tomato. Sprinkle with herbes de Provence, olive oil, salt and pepper.
3. Bake in preheated oven until tomatoes are caramelized and pastry is golden brown, about 35 minutes. Cut into 8 wedges and place on serving plates. Serve immediately.

Mushroom Asparagus Pie

Makes 8 servings

Mushrooms and asparagus make a wonderful combination. Serve next to Black Pepper Goat Cheese Dip (page 20) and Marinated Mushrooms (page 548) or Braised Leeks (page 548) for a decadent brunch, lunch or dinner appetizer.

Tips

To serve: Combine 1 cup (250 mL) crème fraîche or sour cream with 1 tbsp (15 mL) coarsely chopped fresh basil and place a dollop on each pie slice.

You can use a single recipe of Tartlet Pastry dough (page 164), Potato Pastry dough (page 165), or your favorite recipe or store-bought pie pastry dough for this quiche.

- Preheat oven to 400°F (200°C)
- 10-inch (25 cm) metal pie plate, greased

1	recipe Tartlet Pastry (page 164) or store-bought (see Tips, left)	1
2 tbsp	olive oil	30 mL
3 cups	thinly sliced cremini mushrooms	750 mL
1 cup	thinly sliced onions	250 mL
1¼ cups	coarsely chopped asparagus	300 mL
½ cup	finely grated Parmesan cheese	125 mL
1 tbsp	coarsely chopped fresh basil	15 mL
1	egg	1
2 tbsp	heavy or whipping (35%) cream	30 mL

1. On a lightly floured surface or on a sheet of parchment paper, roll out pie pastry dough and fit into pie plate. Pierce pastry all over with a fork and bake in a preheated oven until golden brown, about 12 minutes. (If it starts to puff, press down gently with scrunched up paper towel or spatula.) Let cool.

2. In a large skillet, heat oil over medium-high. Sauté mushrooms and onions until onions are soft, about 5 minutes. Add asparagus and continue to sauté until asparagus turns vibrant green, about 3 minutes. Transfer to a bowl. Let cool to room temperature. Add cheese and basil and set aside.

3. In a bowl, whisk together egg and cream. Add to vegetables and mix well. Transfer to pie shell. Bake until filling is set, 12 to 15 minutes. Let cool. Cut into 8 wedges and serve immediately.

Apple Bacon Tart

Makes 10 appetizers

This incredible plated appetizer is so versatile. Perfect for a brunch appetizer party, afternoon tea party or even a chic dinner party. Add a touch of class with a garnish of soft goat cheese and a small baby greens salad.

Tip

Cooking time for bacon may vary depending on thickness. If you slice your own, a little more time may be needed but use your best judgment as a little over or undercooked will not make that much difference.

- **Preheat oven to 400°F (200°C)**

8 oz	puff pastry, thawed	250 g
1 tbsp	apricot or strawberry jam, warmed	15 mL
2	Granny Smith apples, peeled and thinly sliced	2
1 tbsp	granulated sugar	15 mL
10	slices bacon	10

1. If necessary, on a lightly floured surface, roll out pastry to a 10-inch (25 cm) square. Place pastry on a baking sheet and brush top with apricot jam. Starting from the edge begin to layer apple slices, overlapping slightly, to cover the entire surface. Evenly sprinkle apples with sugar. Bake in preheated oven until apples are caramelized and pastry is golden brown, about 35 minutes. Remove from heat and let cool on pan on a wire rack while bacon is cooking.

2. Place bacon slices on another baking sheet and bake until bottom is golden brown, about 8 minutes. Flip and continue to bake until bacon is crisp, about 10 minutes (see Tip, left). Transfer to paper towels to drain. Roughly chop.

3. Spread bacon evenly over apples. Cut pastry into 10 squares and serve immediately.

Grilled Portobello Stack with Goat Cheese and Roasted Peppers

Makes 4 servings

This recipe is like a big, beautiful mushroom burger... and boy is it filling. A garnish of a very flavorful and fragrant Basil Pesto (page 549) or Chive Parsley "Pistou" (page 550) add the perfect color contrast, creating an eye popping appetizer, especially when served on a white plate.

Tip

Portobello mushrooms are a good staple for your home. They are a versatile mushroom, used as an appetizer, side dish and the main meal in any meal.

• **Preheat greased barbecue grill to high**

4	portobello mushrooms, (see Tip, left) (about 1 lb/500 g)	4
1 tbsp	balsamic vinegar	15 mL
1 tbsp	extra virgin olive oil	15 mL
Pinch	salt	Pinch
Pinch	freshly ground black pepper	Pinch
1/2 cup	thinly sliced sweet onion	125 mL
8	fresh basil leaves	8
2	red bell peppers, roasted (see Tip, page 184) and cut in half, divided, or store-bought	2
1/4 cup	crumbled goat cheese	60 mL

1. Peel tops of mushroom by holding mushroom, stem side away from your body. Grabbing hold of the skin that hangs just beneath the mushroom top, pull toward the center. Rotate the mushroom in your hand, peeling off one section at a time, until fully peeled.

2. In a large bowl, combine mushrooms, vinegar, olive oil and pinch each of salt and pepper. Set aside.

3. Place mushrooms, peeled side down, on a plate and build stacks. Layer onion, then basil, roasted peppers and goat cheese on top of mushroom caps, dividing evenly. Grill, peeled side down, until mushrooms are soft and all ingredients are warmed through, about 10 minutes. Serve immediately or refrigerate for up to 3 days.

Poached Artichokes

Makes 4 servings

This is a great way to enjoy whole artichokes. Enjoy with a Roasted Red Pepper Vinaigrette (page 541), Caper Lemon Rémoulade (page 539) or Basil Pesto (page 549).

Tip

If artichokes scare you, you're not alone. If you love the flavor of artichokes, you're still not alone. I highly recommend poaching your artichokes whole until you are comfortable with peeling prior to cooking. Eating the artichokes whole will give you the opportunity to study the "innards," giving you a comfort level as you progress to the sautéed version.

4	artichokes (each about 12 oz/375 g)	4
10 cups	water	2.5 L
1	lemon, cut in half	1
3	thyme sprigs	3
2	bay leaves	2
1 tbsp	mustard seeds	15 mL
1 tbsp	white wine vinegar	15 mL
1 tsp	herbes de Provence	5 mL
1 tsp	salt	5 mL

1. Using your hands, remove about 5 layers of leaves starting from the base of the artichoke, working your way up by pulling the leaves backward toward the stem and snapping them off, exposing the pale, tender green leaves underneath. Using a sharp knife, cut off the very bottom of the stem, revealing a white core, and trim off the dark green, fibrous flesh from around the stem. Cut $1\frac{1}{2}$ to 2 inches (4 to 5 cm) from the top of the artichoke, exposing hard purple leaves and the hairy choke. Using a spoon, scoop out the purple leaves and choke. While you're working, rub all cut surfaces of the artichoke with lemon to prevent discoloring. Set aside.

2. In a covered stockpot over medium heat, bring water, lemon, thyme sprigs, bay leaves, mustard seeds, vinegar, herbes de Provence and salt to a boil. Add artichokes, reduce heat and simmer until artichoke is fork tender, about 40 minutes. Remove from heat and refrigerate overnight before serving. Serve chilled or bring to room temperature before serving. Serve with suggested condiments in introduction.

Oven-Roasted Artichokes

Makes about 2 cups (500 mL)

Congratulations, you've graduated to oven-roasted artichokes! These are the perfect starters for an evening party and pair wonderfully with a vodka martini.

Tips

If turkey bacon doesn't appeal to you, smoked turkey breast or thighs work just as well. Break up the turkey into small pieces and follow the recipe as written.

For best results, buy good quality Parmesan and grate it yourself. If you must use already-grated cheese, buy it from an Italian market or deli or a good cheese shop and ask to make sure it doesn't contain any "filler."

- **Preheat oven to 400°F (200°C)**
- **Ovenproof sauté pan or skillet**

2	artichokes (each about 12 oz/375 g)	2
1	lemon, cut in half	1
1 tbsp	olive oil	15 mL
¼ cup	diced turkey bacon (see Tips, left)	60 mL
¼ cup	diced sweet onion	60 mL
2	cloves garlic, minced	2
1	thyme sprig	1
2 tbsp	water	30 mL
¼ cup	freshly grated Parmesan cheese	60 mL

1. Using your hands, remove about 5 layers of leaves starting from the base of the artichoke, working your way up by pulling the leaves backward toward the stem and snapping them off, exposing the pale, tender green leaves underneath. Using a sharp knife, cut off the very bottom of the stem, revealing a white core, and trim off the dark green, fibrous flesh from around the stem. Cut 1½ to 2 inches (4 to 5 cm) from the top of the artichoke, exposing hard purple leaves and the hairy choke. Using a spoon, scoop out the purple leaves and choke. While you're working, rub all cut surfaces of the artichoke with lemon to prevent discoloring. Set aside.

2. In ovenproof pan, heat oil over medium heat. Add bacon, onion, garlic and thyme and cook, stirring frequently, until onions are soft, 3 to 4 minutes. Add artichokes. Transfer pan to preheated oven and roast, stirring often, until artichokes are fork tender, about 25 minutes. Remove from heat and add water and Parmesan. Stir well to combine. Let cool to room temperature.

Egg and Sweet Pepper Fried Rice

Makes about 2¹⁄₂ cups (625 mL)

A superb rice appetizer that can be made with almost any vegetables in your fridge. For a fun presentation and conversation starter, serve in Chinese food to-go containers with chopsticks.

Tip

To grate peeled ginger: Use a fine, sharp-toothed grater such as Microplane.

2 tbsp	olive oil, divided	30 mL
1 tbsp	toasted sesame oil	15 mL
¹⁄₂ cup	diced red bell pepper	125 mL
¹⁄₂ cup	diced sweet onion	125 mL
³⁄₄ cup	basmati rice	175 mL
1¹⁄₄ cups	water	300 mL
1 tsp	puréed gingerroot (see Tip, left)	5 mL
2	egg yolks, beaten	2
2 tbsp	soy sauce	30 mL
1 tbsp	thinly sliced green onions	15 mL
¹⁄₂ tsp	salt	2 mL

1. In a saucepan, heat 1 tbsp (15 mL) of the olive oil and sesame oil over medium heat. Add bell pepper and onion and cook, stirring, until onion is translucent, about 5 minutes. Add rice and stir well to incorporate. Add water and cover, reduce heat to low and simmer for 5 minutes. Remove from heat and set aside, covered, until all liquid is absorbed, about 25 minutes.

2. In a large skillet, heat remaining olive oil over high heat. Pour in egg yolks, swirling the pan to spread the eggs into a thin omelet. Cook, without stirring, until eggs are set, 1 to 2 minutes. Add rice mixture and mix well to combine. Cook, without stirring, for 3 minutes. Mix and continue cooking for 5 minutes more. Remove from heat and stir in soy sauce, green onions and salt.

Potato Tortilla with Peppers

Makes 12 to 16 pieces

This variation on tortilla, a traditional Spanish tapas dish resembling an omelet, adds green and red bell peppers, a chile pepper and a liberal amount of sharp cheese to the traditional potato and egg combination. Traditionally it is served cold or at room temperature.

Tip

To microwave potato for this recipe: Place scrubbed potato in a microwave-safe dish. Add cold water to a depth of about $\frac{1}{2}$ inch (1 cm), cover and microwave on High for 3 minutes. Leave the lid on and let cool for at least 5 minutes before running under cold water.

- **Large nonstick ovenproof skillet**

1	potato (8 oz/250 g), cooked in its skin, cooled and cut into $\frac{1}{2}$-inch (1 cm) cubes (see Tip, left)	1
2 tbsp	extra virgin olive oil	30 mL
1	red onion, thinly sliced on the vertical	1
1	red bell pepper, diced	1
1	green bell pepper, diced	1
1	long red chile or jalapeño pepper, seeded and minced	1
2	cloves garlic, minced	2
	Salt and freshly ground black pepper	
6	eggs	6
1 cup	shredded sharp (aged) cheese, such as Cheddar	250 mL

1. In a large nonstick ovenproof skillet, heat oil over medium heat. Add potato, red onion, red and green bell peppers, chile pepper and garlic and cook, stirring, until peppers are softened and potato and onion just begin to brown, about 8 minutes. Season to taste with salt and pepper.

2. Preheat broiler. In a bowl, beat eggs. Pour over onion mixture and sprinkle cheese evenly over top. Reduce heat to low, loosely cover and cook until eggs are set, about 6 minutes. Place under preheated broiler and broil until top is nicely browned. Unmold and cut into wedges. Serve warm or at room temperature.

Variation

Potato Tortilla with Chorizo: Substitute $\frac{1}{2}$ cup (125 mL) shredded Manchego cheese and 6 oz (175 g) cured (hard) chorizo, diced, for the cheese.

Chorizo Tortilla

Makes 8 pieces

If there is one item that is ubiquitous in tapas bars in Spain, it is the tortilla — an omelet that contains potatoes and is usually served at room temperature or cold. Here spicy chorizo sausage bumps up the flavor.

Tip

To microwave potato for this recipe: Place scrubbed potato in a microwave-safe dish. Add cold water to a depth of about 1/2 inch (1 cm), cover and microwave on High for 2 minutes. Leave the lid on and let cook for at least 5 minutes before running under cold water.

1	small potato (4 oz/125 g) cooked in its skin, cooled and cubed (1/2 inch/1 cm) (see Tip, left)	1
2 tbsp	olive oil	30 mL
1/2	onion, thinly sliced on the vertical	1/2
4 oz	soft chorizo sausage, removed from casing	125 g
	Salt and freshly ground black pepper	
4	eggs	4
2 tbsp	freshly grated Parmesan cheese	30 mL

1. In skillet, heat oil over medium heat. Add potato, onion and sausage and cook, stirring, until sausage begins to brown and is cooked through, about 6 minutes. Season to taste with salt and pepper.

2. Preheat broiler. In a bowl, beat eggs. Pour over sausage mixture. Reduce heat to low, loosely cover and cook until eggs are set, about 5 minutes. Sprinkle cheese evenly over top. Place under preheated broiler until top is nicely browned. Unmold and cut into wedges. Serve warm or at room temperature.

Variation

Ham Tortilla: Substitute 3 oz (90 g) julienned ham for the chorizo. Cook potato and onion until softened and just beginning to color, about 6 minutes. Then add the ham and stir well. Continue with Step 2.

Mexican-Style Shrimp Cocktail

Makes 6 to 8 servings

Some old-fashioned dishes are just too good to go away and shrimp cocktail is one of them. Here we've updated it by bathing shrimp in Mexican Sangrita, a spicy homemade tomato juice. If you're looking for a more contemporary version that even more closely resembles the retro version you remember, try Almost Classic Shrimp Cocktail (see Variation, below). For an elegant presentation, spoon into chilled martini glasses and enjoy.

Tips

Sangrita is very easy to make. If you make the full recipe, you'll have leftovers. Enjoy the remainder another night as a pre-dinner shooter or add vodka or tequila for a flavorful cocktail.

If you happen to have chipotle ketchup in your larder and aren't afraid of heat, use it instead of the regular version. It will broaden and intensify the chile experience.

1 lb	cooked salad shrimp	500 g
4	green onions, minced	4
½	English cucumber, diced	½
1 cup	chilled Sangrita (page 99) (see Tips, left)	125 mL
2 tbsp	ketchup (see Tips, left)	30 mL
1 tbsp	Worcestershire sauce	15 mL
1 tbsp	tequila, optional	15 mL
	Finely chopped fresh cilantro	

1. In a bowl, combine shrimp, green onions and cucumber. Mix well. Cover and refrigerate until thoroughly chilled, at least 1 hour.

2. In a measuring cup or bowl with a pouring spout, combine Sangrita, ketchup, Worcestershire sauce, and tequila, if using. Stir well and set aside.

3. Spoon shrimp mixture into chilled martini glasses and add sangrita to cover. Garnish with cilantro. Serve very cold, with spoons for enjoying the sauce.

Variation

Almost Classic Shrimp Cocktail: In a small bowl, combine ¼ cup (60 mL) ketchup, 1 tbsp (15 mL) each freshly squeezed lemon juice and prepared horseradish and half a jalapeño pepper, finely minced. Mix well. Substitute for Sangrita mixture above.

Shrimp-Stuffed Avocado

Makes 4 servings

This is one of the easiest starters there is. It is also elegant and delicious. Look for cooked salad shrimp at your supermarket fish counter.

Tips

Most of the avocados in supermarkets are still unripe and require another 2 or 3 days to ripen. Once home, keep them in a warm, dark place. You'll know they are ripe when they respond to the pressure of your finger. If you need to speed up the ripening process, place them in a brown paper bag with an apple or banana, which generates ethylene gas. Once ripe, avocados should be stored in the refrigerator.

Do not halve avocados until just before serving; otherwise the flesh will turn brown.

Use the tip of a spoon or a grapefruit spoon to remove the pit.

8 oz	cooked salad shrimp, thawed and drained if frozen	250 g
1 tbsp	freshly squeezed lemon juice	15 mL
1/2 cup	finely chopped celery	125 mL
2 tbsp	finely chopped green onion, white part only	30 mL
2 tbsp	finely chopped fresh dill fronds	30 mL
1/4 cup	mayonnaise	60 mL
	Salt and freshly ground black pepper	
2	avocados (see Tips, left)	2

1. In a bowl, combine shrimp and lemon juice. Toss well. Add celery, green onion, dill, mayonnaise, and salt and pepper to taste. Mix well.

2. Cut each avocado in half and remove pits (see Tips, left).

3. Place one avocado half on each plate. Fill with shrimp mixture (it will spill over the sides) and serve immediately.

Variation

Crab-Stuffed Avocado: Substitute an equal quantity of cooked drained crab for the shrimp.

Seared Pickerel with Eggplant and Peppers

Makes 4 appetizers

This appetizer is an amazing way to get your guests' palate ready for the main course.

Tip

Any thick firm white-fleshed fish such as cod or flounder or even monkfish would all substitute well for pickerel in this recipe.

- **Preheat oven to 325°F (160°C)**
- **Large ovenproof skillet**

4	pieces pickerel fillet, skin on, each about 4 oz (125 g) (see Tip, left)	4
¼ tsp	salt, divided	1 mL
1 tbsp	olive oil	15 mL
1 tsp	unsalted butter	5 mL
1	red bell pepper, cut into 1-inch (2.5 cm) wide strips	1
1 cup	large strips eggplant (about ½ inch/ 1 cm wide)	250 mL
3	thyme sprigs	3
1 tbsp	thinly sliced garlic	15 mL
	Freshly ground black pepper	
	Fresh thyme leaves	

1. Season the fish evenly with ⅛ tsp (0.5 mL) salt. In large ovenproof skillet, heat oil and butter over medium-high heat. Add pickerel fillets, skin side down, and fry until crisp, about 5 minutes. Flip over and fry until fish flakes easily with a fork, about 2 minutes. Remove from heat and let cool slightly. Reserve any juices that have been released from fish.

2. Reduce heat to low. In same skillet, add bell pepper and eggplant and cook, stirring often, until pepper begins to soften, 7 to 8 minutes. Add thyme, garlic, remaining salt, and pepper to taste. Transfer skillet to preheated oven and bake until eggplant is soft, about 10 minutes.

3. On a large plate, place eggplant and peppers in a small mound in the middle of plate. Place pickerel fillet on top, skin side facing up, and drizzle with reserved fish juices around mound of peppers and eggplant. Garnish with a few thyme leaves.

Fresh Salmon Macaroni and Cheese Gratin

Makes 3 cups (750 mL)

Yes, we can just hear you asking, "What, salmon in my macaroni and cheese"? But yes, not only is it great but it is quite possibly one of the greatest comfort food dishes you've ever tried!

Tip

For best results, buy good quality Parmesan and grate it yourself. If you must use already-grated cheese, buy it from an Italian market or deli or a good cheese shop and ask to make sure it doesn't contain any "filler."

- **Preheat oven to 450°F (230°C)**
- **Six ½-cup (125 mL) ramekins**

2 cups	penne pasta	500 mL
5 oz	skinless salmon fillet	150 g
1 tbsp	olive oil	15 mL
½ tsp	salt	2 mL
Pinch	freshly ground black pepper	Pinch
2 tbsp	unsalted butter	30 mL
5 tsp	unbleached all-purpose flour	25 mL
1 cup	whole milk	250 mL
½ cup	shredded Cheddar cheese	125 mL
¾ cup	freshly grated Parmesan cheese	175 mL

1. In a large pot of boiling salted water, cook pasta until al dente, about 10 minutes. Drain and set aside.

2. Evenly coat salmon with olive oil, salt and pepper. Place in a baking dish and bake in preheated oven until just slightly rosy inside for medium-rare, 10 to 12 minutes. Let cool to the touch and break into large pieces. Set aside.

3. In a saucepan, melt butter over medium heat. Sprinkle with flour and cook, stirring, for 2 minutes. Gradually whisk in milk. Bring to a simmer, stirring, and cook until bubbling and thickened, about 3 minutes. Remove from heat and stir in Cheddar cheese, ¼ cup (60 mL) at a time, until melted.

4. Preheat broiler. In a large bowl, combine cheese sauce with penne and salmon and fold gently to thoroughly combine. Spoon into ramekins. Garnish with equal amounts of Parmesan cheese. Place under preheated broiler and broil until Parmesan is melted and golden brown, 2 to 3 minutes. Serve immediately.

Variation

Smoked chicken, roasted chicken or other fish would all be lovely as a substitute for salmon.

Cheese Please

Cheese is a great convenience food. Like salumi (page 131) it can be served basically on its own on a cheese plate, perhaps accompanied by fresh berries or fruit. Sliced baguette, crackers or any of the crostini (pages 219 to 220) are all that is needed to complete the course.

But cheese is also very versatile. Cheese has been made for thousands of years from many different kinds of milk, employing a wide variety of techniques, which makes for a great deal of depth in terms of how it can be used. While this chapter is by no means exhaustive, we've tried to showcase some of the many ways that cheese can be used to make delicious appetizers, from simple herb-spiked soft cheese spreads such as Arugula-Spiked Goat Cheese (page 374) to pub-style crock cheese such as Potted Cheddar (page 375) to oozing hot cheese such as Deep-Fried Brie (page 388).

Take Some Cream Cheese 372
Walnut-Dusted Cheese Balls 372
Homemade Herb Cheese 373
Chile-Spiked Cheese and Avocado Spread 373
Arugula-Spiked Goat Cheese 374
Caraway-Spiked Cheese Spread 374
Liptauer 375
Potted Cheddar 375
Quark Claqueret 376
Just the Best Feta 377
Spiced Feta 377
Fingerling Potato Skins 378
Pimento Cheese 379
Marinated Mozzarella 379
Kentucky Beer Cheese 380
Chile Cheese 380
Baked Goat Cheese 381
Baked Marinated Goat Cheese 382
Baked Ricotta 383
Goat Cheese Fritters on Endive 384
Stuffed Mushroom Caps 385
Mushroom Fundido 386
Chorizo-Laced Fundido 387

Greek-Style Fried Cheese 387
Smoked Brie 388
Deep-Fried Brie 388
Plum-Stuffed Brie Cheese 389
Celery Spears and Whipped Brie 389
Strawberry-Topped Brie 390
Perfect Tomato and Cheese Canapés 390
Belgian Endive with Blue Cheese 391
Blue Cheese–Stuffed Dates 391
Cheese and Peach Wontons 392
Cheddar Cheese Crisps 392
Cheese Puffs 393
Mini Goat Cheese Puffs 394
Thyme-Spiked Cheese Sticks 395
Cheddar Cheese Fondue 396
Blue Cheese Fondue 396
Warm Pineapple with Mascarpone Cheese
 and Basil 397
Honey-Glazed Pear and Cheddar Cheese
 Stacks 397
Panko-Crusted Tomato with Camembert
 Cheese 398

Take Some Cream Cheese

No matter how well you plan, there will always be times when unexpected guests drop in. So long as you have an 8 oz (250 g) package of cream cheese in the fridge and some crackers in the cupboard, you'll likely be able to whip up one of these tasty concoctions made from things you're likely to already have in your fridge or pantry. Even if you don't have unexpected guests — you'll want to make them — they are so good. Fresh baguette, Belgian endive spears or cucumber slices are just some of the many delicious partners for these blends. Makes about 1 cup (250 mL).

Horseradish and Dill–Spiked Cream Cheese: (Vegetarian Friendly) In a food processor fitted with metal blade, process 8 oz (250 g) cubed softened cream cheese and ¼ cup (60 mL) each drained prepared horseradish and fresh dill fronds until smoothly blended. Season liberally with freshly ground black pepper and refrigerate until ready to serve.

Anchovy and Caper–Spiked Cream Cheese: In a food processor fitted with metal blade, process 8 oz (250 g) cubed softened cream cheese, 8 coarsely chopped anchovy fillets and 2 tbsp (30 mL) small capers (nonpareils) until smoothly blended.

Artichoke and Roasted Red Pepper–Spiked Cream Cheese: (Vegetarian Friendly) In a food processor fitted with metal blade, process 8 oz (250 g) cubed softened cream cheese, 1 jar (6 oz/170 mL) drained marinated artichoke hearts, 1 quartered roasted red pepper and, if desired, 6 basil leaves, until smoothly blended. Good with warm pita.

Walnut-Dusted Cheese Balls

Makes 4 balls

Vegetarian Friendly

The combination of soft, sweet mascarpone, slightly astringent Gorgonzola and bittersweet walnuts is quite glorious. Spread this on a plain cracker and enjoy with a glass of robust red wine.

4 oz	mascarpone cheese	125 g
4 oz	Gorgonzola cheese	125 g
1 tbsp	minced red onion	15 mL
1	clove garlic, chopped	1
½ cup	finely chopped walnuts	125 mL

1. In a food processor fitted with metal blade, process mascarpone, Gorgonzola, red onion and garlic until smoothly blended. Transfer to a cutting board and shape into 4 balls, each about 1½ inches (4 cm) in diameter.

2. Spread walnuts on a work surface. Roll balls until well covered. Chill for at least 3 hours or up to 2 days, until nicely firm.

Homemade Herb Cheese

Makes about ¾ cup (175 mL)

In the tradition of simple cheese spreads, this is easy to make yet delicious. Serve this flavorful cheese with breadsticks or celery sticks, or on sliced baguette or crackers.

¼ cup	crème fraîche	60 mL
2 tbsp	chopped parsley leaves	30 mL
2 tbsp	snipped chives	30 mL
2	cloves garlic, coarsely chopped	2
1 tsp	cracked black peppercorns	5 mL
4 oz	soft goat cheese	125 g

1. In a food processor fitted with metal blade, process crème fraîche, parsley, chives, garlic and peppercorns until smoothly blended, stopping and scraping down sides of the bowl as necessary. Add goat cheese and process until smooth, about 30 seconds.

Chile-Spiked Cheese and Avocado Spread

Makes about 1½ cups (375 mL)

Creamy yet pleasantly assertive, this glorious spread is chock-full of goodness in addition to being extremely tasty. A slice of cucumber is the perfect finish, but plain crackers work well, too.

Tip

The neutral flavor of long chile peppers or Thai chiles works well in this recipe, but if you can't find them, substitute half a jalapeño, instead. It will change the flavor profile, but still be delicious.

8	fresh basil leaves	8
½	long red or green chile pepper or 1 Thai chile (see Tip, left)	½
1	clove garlic, quartered	1
3 tbsp	freshly squeezed lemon juice	45 mL
2 tbsp	extra virgin olive oil	30 mL
1	large avocado, cut into chunks	1
6 oz	soft goat cheese	175 g
	Salt and freshly ground black pepper	
	Cucumber slices, optional	

1. In a food processor fitted with metal blade, process basil, chile pepper, garlic, lemon juice and olive oil until smoothly blended, about 30 seconds. Add avocado and goat cheese and process until smooth, about 30 seconds. Season to taste with salt and pepper. Spread on cucumber slices, if using.

Arugula-Spiked Goat Cheese

Makes about 1 cup (250 mL)

Use this as a spread or dip. It is terrifically easy to make and very tasty. It's refreshing and summery — a perfect addition to a garden party. Double or triple the quantity to suit your needs. Serve it with sliced baguette or crudités of seasonal vegetables.

2 cups	packed baby arugula	500 mL
½ cup	packed Italian flat-leaf parsley leaves	125 mL
½	small red onion, halved	½
1	clove garlic, quartered	1
4 oz	soft goat cheese	125 g
1 tsp	grated lemon zest	5 mL
2 tbsp	freshly squeezed lemon juice	30 mL
2 tbsp	extra virgin olive oil	30 mL
½ tsp	salt	2 mL
	Freshly ground black pepper	

1. In a food processor fitted with metal blade, pulse arugula, parsley, red onion and garlic until finely chopped, about 10 times. Add goat cheese, lemon zest and juice, olive oil, salt, and pepper to taste and process until blended, about 15 seconds. Cover and refrigerate until thoroughly chilled, for at least 2 hours or up to 2 days.

Caraway-Spiked Cheese Spread

Makes about 1 cup (250 mL)

This is another recipe that demonstrates the versatility of cream cheese. Here the flavors are eastern European — caraway and dill with a soupçon of sour cream. Serve this on thin slices of pumpernickel, dark rye bread or with crudités.

Tip

Grind caraway seeds in a mortar with a pestle or a spice grinder.

8 oz	softened cream cheese	250 g
½ cup	sour cream	125 mL
2 tbsp	finely chopped fresh dill fronds	30 mL
1 tbsp + 1 tsp	sweet paprika, divided	20 mL
1 tbsp	Dijon mustard	15 mL
1 tbsp	ground caraway seeds (see Tip, left)	15 mL
1	clove garlic, chopped	1

1. In a food processor fitted with metal blade, process cream cheese, sour cream, dill, 1 tbsp (15 mL) of the paprika, mustard, caraway and garlic until smooth, about 30 seconds, stopping and scraping down sides of the bowl once or twice. Transfer to a small serving bowl and dust with remaining 1 tsp (5 mL) of paprika. Serve immediately or cover and refrigerate for up to 2 days.

Liptauer

Makes about 1 cup (250 mL)

This is a classic Austrian/Hungarian dish, often made with Camembert, combined with a creamy cottage cheese. Here it's made with cream cheese and Emmental with lively additions such as hot smoked paprika. It is delicious served with thin slices of dark rye bread.

4 oz	Swiss Emmental cheese, shredded	125 g
4 oz	cream cheese, cubed and softened	125 g
¼ cup	mayonnaise	60 mL
1 tbsp	Dijon mustard	15 mL
1	shallot, coarsely chopped	1
2	cornichon or gherkin pickles	2
1 tbsp	drained capers	15 mL
2 tsp	caraway seeds	10 mL
½ tsp	hot smoked paprika	2 mL
	Freshly ground black pepper	

1. In a food processor fitted with metal blade, process Swiss cheese, cream cheese, mayonnaise, Dijon mustard, shallot, cornichons, capers, caraway and paprika until smoothly blended, about 20 seconds. Season to taste with pepper.

Potted Cheddar

Makes about 1 cup (250 mL)

Here's a traditional English technique for turning store-bought cheese into something special.

Tip

When choosing crackers for dips and spreads, look for high-quality versions that don't have strong flavors or too much salt. Pita bread or crisps, flatbreads, thinly sliced pumpernickel and crostini go well with specific recipes. And you can rarely go wrong with a fresh baguette.

8 oz	sharp (aged) Cheddar cheese	250 g
¼ cup	unsalted butter, softened	60 mL
2 tbsp	sweet sherry	30 mL
1 tbsp	freshly grated Parmesan cheese	15 mL
⅛ tsp	freshly grated nutmeg	0.5 mL
	Freshly ground white pepper	
	Walnut halves, optional	

1. In a food processor fitted with shredding blade, shred Cheddar. Replace shredding blade with metal blade. Add butter, sherry, Parmesan, nutmeg, and white pepper to taste. Process until smooth and blended, about 20 seconds.

2. Transfer to a serving bowl or earthenware crock. Flatten top with a spatula and press walnut halves into cheese, if using. Cover and refrigerate until flavors meld, about 2 hours or for up to 1 week.

Quark Claqueret

Makes about 1½ cups (375 mL)

Claqueret is a specialty of Lyons, one of France's gourmet centers. This herb-infused spread is traditionally served with dark rye bread but can also double as a dip for raw vegetables, also known as crudités (see Tips, below).

Tips

Crudites are cut-up vegetables used for dipping. Popular choices are broccoli and cauliflower florets, peeled baby carrots, Belgian endive and cherry tomatoes. And don't forget old standbys such as celery sticks and thinly sliced cucumber (see also page 31).

Quark is a fresh lower-fat cheese, long popular in Europe and gaining traction in North America. Look for it in well-stocked supermarkets and natural food stores.

2	shallots, quartered	2
2	cloves garlic, coarsely chopped	2
½ cup	coarsely snipped chives	125 mL
½ cup	Italian flat-leaf parsley leaves	125 mL
2	green onions, white part only, coarsely chopped	2
1 tbsp	fresh tarragon leaves	15 mL
1 cup	quark cheese (see Tips, left)	250 mL
2 tbsp	dry white wine	30 mL
½ tsp	salt	2 mL
	Freshly ground black pepper	
	Additional fresh herbs for garnishing, optional	

1. In a food processor fitted with metal blade, pulse shallots, garlic, chives, parsley, green onions and tarragon until finely chopped, about 15 times, stopping and scraping down sides of the bowl once or twice. Add quark, wine, salt, and pepper to taste. Process until smooth, about 30 seconds. Spoon into a serving dish, cover and refrigerate overnight or for up to 2 days to allow flavors to meld. Garnish with fresh herbs, if using.

Just the Best Feta

Serves 6 to 8 as part of a mezes platter

Good Greek restaurants will sometimes serve this simple treatment for feta as part of a mezes platter.

Tip

Be sure to use the very best feta you can find — preferably made from sheep's milk.

8 oz	block of good feta, drained (see Tip, left)	250 g
2 tsp	minced fresh oregano leaves	10 mL
2 tbsp	extra virgin olive oil	30 mL
	Freshly ground black pepper	
	Warm grilled pita bread	

1. Place feta on a small serving dish. Sprinkle evenly with oregano and drizzle with olive oil. Season to taste with pepper. Serve with warm pita.

Spiced Feta

Makes about 2 cups (500 mL)

Feta is to some cultures what Philadelphia cream cheese is to North Americans: a tabula rasa upon which to build an infinite number of delicious combinations. Here garden-fresh ingredients and a splash of extra virgin olive oil transform the pleasantly salty cheese into a tasty dip. Serve with warm pita or crudités such as sliced cucumber.

Tips

If you prefer, used chopped cherry tomatoes.

If you don't like heat, seed the chile and remove the veins.

8 oz	feta, crumbled	250 g
1 cup	chopped tomato (see Tips, left)	250 mL
6	green onions, white part with a bit of green, chopped	6
1	long red chile pepper, chopped (see Tips, left)	1
2 tbsp	extra virgin olive oil	30 mL
2 tbsp	fresh dill fronds	30 mL
1 tbsp	freshly squeezed lemon juice	15 mL
	Salt and freshly ground black pepper	

1. In a food processor fitted with metal blade, process feta, tomato, green onions, chile pepper, oil, dill and lemon juice until smooth, about 1 minute, stopping and scraping down sides of the bowl as necessary. Season to taste with salt and black pepper. Transfer to a serving bowl and refrigerate until ready to serve.

Fingerling Potato Skins

Makes 24 skins

There's nothing like a crisp potato with smoky bacon and creamy hot cheese. It's sitting-in-front-of-the-fire comfort food.

- **Preheat oven to 350°F (180°C)**

12	fingerling potatoes	12
1 cup	finely diced smoked bacon	250 mL
1 cup	crumbled soft goat cheese	250 mL
¾ cup	crumbled feta cheese	175 mL
1 tbsp	finely chopped chives	15 mL

1. Place potatoes in a large saucepan and add cold water to cover. Bring to a boil over high heat. Reduce heat and boil gently until potatoes are fork tender, 10 to 15 minutes. Remove from heat and drain thoroughly.

2. In a skillet over medium heat, cook bacon, stirring, until all fat is rendered and bacon is firm, 6 to 7 minutes. Drain on paper towels to remove excess fat.

3. Cut potatoes in half lengthwise and, using a teaspoon, remove half the flesh from potato, reserving for another use. Place skins on a baking sheet. Spoon goat and feta cheeses into each potato cavity, dividing equally. Garnish with bacon. Bake in preheated oven until potatoes are crisp, about 20 minutes. Remove from heat, garnish with chives and serve immediately.

Pimento Cheese

Makes about 1½ cups (375 mL)

Pimento cheese is an old favorite in the southern U.S. Serve this with sliced baguette, crackers, cracker bread or celery sticks.

Tip

If you prefer, substitute ¼ cup (60 mL) coarsely chopped sweet onion, such as Vidalia, for the green or red.

8 oz	sharp (aged) Cheddar cheese	250 g
1	red bell pepper, roasted	1
½ cup	mayonnaise	125 mL
3 tbsp	chopped green or red onion	45 mL
	Hot pepper sauce	
	Freshly ground black pepper	

1. In a food processor fitted with shredding blade, shred Cheddar. Replace shredding blade with metal blade. Add roasted pepper, mayonnaise, onion, and hot pepper sauce and black pepper to taste, and pulse until onion is finely chopped and mixture is blended, about 10 times.

2. Transfer to a small serving bowl or earthenware crock, cover and refrigerate for at least 2 hours or for up to 2 days. Before serving let stand at room temperature to allow the flavors to bloom, about 20 minutes.

Marinated Mozzarella

Makes about 10 servings

This is a dish that you can make days ahead of time, which will give you plenty of time for all of your other tasks.

2	large balls mozzarella (bocconcini), drained	2
2 tbsp	extra virgin olive oil	30 mL
1 tbsp	finely chopped fresh basil leaves	15 mL
¼ tsp	salt	1 mL
¼ tsp	freshly ground black pepper	1 mL
¼ tsp	finely chopped fresh oregano leaves	1 mL
¼ tsp	finely grated lemon zest	1 mL
1 tbsp	freshly squeezed lemon juice	15 mL
30	Grilled Herbed Crostini (page 220)	30

1. In a bowl, combine mozzarella, olive oil, basil, salt, pepper, oregano, lemon zest and lemon juice and coat well. Cover and marinate in the refrigerator for at least 3 hours or for up to 3 days.

2. Remove mozzarella from marinade, reserving marinade. Slice each mozzarella ball into 6 slices and place on a platter. Drizzle with any residual marinade. Serve immediately with Grilled Crostini on the side.

Kentucky Beer Cheese

Makes about 2½ cups (625 mL)

In Kentucky, this spread is an indigenous treat — some call it America's answer to Britain's Welsh rarebit. Serve with sliced baguette, rye bread or celery sticks. Or spread it on toast, garnish with sliced tomatoes and run under the broiler for a delicious lunch.

Tip

Use light or dark beer to suit your preference.

8 oz	extra sharp (aged) Cheddar, cubed	250 g
8 oz	Monterey Jack, cubed	250 g
¾ cup	beer, divided (see Tip, left)	175 mL
2	cloves garlic, coarsely chopped	2
2 tbsp	coarsely snipped chives	30 mL
1 tbsp	vegan or regular Worcestershire sauce	15 mL
1 tbsp	Dijon mustard	15 mL
	Hot pepper sauce	
	Freshly ground black pepper	
	Paprika	

1. In a food processor, process cheeses, ¼ cup (60 mL) of the beer, garlic, chives, Worcestershire, mustard, pepper sauce and pepper to taste until combined. Add remaining beer and process until smooth.

2. Spoon into a serving bowl, cover and refrigerate for at least 2 hours. Dust with paprika before serving.

Chile Cheese

Makes about 1½ cups (375 mL)

Here's a zesty cheese that makes a great addition to a tasting platter. Although the Asian sambal is far from traditional, it's in the British tradition of cheese spreads in crocks, which are a pub staple.

8 oz	Monterey Jack cheese, cubed	250 g
⅓ cup	mayonnaise	75 mL
¼ cup	dry white wine	60 mL
4	green onions, white with a bit of green, cut into chunks	4
1	clove garlic, quartered	1
2 tsp	hot Asian chile sauce, such as sambal oelek	10 mL
½ tsp	cracked black peppercorns	2 mL

1. In a food processor, pulse cheese until finely chopped, about 20 times. Add mayonnaise, wine, onions, garlic, chile sauce and peppercorns and pulse until onion is finely chopped and mixture is blended.

2. Transfer to a small serving bowl or crock, cover and refrigerate for at least 2 hours or for up to 2 days. Before serving let stand at room temperature to allow the flavors to bloom, about 20 minutes.

Baked Goat Cheese

Makes about 1 cup (250 mL)

Soft goat cheese baked with savory enhancements is a theme that can be played with many different variations. Here it's combined with roasted tomatoes and Mediterranean flavorings, a version that is delicious served with crudités, fresh baguette or crostini. Double or triple the recipe to suit your needs.

- **Preheat oven to 400°F (200°C)**

2 tbsp	extra virgin olive oil	30 mL
1	anchovy, finely minced	1
1	clove garlic, finely minced	1
1 tsp	dried oregano	5 mL
¼ tsp	hot pepper flakes, optional	1 mL
12	cherry tomatoes, peeled and halved	12
	Sea salt	
4 oz	soft goat cheese	125 g
	Freshly ground black pepper	
2 tbsp	finely chopped black olives	30 mL

1. In a small bowl, combine olive oil, anchovy, garlic, oregano, and hot pepper flakes, if using. Stir well. Arrange tomatoes on a rimmed baking sheet, cut side up. Drizzle with olive oil mixture. Roast in preheated oven until soft, about 8 minutes. Sprinkle with sea salt to taste. Let cool slightly. Reduce oven heat to 350°F (180°C).

2. Spoon goat cheese into an ovenproof tureen. Add tomato mixture and stir well. Season to taste with pepper. Bake in preheated oven until cheese is bubbling and browning, about 8 minutes. Remove from oven and sprinkle with olives.

Variation

Salsa Baked Goat Cheese: Makes about ¾ cup (175 mL). Omit Step 1. Substitute ⅓ cup (75 mL) tomato or tomatillo-based salsa for the roasted tomato mixture. Substitute an equal quantity of toasted chopped pine nuts for the olives. Serve with tostadas or tortilla chips.

Baked Marinated Goat Cheese

Makes about 8 rounds

These little patties of warm flavor-infused goat cheese are luscious. Serve them on simple crackers. Or, if you're looking for something different, serve as a plated appetizer on top of your favorite arugula or mixed greens salad. Double or triple the recipe to suit your needs.

Tip

To make the bread crumbs for this recipe: Tear 4 slices (1 inch/2.5 cm thick) of French or Italian bread into small pieces and place on a baking sheet in a 350°F (180°C) oven until dry, about 10 minutes. Process in a food processor fitted with metal blade until fine crumbs. Add 1 shallot, coarsely chopped, and 1 tbsp (15 mL) fresh thyme leaves and process until herbs are very finely chopped and well integrated. You'll get about 2 cups (500 mL) of bread crumbs from this quantity. Place excess in a resealable plastic bag and freeze for up to 3 months.

- **Rimmed baking, sheet lined with parchment paper**

½ cup	extra virgin olive oil (approx.)	125 mL
4	cloves garlic, minced	4
4	thyme sprigs, cut crosswise into 3 pieces	4
½ tsp	cracked black peppercorns	2 mL
4 oz	soft goat cheese, cut into 8 rounds	125 g
¾ cup	fresh bread crumbs (see Tip, left)	175 mL

1. In a bowl, combine olive oil, garlic, thyme and peppercorns. Mix well. Spread a thin layer of mixture over a shallow dish just large enough to accommodate the cheese in one layer. Place goat cheese slices on top and pour remaining marinade over cheese. If slices are not completely covered, add olive oil, as necessary. Cover with plastic wrap and refrigerate for 12 hours or for up to 2 days.

2. Preheat oven to 375°F (190°C). Just before you're ready to serve, remove cheese from marinade and set aside. Strain marinade into a small bowl. Discard solids and set liquid aside. Spread bread crumbs on a plate and coat cheese slices on all sides with crumbs. Place on prepared baking sheet and bake in preheated oven, turning once, until crumbs begin to brown and cheese looks softened, about 8 minutes per side. Remove from oven and drizzle with liquid from marinade. Serve immediately.

Baked Ricotta

Makes about 3 cups (750 mL)

Serve this as the centerpiece of an antipasti platter, surrounded by slices of good salumi (for instance, mortadella, prosciutto, salami) or roasted vegetables and black and green olives. Or, if you're not in a particularly Italian mood, some thinly sliced smoked salmon and a small bowl of capers.

Tip

The drier your ricotta, the better the results will be. For best results look for ricotta that has a moisture content of about 65%. (The norm is between 72 and 80%.) Or drain it yourself. *To drain ricotta:* Place ricotta in a clean tea towel, wrap tightly and, using your hands, press against the fabric until excess moisture is absorbed.

- **Preheat oven to 375°F (190°C)**
- **3-cup (750 mL) shallow rectangular baking dish, lightly greased and dusted with dry bread crumbs**

2 cups	whole milk ricotta (see Tip, left)	500 mL
2	eggs, beaten	2
½ cup	freshly grated Parmesan cheese	125 mL
2 tbsp	minced red onion	30 mL
1 tbsp	minced fresh sage leaves	15 mL
½ tsp	cracked black peppercorns	2 mL
	Salt	
2 tbsp	finely chopped Italian flat-leaf parsley leaves	30 mL
	Extra virgin olive oil	

1. In a bowl, combine ricotta, eggs, Parmesan, red onion, sage and peppercorns. Season to taste with salt and mix well. Transfer to prepared dish.

2. Bake in preheated oven until cheese puffs up and mixture looks set, about 30 minutes. Let cool slightly, then invert onto a platter and sprinkle with parsley. Cut into thin slices or small squares and drizzle with oil.

Goat Cheese Fritters on Endive

Makes 16

Served on thin spears of Belgian endive and drizzled with a tarragon-spiked vinaigrette, these tasty tidbits win rave reviews.

Tips

For added flavor, use seasoned goat cheese, such as Roasted Garlic or Herb.

This is more Belgian endive than you will need. For the nicest presentation, use the largest spears and save the remainder to add to salad.

2 tbsp	extra virgin olive oil	30 mL
1 tbsp	white wine vinegar with tarragon	15 mL
1	roll (4 oz/250 g) soft goat cheese (see Tips, left)	1
¼ cup	oil (approx.)	60 mL
1 cup	dry bread crumbs, such as panko	250 mL
¼ cup	all-purpose flour	60 mL
1	egg, beaten with 1 tbsp (15 mL) milk	1
2	Belgian endive (see Tips, left)	2
	Freshly ground black pepper	

1. In a small bowl, whisk olive oil and vinegar. Set aside.
2. Cut cheese in half lengthwise, then cut crosswise into 8 slices, each about ¼ inch (0.5 cm) wide. (You'll have 16 pieces of cheese.) Using your hands, roll each piece into a cylinder about 2 inches (5 cm) long.
3. In a small skillet, heat oil over medium heat.
4. Place panko in a bowl, flour in another bowl and beaten egg in a third bowl. Dip each cheese piece into flour, egg mixture and finally, panko. Refrigerate for at least 30 minutes to firm it up.
5. Add fritters, in batches, to hot oil and cook until bottoms are browned. Turn as necessary to brown remaining sides. Remove with a slotted spoon and drain on a paper towel–lined plate. Repeat until all fritters are fried.
6. Separate endives into leaves. Place 1 fritter on each spear. Drizzle lightly with olive oil mixture and season to taste with pepper. Serve warm or at room temperature.

Stuffed Mushroom Caps

Makes 24

Elegant yet easy to make, these tasty tidbits make great finger food.

Tip

If you have a mini-bowl attachment for your food processor, you can use it to mix the ingredients. Combine coarsely chopped artichokes, tomatoes and garlic and pulse until finely chopped, stopping and scraping down sides of the bowl as necessary. Add goat cheese and pulse to blend.

- **Preheat oven to 400°F (200°C)**

24	large white mushroom caps	24
2 tbsp	olive oil	30 mL
1	jar (6 oz/170 mL) marinated artichokes, drained and finely chopped (see Tip, left)	1
2	reconstituted sun-dried tomatoes, minced	2
2	cloves garlic, minced	2
4 oz	soft goat cheese	125 g
2 tbsp	pine nuts, finely chopped	30 mL

1. Brush mushroom caps all over with olive oil and place, convex side up, on a baking sheet. Bake in preheated oven until nicely softened, for 15 minutes. Let cool slightly. Leave oven on.

2. Meanwhile, in a bowl, combine artichokes, sun-dried tomatoes and garlic. Mix well. Add goat cheese and mix until blended. Spoon about 1 heaping tsp (7 mL) of mixture into each mushroom cap. Sprinkle with pine nuts. Return to oven and bake until cheese is melted and pine nuts are lightly toasted, about 10 minutes. Serve warm.

Mushroom Fundido

Makes about 2 cups (500 mL)

Fundido is, depending on your source, a Spanish or Mexican dip built around melted cheese. It is rich, delicious and quite addictive. Serve it when the first chill of winter is in the air, accompanied by tostadas or tortilla chips.

Tips

If you can't find poblano peppers, substitute 1 large green bell pepper and 1 jalapeño pepper.

To roast peppers: Place peppers under preheated broiler. Broil, turning frequently, until the skins are dark and charred. Transfer to a large bowl and cover with a plate until peppers are cool enough to handle. Lift off the skins and discard. Seed and dice the peppers. Set aside.

- **Preheat oven to 375°F (190°C)**
- **Ovenproof serving bowl or large (2 cup/500 mL) ramekin**

2	roasted poblano peppers, seeded and diced (see Tips, left)	2
1 tbsp	oil	15 mL
1	onion, finely chopped	1
8 oz	mushrooms, trimmed and thinly sliced	250 g
2	cloves garlic, minced	2
1	jalapeño pepper, seeded and minced	1
¼ cup	beer, white wine, chicken or vegetable broth	60 mL
2 cups	shredded Monterey Jack cheese	500 mL
3 tbsp	tomato or tomatillo salsa	45 mL
	Tostadas or tortilla chips	

1. In a skillet, heat oil over medium heat. Add onion and stir well. Increase heat to medium-high. Add mushrooms and cook, stirring, until lightly browned, about 7 minutes. Stir in garlic, jalapeño and roasted peppers. Add beer and cook, stirring, until evaporated, about 3 minutes. Remove from heat.

2. In an ovenproof serving bowl or large ramekin, place half the cheese. Add mushroom mixture. Add remaining cheese. Bake in preheated oven until cheese is melted and bubbling, about 20 minutes. Remove from oven. Add salsa and stir well. Serve immediately with chips.

Chorizo-Laced Fundido

Makes about 4 cups (1 L)

This robustly flavored warm cheese dip is perfect if you're having friends over to watch a sports event. You can assemble it ahead of time and bake when you're ready to eat. This makes a fairly substantial quantity and all it needs is tostadas or tortilla chips.

- **Preheat oven to 375°F (190°C)**
- **4-cup (1 L) baking dish, greased**

8 oz	dry (cured) chorizo, diced	250 g
½ cup	diced red onion	125 mL
¼ cup	sour cream or crème fraîche	60 mL
2 tbsp	tomato salsa	30 mL
2 cups	shredded Monterey Jack cheese	500 mL
	Tostadas or tortilla chips	

1. In a bowl, combine chorizo, red onion, sour cream and salsa. Mix well. Add shredded cheese and toss. Transfer to prepared baking dish. Cover and bake in preheated oven, stirring once, until bubbling and hot, about 20 minutes.

Greek-Style Fried Cheese

Makes about 16 pieces • Serves 8

Vegetarian Friendly

Warm oozing cheese is always a hit. This version is simple, stylish and delicious. Spear this on toothpicks or serve on crackers or sliced baguette.

Tip

Italian flat-leaf parsley is preferred because it has much more flavor than the curly leaf variety.

1	egg	1
1 tbsp	milk	15 mL
½ cup	all-purpose flour	125 mL
8 oz	kasseri cheese, cut into 1-inch (2.5 cm) cubes	250 g
¼ cup	olive oil	60 mL
2 tbsp	finely chopped Italian flat-leaf parsley leaves	30 mL
	Freshly squeezed lemon juice	
	Freshly ground black pepper	

1. In a bowl, combine egg and milk. Mix well. Spread flour on a large plate. Working in batches, coat cheese with egg mixture, then dredge in flour.

2. In a large skillet, heat oil over medium-high heat. Add cheese and cook, turning, until all sides are browned, about 15 seconds per side. Transfer to a platter. Sprinkle with parsley. Drizzle with lemon juice and season to taste with pepper. Serve immediately.

Smoked Brie

Makes 6 servings

A warm, delicately smoked Brie cheese spread over a Grilled Herbed Crostini (page 220) or just a crunchy celery stick is outstanding.

Tip

Typically the wood from any fruit or nut you enjoy eating will work for smoking; apple, cherry and pecan wood chips would all work well in this recipe.

- **Preheat barbecue grill to low for indirect heat (see Tips, page 478)**

4 oz	applewood chips	125 g
6	thyme sprigs	6
6 oz	Brie cheese round	175 g
1 tbsp	packed brown sugar	15 mL

1. Wrap wood chips loosely in foil, sealing edges, and poke holes in the top and bottom. Place package over hot side of preheated grill, close lid and grill until smoke is released from package, about 20 minutes.

2. Place a sheet of foil on a work surface and place thyme sprigs in the middle. Place Brie on top and sprinkle evenly with brown sugar. Pull foil up around Brie into a pyramid shape, leaving top open. Transfer to unlit side of grill, close lid and smoke until cheese is soft to the touch and rind has a yellow hue, 35 to 45 minutes. Transfer to a serving plate and serve immediately.

Deep-Fried Brie

Makes about 24

Deep-frying rich Brie cheese may seem like overkill, but once you taste these warm luscious nuggets, you'll be a convert. Top them with a tiny dollop of your favorite chutney or a homemade coulis such as Two-Tomato Coulis (page 544) or Roasted Red Pepper Coulis (page 543) or even Strawberry and Rhubarb Salsa (page 91).

- **Candy/deep fry thermometer**

1 cup	all-purpose flour	250 mL
1 cup	dry bread crumbs, such as panko	250 mL
2	eggs, beaten	2
1 lb	cold Brie cheese, cut into ¾-inch (2 cm) cubes	500 g
	Oil	

1. Spread flour and bread crumbs on two plates and beat eggs in a bowl. Dip Brie in flour, then eggs, and in bread crumbs, turning to thoroughly coat all sides. Place on a platter and freeze for 10 minutes.

2. Add oil to pan to a depth of $1\frac{1}{2}$ inches (4 cm) and heat to 350°F (180°C). Add Brie in batches (do not crowd) and cook until browned. Carefully transfer to a platter. Spear with toothpicks and serve immediately.

Plum-Stuffed Brie Cheese

Makes 7 to 10 servings

Sure, warm Brie cheese is a classic but wait until you stuff it! This is perfect when served with Grilled Herbed Crostini (page 220).

- **Preheat oven to 300°F (150°C)**

¾ cup	diced plums (about 2 small)	175 mL
¼ cup	white balsamic vinegar	60 mL
2 tbsp	granulated sugar	30 mL
12 oz	cold Brie cheese round	375 g

1. In a saucepan, bring plums, vinegar and sugar to a boil over high heat. Reduce heat and simmer, stirring often, until liquid is evaporated, about 10 minutes. Let cool to room temperature.

2. Slice Brie in half horizontally and separate top from bottom. Spoon plum marmalade onto one half and cover with other. Wrap cheese in foil, place on a baking sheet and bake in a preheated oven until soft, 10 to 15 minutes. Open and roll down the foil, place on a platter and serve immediately.

Celery Spears and Whipped Brie

Makes 12 appetizers

Vegetarian Friendly

This is an elegant spin on a comfort food classic usually made with celery and store-bought cheese sauce. Garnish with Caramelized Onions (page 552) or a dollop of your favorite fruit jam or marmalade.

Tip

Celery is very fibrous and "stringy." Using a vegetable peeler, peel the outside of the celery stalk to reveal a white, delicate flesh. The difference will be appreciated.

¼ cup	heavy or whipping (35%) cream	60 mL
¼ tsp	chopped fresh thyme leaves	1 mL
6 oz	Brie cheese, rind removed and at room temperature	175 g
12	celery sticks, peeled and cut into 3-inch (7.5 cm) lengths (see Tip, left)	12

1. In a bowl, using an electric mixer, whip cream and thyme to stiff peaks.

2. In another bowl, using electric mixer, whip Brie until light and fluffy. Fold cream mixture into Brie, one-third at a time, until fully incorporated. (This should resemble cream cheese.)

3. Spoon Brie mixture into cavity of celery, dividing equally. Using a paring knife, smooth the surface of the cheese. (Presentation does count for something after all.) Serve immediately or store covered in the refrigerator for up to 3 hours.

Strawberry-Topped Brie

Makes 6 canapés

A sensory overload! Frozen ingredients add a wonderful textural and temperature contrast when paired with warm or room temperature ingredients.

Tip

Freezing the strawberry contributes a unique temperature and texture contrast but feel free to use fresh berries. It will impress your guests either way.

• **Baking sheet and pie plate, lined with parchment paper**

1	strawberry	1
3	Black mission figs, cut in half lengthwise	3
1 tsp	granulated sugar	5 mL
2 oz	Brie cheese, cut into 6 cubes	60 g
6	small fresh mint leaves	6

1. Slice strawberry lengthwise into 6 thin slices and place on prepared baking sheet. Freeze for a minimum of 2 hours or overnight. Keep frozen until ready to assemble.

2. Preheat broiler. Place figs, cut side up, on prepared pie plate. Evenly dust figs with sugar. Broil until sugar is caramelized, 2 to 4 minutes. Let cool to the touch.

3. Place fig on a work surface, sugar facing up. Place a slice of frozen strawberry on top, then cube of Brie. Place on a spoon. Garnish with mint leaf and serve immediately.

Perfect Tomato and Cheese Canapés

Makes 24 canapés

This sophisticated appetizer is ready in minutes. Serve on crackers or if you feel like taking it to the next level, use Cheddar Cheese Crisps (page 392) as a base for the tomato and goat cheese.

2 oz	soft goat or blue cheese	60 g
12	large cherry tomatoes, cut in half crosswise	12
1 tsp	finely diced red onion	5 mL
1/4 tsp	thin strips basil leaves	1 mL

1. In a bowl, using an electric mixer, whip goat cheese until creamy, 1 to 2 minutes.

2. Place tomatoes on a platter, cut side facing up. Divide whipped goat cheese into 24 segments and scoop one portion into one spoon. With two spoons in hand, gently press the bowl of the second spoon against the cheese, scooping the contents of the first spoon into the second. Transfer the cheese back to the first spoon in the same way and repeat until three smooth sides are formed. Place quenelle on top of tomato and garnish with red onion and basil. Serve immediately.

Belgian Endive with Blue Cheese

Makes 16 servings

It's possible, dare we say probable, that you will find this salad combination in most restaurants across France. From France to your table, why not?

Tip

Any blue cheese can work for this hors d'oeuvre, from Stilton to Danish Blue — they will all taste amazing.

12	medium-size Belgian endive leaves	12
1½ oz	Roquefort blue cheese, crumbled	45 g
1 tsp	toasted pine nuts	5 mL
1 tbsp	Red Wine Vinaigrette (page 540) or store-bought	15 mL
1 tsp	fresh chervil leaves	5 mL

1. Place endive leave spears with the natural curve facing up on a platter. Place blue cheese and pine nuts at the wide edge of the endive, dividing evenly. Drizzle about ¼ tsp (1 mL) of the vinaigrette along entire length of endive. Garnish with chervil leaves and serve immediately.

Blue Cheese–Stuffed Dates

Makes 24 stuffed dates

The tartness of the blue cheese pairs beautifully with the sweetness of the dates.

Tip

In the absence of a pastry bag, a resealable plastic sandwich bag will work just fine. To use, fill bag with mixture and seal, removing all air. Using scissors, cut one corner of the bag and push mixture toward hole. Pipe away!

- **Small pastry bag (see Tip, left)**

4 oz	crumbled loosely packed blue cheese	125 g
1 tsp	milk	5 mL
24	pitted dates	24

1. In a bowl, combine cheese and milk and mash until smooth. Transfer to a pastry bag and pipe about 1½ tsp (7 mL) into the center of each date. Serve immediately or cover and refrigerate for up to 3 days. Bring to room temperature before serving.

Variation

For a wonderful variation, wrap a thin slice of prosciutto around stuffed dates.

Cheese and Peach Wontons

Makes about 15 wontons

These wontons are like a sweet and tart explosion in your mouth. Serve with Warm Apple Sour Cream (page 522).

- • **Candy/deep fry thermometer**

15	wonton wrappers, about 3 inches (7.5 cm) square	15
6 tbsp	finely diced peaches	90 mL
2 oz	blue cheese, crumbled	60 g
½ tsp	chopped fresh sage leaves	2 mL
	Oil	

1. Place wonton wrappers on a work surface. Place peaches, blue cheese and chopped sage in the center of each wrapper, dividing equally. Wet edges of wonton with water. Working with one square at a time, starting with two opposite corners, bring toward the center over filling and press corners together. Repeat with third and fourth corners, meeting edges of first two to resemble a pyramid, squeezing out air before you press to seal the edges.

2. In a deep skillet, Dutch oven or deep-fryer, heat about 3 inches (7.5 cm) of oil to 325°F (160°C). Fry wontons, in batches, until golden brown and floating to the surface, 2 to 3 minutes. Serve immediately.

Cheddar Cheese Crisps

Makes about 30 crisps

These crisps are so tasty and boy are they easy. They can be formed into many shapes. You can make a cup with them, shape as a large cannoli or just lay flat for the base of a canapé — options are endless.

2 cups	finely grated extra sharp (extra old) Cheddar cheese	500 mL

1. Warm a nonstick skillet over medium heat. Place about 1 tbsp (15 mL) of the cheese in pan and cook until melted and bottom is crisp, about 1 minute. Flip over and cook just until second side is crisp, 30 to 60 seconds. Using a spatula, transfer to a work surface and carefully roll into a cigar shape, if desired or let cool flat. The crisps will harden as they cool. Set aside to cool and repeat with remaining cheese, adjusting heat and wiping out pan as necessary between batches. Serve immediately or store in an airtight container for up to 2 days.

Cheese Puffs

Makes about 4 dozen

In France, their country of origin, these savory pastries are known as gougères. They are a perfect tidbit to enjoy with a glass of wine. Serve them warm from the oven and watch them disappear.

Tip

If you want your cheese puffs to be particularly pretty, use a pastry bag to pipe them onto the baking sheets.

- **Preheat oven to 400°F (200°C)**
- **2 baking sheets, lined with parchment paper**

½ cup	unsalted butter	125 mL
½ cup	milk	125 mL
½ cup	water	125 mL
½ tsp	salt	2 mL
	Freshly ground black pepper	
1 cup	all-purpose flour	250 mL
4	eggs	4
1	clove garlic, grated	1
1 cup	shredded Gruyère cheese	250 mL
¼ cup	freshly grated Parmesan	60 mL

1. In a heavy saucepan, combine butter, milk, water, salt, and pepper to taste. Bring to a boil over medium-high heat, beating to ensure mixture is well blended. Remove from heat and immediately add flour all at once. Beat vigorously with a wooden spoon until mixture becomes smooth and pulls away from the sides of the pan. Return to low heat and beat vigorously for 1 to 2 minutes until mixture begins to dry out.

2. Transfer to a bowl and, using a mixer on high speed, add eggs, one at a time, mixing until each is incorporated before adding the next. Reduce speed to medium-low and add garlic and Gruyère, mixing until just incorporated.

3. Drop batter by heaping teaspoonfuls (7 mL) onto prepared sheets, leaving about 2 inches (5 cm) between each dollop. Sprinkle with Parmesan. Bake for 15 minutes, then reduce heat to 350°F (180°C) and bake until puffs are firm and golden, about 15 minutes. Serve warm.

Mini Goat Cheese Puffs

Makes 24 mini puffs

Many people are intimidated by this simplest of creations — the cheese puff. You'll be amazed how quick they are and can take the credit for preparing such a special treat.

Tip

You can also scoop dough into a piping bag fitted with a large, plain or star tip to fill the muffin cups.

- **Preheat oven to 400°F (200°C)**
- **Mini muffin pan, greased**

½ cup	whole milk	125 mL
¼ cup	unsalted butter, diced	60 mL
¼ tsp	salt	1 mL
7 tbsp	all-purpose flour	105 mL
3 tbsp	crumbled goat cheese, softened	45 mL
2	eggs	2
1 tsp	finely chopped fresh oregano leaves	5 mL
¼ cup	freshly grated Parmesan cheese	60 mL

1. In a saucepan over medium-low heat, combine milk, butter and salt until butter is melted and bubbles form around the edge. Add flour and, using a wooden spoon, stir vigorously until mixture pulls away from sides of pan and forms a ball, 2 to 3 minutes. Remove from heat and stir in goat cheese, 1 egg and oregano until well combined. Add remaining egg and continue to stir until a loose dough is formed.

2. Using two spoons, fill prepared muffin cups two-thirds full, scooping dough with one spoon and scraping into pan with the other. Sprinkle evenly with Parmesan cheese. Bake in preheated oven until puffs have risen and are golden brown, about 12 minutes. Serve immediately.

Thyme-Spiked Cheese Sticks

Makes 10 cheese sticks

These cheese sticks are almost as easy to make as ordering them in your favorite restaurant or pub but you can certainly taste the homemade in every bite. Serve with sweet Warm Apple Sour Cream (page 522) for a lovely contrast of sweet and savory.

Tip

Be creative with your cheese. From Swiss to Oka or even Parmesan, virtually any medium to hard cheese will work for this recipe.

- **Candy/deep fry thermometer**

1 cup	panko bread crumbs	250 mL
1 tbsp	finely grated Parmesan cheese	15 mL
1 tsp	chopped fresh thyme leaves	5 mL
2/3 cup	all-purpose flour	150 mL
2	eggs, beaten	2
3 oz	Cheddar cheese	90 g
	Oil	
1/4 tsp	salt	1 mL

1. In a shallow bowl, combine bread crumbs, Parmesan and thyme. Place flour and eggs in two separate shallow bowls.

2. Cut Cheddar into 10 sticks, each 3 inches (7.5 cm) long by ½ inch (1 cm) thick. Dredge cheese sticks in flour, turning to coat thoroughly. Place into egg to coat and finally the bread crumbs. Discard any excess flour, egg and crumbs.

3. In a deep skillet, Dutch oven or deep-fryer, heat 3 inches (7.5 cm) inches of oil over medium-high heat to 325°F (160°C). In batches as necessary, fry cheese sticks, turning once, until golden brown, 2 to 3 minutes. Transfer to paper towel to drain excess oil and season with salt. Serve immediately.

Cheddar Cheese Fondue

Makes 2 cups (500 mL)

This silky cheesy dip is great for bread, vegetables and perhaps even the new "cheese" for your sliders or on the side. Try it — you and your guests will love it.

1 tbsp	unsalted butter	15 mL
3 tbsp	all-purpose flour	45 mL
1½ cups	whole milk	375 mL
2 cups	shredded Cheddar cheese	500 mL
1 tsp	finely chopped fresh chives	5 mL

1. In a saucepan, melt butter over medium-low heat. Sprinkle with flour and cook, stirring often, until smooth and a nutty brown color, 4 to 5 minutes. Gradually whisk in milk. Cook, stirring, until bubbling and thickened, about 5 minutes. Remove from heat and slowly add cheese, about 1 tbsp (15 mL) at a time, whisking to incorporate. Transfer to a serving dish. Garnish with chives and serve immediately.

Blue Cheese Fondue

Makes 2 cup (500 mL)

This tart fondue is perfect with everything from simple carrot sticks to Classic Buffalo Chicken Wings (page 473).

1 tbsp	unsalted butter	15 mL
3 tbsp	all-purpose flour	45 mL
1½ cups	whole milk	375 mL
8 oz	crumbled loosely packed blue cheese	250 g
1 tsp	finely grated toasted pecans	5 mL

1. In a saucepan, melt butter over medium-low heat. Sprinkle with flour and cook, stirring often, until smooth and a nutty brown color, 4 to 5 minutes. Gradually whisk in milk. Cook, stirring, until bubbling and thickened, about 5 minutes Remove from heat and add cheese, about 1 tbsp (15 mL) at a time, and whisk to incorporate. Repeat until all cheese has been added. Garnish with pecans and serve immediately.

Warm Pineapple with Mascarpone Cheese and Basil

Makes about 16 servings

There's nothing like taste of warm, fresh pineapple on a warm spring or summer day. This flavorful appetizer is a lovely addition to brunch or toward the end of a party as a dessert.

Tip

If time is of the essence, buy a freshly peeled pineapple from your local gourmet or grocery market.

- **16 small dishes or ramekins**

½ cup	water	125 mL
2 tbsp	liquid honey	30 mL
1 cup	diced pineapple (see Tip, left)	250 mL
1 tsp	chopped fresh basil leaves	5 mL
2 cups	mascarpone cheese	500 mL
2 tbsp	coconut-flavored rum	30 mL

1. In a saucepan over high heat, bring water and honey to a boil. Add pineapple, reduce heat and simmer until water is fully evaporated and pineapple is caramelized, about 15 minutes. Remove from heat and stir in basil.

2. Place 2 tbsp (30 mL) mascarpone cheese into each dish. Pour pineapple mixture over top, dividing equally. Drizzle with rum and serve immediately.

Honey-Glazed Pear and Cheddar Cheese Stacks

Makes 12 stacks

An appetizer fit for people of all ages, refined enough to serve adults for a lunch or tea party and tasty enough to please the children in your life. Try dipping this into Cheddar Cheese Fondue (page 396) for a very cheesy variation.

12	1-inch (2.5 cm) cubes pear	12
1 tbsp	freshly squeezed lemon juice	15 mL
3 oz	extra sharp (extra old) Cheddar cheese, cut into twelve 1-inch (2.5 cm) cubes	90 g
1 tsp	honey, warmed	5 mL
½ tsp	fresh thyme leaves	2 mL

1. Place pear cubes on a platter and brush all over with lemon juice. Place Cheddar on top of pear and glaze with honey. With a toothpick, skewer the stack from the top, garnish with thyme leaves and serve.

2. Assemble these hors d'oeuvres ahead of time. Cover and refrigerate for up to 3 hours.

Panko-Crusted Tomato with Camembert Cheese

Makes 16 appetizers

An incredible appetizer with the simplest of ingredients. Try a garnish of Basil Pesto (page 549) or Chive Parsley "Pistou" (page 550) for the perfect fresh accent to the creamy Camembert.

Tip

Green tomatoes work very well in this recipe, too.

1	tomato	1
1 cup	panko bread crumbs	250 mL
½ tsp	finely chopped fresh thyme leaves	2 mL
¼ tsp	salt	1 mL
¼ tsp	freshly ground black pepper	1 mL
5 tsp	all-purpose flour	25 mL
1	egg, beaten	1
2 tbsp	olive oil	30 mL
4 oz	Camembert or Brie cheese, cut into 16 1-inch (2.5 cm) cubes	125 g
½ tsp	fresh thyme leaves	2 mL

1. Using a sharp knife, remove thin slices from top and bottom of tomato to expose some flesh (flour will not stick to skin). Slice tomato crosswise into 4 equal slices and cut each slice into quarters. Set aside.

2. In a shallow bowl, combine bread crumbs, finely chopped thyme, salt and pepper. Mix well. Place flour and egg in a separate shallow bowls. Dredge tomatoes in flour, then egg and finally in bread crumb mixture, turning and pressing to coat. Discard any excess flour, egg and crumbs.

3. In a large nonstick skillet, heat oil over medium heat. Sear tomato slices, turning once, until golden brown, about 2 minutes per side. Drain on paper towels.

4. Place a cube of Camembert on top of each tomato and garnish with thyme leaves. Serve immediately.

Mostly Veggies
and Bar Noshes

In many ways, vegetables are like the Cinderella of the appetizer course — initially so taken for granted that their inherent charms are easily overlooked. But dressed up they can be dazzling. In addition there are many vegetable appetizers that are simple beyond belief but quite mouthwatering, such as Buttered Radishes (page 404) or Salt-Roasted Potatoes (page 405). And vegetables are very versatile. For instance, you can stuff them, eat them raw with a dressing or a dip, or cook them and chill in a zesty marinade.

When serving appetizers focused on vegetables, your best bet is to buy local produce in season whenever possible. The difference in freshness and flavor will produce the finest results. That said, some of the best ready-made appetizers are vegetables: olives, marinated mushrooms or artichokes, roasted peppers, and bottled or tinned white asparagus, to name just a few. Whether you're buying fresh or prepared, always look for quality. Starting with great ingredients is the surest way to guarantee exceptional results.

Mostly Veggies

Asparagus and Cheddar–Topped Toasts 401
Asparagus Toasts with Hollandaise. 402
Grilled Asparagus Spears with Lemon
   and Olive Oil 403
White Asparagus with Tonnato 403
Buttered Radishes 404
Roasted Potato Wedges. 404
Salt-Roasted Potatoes 405
Stewed Potatoes with Truffle 405
Caviar-Stuffed New Potatoes 406
Bacon-Spiked Rösti Cakes. 407
Indian-Style Potato Fritters 408
Truffle-Spiked Potato Croquettes 409
Sweet Pea and Potato Croquettes 410
Mini Potato Croquettes. 411
Potatoes Anna 412
Classic French Fries 413
Diced Potato Gratin 414
Spicy Sweet Potato Wedges
   with Maple Glaze 415
Sweet Potato Cakes. 416
Sweet Potato Galette 417
Crispy Potato Galette 417
Zucchini Fritters 418
Crispy Zucchini Fingers. 419
Classic Coleslaw 419
Quick Zucchini and Jerusalem Artichoke
   Sauté on Grilled Crostini 420

Panko-Crusted Onion Rings 421
Shoestring Onion Rings with Pommery
   Mustard Dip 422
Vegetable Tempura. 423
Fried Zucchini Flowers 424
Sweet-and-Sour Cipollini 425
Spicy Cheese and Onion–Spiked Eggplant. 426
Baby Candy Cane Beets with Fresh Mint 427
Lemony Marinated Beets 428
Cumin-Dusted Cauliflower 429
Cumin-Spiked Carrots with Cilantro 429
Orange-Spiked Cucumbers with Mint 430
Overstuffed Cucumbers with Feta and Dill 430
Dressy Fennel à la Grecque 431
Celery Root Rémoulade 432
Celery Root Avgolemono 433
Roasted Red Peppers with Anchovy-Spiked
   Olive Oil 433
Olive-Studded Roasted Red Peppers
   with Sherry Vinegar. 434
Roasted Garlic and Mushroom Whirl. 434
Cheesy Mushroom Muffins 435
Prosciutto-Stuffed Mushrooms 436
Stuffed Cremini Mushroom Caps 437
King Oyster Mushroom and Asparagus
   Salsa Canapé. 438
Peppery Roasted Squash Pâté. 438
Risotto Balls 439
Cornmeal-Crusted Black Bean Cakes 440

continued on next page

Black Bean Quesadillas 441
Red Bean Quesadillas 442
Polenta Tamales 443
Tomato Basil Polenta Gratin 444
Fried Green Tomatoes 445
Panko-Crusted Tomatillos with
    Summer Tomato Salsa 446
Sweet Pepper and Garlic Marinated Olives 446
Classic Deviled Eggs 447
Classic Edamame. 448
Edamame with Asian Vinaigrette. 448
Fresh Corn Cakes. 449
Marinated Corn on the Cob 450
The Absolute Best Creamed Corn 450
Vegetarian Cabbage Rolls. 451

Bar Noshes
Spicy Almonds 452
Spanish-Style Smoked Almonds. 453
Coconut-Scented Macadamia Nuts 453
Cornflake and Almond Clusters 454
Chile-Spiked Peanuts. 454
Agave and Ginger-Scented Peanuts. 455
Sweet Sesame Snap Squares 455
Cinnamon-Spiked Pumpkin Seeds 456
Curried Cashews with Sultanas 457
Coffee-Scented Hazelnuts 457
Cinnamon-Scented Popcorn 458
Thyme-Scented Popcorn 458

Asparagus and Cheddar–Topped Toasts

Makes about 12

One secret to making this dish is to cut everything extremely thin. It is an elegant appetizer that is very easy to make.

Tips

Peel the stems of the asparagus before slicing and use a sharp knife to cut the asparagus on the diagonal into very thin slices.

If you have access to cloth-wrapped Cheddar, a premium product, by all means use it in this recipe.

6	asparagus spears, peeled and very thinly sliced (approx.) (see Tips, left)	6

Vinaigrette

¼ tsp	salt	1 mL
1 tbsp	freshly squeezed lemon juice	15 mL
2 tbsp	extra virgin olive oil	30 mL
2 oz	very thinly sliced best-quality sharp (aged) Cheddar cheese	60 g
	Toast points or crostini	
	Freshly ground black pepper	

1. In a pot of rapidly boiling salted water, drop sliced asparagus. Return to the boil and boil for 30 seconds. Drain and run under cold running water. Let cool slightly.

2. *Vinaigrette:* Meanwhile, in a small bowl dissolve salt in lemon juice. Whisk in olive oil.

3. Place thinly sliced Cheddar on a toast point, arrange asparagus over top, drizzle with vinaigrette and season liberally with pepper.

Variations

Substitute 1 tbsp (15 mL) of walnut oil for an equal quantity of olive oil in the vinaigrette.

Substitute an equal quantity of Roasted Cherry Tomato Vinaigrette (page 541) for the Vinaigrette.

Asparagus Toasts with Hollandaise

Makes 16

This is a great appetizer to make when asparagus just comes into season and the stalks are still quite thin. It is rich, retro and delicious.

Tip

The one problem with Hollandaise sauce is that it must be kept warm over boiling water and used very soon after it is made. If you are making this recipe, serve it as a finger food starter, then serve Asparagus with Hollandaise (page 358) to start the meal or as a vegetable course with simple grilled salmon to use up the remainder of the batch.

16	thin asparagus spears	16
¼ cup	Foolproof Hollandaise (approx.) (page 539)	60 mL
16	toast points or crostini	16
	Freshly ground black pepper	

1. Trim the ends off the asparagus and peel stalks. Drop in a pot of rapidly boiling salted water and cook until just tender, about 4 minutes. Drain. Cut asparagus to make spears about the same size as the toast points or crostini you are using. Set spears and stalks aside.

2. In a food processor fitted with metal blade, process asparagus stalks and 2 tbsp (30 mL) Hollandaise.

3. Spread each toast with asparagus purée, top with an asparagus spear and a tiny dollop of Hollandaise. Season to taste with pepper. Serve warm.

Variation

If you don't want to make Hollandaise for this recipe, substitute 1 tbsp (15 mL) butter and 2 tsp (10 mL) freshly squeezed lemon juice for the Hollandaise.

Grilled Asparagus Spears with Lemon and Olive Oil

Makes about 6 servings

Mother nature made asparagus the perfect vegetable to serve as an appetizer, no mess at all, just pick up and eat.

Tip

To blanch vegetables: Cook vegetables in boiling salted water until tender-crisp, then plunge into ice water to stop the cooking process. Here it achieves a beautifully vibrant green asparagus tip.

- **Preheat barbecue grill to high**

1 lb	asparagus (about 12 large spears), trimmed	500 g
	Ice water	
1 tsp	extra virgin olive oil	5 mL
½ tsp	minced garlic	2 mL
½ tsp	freshly squeezed lemon juice	2 mL
¼ tsp	salt	1 mL

1. In a large pot of boiling salted water boil asparagus until bright green and slightly tender, 2 to 3 minutes. Drain and immediately plunge into a bowl of ice water (see Tip, left) to stop the cooking. Drain well and pat dry.
2. In a bowl, combine oil, garlic, lemon juice and salt.
3. Place asparagus on preheated barbecue and grill, rolling over the grill often, until charred and warmed through, about 3 minutes. Immediately transfer to the bowl with the oil mixture and toss to coat. Serve immediately.

White Asparagus with Tonnato

Makes 4 servings

Make this in the depths of winter if you live in an area where fresh asparagus is a faint dream. Good quality preserved white asparagus is also a treat.

1	can or jar (16 oz/300 g approx.) white asparagus	1
¼ cup	Tonnato (page 64)	60 mL)

1. Thoroughly chill white asparagus. Drain and arrange on a small platter or serving plate. Top with Tonnato. Serve plated.

Variations

Use cooked chilled fresh green asparagus in season.

You can also turn this into a salad starter by spreading a layer of salad greens over a large platter. Arrange the asparagus over the greens and top with Tonnato.

Buttered Radishes

Makes 4 servings

It's hard to believe such a simple combination of ingredients can produce such appetizing results.

Tip

It is important to use unsalted butter of the best quality you can find.

1	bunch radishes, preferably French breakfast, (about 10), scrubbed and halved lengthwise	1
1 tbsp	best-quality unsalted butter, softened (see Tip, left)	15 mL
	Crunchy sea salt, such as Malden or fleur de sel	

1. Spread cut side of radishes with butter and sprinkle with sea salt to taste. Cover and refrigerate for up to 2 hours.

Roasted Potato Wedges

Makes 16 wedges

This falls under the category of "everyone will love." Serve these great roasted wedges with an assortment of dips, from Black Pepper Goat Cheese Dip (page 20) and Roasted Red Pepper Coulis (page 543) to Truffle Vinaigrette (page 542).

Tip

Play with this recipe to create your own fan favorite. Glaze with maple syrup or drizzle a good-quality white truffle oil over top — or how about some leftover gravy!

- **Preheat oven to 325°F (160°C)**
- **Large ovenproof skillet**

1 lb	russet (Idaho) potatoes (about 2 medium)	500 g
1 tbsp	salt	15 mL
1 tbsp	olive oil	15 mL
1 tbsp	unsalted butter	15 mL
½ tsp	chopped fresh thyme leaves	2 mL
½ tsp	chopped fresh basil leaves	2 mL
½ tsp	freshly ground black pepper	2 mL

1. Using a sharp knife, cut each potato lengthwise into 8 wedges.
2. Place potatoes in a pot and add water to cover. Add salt and bring to a boil over medium heat. Reduce heat and simmer until potatoes are fork tender, about 8 minutes. Drain and pat dry with a towel. Set aside.
3. In skillet, heat oil and butter over medium-high heat. Add potatoes and mix well to coat. Transfer skillet to preheated oven and bake until golden brown and crisp, about 25 minutes. Transfer potatoes to a bowl. Add thyme, basil and pepper. Mix well and serve immediately.

Salt-Roasted Potatoes

Makes 1 serving per potato

Serve these mouthwatering potatoes on their own, topped with a dollop of sour cream and a sprinkling of finely snipped chives or use them as delivery vehicles for many dips.

Tip

You can precook the potatoes and refrigerate until ready to use. Don't cut them in half until you're ready to finish them.

- **Preheat barbecue grill to high or broiler**

1 tbsp	extra virgin olive oil	15 mL
	Fine sea salt	
1 lb	new potatoes, boiled in their skins just until tender (see Tip, left)	500 g
	Sour cream, optional	
	Finely snipped chives, optional	

1. In a bowl large enough to accommodate the potatoes, combine olive oil and salt to taste. Cut cooked potatoes in half. Add to bowl and toss to thoroughly coat with mixture.

2. Place potatoes cut side down on grill or broiling pan and cook until beginning to brown, about 5 minutes per side. Let cool slightly. Spear each half with a toothpick and serve.

Stewed Potatoes with Truffle

Makes 4 cups (1 L)

An easy, yet very decadent pairing of potato and the flavor of truffles.

Tip

Fresh truffles are a glorious treat for the senses if you can find them and, better yet, afford them. Truffle oil is more widely available in your local fine foods or gourmet food shops — just be careful of those synthetic imposters!

- **30 Chinese-style soup spoons**

2 tbsp	unsalted butter	30 mL
4½ cups	cubed unpeeled russet (Idaho) potatoes	1.125 L
¾ cup	white wine	175 mL
1 tsp	salt	5 mL
½ tsp	freshly ground black pepper	2 mL
1 tbsp	white truffle oil (see Tip, left)	15 mL
1 tsp	fresh thyme leaves	5 mL

1. In a large saucepan, melt butter over medium-high heat. Sauté potatoes, stirring often, until slightly tender, about 30 minutes. Add wine and deglaze, stirring up all the browned bits on the bottom. Cover, and reduce heat to low and simmer until potatoes are soft, resembling a very chunky mashed potato, about 20 minutes.

2. Place about 2 tbsp (30 mL) of potato mixture on each spoon and drizzle with a splash of truffle oil and a few thyme leaves. Serve immediately.

Caviar-Stuffed New Potatoes

Makes 12

The addition of caviar, a luxury food, transforms earthy potatoes into a royal treat. We like to make this with salmon roe because the large red eggs look particularly attractive. Also it is pricey enough to lend a festive air to the dish but not so expensive it will break the bank. However, it can be successfully made with any "caviar," from premium sturgeon to supermarket lumpfish. Double or triple the recipe to suit your needs.

- **Preheat oven to 400°F (200°C)**

6	new potatoes, scrubbed and halved	6
2 tbsp	extra virgin olive oil	30 mL
	Crunchy sea salt, such as Malden or fleur de sel	
¼ cup	crème fraîche or sour cream (approx.)	60 mL
2 tbsp	caviar (approx.)	30 mL
	Freshly squeezed lemon juice	
	Freshly ground black pepper	

1. In a bowl, combine potato halves and olive oil. Toss until potatoes are well coated with oil. Transfer to a rimmed baking sheet cut side down and roast in preheated oven until tender, about 20 minutes. Let cool slightly.

2. Using a grapefruit spoon or melon baller, generously scoop out the center of each half. Season potatoes all over liberally with sea salt. Fill indentation with about 1 generous tsp (7 mL) crème fraîche and top with about half that much caviar. Drizzle with lemon juice and season to taste with pepper. Serve immediately.

Bacon-Spiked Rösti Cakes

Makes about 24

If you're a fan of latkes, here's the Swiss equivalent, rejigged to work as an appetizer. These are great on their own, but if you feel so inclined, you can top them with a dollop of Fresh Tomato Salsa (page 70), Two-Tomato Coulis (page 544), sour cream, or even a slice of smoked salmon garnished with crème fraîche and a dusting of chives.

- **Preheat oven to 375°F (190°C)**
- **Baking sheets, lined with parchment paper**

2 lbs	potatoes (4 medium), peeled	1 kg
6	strips bacon	6
1	onion	1
2 tbsp	melted unsalted butter	30 mL
2 tbsp	extra virgin olive oil	30 mL
1 tbsp	fresh thyme leaves or finely chopped rosemary	15 mL
1 tsp	salt	5 mL
	Freshly ground black pepper	

1. In a large pot of boiling salted water, place potatoes. Return to a boil and cook for 5 minutes. Drain well.

2. Meanwhile, in a skillet over medium-high heat, cook bacon until crisp. Remove from pan and drain well on paper towel. Crumble and set aside.

3. In a food processor fitted with shredding blade and working in batches, shred potatoes and onion. Transfer to a large bowl as completed. Add reserved bacon, butter, olive oil, thyme, salt, and pepper to taste to bowl and mix well.

4. Using your hands, shape into patties about 1½ inches (4 cm) in diameter. Place on prepared baking sheets as completed and flatten with a spatula. Bake in preheated oven until edges are browned, about 25 minutes. Turn over and flatten with a spatula. Return to oven and continue cooking until tops are very well browned, about 20 minutes longer.

Indian-Style Potato Fritters

Makes about 12

These fritters resemble pakora, without the chickpea batter. They are very easy to make. They are delicious with Suneeta's Cilantro Mint Chutney (page 93) or you can pass your favorite prepared chutney alongside and urge people to put a small dollop on top. For something a little different, use them as a dipper for Yogurt Mint Chutney (page 94).

Tips

Double or triple the recipe to suit your needs.

For best results, use floury potatoes, which are usually oblong in shape and do not contain as much water as waxy varieties such as thin-skinned red or white potatoes. The most common floury potatoes are russet (Idaho) potatoes.

You'll get the best flavor if you toast and grind cumin and coriander seeds yourself. *To toast cumin and coriander seeds:* Place 1 tsp (5 mL) each seed in a dry skillet over medium heat. Cook, stirring, until fragrant, about 3 minutes. Transfer to a mortar or spice grinder and grind.

1 lb	russet (Idaho) potato (about 1 large), peeled (see Tips, left)	500 g
4	green onions, white part with a bit of green, chopped	4
1	egg	1
1 tsp	salt	5 mL
1 tsp	ground cumin (see Tips, left)	5 mL
1 tsp	ground coriander (see Tips, left)	5 mL
⅛ tsp	cayenne pepper	0.5 mL
¼ cup	oil (approx.)	60 mL
	Chutney	

1. In a food processor fitted with shredding blade, shred potato. Using your hands, squeeze out as much liquid as possible. Place in a clean tea towel and squeeze out more. Keep covered to prevent browning.

2. Replace slicing blade with metal blade. Add green onions, egg, salt, cumin, coriander and cayenne. Pulse until onions are finely chopped, about 3 times, stopping and scraping down sides of the bowl once or twice. Return potatoes to work bowl and pulse to blend, about 5 times.

3. In a large pan, heat oil over medium-high heat. Scoop out a heaping tbsp (20 mL) of potato mixture and drop into pan. Flatten top with back of spoon. Cook, turning once, until golden, about 3 minutes per side. Repeat until all the mixture is used, adding more oil as necessary and cooking fritters in batches (no more than 6 at a time in a large skillet). Transfer to a paper towel lined–platter as completed. Serve hot with chutney.

Truffle-Spiked Potato Croquettes

Makes about sixty ½-inch (1 cm) croquettes

These croquettes are very versatile. Because they are quite rich, they work best as pop-in-your-mouth one-bite canapés.

Tip

We like the flavor delivered by truffle salt but if you can't find it, substitute fine sea salt instead and just make potato croquettes.

- **Rimmed baking sheet, lined with parchment paper or waxed paper**

1 lb	potatoes, cooked in their skins and refrigerated overnight	500 g
1 tbsp	melted butter	15 mL
1	egg yolk	1
1	egg	1
1 tsp	truffle salt (see Tip, left)	5 mL
	Freshly ground black pepper	

Coating

¼ cup	all-purpose flour (approx.)	60 mL
1 cup	dry bread crumbs, such as panko (approx.)	250 mL
2	eggs, beaten	2
¼ cup	unsalted butter, divided	60 mL
¼ cup	olive oil, divided	60 mL

1. Peel potatoes, cut into chunks and place in a food processor fitted with metal blade. Purée until smooth. Add melted butter, egg yolk, egg, truffle salt, and pepper to taste. Pulse until blended. Transfer to a saucepan over low heat and cook, beating constantly with a wooden spoon, until mixture becomes pliable, about 3 minutes. Remove from heat. Let cool to room temperature. Using your hands, flatten into a disk. Wrap tightly in plastic and refrigerate until thoroughly chilled, at least 2 hours or overnight.

2. *Coating:* When you're ready to cook, shape into small balls, about ¾ inch (2 cm) in diameter. Spread flour and bread crumbs on two plates, and beat eggs in a shallow bowl. Roll balls in flour, then eggs, then bread crumbs. Discard any excess coating.

3. In a large skillet, heat 2 tbsp (30 mL) each of the butter and oil over medium-high heat. Add croquettes, in batches, and cook, turning carefully, until crisp and golden, about 3 minutes. As cooked, transfer to a platter and keep warm. Adjust the heat to prevent burning and add more butter and oil between batches as necessary.

Sweet Pea and Potato Croquettes

Makes about 20 croquettes

These bite-size crispy potatoes are accented with the sweetness of sweet peas. They are just spectacular when plunged into Caramelized Red Onion Dip (page 39) or Roasted Red Pepper Hummus (page 55).

Tip

These are wonderful baked in the oven instead of frying but will not be as crisp. Place on a parchment-lined baking sheet and bake in 400°F (200°C) oven until golden brown, about 20 minutes.

- **Preheat oven to 400°F (200°C)**
- **Candy/deep-fry thermometer**

1 lb	russet (Idaho) potatoes (about 2 medium)	500 g
1 tbsp	unsalted butter or duck fat	15 mL
½ cup	frozen sweet green peas, thawed	125 mL
2	cloves garlic	2
½ cup	chicken broth or water	125 mL
½ tsp	salt	2 mL
¼ tsp	freshly ground black pepper	1 mL
	Oil	
1 cup	all-purpose flour	250 mL
1 cup	panko bread crumbs	250 mL
2	eggs, beaten	2

1. Prick potatoes all over with a fork. Bake potatoes in preheated oven until fork tender, about 1 hour. Let cool slightly. Cut potatoes in half and scoop out flesh. Discard skins. Transfer flesh to a food mill or potato ricer and press potatoes into a bowl. Let cool.

2. In a saucepan, melt butter over high heat. Add peas and garlic and cook, stirring, until peas are soft, about 3 minutes. Add broth and bring to a boil. Transfer to a blender (or use an immersion blender in the pan) and purée until smooth. Let cool to room temperature.

3. Add pea purée to potatoes and fold well to combine and season with salt and pepper. (Be sure not to overmix as the potatoes will become glutinous.) For each croquette, shape 1 tbsp (15 mL) into ball and place on a baking sheet. Cover and refrigerate for 1 hour, until firm or for up to 3 hours.

4. In a deep skillet, Dutch oven or deep-fryer, heat 3 inches (7.5 cm) of oil over medium-high heat to 375°F (190°C).

5. Place flour, panko and eggs in separate shallow bowls. Dip balls in flour, turning to coat and shaking off excess, then in egg and into panko pressing to coat. Discard any excess flour, egg and crumbs.

6. Fry croquettes in hot oil in batches, turning once, until golden brown, 2 to 3 minutes. Using a slotted spoon, transfer to paper towels and season with salt.

Mini Potato Croquettes

Makes about 24 croquettes

A very versatile potato appetizer that can be served at any time of day. They are perfect for brunch topped with crisp bacon, for lunch with a garnish of Basil Pesto (page 549) or Creamy Green Onion Dip (page 41) or for a dinner party dipped into Cheddar Cheese Fondue (page 396).

Tip

For a heartier hors d'oeuvres, split croquettes in half after frying and fill with a slice of smoked turkey or smoked salmon, using croquettes as the "bread."

- **Candy/deep-fry thermometer**

6 cups	water	1.5 L
4 cups	diced unpeeled russet (Idaho) potatoes	1 L
2 tsp	salt, divided	10 mL
⅓ cup	finely shredded Cheddar cheese	75 mL
¼ cup	corn kernels	60 mL
4 tsp	stone-ground mustard	20 mL
1 tsp	finely chopped fresh thyme	5 mL
¼ tsp	freshly ground black pepper	1 mL
	Oil	
1 cup	all-purpose flour	250 mL
1 cup	panko bread crumbs	250 mL
3	eggs, beaten	3

1. In a large saucepan, bring water, potatoes and 1 tsp (5 mL) of salt to a boil over medium heat. Reduce heat and simmer until potatoes are fork tender, 5 to 6 minutes. Drain well and return potatoes to the pot. Using a potato masher, slightly mash potatoes. Transfer to a large bowl.

2. Add Cheddar, corn, mustard, thyme, ½ tsp (2 mL) of salt and pepper and mix well to combine. For each croquette, spoon 2 tbsp (30 mL) of potato mixture into your hands and form into a ball. Place on a baking sheet, cover and refrigerate for at least 30 minutes, until firm or for up to 3 hours.

3. In a deep skillet, Dutch oven or deep-fryer, heat 4 inches (10 cm) of oil over medium-high heat to 350°F (180°C).

4. Place flour, bread crumbs and eggs in separate shallow bowls. Dip croquettes in flour, turning to coat and shaking off excess, and then in egg to cover and finally in bread crumbs, pressing to coat. Discard any excess flour, egg and crumbs.

5. Fry croquettes in hot oil, in batches, turning once, until golden brown, 2 to 3 minutes. Using a slotted spoon, transfer to a paper towel–lined plate. Season with a pinch of salt. Serve immediately.

Potatoes Anna

Makes 8 or 16 wedges

Here a few ingredients come together to create a very classic French potato cake formed from the natural starch in potato. Serve each wedge with a garnish of lovely smoked salmon and crème fraîche or a simple dollop of Summer Tomato Salsa (page 70).

Tip

We prefer yellow-fleshed potatoes, such as Yukon Gold because the slightly starchy texture works beautifully.

- **Preheat oven to 425°F (220°C)**
- **10-inch (25 cm) ovenproof skillet**

2 tbsp	unsalted butter, melted	30 mL
1 lb	yellow flesh potatoes, unpeeled and thinly sliced (see Tip, left)	500 g
1 cup	shredded sharp (aged) Cheddar cheese	250 mL
½ tsp	salt	2 mL
½ tsp	freshly ground black pepper	2 mL
¼ tsp	chopped fresh thyme leaves	1 mL

1. In a bowl, combine butter, potatoes, cheese, salt, pepper and thyme and mix well to coat each potato slice. Drain the residual butter into a small bowl.

2. Brush the inside of ovenproof skillet with the butter. Layer the potatoes, starting from the outside of the pan and working toward the middle, overlapping about ¼ inch (0.5 cm) of each potato slice. Cook over medium heat until bottom begins to brown, 6 to 8 minutes.

3. Transfer skillet to preheated oven and bake until golden brown and potatoes are tender, about 30 minutes. Let cool to room temperature. Place a cutting board on top of the skillet, then flip both the cutting board and skillet over to invert potato cake onto board. Cut into 8 or 16 wedges. Serve immediately or let stand at room temperature for up to 2 hours.

Classic French Fries

Makes 4 to 6 servings

Vegetarian Friendly

There is a trick to achieving the perfect crispy french fry — fry them twice! The first fry thoroughly cooks the potato and releases all moisture. The second fry, at a higher temperature, is meant to only crisp the potato, which happens quite quickly. Serve alongside Pommery Mustard Dip (page 61) or Oven-Roasted Cherry Tomato Sauce (page 546) that, when served cold, doubles as homemade ketchup.

- **Candy/deep-fry thermometer**

	Oil	
1 lb	russet (Idaho) potatoes (about 2 medium size potatoes)	500 g
1 tsp	chopped fresh chives	5 mL
¼ tsp	salt	1 mL
¼ tsp	freshly ground black pepper	1 mL

1. In a deep skillet or Dutch oven, heat 5 inches (12.5 cm) of oil over medium-high heat to 300°F (150°C). (You can also use a deep-fryer; follow the manufacturer's instructions).

2. Peel potatoes and cut into sticks 3 inches (7.5 cm) long and ¼ inch (0.5 cm) square. Pat dry.

3. Fry potatoes in oil, in small batches, until they begin to take on a light golden color, about 5 minutes. Using a slotted spoon, transfer to a paper towel–lined baking sheet to drain and let cool to room temperature.

4. Just before serving, heat oil to 375°F (190°C). Fry potatoes in hot oil, in small batches, until crisp and golden brown, 2 to 3 minutes. Using a slotted spoon, transfer to clean paper towel–lined baking sheet to drain. Sprinkle with chives, salt and pepper. Serve hot.

Diced Potato Gratin

Makes 16 servings

This very simple potato recipe is so easy to make and encapsulates the essence of French cuisine; simple ingredients made with lots of love.

Tips

Whole milk is essential to this recipe because its high fat content provides a wonderful richness that cannot be achieved with skim milk.

Cooks are taught to store cut potatoes in water to avoid oxidization. While that is true, water will also draw the starch out of potatoes and in this case, starch is a good thing since it will help thicken the milk. It's best to cut the potatoes just before cooking and avoid soaking them in water.

- **16 small ramekins or other ovenproof dishes**

2½ cups	whole milk (see Tips, left)	625 mL
1 tbsp	unsalted butter	15 mL
2 cups	diced russet (Idaho) potatoes (unpeeled) (see Tips, left)	500 mL
⅔ cup	freshly grated Parmesan cheese	150 mL
1 tbsp	chopped fresh thyme leaves	15 mL
½ tsp	salt	2 mL
½ tsp	freshly ground black pepper	2 mL

1. In a saucepan, bring milk and butter to a simmer over medium heat. Stir in potatoes, reduce heat and simmer until potatoes are fork tender, about 20 minutes. Remove from heat.

2. Meanwhile, preheat broiler.

3. Stir in Parmesan, thyme, salt and pepper. Spoon into ramekins, dividing equally. Place ramekins on a baking sheet and broil until tops are golden brown, 2 to 3 minutes. Serve immediately.

Spicy Sweet Potato Wedges with Maple Glaze

Makes 32 pieces

Simple-to-make with glorious flavors, these are perfect for vegan guests and omnivores, too.

Tip

You'll get the best flavor if you toast and grind cumin and coriander seeds yourself. *To toast cumin and coriander seeds:* Place seeds in a dry skillet over medium heat. Cook, stirring, until fragrant, about 3 minutes. Transfer to a mortar or spice grinder and grind.

- **Preheat oven to 400°F (200°C)**

2	sweet potatoes, peeled or unpeeled	2
2 tbsp	olive oil	30 mL
½ tsp	ground cumin (see Tip, left)	2 mL
½ tsp	ground coriander (see Tip, left)	2 mL
½ tsp	smoked paprika	2 mL
2 tbsp	maple syrup	30 mL

1. Using a large sharp knife, cut each sweet potato in half lengthwise. Place 1 half cut side down on cutting board and slice off ¼ inch (0.5 cm) on each long side to make a flat surface. Cut lengthwise into 4 wedges. Cut each wedge in half crosswise to make 8 pieces in total. Repeat with remaining sweet potato to make 32 pieces. Brush each piece liberally with olive oil and bake in preheated oven for 20 minutes.

2. Meanwhile, in a small bowl, combine cumin, coriander and paprika. Brush potato slices liberally with maple syrup and sprinkle with spice mixture. Return to oven and bake until tender, about 10 minutes. Spear with toothpicks and serve warm.

> ## Variation
> If you are averse to sweetness, try making these without adding the maple syrup. Instead, offer Chipotle Mayo (page 267) as a dipping sauce.

Sweet Potato Cakes

Makes 30 cakes

These pillow-like cakes are very sweet and have a subtle tartness due to the addition of sour cream. Although wonderful on their own, a dollop of Creamy Green Onion Dip (page 41) or Grilled Scallion and Corn Dip (page 42) helps to create an even more enticing appetizer.

- **Preheat oven to 350°F (180°C)**

2	sweet potatoes	2
¾ cup	sour cream	175 mL
1	egg, beaten	1
¼ cup	thinly sliced green onions	60 mL
¼ tsp	salt	1 mL
¼ tsp	freshly ground black pepper	1 mL
2 tbsp	all-purpose flour, divided	30 mL
2 tbsp	olive oil, divided	30 mL
2 tbsp	finely chopped fresh chives	30 mL

1. Prick sweet potatoes all over with a fork. Bake in preheated oven until fork tender, about 1 hour. Let cool slightly. Cut in half and scoop out orange flesh. Discard skins. Press flesh through a food mill or potato ricer into a bowl. Measure 1¼ cups (300 mL), reserving any extra for another use. Let cool to room temperature.

2. Add sour cream, egg, green onions, salt and pepper and mix well to thoroughly combine. Add 1 tbsp (15 mL) of the flour and fold to just incorporate. Fold in remaining flour. Set aside to rest for 10 minutes.

3. In a large nonstick skillet, heat 1 tbsp (15 mL) of the oil over medium heat. Spoon about 1 tbsp (15 mL) of batter for each cake into the pan. Cook, turning once, until golden brown and crisp, 2 to 3 minutes per side. Transfer to a plate. Repeat with remaining batter, adding more oil and adjusting heat as necessary between batches. Garnish with chives and serve hot.

Sweet Potato Galette

Makes 8 wedges

A simple way to enjoy a sweet potato, which is perfect served around the holiday season. Serve with Apple Salsa (page 90) or ground cinnamon and granulated sugar for some added festive cheer.

1½ cups	grated peeled sweet potato	375 mL
½ tsp	salt	2 mL
Pinch	freshly grated nutmeg	Pinch
Pinch	cayenne pepper	Pinch
2 tbsp	olive oil, divided	30 mL

1. In a bowl, combine potato, salt, nutmeg and cayenne and mix thoroughly.

2. In a small nonstick skillet, heat 1 tbsp (15 mL) of the oil over medium heat. Add potato, spreading to evenly cover the entire surface to form what looks like pizza crust. Reduce heat to low and cook until bottom is golden brown, about 12 minutes. Slide galette, crisp side down, onto a plate. Invert skillet over the plate, then flip both the plate and skillet over to invert the galette back into the pan with the uncooked side down. Cook, adding more oil if necessary, until bottom is golden brown and potatoes are tender, about 10 minutes. Transfer to a cutting board and cut into 8 wedges. Serve immediately.

Crispy Potato Galette

Makes 8 servings

Potato galette make wonderful snacks or appetizers in place of store-bought potato chips. This is wonderful when served with smoked salmon and Preserved Lemons (page 554).

2 tbsp	olive oil	30 mL
1 cup	shredded russet (Idaho) potato, skin on	250 mL

1. In a small nonstick skillet, heat oil over high heat. Add potato, spreading to evenly cover the entire surface to form what looks like pizza crust. Reduce heat to low and cook until bottom is golden brown, about 10 minutes. Slide galette, crisp side down, onto a plate. Invert skillet over the plate, then flip both the plate and skillet over to invert the galette back into the pan with the uncooked side down. Cook until bottom is golden brown and potatoes are tender, about 10 minutes. Transfer to a cutting board and cut into 8 wedges. Serve immediately.

Zucchini Fritters

Makes about 24

Serve these fritters as part of an antipasti spread. They are great on their own or, if you like to gild the lily, even better with a bowl of Tzatziki (page 14) alongside.

Tip

To expedite preparation, shred zucchini and set aside to sweat while you prepare the remaining ingredients.

- **Preheat oven to 200°F (100°C)**

4 cups	shredded zucchini (about 3 medium) (see Tip, left)	1 L
2 tsp	coarse salt	10 mL
4 oz	feta, crumbled	125 g
6	green onions, white part with a bit of green, minced	6
½ cup	finely chopped fresh dill fronds	125 mL
2	cloves garlic, minced	2
2	eggs, beaten	2
½ cup	all-purpose flour	125 mL
¼ cup	vegetable oil (approx.)	60 mL

1. In a colander, placed over a sink, combine zucchini and salt. Toss well and set aside for 30 minutes to sweat. Rinse under cold running water and drain. Using your hands, squeeze out as much water as possible. Spread on a clean tea towel and press to soak up as much liquid as possible, using a second tea towel, if necessary.

2. In a bowl, combine feta, green onions, dill and garlic. Add zucchini and eggs and mix well. Sprinkle flour evenly over mixture and toss well.

3. In a large heavy skillet, heat oil over medium-high heat. Scoop out about 1 heaping tbsp (20 mL) of mixture at a time and drop into hot oil. Repeat until pan is full, leaving about 2 inches (5 cm) between fritters. Cook, turning once, until nicely golden, about 5 minutes per batch. Drain on paper towel–lined platter and keep warm in the oven while you complete the frying. Serve warm.

Crispy Zucchini Fingers

Makes 16 fingers

These fingers are so crispy you won't believe it's zucchini until, of course, you bite into the creamy inside, which is nothing but zucchini. Dip these fingers into Roasted Zucchini Dip (page 44) for an exciting combination.

- **Preheat oven to 350°F (180°C)**
- **Baking sheet, lined with parchment paper**

1	medium zucchini	1
1 cup	panko bread crumbs	250 mL
¼ cup	finely grated Parmesan cheese	60 mL
¼ cup	whole wheat flour	60 mL
1	egg, beaten	1
	Salt and freshly ground black pepper	

1. Trim ends off zucchini and cut in half crosswise, then cut each half into 8 fingers.
2. In a bowl, combine bread crumbs and cheese. Place flour and egg in separate bowls. Dip zucchini in flour, turning to coat and shaking off excess, then dip in egg and finally into bread crumbs, pressing to coat.
3. Place at least 2 inches (5 cm) apart on prepared baking sheet and bake until crisp and golden brown, 25 to 30 minutes. Season to taste with salt and pepper.

Classic Coleslaw

Makes about 4 cups (1 L)

You might be thinking, "how am I going to serve coleslaw at an hors d'oeuvres party"? A reasonable question with a simple answer: Chinese soup spoons! Spoon coleslaw in a mound on the spoon and garnish with a slice of grilled rib steak or pulled pork — it's a one-bite Southern barbecue.

4 cups	thinly sliced green cabbage	1 L
½ cup	coarsely grated carrot	125 mL
½ cup	thinly sliced onion	125 mL
1 tbsp	minced fresh red chile pepper	15 mL
1 tbsp	minced garlic	15 mL
2 tbsp	red wine vinegar	30 mL
1½ tbsp	Dijon mustard	22 mL
1 tbsp	extra virgin olive oil	15 mL
½ tsp	each salt and freshly ground pepper	2 mL

1. In a bowl, combine cabbage, carrot, onion, chile pepper and garlic.
2. In a small bowl, whisk vinegar, mustard, oil, salt and pepper until blended. Pour over vegetables and toss well. Let stand for at least 1 hour to marinate or cover and refrigerate overnight.

Quick Zucchini and Jerusalem Artichoke on Grilled Crostini

Makes 30 crostini

This quick sauté of vegetables is perfect served on top of crisp crostini, creating a bruschetta-like appetizer, but if you feel like moving out of your comfort zone, why not serve it atop Beet Chips (page 213) or Taro Root Chips (see Variations, page 213) for something just a little different?

Tips

Jerusalem artichokes, also known as sunchokes, resemble gingerroot and are sweetest when they are 2 to 3 inches (5 to 7.5 cm) wide by 3 to 4 inches (7.5 to 10 cm) long and can be peeled using a regular vegetable peeler.

To create Parmesan curls, gently press a vegetable peeler against the cheese and push the peeler away from your body in one long motion.

- **Preheat oven to 350°F (180°C)**
- **Ovenproof skillet**

1 tbsp	olive oil	15 mL
½ cup	diced Jerusalem artichokes (see Tips, left)	125 mL
1¼ cups	diced zucchini	300 mL
½ cup	diced red onion	125 mL
1 cup	diced roasted red bell pepper (see Tips, page 495)	250 mL
½ cup	sliced cherry tomatoes	125 mL
1 tbsp	thinly sliced garlic	15 mL
½ tsp	finely chopped fresh thyme leaves	2 mL
½ tsp	finely chopped fresh basil leaves	2 mL
1 tsp	salt	5 mL
½ tsp	freshly ground black pepper	2 mL
30	Grilled Herbed Crostini (page 220)	30
¼ cup	Parmesan curls (see Tips, left)	60 mL

1. In ovenproof skillet, heat oil over high heat. Add artichokes and toss to coat. Transfer skillet to a preheated oven and roast until golden brown, about 10 minutes. Add zucchini and red onion and roast in preheated oven until zucchini is tender-crisp, 15 to 20 minutes.

2. Add roasted peppers, tomatoes, garlic, thyme, basil, salt and pepper and toss to combine. Place about 1 tbsp (15 mL) on each crostini and garnish with Parmesan cheese. Serve immediately.

Panko-Crusted Onion Rings

Makes about 24

Warm and crusty yet sweet, onion rings are a perennial favorite. Sprinkle these with good sea salt for a wonderful combination of flavor and texture.

Tips

Make sure the onion rings are well coated with flour, egg and panko for best results.

Be sure to use good sea salt such as fleur de sel to finish the onion rings. Table salt has an unpleasant acrid taste that would diminish the result.

- **Candy/deep-fry thermometer**

1	large Spanish or sweet onion	1
1 cup	all-purpose flour	250 mL
1 tbsp	hot smoked paprika	15 mL
3	eggs, beaten	3
2 cups	panko bread crumbs	500 mL
	Oil	
	Fine sea salt, optional	

1. Cut onion into thick slices (about ¾ inch/2 cm) and separate into rings, discarding smallest center pieces.

2. In a resealable bag, combine flour and paprika. In a wide shallow bowl, beat eggs. In a separate resealable bag, place panko.

3. In a large deep skillet, heat 1½ inches (4 cm) of oil over medium-high heat to 350°F (180°C).

4. Working in batches of about 6 (the number that will fit comfortably in your pan without crowding), toss onion rings in flour mixture, then dip in egg and finally toss in panko. Add to hot oil and fry until crisp and golden, 1½ to 2 minutes. Transfer to a paper towel–lined platter and sprinkle with sea salt, if using. Repeat until all onion rings are used.

Shoestring Onion Rings with Pommery Mustard Dip

Makes 6 to 8 servings

These are so much better than the thick onion rings found in diners across the globe. They're a particularly crispy onion ring.

- **Candy/deep-fry thermometer**

	Oil	
¼ cup	all-purpose flour	60 mL
¾ tsp	salt, divided	3 mL
⅛ tsp	freshly ground black pepper	0.5 mL
3 cups	thinly sliced white onion rings	750 mL
¾ cup	Pommery Mustard Dip (page 61)	175 mL

1. In a deep skillet or Dutch oven, heat 4 inches (10 cm) of oil over medium-high heat to 325°F (160°C). (You can also use a deep fryer; follow the manufacturer's instructions.)

2. In a bowl, combine flour, ½ tsp (2 mL) of the salt and pepper. Add onions and toss to coat. Shake off excess flour.

3. Fry onion rings in hot oil, in batches, until crisp and golden brown, about 5 minutes. Using a slotted spoon, transfer to a paper towel–lined plate. Season with remaining salt and serve with Pommery Mustard Dip.

Variation

Gently fold ½ cup (125 mL) chive pieces (1 to 2 inches/2.5 to 5 cm) with onion rings after the onions have cooled slightly. This not only adds a wonderful color contrast but it also adds a spicy fresh onion note.

Vegetable Tempura

Makes 6 to 8 servings

Vegetables cosseted in batter and fried are absolutely delicious. They are a treat on their own with a sprinkling of good sea salt or one of our Seasoned Salts (page 552). Or, if you prefer, make a soy-based dipping sauce (see Variation, below).

Tip

Many vegetables make excellent tempura. Some such as green onions and shiitake can be trimmed and added to the batter raw. Others require precooking. Green beans should be trimmed and blanched for about 1 minute; carrots need to be cut into sticks (about 1/2 by 3 inches (1 by 7.5 cm) and blanched for about 2 1/2 minutes; beets and potatoes should be sliced and parboiled (or microwaved) just until fork tender: and sweet potatoes should be sliced and roasted at 400°F (200°C) for about 30 minutes just until fork tender. Those are some we've tried, but there are lots of other options.

- **Candy/deep-fry thermometer**

Batter

3/4 cup	cornstarch, divided	175 mL
1/2 cup	all-purpose flour	125 mL
1 tsp	baking powder	5 mL
1/2 tsp	salt	2 mL
3/4 cup	cold soda water or sparkling mineral water	175 mL
1 tsp	sesame seed oil	5 mL
	Vegetables for frying (see Tip, left)	
	Seasoned salt (page 552), optional	

1. *Batter:* In a bowl, combine 1/2 cup (125 mL) of the cornstarch, flour, baking powder and salt. Mix well. Add soda water and oil and mix just until blended. (Don't overmix. It should be a bit lumpy.) Cover and refrigerate for 1 hour.

2. When you're ready to cook, in a Dutch oven or wok, add oil to a depth of about 2 inches (5 cm). Heat over medium-high heat until temperature reaches 350°F (180°C). (You can also use a deep fryer; follow the manufacturer's instructions.)

3. Spread remaining 1/4 cup (60 mL) of cornstarch on a plate and dredge vegetables in it (this helps the batter to adhere). Dip in batter. Add to hot oil in batches (about 4 pieces at a time) and fry until crisp and golden, turning once, about 1 minute per side. Transfer to a paper towel–lined platter to drain. Sprinkle with a Seasoned Salt, if using. Serve warm.

Variation

To make a dipping sauce for vegetable tempura, combine 1/4 cup (60 mL) soy sauce, 2 tbsp (30 mL) each freshly squeezed lime juice and mirin and 1/2 tsp (2 mL) sambal oelek.

Fried Zucchini Flowers

Makes enough for about 24 flowers

If you grow zucchini in your garden, here is a delicious way to cull those plants, which tend to overtake any available space. These are delicious served with just a sprinkling of sea salt or Roasted Salt and Pepper (page 552). But if you're looking for a more festive finish, add a dipping sauce such as Two-Tomato Coulis (page 544) or Roasted Red Pepper Coulis (page 543.) You might even consider stuffing each flower with a tsp (5 mL) of so of fresh cheese such as ricotta or a seasoned goat cheese (see Variation, below).

Tips

You can make these in a deep fryer, if you prefer, but a wok works very well and uses much less oil.

Zucchini flowers come in male and female varieties. The female flowers have baby zucchini attached to them.

The sparkling water adds lightness to the batter.

- **Candy/deep-fry thermometer**

1	egg	1
¾ cup	all-purpose flour	175 mL
⅓ cup	milk	75 mL
⅓ cup	soda water, sparkling mineral water or beer	75 mL
	Salt	
24	zucchini flowers, rinsed and patted dry	24
	Oil	

1. In a small bowl, whisk egg and flour until reasonably well combined. Whisk in milk, soda water, and salt to taste. Cover and refrigerate for 1 hour or for up to 4 hours.

2. When you're ready to cook, in a large wok, add oil to a depth of about 2 inches (5 cm). Heat over medium-high heat until temperature reaches 375°F (190°C). Holding a flower by the stalk dip in batter until well coated. Cook in batches (about 5 at a time if you're using a large wok), turning once, about 1 minute per side. (You can also use a deep fryer; follow the manufacturer's instructions.) Remove from oil and drain on paper towels. Discard any excess batter. Sprinkle with sea salt. Serve warm.

Variation

Cheese-Stuffed Zucchini Flowers: In a small bowl, combine 2 oz (60 g) crumbled soft goat cheese, ¼ cup (60 mL) dry bread crumbs, 2 tbsp (30 mL) finely chopped parsley, 2 cloves minced garlic and, if you like a bit of heat, 1 minced fresh chile pepper. Mix well. Work with about 1 tsp (5 mL) of stuffing at a time. Using your hands, roll stuffing into a thin log about the length of the petal. Place 1 flower on a clean work surface and open the petals. Stuff cheese log into cavity and fold petals back around it. Continue with Step 2.

Sweet-and-Sour Cipollini

Makes about 1½ cups (375 mL)

Cipollini are small squat Italian onions with a mildly bitter flavor. They are increasingly available in well-stocked markets. Although they can be served raw, they are most often cooked to bring out their delicate flavor. This version is traditionally served as part of an antipasti platter. It can be served warm or cold.

1 lb	cipollini onions	500 g
2 tbsp	olive oil	30 mL
1 tbsp	fresh thyme leaves	15 mL
1 tbsp	brown sugar, preferably Demerara or other raw cane sugar	15 mL
3 tbsp	balsamic vinegar	45 mL
1 tsp	tomato paste	5 mL
½ cup	vegetable or chicken broth	125 mL
	Salt and freshly ground black pepper	

1. In a large pot of boiling water, place cipollini. Return to a boil and boil rapidly for 30 seconds. Drain, rinse under cold running water and, using a sharp knife, lift off skins and discard. Pat onions dry.

2. In a heavy skillet large enough to accommodate the onions in a single layer, heat olive oil over medium heat. Add onions and cook until lightly browned on one side, about 5 minutes per side. Reduce heat to low. Sprinkle thyme, brown sugar, vinegar and tomato paste evenly over onions and toss to mix well. Drizzle broth evenly over onions.

3. Cover and cook until fork tender, about 15 minutes. Increase heat to medium-high and cook, stirring, for 1 minute to evaporate liquid and intensify browning. Season to taste with salt and pepper. Serve hot or cold as part of an antipasti table.

Spicy Cheese and Onion–Spiked Eggplant

Makes 24 pieces

A crisp coating surrounding oozing slightly tangy cheese with a hint of onion and hot pepper — what's not to love about these perfect little bites? Add a dash of fresh lemon juice to round out the flavors.

- **Candy/deep-fry thermometer**

1	eggplant (about 1 lb/500 g)	1
1 tbsp	coarse salt	15 mL
2 tbsp	olive oil	30 mL
1 tbsp	mayonnaise	15 mL
1 tbsp	drained minced pickled hot banana pepper	15 mL
1/3 cup	finely chopped Spanish or sweet onion	75 mL
1/2 cup	grated Asiago cheese	125 mL
1/4 cup	all-purpose flour	60 mL
1	egg, beaten	1
1/2 cup	dry bread crumbs, such as panko	125 mL
	Oil	
	Freshly squeezed lemon juice	

1. With a sharp knife, trim top and cut off round bottom of eggplant to make a flat surface. Stand eggplant upright on a cutting board and make 4 thin vertical slices to square off roundness. Remove remaining peel. Cut vertically into 6 thin slices, about 1/2 inch (1 cm) thick. Sprinkle with salt and set aside in a colander for 30 minutes to "sweat." Rinse under cold running water and pat dry with paper towel.

2. Preheat broiler. Brush eggplant on one side with olive oil. Place on broiling pan and broil under preheated broiler until softened, about 2 minutes. Remove from oven, turn over and brush other side with oil. Place under broiler for 2 minutes. Remove from oven.

3. In a small bowl, combine mayonnaise and minced pepper. Mix well and set aside.

4. Cut each eggplant strip in half crosswise. Lay 6 of the pieces on a clean work surface. Brush with mayonnaise mixture and sprinkle generously with onion and cheese. Top with remaining eggplant.

5. In a large deep skillet, add oil to a depth of about $\frac{1}{2}$ inch (1 cm). Heat over medium-high heat until temperature reaches 350°F (180°C). (You can also use a deep fryer; follow the manufacturer's instructions.)

6. Place flour in one small bowl, egg in a second and bread crumbs in a third. Dip each sandwich into flour, then egg, and finally bread crumbs, coating both sides well. Fry in hot oil, in batches, turning once, until golden, 3 to 4 minutes. Drain on a paper towel–lined platter. Cut each piece into quarters and drizzle lightly with lemon juice. Serve warm.

Baby Candy Cane Beets with Fresh Mint

Makes about 1$\frac{1}{4}$ cups (300 mL)

Vegan Friendly

This vegetable is as sweet as candy. Of course, they're candy cane beets. Serve these beets with toothpicks as part of an antipasti platter.

Tip

A creative presentation is to create beet "lollipops" with a beet skewered at the top of a 6-inch (15 cm) wooden skewer.

1$\frac{1}{4}$ cups	baby candy cane beets, halved	300 mL
	Ice water	
2 tsp	pure maple syrup	10 mL
2 tsp	red wine vinegar	10 mL
1 tsp	extra virgin olive oil	5 mL
$\frac{1}{2}$ tsp	coarsely chopped fresh mint leaves	2 mL
$\frac{1}{4}$ tsp	salt	1 mL
	Freshly ground black pepper	

1. Remove tops and stems from beets. Place in a large saucepan and add water to cover. Bring to a boil over medium heat. Reduce heat and boil gently until beets are fork tender, about 45 minutes. Plunge beets into a bowl of ice water and let stand until chilled. Drain and let cool. Peel off skins.

2. In a bowl, combine beets, maple syrup, vinegar, oil, mint, salt, and pepper to taste. Mix well and serve or keep beets refrigerated for up to 3 days before combining with vinaigrette.

Lemony Marinated Beets

Makes about 24 pieces

Roasted beets marinated in an assertive combination of cumin, oregano, garlic, lemon juice and vinegar and thoroughly chilled make a surprisingly tasty appetizer. You can serve them on their own, presented in a small serving bowl, providing cocktail toothpicks for eating, or make small skewers containing a beet chunk and a cube of cheese (see Variation, below).

Tip

Don't be timid when salting this dish. Salt balances the lemon juice and the salty flavor will mitigate with chilling.

- **Preheat oven to 400°F (200°C)**

2	medium beets (about 12 oz/375 g total), scrubbed	2
3 tbsp	freshly squeezed lemon juice	45 mL
2 tbsp	coarsely chopped Italian flat-leaf parsley leaves	30 mL
1 tbsp	red wine vinegar	15 mL
2	cloves garlic, quartered	2
2 tsp	ground cumin	10 mL
2 tsp	dried oregano	10 mL
1 tsp	salt	5 mL
	Freshly ground black pepper	
½ cup	extra virgin olive oil	125 mL

1. Place beets on a rimmed baking sheet or in a baking dish and cover with foil. Roast in preheated oven until tender, about 1 hour. Let beets cool just until they are cool enough to touch, then, using a piece of paper towel, rub off skins.

2. Cut ends off beets to make flat tops and bottoms and discard. Cut beets crosswise into slices, about ¾ inch (2 cm) thick and cut each slice into quarters. (You should get 12 chunks per beet.) Transfer to a bowl.

3. In a food processor fitted with metal blade, process lemon juice, parsley, vinegar, garlic, cumin, oregano, salt, and pepper to taste until smooth. With motor running, slowly add olive oil through the feed tube.

4. Pour over beets and toss well. Cover and refrigerate until thoroughly chilled, at least 3 hours or for up to 3 days.

Variation

Spear 1 beet piece on a cocktail toothpick and add 1 cube (about ¾ inch/2 cm) Manchego or Gouda cheese.

Cumin-Dusted Cauliflower

Makes 6 to 8 servings

This is such a simple idea — borrowed from Middle Eastern cuisine — yet it is absolutely delicious. We've simply roasted cauliflower florets, liberally seasoned with cumin, and served them with a complementary dipping sauce. We particularly like Easy Tahini Dip (page 23) as an accompaniment.

- **Preheat oven to 400°F (200°C)**

3 tbsp	olive oil	45 mL
1 tbsp	ground cumin (see Tip, page 505)	15 mL
4 cups	cauliflower florets (about 1 medium cauliflower)	1 L
	Salt and freshly ground black pepper	

1. In a large bowl, combine olive oil and cumin. Mix well. Add cauliflower and toss until well coated with mixture. Place on a rimmed baking sheet, top side down, and roast in preheated oven, turning once, until softened and nicely charred, about 40 minutes.

2. Remove from oven and season to taste with salt and pepper. Arrange on a platter top side up and spear with toothpicks. Serve warm accompanied by a dipping sauce.

Cumin-Spiked Carrots with Cilantro

Makes about 2 cups (500 mL)

Serve these in a small serving bowl and put cocktail toothpicks alongside so people can spear their own. They are very tasty, surprisingly festive and extremely nutritious to boot.

Tip

Don't be timid when salting this dish. Salt balances the lemon juice and the salty flavor will mitigate with chilling.

3	medium carrots, peeled, sliced (¾ inch/ 2 cm thick) and cooked until tender	3
1 tsp	ground cumin	5 mL
1	clove garlic, quartered	1
¼ cup	packed cilantro leaves	60 mL
¼ cup	extra virgin olive oil	60 mL
3 tbsp	freshly squeezed lemon juice	45 mL
Pinch	granulated sugar	Pinch
	Sea salt and freshly ground pepper	

1. In a food processor fitted with metal blade, process cumin, garlic, cilantro, olive oil, lemon juice and sugar until smooth, about 30 seconds. Season to taste with salt and pepper.

2. In a bowl, combine carrots and cumin mixture. Toss well. Cover and refrigerate until thoroughly chilled, at least 3 hours or for up to 3 days.

Orange-Spiked Cucumbers with Mint

Makes about 2 cups (500 mL)

Here's something to round out an antipasto platter. It's very easy to make and, with the orange flavor, a tad unusual.

Tip

If you like the flavor of orange, add up to 1 tsp (5 mL) orange blossom water, which is available in Middle Eastern markets, to the dressing.

1 tbsp	finely grated orange zest	15 mL
2 tbsp	freshly squeezed orange juice	30 mL
1 tsp	salt	5 mL
3 tbsp	extra virgin olive oil	45 mL
1	English cucumber, peeled	1
	Freshly ground black pepper	
1 tbsp	finely chopped fresh mint leaves	15 mL

1. In a small bowl, combine orange zest and juice and salt, stirring until salt is dissolved. Gradually whisk in olive oil. Set aside.

2. In a food processor fitted with shredding blade, shred cucumber. Transfer to a serving dish. Pour vinaigrette over cucumbers and stir well. Season with pepper to taste and sprinkle with mint.

Overstuffed Cucumbers with Feta and Dill

Makes about 24 hors d'oeuvres

Especially wonderful when cucumbers are in season, this has great flavor and crunch.

Tip

This quantity will fill 1 long English cucumber or 2 shorter field cucumbers. Use whatever looks freshest or suits your taste.

- **Mini bowl food processor attachment**

½ cup	crumbed feta	125 mL
¼ cup	fresh dill fronds	60 mL
2 tbsp	mayonnaise (see Tips, page 536)	30 mL
1	clove garlic, coarsely chopped	1
1 to 2	cucumbers, peeled and halved lengthwise (see Tip, left)	1 to 2

1. In mini bowl of food processor, process feta, dill, mayonnaise and garlic until smooth and blended, about 20 seconds, stopping and scraping down sides of the bowl as necessary.

2. Using a spoon, scrape out cucumber seeds and discard. Fill hollow with feta spread. Cut cucumbers horizontally into ½-inch (1 cm) slices and serve.

Dressy Fennel à la Grecque

Makes 6 servings

Light, flavorful and nutritious, cold cooked vegetables can make delightful hors d'oeuvres. Here, fennel is lightly poached in a court bouillon to soften its slightly bitter edge, thoroughly chilled and tossed in a lemony vinaigrette. This makes a great addition to an antipasti table and the recipe is easily doubled to serve more people.

Tips

To prepare fennel: Chop off celery-like stems and save for making stock or bouillon. Cut bulb in half on the vertical and remove the knobby core. Slice thinly on the vertical.

Not all fennel bulbs retain their fronds. If you are lucky enough to have some, wash them, wrap in paper towel and refrigerate until you're ready to dress the fennel. You likely won't have enough to provide the sole garnish, but they can be chopped along with the other herb(s).

Court Bouillon

4 cups	water	1 L
1	onion, chopped	1
2	stalks celery or fennel stems (see Tips, left), chopped	2
4	parsley sprigs	4
½ cup	white wine or freshly squeezed lemon juice	125 mL
8	peppercorns	8
8	whole coriander seeds	8
1	bay leaf	1
½ tsp	salt	2 mL
1	bulb fennel, thinly sliced on the vertical (see Tips, left)	1

Dressing

½ tsp	salt	2 mL
1½ tbsp	freshly squeezed lemon juice	22 mL
3 tbsp	extra virgin olive oil	45 mL
	Freshly ground white pepper	
2 tbsp	finely chopped chervil, parsley or fennel fronds (see Tips, left)	30 mL

1. *Court Bouillon:* In a large saucepan or stockpot, combine water, onion, celery, parsley, wine, peppercorns, coriander seeds, bay leaf and salt. Bring to a boil over medium-high heat. Reduce heat and simmer for 30 minutes. Strain and discard solids.

2. Return liquid to saucepan and bring to a boil. Add fennel. Stir well, cover, reduce heat to low and simmer until fennel is tender-crisp, about 15 minutes. Transfer fennel and poaching liquid to a bowl. Cover and refrigerate until thoroughly chilled, at least 3 hours or for up to 2 days.

3. When you're ready to serve, strain fennel, discarding liquid. Arrange fennel on a small platter.

4. *Dressing:* In a small bowl, combine salt and lemon juice. Stir until salt is dissolved. Gradually whisk in olive oil. Pour over fennel and toss gently to combine. Season to taste with pepper and garnish with chervil. Serve immediately.

Celery Root Rémoulade

Makes 6 to 8 servings

Part salad, part condiment, in France, Celery Root Rémoulade almost always accompanies charcuterie. It makes an easy transition to a salumi platter (page 131) and is particularly delicious with prosciutto. You can serve this tasty salad as a first course on its own, as part of a buffet, or as a condiment, with sliders (pages 265 to 269), Country Terrine (page 464) or Country-Style Pork Terrine (page 502.)

Tip

Since celery root oxidizes quickly on contact with air, transfer to a bowl of acidulated water (4 cups/1 L water combined with 2 tbsp/30 mL lemon juice) as soon as it has been shredded to prevent discoloration. Drain before adding to pot.

1	small celery root (about 1 lb/500 g), peeled and halved (see Tip, left)	1
¼ cup	mayonnaise (see Tips, page 536)	60 mL
¼ cup	Italian flat-leaf parsley leaves	60 mL
¼ cup	fresh tarragon leaves	60 mL
2 tbsp	freshly squeezed lemon juice	30 mL
1 tbsp	extra virgin olive oil	15 mL
1 tbsp	drained capers	15 mL
1 tbsp	Dijon mustard	15 mL
2	anchovy fillets, optional	2

1. In food processor fitted with shredding blade, shred celery root. Transfer to serving bowl.

2. In a food processor fitted with metal blade (use a mini bowl, if you have one), process mayonnaise, parsley, tarragon, lemon juice, olive oil, capers, mustard, and anchovies, if using, until smooth and blended, stopping and scraping down sides of the bowl as necessary. Add to celery root and mix well. Chill thoroughly before serving.

Celery Root Avgolemono

Makes about 4 cups (1 L)

This might be described as a North African version of Celery Root Rémoulade (page 432). Here the celery root is cooked and tossed in an avgolemono sauce. Serve it thoroughly chilled, as part of a selection of mezes.

1	large (about 2 lbs/1 kg) celery root, peeled	1
3 tbsp	freshly squeezed lemon juice, divided	45 mL
	Salt and freshly ground black pepper	
2	egg yolks	2

1. In a food processor fitted with shredding blade, shred celery root. Transfer to saucepan. Add 1 tbsp (15 mL) of the lemon juice and water barely to cover. Season to taste with salt and pepper. Bring to a boil over high heat. Reduce heat and simmer until celery root is tender, about 10 minutes.

2. In a small bowl, beat egg yolks with remaining 2 tbsp (30 mL) of lemon juice. Beat in 2 tbsp (30 mL) of cooking water. Add to pan, stirring. Heat through, stirring constantly, until mixture is thickened, being careful not to boil. Transfer to a serving dish and refrigerate until thoroughly chilled.

Roasted Red Peppers with Anchovy-Spiked Olive Oil

Makes about 2 cups (500 mL)

Anchovies and a hint of garlic lend pleasant punch to classic roasted sweet peppers. Serve this with sliced baguette — scooping up the peppers with a fork.

Tip

You can make this dish up to 1 day ahead and refrigerate it. Before serving let stand at room temperature for about 20 minutes to allow the flavors to develop.

6	roasted red peppers, peeled, seeded and cut into strips (see Tips, page 495)	6
½ cup	extra virgin olive oil	125 mL
6	anchovy fillets, minced	6
2	cloves garlic, minced	2
¼ cup	Italian flat-leaf parsley or basil leaves, finely chopped	60 mL

1. Place peppers in a serving bowl or small platter.

2. In a small bowl, whisk olive oil, anchovies, garlic and parsley until combined. Pour over peppers. For best results, serve immediately at room temperature.

Variation

Use half yellow or orange bell peppers for a more colorful result.

Olive-Studded Roasted Red Peppers with Sherry Vinegar

Makes 8 to 12 servings

This is a great dish to serve when peppers are in season. It is remarkably easy to make, can be prepared several hours ahead of time, and is fresh and delicious spooned over thin slices of baguette.

4	roasted red bell peppers, peeled, seeded and cut into thin strips (see Tips, page 495)	4
½ cup	pitted black olives, halved (about 30)	125 mL
1 tsp	puréed garlic	5 mL
2 tbsp	extra virgin olive oil	30 mL
1 tbsp	sherry vinegar	15 mL
	Freshly ground black pepper	

1. In a bowl, combine pepper strips, olives, garlic, olive oil and vinegar. Toss to combine. Season to taste with black pepper. Cover and refrigerate until nicely chilled, about 2 hours.

Roasted Garlic and Mushroom Whirl

Makes 1 cup (250 mL)

This tasty spread is robust and incredibly easy-to-make. Serve with crackers or sliced baguette.

Tips

You'll need about 1¼ lbs (625 g) cremini mushrooms to get 1 lb (500 g) mushroom caps.

If you don't have mascarpone, use an equal quantity of heavy cream.

- **Preheat oven to 400°F (200°C)**

1 lb	cremini mushroom caps (see Tips, left)	500 g
8	cloves garlic	8
2 tbsp	olive oil	30 mL
2 tbsp	mascarpone cheese (see Tips, left)	30 mL
1 tbsp	fresh thyme leaves	15 mL
½ tsp	salt	2 mL
	Freshly ground black pepper	

1. In a bowl, combine mushrooms and garlic. Add oil and toss to coat. Transfer to a rimmed baking sheet and bake in preheated oven, stirring once or twice until mushrooms are wizened and garlic is lightly browned, about 20 minutes. Let cool slightly.
2. Transfer to a food processor fitted with metal blade. Add mascarpone, thyme, salt, and pepper to taste. Pulse until finely chopped and blended, about 6 times. Transfer to a serving bowl. Serve warm or chilled.

Cheesy Mushroom Muffins

Makes 24

These "muffins" resemble a dense mushroom flan. They are tasty and satisfying like comfort food.

Tip

We always use Italian flat-leaf parsley because it has so much more flavor than the curly leaf variety. Unless the stems or sprigs are specifically called for in a recipe, be sure to use only the tender leaves.

- **Preheat oven to 350°F (180°C)**
- **24 mini muffin cups, lightly greased**

2 tbsp	unsalted butter	30 mL
4 oz	cremini mushrooms, trimmed and sliced (about 6 medium)	125 g
1	small shallot, chopped	1
1/4 tsp	dried tarragon	1 mL
1 tsp	freshly squeezed lemon juice	5 mL
1/4 cup	Italian flat-leaf parsley leaves (see Tip, left)	60 mL
1 cup	shredded Swiss cheese	250 mL
1/2 cup	heavy or whipping (35%) cream	125 mL
2	eggs	2
2 tbsp	dry bread crumbs, such as panko	30 mL

1. In a skillet, melt butter over medium-high heat. Add mushrooms and shallot and cook, stirring, until mushrooms are lightly browned, about 5 minutes. Add tarragon and cook, stirring, for 1 minute. Remove from heat and drizzle with lemon juice.

2. Transfer to a food processor fitted with metal blade. Add parsley and pulse until chopped and blended, about 10 times. Add cheese, cream, eggs and bread crumbs and pulse to blend, about 10 times. Divide equally among prepared muffin cups. Bake in preheated oven until puffed and browned, about 20 minutes. Serve warm.

Prosciutto-Stuffed Mushrooms

Makes 24

Easy to make, tasty and comforting, warm stuffed mushrooms are always a treat. Here a small amount of prosciutto lends a luxurious note to this simple pleasure.

Tip

Chervil has a slight licorice flavor, which works very well with these ingredients, but if you don't have it, parsley makes a perfectly acceptable substitute.

- **Preheat oven to 350°F (180°C)**

24	cremini mushrooms, stems removed and set aside	24
¼ cup	fine bread crumbs	60 mL
2 tbsp	freshly grated Parmesan cheese	30 mL
2	cloves garlic, chopped	2
2 tbsp	chervil or Italian flat-leaf parsley leaves (see Tip, left)	30 mL
¼ cup	chopped prosciutto	60 mL
2 tbsp	heavy or whipping (35%) cream	30 mL
1 tbsp	freshly squeezed lemon juice	15 mL
	Freshly ground black pepper	
	Extra virgin olive oil	

1. Trim mushroom stems. Place stems in a food processor fitted with metal blade. Add bread crumbs and Parmesan and pulse until stems are chopped and mixture is blended, about 5 times. Add garlic and chervil and pulse until chopped, about 5 times. Add prosciutto, cream and lemon juice. Season to taste with pepper.

2. Spoon mixture into mushroom caps. Place on baking sheet and drizzle lightly with olive oil. Bake in preheated oven until hot and sizzling, about 15 minutes.

Stuffed Cremini Mushroom Caps

Makes 10 caps

Comfort foods have such familiar flavors and are always a hit, but the stuffing in these caps may just knock your socks off. The roasted corn and bacon add a sweet smoky flavor your guests will love.

Tip

To grill corn: Preheat barbecue grill to high. Grill ears of corn, husks on, rotating often until dark brown all over, about 20 minutes. Transfer to a plate and let cool for 5 minutes or until cool enough to handle. Remove husk and silks and, using a serrated knife, cut kernels from cob.

- **Preheat oven to 400°F (200°C)**
- **Baking sheet, lined with parchment paper**

10	cremini mushrooms (each about 2 inches/5 cm)	10
1 tbsp	olive oil	15 mL
¼ cup	finely diced white onion	60 mL
¼ cup	finely diced bacon	60 mL
⅓ cup	roasted corn kernels (see Tip, left)	75 mL
2 tbsp	freshly grated Parmesan cheese	30 mL
1 tbsp	coarsely chopped fresh thyme leaves	15 mL
½ tsp	salt	2 mL
½ tsp	freshly ground black pepper	2 mL

1. Separate the mushroom stems from the caps and finely chop stems. Set caps aside.

2. In a large skillet, heat oil over medium heat. Add onion, bacon and chopped mushroom stems and cook, stirring often, until onions are soft, about 5 minutes. Transfer to a bowl and add corn, Parmesan, thyme, salt and pepper and mix thoroughly.

3. Stuff onion mixture into mushroom caps, dividing evenly, and place on prepared baking sheet. Bake in a preheated oven until caps are soft, about 15 minutes. Serve immediately or keep the stuffed mushrooms covered in the refrigerator for up to 1 day and bake when ready to serve.

King Oyster Mushroom and Asparagus Salsa Canapé

Makes 10 servings

King Oyster mushrooms are so dense and packed with flavor, they make the perfect base for any hors d'oeuvre.

Tip

A suitable substitute for the king oyster mushroom would be a stem of the portobello mushroom. Remove from the cap, and slice the stems into ¾-inch (2 cm) rounds.

2	king oyster mushrooms (see Tip, left)	2
1 tbsp	olive oil	15 mL
1	clove garlic	1
¼ tsp	salt	1 mL
⅛ tsp	freshly ground black pepper	0.5 mL
2 tbsp	Asparagus Salsa (page 79)	30 mL

1. Trim ends off mushrooms. Cut mushrooms crosswise into about ten ¾-inch (2 cm) thick slices.

2. In a skillet, heat oil over medium heat. Add mushrooms and garlic and sear mushrooms until golden brown on the bottom, about 5 minutes. Flip over and cook for 2 minutes or until mushrooms are fork tender. Discard garlic and sprinkle mushrooms with salt and pepper.

3. Spoon Asparagus Salsa in a mound on top of each mushroom round. Serve immediately.

Peppery Roasted Squash Pâté

Makes about 1½ cups (375 mL)

This is very tasty and mildly addictive. Serve on sliced baguette.

Tip

To roast squash: Preheat oven to 400°F (200°C). Cut squash in half lengthwise and scoop out the seeds. Place 1 tbsp (15 mL) butter in each cavity and wrap tightly in foil. Bake in preheated oven until tender, about 45 minutes.

1 cup	puréed roasted acorn or butternut squash or pumpkin (see Tip, left)	250 mL
1 cup	black pepper-flavored fresh cream cheese, such as Boursin	250 mL
½ to 1	jalapeño pepper, seeded and coarsely chopped	½ to 1
½ cup	pecan halves	125 mL
	Salt and freshly ground black pepper	

1. In a food processor fitted with metal blade, pulse squash, cream cheese, jalapeño to taste and pecans until pecans are finely chopped and ingredients are blended, about 15 times. Season to taste with salt and pepper. Transfer to a serving dish, cover and refrigerate until chilled, for at least 2 hours or for up to 2 days.

Risotto Balls

Makes about 30 balls

Risotto balls, also known as arancine, are a classic Sicilian appetizer that easily incorporates your favorite ingredients. Here we have provided a basic recipe but feel free to incorporate asparagus, sweet potato, truffles or even beets to create the perfect seasonal appetizer.

- **Candy/deep-fry thermometer**

2 tbsp	olive oil	30 mL
½ cup	finely diced onion	125 mL
¾ cup	Arborio rice	175 mL
½ cup	white wine	125 mL
3 cups	chicken or vegetable broth, warmed	750 mL
½ cup	freshly grated Parmesan cheese	125 mL
1 tbsp	finely chopped fresh chives	15 mL
¾ tsp	salt	3 mL
½ tsp	freshly ground black pepper	2 mL
	Oil	
1 cup	panko bread crumbs or cornflake crumbs	250 mL
2 tbsp	finely grated lemon zest	30 mL
1 tbsp	extra virgin olive oil	15 mL

1. In a saucepan, heat oil over medium heat. Add onion and cook, stirring often, until translucent, about 5 minutes. Add rice and toast, stirring often, until nutty brown and fragrant, 3 to 5 minutes. Add wine and boil, stirring until all wine is absorbed, about 2 minutes. Reduce heat and simmer gently, adding broth, about ½ cup (125 mL) at a time, and stirring until all broth has been absorbed and rice is al dente, about 20 minutes. Remove from heat and add cheese, chives, salt and pepper and fold gently to combine. Let cool for at least 2 hours, preferably overnight.

2. In a deep skillet or Dutch oven, heat 3 inches (7.5 cm) of oil over medium-high heat to 350°F (180°C). (You can also use a deep fryer; follow the manufacturer's instructions.)

3. Place breads crumbs in a shallow bowl. Working with 2 tsp (10 mL) of the risotto at a time, form into balls. Dip risotto balls in the bread crumbs, turning to coat all over.

4. Fry risotto balls in hot oil, in batches, turning once, until golden brown, 3 to 4 minutes. Using a slotted spoon, transfer to a paper towel–lined plate. Season with lemon zest and extra virgin olive oil. Serve hot.

Cornmeal-Crusted Black Bean Cakes

Makes about 36

These little nuggets of seasoned beans are flavorful and healthful. The addition of a jalapeño pepper imbues them with a bit of zest, so if you're heat averse you can omit it. Serve them warm with the Cumin-Spiked Crema or Guacamole (page 26). Heat seekers might consider Fresh Tomato Salsa or Fresh Salsa Verde (pages 70 and 71) as an accompaniment.

Tips

Be sure to use finely ground cornmeal. Coarser grinds will be unpleasantly mealy in this recipe.

These cakes can be made ahead of time. After they are cooked, place on a baking sheet and let cool. Cover with plastic and refrigerate for up to 2 days. When you are ready to serve, place in a 350°F (180°C) oven until warmed through, about 10 minutes.

Cumin-Spiked Crema, optional

4 oz	crème fraîche or sour cream	125 g
2 tsp	ground cumin (see Tips, page 505)	10 mL
1 tsp	finely grated lime zest	5 mL
	Salt and freshly ground black pepper	

Black Bean Cakes

1/4 cup	fresh cilantro leaves	60 mL
4	green onions, cut into chunks	4
2	cloves garlic, coarsely chopped	2
1	jalapeño pepper, seeded and quartered	1
1 tbsp	ground cumin (see Tips, page 505)	15 mL
2 cups	cooked black beans (see Tips, page 441)	500 mL
	Salt and freshly ground black pepper	
2	eggs, beaten	2
3/4 cup	finely ground cornmeal (see Tips, left)	175 mL
	Oil	

1. *Cumin-Spiked Crema, optional:* In a small serving bowl, combine crème fraîche, cumin and lime zest. Season to taste with salt and pepper. Stir well to blend. Cover and refrigerate for at least 30 minutes or up to overnight to allow flavors to blend.

2. *Black Bean Cakes:* In a food processor fitted with metal blade, pulse cilantro, onions, garlic, jalapeño and cumin until chopped, stopping and scraping down sides of the bowl as necessary. Add beans and process until blended. Season to taste with salt and pepper.

3. Place eggs in a shallow dish and cornmeal in a separate shallow dish. One at a time, scoop out a level tbsp (15 mL) of the bean mixture. Flatten into a small cake about 1 1/2 inches (4 cm) in diameter and 1/4 inch (0.5 cm) thick. Repeat until all beans are used up.

4. When you're ready to cook, add oil to skillet to a depth of about 1 inch (2.5 cm) and heat over medium heat. Dip bean cakes in egg, then in cornmeal and fry in hot oil, in batches, turning once, until light golden, about 2 minutes. Transfer to a paper towel–lined plate to drain.

Black Bean Quesadillas

Makes 12 to 18

Easy to make yet lusciously yummy, quesadillas are always a hit. They are good on their own but even better with a dollop of Cumin-Spiked Crema (page 440) or even plain sour cream. Fresh Tomato Salsa (page 70) makes a great finish, too.

Tips

For this quantity of beans, soak and cook 1 cup (250 mL) dried beans or use 1 can (14 to 19 oz/398 to 540 mL) cooked beans, drained and rinsed.

Use a Mexican chile powder blend or a single chile powder such as ancho or New Mexico.

Be aware that if you are making these ahead of time, the edges of the top tortilla will have a tendency to curl up. You can fix this by removing them from the oven after they have cooked for about 5 minutes and running a spatula around the edges to turn them down. Return to oven to complete cooking.

- **Preheat oven to 400°F (200°C)**

2 cups	cooked black beans (see Tips, left)	500 mL
6	green onions, white parts with a bit of green, cut into chunks	6
½ cup	packed fresh cilantro leaves	125 mL
1	chipotle chile in adobo sauce	1
2	cloves garlic, quartered	2
1 tbsp	ground cumin (see Tips, page 505)	15 mL
1 tbsp	dried oregano	15 mL
4 oz	cream cheese, softened	125 g
	Salt and freshly ground black pepper	
6	7-inch (18 cm) tortillas	6
	Olive oil	
1 tsp	chile powder (see Tips, left)	5 mL
2 tbsp	toasted pumpkin seeds (pepitas), finely chopped, optional	30 mL

1. In a food processor fitted with metal blade, pulse beans, green onions, cilantro, chipotle chile, garlic, cumin and oregano until chopped and blended, about 10 times. Add cream cheese and pulse to blend. Season to taste with salt and black pepper.

2. Place 3 tortillas on a large rimmed baking sheet. Spread with bean mixture, leaving a ½-inch (1 cm) border. Top with remaining tortillas. Brush tops of tortillas lightly with olive oil and dust evenly with chile powder.

3. Bake in preheated oven until top is nicely browned, about 10 minutes. Remove from oven and sprinkle pepitas evenly over tops, if using. Cut each tortilla pair into 4 or 6 wedges. Serve warm.

Red Bean Quesadillas

Makes 12 to 18

Here's a tasty version of quesadillas that can be preassembled and popped in the oven when your guests arrive. These are great on their own, but if you like to guild the lily, serve with a small bowl of sour cream or Guacamole (page 26) or even a robust salsa such as Fresh Tomato Salsa (page 70) or Fresh Salsa Verde (page 71).

Tips

This quantity of jalapeño produces a mildly spiced quesadilla. If you are serving these with a zesty salsa it will be enough but if you like heat, you may want to increase the quantity.

Use a Mexican chile powder blend or a single chile powder such as ancho or New Mexico.

Be aware that if you are making these ahead of time, the edges of the top tortilla will have a tendency to curl up. You can fix this by removing them from the oven after they have cooked for about 5 minutes and running a spatula around the edges to turn them down. Return to oven to complete cooking.

- **Preheat oven to 400°F (200°C)**

2 cups	cooked drained red beans (see Tips, page 441)	500 mL
1	red onion, quartered	1
1 tbsp	dried oregano	15 mL
1 tbsp	drained pickled jalapeño pepper (see Tips, left)	15 mL
	Salt and freshly ground black pepper	
6	7-inch (18 cm) tortillas	6
6 oz	shredded Monterey Jack cheese	175 g
1 tbsp	olive oil (approx.)	15 mL
1 tsp	chile powder (see Tips, left)	5 mL
2 tbsp	finely chopped fresh cilantro	30 mL

1. In a food processor fitted with metal blade, pulse beans, red onion, oregano and jalapeño until chopped and blended, about 10 times. Season to taste with salt and black pepper and pulse to blend, once or twice.

2. Place 3 tortillas on a large rimmed baking sheet. Spread with bean mixture, leaving a $\frac{1}{2}$-inch (1 cm) border. Top beans with shredded cheese and remaining tortillas. Brush tops of tortillas lightly with olive oil and dust evenly with chile powder.

3. Place in preheated oven and bake until top is nicely browned and cheese is melted, about 10 minutes. Remove from oven and sprinkle cilantro evenly over tops. Cut each tortilla pair into 4 or 6 wedges. Serve warm.

Polenta Tamales

Makes 15 tamales

You'll be transported to Mexico with one bite. For a fantastic presentation cut 5- by ½-inch (12.5 by 1 cm) strips of husk and use to tie the top and bottom of the tamale.

Tips

To serve tamales hot, you can reheat in a 400°F (200°C) oven until warmed through, about 10 minutes.

To grill corn: Preheat barbecue grill to high. Grill ears of corn, husks on, rotating often until dark brown all over, about 20 minutes. Transfer to a plate and let cool for 5 minutes or until cool enough to handle. Remove husk and silks and, using a serrated knife, cut kernels from cob.

- **Fifteen 5- by 3-inch (12.5 by 7.5 cm) squares dry corn husk**

1 tbsp	unsalted butter	15 mL
⅓ cup	finely diced onion	75 mL
½ cup	white wine	125 mL
1 cup	chicken or vegetable broth	250 mL
⅔ cup	fine cornmeal	150 mL
¾ cup	grilled corn kernels (see Tips, left)	175 mL
½ cup	finely grated Parmesan cheese	125 mL
2 tbsp	coarsely chopped fresh cilantro leaves	30 mL
½ tsp	salt	2 mL
¼ tsp	freshly ground black pepper	1 mL

1. In a saucepan, melt butter over medium heat. Add onion and cook, stirring, until translucent, 3 to 4 minutes. Add wine and bring to a boil. Reduce heat and simmer until liquid is reduced by one-quarter, about 4 minutes. Add broth and bring to a simmer.

2. Gradually pour in cornmeal, whisking to avoid lumps. Remove from heat. Cover and let stand until cornmeal is soft, about 30 minutes. Stir in corn, cheese, cilantro, salt and pepper.

3. Place the husks on a work surface with natural curve facing up. Spoon polenta onto husks, dividing equally and spreading out in a strip lengthwise, leaving about 1-inch (2.5 cm) border along each long edge of rectangle. Starting at one long edge, roll up husk around filling, forming a cigar shape. Let cool to room temperature and serve, or refrigerate for up to 3 days. Let come to room temperature before serving.

Tomato Basil Polenta Gratin

Makes 16 servings

A classic Italian appetizer that can be made days in advance and heated when guests arrive, which means you have so much more time for you. Enjoy on a cool fall or winter evening and don't forget to make a lot — they will go fast. This recipe is easily doubled and tripled.

Tips

We have a preference for coarsely ground cornmeal because of its wonderful texture but the recipe would work with fine cornmeal as well.

This appetizer can be made up to 3 days in advance. Garnish with cheese and broil just before serving.

- **Sixteen ½-cup (125 mL) ramekins or other ovenproof dishes**

3 cups	chicken or vegetable broth	750 mL
1 cup	Oven-Roasted Cherry Tomato Sauce (page 546)	250 mL
½ cup	coarsely chopped peeled ripe tomatoes	125 mL
½ cup	whole milk	125 mL
1½ cups	coarsely ground cornmeal (see Tips, left)	375 mL
¼ cup	shredded sharp (aged) Cheddar cheese	60 mL
1 tbsp	chopped fresh basil	15 mL
2 tbsp	freshly grated Parmesan cheese	30 mL

1. In a large saucepan, combine broth, tomato sauce, tomatoes and milk and bring to a simmer over medium heat. Gradually pour in cornmeal, whisking constantly to avoid lumps. Cook, whisking constantly, until cornmeal begins to bloom and the mixture begins to bubble, about 3 minutes. Cover with a tight-fitting lid, remove from heat and let stand until cornmeal is soft, about 30 minutes. Add Cheddar and basil and whisk well to incorporate.

2. Just before serving, preheat broiler. Spoon about ¼ cup (60 mL) polenta into each ramekin and smooth tops. Place ramekins on baking sheet and sprinkle with Parmesan, dividing evenly. Broil until cheese is melted and tops are golden brown, about 1 minute. Serve immediately.

Fried Green Tomatoes

Makes 8 appetizers

These wonderfully crispy tomatoes create a refined plated appetizer with a side salad but are also ideal as a base for a canapé. Garnish with Summer Tomato Salsa (page 70) or Roasted Corn Salsa (page 82) for a tasty vegetarian friendly appetizer.

- **Candy/deep-fry thermometer**

2	green tomatoes	2
	Oil	
1 cup	panko bread crumbs	250 mL
1/4 cup	freshly grated Parmesan cheese	60 mL
1/4 tsp	salt	1 mL
1/4 tsp	freshly ground black pepper	1 mL
5 tsp	all-purpose flour	25 mL
1	egg, beaten	1

1. Using a sharp knife, remove thin slices from top and bottom of tomato to expose some flesh (flour will not stick to skin). Slice tomato crosswise into four equal slices and set aside.

2. In a deep skillet or Dutch oven or deep-fryer, heat 3 inches (7.5 cm) of oil over medium-high heat to 375°F (190°C). (You can also use a deep-fryer; follow the manufacturer's instructions.)

3. In a shallow bowl, combine bread crumbs, Parmesan, salt and pepper. Mix well. Place flour and egg in separate shallow bowls. Dip tomatoes in flour, turning to coat, shaking off excess, and then in egg and finally in bread crumb mixture to coat. Discard any excess flour, egg and crumb mixture.

4. Fry in hot oil, in batches, turning once, until golden brown and crisp, about 3 minutes. Using a slotted spoon, transfer to a paper towel–lined plate. Wrap tomatoes in decorative napkins covering only half of the tomatoes and serve immediately.

Panko-Crusted Tomatillos with Summer Tomato Salsa

Makes 12 pieces

Tomatillos have a wonderful acidic flavor and contrast beautifully with a fresh tomato salsa.

¼ cup	panko bread crumbs	60 mL
⅛ tsp	ground cumin (see Tip, page 505)	0.5 mL
⅛ tsp	salt	0.5 mL
6	tomatillos, peeled and cut in half crosswise	6
1 tbsp	unsalted butter	15 mL
2 tbsp	Summer Tomato Salsa (page 70)	30 mL

1. In a bowl, combine bread crumbs, cumin and salt and stir well to combine. Press the flesh-side of the tomatillos into the bread crumbs to coat.

2. In a skillet, melt butter over medium heat. Place tomatillos, crumb side down, into pan and fry until golden brown, 4 to 5 minutes. Transfer to a platter, crumb side up, and garnish with Summer Tomato Salsa. Serve immediately.

Sweet Pepper and Garlic Marinated Olives

Makes 3 cups (750 mL)

This quick-to-prepare appetizer is perfect for dinner and appetizer parties and can be prepared an entire week in advance. The longer olives marinate, the better they are. Also try Truffle Vinaigrette (page 542) or Roasted Red Pepper Vinaigrette (page 541) for the marinade.

¼ cup	olive oil	60 mL
¼ cup	thinly sliced red bell pepper	60 mL
1 tbsp	thinly sliced garlic	15 mL
3 cups	jumbo green olives	750 mL
1 tbsp	freshly squeezed lemon juice	15 mL
1 tbsp	chopped fresh basil leaves	15 mL

1. In a saucepan, heat oil over medium heat. Add bell pepper and garlic and cook, stirring, just until fragrant, about 1 minute. Add olives, lemon juice and basil and toss to evenly coat. Let cool to room temperature, cover and refrigerate and let marinate for at least 24 hours or for up to 1 week before serving.

Classic Deviled Eggs

Makes 12

This old-fashioned appetizer is a staple at picnics as well as cocktail parties. For a pretty presentation, line a platter with lettuce leaves and place the filled eggs on top. Or, if you're from the South, use your special serving plate (see Tips, below).

Tips

In the American South, where deviled eggs are a tradition, hostesses have plates with concave indentations made specially for serving this delicacy. If you don't have a plate for deviled eggs, to keep them from slipping, create a flat surface by cutting a thin piece from the convex bottom of each cooked half before filling.

The greatest challenge in making deviled eggs is evenly peeling the cooked egg. After the egg has cooled (quick cooling helps to eliminate unattractive ring around the yolk; it also facilitates removal of the shell) tap the wide end on the counter to create cracks in the shell. Using your fingers, gently peel away the shell and membrane.

6	eggs	6

Filling

3 tbsp	mayonnaise	45 mL
1 tbsp	Dijon mustard	15 mL
1 tbsp	finely snipped chives	15 mL
1 tbsp	minced drained capers	15 mL
$\frac{1}{4}$ tsp	salt	1 mL
$\frac{1}{8}$ tsp	cayenne pepper	0.5 mL
	Freshly ground black pepper	
	Sweet paprika	

1. In a saucepan, combine eggs and cold water liberally to cover. Bring to a boil over high heat. Cover, remove from heat and let stand for 12 minutes. Drain well. Transfer to a bowl of ice water and let stand for 5 minutes. Carefully peel the eggs (see Tips, left) and rinse well under cold running water.

2. *Filling:* Cut eggs in half lengthwise and carefully scoop out the yolks, keeping the whites intact. In a bowl, combine egg yolks, mayonnaise, mustard, chives, capers, salt, cayenne, and pepper to taste. Mix well. Spoon filling into whites. (For a more elegant presentation, use a pastry tube.) Dust lightly with paprika. Cover and refrigerate until ready to serve.

Variation

Deviled Eggs with Hummus: Eliminate the Dijon mustard and chives. Add $\frac{1}{4}$ cup (60 mL) hummus and 1 tbsp (15 mL) freshly squeezed lemon juice to the yolk mixture.

Classic Edamame

Makes about 3 cups (750 mL)

Edamame is healthy for you and simple to prepare, too.

Tip

Edamame is easy to eat because it has a built-in serving vessel — the pod. Place half of pod in your mouth and with your fingers push beans up toward top. Beans will release easily. Be sure to have an extra dish available for those empty pods.

12 cups	water	3 L
¼ cup	salt, divided	60 mL
3 cups	edamame in the pod, trimmed	750 mL
¼ tsp	toasted sesame oil	1 mL

1. In a saucepan, bring water and 3 tbsp (45 mL) of the salt to a boil over high heat. Add edamame and boil until tender-crisp and vibrant green, about 6 minutes.

2. Drain beans and transfer to a large bowl. Add remaining salt and sesame oil and toss to coat. Serve warm.

Edamame with Asian Vinaigrette

Makes about 3 cups (750 mL)

This recipe is great served warm but the leftovers are even better cold.

Tip

Ginger is very easy to purée if kept whole in the freezer. Remove from the freezer as required and grate with skin on.

12 cups	water	3 L
3 tbsp	salt	45 mL
3 cups	edamame in the pod, trimmed	750 mL
¼ cup	thinly sliced shallots	60 mL
1 tbsp	soy sauce	15 mL
2 tsp	rice vinegar (see Tips, page 344)	10 mL
½ tsp	chopped fresh cilantro leaves	2 mL
¼ tsp	puréed fresh gingerroot (see Tip, left)	1 mL
¼ tsp	toasted sesame oil	1 mL

1. In a saucepan, bring water and salt to a boil over high heat. Add edamame and boil until soybeans are tender-crisp and vibrant green, about 6 minutes.

2. Drain beans and transfer to a large bowl. Add shallots, soy sauce, vinegar, cilantro, ginger and sesame oil and toss to coat. Serve immediately or cover and refrigerate for up to 3 days.

Fresh Corn Cakes

Makes about 25 cakes

What a glorious showcase for one of the sweetest vegetables around — corn. For a fresh pick-me-up, top with a spoon of sour cream or crème fraîche. To take it to the next level, garnish with a dollop of Roasted Corn Salsa (page 82) or Roasted Red Pepper Salsa (page 76).

Tip

Frozen corn is readily available and can be used in place of fresh but should be thoroughly thawed and dried before using.

7 tbsp	all-purpose flour	105 mL
¼ cup	freshly grated Parmesan cheese, preferably Parmigiano-Reggiano	60 mL
½ tsp	baking powder	2 mL
½ tsp	salt	2 mL
2	eggs	2
¼ cup	milk	60 mL
2 cups	fresh corn kernels	500 mL
2 tbsp	finely chopped red bell pepper	30 mL
1 tbsp	minced garlic	15 mL
½ tsp	chopped fresh thyme leaves	2 mL
2	egg whites, at room temperature	2
3 tbsp	unsalted butter, divided	45 mL

1. In a large bowl, combine flour, Parmesan, baking powder and salt. In another bowl, whisk together eggs and milk. Add to flour mixture with corn, bell pepper, garlic and thyme and stir just until blended.

2. In a small bowl, using an electric mixer, beat egg whites until stiff peaks. Fold into batter just until blended. Cover and refrigerate for 1 hour.

3. In a nonstick skillet, melt 1 tbsp (15 mL) of the butter over medium heat. Spoon about 1½ tbsp (22 mL) of batter per cake into the pan. Cook, turning once, until golden brown, 3 to 4 minutes per side. Transfer to a plate. Repeat with remaining batter, adding butter and adjusting heat as necessary between batches. Serve hot.

Marinated Corn on the Cob

Makes 18 servings

A wonderful summertime barbecue party appetizer.

Tip

Corn picks or corn holders are perfect for this appetizer, your guests will love you for keeping their hands and clothing clean.

- **Preheat barbecue grill to high**

1 tbsp	unsalted butter	15 mL
1 tsp	chopped fresh thyme leaves	5 mL
1 tsp	Dijon mustard	5 mL
$\frac{1}{2}$ tsp	salt	2 mL
$\frac{1}{4}$ tsp	granulated sugar	1 mL
6	cobs corn, husked and cut crosswise into thirds	6

1. In a large bowl, combine butter, thyme, mustard, salt and sugar and, using the back of a spoon, mash until blended. Set aside.
2. In a large pot of boiling salted water, boil corn until slightly tender, about 3 minutes. Drain well and add to the bowl with butter mixture. Toss to coat.
3. Place corn on preheated barbecue and grill, turning often, until caramelized and kernels are tender, about 5 minutes. Serve immediately.

The Absolute Best Creamed Corn

Makes about 25 servings

This is a very simple yet elegant appetizer. Best known for being a side dish, this very sweet creamed corn is served as a one- or two-bite appetizer that explodes with flavor.

Tip

To serve, spoon about 1$\frac{1}{2}$ tbsp (22 mL) onto a Chinese soup spoon and garnish with fresh thyme.

- **Chinese soup spoon or large decorative spoon**

1 tbsp	unsalted butter	15 mL
2$\frac{1}{4}$ cups	corn kernels	550 mL
$\frac{3}{4}$ cup	whole milk, divided	175 mL
$\frac{1}{4}$ tsp	cornstarch	1 mL
1 tsp	agave syrup or liquid honey	5 mL
$\frac{1}{4}$ tsp	each salt and freshly ground black pepper	1 mL

1. In a saucepan, melt butter over medium heat. Add corn and cook, stirring often, until soft, about 10 minutes.
2. In a small bowl, combine 1 tbsp (15 mL) of the milk with cornstarch and stir well to remove lumps. Stir remaining milk, agave and cornstarch mixture into pan. Reduce heat to low, and simmer, stirring, until thick, about 5 minutes. Remove from heat and season with salt and pepper.

Vegetarian Cabbage Rolls

Makes 20 rolls

This fresh roll is a perfect vegetarian appetizer or a great addition to any hors d'oeuvre party.

Tip

Although red cabbage would work perfectly in a sit-down environment, it may not be the best vessel for hors d'oeuvres because it tends to bleed and your guests may not like it one bit.

5	green cabbage leaves, each cut into 4 wedges	5
	Ice water	
1½ cups	coarsely grated carrots	375 mL
1 cup	grilled corn kernels (see Tips, page 443)	250 mL
1 cup	drained rinsed cooked or canned chickpeas	250 mL
½ cup	coarsely chopped Shoestring Onion Rings (page 422)	125 mL
¼ cup	freshly squeezed lemon juice	60 mL
3	cloves garlic, minced	3
1 tbsp	thinly sliced green onions	15 mL
¾ tsp	salt	3 mL
½ tsp	chipotle powder	2 mL

1. In a pot of boiling salted water, blanch cabbage until pliable, about 3 minutes. Drain and plunge into a bowl of ice water and let stand until chilled.

2. In a bowl, combine carrots, corn, chickpeas, onion rings, lemon juice, garlic, green onions, salt and chipotle and mix well to combine.

3. Place cabbage on a flat surface with natural curve facing up to form a bowl shape and spoon carrot mixture on top, dividing equally. Spread filling lengthwise along the center of the wedge, leaving a 1-inch (2.5 cm) border on each long side. Fold the sides of cabbage in toward middle to enclose the stuffing and, starting from the wide edge, roll up tightly to form a roll. Serve immediately or cover and refrigerate for up to 1 day.

Bar Nosh

To nosh means to snack. Who doesn't enjoy standing around tasting little tidbits while chatting with friends? The following are a selection of our favorites.

Spicy Almonds

Makes 1 cup (250 mL)

Vegan Friendly

A small bowl of seasoned nuts is always a welcome addition to a selection of mezes. Slightly Middle Eastern in their flavoring, these are pleasantly spicy and mildly addictive.

Tips

For the best flavor, buy almonds with the skin on and blanch them yourself. *To blanch almonds:* Drop almonds in a pot of rapidly boiling water and boil until the skins start to pucker. Transfer to a colander and rinse well under cold running water. Using your hands, pop the almonds out of their skins. Place on paper towels and let dry for at least 10 minutes, changing the paper towels, if necessary.

Aleppo pepper is a moderately hot, beautifully fruity pepper that is Syrian in origin. If you can't find it, substitute sweet paprika and increase the quantity of cayenne pepper by $\frac{1}{8}$ tsp (0.5 mL).

1 cup	blanched almonds (see Tips, left)	250 mL
2 tbsp	extra virgin olive oil	30 mL
1 tsp	fine sea salt	5 mL
1 tsp	Aleppo pepper (see Tips, left)	5 mL
$\frac{1}{4}$ tsp	ground coriander	1 mL
$\frac{1}{4}$ tsp	cayenne pepper	1 mL
Pinch	ground cinnamon	Pinch

1. In a skillet just large enough to accommodate almonds in a single layer, heat oil over medium-low heat. Add almonds and cook, stirring occasionally, until they begin to brown. At that point, begin to stir frequently to ensure even browning. When finished, nuts should be a caramel brown and the process will take about 10 minutes. Using a slotted spoon, transfer to a paper towel–lined dish and drain well. Transfer to a small serving bowl.

2. Meanwhile, in a small bowl, combine salt, Aleppo pepper, coriander, cayenne and cinnamon. Mix well. Add to almonds and stir well.

Spanish-Style Smoked Almonds

Makes 1 cup (250 mL)

Here's a very simple way to make spicy almonds. Adjust the quantity of smoked paprika to suit your taste. Half a teaspoon (2 mL) produces a mild result, but smoked paprika can easily overwhelm, so increase the quantity cautiously.

- **Preheat oven to 325°F (160°C)**

1 cup	whole blanched almonds (see Tips, page 452)	250 mL
1 tsp	extra virgin olive oil	5 mL
½ to 1 tsp	hot smoked paprika	2 to 5 mL
	Sea salt	

1. On a rimmed baking sheet, roast almonds in preheated oven, stirring several times, until golden brown, 15 to 20 minutes.
2. In a bowl, combine olive oil and smoked paprika to taste. Add almonds and toss well. Return to baking sheet and sprinkle evenly with salt to taste. Toss well. Transfer to a serving bowl.

Coconut-Scented Macadamia Nuts

Makes 2 cups (500 mL)

These are perfect to accompany any Pacific Rim or Caribbean-inspired meal or all on their own to accompany an aperitif, coffee and tea.

- **Preheat oven to 250°F (120°C)**

2 cups	macadamia nuts	500 mL
2 tbsp	agave syrup	30 mL
½ tsp	vanilla extract	2 mL
3 tbsp	unsweetened desiccated coconut	45 mL
½ tsp	fine sea salt	2 mL

1. On a rimmed baking sheet, roast nuts in preheated oven, stirring often, until fragrant and golden brown, 10 to 12 minutes. Drizzle agave syrup and vanilla over nuts, mixing well to coat. Return to oven for 2 minutes longer.
2. Transfer to a bowl and add coconut and salt. Toss well to coat. Spread on baking sheet and let cool to room temperature before serving or store in an airtight container for up to 1 week.

Cornflake and Almond Clusters

Make about 1 cup (250 mL)

Cornflakes add crunchy texture to the almonds, which are just wonderful served alongside coffee or tea.

1 cup	slivered almonds	250 mL
2 tbsp	cornflake crumbs	30 mL
2 tbsp	agave syrup	30 mL
¼ tsp	cayenne pepper	1 mL
¼ tsp	fine sea salt	1 mL

1. In a skillet over medium-high heat, toast almonds, stirring often, until fragrant and golden brown, about 5 minutes. Add cornflake crumbs, agave, cayenne and salt and stir well to combine. Immediately transfer to a bowl and let cool to room temperature. Break into random clusters. Serve immediately or store in an airtight container for up to 1 week.

Chile-Spiked Peanuts

Makes about 2 cups (500 mL)

Even if you're not normally a fan of peanuts, you'll love these flavorful nuggets.

Tip

Sea salt is available in most supermarkets. It is much sweeter than table salt and is essential for these recipes as table salt would impart an unpleasant acrid taste to the nuts. Be sure to buy sea salt without additives, such as iodine or anti-caking agents.

2 cups	shelled raw peanuts, with or without skins	500 mL
1 cup	peanut oil (approx.)	250 mL
2 tsp	ancho chile powder	10 mL
Pinch	cayenne pepper	Pinch
1 tsp	fine sea salt (see Tip, left)	5 mL

1. In a deep skillet, heat oil over medium heat. Add peanuts and cook, stirring, until nicely browned, about 5 minutes. Using a slotted spoon, transfer to a paper towel–lined bowl. Sprinkle with chile powder, cayenne and salt. Lift out paper and toss well.

Agave and Ginger-Scented Peanuts

Makes about 1½ cups (375 mL)

These versatile sweet and spicy nuts are delicious and make a wonderful nosh for an Asian-inspired party.

1½ cups	whole skinless unsalted peanuts	375 mL
1 tbsp	agave syrup	15 mL
1 tsp	finely puréed gingerroot	5 mL
¼ tsp	fine sea salt	1 mL

1. In a large skillet over high heat, toast peanuts, stirring often, until fragrant and golden brown, 5 to 7 minutes. Add agave syrup, ginger and salt and stir well to coat. Immediately transfer to a bowl and let cool to room temperature. Serve immediately or store in an airtight container for up to 1 week.

Sweet Sesame Snap Squares

Makes about 2 cups (500 mL)

This highly addictive nosh is a perfect addition to an Asian-inspired party.

Tip

Toasting sesame seeds are quite easy and only takes minutes. *To toast seeds:* In a large skillet over medium-high heat, toast sesame seeds, stirring often, until fragrant and golden brown, 3 to 4 minutes.

- **Baking sheet, lined with parchment paper**

2 tbsp	packed brown sugar	30 mL
2 tbsp	pure maple syrup	30 mL
1 tbsp	corn syrup	15 mL
2 cups	toasted sesame seeds (see Tip, left)	500 mL
¼ tsp	toasted sesame oil	1 mL

1. In a skillet over medium-low heat, warm brown sugar, maple syrup and corn syrup, stirring, until sugar is dissolved and mixture resembles caramel sauce, 3 to 4 minutes. Add sesame seeds and oil and mix well to combine.

2. Spread onto prepared baking sheet and let cool to room temperature. Transfer to a cutting board and cut into bite-size pieces, about ½-inch (1 cm) square. Serve immediately or store in an airtight container for up to 1 week.

Cinnamon-Spiked Pumpkin Seeds

Makes 2 cups (500 mL)

And to think you threw away all of those pumpkin seeds every Halloween. With this recipe you'll never discard those seeds again.

Tip

If you don't have fresh pumpkin seeds, you can use store-bought unsalted, raw pumpkin seeds in the shell instead. Skip Step 1 and season and bake as directed in Step 2.

- **Preheat oven to 350°F (180°C)**
- **Baking sheet, lined with parchment paper**

1 cup	pumpkin seeds (in the shell), rinsed and patted dry (see Tip, left)	250 mL
1	egg white	1
1 tbsp	granulated sugar	15 mL
¼ tsp	ground cinnamon	1 mL
¼ tsp	fine sea salt	1 mL

1. If using seeds straight from a pumpkin, thoroughly rinse under cold water and pat dry on paper towel. Spread pumpkin seeds on a baking sheet and bake in preheated oven until all moisture has been removed and seeds are not sticking to each other, about 15 minutes. Let cool to room temperature. Leave oven on.

2. In a bowl, using a whisk or an electric mixer, whisk egg white and sugar to soft peaks. Add cinnamon, salt and seeds and fold well to evenly coat seeds. Return to prepared baking sheet and bake in oven until seeds are golden brown and begin to split open, about 15 minutes. Serve immediately or let cool and store in an airtight container for up to 1 week.

Curried Cashews with Sultanas

Makes about 2 cups (500 mL)

This Indian-influenced spice mixture creates the perfect savory cashew nosh. Combined with naturally sweet sultanas, this is just the combination to begin any appetizer party. Pass around in individual cups or small bowls and enjoy!

Tip

Store nuts in an airtight container for up to 1 week.

¼ tsp	each hot pepper flakes and curry powder	1 mL
¼ tsp	each cumin and coriander seeds	1 mL
1	cardamom pod	1
1 tbsp	unsalted butter	15 mL
1 tbsp	packed brown sugar	15 mL
2 cups	roasted unsalted cashews	500 mL
¼ cup	sultana raisins	60 mL

1. In a mortar and pestle or spice grinder, combine hot pepper flakes, curry powder, cumin, coriander and cardamom pod and grind to a powder. Set aside.

2. In a skillet over medium-low heat, melt butter with brown sugar until sugar is dissolved, 3 to 4 minutes. Add spice mixture and cook, stirring, until fragrant, about 1 minute. Remove from heat.

3. Add cashews and stir well to coat. Transfer to a bowl and let cool to room temperature. Stir in sultanas.

Coffee-Scented Hazelnuts

Makes 2 cups (500 mL)

These are a wonderful dessert nosh. For something a little whimsical, serve your guests the hazelnuts in espresso cups. To take this presentation one step further, crush the hazelnuts and sprinkle on a coffee-flavored ice cream as a dessert for an appetizer party. It's delicious and perhaps just the caffeine fix your guests were looking for.

- **Preheat oven to 250°F (120°C)**

3 tbsp	water	45 mL
2 tbsp	granulated sugar	30 mL
1 tbsp	brewed espresso coffee	15 mL
1 tsp	finely grated semisweet chocolate	5 mL
2 cups	hazelnuts	500 mL

1. In a saucepan over medium heat, combine water, sugar and coffee and bring to a boil. Reduce heat to low and simmer until syrupy, about 2 minutes. Remove from heat and swirl in chocolate until melted. Set aside.

2. Spread nuts on a baking sheet and bake in preheated oven, stirring often, until fragrant and golden brown, 12 to 15 minutes. Let cool to the touch. Rub nuts in small batches between two tea towels to remove skins and drizzle simple syrup over nuts, mixing well to coat. Let cool to room temperature.

Cinnamon-Scented Popcorn

Makes about 6 cups (1.5 L)

Popcorn is comfort food we often associate with a favorite movie, camping trip or special family time. Here, the addition of cinnamon and sugar creates a subtle sophistication, which can accompany an aperitif, espresso or coffee. Time to create those new memories.

1 tbsp	olive oil	15 mL
1/2 cup	popping corn	125 mL
2 tbsp	unsalted butter, melted	30 mL
1/2 tsp	fine sea salt	2 mL
1/2 tsp	ground cinnamon	2 mL
1/4 tsp	granulated sugar	1 mL

1. In a large deep saucepan, heat oil over medium heat. Add popping corn and stir well to coat. Cover pan and, shaking pan often, cook until corn stops popping, about 5 minutes. Immediately transfer to a large bowl.

2. Add butter, salt, cinnamon and sugar and toss to coat. Serve immediately.

Variation

Substitute 1/8 tsp (0.5 mL) ground nutmeg for the cinnamon for a festive wintery variation.

Thyme-Scented Popcorn

Makes about 6 cups (1.5 L)

A subtle fresh herb-flavored popcorn, which is wonderful as an appetizer passed to guests in paper bags or popcorn bags. Also try savory-flavored popcorn as a perfect crunchy addition to salads.

1 tbsp	olive oil	15 mL
1/2 cup	popping corn	125 mL
2 tbsp	unsalted butter, melted	30 mL
1/2 tsp	fine sea salt	2 mL
1/2 tsp	finely chopped fresh thyme	2 mL
1/4 tsp	granulated sugar	1 mL

1. In a large saucepan, heat oil over medium heat. Add popcorn and stir well to coat. Cover pan and, shaking pan often, cook until corn stops popping, about 5 minutes. Transfer to a bowl. Add butter, salt, thyme and sugar and toss well. Serve immediately.

Poultry and Meat

From *Classic Cocktail Meatballs* (page 470) to *Duck Confit Canapés* (page 479), *Citrus BBQ-Glazed Ribs* (page 468) to *Classic Buffalo Chicken Wings* (page 473), *appetizers made with poultry or meat often cater to our desire for decadent, finger-lickin' goodness. Because they are high in protein, meat-based appetizers are more filling than most, which means they are probably best-served at events such as a Super Bowl party, where dinner won't be served. Some, like pâtés (pages 462, 463 and 471), terrines (page 464) and rillettes (page 465) are on the rich side, so when planning quantity assume your guests will want only a few very satisfying tastes.*

Because meat is a pricey ingredient, it tends to be associated with luxury even though some appetizers such as chopped liver (page 475) and Tinga (page 466) are quite economical.

Japanese-Style Stuffed Mushroom Caps 460
Panko-Crusted Beef Marrow 461
Squash-Spiked Chicken Liver Pâté. 462
Bacon-Spiked Mushroom and
   Chicken Liver Pâté 463
Country Terrine. 464
Pork Rillettes 465
Tinga 466
Spice-Rubbed Rack of Lamb 467
Deviled Ham. 467
Citrus BBQ-Glazed Ribs. 468
Asian-Seared Beef Tenderloin. 468
Lebanese Meatballs with Garlic Dipping Sauce. . . 469
Classic Cocktail Meatballs 470
Potted Beef 471
Instant Pâté 471
Coconut-Crusted Mini Drumsticks 472
Classic Buffalo Chicken Wings 473

Pecan-Crusted Lamb Chops 474
Bacon-Spiked Chopped Liver Spread
   with Grilled Crostini. 475
Chicken and Black Bean Quesadillas 476
Tortilla Chip–Crusted Chicken with
   Avocado Ancho Chile Dip 477
Smoked Chicken 478
Smoked Chicken–Stuffed Yellow Pepper 479
Duck Confit Canapés 479
Maple-Glazed Bacon 480
Angel and Devil Grilled Salami with
   Cheddar Cheese Dip 480
Crisp Pancetta Canapés with
   Roasted Corn Salsa 481
Crispy Prosciutto Cups with
   Classic Mango Salsa 481
Sliced Steak with Horseradish and
   Roquefort Cheese. 482

Japanese-Style Stuffed Mushroom Caps

Makes about 40

The flavors in this reflect Chicken Tsukune, a Japanese meatball. Here a robustly flavored ground chicken mix is used to fill shiitake mushroom caps. All is brushed with a sweet soy-based glaze and baked. These are different and delicious.

Tips

When soaking the diced mushrooms, weigh down with a cup to ensure they remain submerged.

The shiitake mushrooms should be about average size. If they are too small, they will overcook in the time it takes to cook the chicken, becoming shriveled and dry.

To purée garlic: Use a sharp-toothed grater such as those made by Microplane.

- **Preheat oven to 400°F (200°C)**
- **2 baking sheets, lined with parchment paper**

4	black Chinese mushroom caps	4
1 tbsp	white miso	15 mL
1 tbsp	soy sauce	15 mL
1 tbsp	sake	15 mL
2 tsp	puréed gingerroot	10 mL
1	egg, beaten	1
2 tbsp	cornstarch	30 mL
4	green onions, white parts with a bit of green, minced	4
1 lb	ground chicken	500 g

Sauce

¼ cup	soy sauce	60 mL
2 tbsp	liquid honey	30 mL
1 tbsp	sake	15 mL
1 tbsp	mirin	15 mL
1 tsp	puréed garlic (see Tips, left)	5 mL
	Freshly ground black pepper	
40	fresh shiitake mushroom caps (see Tips, left)	40

1. In a small bowl, cover mushrooms with very hot water. Set aside for at least 20 minutes, until mushrooms are soft. Drain, remove stems and chop finely. Discard soaking liquid.

2. In a bowl, combine miso, soy sauce, sake, ginger, egg and cornstarch. Mix well. Stir in green onions and chopped dried mushrooms. Add chicken and mix well.

3. *Sauce:* In a small saucepan over medium heat, combine soy sauce, honey, sake, mirin, garlic, and pepper to taste. Bring to a boil and cook, stirring, until syrupy, about 3 minutes. Brush shiitake mushroom caps lightly on both sides and place on prepared baking sheets.

4. Place about 1 tbsp (15 mL) of chicken mixture on each mushroom cap and brush tops lightly with sauce. Bake in preheated oven until meat is no longer pink inside, about 15 minutes. Serve warm.

Panko-Crusted Beef Marrow

Makes about 10 servings

Marrow is vastly underused but is one of the most decadent flavors known to man. Marrow is to beef what foie gras is to goose.

Tip

You butcher can be your best friend. Be nice; be very nice and maybe they will remove the marrow from the bone for you. *To remove marrow yourself:* It requires a bit of work but is quite easy. Using a paring knife, gently cut around the marrow on one side of the bone ensuring not to cut into the marrow. Flip and repeat on the other side. Using a long flat-ended utensil gently push the marrow from the narrowest end until the marrow is released.

- **Preheat oven to 350°F (180°C)**
- **Ovenproof skillet**

2	pieces boneless beef marrow (each about 1½ to 2 oz/45 to 60 g) (see Tip, left)	2
¼ tsp	kosher salt	1 mL
Pinch	freshly ground black pepper	Pinch
1	egg, beaten	1
2 tbsp	panko bread crumbs	30 mL
1 tbsp	finely grated Parmesan cheese	15 mL
1 tbsp	olive oil	15 mL
10	Grilled Herbed Crostini (page 220)	10

1. Sprinkle marrow all over with salt and pepper. Place egg in a shallow bowl. In another shallow bowl, combine bread crumbs and Parmesan. Dip marrow in egg, turning to coat, then dip in crumb mixture, turning and pressing to coat. Discard any excess egg and crumbs.

2. In ovenproof skillet, heat oil over medium heat. Sear marrow until golden brown, about 2 minutes. Flip and transfer skillet to preheated oven and bake until marrow is soft to the touch and golden brown, 2 to 3 minutes. Transfer to a cutting board and cut each piece of marrow into 5 slices. Serve on grilled crostini.

Squash-Spiked Chicken Liver Pâté

Makes about 2 cups (500 mL)

Chicken liver pâtés are so easy to make, yet seem so impressive. This version is lightened up with the addition of roasted squash and herb-infused fresh cheese. A splash of eau de vie or cognac completes the flavor profile. Strongly flavored, this is best served on plain crackers or sliced baguette.

Tips

For best results, roast the squash, rather than steaming it. (The flavor will be more intense and the squash will be less watery.) You will need half of a good size acorn or butternut squash. Simply cut the squash in half, scoop out the seeds and cover in foil. Place in preheated oven (400°F/200°C) until flesh is soft, about 45 minutes. Set aside until cool enough to handle. Scoop out flesh, transfer to work bowl fitted with metal blade and purée. Measure out 1 cup (250 mL) of purée and return to work bowl. Complete the recipe.

Use a prepared cheese such as Boursin or leftover Quark Claqueret (page 376).

1 cup	puréed roasted squash (see Tips, left)	125 mL
1 tbsp	olive oil	15 mL
1	small onion, chopped	1
2	cloves garlic, coarsely chopped	2
8 oz	chicken livers, trimmed and coarsely chopped	250 g
½ cup	herb-infused cream cheese (see Tips, left)	125 mL
1 tbsp	eau de vie, such as kirsch or Poire Williams or cognac, optional	15 mL
½ tsp	salt	2 mL
½ tsp	cracked black peppercorns	2 mL
	Finely chopped Italian flat-leaf parsley	

1. In a skillet, heat oil over medium heat. Add onion and cook, stirring, until softened, about 3 minutes. Add garlic and chicken livers and cook until lightly browned and just a hint of pink remains in the center of livers, about 5 minutes. Let cool slightly.

2. In a food processor fitted with metal blade, process chicken liver mixture, squash, cream cheese, eau de vie, if using, salt and peppercorns until smooth. Transfer to a serving bowl. Garnish with chopped parsley. Cover and refrigerate for at least 3 hours or for up to 2 days.

Bacon-Spiked Mushroom and Chicken Liver Pâté

Makes about 2 cups (500 mL)

Mushrooms, bacon and a good dash of cognac add oomph to what is basically a simple chicken liver pâté. Serve with sliced baguette or crostini.

Tips

Cremini mushrooms have more robust flavor than white mushrooms, which works well with the chicken livers in this recipe. But white mushrooms can easily be substituted.

Italian flat-leaf parsley is preferred because it has much more flavor than the curly leaf variety.

1 tbsp	oil (approx.)	15 mL
2	strips thick-cut bacon, diced	2
1	onion, chopped	1
2	cloves garlic, chopped	2
8 oz	cremini mushrooms, trimmed and sliced (see Tips, left)	250 g
1 lb	chicken livers, trimmed and patted dry	500 g
1/4 cup	brandy	60 mL
1 tsp	salt	5 mL
1 tsp	cracked black peppercorns	5 mL
1/2 cup	Italian flat-leaf parsley leaves	125 mL

1. In a skillet, heat oil over medium-high heat. Add bacon and cook, stirring, until browned and crispy. Using a slotted spoon, transfer to a paper towel–lined plate to drain. Set aside.

2. Add onion and garlic to pan and cook, stirring, just until softened, about 2 minutes. Add mushrooms and cook, stirring, until they brown and lose their liquid, about 7 minutes. Using a slotted spoon, transfer to a food processor fitted with metal blade.

3. Add chicken livers to pan, adding more oil, if necessary, and cook, stirring, until browned on the exterior and just a hint of pink remains in the center, about 5 minutes. Add brandy, salt and peppercorns and cook, stirring, for 2 minutes. Transfer to food processor and process until smooth. Add parsley and reserved bacon and process until finely chopped and blended. Transfer to a serving bowl. Cover and refrigerate for at least 3 hours or for up to 3 days.

Country Terrine

Makes about 1½ lbs (750 g)

*Why pay a fortune
for prepared pâtés or
terrines when you can
so easily make your
own? This one has a
beautiful mild flavor,
and the dots of green
pistachio add great
visual appeal. Serve
on sliced baguette
with thin slices of
gherkins or cornichons
and/or a small bowl
of the best Dijon
mustard. Celery Root
Rémoulade (page 432)
also makes a good
accompaniment.*

Tip

You can buy pistachios shelled and peeled or peel them yourself. *To peel pistachios:* Drop shelled nuts into a saucepan of rapidly boiling water. Return to a boil and boil for 1 minute. Transfer to a colander and drain. Spread nuts on a clean tea towel and rub until the skins come off.

- **6-cup (1.5 L) loaf pan or crockery terrine, lightly greased**
- **Instant-read thermometer**

4 oz	pancetta, coarsely chopped	125 g
½ cup	whole peeled pistachios (see Tip, left)	125 mL
1 lb	lean ground pork	500 g
1 lb	ground veal	500 g
¼ cup	brandy or cognac	60 mL
2 tbsp	fresh thyme leaves	30 mL
1 tsp	salt	5 mL
1 tsp	cracked black peppercorns	5 mL
2	eggs, beaten	2

1. In a food processor with metal blade, pulse pancetta and pistachios until finely chopped, about 8 times. Add pork, veal, brandy, thyme, salt, peppercorns and eggs and pulse until blended, about 15 times. Transfer to a bowl, cover and refrigerate overnight to allow flavors to blend.

2. Preheat oven to 400°F (200°C). Transfer meat mixture to prepared loaf pan and pack tightly. Place in a larger pan filled with enough boiling water to come halfway up to the top of the dish. Cover tightly with foil.

3. Bake in preheated oven until an instant-read thermometer inserted into the center reads 165°F (74°C), about 1½ hours. Let cool in pan on a rack for 15 minutes then refrigerate for at least 3 hours until thoroughly chilled before serving. Store in refrigerator for up to 3 days.

Pork Rillettes

Makes about 4 cups (1 L)

If you are fat phobic, move on to the next recipe. Rillettes are, basically, lightly seasoned pork cooked in fresh lard. It is a classic French country dish and, if you're a fan, it is delicious. Serve cold with sliced baguette or country bread, accompanied by grainy mustard and good cornichons.

Tip

The liquid (wine) should have evaporated during cooking. If that didn't happen, boil the fat down for about 10 minutes to evaporate the wine.

● **Preheat oven to 275°F (140°C)**

2 cups	dry white wine	500 mL
6 oz	pork fat	175 g
2	onions, sliced	2
4	cloves garlic, halved	4
4	thyme sprigs	4
1 tsp	black peppercorns	5 mL
2	bay leaves	2
6	whole cloves	6
2 lbs	pork shoulder, cut into 4 pieces	1 kg
	Sea salt and freshly ground black pepper	

1. In a Dutch oven, combine wine, fat, onions, garlic, thyme, peppercorns, bay leaves and cloves. Heat over low heat until fat is rendered. Add pork and toss to coat. Cover and cook in preheated oven, turning the meat several times, until meat is very tender and most of the liquid is evaporated, about 4 hours.

2. Lift out meat and transfer to a cutting board. Scrape off any seasonings and, using two forks, shred. Set aside.

3. Place a strainer over a bowl and add contents of Dutch oven. Strain and discard solids. Scoop off about ¼ cup (60 mL) of the fat and set aside. Add shredded pork to bowl and toss well. Season to taste with salt and pepper. Pack pork (with fat) into an earthenware pot and cover with reserved fat. Cover tightly with plastic and let cool. Refrigerate for at least 2 days to allow flavor to mellow or for up to 10 days. Before serving, let stand at room temperature for 20 minutes to allow flavors to bloom.

Tinga

Makes about 6 cups (1.5 L)

This dish, which is Mexican in origin, is basically a pork stew seasoned with chorizo and chipotle pepper. It is traditionally served with homemade tostadas (deep-fried tortillas) and topped with queso fresco, but here Monterey Jack cheese is used. It makes a hearty dip for tortilla chips. It's a bit of work to prepare, but actually improves if made a day or so ahead and reheated (see Tips, below).

Tips

If you are making this ahead of time, do not stir in the cheese until you have reheated the mixture and are ready to serve.

Many butchers sell cut up pork stewing meat, which is fine to use in this recipe.

You can buy ready-made tostadas or you can make your own. Simply fry fresh tortillas in oil until crisp and brown, about 1 minute. Drain on paper towel and season with salt.

2 tbsp	oil or good-quality lard, divided	30 mL
1 lb	trimmed boneless pork shoulder or blade (butt), cut into 1½-inch (4 cm) cubes and patted dry (see Tips, left)	500 g
2	cloves garlic, minced	2
1 tsp	dried thyme leaves or 2 thyme sprigs	5 mL
1 tsp	salt	5 mL
1 tsp	cracked black peppercorns	5 mL
2	onions, finely chopped	2
4 oz	fresh chorizo, removed from casings	125 mL
1 tsp	dried oregano	5 mL
1	can (28 oz/796 mL) diced tomatoes with juice	1
1	chipotle pepper in adobo sauce, minced	1
2 cups	shredded Monterey Jack cheese	500 mL
	Salt and freshly ground black pepper	
	Tostadas or tortilla chips	

1. In a Dutch oven, heat 1 tbsp (15 mL) of the oil over medium-high heat. Add pork and cook, stirring, until nicely browned. Add garlic, thyme, salt and peppercorns and cook, stirring, for 1 minute. Add water to cover and bring to a boil. Skim off any foam. Reduce heat to low, cover and simmer until meat is fork tender, about 40 minutes. Remove lid and simmer until pork is almost falling apart, about 20 minutes longer. Using a slotted spoon, transfer pork to a cutting board and shred. Set liquid aside.

2. In a skillet, heat remaining tbsp (15 mL) oil over medium-high heat. Add pork, onions and chorizo and cook, stirring, until pork is well browned, about 10 minutes. Add oregano and cook, stirring, for 1 minute. Add tomatoes with juice, chipotle pepper and reserved cooking liquid and simmer, stirring and scraping up brown bits from bottom of the pan, until mixture is reduced and thickened, about 10 minutes. Stir in cheese (see Tips, left). Season to taste with salt and pepper. Serve warm with tortilla chips.

Spice-Rubbed Rack of Lamb

Makes about 8 servings

Rack of lamb is nature's gift to the appetizer — they're like lamb lollipops! Serve with a cool Tzatziki (page 14) or Smoky Eggplant Dip with Yogurt (page 17).

Tip

Having various spice mixtures labeled and ready to go for everyday use in a pepper mill makes creating meals so easy. For this recipe, combine equal parts whole coriander seeds, cumin seeds and fennel seeds in a pepper mill and grind when ready for use.

- **Preheat oven to 450°F (230°C)**
- **Ovenproof skillet**

1 tsp	ground spice mixture (see Tip, left)	5 mL
1	rack of lamb (about 8 oz/250 g)	1
1 tbsp	extra virgin olive oil	15 mL
Pinch	salt	Pinch

1. On a plate, press ground spice mixture evenly over meaty side of the lamb.
2. In ovenproof skillet, heat oil over medium-high heat. Sear lamb, meat side down, until a nice crust has developed, about 5 minutes. Transfer skillet to preheated oven and roast until lamb is firm to the touch, about 15 minutes for medium-rare. Season with salt.
3. Transfer to a cutting board and let rest for 10 minutes. Slice into chops and serve hot.

Deviled Ham

Makes about 2 cups (500 mL)

This retro-style spread can round out an appetizer tray. It tastes great on simple sliced baguette, celery sticks, Belgian endive or, for something a little different, leaves of radicchio. Leftovers make a delicious sandwich spread.

Tip

For a mildly spicy spread, use 2 tbsp (30 mL) of banana peppers. If you like more punch, use the larger quantity.

8 oz	ham, cut into chunks	250 mL
6	gherkins (sweet or sour)	6
1	roasted red pepper	1
3 tbsp	mayonnaise	45 mL
2 to 3 tbsp	chopped pickled banana peppers (see Tip, left)	30 to 45 mL
1 tsp	Dijon mustard	5 mL
Dash	Worcestershire sauce	Dash

1. In a food processor fitted with metal blade, pulse ham, gherkins, roasted pepper, mayonnaise, banana peppers to taste, Dijon mustard and Worcestershire sauce until chopped and blended, about 30 times. Cover and refrigerate for at least 1 hour or for up to 3 days.

Citrus BBQ-Glazed Ribs

Makes about 5 servings

Individual ribs are a welcome hors d'oeuvre for any appetizer party.

Tips

Use Basic Barbecue Sauce (page 553) or your own homemade or favorite store-bought version.

To take the flavor to the next level, preheat a barbecue to high and grill whole racks of ribs until caramelized on one side, 3 to 4 minutes per side. Transfer to a cutting board and cut into individual or two-rib portions and serve.

- **Preheat oven to 300°F (150°C)**
- **Roasting pan**

¾ cup	barbecue sauce (see Tips, left)	175 mL
½ cup	minced green onions	125 mL
¼ cup	each freshly squeezed lemon and orange juice	60 mL
1 tbsp	liquid honey	15 mL
1	rack pork baby back ribs (about 1½ lbs/750 g)	1

1. In a bowl combine barbecue sauce, green onions, lemon juice, orange juice and honey and mix well.

2. In roasting pan, combine ribs with sauce and, with your hands, rub the sauce into every nook and cranny. Bake in preheated oven until caramelized and meat is beginning to pull away from the bone, about 1½ hours. Transfer to a cutting board and cut ribs into individual or two-rib portions and serve.

Asian-Seared Beef Tenderloin

Makes about 20 slices

If you love the taste of Asian ingredients you will love this simply prepared beef appetizer that will melt in your mouth.

Tip

This recipe could be used with other prime cuts of beef, namely strip loin and rib steak.

½ tsp	toasted sesame oil	2 mL
2	medallions beef tenderloin, each 4 oz (125 g) (see Tip, left)	2
1 tsp	soy sauce	5 mL
1 tsp	thinly sliced green onions	5 mL
½ tsp	puréed gingerroot	2 mL

1. In a skillet, heat oil over medium-high heat. Sear beef, flat side down, until bottom is caramelized, 2 to 3 minutes per side. Turn medallions on side and sear, turning often, until caramelized all over, about 5 minutes. Transfer to a cutting board and let rest for 10 minutes. Cut into 20 thin slices and lay flat on a decorative platter. Drizzle with soy sauce and garnish with green onions and ginger. Serve immediately or keep beef on a platter, without garnish, covered in the refrigerator for up to 3 hours and garnish just before serving.

Lebanese Meatballs with Garlic Dipping Sauce

Makes about 36

Enjoy these yummy little meatballs with their mildly Middle Eastern flavors not only because they taste so good but also because the addition of bulgur, a whole grain, makes them more healthful than if they were made exclusively from meat. The garlic-spiked dipping sauce provides a delicious finish but if you're looking for something a little different, substitute Easy Tahini Dip (page 23).

Tip

Za'atar is a blend of dried herbs and sesame seeds that is used in Middle Eastern cuisine. It is available in specialty shops but if you can't find it, you can make your own. *To make za'atar:* In a small bowl, combine 2 tbsp (30 mL) fresh thyme leaves, 1 tbsp (15 mL) toasted sesame seeds and 1 tsp (5 mL) each ground sumac and coarse sea salt.

- **Preheat oven to 350°F (180°C)**
- **Rimmed baking sheet, lined with parchment paper**

1/3 cup	fine bulgur	75 mL
3/4 cup	cold water	175 mL
1 lb	lean ground beef or lamb	500 g
1/2 cup	finely chopped Italian flat-leaf parsley	125 mL
1	onion, grated	1
1 tbsp	ground cumin	15 mL
1 tsp	salt or to taste	5 mL
1/2 tsp	hot paprika	2 mL
	Freshly ground black pepper	

Garlic Dipping Sauce

1/4 cup	plain Greek-style (pressed) yogurt (see Tips, page 341)	60 mL
2 tbsp	freshly squeezed lemon juice	30 mL
4	cloves garlic, quartered	4
2 tsp	za'atar (see Tips, left)	10 mL
1/2 tsp	salt	2 mL
1/4 cup	extra virgin olive oil	60 mL

1. In a bowl, combine bulgur and water. Stir well and set aside until water is absorbed, about 10 minutes. Stir well. Drain off any excess water, if necessary.

2. In a bowl, combine soaked bulgur, beef, parsley, onion, cumin, salt, paprika, and pepper to taste. Using your hands, mix well. Shape into about 36 meatballs, each about the size of a walnut and place on prepared baking sheet. Bake in preheated oven until meat is no longer pink inside, about 15 minutes.

3. *Garlic Dipping Sauce:* Meanwhile, in a food processor fitted with metal blade, pulse yogurt, lemon juice, garlic, za'atar and salt to chop and blend garlic, about 5 times. With motor running, add olive oil through the feed tube until blended. Transfer to a small serving bowl. Serve warm meatballs on toothpicks accompanied by dipping sauce.

Classic Cocktail Meatballs

Makes about 25 meatballs

Classics are just that for a reason. Meatballs are timeless and easily satisfy those carnivorous guests.

Tip

These hors d'oeuvres could easily be turned into plated appetizers. Preheat the broiler. Soak eight 6-inch (15 cm) bamboo skewers for 30 minutes. Skewer 3 meatballs on each and place on a parchment paper–lined baking sheet. Sprinkle meatballs evenly with 1 tbsp (15 mL) Parmesan cheese and broil until cheese is melted, about 1 minute. Place each skewer on a plate and garnish with sauce.

1	slice egg bread, crusts removed	1
2 tbsp	whole milk	30 mL
12 oz	lean ground beef	375 g
1 tbsp	pure maple syrup	15 mL
1 tbsp	stone-ground mustard	15 mL
½ tsp	salt	2 mL
¼ tsp	freshly ground black pepper	1 mL
2 tbsp	olive oil	30 mL
1 cup	tomato sauce	250 mL
½ cup	water	125 mL

1. In a bowl, combine bread and milk and, using your hands crumble the bread into milk, creating something resembling a bread purée. Add beef, maple syrup, mustard, salt and pepper and mix to combine. Scoop 1 tbsp (15 mL) of the meat mixture and shape into ball. Continue with the rest of the mixture. Place on a baking sheet, cover and refrigerate until firm, about 1 hour or overnight.

2. In a large skillet, heat oil over medium heat. Sear meatballs until bottoms are golden brown, about 3 minutes. Flip over and cook until golden brown, about 2 minutes. Add tomato sauce and water and bring to a boil. Reduce heat to low and simmer until meatballs are no longer pink inside, about 5 minutes. Serve immediately with toothpicks.

Potted Beef

Makes about 3 cups (750 mL)

Whenever you serve roast beef, make extra so you can prepare this delicious nibble. It is spicy and intriguing and people gobble it up. It is also a great way to use up almost any leftover beef, including steak. Serve it on toast points, accompanied by cornichons, or crackers and plain baguette.

8	anchovy fillets	8
1	small red onion, quartered	1
2	cloves garlic, coarsely chopped	2
1 tsp	salt	5 mL
½ tsp	cracked black peppercorns	2 mL
1	piece (about 1 by ¼ inch/2.5 by 0.5 cm) mace, crumbled, or ¼ tsp (1 mL) freshly grated nutmeg, optional	1
2 cups	cubed (½ inch/1 cm) cooked beef	500 mL
½ cup	melted or clarified butter	125 mL

1. In a food processor fitted with metal blade, pulse anchovies, red onion, garlic, salt, peppercorns and mace, if using, until finely chopped, about 10 times, stopping and scraping down sides of the bowl once or twice. Add beef and melted butter and process until smooth, about 30 seconds. Cover and refrigerate for up to 3 days.

Instant Pâté

Makes about 2 cups (500 mL)

This is a classic because it's so easy to make and delicious. Put a small terrine of this out for a party and watch it disappear. Serve on sliced baguette or your favorite crackers.

1 lb	chicken livers, trimmed	500 g
6 oz	unsalted butter, softened	175 g
¼ cup	coarsely chopped sweet onion, such as Vidalia	60 mL
2	cloves garlic	2
2 tbsp	fresh thyme leaves	30 mL
2 tbsp	cognac or brandy	30 mL
1 tsp	salt	5 mL
1 tsp	cracked black peppercorns	5 mL
	Baguette or crackers	

1. In a pot of boiling water, cook chicken livers until just a hint of pink remains in the center, about 3 minutes. Drain. Transfer to a food processor fitted with metal blade. Add butter, onion and garlic. Purée until smooth. Add thyme, cognac, salt and peppercorns and process until blended. Transfer to a serving dish. Cover and refrigerate for at least 3 hours or for up to 2 days.

Coconut-Crusted Mini Drumsticks

Makes 12 drumsticks

Here's a perfect alternative to Classic Buffalo Chicken Wings (page 473). These drumsticks will be loved by guests of all ages. Serve for lunch or dinner parties.

Tips

Chicken wing drumsticks are the thicker, drumstick-shaped portion of the wing; they are sometimes called drumettes. *To split a chicken wing:* Using a sharp knife, cut the chicken wing at the joint and separate the wing portion, also known as the wingette, and the drumstick portion, which is the drumette.

Pair coconut with any tropical fruit dip such as Mango Dip (page 68). It would be wonderful with these drumsticks.

- **Baking sheet, lined with parchment paper**

1¼ lbs	chicken wing drumsticks (see Tips, left)	625 g
2 tbsp	unsweetened coconut milk	30 mL
2 tbsp	tomato ketchup	30 mL
1 tbsp	packed brown sugar	15 mL
2 tsp	hot Asian chile sauce, such as sambal oelek	10 mL
½ cup	desiccated unsweetened coconut	125 mL
½ tsp	salt	2 mL

1. On a cutting board, using a sharp knife, remove knuckle of each chicken wing. Scrape and pull the meat down toward the opposite end of bone, revealing a clean bone resembling a chicken "lollipop."

2. In a bowl, combine coconut milk, ketchup, brown sugar and hot sauce. Add chicken and toss to evenly coat. Cover and refrigerate for at least 3 hours or for up to 1 day.

3. Preheat oven to 475°F (240°C).

4. Remove chicken from marinade and pat dry to remove excess marinade. Discard marinade. Place chicken in a clean bowl and add coconut. Toss to evenly coat. Place at least 1 inch (2.5 cm) apart on prepared baking sheet. Bake in preheated oven until coating is crisp and golden brown and juices run clear when chicken is pierced, about 15 minutes. Season with salt and serve immediately.

Classic Buffalo Chicken Wings

Makes about 12 wings

Not just for the Super Bowl! These wings can be served at an elegant cocktail party, too, just supply some extra napkins!

Tips

These wings are wonderful on their own but are fantastic when served with Blue Cheese Dip (page 38).

Chipotle powder is made from finely grated smoked jalapeños and adds a wonderful smoky and spicy flavor to your foods. It can be found in the dry herb and spice sections of most large supermarkets. Smoked paprika or ancho chile powder would also substitute nicely here.

Often times your butcher will either have split chicken wings available or they will offer to split them for you while you wait. This is quite easy to do yourself, too. Using a sharp knife, split the drumette from the wing right at the joint and remove the wing tip. Discard the wing tip or reserve for another use.

- **Candy/deep-fry thermometer**

	Oil	
	Oil	
1/3 cup	all-purpose flour	75 mL
1/2 tsp	salt	2 mL
1/4 tsp	freshly ground black pepper	1 mL
1/4 tsp	cayenne pepper	1 mL
2 tbsp	tomato ketchup	30 mL
1 tbsp	unsalted butter, melted	15 mL
1/4 tsp	hot pepper sauce	1 mL
1/4 tsp	chipotle powder (see Tips, left)	1 mL
1 lb	chicken wings, split (see Tips, left)	500 g

1. In a Dutch oven, heat 4 inches (10 cm) of oil over medium-high heat to 350°F (180°C). (You can also use a deep fryer; follow the manufacturer's instructions.)

2. In a bowl, combine flour, salt, black pepper and cayenne pepper. Set aside.

3. In a large bowl, combine ketchup, butter, hot pepper sauce and chipotle powder. Set aside at room temperature.

4. Dredge wings in the flour mixture, shaking off excess. Fry wings in hot oil, in batches, until golden brown and juices run clear when chicken is pierced, about 10 minutes. Using a slotted spoon, remove from oil and carefully shake off excess oil. Immediately add to sauce and toss to coat. Serve hot.

Pecan-Crusted Lamb Chops

Makes 8 to 9 chops

*Mustard and lamb
work very well
together. Serve
with a selection
of your favorite
mustards or try our
Pommery Mustard
Dip (page 61) or
Honey Mustard Dip
(page 60).*

Tip

Rack of lamb comes in
many different sizes, from
the smallest being 8 oz
(250 g) to the largest
2½-lb (1.25 kg) racks.
Any size would do for
this recipe but you will
need to adjust cooking
time and amount of crust
ingredients accordingly.

- **Large ovenproof skillet**

1 tbsp	extra virgin olive oil	15 mL
1 tsp	minced garlic	5 mL
½ tsp	freshly ground black pepper	2 mL
1 lb	rack of lamb	500 g
2 tbsp	unsalted butter, divided	30 mL
1 tsp	olive oil	5 mL

Crust

½ cup	ground pecans	125 mL
1 tsp	granulated sugar	5 mL
Pinch	salt	Pinch
Pinch	freshly ground black pepper	Pinch
3 tbsp	Dijon mustard	45 mL

1. In a shallow dish, combine extra virgin olive oil, garlic and pepper. Add lamb and spread marinade over to evenly coat. Cover and refrigerate for at least 3 hours or preferably overnight.

2. Preheat oven to 450°F (230°C).

3. In a skillet, heat 1 tbsp (15 mL) of the butter and oil over medium-high heat. Add lamb, meaty side down, and sear until caramelized, about 5 minutes. Transfer to a cutting board and let cool to room temperature, about 15 minutes. Cut into individual chops.

4. *Crust:* In a bowl, combine pecans, sugar, salt and pepper and mix well to combine. Place mustard in another bowl. Dip chops first into mustard to evenly coat, then brush off excess. Dip into pecan crust, turning and pressing to coat evenly. Discard any excess mustard and crust mixture.

5. In large ovenproof skillet, melt remaining butter over medium heat. Sear lamb until golden brown, about 2 minutes. Transfer skillet to preheated oven and roast until crust is golden brown and lamb is just pink inside, 6 to 8 minutes for medium. Let rest for 5 minutes before serving.

Bacon-Spiked Chopped Liver Spread with Grilled Crostini

Makes 30 crostini

The bubbies of the world may disagree, but the addition of bacon creates an additional layer of flavor that transports this recipe from a classic Shabbat dinner meal to a five-star pâté.

Tip

A wonderful way to serve this is with Caramelized Onions (page 552) spooned on top of the liver.

1 tbsp	olive oil	15 mL
1½ cups	diced onions	375 mL
1 lb	chicken livers	500 g
2	slices bacon	2
2	hard-cooked eggs, peeled (see Tips, page 63)	2
½ tsp	kosher salt	2 mL
¼ tsp	freshly ground black pepper	1 mL
30	Grilled Herbed Crostini (page 220)	30
2 tbsp	finely chopped Italian parsley	30 mL

1. In a skillet, heat oil over medium-low heat. Add onions and cook, stirring, until translucent, about 10 minutes. Transfer onions to a bowl and set aside.

2. Return skillet to medium heat. Add chicken livers and bacon to skillet and cook, stirring, until livers are a bit pink inside, 6 to 8 minutes. Remove from heat.

3. In a food processor fitted with a metal blade, combine livers, bacon, onions, eggs, salt and pepper. Pulse about 20 times, stopping every five pulses to scrape down the sides, until smooth. Transfer to a bowl, cover and refrigerate for at least 3 hours until chilled or up to 3 days.

4. Place crostini on a platter and dollop about 1 tbsp (15 mL) liver spread on top. Garnish with a pinch of chopped parsley. Serve immediately.

Chicken and Black Bean Quesadillas

Makes 16 wedges

This Mexican appetizer is casual enough to be served for lunch and can be refined enough to serve as an evening party appetizer. For a more elegant presentation garnish each wedge with a dollop of Avocado Corn Salsa (page 83).

4 cups	chicken broth or water	1 L
2 tbsp	barbecue sauce	30 mL
1	lime, cut in half	1
2	skinless boneless chicken breasts	2
8	8-inch (20 cm) whole wheat flour tortillas	8
1¼ cups	Black Bean Spread (page 57)	300 mL
2 cups	shredded Manchego cheese	500 mL
4 tsp	olive oil, separated	20 mL
1½ cups	Roasted Red Pepper Coulis (page 543)	375 mL

1. In a saucepan, bring broth, barbecue sauce and lime to a simmer over medium-high heat. Add chicken and simmer until firm to the touch and no longer pink inside, about 20 minutes. Remove chicken from broth, transfer to a cutting board and let rest for 10 minutes. Discard poaching liquid. Thinly slice chicken.

2. Place 4 of the tortillas on a work surface and spoon Black Bean Spread on tortillas, dividing equally. Spread evenly over tortillas. Sprinkle with cheese and arrange chicken on top. Cover with remaining tortillas and press to seal.

3. In a large skillet, heat 1 tsp (5 mL) of the oil over medium heat. Add quesadilla and cook until bottom is crisp, about 3 minutes. Flip over and cook until crisp and cheese is melted, about 2 minutes. Transfer to a cutting board and cut into quarters. Repeat with remaining quesadillas, adjusting heat and adding oil as necessary between batches. Serve hot with Roasted Red Pepper Coulis.

Tortilla Chip–Crusted Chicken with Avocado Ancho Chile Dip

Makes 6 servings

This simple Mexican-inspired hors d'oeuvre is perfect for a casual lunch party and tasty enough to be served with a small side salad as a plated dinner appetizer.

Tip

If the tortilla chips are salted you may want to reduce the salt in the recipe. Use your judgment.

- **Preheat oven to 350°F (180°C)**
- **Baking sheet, lined with parchment paper**

2 tsp	Dijon mustard	10 mL
½ tsp	chipotle powder (see Tips, page 473)	2 mL
½ tsp	salt	2 mL
1½ cups	crushed tortilla chips (see Tip, left)	375 mL
1 lb	boneless skinless chicken thighs (about 6 thighs), cut in half	500 g
2 tbsp	olive oil	30 mL
½ cup	Avocado Ancho Chile Dip (page 28)	125 mL

1. In a bowl, combine mustard, chipotle powder and salt and mix well to combine. Place crushed tortilla chips in another bowl.

2. Add chicken to mustard mixture and toss to coat. Dip into tortilla chips, turning and pressing to coat. Place on prepared baking sheet, at least 2 inches (5 cm) apart. Bake in preheated oven until golden brown and juices run clear when chicken is pierced, 7 to 8 minutes. Serve immediately with Avocado Ancho Chile Dip.

Smoked Chicken

Makes 3 cups (750 mL) shredded

This versatile ingredient can take the place of a roasted chicken in most recipes.

Tips

To prepare a gas barbecue grill for indirect heat, you need a grill with 2 or more burners. Preheat one burner of grill to medium-low heat and leave the other off (if you have 3 burners, heat 2 of them to low). Place food on grill over unlit burner. For a charcoal barbecue grill, heat coals, then push warm coals to one side of pit. Place food on grill over opposite side of pit.

Typically the wood from any fruit or nut you enjoy eating will work for smoking; apple, cherry and pecan wood chips would all work well in this recipe.

For the easiest way to truss a chicken, cut two pieces of butcher's twine about 10 inches (25 cm) long. Tuck wings under the chicken and wrap one piece of string around the wings pulling tight against the chicken and tie to secure. Wrap the second string around the thighs pushing the legs against the chicken and tie the string to secure.

- **Instant-read thermometer**
- **Shallow foil pan or double-layer of heavy-duty foil shaped into a shallow pan**

1 lb	applewood chips	500 g
2 cups	water	500 mL
3 lb	whole chicken	1.5 kg
1	head garlic, cut in half crosswise	1
6	thyme sprigs	6
3	rosemary sprigs	3
½ tsp	salt	2 mL

1. In a bowl, combine half of the wood chips with water and let soak for 1 hour.

2. Meanwhile, preheat barbecue grill to medium-low heat for indirect heat (see Tips, left).

3. Drain water off wood chips and add dry chips to bowl. Place one-third of the chips into foil pan. Place pan over hot side of preheated grill, close lid and grill until smoke is released from package, about 20 minutes.

4. Meanwhile, stuff garlic, thyme and rosemary into chicken cavity and truss (see Tips, left). Sprinkle outside of chicken with salt. Transfer to unlit side of grill, close lid and smoke, replacing the wood chips every 45 minutes in equal portions, until thermometer inserted in the thigh of chicken registers 165°F (74°C), about 2 hours. Transfer to a cutting board and let cool for up to 30 minutes.

5. When chicken is cool enough to handle, remove and discard skin and bones. Using your fingers, shred chicken into pieces.

Smoked Chicken–Stuffed Yellow Pepper

Makes 8 servings

This makes a perfect hand-held appetizer. The sweetness of the yellow pepper contrasts with the smoked chicken beautifully.

Tip

For this recipe, your hands are your best tools to arrange the ingredients on the pepper strips.

1 cup	coarsely chopped smoked chicken (page 478)	250 mL
1 tbsp	finely chopped drained oil-packed sun-dried tomato	15 mL
1 tbsp	finely diced red onion	15 mL
1 tbsp	mayonnaise	15 mL
1 tsp	Dijon mustard	5 mL
1	yellow bell pepper, cut lengthwise into 8 strips (see Tip, left)	1
1 tsp	finely chopped fresh parsley leaves	5 mL

1. In a bowl, combine chicken, sun-dried tomato, onion, mayonnaise and mustard and mix well to combine. Place pepper strips on a platter with natural curve facing up. Arrange chicken mixture on top, dividing equally. Garnish with parsley and serve. To make ahead, assemble, cover and refrigerate for up to 3 hours ahead and garnish with parsley just before serving.

Duck Confit Canapés

Makes 12 canapés

Duck and fruit are a classic pairing. Here crisp Granny Smith apples add a wonderful tartness to the duck — a perfect marriage of flavors.

Tip

Duck confit is a delightful French recipe in which the duck legs are cooked slowly in their own fat. Today, however, very good quality confit can be found in gourmet food shops.

12	Grilled Herbed Crostini (page 220)	12
¾ cup	coarsely chopped duck confit (see Tip, left)	175 mL
1 tbsp	thinly sliced green onions	15 mL
1 tbsp	finely diced peeled Granny Smith apple	15 mL
1 tbsp	Roasted Red Pepper Vinaigrette (page 541)	15 mL

1. Place crostini on a surface and spoon confit on top, dividing equally. Garnish with green onions and apple and drizzle with about ¼ tsp (1 mL) vinaigrette. Repeat with remaining crostini and ingredients. Serve immediately.

Maple-Glazed Bacon

Makes 12 hors d'oeuvres

The amazing contrast of salty and sweet will arouse your senses for sure!

Tip

Although maple syrup is the sweet ingredient of choice, other ingredients would work just as well. Palm sugar, brown sugar, liquid honey or agave syrup would all be perfect.

- **Preheat oven to 400°F (200°C)**
- **Ovenproof skillet**

2 tbsp	water	30 mL
6 oz	salted pork belly	175 g
1 tbsp	pure maple syrup (see Tip, left)	15 mL

1. In ovenproof skillet, combine water and pork and bring to a boil over medium heat. Transfer skillet to preheated oven. Bake, flipping pork every 5 minutes, until golden brown, 20 to 25 minutes. Add maple syrup and turn to coat. Let stand until cool to the touch. Leave oven on.

2. On a cutting board, cut the belly into 6 equal slices and then cut each in half to make 12 squares. Return to skillet and bake until golden brown, about 10 minutes. Serve immediately.

Angel and Devil Grilled Salami with Cheddar Cheese Dip

Makes 8 servings

Here's a very sweet and spicy treat for your senses.

Tip

This makes a perfect appetizer for children, but you may want to omit the hot pepper sauce and choose a mild salami.

1 tsp	agave syrup	5 mL
¼ tsp	hot pepper sauce	1 mL
8	slices salami, each ½ inch (1 cm) thick	8
½ cup	Cheddar Cheese Fondue (page 396)	125 mL

1. In a bowl, combine agave syrup and hot sauce. Add salami and toss to coat. Cover and refrigerate for at least 1 hour or overnight.

2. Meanwhile, preheat barbecue grill to high.

3. Grill salami, until grill marks appear, for 1 minute. Turn each slice 45 degrees to create the restaurant style hatch marks and grill for 1 minute until caramelized. Flip over and grill until second side is caramelized, about 2 minutes. Serve immediately with Cheddar Cheese Fondue.

Crisp Pancetta Canapés with Roasted Corn Salsa

Makes 6 canapés

Pancetta makes the ideal base for canapés. Here the salty-sweet combination of pancetta with freshly roasted corn is delicious.

Tip

To blanch vegetables: Cook in boiling salted water until tender-crisp, then plunge into ice water to stop the cooking process. Here it achieves a beautifully vibrant green asparagus tip.

- **Preheat oven to 350°F (180°C)**
- **Baking sheet, lined with parchment paper**

6	slices pancetta	6
6 tbsp	Roasted Corn Salsa (page 82)	90 mL
6	asparagus tips, blanched and cut in half lengthwise (see Tip, left)	6

1. Place pancetta slices on prepared baking sheet, at least 2 inches (5 cm) apart. Bake in preheated oven until crisp, 15 to 20 minutes. Transfer to a paper towel–lined plate to drain off excess fat. Place pancetta crisps on a serving platter and top with corn salsa and two asparagus pieces. Serve immediately.

Crispy Prosciutto Cups with Classic Mango Salsa

Makes 20 cups

A very salty and sweet combination that you'll never forget.

Tip

Instead of deep-frying, the prosciutto can easily be crisped on the stovetop by warming a nonstick pan over medium heat and cooking until crisp on one side, about 3 minutes. Turn and cook another 3 minutes. (Baking will not cause the prosciutto to curl as much but will create a great base.) Remove and serve.

- **Candy/deep-fry thermometer**

	Oil	
10	slices prosciutto (about 5 oz/150 g)	10
1 cup	Classic Mango Salsa (page 88)	250 mL
½ tsp	toasted sesame seeds	2 mL

1. In a Dutch oven or deep fryer, heat 3 inches (7.5 cm) of oil over medium-high heat to 325°F (160°C).

2. Cut each slice of prosciutto in half crosswise. Fry in hot oil, in batches, turning often, until crisp, about 2 minutes (it will curl into a freeform cup). Using a slotted spoon, transfer to a paper towel–lined plate to drain of excess oil.

3. Spoon Classic Mango Salsa into the deep valleys of the crisp prosciutto cups. Garnish with sesame seeds and serve immediately.

Sliced Steak with Horseradish and Roquefort Cheese

Makes about 8 servings

This appetizer is so easy but your guests will think you've hired a five-star chef to cook it!

Tips

One of the most important lessons one can learn in cooking is to rest meat and poultry after cooking. General rule of thumb is to rest your chickens, roasts, steaks etc. for at least 1/3 the cooking time. For example, if a steak takes you 30 minutes to cook, rest the meat for a minimum of 10 minutes prior to slicing, this gives juices ample time to disperse throughout the meat instead of having them in a puddle on your plate. Don't let any meats rest longer than 30 minutes.

Fresh horseradish adds a wonderful spicy note to foods and can usually be found in many large grocery chains or specialty food markets. Using a vegetable peeler, peel the tough skin and grate the root with windows open as the fumes can be quite harsh. Prepared horseradish can be used in place of fresh by rinsing thoroughly under cold water.

1 lb	boneless beef top loin or strip loin steak, about 1½ inches (4 cm) thick	500 g
	Salt and freshly ground black pepper	
1 tbsp	unsalted butter, divided	15 mL
1 tsp	olive oil	5 mL
¼ cup	chicken or beef broth or water	60 mL
1 tbsp	crumbled Roquefort or other blue cheese	15 mL
1 tbsp	finely grated fresh horseradish (see Tips, left)	15 mL

1. Sprinkle steak on both sides with salt and pepper. In a skillet, heat butter and oil over medium-high heat. Sear steak until nicely caramelized and golden brown, about 10 minutes. Flip over and cook another 5 minutes to achieve a perfect medium-rare (if you prefer the steak more well done, leave it in the pan for another 5 minutes for medium or 15 for well done). Transfer to a cutting board plate and let rest (see Tips, left).

2. Using the same skillet, bring broth to a boil over medium-low heat. Add cheese and stir to incorporate. Boil until sauce is reduced by half, about 5 minutes. Pour into a ramekin or other serving vessel.

3. Cut steak across the grain into thin slices and place one or two slices in the middle of each small plate. Garnish with Roquefort sauce and horseradish, dividing equally and serve.

Slow Cooker

The slow cooker is usually thought of in terms of robust big-batch dishes such as soups and stews, chilis, pot roasts and briskets. But it is equally adept at cooking appetizers, freeing you up to do other things while the nibblies simmer away. Hot dips, warm spiced nuts, roasted garlic, even a braised tomato bruschetta are all delicious prepared in the slow cooker. And once you put on the lid, you can probably forget about it until you're ready to serve.

Slow-Roasted Garlic. 484
Spicy Artichoke Dip 484
Sumptuous Spinach and Artichoke Dip 485
Chile Artichoke Dip. 486
Creamy Jalapeno-Spiked Mushroom
   and Artichoke Dip. 487
Bubbling Bacon and Horseradish Dip. 488
Sizzling Shrimp and Dill Pickle Dip 489
Nippy Oyster and Bacon Dip 490
Hot Curried Crab 491
Hot and Smoky Shrimp 492
Cheddar-Onion Melt. 492
Pimento-Spiked Cheesy Ham Melt
   with Potato Dippers 493
Caramelized Onion Dip. 494
Chile con Queso. 495
Santorini-Style Fava Spread 496

Chilly Dilly Eggplant. 497
Caper-Studded Caponata 498
Slow Cooker Eggplant Caviar. 499
Braised Tomato Bruschetta 500
Balsamic-Spiked Caramelized Onions
   with Shaved Parmesan. 501
Country-Style Pork Terrine 502
Oh-So-Retro Swedish Meatballs. 503
Black Bean and Salsa Dip 504
Spicy Black Bean Dip. 505
Black Bean Nachos 506
Salty Almonds with Thyme 506
Spicy Tamari Almonds 507
Cajun-Spiced Peanuts 507
Buttery Peanuts 508
Spicy Cashews. 508

Slow-Roasted Garlic

Makes 2 heads

If you like to have roasted garlic on hand to use as a condiment to spread on crackers or in recipes such as Roasted Garlic Polenta Crostini (page 228) or Roasted Garlic Aïoli (see Variations, page 538) here is a very easy way to make it.

- **Small (approx. 2 quart) slow cooker**
- **Large sheet of parchment paper**

30	cloves peeled garlic (about 2 heads)	30
2 tbsp	olive oil	30 mL

1. Lay parchment on a flat work surface and mound garlic in the middle. Spoon olive oil over garlic. Lift 2 opposite sides of parchment to meet in the middle, then fold them over to form a seal. Continue folding until flush with garlic. Fold remaining sides over to form a package. Place in stoneware, seam side down. Cover and cook on High for 4 hours, until garlic is nicely caramelized.

Spicy Artichoke Dip

Makes about 3 cups (750 mL)

This creamy dip with an intriguing hint of spice is flavorful and light if made with lower-fat cheeses and mayonnaise. Serve with tostadas, tortilla or pita chips.

Tip

Use a blended chile powder, or ancho or New Mexico chile powder, both of which are available in many supermarkets or specialty stores.

- **Small (maximum 3½ quart) slow cooker**

1	can (14 oz/398 mL) artichokes, drained and chopped	1
8 oz	cream cheese, softened	250 g
½ cup	shredded lower-fat mozzarella cheese	125 mL
4	green onions, white part only, finely chopped	4
1	clove garlic, minced	1
1	jalapeño pepper, minced	1
2 tbsp	mayonnaise	30 mL
1 tbsp	Dijon mustard	15 mL
1 tbsp	chile powder (see Tip, left)	15 mL
1 tsp	Worcestershire sauce	5 mL
½ tsp	salt	2 mL
¼ tsp	freshly ground black pepper	1 mL

1. In slow cooker stoneware, combine artichokes, cream cheese, mozzarella, green onions, garlic, jalapeno, mayonnaise, mustard, chile powder, Worcestershire sauce, salt and black pepper. Cover and cook on High for 2 hours, until hot and bubbly. Stir well and serve.

Sumptuous Spinach and Artichoke Dip

Makes 6 to 8 servings

Spinach and artichoke dip has become a classic. Serve with toast points, Basic Crostini (page 219), tortilla chips or sliced baguette.

Tips

If you are using fresh spinach leaves in this recipe, take care to wash them thoroughly, as they can be quite gritty. *To wash spinach:* Fill a clean sink with lukewarm water. Remove the tough stems and submerge the tender leaves in the water, swishing to remove the grit. Rinse thoroughly in a colander under cold running water, checking carefully to ensure that no sand remains. If you are using frozen spinach in this recipe, thaw and squeeze the excess moisture out before adding to the slow cooker.

If you prefer a smoother dip, place spinach and artichokes in a food processor, in separate batches, and pulse until desired degree of fineness is achieved. Then combine with remaining ingredients in slow cooker stoneware.

- Works best in a small (maximum 3½ quart) slow cooker

1 cup	shredded mozzarella cheese	250 mL
8 oz	cream cheese, cubed	250 g
¼ cup	freshly grated Parmesan cheese	60 mL
1	clove garlic, minced	1
¼ tsp	freshly ground black pepper	1 mL
1	can (14 oz/398 mL) artichokes, drained and finely chopped	1
1 lb	fresh spinach, stems removed, or 1 package (10 oz/300 g) spinach leaves, thawed if frozen (see Tips, left)	500 g
	Tostadas or tortilla chips	

1. In slow cooker stoneware, combine cheese, cream cheese, Parmesan, garlic, pepper, artichokes and spinach. Cover and cook on High for 2 hours, until hot and bubbly. Stir well and serve with tostadas or tortilla chips.

Chile Artichoke Dip

Makes about 3 cups (750 mL)

This mild-tasting dip has just a hint of spice balanced by the tang of citrus. This very enjoyable combination of flavors marries well with tostadas or celery sticks.

Make Ahead

Complete Step 1, combining ingredients in a mixing bowl rather than the stoneware. Cover and refrigerate overnight. When you're ready to cook, transfer to the stoneware and complete the recipe.

- **Small (2 to 3$\frac{1}{2}$ quart) slow cooker**

8 oz	cream cheese, cubed	250 g
1 cup	shredded mozzarella	250 mL
$\frac{1}{4}$ cup	mayonnaise	60 mL
1	clove garlic, minced	1
2 tsp	finely grated lemon zest	10 mL
1	can (14 oz/398 mL) artichokes, drained and chopped	1
1	can (4$\frac{1}{2}$ oz/127 mL) minced green chiles, drained	1
	Freshly ground black pepper	
	Tostadas or tortilla chips	

1. In slow cooker stoneware, combine cream cheese, mozzarella, mayonnaise, garlic, lemon zest, artichokes and chiles. Season with black pepper to taste. Cover and cook on High for 2 hours, until hot and bubbly. Stir well and serve. Serve with tostadas or tortilla chips.

Vegan Alternative

Substitute an equal quantity of vegan cream cheese, vegan mozzarella and vegan mayonnaise for the non-vegan products.

Creamy Jalapeño-Spiked Mushroom and Artichoke Dip

Makes about 2 cups (500 mL)

If you're looking for something a little different but are still hankering for comfort food, try this. It's a great combination of flavors and textures. Serve it with whole-grain tortilla chips for a great treat but sliced baguette works well, too.

Tip

If you prefer, use frozen artichokes, thawed, to make this recipe. You will need 6 artichoke hearts.

Make Ahead

Complete Step 1. Cover and refrigerate for up to 2 days. When you're ready to cook, complete the recipe.

- **Small (approx. 2 quart) slow cooker**

2 tbsp	olive oil, divided	30 mL
1 tbsp	butter	15 mL
4 oz	cremini mushrooms, stemmed and quartered	125 g
3 tbsp	diced onion	45 mL
3 tbsp	diced celery	45 mL
1 tbsp	minced garlic	15 mL
½ tsp	salt	2 mL
½ tsp	cracked black peppercorns	2 mL
1	can (14 oz/398 mL) artichoke hearts, drained (see Tip, left)	1
2	jalapeño peppers, seeded and diced	2
1 cup	shredded mozzarella cheese	250 mL
½ cup	mayonnaise	125 mL
½ cup	freshly grated Parmesan cheese	125 mL

1. In a skillet, heat 1 tbsp (15 mL) of the oil and butter over medium-high heat. Add mushrooms and cook, stirring, until browned, about 5 minutes. Transfer to a food processor fitted with a metal blade and set aside. Reduce heat to medium. Add remaining olive oil, onion and celery to pan and cook, stirring, until softened, about 3 minutes. Add garlic, salt and peppercorns and cook, stirring, for 1 minute. Transfer to food processor, along with artichokes and jalapeño peppers. Pulse until desired consistency is achieved.

2. Transfer to slow cooker stoneware. Add mozzarella, mayonnaise and Parmesan. Stir well. Cover and cook on Low for 4 hours or on High for 2 hours, until hot and bubbly.

Bubbling Bacon and Horseradish Dip

Makes 6 servings

There's nothing like a good dollop of horseradish to add zest to a dish. On a cold winter's day, a bubbling pot of this savory blend is very inviting. Open a big bag of potato chips and have some ready for après-ski or, for a more elegant presentation, serve on crisp spears of Belgian endive.

Tip

If you want to avoid stirring the dip after an hour, place all the ingredients in a food processor and pulse two or three times until well blended. Transfer to slow cooker stoneware and cook on High as directed.

- **Works best in a small (maximum 3½ quart) slow cooker**

2	slices bacon, finely chopped	2
8 oz	cream cheese, softened	250 g
¼ cup	sour cream	60 mL
2 tbsp	mayonnaise	30 mL
2 tbsp	prepared horseradish	30 mL
2 tbsp	finely chopped green onion	30 mL
1	clove garlic, minced	1
¾ cup	shredded Cheddar cheese, preferably sharp (aged)	175 mL
¼ tsp	freshly ground black pepper	1 mL
	Potato chips, optional	
	Belgian endive, optional	

1. In a skillet over medium-high heat, cook bacon until crisp. Remove with a slotted spoon and drain thoroughly on paper towel.

2. In slow cooker stoneware, combine bacon, cream cheese, sour cream, mayonnaise, horseradish, green onion, garlic, cheese and pepper. Stir well. Cover and cook on High for 1 hour. Stir again and cook on High for an additional 30 minutes, until hot and bubbly. Serve immediately or set temperature at Low until ready to serve. Serve with potato chips or Belgian endive, if desired.

Sizzling Shrimp and Dill Pickle Dip

Makes 6 servings

This is a great all-season dip, which works well with both light and regular cream cheese and mayonnaise. Serve with celery or carrot sticks, spears of Belgian endives, crackers, biscuits, melba toast or potato chips. Refrigerate any leftovers for future snacks. It keeps well and reheats nicely in the microwave.

Tip

If you prefer, substitute 2 cans (each approx. 3¾ oz/106 g) shrimp, drained.

- **Works best in a small (maximum 3½ quart) slow cooker**

8 oz	cream cheese, softened	250 g
¼ cup	mayonnaise	60 mL
1 tbsp	Dijon mustard	15 mL
½ cup	cooked salad shrimp (see Tip, left)	125 mL
¼ cup	finely chopped dill pickle	60 mL
2 tbsp	finely chopped green onion	30 mL
2 tbsp	chopped fresh dill	30 mL

1. In slow cooker stoneware, combine cream cheese, mayonnaise and mustard. Cover and cook on Low for 2 hours or on High for 1 hour.

2. Add shrimp, dill pickle, green onion and dill and stir well to combine. Cover and cook on Low for 1 hour or on High for 30 minutes, until bubbly.

Nippy Oyster and Bacon Dip

Makes about 2 cups (500 mL)

One advantage to this rich, creamy infusion is its versatility. For an impressive presentation, spoon into a serving bowl and surround with a big platter of vegetables for dipping, such as blanched broccoli, cauliflower or Brussels sprouts and crispy potato wedges. If simplicity is the order of the day, open a bag of potato chips. Either way, this dip always earns rave reviews.

Tip

To make Crispy Potato Wedges: Bake the desired number of baking potatoes in a 400°F (200°C) oven for 1 hour. Set aside to cool. Thirty minutes before serving the dip, cut each potato into 8 wedges. Brush with olive oil, place in 400°F (200°C) oven and roast until crisp and golden.

- **Small (maximum 3½ quart) slow cooker**

2	slices bacon, cooked to crisp, then crumbled	2
8 oz	cream cheese, softened	250 g
1 cup	shredded Cheddar cheese, preferably sharp (aged)	250 mL
2 tbsp	mayonnaise	30 mL
¼ tsp	freshly ground black pepper	1 mL
½ to 1	jalapeño pepper, seeded and finely chopped	½ to 1
1	can (4 oz/85 g) smoked oysters, drained and cut in half	1
1	roasted red bell pepper, finely chopped (see Tips, page 495)	1
	Potato chips, optional	
	Crispy Potato Wedges (see Tip, left), optional	
	Brussels sprouts, cooked until slightly underdone, optional	
	Blanched broccoli spears or cauliflower florets, optional	

1. In slow cooker stoneware, combine bacon, cream cheese, Cheddar, mayonnaise, black pepper and jalapeño pepper. Stir well. Cover and cook on High for 1 hour. Add oysters and bell pepper and stir again. Cook on High for an additional 30 minutes, until hot and bubbly. Serve immediately with desired vegetables or set temperature to Low until ready to serve.

Vegan Alternative

Nippy Clam and Bacon Dip: Substitute 1 can (5 oz/142 g) drained clams for the smoked oysters. Add along with the bacon.

Hot Curried Crab

Makes about 2 cups (500 mL)

This is a great dish for a party. Serve it with pieces of warm naan, sliced baguette or rice crackers.

Tip

Our preference is the pasteurized crabmeat, which you can find in cans in the refrigerated section of supermarkets. But regular canned or thawed drained frozen crabmeat works well, too.

- **Small (2 to 3½ quart) slow cooker**

8 oz	cooked crabmeat, chopped (see Tip, left)	250 g
2 tbsp	finely chopped fresh cilantro	30 mL
1 tbsp	extra virgin olive oil	15 mL
½ tsp	grated lime zest	2 mL
1 tbsp	freshly squeezed lime juice	15 mL
1 tsp	Asian chile sauce, such as sambal oelek	5 mL
8 oz	cream cheese, cubed	250 mL
2 tbsp	mayonnaise	30 mL
4	green onions, white part with just a hint of green, finely chopped	4
1 tsp	Thai red curry paste	5 mL

1. In a bowl, combine crabmeat, cilantro, olive oil, lime zest and juice and chile sauce. Stir well. Cover and refrigerate until ready to use.

2. In slow cooker stoneware, combine cream cheese, mayonnaise, green onions and curry paste. Cover and cook on Low for 2 hours or High for 1 hour, until cheese is melted. Stir in crab mixture. Cover and cook on High for 30 minutes, until hot and bubbly. Stir well.

Hot and Smoky Shrimp

Makes about 2 cups (500 mL)

This warm and oh-so-soothing mélange, with just an intriguing hint of spice, makes a perfect starter for any meal — from casual to elegant. Spread on thin slices of crusty baguette or celery sticks. Plain crackers work well, too.

Make Ahead

Complete Steps 1 and 2. Cover and refrigerate shrimp and cheese mixtures separately overnight. When you're ready to cook, complete the recipe.

- **Small (2 to 3½ quart) slow cooker**

8 oz	cooked salad shrimp, chopped	250 g
2 tbsp	finely chopped parsley	30 mL
1 tbsp	freshly squeezed lemon juice	15 mL
1 tbsp	extra virgin olive oil	15 mL
	Freshly ground black pepper	
8 oz	cream cheese, softened	250 g
¼ cup	mayonnaise	60 mL
2	green onions, white part with just a hint of green, finely chopped	2
1 tsp	smoked hot paprika	5 mL

1. In a bowl, combine shrimp, parsley, lemon juice, olive oil, and pepper to taste. Stir well. Cover and refrigerate until ready to use.

2. In slow cooker stoneware, combine cream cheese, mayonnaise, green onions and paprika. Cover and cook on Low for 2 hours or High for 1 hour, until cheese is melted. Stir in shrimp mixture. Cover and cook on High for 30 minutes, until hot and bubbly. Stir well.

Cheddar-Onion Melt

Makes about 2 cups (500 mL)

Vegetarian Friendly

This is one of those classics that just about everyone adores. Serve this with sliced baguette, flatbread or even celery sticks and watch it disappear right to the last drop.

Make Ahead

See page 493.

- **Small (2 to 3½ quart) slow cooker**

3 cups	shredded medium or sharp (aged) Cheddar cheese	750 mL
2	onions, grated	2
½ cup	mayonnaise	125 mL
2 tbsp	sour cream	30 mL
½ tsp	dry mustard	2 mL
⅛ tsp	cayenne pepper, optional	0.5 mL

1. In slow cooker stoneware, combine cheese, onions, mayonnaise, sour cream, mustard, and cayenne, if using. Cover and cook on Low for 2 hours or on High for 1 hour, until cheese is melted. Stir well and serve.

Pimento-Spiked Cheesy Ham Melt with Potato Dippers

Makes about 2 cups (500 mL)

Served on baked potato sticks, this makes a substantial starter, just the thing to greet active outdoorsy folks coming in from the cold. For a more conventional presentation, serve the melt with sliced baguette or spread over toast points and run under the broiler.

Tip

To make baked potato sticks: Cut a baked potato in half and cut each half into quarters. Brush cut sides with olive oil and run under preheated broiler until nicely browned. Sprinkle with sea salt, if desired. Place on a platter and cover with cheese mixture.

Make Ahead

You can make this up to 2 days ahead of serving it. Cover and refrigerate in an ovenproof ramekin. When you're ready to serve, uncover and place in a preheated 400°F (200°C) oven until bubbly and top is browning, about 10 minutes. If the mixture gets overheated, it might start to separate. No problem, just stir well before serving.

- **Small (2 to 3 1/2 quart) slow cooker**

2 cups	shredded Cheddar cheese (about 4 oz/125 g)	500 mL
2 tbsp	minced green onion	30 mL
2 tbsp	mayonnaise	30 mL
2 tbsp	sour cream	30 mL
1 tsp	Dijon mustard	5 mL
1/8 tsp	cayenne pepper	0.5 mL
1/2 cup	finely minced smoked ham (about 4 oz/125 g)	125 mL
1 tbsp	minced pimento	15 mL
	Freshly ground black pepper	
	Baked potato sticks (see Tips, left)	

1. In slow cooker stoneware, combine cheese, green onion, mayonnaise, sour cream, mustard and cayenne. Cover and cook on Low for 2 hours or on High for 1 hour, until cheese is melted. Stir in ham and pimento. Cover and cook on High for 30 minutes, until flavors meld. Season to taste with pepper. Serve with potato sticks for dipping.

Variation

If you prefer, omit the baked potato sticks and serve the melt with sliced baguette.

Caramelized Onion Dip

Makes about 1½ cups (375 mL)

This dip is one of life's guilty pleasures. Serve it with good potato chips and you'll be amazed: It will disappear to the very last drop.

Tip

The amount of salt you'll need to add depends upon the accompaniment. If you're serving this with salty potato chips, err on the side of caution.

• **Small (approx. 2 quart) slow cooker**

2	onions, thinly sliced on the vertical	2
4	cloves garlic, chopped	4
1 tbsp	melted butter	15 mL
4 oz	cream cheese, cubed and softened	125 g
½ cup	sour cream	125 mL
1 tbsp	dark miso	15 mL
	Salt and freshly ground black pepper (see Tip, left)	
	Finely snipped chives	
	Natural potato chips, optional	
	Belgian endive, optional	

1. In slow cooker stoneware, combine onions, garlic and butter. Toss well to ensure onions are thoroughly coated. Place a clean tea towel, folded in half (so you will have two layers), over top of stoneware to absorb moisture. Cover and cook on High for 5 hours, stirring two or three times to ensure onions are browning evenly, replacing towel each time, until onions are nicely caramelized.

2. Transfer mixture to a food processor fitted with a metal blade. Add cream cheese, sour cream, miso, and salt and black pepper to taste. Process until well blended. Transfer to a serving dish and garnish with chives. Serve with potato chips or leaves of Belgian endive, if using.

Variation

For a more herbal flavor, add 2 tbsp (30 mL) fresh thyme leaves along with the cream cheese.

Chili con Queso

Makes about 4 cups (1 L)

This is a delicious combination of hot peppers, tomatoes, corn and melted cheese Team it up with tortilla chips or crudités for a great dip.

Tips

If you don't have time to roast a pepper, use good-quality bottled roasted peppers.

To roast peppers: Preheat broiler. Place pepper(s) on a baking sheet and broil, turning two or three times, until skin on all sides is blackened, about 25 minutes. Transfer to a heatproof bowl. Cover with a plate and let stand until cool. Remove and, using a sharp knife, lift skins off. Discard skins, core and seeds.

- **Small (maximum 3½ quart) slow cooker**

1 tbsp	vegetable oil	15 mL
2	onions, finely chopped	2
4	cloves garlic, minced	4
1 to 2	jalapeño peppers, minced	1 to 2
2 tsp	chili powder	10 mL
1 tsp	dried oregano	5 mL
1 tsp	cracked black peppercorns	5 mL
1 tsp	salt	5 mL
2	tomatoes, peeled and diced	2
1 cup	corn kernels, thawed if frozen	250 mL
2 cups	shredded Monterey Jack or Cheddar cheese	500 mL
¼ cup	sour cream	60 mL
1	roasted red bell pepper, chopped, optional (see Tips, left)	1

1. In a skillet, heat oil over medium heat. Add onions and cook, stirring, until softened, about 3 minutes. Add garlic, jalapeño pepper to taste, chili powder, oregano, peppercorns and salt and cook, stirring, for 1 minute. Stir in tomatoes and corn and cook until mixture is bubbly. Transfer to slow cooker stoneware.

2. Add cheese, sour cream and roasted pepper, if using. Stir well. Cover and cook on High for 1½ hours, until hot and bubbly.

Santorini-Style Fava Spread

Makes about 2 cups (500 mL)

This spread, which is Greek in origin, is unusual and particularly delicious. Although fava beans do figure in Greek cuisine, for most Greek people fava is synonymous with yellow split peas, one of the major indigenous foods of the island of Santorini, from which they make many dishes, including variations of this spread. Serve this with warm toasted pita and wait for the compliments.

Tip

Italian flat-leaf parsley is preferred because it has much more flavor than the curly leaf variety.

Make Ahead

Complete Step 1. Cover and refrigerate for up to 2 days. When you're ready to serve, heat peas on the stovetop until bubbles form about the edges. Complete the recipe.

- **Small (1½ to 2 quart) slow cooker**

½ cup	extra virgin olive oil, divided	125 mL
½ cup	diced shallots (about 2 large)	125 mL
2 tsp	dried oregano	10 mL
1 tsp	salt	5 mL
½ tsp	cracked black peppercorns	2 mL
1 cup	yellow split peas	250 mL
4 cups	water	1 L
6	oil-packed sun-dried tomato halves, drained and coarsely chopped	6
4	cloves garlic, chopped	4
¼ cup	coarsely chopped Italian flat-leaf parsley (see Tip, left)	60 mL
4	fresh basil leaves, hand-torn	4
3 tbsp	red wine vinegar	45 mL
	Salt and freshly ground black pepper	
	Toasted pita bread	

1. In a skillet, heat 1 tbsp (15 mL) of the oil over medium heat. Add shallots and cook, stirring, until softened, about 3 minutes. Add oregano, salt and peppercorns and cook, stirring, for 1 minute. Add split peas and cook, stirring, until coated. Add water and bring to a boil. Boil for 2 minutes.

2. Transfer to slow cooker stoneware. Cover and cook on Low for 8 hours or on High for 4 hours, until peas have virtually disintegrated. Drain off excess water, if necessary. Transfer solids to a food processor. Add sun-dried tomatoes, garlic, parsley, basil and vinegar. Pulse 7 or 8 times to chop and blend ingredients. With motor running, add remaining olive oil in a steady stream through the feed tube. Season to taste with additional salt and pepper and drizzle with additional olive oil, if desired. Serve warm with toasted pita.

Chilly Dilly Eggplant

Makes about 4 cups (1 L)

This is delicious as a dip with raw vegetables or on pita triangles and makes a wonderful addition to a mezes or tapas-style meal. Although it is tasty warm, the flavor dramatically improves if it is thoroughly chilled before serving. This makes a big batch — perfect for a party.

Tip

Sprinkling the eggplant pieces with salt and leaving them to "sweat" for an hour or two draws out any bitter juice. If time is short, blanch the pieces for a minute or two in heavily salted water. In either case, rinse thoroughly in fresh cold water and, using your hands, squeeze out the excess moisture. Pat dry with paper towels and it's ready for cooking.

Make Ahead

You'll achieve the best results if you make this a day ahead and chill thoroughly before serving, or cook overnight, purée in the morning and chill.

- **Works best in a small (maximum 3½ quart) slow cooker**

2	large eggplants, peeled, cut into 1-inch (2.5 cm) cubes and drained of excess moisture (see Tip, left)	2
2 to 3 tbsp	olive oil	30 to 45 mL
2	onions, chopped	2
4	cloves garlic, chopped	4
1 tsp	dried oregano	5 mL
1 tsp	salt	5 mL
½ tsp	freshly ground black pepper	2 mL
1 tbsp	balsamic or red wine vinegar	15 mL
½ cup	chopped fresh dill	125 mL
	Dill sprigs, optional	
	Finely chopped black olives, optional	

1. In a skillet, heat 2 tbsp (30 mL) of the oil over medium-high heat. Add eggplant, in batches, and cook, stirring and tossing, until it begins to brown, about 3 minutes per batch. Transfer to slow cooker stoneware.

2. Reduce heat to medium. Add more oil if necessary and cook onions, stirring, until softened, about 3 minutes. Add garlic, oregano, salt and pepper and cook, stirring, for 1 minute. Transfer to stoneware and stir to combine thoroughly. Cover and cook on Low for 7 to 8 hours or on High for 4 hours, until eggplant is tender.

3. Transfer contents of slow cooker (in batches, if necessary) to a blender or food processor. Add vinegar and dill and process until smooth, scraping down sides of bowl at halfway point. Taste for seasoning and adjust. Spoon into a small serving bowl and chill thoroughly. Garnish with sprigs of dill and chopped black olives, if using.

Caper-Studded Caponata

Makes about 2 cups (500 mL)

This recipe differs from most caponata because it uses tomato paste rather than tomatoes and contains a sweet pepper and capers. It makes a great topping for bruschetta but if you don't feel like toasting bread, it is also great spread on crackers.

Tip

You can also use salt-cured capers in this recipe, but they will need to soak in cold water for about 30 minutes, then thoroughly rinsed under cold running water before adding to the recipe.

Make Ahead

Complete Step 2. Cover and refrigerate for up to 2 days. When you're ready to cook, complete the recipe.

- **Small (approx. 2 quart) slow cooker**
- **Large sheet of parchment paper**

1	medium eggplant, peeled, cut into 1/2-inch (1 cm) cubes and drained of excess moisture (see Tip, page 497)	1
3 tbsp	red wine vinegar	45 mL
1 tsp	granulated sugar	5 mL
2 to 3 tbsp	olive oil	30 to 45 mL
4	cloves garlic, minced	4
1 tsp	cracked black peppercorns	5 mL
1/2 tsp	salt	2 mL
4 tbsp	tomato paste	60 mL
1/2	red bell pepper, seeded and diced	1/2
2 tbsp	drained capers (see Tip, left)	30 mL
1/4 cup	finely chopped fresh Italian flat-leaf parsley	60 mL
	Bruschetta (page 231), optional	

1. In a small bowl, combine vinegar and sugar. Stir until sugar dissolves. Set aside.

2. In a skillet, heat 2 tbsp (30 mL) of the oil over medium-high heat. Add eggplant, in batches, if necessary, and cook, stirring and tossing, until it begins to brown, adding more oil as necessary, about 3 minutes per batch. Transfer to slow cooker stoneware. Add garlic, peppercorns and salt to pan and cook, stirring, for 1 minute. Add tomato paste and vinegar mixture and stir to combine. Stir into stoneware.

3. Place a large piece of parchment over the eggplant mixture, pressing it down to brush the food and extending up the sides of the stoneware so it overlaps the rim. Cover and cook on Low for 6 hours or High for 3 hours, until mixture is hot and bubbly. Lift out parchment and discard, being careful not to spill the accumulated liquid into the mixture. Stir in bell pepper and capers. Cover and cook on High for 15 minutes, until bell pepper is soft and flavors blend. Transfer to a serving bowl and garnish with parsley. Serve warm or at room temperature, spooned onto Bruschetta, if using.

Slow Cooker Eggplant Caviar

Makes about 3 cups (750 mL)

Although its origins are Mediterranean, this flavorful spread has become a favorite around the world. What's more, it's loaded with nutrition. Serve it well chilled with warm pita bread or sliced veggies, or as a topping for Bruschetta (page 231).

Tips

For the diced peeled tomatoes you can use a fresh tomato or well-drained canned diced tomatoes.

To toast cumin: In a large dry skillet over medium heat, toast cumin seeds, stirring, until fragrant, about 3 minutes. Transfer to a mortar and pestle or a spice grinder and pound or grind as finely as you can.

Make Ahead

You can make Eggplant Caviar up to 2 days ahead. Cover and refrigerate until you're ready to serve.

- **Small (2 to 3½ quart) slow cooker**

1	medium eggplant (about 1 lb/500 g) peeled and cut into 2-inch (5 cm) cubes	1
1	roasted red bell pepper, seeded and chopped (see Tips, page 495)	1
1 tsp	salt	5 mL
1 tbsp	ground cumin seeds (see Tips, left)	15 mL
2 tbsp	extra virgin olive oil, divided (approx.)	30 mL
½ tsp	cracked black peppercorns	2 mL
4	cloves garlic, minced	4
½ cup	diced peeled tomatoes (see Tip, left)	125 mL
4	green onions, white part only with just a hint of green, chopped	4
2	sun-dried tomatoes packed in oil, drained and chopped	2
½ cup	coarsely chopped Italian flat-leaf parsley leaves	125 mL
2 tbsp	red wine vinegar	30 mL
	Salt and freshly ground black pepper	

1. In a colander over a sink, combine eggplant and salt. Toss and let stand for 30 minutes. Rinse thoroughly under cold running water. Lay a clean tea towel on a work surface. Working in batches over the sink and using your hands, squeeze liquid out of eggplant. Transfer to tea towel. When batches are complete, roll the towel up and press down to remove remaining liquid.

2. In same skillet, heat 1 tbsp (15 mL) of the oil over medium heat. Add sweated eggplant, in batches, and cook until browned, adding more oil as necessary, about 3 minutes per batch. Transfer to slow cooker stoneware. Add reserved cumin, peppercorns, garlic and tomatoes. Cover and cook on Low for 4 hours or High for 2 hours.

3. Transfer to a food processor and process until smooth. Add green onions, roasted pepper, sun-dried tomatoes, parsley and vinegar and pulse until blended. Season to taste with salt and pepper. Refrigerate until thoroughly chilled.

Braised Tomato Bruschetta

Makes about 2 cups (500 mL)

When they are in season, there are few things more delicious than bruschetta overflowing with fresh chopped tomatoes (see pages 231 and 232). This is an adaptation of a recipe from Seattle's Café Lago, which demonstrates that a braised version of this summertime treat can be made using canned tomatoes. It is simply delicious and a wonderful treat in the midst of winter, when succulent local field tomatoes are only a faint memory.

Make Ahead

Complete the recipe. Cover and refrigerate bruschetta mixture for up to 3 days. Bring to room temperature before serving.

- **Small to medium (1½ to 3½ quart) slow cooker**
- **Large sheet of parchment paper**

¼ cup	extra virgin olive oil, divided	60 mL
1	can (28 oz/796 mL) diced tomatoes, drained	1
2	cloves garlic, minced	2
2 tsp	dried oregano	10 mL
1 tsp	granulated sugar	5 mL
1 tsp	salt	5 mL
2 tbsp	finely chopped fresh Italian flat-leaf parsley	30 mL
	Freshly ground black pepper	
6	slices of warm Bruschetta (page 231), cut in half country-style bread or 12 slices of baguette, grilled or lightly toasted	6

1. In slow cooker stoneware, place 2 tbsp (30 mL) of the olive oil and swirl to coat bottom. Add tomatoes and sprinkle with garlic, oregano, sugar and salt. Drizzle with remaining olive oil. Place a large piece of parchment over the tomatoes, pressing it down to brush the food and extending up the sides of the stoneware so it overlaps the rim.

2. Cover and cook on Low for 6 hours or High for 3 hours, until mixture is hot and bubbly. Lift out parchment and discard, being careful not to spill the accumulated liquid into the tomato mixture. Stir in parsley and season to taste with pepper. Transfer to a serving dish and let cool to room temperature. To serve, spoon onto toasted or grilled bread Bruschetta.

Variation

If you prefer, spread the warm toasted bread with a thin layer of soft goat cheese before topping with the bruschetta.

Balsamic-Spiked Caramelized Onions with Shaved Parmesan

Makes 6 servings

This is an elegant and delicious starter. Serve it plated or as a topping for crostini (pages 219 and 220).

Make Ahead

After adding vinegar and sugar, refrigerate onions. Warm on the stovetop in a saucepan.

- **Small to medium (2 to 3½ quart) slow cooker**

4	onions, thinly sliced on the vertical	4
2 tsp	dried thyme	10 mL
1 tsp	cracked black peppercorns	5 mL
¼ cup	olive oil	60 mL
2 tbsp	balsamic vinegar	30 mL
1 tsp	Demerara or other raw cane sugar	5 mL
	Thinly sliced prosciutto, optional	
	Freshly grated Parmesan cheese	
	Crostini, optional	

1. In slow cooker stoneware, combine onions, thyme, peppercorns and olive oil. Stir well. Place a clean tea towel, folded in half (so you will have 2 layers), over top of stoneware to absorb moisture. Cover and cook on High for 3 hours, stirring every hour and replacing the towel each time, until onions are nicely caramelized.

2. In a small bowl or measuring cup, combine vinegar and brown sugar. Stir until sugar dissolves. Add to onions and stir well. Transfer onions with juices to a small serving dish.

3. To serve, spoon onions with sauce onto small plates. Top with a piece of prosciutto, if using, and garnish with Parmesan. Or use Crostini as a base and make smaller portions.

Vegan Alternative

Substitute vegan Parmesan cheese for the regular version and omit prosciutto.

Country-Style Pork Terrine

Makes about 2 lbs (1 kg)

This is a simple terrine, mildly flavored and nicely moist. Served with crusty bread and a spirited condiment such as Dijon mustard or some cornichons, it's a real treat.
It makes a great companion for a leisurely glass of wine.

Tips

This terrine can be made in almost any kind of baking dish that will fit into your slow cooker. A variety of baking pans work well: a small loaf pan, approximately 8 by 5 inches (20 by 12.5 cm), makes a traditionally shaped terrine; a round 4-cup (1 L) soufflé dish or a square 7-inch (18 cm) baking dish produces slices of different shapes.

To purée garlic, use a fine-tooth grater such as Microplane.

Placing a weight on a terrine while it cools compacts the meat and ensures it has a uniform texture. Keep a brick wrapped in plastic wrap for this purpose. It fits nicely into a loaf pan.

- **Large (minimum 5 quart) oval slow cooker**
- **Loaf pan, earthenware terrine or soufflé dish, lightly greased (see Tips, left)**
- **Instant-read thermometer**

1½ lbs	boneless pork shoulder, including fat, coarsely chopped	750 g
8 oz	stewing veal, coarsely chopped	250 g
4 oz	smoked bacon, trimmed of rind, cubed	125 g
2 tsp	cracked black peppercorns	10 mL
1 tsp	salt	5 mL
3 tbsp	brandy or cognac	45 mL
1	onion, grated	1
2	cloves garlic, puréed (see Tips, left)	2
2 tbsp	fresh thyme leaves	30 mL

1. In a meat grinder (or food processor in batches), grind pork, veal and bacon, transferring to a bowl as completed. Mix well. Add peppercorns, salt, brandy, onion, garlic and thyme and mix well. Cover and refrigerate overnight.

2. When you're ready to cook, transfer mixture to prepared pan. Cover tightly with foil and secure with a string. Place in stoneware and add hot water to come about halfway up the sides of the pan.

3. Cover and cook on High about 4 hours, until juices run clear or an instant-read thermometer inserted into the center of the terrine registers 160°F (71°C). Refrigerate overnight, weighted down (see Tips, left) before serving.

Oh-So-Retro Swedish Meatballs

Makes about 30 meatballs

These were a cocktail party standard way back when. Serve them in a shallow serving dish or a deep platter, speared with cocktail toothpicks. They will disappear in a flash. Make sure your guests have napkins or a plate to catch any drips.

Tip

You may want to use a whisk while combining the flour mixture and hot stock, to minimize the possibility of lumps.

- **Small to medium (2 to 3½ quart) slow cooker**

1 lb	lean ground beef, preferably sirloin	500 g
1 cup	fine dry bread crumbs	250 mL
1	onion, grated	1
1	egg, beaten	1
2 tsp	finely grated lemon zest	10 mL
2 tbsp	freshly squeezed lemon juice	30 mL
½ tsp	salt	2 mL
½ tsp	allspice	2 mL
	Freshly ground black pepper	
2 tbsp	olive oil	30 mL
3 tbsp	all-purpose flour	45 mL
½ tsp	cracked black peppercorns	2 mL
2 cups	beef broth, heated to the boiling point	500 mL
½ cup	sour cream	125 mL
½ cup	finely chopped dill fronds	125 mL

1. In a bowl, combine ground beef, bread crumbs, onion, egg, lemon zest and juice, salt, allspice, and pepper to taste. Mix well. Using your hands, shape into balls about ½ inch (1 cm) in diameter.

2. In a large skillet, heat oil over medium-high heat. Add meatballs in batches and cook, stirring, until nicely browned, about 4 minutes per batch. Transfer to slow cooker stoneware as completed. Add flour to pan and cook, stirring, until frothy but not browning, about 2 minutes. Stir in peppercorns. Add beef broth and cook, stirring, until mixture comes to a boil and thickens, about 2 minutes (see Tips, left). Pour over meatballs.

3. Cover and cook on Low for 6 hours or on High for 3 hours, until meatballs are cooked through. Using a slotted spoon, transfer meatballs to a serving dish. Add sour cream and dill to stoneware and stir well. Pour over meatballs and serve.

Black Bean and Salsa Dip

Makes about 3 cups (750 mL)

This tasty Cuban-inspired dip can be made from ingredients you're likely to have on hand. Serve with tortilla chips, tostadas, crisp crackers or crudités.

Tips

For this quantity of beans, soak, cook and drain 1 cup (250 mL) dried black beans or drain and rinse 1 can (14 to 19 oz/398 to 540 mL) black beans.

For a smoother dip, purée the beans in a food processor or mash with a potato masher before adding to stoneware.

If you use a five-alarm salsa in this dip, you may find it too spicy with the addition of jalapeño pepper.

If you don't have time to roast your own pepper, use a bottled roasted red pepper.

- **Works best in a small (maximum 3½ quart) slow cooker**

2 cups	cooked black beans (see Tips, left)	500 mL
8 oz	cream cheese, cubed	250 g
½ cup	tomato salsa	125 mL
¼ cup	sour cream	60 mL
2 tsp	cumin seeds, toasted and ground (see Tip, page 505)	10 mL
1 tsp	chili powder	5 mL
1 tsp	cracked black peppercorns	5 mL
1	jalapeño pepper, finely chopped, optional (see Tips, left)	1
1	roasted red bell pepper, finely chopped, optional (see Tips, page 495)	1
	Finely chopped green onion, optional	
	Finely chopped cilantro leaves, optional	

1. In slow cooker stoneware, combine beans, cream cheese, salsa, sour cream, cumin, chili powder, peppercorns, jalapeño pepper and roasted pepper, if using. Cover and cook on High for 1 hour. Stir again and cook on High for an additional 30 minutes, until mixture is hot and bubbly. Serve immediately or set temperature at Low until ready to serve. Garnish with green onion and/or cilantro, if desired.

Spicy Black Bean Dip

Makes about 3 cups (750 mL)

Simple, yet delicious and nutritious to boot. What more could you want? Serve this with blue corn tortilla chips for something a little different. Regular ones are perfect, too.

Tip

For the best flavor, toast and grind whole cumin seeds rather than buying ground cumin. *To toast cumin seeds:* Simply stir seeds in a dry skillet over medium heat until fragrant, about 3 minutes. Immediately transfer to a spice grinder or mortar and grind.

Make Ahead

Complete Step 1. Cover and refrigerate for up to 2 days. When you're ready to cook, complete the recipe.

• **Small to medium (1½ to 3½ quart) slow cooker**

1	small red or sweet onion, coarsely chopped	1
2	cloves garlic, chopped	2
1 to 2	canned chipotle pepper in adobo sauce	1 to 2
2 cups	cooked black beans (see Tips, page 504)	500 mL
2 tsp	ground cumin (see Tip, left)	10 mL
1 tsp	finely grated lime zest	5 mL
1 tsp	salt	5 mL
½ tsp	cracked black peppercorns	2 mL
2 cups	shredded Monterey Jack cheese or vegan alternative (about 8 oz/250 g)	500 mL
	Finely chopped cilantro leaves	

1. In a food processor fitted with a metal blade, process onion, garlic and chipotle pepper to taste until finely chopped. Add beans, cumin, lime zest, salt and peppercorns and process until desired consistency is achieved.

2. Transfer to slow cooker stoneware. Stir in cheese. Cover and cook on High for 1 hour. Stir well. Cover and cook on High for 30 minutes, until mixture is hot and bubbly. Garnish with cilantro. Serve immediately or set temperature at Warm until ready to serve.

Black Bean Nachos

Makes about 3 cups (750 mL)

This dip is a perennial hit.

Tips

If you're using sweet peppers rather than poblano and want a zestier result, add an extra jalapeño or chipotle pepper.

Use your favorite store-bought tomato-based mild or spicy, salsa to make this dip.

- **Small (2 to 3½ quart) slow cooker**

1	can (14 to 19 oz/398 to 540 mL) black beans, drained, rinsed and mashed	1
1 cup	salsa (see Tips, left)	250 mL
4	green onions, finely chopped	4
2	roasted peppers (poblanos or sweet), peeled and diced	2
1	roasted jalapeño, seeded and diced, or 1 chipotle pepper in adobo sauce	1
2 cups	shredded Cheddar or Monterey Jack cheese	500 mL
	Tortilla chips	

1. In slow cooker stoneware, combine beans, salsa, green onions, poblano and jalapeño peppers and cheese. Stir well. Cover and cook on High for 1½ hours, until mixture is hot and bubbly. Serve with tortilla chips.

Salty Almonds with Thyme

Makes 2 cups (500 mL)

The combination of good sea salt, fresh thyme and flavorful almonds is irresistible.

Tip

A small slow cooker is recommended when making this recipe (and others using nuts) because the nuts are less likely to burn.

- **Small (maximum 3½ quart) slow cooker (see Tip, left)**

2 cups	unblanched almonds	500 mL
½ tsp	ground white pepper	2 mL
1 tbsp	fine sea salt, or more to taste (see Tip, page 507)	15 mL
2 tbsp	extra virgin olive oil	30 mL
2 tbsp	fresh thyme leaves	30 mL

1. In slow cooker stoneware, combine almonds and white pepper. Cover and cook on High for 1½ hours, stirring every 30 minutes, until nuts are nicely toasted.

2. In a bowl, combine salt, olive oil and thyme. Add to hot almonds in stoneware and stir thoroughly to combine. Spoon mixture into a small serving bowl and serve hot or let cool.

Spicy Tamari Almonds

Makes about 2 cups (500 mL)

These tasty tidbits make a fabulous pre-dinner nibble with a glass of cold white wine. Tamari is a wheat-free soy sauce, so you can serve this snack to people who are unable to tolerate gluten.

- **Small (2 to 3½ quart) slow cooker**

2 cups	whole almonds	500 mL
¼ tsp	cayenne pepper	1 mL
2 tbsp	tamari sauce	30 mL
1 tbsp	extra virgin olive oil	15 mL
	Fine sea salt (see Tip, below)	

1. In slow cooker stoneware, combine almonds and cayenne. Place a clean tea towel, folded in half (so you will have 2 layers), over top of stoneware to absorb moisture. Cover and cook on High for 45 minutes.

2. In a small bowl, combine tamari and olive oil. Add to hot almonds and stir thoroughly to combine. Replace tea towel. Cover and cook on High for 1½ hours, until nuts are hot and fragrant, stirring every 30 minutes and replacing towel each time. Sprinkle with salt to taste. Store in an airtight container.

Cajun-Spiced Peanuts

Makes about 2 cups (500 mL)

Eaten warm, these aromatic treats are positively luscious.

Tip

Sea salt is available in most supermarkets. It is much sweeter than table salt and is essential for these recipes as table salt would impart an unpleasant acrid taste to the nuts. Be sure to buy sea salt without additives, such as iodine or anti-caking agents.

- **Small (2 to 3½ quart) slow cooker**

2 cups	raw peanuts	500 mL
2 tbsp	unrefined peanut or extra virgin olive oil	30 mL
2 tsp	Cajun spice	10 mL
Pinch	cayenne pepper	Pinch
1 tsp	fine sea salt (see Tip, left)	5 mL

1. In slow cooker stoneware, combine peanuts, oil, Cajun spice and cayenne. Place a clean tea towel, folded in half (so you will have 2 layers), over top of stoneware to absorb moisture. Cover and cook on High for 2 to 2½ hours, stirring occasionally, until peanuts are nicely roasted. Drain on paper towel. Place in a serving bowl, sprinkle with salt and stir to combine. Serve warm or cool.

Buttery Peanuts

Makes 2 cups (500 mL)

Everyone loves these hot buttery peanuts. Use peanuts with skins on or buy them peeled, to suit your preference. Both work well in this recipe.

- **Small (maximum 3½ quart) slow cooker**

2 cups	raw peanuts	500 mL
¼ cup	melted butter	60 mL
2 tsp	fine sea salt	10 mL

1. In stoneware, combine peanuts and butter. Cover and cook on High for 2 to 2½ hours, stirring occasionally, until peanuts are nicely roasted. Drain on paper towels. Place in a bowl, sprinkle with salt and stir.

Variation

Curried Buttery Peanuts: In a small bowl, combine salt with 2 tsp (10 mL) curry powder and pinch cayenne pepper. Sprinkle hot peanuts with this mixture instead of plain salt and stir to combine.

Spicy Cashews

Makes 2 cups (500 mL)

Only slightly nippy, with just a hint of cinnamon, these cashews are a tasty and nutritious treat any time of the year.

Tip

Sea salt is available in most supermarkets. It is much sweeter than table salt and is essential for these recipes as table salt would impart an unpleasant acrid taste to the nuts. Be sure to buy sea salt without additives, such as iodine or anti-caking agents.

- **Small (maximum 3½ quart) slow cooker**

2 cups	raw cashews	500 mL
1 tsp	chili powder	5 mL
½ tsp	cayenne pepper	2 mL
¼ tsp	ground cinnamon	1 mL
2 tsp	fine sea salt	10 mL
1 tbsp	extra virgin olive oil	15 mL

1. In stoneware, combine cashews, chili powder, cayenne and cinnamon. Stir to combine thoroughly. Cover and cook on High for 1½ hours, stirring every 30 minutes, until nuts are nicely toasted.

2. In a small bowl, combine salt and oil. Add to nuts and stir to combine. Transfer to a bowl. Serve hot or cool.

Variation

Sweet and Spicy Cashews: Substitute 1 tbsp (15 mL) butter for the olive oil and add along with 2 tbsp (30 mL) brown sugar.

Desserts

You may be asking yourself, "What do desserts have to do with appetizers?" Fair question. But if you've ever been to a cocktail party where the only items on the menu are sweet and flaky, fruity or chocolaty, or some combination thereof, you know they fit in. We call them Hors D'esserts or Dessappetizers. Sometimes dessert appetizers will be paired with wines and alcoholic beverages that heighten the experience. Just think of the possibilities!

After every great meal there is usually an equally wonderful dessert to follow. Instead of preparing just one, how about serving a sampling of Dessappetizers? Your guests will be able to choose from a wider sample of sweet indulgences and to try small bites of the most tempting. From child-inspired Jelly Shots (page 511) to Agave-Glazed Pineapple (page 527) to Caramel and Chocolate-Covered Apples (page 532), the opportunities are endless.

Chocolate Meringue Drops 510
Chocolate Toasts 510
Classic Raspberry Jelly Shots 511
Chocolate Popcorn Clusters 511
Fried Green Bananas 512
Almond Cranberry Chocolate "Brittle" 513
Five-Ingredient Molten Chocolate Cakes 514
Quick Chocolate Mousse 515
Strawberries and Cream 515
Kickin' Chocolate Almond Clusters 516
Blueberry Chocolate Brochettes 516
Rhubarb and Blueberry Compote
   with Vanilla Ice Cream 517
Sesame-Scented Apricots 517
Cinnamon-Sugar Phyllo Bunches 518
Apple-Cinnamon Phyllo Purses 519
Mini Sweet Potato Muffins
   with Maple Syrup Glaze 520
Mini Chocolate Chunk Banana Sandwiches 521
Quick Blueberry "Sorbet" 522
Warm Apple Sour Cream 522

Frozen Mango Mousse 523
Tropical Fruit Soup 523
World's Greatest Applesauce 524
Chocolate Macaroons 524
Mini French Toast with Fresh Peaches
   and Peach Maple Syrup 525
Sweet Wontons 526
Mini Peach Bread Pudding 526
Brown Sugar and Peach Sabayon 527
Agave-Glazed Pineapple 527
Sugar-Coated Concord Grapes 528
Easy-Peasy Chocolate Pudding 528
Homemade Marshmallows 529
Frozen Pecan and Caramel Log 530
Raspberry Puff Pastry Fingers 531
Frozen Dulce Leche 531
Caramel and Chocolate–Covered Apples 532
Fried Banana Spring Rolls 533
Chocolate and Cinnamon Dessert Pizza 534
Blended Iced Coffee Shooter 534

Chocolate Meringue Drops

Makes about 4 dozen cookies

Make more of these than you think you'll need — they are addictive.

- **Preheat oven to 300°F (150°C)**
- **Baking sheets, lined with parchment paper**

3	egg whites	3
Pinch	salt	Pinch
1 tsp	vanilla extract	5 mL
¾ cup	granulated sugar	175 mL
¾ cup	mini chocolate chips	175 mL
	Unsweetened cocoa powder	

1. In a large bowl, using an electric mixer, beat egg whites and salt until soft peaks form. Beat in vanilla, then gradually beat in sugar until stiff peaks form. Fold in chocolate chips.

2. Drop by tablespoonfuls (15 mL) onto prepared baking sheet, leaving about 2 inches (5 cm) between cookies. Bake in preheated oven until lightly browned, about 45 minutes. Turn off oven and let cookies stand for 1 hour. Transfer to a wire rack and dust lightly with cocoa. Let cool before serving. Drops will keep for up to 1 week in an airtight container.

Chocolate Toasts

Makes 12 toasts

These are so easy to make and so good. Buy the best chocolate you can find.

Tips

Depending upon the size of your bread, you may find it preferable to cut the slices into squares or triangles. You want the chocolate to be more or less centered on the bread.

- **Preheat oven to 350°F (180°C)**
- **Rimmed baking sheet, lined with parchment paper**

6	slices raisin bread, crusts removed and toasted (approx.) (see Tips, left)	6
2½ oz	plain chocolate bar, about ¼ inch (0.5 cm) thick, broken into 12 pieces (approx.)	75 g

1. Cut toasted crustless bread in half lengthwise. (You want each rectangle to be about 2½ by 1½ inches/ 6 by 4 cm). Place on prepared baking sheet. Place 1 piece of chocolate on top of each square. Place in preheated oven just until chocolate begins to melt, about 2 minutes. Serve immediately.

Classic Raspberry Jelly Shots

Makes 16 shots

For whatever reason, jelly unleashes the child in all of us.

Tips

The best way to work with gelatin is "bloom" the powder in water prior to adding to a large mixture. This will help to avoid a lumpy mixture.

These are wonderful as is but for a more adult version float a ½ tsp (2 mL) of vodka on the surface of the firmed jelly.

- **16 shot glasses**

1 tbsp	unflavored gelatin powder	15 mL
1 tbsp	cold water	15 mL
3 cups	raspberries, divided	750 mL
2 cups	water	500 mL
2 tbsp	granulated sugar	30 mL
1 tsp	chopped fresh basil leaves	5 mL

1. In a small bowl, sprinkle gelatin over 1 tbsp (15 mL) cold water. Let stand for 5 minutes, until softened.

2. In a saucepan, bring 2 cups (500 mL) of the raspberries, water and sugar to a boil over medium heat. Reduce heat and simmer until berries are falling apart, 3 to 5 minutes. Strain through a fine-mesh sieve into a bowl, pressing to remove seeds and pulp. Discard solids and reserve the liquid. Add 1 tbsp (15 mL) of the strained liquid to gelatin mixture and stir well. Stir into remaining strained liquid. Add remaining raspberries and stir well. Pour into shot glasses and refrigerate for at least 3 hours, until set, or overnight. Garnish with basil before serving.

Chocolate Popcorn Clusters

Makes 30 to 35 clusters

What a wonderful way to enjoy a childhood favorite. These are perfect frozen, too.

Tip

To freeze, remove refrigerated clusters after 1 hour, cover and freeze for a minimum of 3 hours or for up to 1 day.

- **Baking sheet, lined with parchment paper**

1 cup	semisweet chocolate chips	250 mL
4 cups	popped popcorn, cooled	1 L
1 tbsp	packed brown sugar	15 mL

1. In the top of a double boiler, or in a heatproof bowl, set over a pan of hot, not boiling water, melt chocolate chips, stirring until smooth. Remove from heat, add popcorn and fold to coat well.

2. Spoon about 1 tbsp (15 mL) popcorn in a pile on prepared baking sheet to form small clusters. Garnish each with brown sugar. Refrigerate for at least 1 hour, until firm, or for up to 1 day. Clusters will become stale after 24 hours.

Fried Green Bananas

Makes 10 bananas

Green bananas are similar to a plantain; unpalatable when eaten raw but simply divine when battered and fried.

Tip

Serve this wonderful dessert with Mango Dip (page 68) for a tropical fruit overload!

- **Candy/deep-fry thermometer**

6 tbsp	all purpose flour, divided	90 mL
1 tsp	granulated sugar	5 mL
¼ tsp	baking powder	1 mL
¼ tsp	baking soda	1 mL
6 tbsp	cold water	90 mL
	Oil	
1	large green banana, cut into ¾-inch (2 cm) slices	1
1 tsp	confectioner's (icing) sugar	5 mL

1. In a bowl, whisk together ⅓ cup (75 mL) of the flour, granulated sugar, baking powder and baking soda. Gradually whisk in cold water until fully incorporated, mix well to avoid lumps. Refrigerate for 20 minutes before using.

2. Meanwhile, in a large, deep saucepan or Dutch oven, heat 3 inches (7.5 cm) of oil over medium-high to 325°F (160°C). (You can also use a deep fryer; follow the manufacturer's instructions.)

3. Place remaining flour in a shallow bowl. Dip banana slices into flour, turning to lightly coat, and shaking off excess flour. Dip bananas into batter. Fry in hot oil, in batches, turning once, until crisp and golden brown, 3 to 4 minutes. Using a slotted spoon, place on a paper towel–lined plate to drain off excess oil. Place on a serving platter and sprinkle with confectioner's sugar. Serve hot.

Almond Cranberry Chocolate "Brittle"

Makes about 10 servings

Cranberries and chocolate make a spectacular marriage; give this a shot, you'll love it.

Tip

This recipe can be considered a base recipe to be used with whatever ingredients you like. If dried fruit isn't to your liking feel free to omit. If cranberries aren't your thing, try dried apricots or cherries. If you aren't crazy for almonds, try any nut you like — they'll all be great.

- **Baking sheet, lined with parchment paper**

¼ cup	coarsely chopped toasted almonds	60 mL
¼ cup	coarsely chopped dried cranberries	60 mL
4 oz	unsweetened chocolate, coarsely chopped	125 g
3 oz	semisweet chocolate, coarsely chopped	90 g
½ cup	granulated sugar	125 mL
2 tbsp	water	30 mL

1. Spread almonds and cranberries evenly over prepared baking sheet.

2. In the top of a double boiler, or in a heatproof bowl, set over a saucepan of hot, not boiling water, melt unsweetened and semisweet chocolate, stirring until smooth. Drizzle over almonds and cranberries and set aside to cool.

3. In a saucepan, combine sugar and water. Heat over medium heat, stirring gently, just until sugar is dissolved, then bring to a boil, without stirring. Boil gently (reducing heat if necessary), without stirring, until syrup turns a caramel color. Remove from heat and drizzle over chocolate, cranberries and almonds, filling in any empty spots. Let cool until set, preferably overnight or for up to 3 days. Break into serving-size pieces.

Five-Ingredient Molten Chocolate Cakes

Makes about 12 mini cakes

These incredible one-bite decadent chocolate treats will delight your senses every time you eat one, and trust us — you'll have a few, they're that good. Serve at the end of an appetizer party topped with a dollop of whipped cream or for a wonderful tart contrast, garnish with Blueberry and Yogurt Dip (page 67).

Tips

When adding the melted chocolate to the yolk mixture, be sure to add it gradually, in a thin stream and whisking constantly, to temper the eggs (warm them gradually) and avoid scrambling them.

These delightful cakes make a great frozen snack, too. Freeze them in an airtight container for up to 1 month. Let them stand at room temperature for 5 minutes before serving.

- **Preheat oven to 400°F 200°C**
- **Mini muffin pan, buttered**

1 cup	semisweet chocolate chips	250 mL
2	eggs, separated, at room temperature	2
¼ tsp	freshly squeezed lemon juice	1 mL
2 tsp	unsalted butter, melted	10 mL
1 tsp	granulated sugar	5 mL
1 tsp	all-purpose flour	5 mL

1. In the top of a double boiler, or in a heatproof bowl, set over a saucepan of hot, not boiling water, melt chocolate chips, stirring until smooth. Remove from heat and set aside.

2. In a small bowl, using an electric mixer, beat egg whites and lemon juice until stiff peaks.

3. In a medium bowl, whisk together egg yolks, butter and sugar until well blended. Gradually pour in melted chocolate, whisking constantly, until fully incorporated. Fold in flour just until blended. Fold in egg whites, one-third at a time, just until combined.

4. Spoon the batter into prepared muffin pan, leaving enough space in each cup to allow the batter to rise. Bake preheated oven until tops are firm to touch, 7 to 8 minutes. Let cool in pans on a wire rack until just cool to the touch. Serve immediately or let cool completely and store in an airtight container for up to 3 days.

Quick Chocolate Mousse

Makes about 1¼ cups (300 mL)

Enjoy this fluffy mousse in small glasses or espresso cups with cappuccino spoons or as dessert canapés (see Tip, below).

Tip

Surprise those surprise guests with an elegant and fun dessert canapé of your favorite cookie topped with a small quenelle of Quick Chocolate Mousse and some shaved chocolate curls.

¾ cup	heavy or whipping (35%) cream	175 mL
1 tbsp	granulated sugar	15 mL
⅓ cup	semisweet chocolate chips	75 mL
1 tbsp	unsalted butter, finely diced	15 mL

1. In a bowl, using an electric mixer or whisk, beat cream and sugar to stiff peaks. Set aside.

2. In the top of a double boiler, or in a heatproof bowl, set over a saucepan of hot, not boiling water, melt chocolate chips, stirring until smooth. Remove from heat and whisk chocolate to cool slightly, about 1 minute. Whisk in butter until melted and blended.

3. Fold whipped cream into the chocolate, one-third at a time, until just blended. Cover and refrigerate for at least 3 hours or until set or for up to 6 hours.

Strawberries and Cream

Makes 15 servings

The contrast of textures of the cold, hard strawberry and the "pillow-like" whipping cream will be a favorite on warm summer days.

Tips

All produce should be thoroughly rinsed before using. For strawberries, place them in a colander (with the hulls still attached) and rinse well under cool running water, rubbing gently to remove all grit. Drain well, then pat dry and remove hulls.

- **Baking sheet, lined with parchment paper**
- **15 Chinese-style soup spoons**

1 cup	strawberries, hulled	250 mL
1 cup	heavy or whipping (35%) cream	250 mL
1 tbsp	packed brown sugar	15 mL
1 tbsp	unsweetened shredded coconut, toasted	15 mL

1. Cut the strawberries lengthwise into quarters and place on prepared baking sheet, leaving space between each to avoid pieces sticking together. Freeze until the berries are solid, about 5 hours. If desired, transfer to an airtight container and freeze for up to 6 months.

2. Just before serving, in a chilled bowl, using an electric mixer or whisk, whip cream and sugar until stiff peaks form. Whisk in coconut. Spoon cream, dividing equally onto each spoon and garnish with 2 pieces of strawberry. Serve immediately.

Kickin' Chocolate Almond Clusters

Makes about 20 clusters

A very easy, yet elegant, way to pair almonds, chocolate and a smoky heat.

Tip

You can replace the almonds with your nut of choice.

- **Baking sheet, lined with parchment paper**

1½ cups	slivered almonds	375 mL
¼ cup	semisweet chocolate chips	60 mL
½ tsp	chipotle powder	2 mL

1. Warm a large skillet over medium heat. Add almonds and toast, stirring and shaking pan constantly, until fragrant and golden brown, 5 to 6 minutes. Remove from heat, add chocolate and chipotle powder and stir to combine until chocolate is fully melted.

2. Spoon almond mixture into small clusters onto prepared baking sheet, piling the clusters as high as you can. Refrigerate at least 3 hours, until set, before serving. Once set, store in an airtight container for up to 3 days. Serve cold.

Blueberry Chocolate Brochettes

Makes 10 brochettes

If you're in search of a simply prepared elegant "dessappetizer," search no more! Presented like a flower bouquet, the beautiful brochettes can sit blueberry side up in a tall clear glass or vase.

Tip

Use the larger, cultivated blueberries for this recipe, rather than the tiny wild blueberries.

- **Ten 6-inch (15 cm) wooden skewers**
- **Baking sheet, lined with parchment paper**

¾ cup	blueberries (see Tip, left)	175 mL
¾ cup	semisweet chocolate chips	175 mL
1 tsp	unsalted butter, at room temperature	5 mL

1. Skewer blueberries through the center of the berry onto the top portion of the skewer, ensuring point is not exposed and dividing blueberries equally among skewers. Place on a wire rack set over prepared baking sheet, or directly on sheet.

2. In the top of a double boiler, or in a heatproof bowl, set over a saucepan of hot, not boiling water, melt chocolate chips, stirring until smooth. Remove from heat and whisk in butter until melted and blended. Spoon chocolate over the blueberries, turning skewers to coat all sides. Refrigerate for at least 1 hour, until set, or up to 2 hours.

Rhubarb and Blueberry Compote with Vanilla Ice Cream

Makes 12 servings

This is like eating a rhubarb crumble without the crumble!

Tip

For a wonderfully minty flavor, pour ½ tsp (2 mL) mint-flavored liqueur on top of each quenelle.

- **12 martini glasses**

1 cup	coarsely chopped rhubarb	250 mL
2 tbsp	pure maple syrup	30 mL
1 tbsp	white wine	15 mL
2 tbsp	fresh or frozen blueberries	30 mL
Pinch	chipotle powder	Pinch
¾ cup	good-quality vanilla ice cream	175 mL
12	fresh mint leaves	12

1. In a medium saucepan, bring rhubarb, syrup and wine to a simmer over medium-high heat. Reduce heat and simmer, stirring often, until rhubarb is very soft, 8 to 10 minutes. Stir in blueberries and chipotle powder. Transfer to a bowl and let cool to room temperature.

2. Spoon compote into martini glasses and top with scoop of ice cream. Garnish with mint leaf and serve immediately.

Sesame-Scented Apricots

Makes 10 servings

These apricots offer a savory and sweet contrast with an Asian twist. Whipped cream would be lovely or even a dollop of Brown Sugar-Scented Peach Sabayon (page 527) but believe us, served all on their own, this will be one of those very simple recipes you'll want to make over and over again.

- **Preheat oven to 300°F (150°C)**
- **Shallow baking dish or ovenproof skillet**

5	apricots, halved	5
1 tsp	packed brown sugar, packed	5 mL
¼ tsp	sesame seeds	1 mL
¼ tsp	toasted sesame oil	1 mL
¼ cup	whipped cream, optional	60 mL

1. In a bowl, combine apricots, sugar, sesame seeds and sesame oil and toss to coat. Place in baking dish, skin side down. Bake in preheated oven until caramelized but not falling apart, about 20 minutes. Let cool to room temperature. Serve in a martini glass or other small dish. Top each with about 1 tsp (5 mL) whipped cream, if using.

Cinnamon-Sugar Phyllo Bunches

Makes 16 bundles

Crisp, sweet and light as a feather — these are almost guilt free!

Tip

For this recipe, we used sheets of phyllo pastry about 16 by 12 inches (40 by 30 cm) in size. If you have slightly larger sheets, you may need a bit more butter to cover them. If you have sheets about half the size, use 8 and after stacking 4 sheets, cut into 8 rectangles then repeat with a second stack of 4 sheets.

- **Preheat oven to 350°F (180°C)**
- **Baking sheet, lined with parchment paper**

1 tbsp	granulated sugar	15 mL
1 tsp	ground cinnamon	5 mL
4	sheets phyllo pastry (see Tip, left)	4
2 tbsp	unsalted butter, melted	30 mL
1 tsp	confectioner's (icing) sugar	5 mL

1. In a small bowl, combine sugar and cinnamon.

2. Place one sheet of phyllo pastry on a large cutting board and brush lightly with butter, covering the entire surface. Sprinkle evenly with 1 tsp (5 mL) cinnamon sugar. Stack another sheet of pastry on top, brush with butter and sprinkle with cinnamon sugar. Repeat until all four sheets are stacked, brushing each with butter and sprinkling with cinnamon sugar. Cut stack into 16 rectangles and, using your hands, scrunch each rectangle into a ball. Place on prepared baking sheet, at least 2 inches (5 cm) apart.

3. Bake in preheated oven until crispy and golden brown, 6 to 7 minutes. Dust with confectioner's sugar and serve warm. Alternatively, let cool to room temperature and store in an airtight container at room temperature for up to 3 days. Dust with confectioners' sugar just before serving.

Variation

How about a savory twist? Replace the cinnamon sugar with a combination of $\frac{1}{4}$ cup (60 mL) finely grated Parmesan cheese and 1 tbsp (15 mL) finely chopped thyme leaves and follow recipe accordingly. These would be perfect served with a cheese platter.

Apple-Cinnamon Phyllo Purses

Makes 12 purses

This is like a one-bite apple pie.

Tips

For this recipe, we used sheets of phyllo pastry about 16 by 12 inches (40 by 30 cm) in size. If you have slightly larger sheets, you may need a bit more butter to cover them. If you have sheets about half the size, use 6 and after stacking 3 sheets, cut into 6 squares then repeat with a second stack of 3 sheets.

When assembling the purses, pinch tightly to ensure purse is closed to avoid leakage.

To make Cinnamon Sugar: Combine ½ cup (125 mL) granulated sugar with 1 tbsp (15 mL) ground cinnamon and grind together in a spice grinder until powder. Store in airtight container in a dry, dark place for up to 1 month.

- **Preheat oven to 400°F (200°C)**

2 tbsp	unsalted butter, divided	30 mL
1½ cups	diced peeled Granny Smith or other tart cooking apples	375 mL
1 tbsp	dried cranberries, chopped	15 mL
1 tbsp	packed brown sugar	15 mL
⅛ tsp	ground cinnamon	0.5 mL
3	sheets phyllo pastry (see Tips, left)	3
	Cinnamon Sugar (see Tips, left)	

1. In a saucepan, melt 1 tbsp (15 mL) of the butter over medium-low heat. Add apples, cranberries, brown sugar and cinnamon and, cook, stirring often, until apples begin to break down and are tender, about 15 minutes. Remove from heat and let cool to room temperature.

2. In a glass bowl in the microwave on Medium-Low (30%) power or in a small saucepan over low heat, melt remaining 1 tbsp (15 mL) butter. Place one sheet of phyllo on a large cutting board and brush lightly with butter, covering the entire surface. Stack remaining sheets on top, brushing with butter. Cut phyllo stack into 12 squares, each about 4 inches (10 cm).

3. Spoon apple filling onto the center of each phyllo square, dividing equally. Working with one square at a time, bring the four corners together above the filling and pinch the dough into a purse, encasing the filling. Repeat with remaining purses. Place on a baking sheet, at least 2 inches (5 cm) apart. Bake in preheated oven until golden brown, about 15 minutes. Dust with cinnamon sugar just before serving. Store the cooked purses, uncovered, for up to 2 hours. These can also be left at room temperature for up to 3 hours and reheated just before serving.

Mini Sweet Potato Muffins with Maple Syrup Glaze

Makes 36 muffins

Even though there is a minimal amount of sugar in this recipe your guests, both young and old, will be coming back for seconds. Serve as a brunch or lunch treat or perhaps paired with a dessert wine for an evening appetizer party.

Tip

To make roasted sweet potato purée: Pierce a large sweet potato all over with a fork and roast in a 350°F (180°C) oven until fork tender, about 1 hour. Let cool to room temperature. Press through a potato ricer or a food mill, or peel and mash in a bowl, until smooth. Measure 1 cup (250 mL) and reserve any extra for another use.

- **Preheat oven to 300°F (150°C)**
- **36 mini muffin tins, greased**

Muffins

1 cup	sifted unbleached all-purpose flour	250 mL
1 tsp	baking powder	5 mL
Pinch	salt	Pinch
¾ cup	roasted sweet potato purée (see Tip, left)	175 mL
½ cup	agave syrup or liquid honey	125 mL
½ cup	milk	125 mL
1 tsp	melted unsalted butter	5 mL
1	egg	1
1 tsp	vanilla seeds (about 1 vanilla pod) or 1 tsp (5 mL) vanilla extract	5 mL

Glaze

½ cup	confectioner's (icing) sugar	125 mL
¼ cup	roasted sweet potato purée (see Tip, left)	60 mL
1 tbsp	maple syrup	15 mL
1 tsp	milk	5 mL

1. *Muffins:* In a bowl, whisk together flour, baking powder and salt. Set aside.

2. In a separate bowl, whisk together sweet potato, agave syrup, milk and melted butter until combined. Add egg and vanilla and whisk until integrated. Fold in dry ingredients into wet, mixing just until incorporated. Do not overmix.

3. Spoon batter into prepared muffin tins until they are about two-thirds full. Bake in preheated oven until muffins have risen and a toothpick comes out clean when inserted into the center, about 10 minutes. Let cool until warm to the touch.

4. *Glaze:* In a bowl, whisk together confectioner's sugar, sweet potato purée, maple syrup and milk until glossy and thick. Cover and refrigerate until ready to use. When ready to serve, dip tops of the muffins into the glaze.

Mini Chocolate Chunk Banana Sandwiches

Makes 18 cookies

This cake-like cookie is amazing by itself and works beautifully to create a "dessapetizer" sandwich.

Tip

Chocolate chips are a fine substitute for chunks, but to make chunks buy baking chocolate, which comes in small "bricks" from the grocery store, and roughly cut with a knife into desired consistency.

- **Preheat oven to 300°F (150°C)**
- **Baking sheet, lightly greased**

Cookies

1¼ cups	sifted pastry flour	300 mL
½ tsp	baking powder	2 mL
Pinch	salt	Pinch
1 cup	packed brown sugar	250 mL
¼ cup	unsalted butter	60 mL
2	eggs	2
1 tsp	vanilla seeds (about 1 vanilla pod) or 1 tsp (5 mL) vanilla extract	5 mL
¼ cup	bittersweet chocolate chunks (see Tip, left)	60 mL
2	ripe bananas, peeled and thinly sliced	2
2 tbsp	maple syrup	30 mL

1. *Cookies:* In a bowl, combine flour, baking powder and salt.

2. In a separate bowl, using an electric mixer on medium speed, beat brown sugar and butter until light and fluffy, about 3 minutes. Add eggs and vanilla, mixing until fully incorporated. On low speed add dry ingredients, mixing just until combined. Stir in chocolate chunks.

3. Drop dough by tablespoonfuls (15 mL), about 2 inches (5 cm) apart onto prepared baking sheet. Bake in preheated oven until golden brown, about 10 minutes. Let cool for 5 minutes on baking sheet then transfer to rack to completely cool.

4. In a bowl, combine bananas and maple syrup and mix to coat. To make sandwiches, slice cookies in half along the "equator." Place a few slices of banana on one side and place the other half on top enclosing the bananas. Serve immediately.

Quick Blueberry "Sorbet"

Makes about 20 servings

Having frozen berries in your freezer at all times makes this a wonderful refreshing dessert a cinch that can be made in minutes!

Tip

All produce should be thoroughly rinsed before using. For blueberries, place them in a colander and rinse well under cool running water, stirring gently. Drain well, then pat dry.

- **Rimmed baking sheet, lined with parchment paper**

2 cups	fresh or frozen blueberries	500 mL
¼ cup	agave syrup	60 mL
¼ cup	heavy or whipping (35%) cream	60 mL
	Blueberries, optional	
	Chopped fresh mint, optional	

1. Spread blueberries on prepared sheet and freeze until blueberries are solid, about 5 hours. If using frozen blueberries, omit this step.

2. In a food processor fitted with a metal blade, pulse berries, syrup and cream until smooth. Transfer to an airtight container and freeze until firm, at least 3 hours. About 20 minutes before serving, let sorbet stand at room temperature to temper. Scrape surface with a tines of a fork to loosen mixture (or break into chunks and transfer to a food processor and pulse quickly). Spoon into martini glasses or shallow serving dishes and garnish with fresh berries or mint, if desired.

Warm Apple Sour Cream

Makes about 1½ cups (375 mL)

Caution: highly addictive! This is the perfect dessert dip. Serve with fresh strawberries, apple, pear or pineapple wedges.

Tips

Spread ¼ cup (60 mL) of dip in the middle of a plate to make a wonderful base for warm apple pie.

2 cups	chopped Granny Smith apples	500 mL
1 tbsp	freshly squeezed lemon juice	15 mL
1 tbsp	unsweetened apple juice or water	15 mL
1 tbsp	unsalted butter	15 mL
¾ cup	sour cream, at room temperature	175 mL
1 tsp	coarsely chopped fresh mint leaves	5 mL
⅛ tsp	salt	0.5 mL

1. In a saucepan, combine apples, lemon juice, apple juice and butter and bring to a simmer over medium heat. Reduce heat and boil gently until apples are breaking down, about 10 minutes. Transfer to a food processor and purée until smooth.

2. Transfer to a bowl and let cool. Stir in sour cream, mint and salt until smooth. Serve immediately.

Frozen Mango Mousse

Makes about 2 cups (500 mL)

A cross between sorbet and granita (a granular Italian frozen ice dessert), this wonderful dessert is good for you, too.

Tip

To make mango purée: Bring 1 large mango, chopped (or 2 small) and 1 cup (250 mL) water to a boil over medium heat. Reduce heat to low and simmer until soft, about 5 minutes. Purée until smooth. Let cool to room temperature.

¼ cup	pasteurized egg whites, at room temperature	60 mL
1 tbsp	granulated sugar	15 mL
1¾ cups	mango purée (see Tip, left)	425 mL
1 tsp	liquid honey	5 mL

1. In a bowl, vigorously whisk together egg whites and sugar until stiff peaks (or beat with an electric mixer). In a freezer-safe bowl, whisk together mango purée and honey. Fold the egg whites into the mango mixture until well blended.

2. Freeze until firm, for at least 4 hours, removing 5 or 6 times and scraping the mixture with the tines of a fork, creating little "pebbles," or for up to 5 hours. About 10 minutes before serving, let stand at room temperature just until soft enough to scoop. Spoon into bowls and serve immediately.

Tropical Fruit Soup

Makes about 12 servings

What a refreshing way to enjoy tropical fruits on a warm day, one "slurp" and you'll be transported to your favorite tropical paradise.

Tip

This is a recipe in which the fruits are interchangeable. Use what tropical fruit you have available; kiwifruit or papaya would substitute very well for either the mango or pineapple.

- **12 espresso cups or other small dishes**

4 cups	coarsely chopped pineapple	1 L
1	mango, diced	1
1 cup	orange juice	250 mL
¼ cup	freshly squeezed lime juice	60 mL
1 tbsp	liquid honey	15 mL
6	mint leaves	6
Pinch	salt	Pinch

1. In a food processor fitted with a metal blade, combine pineapple, mango, orange juice, lime juice, honey, mint and salt and pulse until smooth. Strain through a fine mesh strainer into a large bowl. Press a wooden spoon against solids to extract as much liquid as possible. Discard any remaining solids. Cover and refrigerate until thoroughly chilled, for at least 3 hours or up to 3 days. Stir well, then ladle into espresso cups and serve immediately.

World's Greatest Applesauce

Makes about 3 cups (750 mL)

A lovely way to serve freshly picked apples from the orchard or those store-bought apples you just had to buy. Serve in clear serving dishes with a dollop of freshly whipped cream or crème fraîche or Stewed Bing cherries (page 546) and a dusting of freshly grated cinnamon.

6 cups	chopped McIntosh or other soft, tart apples (about 2 lbs/1 kg)	1.5 L
2	chopped nectarines	2
½ cup	granulated sugar	125 mL
1	piece (2 inches/5 cm) cinnamon stick	1
½ cup	freshly squeezed grapefruit juice	125 mL

1. In a saucepan, combine apples, nectarines, sugar, cinnamon stick and grapefruit juice and bring to a boil over medium heat. Reduce heat and simmer, stirring occasionally, until all apples are very soft, about 1½ hours. Discard cinnamon stick.

2. Press through a food mill or transfer to a food processor fitted with a metal blade (see Tips, left) and pulse until smooth. Let cool to room temperature before serving.

Chocolate Macaroons

Makes about 18 macaroons

These macaroons are on the smallish side, almost one-biters — make a lot because they'll go fast!

Tip

When egg whites are whisked to "stiff peaks" this literally means to whip them until they resemble a mountain range — stiff, with zero movement when you slowly lift the whisk out of the whites.

- **Preheat oven to 350°F (180°C)**
- **Baking sheet, lined with parchment paper**

2	egg whites, at room temperature	2
1 tsp	agave syrup	5 mL
1 tsp	granulated sugar	5 mL
1 cup	sweetened shredded coconut	250 mL
½ cup	milk chocolate chips	125 mL

1. In a bowl, whisk egg whites, agave syrup and sugar and whisk to stiff peaks (or use an electric mixer). Stir in coconut and chocolate chips, mix thoroughly to combine.

2. Drop tablespoonfuls (15 mL) of batter onto prepared baking sheets, at least 2 inches (5 cm) apart. Bake in preheated oven until golden brown, about 10 minutes. Transfer to a wire rack and let cool to room temperature before serving. Enjoy immediately or store in airtight container at room temperature for up to 5 days.

Mini French Toast with Fresh Peaches and Peach Maple Syrup

Makes about 6 Servings

Really, could there be a better way to start your guests' meal than with a familiar food like French toast showcasing gorgeous ripe peaches? You should make a lot because they become addictive.

Tip

Our favorite bread to use for French toast is challah or egg bread. The texture is a little softer and more the finished product is moister than their whole wheat counterpart.

3	eggs	3
¼ cup	whole milk	60 mL
1 tsp	granulated sugar	5 mL
1 tsp	vanilla extract	5 mL
18	1½-inch (4 cm) cubes whole wheat bread (see Tip, left)	18
1 tbsp	unsalted butter	15 mL
1 tsp	peach preserves or jam	5 mL
¼ cup	pure maple syrup	60 mL
18	small cubes fresh peaches	18

1. In a bowl, whisk together eggs, milk, sugar and vanilla.

2. In a nonstick skillet, melt butter over medium heat. Dip the bread cubes into egg mixture, letting excess drip off. Fry until golden brown on bottom, about 1 minute. Cook, turning often, until every side is golden brown, about 3 to 4 minutes. Transfer to a plate.

3. In the same pan over low heat, warm peach preserves and maple syrup, stirring constantly, about 30 seconds. Remove from heat. Place 1 cube of peach on top of each French toast cube and pierce with a toothpick. Drizzle the peach syrup over top and serve immediately.

Sweet Wontons

Makes 20 wontons

A versatile canvas for fruit salsas like Minty Mango Salsa (page 87) or Tropical Fruit Salsa (page 92).

- • **Preheat oven to 475°F (240°C)**
- • **Baking sheet, lined with parchment paper**

10	wonton skins, each about 3 inches (7.5 cm) square	10
1	egg, beaten	1
1 tbsp	granulated sugar	15 mL

1. Cut the wrappers in half diagonally, creating triangles. Place on prepared baking sheets, at least 1 inch (2.5 cm) apart. Brush the wontons with egg and sprinkle evenly with sugar.

2. Bake in preheated oven until golden brown, about 20 minutes. Let cool on pan or wire rack. Store in an airtight container at room temperature for up to 1 week.

Mini Peach Bread Pudding

Makes 9 puddings

Bread pudding is not a guilt-free dessert but the peaches sure help to justify those calories.

Tip

A bain marie, also known as a water bath, is used to evenly disperse the heat to gently cook delicate custard-based desserts such as pudding, soufflé or crème brûlée.

- • **Nine ½-cup (125 mL) ramekins**
- • **Roasting pan or baking pan large enough to fit ramekins**

¼ cup	granulated sugar	60 mL
3½ cups	whole milk	875 mL
4	eggs	4
¼ tsp	vanilla extract	1 mL
4½ cups	diced dried bread	1.125 L
1 cup	diced peaches	250 mL
	Hot water	

1. In a bowl, whisk together sugar, milk, eggs and vanilla until smooth. Fold in bread and peaches and mix well. Cover and refrigerate for 1 hour.

2. Preheat oven to 300°F (150°C).

3. Spoon bread mixture into ramekins. Place ramekins in roasting pan and pour in hot water to come a quarter of the way up the sides of ramekins. Bake in preheated oven until golden brown and toothpick inserted in the center comes out clean, about 50 minutes. Serve hot or let cool slightly.

Brown Sugar and Peach Sabayon

Makes about 2½ cups (625 mL)

Sabayon has a velvety texture that you really must try at least once in your life.

Tip

Serve this sabayon in a Chinese soup spoon with a garnish of mint leaves and diced peaches.

3 cups	diced peaches	750 mL
⅓ cup	packed brown sugar	75 mL
1 cup	sweet white wine	250 mL
1 cup	water	250 mL
1 tbsp	granulated sugar	15 mL
6	egg yolks	6
⅛ tsp	vanilla extract	0.5 mL

1. In a saucepan combine peaches, brown sugar, wine and water and bring to a boil over medium heat, stirring until sugar is dissolved. Reduce heat and simmer until liquid has reduced to syrup, about 15 minutes. Transfer to a blender, or use an immersion blender in the pot, and purée until smooth. Set aside.

2. In the top of a double boiler or a heatproof bowl, whisk together granulated sugar, egg yolks and vanilla. Cook over simmering water, whisking constantly, until pale and thick and ribbons form when whisk is lifted. Remove from heat and fold in peach purée. Return to saucepan and cook, whisking until thick, about 2 minutes. Serve immediately.

Agave-Glazed Pineapple

Makes 12 pieces

This incredibly sweet dessert is simple to make and packed full of wonderful flavor.

Tip

Place the cubes on Chinese-style soup spoons and garnish with whipped cream.

1 tbsp	unsalted butter	15 mL
12	1½-inch (4 cm) cubes pineapple	12
1 tbsp	agave syrup	15 mL
1 tbsp	toasted sliced almonds	15 mL

1. In a large skillet, melt butter over high heat until browned, about 1 minute. Add pineapple and cook, stirring often, until caramelized, about 5 minutes. Add agave syrup and toss to coat. Remove from heat. Garnish with almonds and serve immediately.

Sugar-Coated Concord Grapes

Makes 6 servings

An elegant dessert that pairs wonderfully with a dessert wine.

Tip

A wonderful alternative is to freeze the bunches of grapes overnight, omitting the sugar syrup and sugar, and serve as a cool summer treat.

Cardamom-Scented Simple Syrup

1 cup	granulated sugar, divided	250 mL
½ cup	water	125 mL
1	cardamom pod	1
6	small bunches Concord or other seedless grapes (10 to 15 grapes per bunch)	6

1. *Cardamom-Scented Simple Syrup:* Place ½ cup (125 mL) of the sugar in the middle of a saucepan. Pour water around the sugar. Add cardamom and bring to a boil over medium heat, stirring, until sugar is dissolved. Remove from heat and let cool to the touch.

2. One bunch at a time, dip the grapes into the simple syrup, letting excess drip off. Holding the grapes over a bowl and using a spoon, shake sugar onto the grapes to evenly cover. Gently shake off excess sugar. Repeat to cover all bunches. Serve immediately.

Easy-Peasy Chocolate Pudding

Makes 2 cups (500 mL)

As we get older it's these familiar comfort food desserts that bring out our inner child and help to keep us young.

Tip

To refrigerate overnight, place plastic wrap on top of pudding, actually touching, to prevent a skin from forming. When removing plastic some chocolate may get on rim of serving dishes, be sure to wipe clean with a damp tea towel.

4 oz	semisweet chocolate, coarsely chopped	125 g
2½ tbsp	cornstarch	37 mL
2 tbsp	granulated sugar	30 mL
¼ tsp	salt	1 mL
2 cups	whole milk	500 mL

1. Place chocolate in a heatproof bowl. In the top of a double boiler, or in a heatproof bowl, whisk together cornstarch, sugar and salt. Gradually whisk in milk to ensure no lumps. Place over a saucepan of simmering water and cook, whisking constantly, until thick enough to coat the back of a spoon, about 15 minutes.

2. Strain through a fine-mesh strainer into the chocolate. Stir well until melted and pour into individual serving dishes. Serve immediately or let cool to room temperature. Cover and refrigerate for at least 3 hours, until set, or overnight before serving. Good both hot or cold.

Homemade Marshmallows

Makes 36 marshmallows

Who needs store-bought when homemade marshmallows are so easy to make? Serve with a variety of jams or marmalade and suggest your guests put a dollop on top for a fruity note.

Tips

Although a stand mixer is really the easiest way to whip the mixture to stiff peaks, it is not absolutely essential. A hand-held electric mixer would work well, too, but will take longer to get stiff peaks.

A wonderful variation is to dip half of the marshmallow into melted chocolate and let stand until set before serving, it's yummy. It's best to avoid humid weather when making these marshmallows; choose a dry day to avoid sticky marshmallows.

- **Stand mixer with whisk attachment or hand mixer (see Tips, left)**
- **9- by 5-inch (23 by 12.5 cm) metal loaf pan, greased**

1 tbsp	unflavored gelatin	15 mL
¾ cup	water, divided	175 mL
½ cup	granulated sugar	125 mL
3 tbsp	corn syrup	45 mL
2 tsp	vanilla extract	10 mL
1 cup	confectioner's (icing) sugar	250 mL

1. In a small bowl, sprinkle gelatin over ¼ cup (60 mL) of the water. Let stand for 5 minutes, until softened.

2. In a saucepan, combine remaining ½ cup (125 mL) water and granulated sugar and bring to a boil over medium heat, stirring until sugar is dissolved. Reduce heat and simmer until syrup consistency, about 3 minutes. Remove from heat. Stir in gelatin mixture, stirring until gelatin is dissolved.

3. Transfer to the bowl of stand mixer and add corn syrup and vanilla. Beat on high speed until stiff peaks form, 10 to 20 minutes. Spread in prepared pan, smoothing top. Let cool completely and then cover loosely and let stand overnight to firm up.

4. Sift confectioner's sugar onto a cutting board. Invert set marshmallow on to the sugar, removing pan, and turn block of marshmallow to evenly coat with sugar to prevent sticking to the board. Dip the knife into sugar to lightly coat and cut into 36 squares. Turn each square several times, dipping in the sugar to coat each side. Serve immediately or store in airtight container at room temperature for up to 1 week.

Frozen Pecan and Caramel Log

Makes about 16 to 20 cookies

This wonderful frozen appetizer can be made well in advance of your guests' arrival. Serve as a dessert cookie all on its own or garnish with a dollop of whipped cream or crème fraîche and a mint leaf and create a dessert canapé.

Tip

When adding the cream to the caramel there is quite a bit of steam that is released, so be sure to not have your face or arms over the pan to avoid severe burns.

2 oz	bittersweet chocolate, coarsely chopped	60 g
2 cups	coarsely chopped toasted pecans	500 mL
1 cup	granulated sugar	250 mL
¼ cup	water	60 mL
⅓ cup	heavy or whipping (35%) cream	75 mL

1. In a heatproof bowl, combine chocolate and pecans. Set aside.

2. In a saucepan, combine sugar and water. Heat over medium heat, stirring gently, just until sugar is dissolved, then bring to a boil, without stirring. Boil gently (reducing heat if necessary), without stirring, until syrup turns a caramel color. Remove from heat and let bubbles subside. Carefully pour in cream (see Tip, left) and swirl to incorporate.

3. Immediately pour caramel over the nuts and chocolate and mix to combine. Place a 12-inch (30 cm) square of parchment paper on a work surface. Pour the nut mixture over the paper. Starting with the edge closest to you, using the parchment to lift the nut mixture as you would a sushi rolling mat, roll up to form a log about 2 inches (5 cm) in diameter and 8 to 10 inches (20 to 25 cm) long. Place the wrapped log on a square of plastic wrap and wrap up tightly, twisting both ends to make the log as tight as possible. Freeze for at least 3 hours, until firm, or for up to 2 weeks.

4. Remove from plastic wrap and place log (leaving the paper on) on a cutting board. Cut into ½-inch (1 cm) thick cookies and serve immediately.

Raspberry Puff Pastry Fingers

Makes 24 fingers

This very simple and elegant dessert is perfect to accompany an espresso or aperitif or even a small scoop of ice cream.

Tip

Pricking the pastry with a fork or a docker (a tool that looks like a spiked paint roller) before baking is called, "docking." It allows steam to escape from the pastry during baking, preventing the pastry dough from rising too much and helps make it crisp.

- **Preheat oven to 325°F (160°C)**
- **Baking sheet, lined with parchment paper**

8 oz	puff pastry, thawed (see Tip, left)	250 g
¼ cup	raspberry jam	60 mL
2 tbsp	sesame seeds, toasted	30 mL

1. On a lightly floured surface, roll out pastry to a 12-inch (30 cm) square. Using a fork, prick pastry all over. Spread jam evenly over the pastry. Using a pizza cutter or large knife, cut into 32 equal "fingers."

2. Place on prepared baking sheet, at least 1 inch (2.5 cm) apart. Bake in preheated oven until pastry is golden brown and flaky, about 15 minutes. Sprinkle with sesame seeds. Let cool on pan on a wire rack before serving. Store in an airtight container for up to 3 days.

Frozen Dulce de Leche

Makes 10 to 12 servings

If you're like us or most people — you love ice cream. This dessert will remind you of a decadent, very dense ice cream or gelato that is very simple to make and lasts for up to one week. This is a wonderful refreshing dessert to make in advance of any appetizer party, especially in the summer months.

2 tbsp	granulated sugar	30 mL
1	can (12 oz or 370 mL) evaporated milk	1
1 tbsp	sliced almonds, toasted	15 mL

1. In the top of a double boiler, or in a heatproof bowl, set over a saucepan of simmering water, whisk together sugar and milk. Cook, whisking often, until the mixture turns caramel color and is thick enough to coat the back of a spoon, about 45 minutes. Let cool slightly, then transfer to a freezer-safe, sealable container and let cool completely. Once cooled, cover and freeze for at least 3 hours, until firm, or for up to 1 week.

2. Warm a teaspoon under hot water, pat dry, then skim the surface of the dulce de leche to form a quenelle (a football shape). Place the spoons on a serving platter. Garnish with almonds and serve immediately.

Caramel and Chocolate–Coated Apples

Makes 12 servings

A gorgeous "dessappetizer" that children and adults of all ages will enjoy. Freshly picked apples aren't just for pies any more! Be creative with your toppings; virtually any sweets would make a lovely garnish.

Tip

When adding the cream to the caramel there is quite a bit of steam that is released, so be sure to not have your face or arms over the pan to avoid severe burns.

- **Baking sheet, lined with parchment paper**

4 oz	semisweet chocolate, coarsely chopped	125 g
2	Gala or other sweet apples, each cut into 6 wedges	2
1 tsp	freshly squeezed lemon juice	5 mL
½ cup	granulated sugar	125 mL
2 tbsp	water	30 mL
¼ cup	heavy or whipping (35%) cream	60 mL
¼ cup	toffee bits, such as Skor	60 mL

1. In the top of a double boiler, or in a heatproof bowl, set over a pan of hot, not boiling water, melt chocolate, stirring until smooth. Remove from heat.

2. Meanwhile, in a separate bowl, combine apples with lemon juice and toss to coat. Drain off excess juice and pat apples dry. Dip apple wedges in chocolate, covering about ¾ of the wedge. Place on prepared baking sheet and refrigerate until chocolate is set, about 30 minutes.

3. In a saucepan, combine sugar and water. Heat over medium heat, stirring gently, just until sugar is dissolved, then bring to a boil, without stirring. Boil gently (reducing heat if necessary), without stirring, until syrup turns a caramel color. Remove from heat and let bubbles subside. Carefully pour in cream (see Tip, left) and swirl to incorporate. Remove from heat and let cool for 5 to 10 minutes. Dip chocolate-dipped portion of the apples into the caramel, covering about half of the wedge and return to baking sheet. Sprinkle wet caramel with toffee bits. Let stand at room temperature for 2 hours before serving or overnight.

Fried Banana Spring Rolls

Makes 12 rolls

Crispy on the outside and melt-in-your-mouth delicious on the inside.

- **Candy/deep-fry thermometer**

	Oil	
3	ripe bananas	3
1 tbsp	packed brown sugar	15 mL
1/4 tsp	ground cinnamon	1 mL
2 tsp	freshly squeezed lemon juice	10 mL
12	spring roll wrappers, each about 6 inches (15 cm) square	12
1	egg, beaten	1

1. In a deep skillet or Dutch oven, heat 3 inches (7.5 cm) of oil over medium-high to 350°F (180°C). (You can also use a deep fryer; follow the manufacturer's instructions.)

2. On a cutting board, slice the peeled banana in half lengthwise and then cut each in half crosswise. In a bowl, combine brown sugar, cinnamon and lemon juice and stir well. Add the bananas and toss gently to coat.

3. Working with one spring roll wrapper at a time and keeping remaining wrappers covered to prevent drying out, place on a work surface and brush egg around the perimeter of the wrapper. Place 1 piece of banana lengthwise on wrapper, about 1/2 inch (1 cm) from the edge closest to you. Fold the two sides in toward the center over the banana. Roll the wrapper away from you until banana is fully encased. Fry, in batches, in hot oil, turning once, until spring rolls are floating and golden brown, 5 to 6 minutes. Using a slotted spoon, transfer to a paper towel–lined plate to drain. Serve hot.

Chocolate and Cinnamon Dessert Pizza

Makes 8 servings

There's no way your pizza man has ever delivered this type of pizza to your door!

Tip

Be creative with your toppings. If cinnamon sugar isn't to your liking, warm your favorite jam or marmalade and brush liberally over the surface of the cooked crust.

- **Preheat oven to 325°F (160°C)**
- **Ovenproof skillet**

7 oz	pizza dough	210 g
1 tbsp	unsalted butter	15 mL
1 tbsp	Cinnamon Sugar (see Tips, page 519)	15 mL
1 cup	chocolate shavings	250 mL
1 tsp	chopped fresh mint leaves	5 mL

1. On a lightly floured surface, roll out pizza dough to an 8-inch (20 cm) round.
2. In ovenproof skillet, melt butter over medium heat. Carefully place dough in bottom of skillet and transfer skillet to oven. Bake until edges are crisp and golden brown, 7 to 10 minutes. Flip dough and bake until dough is golden and firm, about 7 minutes. Sprinkle evenly with Cinnamon Sugar. Let cool in pan until cool enough to work with. Transfer to a cutting board and cut into 8 wedges. Sprinkle each wedge with chocolate shavings and garnish with mint. Serve immediately.

Blended Iced Coffee Shooter

Makes about 4 cups (1 L)

Here's a refreshing way to finish any appetizer party in the heat of summer. Be sure to make extras for those coffee refills.

Tip

Serve in a shot glass with Coffee Scented Hazelnuts (page 457) as a whimsical coffee offering to your guests.

- **Shooter glasses or espresso cups and spoons**

2 tbsp	packed brown sugar, packed	30 mL
2 cups	crushed ice	500 mL
1⅓ cups	heavy or whipping (35%) cream	325 mL
1 cup	cold brewed coffee	250 mL
2 tbsp	chocolate-flavored liqueur	30 mL
2 tbsp	chocolate syrup	30 mL

1. In a blender, combine sugar, ice, cream, coffee, liqueur and chocolate syrup and blend until smooth. If the mixture is too thick to blend, gradually add just enough cold water until desired consistency. Serve immediately.

Basics and Condiments

This chapter contains basic recipes such as vinaigrettes, which can be used for various recipes. It also contains recipes for condiments such as *Seasoned Salts (page 552), Enhanced Mayonnaise (page 538)or Roasted Red Pepper Coulis (page 543), which can provide a finishing touch for many recipes. We've given you some ideas of how to use the condiments here and you'll find further references in the recipes scattered throughout the book.*

Instant Aïoli	536
Chile-Spiked Aïoli	536
Lemon Horseradish Aïoli	537
Wasabi Aïoli	537
Cooked Egg Mayonnaise	538
Enhanced Mayonnaise	538
Foolproof Hollandaise	539
Caper Lemon Rémoulade	539
Red Wine Vinaigrette	540
Tomatillo Vinaigrette	540
Roasted Cherry Tomato Vinaigrette	541
Roasted Red Pepper Vinaigrette	541
Maple Vinaigrette	542
Truffle Vinaigrette	542
Roasted Red Pepper Coulis	543
Smoky Red Pepper Coulis	543
Two-Tomato Coulis	544
Sauce Vierge	544
Jalapeño-Spiked Onion Marmalade	545
Grape Mignonette	545
Stewed Bing Cherries	546
Oven-Roasted Cherry Tomato Sauce	546
Basic Sweet-and-Sour Sauce	547
Cocktail Sauce	547
Braised Leeks	548
Marinated Mushrooms	548
Sautéed Garlic Scapes	549
Basil Pesto	549
Chive Parsley "Pistou"	550
The Perfect Barbecue Coleslaw	550
Refrigerated Dill Pickles	551
Pickled Onions	551
Seasoned Salts	552
Caramelized Onions	552
Basic Barbecue Sauce	553
Preserved Lemons	554
Peanut Sauce	554
Ian's Dukkah	555

Instant Aïoli

Makes about ¾ cup (175 mL)

Here's a perfect solution to finishing a simple appetizer such as Grilled Shrimp (page 303). It's effortless and surprisingly delicious.

Tips

The quantity of garlic depends upon how strong you want the aïoli to taste and the size of the garlic cloves. Four produces a nicely garlicky aïoli.

Don't confuse real mayonnaise with "mayonnaise-type" salad dressings. Mayonnaise is a combination of egg yolks, vinegar or lemon juice, olive oil and seasonings. Imitators will contain additional ingredients, such as sugar, flour or milk.

½ cup	store-bought mayonnaise (see Tips, left)	125 mL
4 to 6	cloves garlic, coarsely chopped (see Tips, left)	4 to 6
2 tbsp	extra virgin olive oil	30 mL
2 tbsp	freshly squeezed lemon juice	30 mL
1 tsp	Dijon mustard	5 mL
1 tsp	salt	5 mL
½ tsp	freshly ground black pepper	2 mL
Pinch	cayenne pepper, optional	Pinch

1. In a food processor fitted with metal blade, process mayonnaise, garlic, olive oil, lemon juice, mustard, salt, black pepper, and cayenne, if using, until mixture is smooth and well blended, about 1 minute. Cover and chill until ready to use.

Variations

Dill Aïoli: Add 2 tbsp (30 mL) chopped dill along with the mayonnaise.

Spicy Aïoli: Add 2 tbsp (30 mL) hot Asian chile sauce, such as sambal oelek or Sriracha. Pulse to blend.

Chile-Spiked Aïoli

Makes about ½ cup (125 mL)

If you're feeling the need to add a little spice to a traditional sandwich or simple boiled or grilled shrimp, try this.

½ cup	mayonnaise (see Tips, above)	125 mL
2 tsp	hot Asian chile sauce, such as sambal oelek	10 mL
1	clove garlic, puréed	1

1. In a small bowl, combine mayonnaise, chile sauce and garlic. Mix well. Refrigerate until ready to use.

Lemon Horseradish Aïoli

Makes ¼ cup (60 mL)

This spicy condiment is so versatile it can accompany anything from Salmon Sliders (page 266) to Crispy Zucchini Fingers (page 419).

2 tbsp	mayonnaise	30 mL
1 tbsp	freshly grated horseradish or drained prepared horseradish	15 mL
1 tsp	chopped drained capers, rinsed thoroughly	5 mL
1 tsp	freshly grated lemon zest	5 mL
1 tbsp	freshly squeezed lemon juice	15 mL
Pinch	freshly ground black pepper	Pinch
Pinch	salt	Pinch

1. In a bowl, combine mayonnaise, horseradish, capers, lemon zest and juice, pepper and salt and mix well to combine. Cover and refrigerate overnight to allow flavors to meld or for up to 3 days.

Wasabi Aïoli

Makes ½ cup (125 mL)

Spicy wasabi is a sensational addition to velvety mayonnaise.

Tip

Wasabi, also called Japanese horseradish, can be found in most large grocery chains in the Asian foods section or in the Asian markets. It is usually found in two forms; powdered in tins or as a paste in tubes. If you're very lucky, you will come across the actual wasabi root, similar to horseradish, which can be grated fresh. For this recipe, grate 1 tbsp (15 mL) fresh horseradish into mayonnaise and omit water altogether.

2 tbsp	cold water	30 mL
1 tsp	wasabi powder (see Tip, left)	5 mL
½ cup	mayonnaise	125 mL
½ tsp	puréed gingerroot	2 mL

1. In a small bowl, combine water and wasabi powder, stirring until smooth. Add mayonnaise and ginger and stir to thoroughly combine. Serve immediately or cover and refrigerate for up to 3 days. It's important to note that this aïoli will become hotter as it sits in the refrigerator so watch out!

Cooked Egg Mayonnaise

Makes about 1¼ cups (300 mL)

If you are using a lot of mayonnaise, it is worth the trouble to make your own. It is tastier, better for you and more economical.

Tip

Canola oil is relatively flavorless and is used here to neutralize the strong flavors in the olive oil. A cold-pressed version is a healthy alternative to the conventional product, which is refined. Look for it in natural foods stores.

2	egg yolks	2
2 tbsp	freshly squeezed lemon juice	30 mL
2 tbsp	water	30 mL
2 tsp	Dijon mustard	10 mL
1 tsp	salt	5 mL
Pinch	cayenne pepper	Pinch
½ cup	extra virgin olive oil	125 mL
½ cup	cold-pressed canola oil (see Tip, left)	125 mL

1. In a small saucepan over low heat, combine egg yolks, lemon juice and water. Cook, whisking constantly, until eggs begin to thicken, about 1 minute. Whisk rapidly for about 5 seconds longer to ensure the yolks are cooked, then immediately transfer to a food processor fitted with metal blade. (If you have a mini-bowl attachment, it is ideal for this recipe.)

2. Add Dijon mustard, salt and cayenne and process for 30 seconds, stopping and scraping down sides of the bowl once or twice. (You want the mixture to be well beaten.) With motor running, slowly add olive oil and canola oil through the feed tube in a small stream, processing until mixture is smooth and creamy. Use immediately or transfer to a clean container, cover and refrigerate for up to 1 week.

Variations

Garlicky Aïoli: Add 4 cloves coarsely chopped garlic to egg mixture after it has been processed for 30 seconds.

Roasted Garlic Aïoli: Add roasted garlic (page 228 or 484) to taste, to egg mixture after it has been processed for 30 seconds.

Enhanced Mayonnaise

There are many kinds of enhanced mayonnaise, such as Easy Tartar Sauce (page 266), Louis Sauce (page 284) and Instant Aïoli (page 536) that can be created in a flash and used to dress up plain ingredients. For instance, aïoli can anchor a tasting platter, surrounded by hard-cooked eggs, boiled new potatoes, blanched green beans, cauliflower and/or broccoli florets.

Foolproof Hollandaise

Makes about 1 cup (250 mL)

Hollandaise is one of the classic sauces in French cuisine. The one problem with Hollandaise is that it doesn't keep. So if you're using only a small amount consider serving simple roasted or grilled salmon for a main course.

Tip

To make the clarified butter for this recipe: Heat ²⁄₃ cup (150 mL) butter in a saucepan over medium heat until melted. Remove from heat and, using a small slotted spoon, skim off the foam. Carefully pour off the yellow butterfat and discard the remaining milk solids that sank to the bottom.

3	egg yolks	3
3 tbsp	water	45 mL
1 tbsp	freshly squeezed lemon juice	15 mL
½ cup	warm clarified butter (see Tip, left)	125 mL
½ tsp	salt	2 mL
	Cayenne pepper	

1. In a small saucepan over low heat, combine egg yolks, water and lemon juice. Cook, whisking constantly, until eggs begin to thicken, about 1 minute. Whisk rapidly for about 5 seconds longer to ensure the yolks are cooked. If they start to curdle whisk in 1 tbsp (5 mL) boiling water. Immediately transfer to a food processor fitted with metal blade.

2. With motor running, slowly add clarified butter through the feed tube in a small stream, processing until mixture is smooth and creamy. Add salt and cayenne to taste and process until smooth. Serve immediately.

Variations

Chive Hollandaise: Add ¼ cup (60 mL) coarsely chopped chives along with the salt and process until smoothly blended.

Dill Hollandaise: Add ¼ cup (60 mL) coarsely chopped fresh dill along with the salt and process until smoothly blended.

Caper Lemon Rémoulade

Makes ½ cup (125 mL)

A wonderful complement to any fish or seafood appetizer.

½ cup	mayonnaise	125 mL
1 tsp	minced drained capers	5 mL
1 tsp	grated lemon zest	5 mL
1 tsp	freshly squeezed lemon juice	5 mL
1 tsp	minced gherkins	5 mL

1. In a bowl, combine mayonnaise, capers, lemon zest and juice and gherkins and mix well to combine. Serve immediately or cover and refrigerate for up to 3 days.

Red Wine Vinaigrette

Makes about ¾ cup (175 mL)

A very tasty, very versatile vinaigrette. Garnish fresh shucked oysters or dip a fresh roll or salad roll or simply dress an appetizer salad. You may have found another addition to your culinary arsenal.

¼ cup	red wine vinegar	60 mL
1 tbsp	Dijon mustard	15 mL
¼ tsp	salt	1 mL
¼ tsp	freshly ground black pepper	1 mL
½ cup	extra virgin olive oil	125 mL

1. In a bowl, whisk together vinegar, mustard, salt and pepper. Slowly drizzle in oil, whisking vigorously, until all oil is incorporated and vinaigrette is thick. Use immediately or transfer to a jar or airtight container and refrigerate for up to 3 days.

Tomatillo Vinaigrette

Makes ¾ cup (175 mL)

Tomatillo's citrusy acidic flavor balances quite well with marbled meats like beef strip loin or prime rib and fatty fish like salmon or black cod.

Tips

To prepare tomatillos, peel back skin and wash thoroughly under cold water to remove the sticky, waxy coating.

Roasting tomatillos yields a sweeter flavor to the vinaigrette. To roast, place tomatillos (in the husks) in a pan and roast in 500°F (260°C) oven until soft, 20 to 25 minutes. Let cool. Peel off husks, chop and measure 1 cup (250 mL) then follow the recipe.

¼ tsp	ground cumin	1 mL
1 cup	coarsely chopped tomatillos (see Tips, left)	250 mL
½ cup	rice vinegar	125 mL
1 tbsp	minced red onion	15 mL
¼ tsp	salt	1 mL
¼ cup	extra virgin olive oil	60 mL

1. In a saucepan over medium heat, toast cumin, stirring constantly, until fragrant, about 2 minutes. Add tomatillos, vinegar and onion and bring to a boil. Reduce heat and simmer, stirring often, until tomatillos are breaking down, about 10 minutes. Remove from heat.

2. Add salt and transfer to a blender, or use an immersion blender in the pan, and purée until smooth. With the motor running, slowly drizzle in oil through the feed tube, mixing until emulsified. Use immediately or transfer to a jar or airtight container and refrigerate for up to 3 days.

Roasted Cherry Tomato Vinaigrette

Makes 1¼ cups (300 mL)

Store-bought salad dressings and vinaigrettes are staples in most households, but why not try making your own? They're yummy and quite simple to make.

¾ cup	Oven-Roasted Cherry Tomato Sauce (page 546)	175 mL
1½ tsp	minced garlic	7 mL
1 tsp	finely chopped fresh basil	5 mL
¼ cup	extra virgin olive oil	60 mL
¼ cup	sherry vinegar	60 mL
½ tsp	salt	2 mL
¼ tsp	freshly ground black pepper	1 mL

1. In a bowl, whisk together tomato sauce, garlic, basil, olive oil, sherry vinegar, salt and pepper. Use immediately or store in a jar or airtight container in the refrigerator for up to 3 days. Whisk well before serving.

Roasted Red Pepper Vinaigrette

Makes 2¼ cups (550 mL)

Not only does this vinaigrette have tremendous depth of flavor, it's also very versatile...try it on salads, as a dip or spread on sandwiches.

1 cup	packed chopped roasted red peppers (see Tips, page 495)	250 mL
½ cup	extra virgin olive oil	125 mL
⅓ cup	red wine vinegar	75 mL
1 tbsp	liquid honey or agave syrup	15 mL
1 tsp	salt	5 mL
1 tsp	freshly ground black pepper	5 mL
½ tsp	finely chopped fresh thyme leaves	2 mL

1. In a blender, combine red peppers, olive oil, vinegar, honey, salt, pepper and thyme and purée until smooth and emulsified, about 1 minute. Use immediately or transfer to a jar or airtight container and refrigerate up to 3 days.

Maple Vinaigrette

Makes ⅔ cup (150 mL)

This lovely vinaigrette can double as a dip for Maple-Glazed Bacon (page 480) or Roasted Potato Wedges (page 404).

Tip

We suggest a good quality pure dark maple syrup.

6 tbsp	extra virgin olive oil	90 mL
¼ cup	white balsamic vinegar	60 mL
3 tbsp	pure maple syrup (see Tip, left)	45 mL
1 tbsp	minced garlic	15 mL
1 tbsp	minced shallots	15 mL
1 tsp	chopped fresh basil leaves	5 mL

1. In a jar or a bowl, combine olive oil, vinegar, syrup, garlic, shallots and basil. Cover jar and shake vigorously to emulsify (or whisk in the bowl). Serve immediately or refrigerate up to 3 days.

Truffle Vinaigrette

Makes about 1 cup (250 mL)

Truffles: a finer flavor there will never be. Bring a little sophistication to Smoked Turkey and Asparagus Rolls (page 132) or a drizzle on Mini Caramelized Onion Tartlets (page 167) or just on an appetizer salad.

Tip

Fresh truffles are a glorious treat for the senses if you can find them and, better yet, afford them. Truffle oil is more widely available in your local fine foods or gourmet food shops — just be careful of those synthetic imposters!

½ cup	sunflower or other mild-flavored oil	125 mL
2 tbsp	finely diced shallots	30 mL
1 tsp	minced garlic	5 mL
⅓ cup	Champagne vinegar or apple cider vinegar	75 mL
2 tbsp	pure white truffle oil	30 mL
1 tbsp	olive oil	15 mL
1 tsp	finely chopped fresh chives	5 mL

1. In a saucepan, combine sunflower oil, shallots and garlic and bring to a simmer over medium heat. Remove from heat, transfer to a bowl and let cool to room temperature.

2. Whisk in vinegar, truffle oil, olive oil and chives. Serve immediately or transfer to a jar or airtight container and refrigerate for up to 1 week.

Roasted Red Pepper Coulis

Makes about 1¾ cups (425 mL)

Vegan Friendly

This coulis is easy to make, packs a lot of flavor and can be used to enhance many dishes. Slightly tart, it is perfect for the glorious overkill of Deep-Fried Brie (page 388) or the crunchy richness of Bacon-Spiked Rösti Cakes (page 407) to name just two.

2	roasted red bell peppers (see Tips, page 495)	2
3	oil-packed sun-dried tomatoes	3
2 tbsp	extra virgin olive oil	30 mL
1 tbsp	balsamic vinegar	15 mL
10	fresh basil leaves	10
	Salt and freshly ground black pepper	

1. In a food processor fitted with metal blade, process roasted peppers, sun-dried tomatoes, oil, balsamic vinegar and basil until smooth. Season to taste with salt and pepper. Serve immediately or cover and store for up to 2 days.

Smoky Red Pepper Coulis

Makes about 1½ cups (375 mL)

Vegan Friendly

This colorful purée can add a shot of color to a plate and bright flavor to countless dishes. Spread on a smoky Grilled Herbed Crostini (page 220) or use as a dip for crudités and Classic French Fries (page 413).

Tips

This recipe will work with any color pepper. Green peppers may not yield the color you're looking for but the addition of fresh basil or parsley will enhance the color.

1 tbsp	olive oil	15 mL
2 cups	coarsely chopped red bell peppers	500 mL
¼ tsp	chipotle powder	1 mL
¼ tsp	ancho chile powder	1 mL
2 cups	water or chicken or vegetable broth	500 mL
½ tsp	sherry vinegar	2 mL
½ tsp	salt	2 mL

1. In a saucepan, heat oil over medium heat. Add peppers, chipotle powder and ancho chile powder and cook, stirring often, until soft, about 5 minutes. Add water and bring to a boil. Reduce heat and simmer until liquid is reduced by one quarter, about 10 minutes.

2. Transfer to a blender, or use an immersion blender in the pan, and purée until smooth. Transfer back to saucepan and bring to a boil over medium heat. Reduce heat and boil until reduced by half, about 20 minutes. Stir in vinegar and salt. Serve immediately or transfer to an airtight container and refrigerate for up to 3 days.

Two-Tomato Coulis

Makes about 1 cup (250 mL)

This light, fresh-tasting sauce is delicious on Corn Cakes (page 199), Spicy Seared Calamari (page 312) or even as a substitute for Aïoli in the Grilled Shrimp with Aïoli (page 303).

Tip

Sun-dried tomatoes are packed in olive oil or packaged dry. Those packed in olive oil are already reconstituted. If yours are the dry variety, blanch in boiling water for 4 minutes and drain before adding to recipe.

1 cup	cherry tomatoes	250 mL
2	reconstituted sun-dried tomatoes (see Tips, left)	2
¼ cup	chicken or vegetable broth	60 mL
1 tbsp	balsamic vinegar	15 mL
15	fresh tarragon leaves or ¼ cup (60 mL) fresh dill fronds	15
½ tsp	salt	2 mL
	Freshly ground black or white pepper	

1. In a food processor fitted with metal blade, pulse cherry and sun-dried tomatoes, broth, vinegar, tarragon, salt, and pepper to taste, until chopped and blended, stopping and scraping down sides of the bowl once or twice, about 15 times.

Sauce Vierge

Makes about 1¾ cups (425 mL)

This sauce is surprisingly light, given that it is so flavorful. It is delicious with fish, particularly shellfish. Try substituting it for the Aïoli in Grilled Shrimp with Aïoli (page 303) or if you're a vegan, try serving it over Bruschetta (page 231) or your favorite roasted vegetables.

20	fresh basil leaves	20
1	clove garlic, coarsely chopped	1
1 tsp	finely grated lemon zest	5 mL
3 tbsp	freshly squeezed lemon juice	45 mL
½ cup	extra virgin olive oil	125 mL
15	cherry or grape tomatoes	15
15	pitted black olives	15
	Salt and freshly ground black pepper	

1. In a food processor fitted with metal blade, process basil, garlic, lemon zest and juice and olive oil until basil and garlic are minced. Add tomatoes and olives and pulse to coarsely chop. Season to taste with salt and pepper.

Jalapeño-Spiked Onion Marmalade

Makes about 1 cup (250 mL)

This tasty condiment is very easy to make and is an impressive addition to any table. Use it to top Crêpes Parmentier (page 200) or as a finish for Bacon-Spiked Rösti Cakes (page 407), among other things.

Tip

After refrigeration, the mixture will thicken even more. If yours becomes too solid, before using simply heat it in a microwave oven for 1 minute or over low heat on top of the stove until desired consistency is reached.

1½ cups	granulated sugar	375 mL
½ cup	apple cider vinegar	125 mL
2 tsp	caraway seeds	10 mL
1 to 2	jalapeño peppers, seeded and minced	1 to 2
1 tsp	salt	5 mL
2	onions (about 1 lb/500 g total), thinly sliced	2

1. In a large saucepan, combine sugar and vinegar. Bring to a boil and simmer until sugar is dissolved and mixture begins to become syrupy, about 5 minutes. Add caraway seeds, jalapeño pepper to taste and salt and stir well. Stir in onions and bring to a boil. Reduce heat and simmer, stirring occasionally, until onions are caramelized and mixture is thick, about 1 hour. Transfer to a serving bowl, cover and refrigerate for up to 1 month.

Grape Mignonette

Makes about ⅔ cup (150 mL)

A perfect garnish to accompany any raw fish or bivalve. It can also be used to garnish Fresh Corn Cakes (page 449) or Zucchini Fritters (page 418).

6 tbsp	finely diced English cucumber	90 mL
¼ cup	finely diced seedless green grapes	60 mL
¼ cup	rice vinegar (see Tips, page 344)	60 mL
½ tsp	chopped fresh dill	2 mL
⅛ tsp	salt	0.5 mL
⅛ tsp	freshly ground black pepper	0.5 mL

1. In a bowl, combine cucumber, grapes, vinegar, dill, salt and pepper and mix to combine. Cover and refrigerate for at least 1 hour or for up to 3 hours.

Stewed Bing Cherries

Makes about ½ cup (125 mL)

There are only a few months of the year when fresh cherries are at their peak of flavor. Eaten raw they're just lovely but when stewed, the flavor is over-the-top cherry! Enjoy these cherries with ice cream, Sweet Wontons (page 526) or on a crostini.

1 cup	pitted Bing or other sweet cherries	250 mL
¼ cup	unsweetened apple juice	60 mL
1 tsp	pure maple syrup	5 mL
½ tsp	balsamic vinegar	2 mL
½ tsp	finely chopped fresh basil leaves	2 mL
¼ tsp	finely chopped fresh mint leaves	1 mL

1. In a saucepan, bring cherries, apple juice, syrup and vinegar to a simmer over medium heat. Boil, stirring occasionally, until liquid is reduced by half and a syrupy consistency, about 10 minutes. Remove from heat and stir in basil and mint. Serve immediately or let cool to room temperature or transfer to an airtight container and refrigerate for up to 3 days.

Oven-Roasted Cherry Tomato Sauce

Makes 1½ cups (375 mL)

You'll want to make this your new staple tomato sauce and get rid of your store-bought imposters.

Tip

Virtually any cherry, grape or small ripe tomato will work perfectly for this recipe.

- **Preheat oven to 350°F (180°C)**
- **Ovenproof saucepan or a glass baking dish**

1 lb	cherry tomatoes (about 2 cups/500 mL)	500 g
1 tsp	olive oil	5 mL
2	thyme sprigs	2
1 tsp	chopped fresh basil leaves	5 mL
1 tsp	chopped garlic	5 mL
¼ tsp	salt	1 mL
Pinch	freshly ground black pepper	Pinch

1. In ovenproof saucepan, combine tomatoes, oil and thyme. Roast in preheated oven until tomatoes are soft and golden brown, about 30 minutes. Discard thyme sprigs.
2. Add basil, garlic, salt and pepper and transfer to a blender, or use an immersion blender in the pan, and purée until smooth. Use immediately or transfer to an airtight container and refrigerate for up to 3 days.

Basic Sweet-and-Sour Sauce

Makes about ¾ cup (175 mL)

This sauce will become a staple for all your parties. Serve with everything from Thyme-Spiked Cheese Sticks (page 395) to Coconut-Crusted Mini Drumsticks (page 472).

¼ cup	finely diced onion	60 mL
¼ cup	extra virgin olive oil	60 mL
2 tbsp	rice vinegar (see Tip, page 344)	30 mL
2 tbsp	liquid honey or agave syrup	30 mL
2 tbsp	soy sauce	30 mL
1 tbsp	finely grated parsnip	15 mL
1 tbsp	finely grated carrot	15 mL
1 tbsp	freshly squeezed lemon juice	15 mL
1 tsp	minced garlic	5 mL
1 tsp	toasted sesame oil	5 mL
½ tsp	puréed gingerroot	2 mL

1. In a bowl, combine onion, olive oil, vinegar, honey, soy sauce, parsnip, carrot, lemon juice, garlic, sesame oil and ginger and mix well. Cover and refrigerate overnight to allow flavors to meld or for up to 3 days.

Cocktail Sauce

Makes about 1¼ cups (300 mL)

The classics are the classics for a reason. Cocktail sauce is not only for dipping poached shrimp for the classic shrimp cocktail. Try this sauce with any seafood, from fresh oysters to grilled salmon, it's the perfect accompaniment.

¾ cup	tomato ketchup	175 mL
¼ cup	stone-ground mustard	60 mL
¼ cup	freshly squeezed lemon juice	60 mL
¼ cup	finely grated fresh horseradish or drained prepared horseradish	60 mL

1. In a bowl, combine ketchup, mustard, lemon juice and horseradish and mix well to combine. Serve immediately or cover and refrigerate for up to 3 days.

Braised Leeks

Makes about 1½ cups (375 mL)

A very sweet condiment with many uses. Use on top of Lamb and Red Onion Sliders (page 269) for an another sweet onion flavor or simply spread on a Grilled Herbed Crostini (page 220), either way you'll love it!

Tip

Reserve the green part of the leeks to make chicken, beef or vegetable stock.

1 tbsp	olive oil	15 mL
2½ cups	finely chopped leeks, white part only	625 mL
¼ cup	white wine	60 mL
1 tsp	minced drained capers	5 mL
¼ tsp	finely chopped fresh thyme leaves	1 mL
¼ tsp	salt	1 mL
¼ tsp	freshly ground black pepper	1 mL

1. In a saucepan, heat oil over medium-low heat. Add leeks and cook, stirring often, until soft but not browned, about 12 minutes. Add wine and cook, stirring often, until evaporated. Remove from heat and stir in capers, thyme, salt and pepper. Serve immediately or let cool, then transfer to an airtight container and refrigerate for up to 3 days.

Marinated Mushrooms

Makes about 1 cup (250 mL)

As a stand-alone antipasti or a condiment on an appetizer sandwich or Grilled Herbed Crostini (page 220), these will be an excellent addition to most parties.

1 tbsp	olive oil	15 mL
¼ cup	diced smoked bacon	60 mL
3 cups	quartered button mushrooms	750 mL
1	rosemary sprig	1
¼ tsp	salt	1 mL
¼ cup	white balsamic vinegar	60 mL
1 tbsp	agave syrup	15 mL

1. In a saucepan, heat oil over medium heat. Add bacon and cook, stirring often, until fat is slightly rendered, about 2 minutes. Add mushrooms, rosemary and salt and cook, stirring often, until mushrooms are soft, 5 to 6 minutes. Add vinegar and agave syrup and bring to a simmer. Boil until liquid is evaporated, about 8 minutes. Let cool to room temperature, cover and refrigerate for at least 3 hours or for up to 3 days before serving. Discard rosemary sprig.

Sautéed Garlic Scapes

Makes about 1½ cups (375 mL)

Try garlic scapes (garlic shoots) in place of spinach or other greens on any of your favorite appetizer sandwich or canapés.

1 tbsp	unsalted butter	15 mL
2 cups	coarsely chopped garlic scapes	500 mL
¼ tsp	salt	1 mL

1. In a skillet, melt butter over medium heat. Add garlic scapes and salt and cook, tossing often, until scapes are tender-crisp, about 5 minutes. Serve immediately.

Basil Pesto

Makes about ¾ cup (175 mL)

This is a fantastic spread on crostini, garnish for shooters or a dip for crudités. We suggest uses for Basil Pesto throughout this book on such recipes as Grilled Vegetable Skewers (page 326), Poached Artichokes (page 362) and Basil and White Bean Spread (page 50) to name a few.

Tips

Different herbs can be used, in addition to, or as a substitute for the basil. Try cilantro, parsley or thyme.

Try freezing pesto in ice cube trays, then transfer to a freezer bag or airtight container once solid.

2 cups	coarsely chopped fresh basil leaves	500 mL
⅔ cup	pine nuts, toasted	150 mL
½ cup	freshly grated Parmesan cheese, preferably Parmigiano-Reggiano	125 mL
½ cup	extra virgin olive oil	125 mL
3	cloves garlic	3
½ tsp	salt	2 mL
¼ tsp	freshly ground black pepper	1 mL

1. In a food processor fitted with metal blade, combine basil, pine nuts, Parmesan, oil, garlic, salt and pepper and pulse until smooth. Use immediately or transfer to a jar or airtight container and refrigerate for up to 3 days.

Chive Parsley "Pistou"

Makes about ½ cup (125 mL)

This is a spin off a classic Italian basil pesto, which includes pine nuts. Here, in the more French version, it's nothing but the clean flavors of parsley, chives, garlic and olive oil. Use to garnish Classic Garlic Bread (page 210), grilled pizza or even Margarita Pizza Pockets (page 253).

¾ cup	coarsely chopped fresh parsley leaves	175 mL
½ cup	extra virgin olive oil	125 mL
¼ cup	coarsely chopped fresh chives	60 mL
2	cloves garlic	2

1. In a blender, combine parsley, olive oil, chives and garlic and purée until smooth. Use immediately or cover and refrigerate for up to 3 days.

The Perfect Barbecue Coleslaw

Makes about 4 cups (1 L)

This is an amazing garnish on appetizer sandwiches like Turkey Sliders with Chipotle Mayo (page 267), or all on its own. You will love the versatility of this coleslaw.

Tip

Although we love the recipe for Basic Barbecue Sauce on page 553, feel free to use any barbecue sauce you're comfortable with — the coleslaw will be great no matter which of your favorites you choose.

4 cups	packed thinly sliced green cabbage	1 L
1 cup	julienned green apples	250 mL
½ cup	thinly sliced red onion	125 mL
3 tbsp	Basic Barbecue Sauce (page 553) or store-bought	45 mL
2 tbsp	red wine vinegar	30 mL
2 tbsp	thinly sliced green onion	30 mL
1 tsp	Dijon mustard	5 mL
1 tsp	minced garlic	5 mL
½ tsp	salt	2 mL

1. In a bowl, combine cabbage, apples, red onion, barbecue sauce, vinegar, green onion, mustard, garlic and salt and mix well to combine. Cover and refrigerate for at least 3 hours to allow flavors to meld or overnight before serving.

Refrigerated Dill Pickles

Makes about 1 quart (1 L)

There are wonderful pickles on the market but making your own allows you to add all of the different flavors you like...and the best part is that they're so easy to make.

Tip

These dill pickles are not preserved, therefore aren't shelf stable and must be stored in the refrigerator.

- **1 quart (1 L) mason jar with lid**

1 lb	3 to 4 inch (7.5 to 10 cm) pickling cucumbers, cut in half lengthwise	500 g
1 cup	water	250 mL
¼ cup	sherry vinegar	60 mL
2	cloves garlic, thinly sliced	2
1 tbsp	kosher or pickling salt	15 mL
1 tbsp	granulated sugar	15 mL
½ tsp	dill seeds	2 mL
¼ tsp	black peppercorns	1 mL
1	bay leaf	1

1. Pack cucumbers into the mason jar.

2. In a saucepan, combine water, vinegar, garlic, salt, sugar, dill, pepper and bay leaf and bring to a boil over medium heat. Pour over cucumbers in jar and let cool to room temperature. Cover and refrigerate for at least 2 days to allow flavors to meld before serving or for up to 1 week.

Pickled Onions

Makes about 1¼ cups (300 mL)

Pickled onions make a fantastic garnish on salads and appetizer sandwiches.

½ cup	sherry vinegar	125 mL
1 tsp	granulated sugar	5 mL
¼ tsp	dill seeds	1 mL
¼ tsp	salt	1 mL
2 cups	thinly sliced red onions	500 mL

1. In a saucepan, combine vinegar, sugar, dill and salt and bring to a boil over medium heat. Place red onions in an airtight container. Pour vinegar mixture over top. Let cool to room temperature. Refrigerate overnight or for up to 3 days.

Seasoned Salts

Seasoned salts are an easy way to add flavor to any dish. You can make them in small batches and use them up, as needed. Don't balk at the extra cost of good sea salt. It's more than worth it. At its most basic it is healthier because it shouldn't contain anti-caking additives or ingredients such as sugar — check the packaging. Also it contains a very small amount of minerals. Table salt is not, in our opinion, real salt. It is a refined product — pure sodium chloride with additives.

Roasted Pepper and Salt: In a dry skillet, combine 1 tsp (5 mL) black or Szechuan peppercorns and 1 tsp (5 mL) coarse sea salt. Cook, stirring, over medium heat until fragrant and pepper begins to pop. Immediately transfer to a mortar or spice grinder and grind.

Green Tea Salt: In a mortar or a spice grinder, combine 2 tbsp (30 mL) coarse sea salt and 2 tsp (10 mL) loose leaf green tea. Grind to desired consistency.

Chile Salt: In a mortar or spice grinder, combine 2 tbsp (30 mL) coarse sea salt and 4 dried red chiles. Grind until desired consistency is reached. Transfer to a small bowl. Stir in 2 tsp (10 mL) finely grated lemon zest.

Caramelized Onions

Makes ½ cup (125 mL)

Vegetarian Friendly

A condiment for all occasions. Serve atop Bacon-Spiked Chopped Liver with Grilled Crostini (page 475), use as a garnish for cheese or spread on a grilled pizza — you'll find many more great uses for Caramelized Onions.

Tip

Any type of onion will work for this recipe; from red to cipollini to shallots, they will all be delicious.

1 tbsp	unsalted butter	15 mL
½ tsp	olive oil	2 mL
2 cups	thinly sliced onions (see Tip, left)	500 mL
¼ tsp	salt	1 mL
⅛ tsp	freshly ground black pepper	0.5 mL

1. In a skillet, heat butter and oil over medium heat. Add onions and cook, stirring often, adjusting the heat as necessary to prevent burning, until soft and golden brown, about 25 minutes. Season with salt and pepper. Serve immediately or transfer to an airtight container and refrigerate for up to 3 days.

Basic Barbecue Sauce

Makes 3 cups (750 mL)

When we think of condiments there are a few that always come up — barbecue sauce is one. Perhaps you have a sauce passed down through generations or just love that store-bought sauce you've been using for years, but trust us, you're going to want to try this sauce. Try as a dip for Smoked Chicken (page 477) or a topping on Beef and Parmesan Sliders (page 268).

Tip

Good quality liquid smoke is made from actual smoke from familiar woods like mesquite and hickory and usually barrel-aged and filtered to dispense of any harmful contaminants. It is often used to replicate that Southern smokehouse smell and flavor, but remember — a little bit goes a very long way.

1½ cups	coarsely chopped plum (Roma) tomatoes	375 mL
1 cup	tomato ketchup	250 mL
1 cup	water	250 mL
½ cup	chopped onion	125 mL
2	cloves garlic, halved	2
2 tbsp	sherry or red wine vinegar	30 mL
1 tbsp	soy sauce	15 mL
1 tbsp	Dijon mustard	15 mL
1 tbsp	packed brown sugar	15 mL
½ tsp	vegan or regular Worcestershire sauce	2 mL
¼ tsp	chipotle powder	1 mL
1 tsp	liquid smoke, optional	5 mL

1. In a deep saucepan, combine tomatoes, ketchup, water, onion, garlic, vinegar, soy sauce, Dijon mustard, brown sugar, Worcestershire sauce and chipotle powder. Cover and bring to a simmer over medium heat. Reduce heat to low and simmer, covered, stirring occasionally, until onions are soft, about 15 minutes.

2. Add liquid smoke and transfer to a blender, or use an immersion blender in the pan, and purée until smooth. Use immediately or let cool to room temperature, then transfer to an airtight container and refrigerate for up to 3 weeks.

Preserved Lemons

Makes 2 lemons

A uniquely tart and salty flavor and aroma that's going to contribute to so many of your appetizers and other dishes.

Tips

Meyer lemons are exceptional in this recipe. They are rounder in shape and much more fragrant than regular lemons.

Every bit of the preserved lemon is edible.

- **1 pint (250 mL) mason jar with plastic lid**

3	lemons	3
3 tbsp	kosher or sea salt	45 mL
1	sprig fresh mint	1

1. On a cutting board, slice 2 of the lemons into 8 wedges each. Squeeze juice from remaining lemon.

2. Spoon 1 tbsp (15 mL) salt into mason jar and pour in lemon juice. Pack 8 lemon wedges into jar and push to release juice. Spoon another tbsp (15 mL) salt on top of lemons and repeat with remaining lemon wedges and salt. Seal jar and store in a cool, dark place for about 1 month or until rind is translucent and soft. Store in the refrigerator for about 6 months. Just before serving, rinse lemons under cold water to remove excess salt and chop or slice to desired consistency.

Peanut Sauce

Makes about 1 cup (250 mL)

This is a great dipping sauce for satay, among other things. Try it with Traditional Chicken Satay (page 342), Coconut-Spiked Chicken Satay (page 343) or Peanut-Crusted Beef Tenderloin Satay (page 351), just to get you started.

½ cup	smooth peanut butter	125 mL
¼ cup	warm water	60 mL
1 tbsp	each soy sauce and rice vinegar	15 mL
2 tsp	toasted sesame oil	10 mL
1	piece (about 2 inches/5 cm) peeled gingerroot, cut into quarters	1
2	cloves garlic, coarsely chopped	2
1 tsp	granulated sugar	5 mL
2 tbsp	chopped cilantro, optional	30 mL
1	long red chile pepper, minced, optional	1
1 tbsp	finely chopped roasted peanuts, optional	15 mL

1. In a blender or food processor, process peanut butter, water, soy, vinegar, oil, ginger, garlic, sugar, and cilantro and/or chile, if using until mixture is smooth. Serve in bowls for dipping and garnish with peanuts, if using.

Ian's Dukkah

Makes about 1½ cups (375 mL)

Thanks to Ian Hemphill, author of The Spice and Herb Bible *for his dukkah recipe, from which this is adapted. Dukkah is a flavorful mix of nuts, seeds and spices that originated in Egypt and is used in many different ways throughout the Middle East. For a instant appetizer, try sprinkling dukkah over fresh cheese such as feta, mozzarella or soft goat cheese and drizzle with extra virgin olive oil. The most common use for dukkah is as an accompaniment to pita or crusty bread. For a simple appetizer, provide each of your guests with two little bowls, one containing extra virgin olive oil and the other dukkah. Dip pita bread into the oil, then the dukkah for a deliciously different treat. For a more sophisticated approach make Crisp Pita Bread with Dukkah (see Variations, page 216) and serve it with Roasted Carrot and Yogurt Dip (page 20).*

- **Preheat oven to 350°F (180°C)**

¼ cup	hazelnuts	60 mL
¼ cup	pistachio nuts	60 mL
⅔ cup	white sesame seeds	150 mL
⅓ cup	ground coriander seeds (see Tip, page 415)	75 mL
2½ tbsp	ground cumin seeds (see Tip, page 415)	37 mL
1 tsp	salt, or to taste	5 mL
½ tsp	freshly ground black pepper	2 mL

1. Place hazelnuts and pistachio nuts on separate baking sheets and roast in preheated oven for 15 minutes until they are fragrant. When the hazelnuts are toasted, place them in a kitchen towel on a cutting board and rub to remove the skins. In a food processor fitted with metal blade, coarsely chop hazelnuts and pistachio nuts.

2. In a dry skillet over medium heat, toast sesame seeds, stirring constantly, just until they begin to brown, 3 to 4 minutes. Immediately remove from heat and transfer to a small bowl. Combine with coriander and cumin seeds, hazelnuts, pistachio nuts and salt and pepper. Refrigerate in an airtight container for up to 3 months.

Acknowledgments

As always, thanks to my husband and greatest fan, Bob Dees. Life wouldn't be nearly as much fun without you. Also to Marian Jarkovich, Nina McCreath and Martine Quibell for their professional commitment, which is always above and beyond the call of duty. Also to Audrey King, my longtime recipe tester, whose exactitude is consistently exemplary. To the team at PageWave Graphics — Kevin Cockburn, Joseph Gisini and Daniella Zanchetta, food stylist Kathryn Robertson, prop stylist Charlene Erricson and photographer Colin Erricson, for making my recipes look so delicious and my books look so beautiful. And last, but certainly not least, to my editor Carol Sherman, who always manages to maintain her poise and terrific sense of humor, even in the middle of impending catastrophe.

— Judith Finlayson

Without question this book has been a labor of love. I have a newfound respect for authors. A huge thank you to Bob Dees for this exceptional opportunity. To Judith Finlayson and Carol Sherman, thank you for your patience and direction throughout this process. To my friends who are fighting, keep up the good fight, you're stronger than I could ever be. To those friends who have lost their fight you will be in our hearts always.

To Tamar, Jonah and Jamie, thank you for putting up with the good, bad and ugly (read cranky) me. I love you very much. You are my life.

— Chef Jordan Wagman

Library and Archives Canada Cataloguing in Publication

Finlayson, Judith
    750 best appetizers : from dips & salsas to spreads & shooters / Judith Finlayson, Jordan Wagman.

Includes index.
ISBN 978-0-7788-0272-3

1. Appetizers. 2. Cookbooks. I. Wagman, Jordan II. Title. III. Title: Seven hundred and fifty best appetizers.

TX740.F5295 2011   641.8'12   C2011-903204-X

Index

(v) = variation

A

The Absolute Best Creamed Corn, 450
Acorn Squash Sage Shooter, 119
agave syrup
Agave and Ginger Scented Peanuts, 455
Agave-Glazed Pineapple, 527
Honey Mustard Dip, 60
Mini Sweet Potato Muffins with Maple Syrup Glaze, 520
Sweet-and-Sour Sauce, Basic, 547
aïolis, 536–37
alcoholic beverages. *See also* beer; wine
Bacon-Spiked Mushroom and Chicken Liver Pâté, 463
Chicken Yakitori, 340
Country Terrine, 464
Martini-Marinated Salmon, 290
Rum-Spiked Watermelon Shooter, 112
Tipsy Tomato Shooter, 104
Vodka-Spiked Gravlax with Honey Mustard Sauce, 287
almonds
Almond Cranberry Chocolate "Brittle", 513
Almond Gazpacho, 103
Anchoyade de Croze, 47
Asparagus Salsa, 79
Chicken Pinwheels with Couscous, 151
Chocolate Almond Clusters, Kickin', 516
Cornflake and Almond Clusters, 454
Greek-Style Garlic-Spiked Potato Dip, 38
Roasted Beet Salsa, 74
Salty Almonds with Thyme, 506
Savory Almond Shooter, 116
Spanish-Style Smoked Almonds, 453
Spicy Almonds, 452
Spicy Tamari Almonds, 507
Thandai, 109
Almost-Indian Chicken Kabobs, 345

anchovies and anchovy paste
Anchovy and Caper–Spiked Cream Cheese, 372
Anchovy Crostini, 225
Anchovy-Spiked Avocado Dip, 29
Anchovy-Spiked Leek and Tomato Galettes, 172
Anchovy-Spiked Roasted Pepper and Feta Roll-Ups, 145
Anchoyade de Croze, 47
Anchoyade on Pita, 247
Artichoke and Olive Tapenade, 45
Baked Goat Cheese, 381
Cheesy Anchovy Crostini, 225
Deconstructed Caesar Salad, 155
Easy Roasted Red Pepper Dip, 16
Egg and Anchovy Crostini, 222
Green Goddess Dipping Sauce, 9
Parsley-Laced Tapenade, 46
Potted Beef, 471
Roasted Peppers with Anchovy-Spiked Olive Oil, 433
Roasted Red Pepper and White Bean Bruschetta, 238
Roasted Tomato Crostini, 226
Tuna Tapenade, 46
Warm Anchovy Dip, 29
Angel and Devil Grilled Salami with Cheddar Cheese Dip, 480
apples
Apple and Dried Cranberry Salsa, 91
Apple and Goat Cheese "Sandwiches", 275
Apple Bacon Tart, 360
Apple-Cinnamon Phyllo Purses, 519
Apple Salsa, 90
Applesauce, World's Greatest, 524
Barbecue Coleslaw, The Perfect, 550
Berry-Glazed Fig Tart, 169
Caramel and Chocolate–Coated Apples, 532
Fruit Skewers, 330
Warm Apple Sour Cream, 522

apricots
Carrot Ginger Shooter, 120
Sesame-Scented Apricots, 517
Warm Banana Salsa, 85
arepas, 186–87
artichokes
Artichoke and Olive Tapenade, 45
Artichoke and Roasted Red Pepper–Spiked Cream Cheese, 372
Chile Artichoke Dip, 486
Creamy Jalapeño-Spiked Mushroom and Artichoke Dip, 487
Easy Artichoke and Mushroom Pizza, 249
Oven-Roasted Artichokes, 363
Oyster and Artichoke Gratin, 315
Poached Artichokes, 362
Spicy Artichoke Dip, 484
Spinach and Artichoke Dip, Sumptuous, 485
Spinach and Artichoke Tartlets, 162
Stuffed Mushroom Caps, 385
Tuna and Artichoke Scoop, 63
arugula
Arugula-Ricotta Bruschetta, 233
Arugula-Spiked Goat Cheese, 374
Arugula-Spiked Tuna Bruschetta, 236
Feta-Spiked Edamame Dip, 49
Green Gazpacho, 101
Mushroom, Spinach and Feta Crostini (v), 227
Asian-Inspired Salmon Tartare, 286
Asian-Seared Beef Tenderloin, 468
asparagus
Asparagus and Cheddar–Topped Toasts, 401
Asparagus Salsa, 79
Asparagus Toasts with Hollandaise, 402
Asparagus with Hollandaise, 358
Crisp Pancetta Canapés with Roasted Corn Salsa, 481
Grilled Asparagus Spears with Lemon and Olive Oil, 403

asparagus (*continued*)
Mushroom Asparagus Pie, 359
Prosciutto-Wrapped Asparagus, 128
Salmon Asparagus Wraps, 133
Smoked Turkey and Asparagus Rolls, 132
Tonnato (v), 64
Vegetarian Vietnamese Fresh Rolls, 138
White Asparagus with Tonnato, 403
avocado
Avocado Ancho Chile Dip, 28
Anchovy-Spiked Avocado Dip, 29
Avocado Black Bean Salsa, 84
Avocado Corn Salsa, 83
Avocado Cream Cheese Dip, 27
Avocado Party Sandwiches, 270
Avocado Salsa Dip, 27
Avocado-Topped Squares, 270
Ceviche, Classic, 283
Cheesy Avocado Dip, 28
Chile-Spiked Cheese and Avocado Spread, 373
Cucumber Avocado Shooter, 105
Dill-Spiked Crab Scoop (v), 65
Guacamole, 26
Honey Mustard–Glazed Salmon with Avocado, 291
Japanese-Style Fried Chicken, 339
Mango-Spiked Salmon Ceviche, 283
Oysters on the Half Shell with Avocado Mignonette, 316
Shrimp Salsa, 96
Shrimp-Stuffed Avocado, 368
Smoked Salmon and Avocado Tartare, 285
Smoked Salmon and Avocado Tea Sandwiches, 275
Tomato Avocado Shooter, 112

B

Baba Ghanouj, 18
Baby Bok Choy and Tofu Bundles with Peanut Sauce, 157
Baby Candy Cane Beets with Fresh Mint, 427
bacon. *See also* pancetta
Apple Bacon Tart, 360
Bacon-Spiked Chopped Liver Spread with Grilled Crostini, 475

Bacon-Spiked Mushroom and Chicken Liver Pâté, 463
Bacon-Spiked Rösti Cakes, 407
Bacon-Studded Cheese and Onion Tart, 245
Bacon-Wrapped Sausage Rolls, 355
Baltimore Oysters, 314
BTs on Lettuce, 59
Bubbling Bacon and Horseradish Dip, 488
Country-Style Pork Terrine, 502
Fingerling Potato Skins, 378
Maple-Glazed Bacon and Tomato Lettuce Wraps, 156
Marinated Mushrooms, 548
Mofongo, 31
Nippy Oyster and Bacon Dip, 490
Oven-Roasted Artichokes, 363
Potato and Smoked Bacon Purée, 114
Stuffed Cremini Mushroom Caps, 437
Tomato-Stuffed Bacon Rolls, 136
Bagel Chips, 215
Balsamic-Spiked Caramelized Onions with Shaved Parmesan, 501
Baltimore Oysters, 314
bananas
Banana Lassi, 110
Fried Banana and Cheese, 332
Fried Banana Spring Rolls, 533
Fried Green Bananas, 512
Mini Chocolate Chunk Banana Sandwiches, 521
Pineapple Banana Salsa, 86
Warm Banana Salsa, 85
Barbecue Coleslaw, The Perfect, 550
Barbecue Rib Steak with Onion Sprouts and Truffle Vinaigrette, 137
Barbecue Sauce, Basic, 553
bar noshes, 452–58
Basic Crostini, 219
basil (fresh)
Apple and Goat Cheese "Sandwiches", 275
Basil and White Bean Spread, 50
Basil Pesto, 549
Butternut Galette with Basil Drizzle, 173
Eggplant, Tomato and Basil Rolls, 139

Green Olive Tapenade, 45
Mini Grilled Cheese with Havarti, Fresh Basil and Tomato, 272
Sauce Vierge, 544
beans. *See also* beans, green; edamame; peas, dried
Arugula-Spiked Tuna Bruschetta, 236
Avocado Black Bean Salsa, 84
Basil and White Bean Spread, 50
Black Bean and Feta Shooter, 113
Black Bean and Pineapple Salsa, 85
Black Bean and Salsa Dip, 504
Black Bean Nachos, 506
Black Bean Quesadillas, 441
Black Bean Spread, 57
Chicken and Black Bean Quesadillas, 476
Chive and Navy Bean Dip, 58
Cornmeal-Crusted Black Bean Cakes, 440
Kidney Bean Salsa, 77
Lemon-Laced Butterbean Dip, 48
Navy Bean Salsa, 77
Red Bean Quesadillas, 442
Refried Nachos, 50
Roasted Cubanelle Pepper and Black Bean Salsa, 80
Roasted Red Pepper and White Bean Bruschetta, 238
Roasted Tomato and Pumpkin Seed Dip, 22
Spicy Black Bean Dip, 505
White Bean Bruschetta, 237
beans, green
Clam Tomato Chowder, 126
Green Bean Salsa, 80
beef
Asian-Seared Beef Tenderloin, 468
Barbecue Rib Steak with Onion Sprouts and Truffle Vinaigrette, 137
Beef and Parmesan Sliders, 268
Beef Crostini with Wasabi Mayo, 221
Beef Knishes, 189
Beef Sushi, 154
Beef Tenderloin Salad Rolls, 134
Cocktail Meatballs, Classic, 470
Ground Beef and Chile-Laced Empanaditas, 185

Kimchi-Spiked Beef Crostini, 221
Korean-Style Beef Kabobs, 350
Lebanese Meatballs with Garlic Dipping Sauce, 469
Meatballs in Lemon Sauce, 354
Meat Samosas, 193
Panko-Crusted Beef Marrow, 461
Peanut-Crusted Beef Tenderloin Satays, 351
Potted Beef, 471
Sliced Steak with Horseradish and Roquefort Cheese, 482
Sugarcane with Marinated Beef, 352
Swedish Meatballs, Oh-So-Retro, 503
beer
  Beer-Battered Clams, 338
  Kentucky Beer Cheese, 380
  Sesame-Dusted Beer-Battered Shrimp with Roasted Pepper, 336
beets
  Baby Candy Cane Beets with Fresh Mint, 427
  Beet and Goat Cheese Shooter, 116
  Beet and Goat Cheese Spread, 21
  Beet Chips, 213
  Lemony Marinated Beets, 428
  Roasted Beet Salsa, 74
  Summer Borscht, 106
  Tahini-Spiked Beet Spread, 21
Belgian Endive with Blue Cheese, 391
Berry-Glazed Fig Tart, 169
black beans. See beans
Black Pepper Goat Cheese Dip, 20
Blended Iced Coffee Shooter, 534
Bloody Mary Salsa, 73
blueberries
  Berry-Glazed Fig Tart, 169
  Blueberry and Yogurt Dip, 67
  Blueberry Chocolate Brochettes, 516
  Quick Blueberry "Sorbet", 522
  Rhubarb and Blueberry Compote with Vanilla Ice Cream, 517
  Strawberry and Rhubarb Salsa, 91
blue cheese. See cheese, blue
bok choy
  Baby Bok Choy and Tofu Bundles with Peanut Sauce, 157

Vegetarian Vietnamese Fresh Rolls, 138
brandy
  Bacon-Spiked Mushroom and Chicken Liver Pâté, 463
  Country Terrine, 464
bread (as ingredient)
  for dipping, 35
  Garlic Bread, Classic, 210
  Garlic Bread, Not-Your-Average, 210
  Mini Peach Bread Pudding, 526
broccoli
  Broccoli Pesto Shooter, 122
  Chicken and Broccoli Crystal Fold, 150
  Broccoli Raab Bruschetta, 234
  Brown Sugar and Peach Sabayon, 527
Bruschetta, 231
bruschetta recipes, 231–38, 500
BTs on Lettuce, 59
Bubbling Bacon and Horseradish Dip, 488
Buckwheat Blinis, 198
Buffalo Chicken Wings, 346
Buffalo Chicken Wings, Classic, 473
Butter-Crusted Black Cod, 319
Butter-Crusted Oysters, 316
Buttered Radishes, 404
buttermilk
  Banana Lassi, 110
  Mango Lassi, 110
Butternut Galette with Basil Drizzle, 173
Buttery Peanuts, 508

C

cabbage
  Barbecue Coleslaw, The Perfect, 550
  Cabbage and Duck Confit Rolls, 155
  Classic Coleslaw, 419
  Crispy Vegetarian Spring Rolls, 141
  Vegetarian Cabbage Rolls, 451
Cajun-Spiced Peanuts, 507
calamari
  Fried Calamari, 311
  Marinated Calamari Antipasti, 312
  Shrimp Tempura (v), 302
  Spicy Seared Calamari, 312
Canary Island Red Pepper Mojo, 15

Candied Salmon, 286
cantaloupe. See melon
Caper Lemon Rémoulade, 539
Caper-Studded Caponata, 498
Caramel and Chocolate–Coated Apples, 532
Caramel-Glazed Sweet Potato Skewers, 328
Caramelized Onion Crostini, 223
Caramelized Onion Dip, 494
Caramelized Onions, 552
Caramelized Pineapple Satays, 330
Caramelized Red Onion Dip, 39
caraway seeds
  Caraway-Spiked Cheese Spread, 374
  Liptauer, 375
Carnitas, 343
carrots
  Carrot Ginger Shooter, 120
  Classic Coleslaw, 419
  Crispy Vegetarian Spring Rolls, 141
  Cumin-Spiked Carrots with Cilantro, 429
  Mini Falafel Sandwiches, 276
  Red Pepper Chive Shooter, 123
  Roasted Carrot and Yogurt Dip, 20
  Spicy Carrot Cooler, 107
  Vegetarian Cabbage Rolls, 451
  Vegetarian Vietnamese Fresh Rolls, 138
cashews
  Curried Cashews with Sultanas, 457
  Spicy Cashews, 508
  Thandai, 109
cauliflower
  Cauliflower and Lentil Hummus Spiked with Cumin, 53
  Cumin-Dusted Cauliflower, 429
  Vegetable Samosas, 196
caviar and roe
  Caviar-Stuffed New Potatoes, 406
  Mini Potato Galettes with Caviar and Crème Fraîche, 176
  Roasted Fingerling Potatoes with Caviar and Crème Fraîche, 320
  Smoked Salmon Mousse, 297
  Sushi Pizza, 317
  Taramasalata, 60

celery
Celery Root Avgolemono, 433
Celery Root Rémoulade, 432
Celery Spears and Whipped
Brie, 389
Dill-Spiked Crab Scoop, 65
Dill-Spiked Smoked Trout
Spread, 297
Navy Bean Salsa, 77
Shrimp Bisque, 125
Ceviche, Classic, 283
Champagne and Raspberry Dip,
68
Cheddar cheese. *See* cheese,
Cheddar
cheese. *See also* cottage cheese;
cream cheese; ricotta cheese;
specific types of cheese below
Anchovy-Spiked Leek and
Tomato Galettes, 172
Black Bean Nachos, 506
Butter-Crusted Black Cod,
319
Cheese Arepas, 186
Cheese Puffs, 392
Cheese Quesadilla, Classic,
152
Chicken and Black Bean
Quesadillas, 476
Chili con Queso, 495
Corn and Cheese Empanaditas,
183
Creamy Jalapeño-Spiked
Mushroom and Artichoke
Dip, 487
Crostini, Super Simple, 221
Easy Artichoke and Mushroom
Pizza, 249
Fingerling Potato Skins, 378
Fontina Cheese Polenta
Crostini, 228
Fried Banana and Cheese, 332
Greek-Style Fried Cheese, 387
Kentucky Beer Cheese, 380
Liptauer, 375
Marinated Mushroom Squares,
259
Mini Grilled Cheese with
Havarti, Fresh Basil and
Tomato, 272
Mini Muffulettas, 256
Potato Pizza, 248
Potato Tortilla with Peppers,
365
Quark Claqueret, 376
Refried Nachos, 50
Roasted Leek Crostini, 226
Salmon Macaroni and Cheese
Gratin, Fresh, 370

Salsa and Chicken
Empanaditas, 183
Smoky Baked Onion Dip, 40
Spinach and Artichoke Dip,
Sumptuous, 485
Spinach and Artichoke Tartlets,
162
Thyme-Spiked Cheese Sticks,
395
Tomato and Cheese Canapés,
Perfect, 390
Walnut-Dusted Cheese Balls,
372
Warm Pineapple with
Mascarpone Cheese and
Basil, 397
Warm Spinach Dip, 37
cheese, Asiago
Butternut Galette with Basil
Drizzle, 173
Easy Chorizo Pizza, 249
Mushroom Polenta Crostini,
230
Spicy Cheese and Onion–
Spiked Eggplant, 426
cheese, blue
Belgian Endive with Blue
Cheese, 391
Blue Cheese Dip, 38
Blue Cheese Fondue, 396
Blue Cheese Sauce, 346
Blue Cheese–Stuffed Dates,
391
Cheese and Peach Wontons,
392
Creamy Gorgonzola with
Walnut Polenta Crostini,
228
Creamy Roquefort Dip, 33
Sliced Steak with Horseradish
and Roquefort Cheese, 482
Walnut-Laced Gorgonzola and
Leek Roll-Ups, 147
Walnut-Spiked Blue Cheese
Bundles, 177
cheese, Brie and Camembert
Celery Spears and Whipped
Brie, 389
Chicken Sliders with Brie, 265
Deep-Fried Brie, 388
Panko-Crusted Tomato with
Camembert Cheese, 398
Pear and Brie Cheese "Rolls",
140
Pizza with Grape Jelly and Brie,
253
Plum-Stuffed Brie Cheese, 389
Smoked Brie, 388
Strawberry-Topped Brie, 390

Warm Croissant, Brie and
Caramelized Onion
Sandwiches, 271
cheese, Cheddar
Angel and Devil Grilled Salami
with Cheddar Cheese Dip,
480
Asparagus and Cheddar–
Topped Toasts, 401
Avocado Party Sandwiches, 270
Bacon-Studded Cheese and
Onion Tart, 245
Bubbling Bacon and
Horseradish Dip, 488
Cheddar Cheese Crisps, 392
Cheddar Cheese Fondue, 396
Cheddar-Onion Melt, 492
Cheese Straws, 209
Cheese Toasts with Pickled
Onions, 261
Cheesy Spinach Dip, 36
French-Style Grilled Cheese,
272
Honey-Glazed Pear and
Cheddar Cheese Stacks, 397
Hot and Smoky Bean Dip, 58
Mini Potato Croquettes, 411
Nippy Oyster and Bacon Dip,
490
Pimento Cheese, 379
Pimento-Spiked Cheesy Ham
Melt with Potato Dippers,
493
Potatoes Anna, 412
Potato Knishes, 189
Potted Cheddar, 375
Tomato Basil Polenta Gratin,
444
Zesty Cheddar Crisps, 207
cheese, feta
Anchovy-Spiked Roasted
Pepper and Feta Roll-Ups,
145
Black Bean and Feta Shooter,
113
Cheesy Avocado Dip, 28
Feta and Roasted Red Pepper
Dip, 15
Feta and Yogurt Dip, 16
Feta Cucumber Dip, 13
Feta-Spiked Edamame Dip, 49
Feta-Spiked Watermelon Salsa
with Chile, 92
Greek Salad Dip, 59
Just the Best Feta, 377
Mushroom, Spinach and Feta
Crostini, 227
Overstuffed Cucumbers with
Feta and Dill, 430

Portobello Mushroom and Feta Cheese Salsa, 81
Spiced Feta, 377
Spinach and Feta Roll-Ups, 144
Zucchini Fritters, 418
cheese, goat
Apple and Goat Cheese "Sandwiches", 275
Arugula-Spiked Goat Cheese, 374
Baked Goat Cheese, 381
Baked Marinated Goat Cheese, 382
Beet and Goat Cheese Shooter, 116
Beet and Goat Cheese Spread, 21
Black Pepper Goat Cheese Dip, 20
Chile-Spiked Cheese and Avocado Spread, 373
Goat Cheese and Caramelized Onion Vol-au-Vent, 170
Goat Cheese and Sun-Dried Tomato Crostini, 224
Goat Cheese Fritters on Endive, 384
Grilled Goat Cheese Baguette, 271
Grilled Portobello Stack with Goat Cheese and Roasted Peppers, 361
Homemade Herb Cheese, 373
Mini Goat Cheese Puffs, 394
Mushroom Tomato Spread, 44
Portobello Mushroom Skewers with Black Pepper Goat Cheese Dip, 329
Red Radish and Goat Cheese Salsa, 78
Roasted Garlic and Goat Cheese Crostini, 221
Stuffed Mushroom Caps, 385
cheese, Gruyère. See cheese, Swiss
cheese, halloumi
Greek-Style Pizza, 250
Grilled Halloumi on Pita, 264
Oregano and Cheese Bundles, 180
cheese, Jack
Baked Crab Dip, 306
Chile Cheese, 380
Chipotle Cheese Toasts, 239
Chorizo-Laced Fundido, 387
Mushroom Fundido, 386
Nachos, Ultimate, 212
Red Bean Quesadillas, 442

Roasted Pepper and Cheese Empanaditas, 184
Salsa-Spiked Cheese Crisps, 208
Salsa-Spiked Cheese Tartlets, 161
Spicy Black Bean Dip, 505
Tinga, 466
cheese, mozzarella
Cheesy Anchovy Crostini, 225
Chile Artichoke Dip, 486
Grilled Pizza with Swiss Chard and Mozzarella, 251
Margherita Pizza Pockets, 253
Marinated Mozzarella, 379
Mozzarella en Carozza, The Ultimate, 263
Prosciutto and Smoked Mozzarella Eggplant Rolls, 135
Spinach Polenta Crostini, 230
Tomato and Cheese Skewers, 327
Tomato-Mozzarella Bruschetta, 232
Tomato Mozzarella Galettes, 174
cheese, Parmesan
Balsamic-Spiked Caramelized Onions with Shaved Parmesan, 501
Basil Pesto, 549
Beef and Parmesan Sliders, 268
Corn Cakes, Fresh, 449
Crispy Zucchini Fingers, 419
Diced Potato Gratin, 414
Eggplant, Tomato and Basil Rolls, 139
Eggplant Parmesan Brochettes, 331
Fried Green Tomatoes, 445
Grilled Pizza with Braised Leeks and Tomato, 252
Meatballs in Lemon Sauce, 354
Mushroom Asparagus Pie, 359
Oven-Roasted Artichokes, 363
Oyster and Artichoke Gratin, 315
Panko-Crusted "Fish Sticks", 322
Parmesan Crackers, 206
Parmesan Crisps, 208
Parmesan Crostini, 221
Polenta Tamales, 443
Risotto Balls, 439
Salmon Nuggets, Fresh, 296
Sesame and Parmesan Pizza Sticks, 254

cheese, Swiss
Caramelized Onion Crostini, 223
Cheesy Mushroom Muffins, 435
Fondue Toasts, 238
Ham and Cheese Crostini, 222
Ham and Cheese Phyllo Bundles, 177
Ham and Cheese Toasts, 239
Hot and Creamy Crab Toasts, 241
Uptown Ham and Cheese, 262
cherries
Chicken Pinwheels with Couscous, 151
Jicama Strawberry Salsa, 95
Stewed Bing Cherries, 546
chicken. See also liver; turkey
Almost-Indian Chicken Kabobs, 345
Buffalo Chicken Wings, 346
Buffalo Chicken Wings, Classic, 473
Chicken and Black Bean Quesadillas, 476
Chicken and Broccoli Crystal Fold, 150
Chicken and Sun-Dried Tomato Croquettes, 347
Chicken Dogs and Pickled Onions, 152
Chicken Kabobs with Tahini Sauce, 341
Chicken Pinwheels with Couscous, 151
Chicken Samosas, 195
Chicken Satays, Traditional, 342
Chicken Sliders with Brie, 265
Chicken Yakitori, 340
Cilantro Chicken Kabobs, 344
Coconut-Crusted Chicken Satays, 343
Coconut-Crusted Mini Drumsticks, 472
Japanese-Style Fried Chicken, 339
Japanese-Style Stuffed Mushroom Caps, 460
Salsa and Chicken Empanaditas, 183
Smoked Chicken, 478
Smoked Chicken–Stuffed Yellow Pepper, 479
Tortilla Chip–Crusted Chicken with Avocado Ancho Chile Dip, 477

chickpeas. *See also* hummus (as ingredient)
  Chickpea Bruschetta, 236
  Easy Hummus, 52
  Hummus from Scratch, 51
  Mini Falafel Sandwiches, 276
  Oil-Poached Garlic Hummus, 56
  Roasted Red Pepper Hummus, 55
  Smoked Oyster Hummus, 52
  Vegetarian Cabbage Rolls, 451
Chile Cheese, 380
chile peppers. *See* peppers, chile
Chile-Spiked Aïoli, 536
Chile-Spiked Peanuts, 454
Chile-Spiked Shrimp Kabobs, 335
Chili con Queso, 495
Chilly Dilly Eggplant, 497
chipotle peppers. *See* peppers, chile
chips, 211–15
chives (fresh)
  Chive and Navy Bean Dip, 58
  Chive Parsley "Pistou", 550
  Egg and Olive Spread (v), 34
  Foolproof Hollandaise (v), 539
  Red Pepper Chive Shooter, 123
  Shoestring Onion Rings with Pommery Mustard Dip (v), 422
chocolate
  Almond Cranberry Chocolate "Brittle", 513
  Beet Chips (v), 213
  Blueberry Chocolate Brochettes, 516
  Caramel and Chocolate–Coated Apples, 532
  Chocolate Almond Clusters, Kickin', 516
  Chocolate and Cinnamon Dessert Pizza, 534
  Chocolate Macaroons, 524
  Chocolate Meringue Drops, 510
  Chocolate Popcorn Clusters, 511
  Chocolate Toasts, 510
  Coffee-Scented Hazelnuts, 457
  Easy-Peasy Chocolate Pudding, 528
  Five-Ingredient Molten Chocolate Cakes, 514
  Frozen Pecan and Caramel Log, 530
  Mini Chocolate Chunk Banana Sandwiches, 521
  Quick Chocolate Mousse, 515
chorizo. *See* sausage

chutneys, 93–94
cilantro
  Almost-Indian Chicken Kabobs, 345
  Black Bean and Feta Shooter, 113
  Black Bean Quesadillas, 441
  Ceviche, Classic, 283
  Cilantro Chicken Kabobs, 344
  Cilantro Lime Dip, 11
  Cilantro-Lime Dipping Sauce, 301
  Cilantro Mint Chutney, Suneeta's, 93
  Cold Pineapple Cilantro Shooter, 108
  Corn Cakes, 199
  Cumin-Spiked Carrots with Cilantro, 429
  Green Plantain Chips (v), 211
  Grilled Scallion and Corn Dip, 42
  Guacamole, 26
  Mini Falafel Sandwiches, 276
  Mojo de Cilantro, 11
  Roasted Tomato and Pumpkin Seed Dip, 22
  Salsa Verde, Fresh, 71
  Sangrita, 99
  Tomato Salsa, Fresh, 70
  Yogurt Mint Chutney, 94
Cinnamon-Spiked Pumpkin Seeds, 456
Cinnamon-Sugar Phyllo Bunches, 518
Citrus BBQ-Glazed Ribs, 468
clams
  Beer-Battered Clams, 338
  Clam Tomato Chowder, 126
  Nippy Oyster and Bacon Dip (v), 490
Cocktail Meatballs, Classic, 470
Cocktail Sauce, 547
coconut. *See also* coconut milk
  Chocolate Macaroons, 524
  Coconut-Crusted Chicken Satays, 343
  Coconut-Crusted Mini Drumsticks, 472
  Coconut-Scented Macadamia Nuts, 453
  Coconut Shrimp with Cilantro-Lime Dipping Sauce, 301
  Fried Banana and Cheese, 332
  Minced Pork and Pineapple Skewers, 349
coconut milk
  Chicken Satays, Traditional (v), 342

Thai Coconut Shooter, 124
coffee
  Blended Iced Coffee Shooter, 534
  Coffee-Scented Hazelnuts, 457
Coleslaw, Classic, 419
Coleslaw, The Perfect Barbecue, 550
coleslaw (as ingredient)
  Beef and Parmesan Sliders, 268
  Seared Tuna on Brioche, 273
corn. *See also* cornmeal; popcorn
  Asparagus Salsa, 79
  Avocado Corn Salsa, 83
  Chili con Queso, 495
  Clam Tomato Chowder, 126
  Corn and Cheese Empanaditas, 183
  Corn Arepas, 187
  Corn Cakes, 199
  Creamed Corn, The Absolute Best, 450
  Cucumber with Smoked Salmon, 290
  Fresh Corn Cakes, 449
  Grilled Scallion and Corn Dip, 42
  Kidney Bean Salsa, 77
  Marinated Corn on the Cob, 450
  Mini Potato Croquettes, 411
  Polenta Tamales, 443
  Roasted Corn Salsa, 82
  Stuffed Cremini Mushroom Caps, 437
  Sweet Corn Shooter, 117
  Vegetarian Cabbage Rolls, 451
Cornflake and Almond Clusters, 454
cornmeal
  Cornmeal-Crusted Black Bean Cakes, 440
  One-Bite Corn Dogs, 353
  Polenta Crostini, 229
  Polenta Tamales, 443
  Smoked Salmon and Grits Cakes, 294
  Tomato Basil Polenta Gratin, 444
cottage cheese
  Avocado-Topped Squares, 270
  Cucumber Cottage Cheese Dip, 12
  Garlic Bread, Not-Your-Average, 210
  Lemon Garlic Dip, 12
coulis, 543–44
Country-Style Pork Terrine, 502
Country Terrine, 464

Couscous, Chicken Pinwheels with, 151
crabmeat
Baked Crab Dip, 306
Crab and Sweet Potato Canapé, 308
Crab Cakes, Classic, 307
Crab Louis, 284
Crab Tartlets, 160
Dill-Spiked Crab Scoop, 65
Hot and Creamy Crab Toasts, 241
Hot Curried Crab, 491
Shrimp-Stuffed Avocado (v), 368
crackers, crisps and chips, 206–8, 211–15
cranberries (dried)
Almond Cranberry Chocolate "Brittle", 513
Apple and Dried Cranberry Salsa, 91
Apple Salsa, 90
Asparagus Salsa, 79
Walnut-Spiked Blue Cheese Bundles, 177
cream. See also cream cheese; crème fraîche; milk; sour cream
Bacon-Studded Cheese and Onion Tart, 245
Blended Iced Coffee Shooter, 534
Carrot Ginger Shooter, 120
Celery Spears and Whipped Brie, 389
Champagne and Raspberry Dip, 68
Cheesy Mushroom Muffins, 435
Crab Tartlets, 160
Creamy Roquefort Dip, 33
Greek Salad Dip, 59
Mango Dip, 68
Prosciutto-Spiked Spinach and Ricotta Tartlets, 163
Quick Chocolate Mousse, 515
Roasted Pepper and Cheese Empanaditas, 184
Salsa-Spiked Cheese Tartlets, 161
Samosa Pastry, 192
Smoked Salmon and Grits Cakes, 294
Smoked Salmon Mousse, 297
Strawberries and Cream, 515
Tipsy Tomato Shooter, 104
cream cheese. See also cheese
Anchovy and Caper–Spiked Cream Cheese, 372

Artichoke and Roasted Red Pepper–Spiked Cream Cheese, 372
Avocado Cream Cheese Dip, 27
Black Bean and Salsa Dip, 504
Black Bean Quesadillas, 441
BTs on Lettuce, 59
Caramelized Onion Dip, 494
Caramelized Red Onion Dip, 39
Caraway-Spiked Cheese Spread, 374
Cheese Knishes, 190
Creamy Watercress Dip, 9
Cubano, Elena Ruz, 260
Dill-Spiked Mushroom and Cheese Roll-Ups, 146
Horseradish and Dill–Spiked Cream Cheese, 372
Hot and Smoky Shrimp, 492
Hot Curried Crab, 491
Knish Pastry, 188
Martini-Marinated Salmon, 290
Peppery Roasted Squash Pâté, 438
Sizzling Shrimp and Dill Pickle Dip, 489
Smoked Salmon Crostini, 221
Smoked Salmon Spread, 296
Spicy Artichoke Dip, 484
Spinach and Water Chestnut Dip, Classic, 35
Squash-Spiked Chicken Liver Pâté, 462
Creamed Corn, The Absolute Best, 450
Creamy Green Onion Dip, 41
Creamy Jalapeño-Spiked Mushroom and Artichoke Dip, 487
Creamy Mushroom Vol-au-Vent, 171
crème fraîche. See also sour cream
Caviar-Stuffed New Potatoes, 406
Cornmeal-Crusted Black Bean Cakes, 440
Herb Cheese, Homemade, 373
Lobster Salad Mille Feuille, 321
Mini Potato Galettes with Caviar and Crème Fraîche, 176
Pommery Mustard Dip, 61
Roasted Fingerling Potatoes with Caviar and Crème Fraîche, 320

Smoked Trout Crostini, 221
Crêpes Parmentier, 200
Crisp Pancetta Canapés with Roasted Corn Salsa, 481
Crisp Pita Bread, 216
Crispy Potato Galette, 417
Crispy Prosciutto Cups with Classic Mango Salsa, 481
Crispy Vegetarian Spring Rolls, 141
Crispy Zucchini Fingers, 419
Croissant, Brie and Caramelized Onion Sandwiches, Warm, 271
croquettes, 409–11
Crostini, Basic, 219
crostini recipes, 219–30, 288, 379, 420, 461, 475, 479
polenta crostini, 228–30
crudités, 31
Crust for Empanaditas, 182
Cubano, Elena Ruz, 260
cucumber
Cucumber and Roasted Corn Salsa, 83
Cucumber Avocado Shooter, 105
Cucumber Cottage Cheese Dip, 12
Cucumber Crostini, 223
Cucumber Watermelon Salsa, 90
Cucumber with Smoked Salmon, 290
Dill Cucumber Dip, 13
Edamame Salsa, 78
Feta Cucumber Dip, 13
Grape Mignonette, 545
Greek Salad Dip, 59
Green Gazpacho, 101
Indian-Spiced Tofu with Cucumber Raita, 325
Mexican-Style Shrimp Cocktail, 367
Middle Eastern Salad Rolls, 136
Mini Falafel Sandwiches, 276
Open-Faced Shrimp and Cucumber Sandwiches, 258
Orange-Spiked Cucumbers with Mint, 430
Overstuffed Cucumbers with Feta and Dill, 430
Pepper Confetti Salsa, 84
Refrigerated Dill Pickles, 551
Roasted Red Pepper Tzatziki, 14
Shrimp Rolls, Fresh, 142
Summer Borscht, 106

cucumber (*continued*)
Tomato Gazpacho, 102
Tzatziki, 14
Vegetarian Vietnamese Fresh
Rolls, 138
Cumin-Dusted Cauliflower, 429
Cumin Mint Cooler, 98
Cumin-Spiked Carrots with
Cilantro, 429
Curried Cashews with Sultanas,
457

D

dates
Blue Cheese–Stuffed Dates,
391
Chicken Pinwheels with
Couscous, 151
Date and Tamarind Chutney, 94
Eggplant and Date Salsa, 75
Warm Prosciutto-Wrapped
Dates, 130
Deconstructed Caesar Salad, 155
Deep-Fried Brie, 388
Deviled Eggs, Classic, 447
Deviled Ham, 467
dill
Chilly Dilly Eggplant, 497
Dill Cucumber Dip, 13
Dill-Spiked Crab Scoop, 65
Dill-Spiked Mushroom and
Cheese Roll-Ups, 146
Dill-Spiked Smoked Trout
Spread, 297
Foolproof Hollandaise (v), 539
Honey Mustard Sauce, 287
Horseradish and Dill–Spiked
Cream Cheese, 372
Swedish Meatballs, Oh-So-
Retro, 503
Tahini-Spiked Beet Spread, 21
Zucchini Fritters, 418
dippers, 42, 493
dips and spreads, 7–68, 484–99,
504–5
sweet, 67–68, 522
Down-Home Hummus, 54
Dressy Fennel à la Grecque, 431
Duck Confit Canapés, 479
Duck Confit Rolls, Cabbage and,
155
Dukkah, Ian's, 555

E

edamame
Classic Edamame, 448
Edamame Salsa, 78
Edamame with Asian
Vinaigrette, 448
Feta-Spiked Edamame Dip, 49
eggplant
Baba Ghanouj, 18
Caper-Studded Caponata, 498
Chilly Dilly Eggplant, 497
Eggplant, Tomato and Basil
Rolls, 139
Eggplant and Date Salsa, 75
Eggplant Caviar, 19
Eggplant Parmesan Brochettes,
331
Greek-Style Eggplant Dip, 19
Grilled Vegetable Bruschetta,
235
Grilled Vegetable Skewers, 326
Hummus from Scratch (v), 51
Prosciutto and Smoked
Mozzarella Eggplant Rolls,
135
Seared Pickerel with Eggplant
and Peppers, 369
Slow Cooker Eggplant Caviar,
499
Smoky Eggplant Dip with
Yogurt, 17
Spicy Cheese and Onion–
Spiked Eggplant, 426
Warm Eggplant Salsa, 76
eggs
Bacon-Spiked Chopped Liver
Spread with Grilled Crostini,
475
Brown Sugar and Peach
Sabayon, 527
Chocolate Macaroons, 524
Chocolate Meringue Drops,
510
Chorizo Tortilla, 366
Cooked Egg Mayonnaise, 538
Deconstructed Caesar Salad,
155
Deviled Eggs, Classic, 447
Egg and Anchovy Crostini, 222
Egg and Olive Spread, 34
Egg and Sweet Pepper Fried
Rice, 364
Egg and Watercress Rounds, 259
Foolproof Hollandaise, 539
Genoa Salami Rolls, 132
Mini French Toast with Fresh
Peaches and Peach Maple
Syrup, 525
Mini Peach Bread Pudding, 526
Potato Tortilla with Peppers,
365
Salmorejo, 30
Spicy Tuna-Stuffed Eggs, 279
Tonnato (v), 64
Tuna and Artichoke Scoop, 63
Elena Ruz Cubano, 260
empanaditas, 182–85
endive (Belgian)
Belgian Endive with Blue
Cheese, 391
Goat Cheese Fritters on
Endive, 384
Enoki Wraps, 129

F

fennel
Dressy Fennel à la Grecque, 431
Roasted Fennel Dip, 33
feta. *See* cheese, feta
figs
Anchoyade de Croze, 47
Berry-Glazed Fig Tart, 169
Fig Yogurt Dip, 67
Strawberry-Topped Brie, 390
Warm Prosciutto-Wrapped
Dates (v), 130
Fingerling Potato Skins, 378
fish. *See also* salmon; seafood;
tuna
Beer-Battered Clams (v), 338
Butter-Crusted Black Cod, 319
Ceviche, Classic, 283
Dill-Spiked Smoked Trout
Spread, 297
Panko-Crusted "Fish Sticks",
322
Seared Pickerel with Eggplant
and Peppers, 369
Smoked Trout Crostini, 221
Five-Ingredient Molten Chocolate
Cakes, 514
flatbreads, 216–18
flatbreads (as ingredient)
Easy Artichoke and Mushroom
Pizza, 249
Easy Chorizo Pizza, 249
Greek-Style Pizza, 250
Potato Pizza (v), 248
Tomato Pizza, Not-Your-
Average, 250
Fondue Toasts, 238
Foolproof Hollandaise, 539
frankfurters. *See* sausage
French Fries, Classic, 413
French-Style Grilled Cheese, 272
French Toast with Fresh Peaches
and Peach Maple Syrup,
Mini, 525
Fresh Salsa Verde, 71
Fresh Tomato Salsa, 70
fritters, 408, 418

Frozen Dulce de Leche, 531
Frozen Mango Mousse, 523
Frozen Pecan and Caramel Log, 530
Fruit Skewers, 330

G

galettes, 172–76, 417
 pastry for, 175
garlic
 Basil Pesto, 549
 Broccoli Raab Bruschetta, 234
 Canary Island Red Pepper Mojo, 15
 Caramelized Red Onion Dip, 39
 Chile-Spiked Aïoli, 536
 Chive Parsley "Pistou", 550
 Cooked Egg Mayonnaise (v), 538
 Easy Hummus, 52
 Eggplant Caviar, 19
 Garlic Bread, Classic, 210
 Garlic Bread, Not-Your-Average, 210
 Garlic Dipping Sauce, 469
 Garlic-Infused Olive Oil, 231
 Greek-Style Garlic-Spiked Potato Dip, 38
 Green Olive Tapenade, 45
 Instant Aïoli, 536
 Mini Caramelized Onion Puff Pastry Tartlets, 167
 Mojo de Cilantro, 11
 Oil-Poached Garlic Hummus, 56
 Pancetta and Potato Bundles, 181
 Peanut Sauce, 554
 Roasted Garlic and Goat Cheese Crostini, 221
 Roasted Garlic and Mushroom Whirl, 434
 Roasted Garlic Polenta Crostini, 228
 Roasted Garlic Sour Cream Dip, 61
 Santorini-Style Fava Spread, 496
 Sautéed Garlic Scapes, 549
 Slow-Roasted Garlic, 484
 Smoked Chicken, 478
 White Bean Bruschetta (v), 237
gazpacho, 101–3
Genoa Salami Rolls, 132
gingerroot
 Agave and Ginger Scented Peanuts, 455
 Almost-Indian Chicken Kabobs, 345
 Carrot Ginger Shooter, 120

Chicken Satays, Traditional (v), 342
 Korean-Style Beef Kabobs, 350
 Peanut Sauce, 554
goat cheese. See cheese, goat
grains
 Chicken Pinwheels with Couscous, 151
 Lebanese Meatballs with Garlic Dipping Sauce, 469
grapefruit and grapefruit juice
 Applesauce, World's Greatest, 524
 Tropical Fruit Salsa, 92
grapes
 Almond Gazpacho, 103
 Concord Grape Jelly, 274
 Grape Mignonette, 545
 Sugar-Coated Concord Grapes, 528
Gravlax with Crostini and Capers, Homemade Spiced, 288
Gravlax with Honey Mustard Sauce, Vodka-Spiked, 287
Greek Salad Dip, 59
Greek-Style Eggplant Dip, 19
Greek-Style Fried Cheese, 387
Greek-Style Garlic-Spiked Potato Dip, 38
Greek-Style Pizza, 250
Green Bean Salsa, 80
Green Gazpacho, 101
Green Goddess Dipping Sauce, 9
Green Olive Tapenade, 45
Green Plantain Chips, 211
Green Tea Salt, 552
Green Tomato Salsa, 71
grits. See cornmeal
Guacamole, 26

H

ham. See also prosciutto
 Chorizo Tortilla (v), 366
 Cubano, Elena Ruz (v), 260
 Deviled Ham, 467
 Ham and Cheese Crostini, 222
 Ham and Cheese Phyllo Bundles, 177
 Ham and Cheese Toasts, 239
 Ham and Roasted Pepper Spread with Hearts of Palm, 66
 Mini Muffulettas, 256
 Pimento-Spiked Cheesy Ham Melt with Potato Dippers, 493
 Salmorejo, 30
 Uptown Ham and Cheese, 262

Hawaiian Shiitake Shooter, 119
hazelnuts
 Coffee-Scented Hazelnuts, 457
 Ian's Dukkah, 555
hearts of palm
 Ham and Roasted Pepper Spread with Hearts of Palm, 66
 Spinach and Artichoke Tartlets (v), 162
herbs. See also specific herbs
 Celery Root Rémoulade, 432
 Creamy Roquefort Dip, 33
 Feta and Yogurt Dip, 16
 Green Goddess Dipping Sauce, 9
 Grilled Herb Crostini, 220
 Herb-Spiked Ricotta Galettes, 175
 Homemade Herb Cheese, 373
 Oregano and Cheese Bundles, 180
 Quark Claqueret, 376
 Smoked Chicken, 478
Hollandaise, Foolproof, 539
Homemade Marshmallows, 529
honey
 Honey-Glazed Pear and Cheddar Cheese Stacks, 397
 Honey Mustard Dip, 60
 Honey Mustard–Glazed Salmon with Avocado, 291
 Honey Mustard Sauce, 287
 Mini Sweet Potato Muffins with Maple Syrup Glaze, 520
 Sweet-and-Sour Sauce, Basic, 547
 Thandai, 109
horseradish
 Bubbling Bacon and Horseradish Dip, 488
 Cocktail Sauce, 547
 Horseradish and Dill–Spiked Cream Cheese, 372
 Lemon Horseradish Aïoli, 537
 Smoked Trout Crostini, 221
hummus, 49, 51–57. See also chickpeas
hummus (as ingredient)
 Deviled Eggs, Classic (v), 447
 Middle Eastern Salad Rolls, 136
 Mini Falafel Sandwiches, 276

I

Ian's Dukkah, 555
Ice Cream, Rhubarb and Blueberry Compote with Vanilla, 517

Indian Chicken Kabobs, Almost-, 345
Indian-Spiced Shrimp Kabobs, 334
Indian-Spiced Sweet Potato Chips, 214
Indian-Spiced Tofu with Cucumber Raita, 325
Indian-Spiced Tomato Cooler, 98
Indian-Style Potato Fritters, 408
Indian-Style Roti, 201
Indonesian Pork Satays, 348
Instant Aïoli, 536
Instant Pâté, 471

J

jalapeños. *See* peppers, jalapeño
jams and jellies (as ingredient)
    Pizza with Grape Jelly and Brie, 253
    Raspberry Puff Pastry Fingers, 531
Japanese-Style Fried Chicken, 339
Japanese-Style Stuffed Mushroom Caps, 460
Jelly Shots, Classic Raspberry, 511
Jerusalem Artichoke Crostini, Quick Zucchini and, 420
jicama
    Jicama Salsa, 93
    Jicama Strawberry Salsa, 95
Just the Best Feta, 377

K

kabobs, 334–35, 340–41, 344–45, 350
Kale Chips, Spicy, 212
Kasha Knishes, 191
Kentucky Beer Cheese, 380
Kickin' Chocolate Almond Clusters, 516
Kidney Bean Salsa, 77
Kimchi-Spiked Beef Crostini, 221
King Oyster Mushroom and Asparagus Salsa Canapé, 438
kiwifruit
    Fruit Skewers, 330
    Tropical Fruit Salsa, 92
knishes, 188–91
Knish Pastry, 188
Korean-Style Beef Kabobs, 350

L

lamb
    Lamb and Red Onion Sliders, 269

Lebanese Meatballs with Garlic Dipping Sauce, 469
    Meat Samosas, 193
    Pecan-Crusted Lamb Chops, 474
    Spice-Rubbed Rack of Lamb, 467
Lebanese Meatballs with Garlic Dipping Sauce, 469
leeks. *See also* ramps
    Anchovy-Spiked Leek and Tomato Galettes, 172
    Braised Leeks, 548
    Butternut Galette with Basil Drizzle, 173
    Grilled Pizza with Braised Leeks and Tomato, 252
    Potato and Smoked Bacon Purée, 114
    Roasted Leek Crostini, 226
    Spinach and Water Chestnut Dip, Classic, 35
    Steamed Leek and Smoked Salmon Pinwheels, 143
    Walnut-Laced Gorgonzola and Leek Roll-Ups, 147
lemon
    Caper Lemon Rémoulade, 539
    Chile Salt, 552
    Cocktail Sauce, 547
    Easy Tahini Dip, 23
    Lemon and Soy-Scented Tuna Slices, 280
    Lemon Garlic Dip, 12
    Lemon Horseradish Aïoli, 537
    Lemon-Laced Butterbean Dip, 48
    Lemon Sauce, 354
    Lemony Marinated Beets, 428
    Preserved Lemons, 554
    Sauce Vierge, 544
    Taramasalata, 60
lettuce
    BTs on Lettuce, 59
    Cabbage and Duck Confit Rolls, 155
    Chicken and Broccoli Crystal Fold, 150
    Deconstructed Caesar Salad, 155
    Maple-Glazed Bacon and Tomato Lettuce Wraps, 156
    Middle Eastern Salad Rolls, 136
    Mini Braised Pork Tacos, 158
    Shrimp Rolls, Fresh, 142
    Smoked Salmon and Pickled Onion Lettuce Wraps, 156
    Tomato-Stuffed Bacon Rolls, 136

lime
    Ceviche, Classic, 283
    Cilantro Lime Dip, 11
    Cilantro-Lime Dipping Sauce, 301
    Hot Curried Crab, 491
    Shrimp Satays, 333
    Tropical Fruit Soup, 523
    Watermelon Cooler, 105
Liptauer, 375
liquor. *See* alcoholic beverages; beer; wine
liver
    Bacon-Spiked Chopped Liver Spread with Grilled Crostini, 475
    Bacon-Spiked Mushroom and Chicken Liver Pâté, 463
    Chopped Liver Crostini with Onion Marmalade, 221
    Instant Pâté, 471
    Squash-Spiked Chicken Liver Pâté, 462
Lobster Salad Mille Feuille, 321

M

macadamia nuts
    Coconut-Scented Macadamia Nuts, 453
    Tuna Poke, 278
Macaroni and Cheese Gratin, Fresh Salmon, 370
mango
    Crispy Prosciutto Cups with Classic Mango Salsa, 481
    Frozen Mango Mousse, 523
    Lobster Salad Mille Feuille, 321
    Mango Dip, 68
    Mango Lassi, 110
    Mango Salsa, Classic, 88
    Mango-Spiked Salmon Ceviche, 283
    Mango Water Chestnut Salsa, 88
    Margarita Mango Salsa, 89
    Minty Mango Salsa, 87
    Pineapple Mango Salsa, 87
    Shrimp Rolls, Fresh, 142
    Spicy Mango Purée, 310
    Thai-Inspired Green Mango Salsa, 89
    Tropical Fruit Salsa, 92
    Tropical Fruit Soup, 523
    Vegetarian Vietnamese Fresh Rolls, 138
maple syrup
    Baby Candy Cane Beets with Fresh Mint, 427

Candied Salmon, 286
Fig Yogurt Dip, 67
Maple-Glazed Bacon, 480
Maple-Glazed Bacon and
  Tomato Lettuce Wraps, 156
Maple Vinaigrette, 542
Mini French Toast with Fresh
  Peaches and Peach Maple
  Syrup, 525
Spicy Sweet Potato Wedges
  with Maple Glaze, 415
Sweet Sesame Snap Squares,
  455
Vodka-Spiked Gravlax with
  Honey Mustard Sauce, 287
Margarita Mango Salsa, 89
Margherita Pizza Pockets, 253
Marinated Calamari Antipasti,
  312
Marinated Corn on the Cob,
  450
Marinated Mozzarella, 379
Marinated Mushrooms, 548
Marinated Mushroom Squares,
  259
Marshmallows, Homemade, 529
Martini-Marinated Salmon, 290
Mayonnaise, Cooked Egg, 538
mayonnaise (as ingredient), 538
  Avocado Ancho Chile Dip, 28
  Beef Crostini with Wasabi
    Mayo, 221
  Blue Cheese Sauce, 346
  Caper Lemon Rémoulade, 539
  Celery Root Rémoulade, 432
  Cheddar-Onion Melt, 492
  Chile Cheese, 380
  Chile-Spiked Aïoli, 536
  Chipotle Mayo, 267
  Creamy Green Onion Dip, 41
  Deviled Eggs, Classic, 447
  Dill-Spiked Crab Scoop, 65
  Easy Tartar Sauce, 266
  Green Goddess Dipping Sauce,
    9
  Instant Aïoli, 536
  Lemon Horseradish Aïoli, 537
  Liptauer, 375
  Louis Sauce, 284
  Martini-Marinated Salmon,
    290
  Pimento Cheese, 379
  Springtime Dill Dip, 10
  Tonnato, 64
  Tuna and Roasted Red Pepper
    Dip, 62
  Wasabi Aïoli, 537
meatballs, 354, 356, 469–70, 503
Meatballs in Lemon Sauce, 354

melon
  Cold Cantaloupe Shooter, 108
  Cucumber Watermelon Salsa,
    90
  Feta-Spiked Watermelon Salsa
    with Chile, 92
  Fruit Skewers, 330
  Melon-Spiked Mexican Rice
    Milk, 100
  Prosciutto-Wrapped
    Caramelized Cantaloupe, 130
  Rum-Spiked Watermelon
    Shooter, 112
  Watermelon Cooler, 105
Mexican-Style Shrimp Cocktail,
  367
Middle Eastern Salad Rolls, 136
milk. *See also* cream
  Blue Cheese Fondue, 396
  Cheddar Cheese Fondue, 396
  Creamed Corn, The Absolute
    Best, 450
  Diced Potato Gratin, 414
  Easy-Peasy Chocolate Pudding,
    528
  Fresh Salmon Macaroni and
    Cheese Gratin, 370
  Frozen Dulce de Leche, 531
  Mini Peach Bread Pudding,
    526
  Thandai, 109
Mini Potato Croquettes, 411
Mini Potato Galettes with Caviar
  and Crème Fraîche, 176
Mini Sweet Potato Muffins with
  Maple Syrup Glaze, 520
mint (fresh)
  Cilantro Mint Chutney,
    Suneeta's, 93
  Cumin Mint Cooler, 98
  Dill Cucumber Dip (v), 13
  Minty Mango Salsa, 87
  Strawberry-Topped Brie, 390
  Yogurt Mint Chutney, 94
Mofongo, 31
Mojo de Cilantro, 11
Molten Chocolate Cakes, Five-
  Ingredient, 514
muffins, 435, 520
Muffulettas, Mini, 256
Muhummara, 24
mushrooms
  Bacon-Spiked Mushroom and
    Chicken Liver Pâté, 463
  Cheesy Mushroom Muffins,
    435
  Creamy Jalapeño-Spiked
    Mushroom and Artichoke
    Dip, 487

Creamy Mushroom Vol-au-
  Vent, 171
Crispy Vegetarian Spring Rolls,
  141
Dill-Spiked Mushroom and
  Cheese Roll-Ups, 146
Easy Artichoke and Mushroom
  Pizza, 249
Enoki Wraps, 129
Grilled Portobello Stack with
  Goat Cheese and Roasted
  Peppers, 361
Hawaiian Shiitake Shooter, 119
Japanese-Style Stuffed
  Mushroom Caps, 460
Kasha Knishes, 191
King Oyster Mushroom and
  Asparagus Salsa Canapé,
  438
Marinated Mushrooms, 548
Marinated Mushroom Squares,
  259
Mini Salmon en Croûte, 292
Mushroom, Spinach and Feta
  Crostini, 227
Mushroom Asparagus Pie, 359
Mushroom Fundido, 386
Mushroom Knishes, 190
Mushroom Phyllo Triangles
  with Grilled Scallion and
  Corn Dip, 204
Mushroom Polenta Crostini,
  230
Mushroom Shooter, 118
Mushroom Tomato Spread, 44
Paprika-Spiked Mushroom
  Bundles, 179
Portobello Mushroom and Feta
  Cheese Salsa, 81
Portobello Mushroom Skewers
  with Black Pepper Goat
  Cheese Dip, 329
Prosciutto-Stuffed Mushrooms,
  436
Roasted Garlic and Mushroom
  Whirl, 434
Stuffed Cremini Mushroom
  Caps, 437
Stuffed Mushroom Caps, 385
Warm Mushroom Salsa, 82
Mussels on the Half Shell, 319
mustard
  Cocktail Sauce, 547
  Honey Mustard Dip, 60
  Honey Mustard–Glazed
    Salmon with Avocado, 291
  Honey Mustard Sauce, 287
  Pigs in a Blanket, 148
  Pommery Mustard Dip, 61

N

Nachos, Ultimate, 212
navy beans. *See* beans
nectarines. *See also* peaches
Applesauce, World's Greatest, 524
Spicy Nectarine Salsa, 95
nori
Beef Sushi, 154
Classic Tuna Sushi, 153
Tuna Poke, 278
Not-Your-Average Garlic Bread, 210
Not-Your-Average Tomato Pizza, 250
nuts. *See specific types of nuts*

O

Oh-So-Retro Swedish Meatballs, 503
Oil-Poached Garlic Hummus, 56
Old-South Shrimp Paste, 306
olive oil
Canary Island Red Pepper Mojo, 15
Cooked Egg Mayonnaise, 538
Garlic-Infused Olive Oil, 231
Hummus from Scratch, 51
Oil-Poached Garlic Hummus, 56
Taramasalata, 60
Warm Anchovy Dip, 29
olives. *See also* olive oil
Artichoke and Olive Tapenade, 45
Egg and Olive Spread, 34
Green Olive Tapenade, 45
Ham and Cheese Toasts, 239
Marinated Calamari Antipasti, 312
Middle Eastern Salad Rolls, 136
Mini Muffulettas, 256
Mini Tomato and Olive Tapenade Puff Pastry Tartlets, 168
Olive Paste, 233
Olive-Spiked Ricotta Crostini, 224
Olive-Stuffed Roasted Red Peppers with Sherry Vinegar, 434
Parsley-Laced Tapenade, 46
Roasted Tomato Crostini, 226
Sauce Vierge, 544
Sweet Pepper and Garlic Marinated Olives, 446

Tapenade-Topped Polenta Crostini, 228
Tuna Tapenade, 46
One-Bite Corn Dogs, 353
onions. *See also* onions, green; shallots
Bacon-Studded Cheese and Onion Tart, 245
Balsamic-Spiked Caramelized Onions with Shaved Parmesan, 501
Caramelized Onion Crostini, 223
Caramelized Onion Dip, 494
Caramelized Onions, 552
Caramelized Red Onion Dip, 39
Cheddar-Onion Melt, 492
Cheese Knishes, 190
Cheese Toasts with Pickled Onions, 261
Chicken Dogs and Pickled Onions, 152
Chopped Liver Crostini with Onion Marmalade, 221
Goat Cheese and Caramelized Onion Vol-au-Vent, 170
Jalapeño-Spiked Onion Marmalade, 545
Lamb and Red Onion Sliders, 269
Mini Caramelized Onion Puff Pastry Tartlets, 167
Mofongo, 31
Panko-Crusted Onion Rings, 421
Pickled Onions, 551
Potato Knishes, 189
Roasted Onion Dip, 41
Roasted Onion Salsa, 73
Shoestring Onion Rings with Pommery Mustard Dip, 422
Smoked Salmon and Pickled Onion Lettuce Wraps, 156
Smoky Baked Onion Dip, 40
Spicy Cheese and Onion–Spiked Eggplant, 426
Sweet-and-Sour Cipollini, 425
Sweet Onion Shooter, 115
Warm Croissant, Brie and Caramelized Onion Sandwiches, 271
onions, green (scallions)
Creamy Green Onion Dip, 41
Grilled Scallion and Corn Dip, 42
Red Pepper and Onion Skewers, 327
Sautéed Scallops with Scallion-Spiked Mashed Potato, 309

Spring Scallion and Tomato Shooter, 121
orange
Cold Cantaloupe Shooter, 108
Jicama Salsa, 93
Mini Braised Pork Tacos, 158
Orange-Spiked Cucumbers with Mint, 430
Sangrita, 99
Tropical Fruit Soup, 523
oregano
Oregano and Cheese Bundles, 180
Oregano-Spiked Pork Meatballs, 356
Oven-Roasted Artichokes, 363
Oven-Roasted Cherry Tomato Sauce, 546
Overstuffed Cucumbers with Feta and Dill, 430
oysters
Baltimore Oysters, 314
Beer-Battered Clams (v), 338
Broiled Oysters with Seasoned Bread Crumbs, 313
Butter-Crusted Oysters, 316
Nippy Oyster and Bacon Dip, 490
Oyster and Artichoke Gratin, 315
Oysters on the Half Shell with Avocado Mignonette, 316
Smoked Oyster Hummus, 52

P

Pacific Salmon Cakes, 295
Pan Bagna, 257
pancetta. *See also* bacon
Country Terrine, 464
Crab Tartlets (v), 160
Crisp Pancetta Canapés with Roasted Corn Salsa, 481
Pancetta and Potato Bundles, 181
Pancetta-Spiked Ricotta Pizza, 246
Pancetta-Wrapped Scallops, 337
Prosciutto and Smoked Mozzarella Eggplant Rolls, 135
panko
Panko-Crusted Beef Marrow, 461
Panko-Crusted "Fish Sticks", 322
Panko-Crusted Onion Rings, 421

Panko-Crusted Tomatillos with Summer Tomato Salsa, 446
Panko-Crusted Tomato with Camembert Cheese, 398
Paprika-Spiked Mushroom Bundles, 179
Parmesan cheese. *See* cheese, Parmesan
parsley (fresh)
Basil and White Bean Spread, 50
Chive Parsley "Pistou", 550
Easy Tahini Dip, 23
Eggplant Caviar, 19
Enoki Wraps, 129
Lemon-Laced Butterbean Dip, 48
Parsley-Laced Tapenade, 46
Slow Cooker Eggplant Caviar, 499
White Bean Bruschetta, 237
parsnips
Beet Chips (v), 213
Sweet Onion Shooter, 115
pastry. *See also* phyllo pastry; puff pastry
for empanadas, 182
for galettes, 175
for knishes, 188
for samosas, 192
for tartlets, 164–65
peaches. *See also* nectarines
Brown Sugar and Peach Sabayon, 527
Cheese and Peach Wontons, 392
Mini French Toast with Fresh Peaches and Peach Maple Syrup, 525
Mini Peach Bread Pudding, 526
peanuts and peanut butter
Agave and Ginger Scented Peanuts, 455
Buttery Peanuts, 508
Cajun-Spiced Peanuts, 507
Chile-Spiked Peanuts, 454
Chive and Navy Bean Dip, 58
Down-Home Hummus, 54
Indonesian Pork Satays, 348
Peanut-Crusted Beef Tenderloin Satays, 351
Peanut Sauce, 554
Peppery Peanut Dip, 43
Shrimp Rolls, Fresh, 142
Thai-Inspired Green Mango Salsa, 89
Thai Peanut Dip, 43
Vegetarian Vietnamese Fresh Rolls, 138

pears
Honey-Glazed Pear and Cheddar Cheese Stacks, 397
Pear and Brie Cheese "Rolls", 140
peas, dried. *See also* beans; chickpeas; peas, green
Down-Home Hummus, 54
Hot and Smoky Bean Dip, 58
Santorini-Style Fava Spread, 496
peas, green
Avocado Salsa Dip, 27
Chicken Samosas, 195
Crab Tartlets (v), 160
Sweet Pea and Potato Croquettes, 410
Vegetable Samosas, 196
pecans
Frozen Pecan and Caramel Log, 530
Pecan-Crusted Lamb Chops, 474
Peppery Roasted Squash Pâté, 438
Zesty Cheddar Crisps, 207
pepitas. *See* pumpkin seeds
peppers, bell. *See also* peppers, roasted red
Caper-Studded Caponata, 498
Crispy Vegetarian Spring Rolls, 141
Down-Home Hummus, 54
Egg and Sweet Pepper Fried Rice, 364
Green Gazpacho, 101
Grilled Vegetable Bruschetta, 235
Grilled Vegetable Skewers, 326
Old-South Shrimp Paste, 306
Pepper Confetti Salsa, 84
Pepper-Spiked Plantain Dip, 32
Potato Tortilla with Peppers, 365
Red Pepper Chive Shooter, 123
Roasted Onion Salsa, 73
Roasted Pepper and Sweet Potato Dip, 25
Seared Pickerel with Eggplant and Peppers, 369
Smoked Chicken–Stuffed Yellow Pepper, 479
Smoky Red Pepper Coulis, 543
Spanish-Style Pizza, 244
Sweet Pepper and Garlic Marinated Olives, 446
Tomato Gazpacho, 102
Warm Salami and Red Pepper Salsa, 96

peppers, chile. *See also* peppers, jalapeño
Avocado Black Bean Salsa, 84
Avocado Corn Salsa, 83
Avocado Salsa Dip, 27
Baked Crab Dip, 306
Black Bean Nachos, 506
Black Bean Quesadillas, 441
Bloody Mary Salsa, 73
Broccoli Raab Bruschetta, 234
Butternut Galette with Basil Drizzle, 173
Canary Island Red Pepper Mojo, 15
Ceviche, Classic, 283
Cheese Arepas, 186
Chicken Samosas, 195
Chile Artichoke Dip, 486
Chile-Fried Tofu, 324
Chile Salt, 552
Chile-Spiked Cheese and Avocado Spread, 373
Chile-Spiked Tuna Tartare, 280
Chili con Queso, 495
Chipotle Cheese Toasts, 239
Chipotle Mayo, 267
Cilantro-Lime Dipping Sauce, 301
Cilantro Mint Chutney, Suneeta's, 93
Corn and Cheese Empanaditas, 183
Corn Cakes, 199
Cornmeal-Crusted Black Bean Cakes, 440
Cubano, Elena Ruz, 260
Cucumber Avocado Shooter, 105
Cumin Mint Cooler, 98
Date and Tamarind Chutney, 94
Deviled Ham, 467
Grilled Shrimp with Aïoli, 303
Ground Beef and Chile-Laced Empanaditas, 185
Guacamole, 26
Ham and Roasted Pepper Spread with Hearts of Palm, 66
Indian-Spiced Tomato Cooler, 98
Indian-Style Roti, 201
Japanese-Style Fried Chicken, 339
Mojo de Cilantro, 11
Pepper-Spiked Plantain Dip, 32
Pineapple Banana Salsa, 86
Pineapple Mango Salsa, 87

peppers, chile (*continued*)
  Potato Tortilla with Peppers, 365
  Potted Salmon, 289
  Potted Tuna, 278
  Refried Nachos, 50
  Roasted Cubanelle Pepper and Black Bean Salsa, 80
  Salsa Verde, Fresh, 71
  Shrimp Samosas, 194
  Shrimp Satays, 333
  Spiced Feta, 377
  Spicy Black Bean Dip, 505
  Spicy Cheese and Onion–Spiked Eggplant, 426
  Spinach and Water Chestnut Dip, Classic, 35
  Tinga, 466
  Tomato Pizza, Not-Your-Average, 250
  Tomato Salsa, Fresh, 70
  Vegetable Samosas, 196
  Yogurt Mint Chutney, 94
peppers, jalapeño. *See also* peppers, chile
  Creamy Jalapeño-Spiked Mushroom and Artichoke Dip, 487
  Jalapeño-Spiked Onion Marmalade, 545
  Mango-Spiked Salmon Ceviche, 283
  Mango Water Chestnut Salsa, 88
  Minty Mango Salsa, 87
  Mofongo, 31
  Mushroom Fundido, 386
  Nippy Oyster and Bacon Dip, 490
  Peppery Peanut Dip, 43
  Peppery Roasted Squash Pâté, 438
  Roasted Tomato and Pumpkin Seed Dip, 22
  Sangrita, 99
  Shrimp Salsa, 96
  Spicy Artichoke Dip, 484
  Spicy Mango Purée, 310
  Tomato Gazpacho, 102
peppers, roasted red
  Anchovy-Spiked Roasted Pepper and Feta Roll-Ups, 145
  Anchoyade de Croze, 47
  Artichoke and Roasted Red Pepper–Spiked Cream Cheese, 372
  Canary Island Red Pepper Mojo, 15

Chicken and Black Bean Quesadillas, 476
Deviled Ham, 467
Easy Chorizo Pizza, 249
Easy Roasted Red Pepper Dip, 16
Egg and Olive Spread (v), 34
Feta and Roasted Red Pepper Dip, 15
Grilled Halloumi on Pita, 264
Grilled Portobello Stack with Goat Cheese and Roasted Peppers, 361
Ham and Roasted Pepper Spread with Hearts of Palm, 66
Hot and Smoky Bean Dip, 58
Mozzarella en Carozza, The Ultimate, 263
Muhummara, 24
Nippy Oyster and Bacon Dip, 490
Olive-Stuffed Roasted Red Peppers with Sherry Vinegar, 434
Parsley-Laced Tapenade, 46
Pepper-Wrapped Chorizo, 149
Pigs in a Blanket, 148
Pimento Cheese, 379
Quick Zucchini and Jerusalem Artichoke Crostini, 420
Red Pepper and Onion Skewers, 327
Roasted Pepper and Cheese Empanaditas, 184
Roasted Peppers with Anchovy-Spiked Olive Oil, 433
Roasted Red Pepper and White Bean Bruschetta, 238
Roasted Red Pepper Coulis, 543
Roasted Red Pepper Hummus, 55
Roasted Red Pepper Salsa, 76
Roasted Red Pepper Tzatziki, 14
Roasted Red Pepper Vinaigrette, 541
Slow Cooker Eggplant Caviar, 499
Smoked Oyster Hummus, 52
Tuna and Artichoke Scoop, 63
Tuna and Roasted Red Pepper Dip, 62
Warm Eggplant Salsa, 76
Peppery Shrimp, 300
Pesto, Basil, 549
pesto (as ingredient)
  Basil and White Bean Spread, 50

Broccoli Pesto Shooter, 122
phyllo pastry
  Anchovy-Spiked Roasted Pepper and Feta Roll-Ups, 145
  Apple-Cinnamon Phyllo Purses, 519
  Cinnamon-Sugar Phyllo Bunches, 518
  Dill-Spiked Mushroom and Cheese Roll-Ups, 146
  Ham and Cheese Phyllo Bundles, 177
  Mushroom Phyllo Triangles with Grilled Scallion and Corn Dip, 204
  Oregano and Cheese Bundles, 180
  Paprika-Spiked Mushroom Bundles, 179
  Phyllo Bundles, 176
  Spinach and Feta Roll-Ups, 144
  Spinach and Pine Nut Bundles, 178
  Walnut-Laced Gorgonzola and Leek Rolls, 147
  Walnut-Spiked Blue Cheese Bundles, 177
Pickled Onions, 551
Pickles, Refrigerated Dill, 551
pickles (as ingredient)
  Caper Lemon Rémoulade, 539
  Cubano, Elena Ruz (v), 260
  Deviled Ham, 467
  Genoa Salami Rolls, 132
  Liptauer, 375
  Nachos, Ultimate, 212
  Roast Turkey Pinwheel "Logs", 273
  Sizzling Shrimp and Dill Pickle Dip, 489
Pigs in a Blanket, 148
Pimento Cheese, 379
Pimento-Spiked Cheesy Ham Melt with Potato Dippers, 493
pineapple and pineapple juice
  Agave-Glazed Pineapple, 527
  Black Bean and Pineapple Salsa, 85
  Caramelized Pineapple Satays, 330
  Chipotle Pineapple Salsa, 86
  Cold Cantaloupe Shooter, 108
  Cold Pineapple Cilantro Shooter, 108
  Minced Pork and Pineapple Skewers, 349

Pineapple Banana Salsa, 86
Pineapple Mango Salsa, 87
Tropical Fruit Salsa, 92
Tropical Fruit Soup, 523
Warm Pineapple with
  Mascarpone Cheese and
  Basil, 397
pine nuts
  Basil Pesto, 549
  Pine Nut Butter and Jelly
    Fingers, 274
  Spinach and Pine Nut Bundles,
    178
  Tuna Tartare with Toasted Pine
    Nuts, 281
pistachios
  Country Terrine, 464
  Ian's Dukkah, 555
pita breads
  Anchoyade on Pita, 247
  Crisp Pita Bread, 216
  Grilled Halloumi on Pita, 264
  Mini Falafel Sandwiches, 276
  Potato Pizza (v), 248
pizzas, 242–53
pizza dough (as ingredient)
  Bacon-Studded Cheese and
    Onion Tart, 245
  Chocolate and Cinnamon
    Dessert Pizza, 534
  Grilled Pizza with Braised
    Leeks and Tomato, 252
  Grilled Pizza with Swiss Chard
    and Mozzarella, 251
  Margherita Pizza Pockets, 253
  Pancetta-Spiked Ricotta Pizza,
    246
  Pizza with Grape Jelly and Brie,
    253
  Potato Pizza, 248
  Sesame and Parmesan Pizza
    Sticks, 254
  Spanish-Style Pizza, 244
plantains
  Green Plantain Chips, 211
  Mofongo, 31
  Pepper-Spiked Plantain Dip,
    32
Plum-Stuffed Brie Cheese, 389
polenta. See cornmeal
Pommery Mustard Dip, 61
popcorn
  Chocolate Popcorn Clusters,
    511
  Cinnamon-Scented Popcorn,
    458
  Thyme-Scented Popcorn, 458
Poppy Seed–Crusted Yellowfin
    Tuna, 282

pork
  Carnitas, 343
  Citrus BBQ-Glazed Ribs, 468
  Country-Style Pork Terrine, 502
  Country Terrine, 464
  Indonesian Pork Satays, 348
  Maple-Glazed Bacon, 480
  Minced Pork and Pineapple
    Skewers, 349
  Mini Braised Pork Tacos, 158
  Oregano-Spiked Pork
    Meatballs, 356
  Pork Rillettes, 465
  Steamed Pork Dumplings, 202
  Tinga, 466
potatoes. See also sweet potatoes
  Bacon-Spiked Rösti Cakes, 407
  Beef Knishes, 189
  Caviar-Stuffed New Potatoes,
    406
  Chicken Samosas, 195
  Chorizo Tortilla, 366
  Corn and Cheese Empanaditas,
    183
  Crêpes Parmentier, 200
  Crispy Potato Galette, 417
  Diced Potato Gratin, 414
  Easy Potato Crisps, 214
  Fingerling Potato Skins, 378
  French Fries, Classic, 413
  Greek-Style Garlic-Spiked
    Potato Dip, 38
  Ground Beef and Chile-Laced
    Empanaditas, 185
  Homemade Potato Chips, 215
  Indian-Style Potato Fritters,
    408
  Indian-Style Roti, 201
  Mini Potato Croquettes, 411
  Mini Potato Galettes with
    Caviar and Crème Fraîche,
    176
  Pancetta and Potato Bundles,
    181
  Potato and Smoked Bacon
    Purée, 114
  Potatoes Anna, 412
  Potato Knishes, 189
  Potato Pastry, 165
  Potato Pizza, 248
  Potato Tortilla with Peppers,
    365
  Roasted Fingerling Potatoes
    with Caviar and Crème
    Fraîche, 320
  Roasted Fingerling Wraps, 128
  Roasted Potato Dip, 37
  Roasted Potato Wedges, 404
  Salt-Roasted Potatoes, 405

Sautéed Scallops with Scallion-
    Spiked Mashed Potato, 309
  Shrimp Samosas, 194
  Stewed Potatoes with Truffle,
    405
  Sweet Pea and Potato
    Croquettes, 410
  Truffle-Spiked Potato
    Croquettes, 409
  Vegetable Samosas, 196
Potted Beef, 471
Potted Cheddar, 375
Potted Salmon, 289
Potted Shrimp, 304
Potted Tuna, 278
Preserved Lemons, 554
prosciutto. See also ham
  Cheese Toasts with Pickled
    Onions (v), 261
  Crispy Prosciutto Cups with
    Classic Mango Salsa, 481
  Enoki Wraps, 129
  Nachos, Ultimate, 212
  Prosciutto and Smoked
    Mozzarella Eggplant Rolls,
    135
  Prosciutto-Spiked Spinach and
    Ricotta Tartlets, 163
  Prosciutto-Stuffed Mushrooms,
    436
  Prosciutto-Wrapped Asparagus,
    128
  Prosciutto-Wrapped
    Caramelized Cantaloupe,
    130
  Roasted Fingerling Wraps, 128
  Salmorejo, 30
  Salumi, 131
  Warm Prosciutto-Wrapped
    Dates, 130
puff pastry
  Anchovy-Spiked Leek and
    Tomato Galettes, 172
  Apple Bacon Tart, 360
  Berry-Glazed Fig Tart, 169
  Butternut Galette with Basil
    Drizzle, 173
  Chicken Dogs and Pickled
    Onions, 152
  Creamy Mushroom Vol-au-
    Vent, 171
  Goat Cheese and Caramelized
    Onion Vol-au-Vent, 170
  Herb-Spiked Ricotta Galettes,
    175
  Lobster Salad Mille Feuille,
    321
  Mini Caramelized Onion Puff
    Pastry Tartlets, 167

puff pastry (*continued*)
Mini Salmon en Croûte, 292
Mini Smoked Salmon and Sour
Cream Puff Pastry Tartlets,
166
Mini Tomato and Olive
Tapenade Puff Pastry
Tartlets, 168
Pigs in a Blanket, 148
Puff Pastry Tomato Tart, 358
Raspberry Puff Pastry Fingers,
531
Salsa-Spiked Cheese Crisps,
208
Tomato Mozzarella Galettes, 174
Uptown Ham and Cheese, 262
pumpkin seeds (pepitas)
Cinnamon-Spiked Pumpkin
Seeds, 456
Roasted Tomato and Pumpkin
Seed Dip, 22

Q

Quark Claqueret, 376
quesadillas, 152, 441–42, 476
Quick Blueberry "Sorbet", 522
Quick Chocolate Mousse, 515
Quick Zucchini and Jerusalem
Artichoke Crostini, 420
Quince-Topped Cheese Crostini,
221

R

radishes
Buttered Radishes, 404
Red Radish and Goat Cheese
Salsa, 78
ramps
Creamy Green Onion Dip (v), 41
Spring Scallion and Tomato
Shooter, 121
raspberries
Champagne and Raspberry
Dip, 68
Classic Raspberry Jelly Shots,
511
Red Wine Vinaigrette, 540
Refried Nachos, 50
Refrigerated Dill Pickles, 551
rhubarb
Rhubarb and Blueberry
Compote with Vanilla Ice
Cream, 517
Strawberry and Rhubarb Salsa,
91
Strawberry Rhubarb Shooter,
111

rice
Beef Sushi, 154
Egg and Sweet Pepper Fried
Rice, 364
Melon-Spiked Mexican Rice
Milk, 100
Risotto Balls, 439
Salmon Nigiri Sushi, Classic,
293
Sushi Pizza, 317
Sushi Rice–Stuffed Shrimp,
305
Tuna Sushi, Classic, 153
rice paper wrappers
Crispy Vegetarian Spring Rolls,
141
Fried Banana Spring Rolls, 533
Shrimp Rolls, Fresh, 142
Vegetarian Vietnamese Fresh
Rolls, 138
ricotta cheese
Arugula-Ricotta Bruschetta,
233
Baked Ricotta, 383
Herb-Spiked Ricotta Galettes,
175
Olive-Spiked Ricotta Crostini,
224
Pancetta-Spiked Ricotta Pizza,
246
Prosciutto-Spiked Spinach and
Ricotta Tartlets, 163
Roasted Tomato Crostini, 226
Tomato–Ricotta Salata
Bruschetta, 232
Risotto Balls, 439
Roasted Pepper and Salt, 552
roe. *See* caviar and roe
Rum-Spiked Watermelon Shooter,
112

S

sage (fresh)
Bacon-Wrapped Sausage Rolls,
355
Meatballs in Lemon Sauce,
354
White Bean Bruschetta (v), 237
salami. *See* sausage
salmon. *See also* salmon, smoked
Asian-Inspired Salmon Tartare,
286
Candied Salmon, 286
Classic Salmon Nigiri Sushi,
293
Classic Salmon Tartare, 285
Fresh Salmon Macaroni and
Cheese Gratin, 370

Fresh Salmon Nuggets, 296
Homemade Spiced Gravlax
with Crostini and Capers,
288
Honey Mustard–Glazed
Salmon with Avocado, 291
Mango-Spiked Salmon
Ceviche, 283
Mini Salmon en Croûte, 292
Pacific Salmon Cakes, 295
Potted Salmon, 289
Salmon Sliders, 266
Vodka-Spiked Gravlax with
Honey Mustard Sauce, 287
salmon, smoked. *See also* salmon
Cucumber with Smoked
Salmon, 290
Martini-Marinated Salmon, 290
Mini Smoked Salmon and Sour
Cream Puff Pastry Tartlets,
166
Salmon Asparagus Wraps, 133
Smoked Salmon and Avocado
Tartare, 285
Smoked Salmon and Avocado
Tea Sandwiches, 275
Smoked Salmon and Grits
Cakes, 294
Smoked Salmon and Pickled
Onion Lettuce Wraps, 156
Smoked Salmon Crostini, 221
Smoked Salmon Mousse, 297
Smoked Salmon Sour Cream
Spread, 62
Smoked Salmon Spread, 296
Steamed Leek and Smoked
Salmon Pinwheels, 143
Salmorejo, 30
salsa recipes, 70–93, 95–96
salsa (as ingredient)
Avocado Salsa Dip, 27
Baked Goat Cheese (v), 381
Black Bean and Salsa Dip, 504
Black Bean Nachos, 506
King Oyster Mushroom and
Asparagus Salsa Canapé, 438
Refried Nachos, 50
Salsa and Chicken
Empanaditas, 183
Salsa-Spiked Cheese Crisps,
208
Salsa-Spiked Cheese Tartlets,
161
salt
Roasted Pepper and Salt, 552
Salt-Roasted Potatoes, 405
Salty Almonds with Thyme,
506
Seasoned Salts, 552

Salumi, 131
Samosa Pastry, 192
samosa recipes, 192–96
Sangrita, 99
Santorini-Style Fava Spread, 496
satays, 330, 333, 340, 342–43,
    348, 351
sauces, 266, 284, 544, 546–47,
    553–54. *See also* dips and
    spreads
Sauce Vierge, 544
sausage
    Angel and Devil Grilled Salami
        with Cheddar Cheese Dip,
        480
    Bacon-Wrapped Sausage Rolls,
        355
    Chicken Dogs and Pickled
        Onions, 152
    Chorizo-Laced Fundido, 387
    Chorizo Tortilla, 366
    Easy Chorizo Pizza, 249
    Genoa Salami Rolls, 132
    Mini Muffulettas, 256
    One-Bite Corn Dogs, 353
    Pancetta-Spiked Ricotta Pizza,
        246
    Pepper-Wrapped Chorizo, 149
    Pigs in a Blanket, 148
    Potato Tortilla with Peppers (v),
        365
    Prosciutto and Smoked
        Mozzarella Eggplant Rolls,
        135
    Salumi, 131
    Tinga, 466
    Warm Salami and Red Pepper
        Salsa, 96
    White Bean Bruschetta (v), 237
scallions. *See* onions, green
seafood. *See also* crabmeat; fish;
    oysters; shrimp
    Beer-Battered Clams, 338
    Clam Tomato Chowder, 126
    Fried Calamari, 311
    Lobster Salad Mille Feuille,
        321
    Marinated Calamari Antipasti,
        312
    Mussels on the Half Shell, 319
    Pancetta-Wrapped Scallops,
        337
    Pan-Seared Scallops with Spicy
        Mango Purée, 310
    Sautéed Scallops with Scallion-
        Spiked Mashed Potato, 309
    Sliced Scallop "Ceviche", 284
    Spicy Seared Calamari, 312
    Sweet Scallop Appetizer, 318

Seasoned Salts, 552
seaweed. *See* nori
sesame seeds. *See also* tahini
    Ian's Dukkah, 555
    Sesame and Parmesan Pizza
        Sticks, 254
    Sesame-Dusted Beer-Battered
        Shrimp with Roasted Pepper,
        336
    Sesame-Scented Apricots, 517
    Sweet Sesame Snap Squares,
        455
shallots
    Edamame with Asian
        Vinaigrette, 448
    Poppy Seed–Crusted Yellowfin
        Tuna, 282
    Roasted Onion Dip (v), 41
    Santorini-Style Fava Spread, 496
    Summer Tomato Salsa, 70
Shoestring Onion Rings with
    Pommery Mustard Dip, 422
shooters, 97–126, 534
shrimp, 299
    Chile-Spiked Shrimp Kabobs,
        335
    Coconut Shrimp with Cilantro-
        Lime Dipping Sauce, 301
    Fresh Shrimp Rolls, 142
    Grilled Shrimp with Aïoli, 303
    Hot and Smoky Shrimp, 492
    Hot Curried Shrimp Toasts,
        240
    Indian-Spiced Shrimp Kabobs,
        334
    Mexican-Style Shrimp
        Cocktail, 367
    Old-South Shrimp Paste, 306
    Open-Faced Shrimp and
        Cucumber Sandwiches, 258
    Pancetta-Wrapped Scallops (v),
        337
    Peppery Shrimp, 300
    Potted Shrimp, 304
    Savory Fried Shrimp Wontons,
        203
    Sesame-Dusted Beer-Battered
        Shrimp with Roasted Pepper,
        336
    Shrimp Bisque, 125
    Shrimp in Piri-Piri Butter, 298
    Shrimp Salsa, 96
    Shrimp Samosas, 194
    Shrimp Satays, 333
    Shrimp-Stuffed Avocado, 368
    Shrimp Tempura, 302
    Shrimp Toasts, 240
    Sizzling Shrimp and Dill Pickle
        Dip, 489

Spicy Sizzling Shrimp, 299
Steamed Pork Dumplings (v),
    202
Sushi Rice–Stuffed Shrimp,
    305
Twisted Butterfly Shrimp, 304
sliders, 265–69
Smoked Brie, 388
Smoked Chicken, 478
Smoked Chicken–Stuffed Yellow
    Pepper, 479
Smoked Oyster Hummus, 52
smoked salmon. *See* salmon,
    smoked
Smoked Trout Crostini, 221
Smoked Trout Spread, Dill-
    Spiked, 297
Smoked Turkey and Asparagus
    Rolls, 132
Smoky Baked Onion Dip, 40
Smoky Eggplant Dip with Yogurt,
    17
Smoky Red Pepper Coulis, 543
Socca de Nice, 197
sour cream. *See also* crème
    fraîche; yogurt
    Beet and Goat Cheese Spread,
        21
    Caramelized Onion Dip, 494
    Caramelized Red Onion Dip, 39
    Caraway-Spiked Cheese
        Spread, 374
    Dill Cucumber Dip, 13
    Lemon Garlic Dip, 12
    Mini Smoked Salmon and Sour
        Cream Puff Pastry Tartlets,
        166
    Paprika-Spiked Mushroom
        Bundles, 179
    Roasted Fennel Dip, 33
    Roasted Garlic Sour Cream
        Dip, 61
    Roasted Potato Dip, 37
    Roasted Zucchini Dip, 44
    Smoked Salmon Sour Cream
        Spread, 62
    Smoked Salmon Spread, 296
    Swedish Meatballs, Oh-So-
        Retro, 503
    Sweet Potato Cakes, 416
    Warm Apple Sour Cream, 522
    Warm Spinach Dip, 37
soy sauce
    Chicken Satays, Traditional,
        342
    Chicken Yakitori, 340
    Cilantro Chicken Kabobs, 344
    Lemon and Soy-Scented Tuna
        Slices, 280

soy sauce (*continued*)
Ponzo-Style Dipping Sauce, 338
Spicy Soy-Marinated Tuna, 281
Sweet-and-Sour Sauce, Basic, 547
Thai Peanut Dip, 43
Vegetable Tempura (v), 423
Spanish-Style Pizza, 244
Spanish-Style Smoked Almonds, 453
Spiced Feta, 377
Spice-Rubbed Rack of Lamb, 467
Spicy Almonds, 452
Spicy Artichoke Dip, 484
Spicy Black Bean Dip, 505
Spicy Carrot Cooler, 107
Spicy Cashews, 508
Spicy Cheese and Onion–Spiked Eggplant, 426
Spicy Kale Chips, 212
Spicy Nectarine Salsa, 95
Spicy Seared Calamari, 312
Spicy Sizzling Shrimp, 299
Spicy Soy-Marinated Tuna, 281
Spicy Sweet Potato Wedges with Maple Glaze, 415
Spicy Tamari Almonds, 507
Spicy Tuna-Stuffed Eggs, 279
spinach
Cheesy Spinach Dip, 36
Mushroom, Spinach and Feta Crostini, 227
Prosciutto-Spiked Spinach and Ricotta Tartlets, 163
Spinach and Artichoke Dip, Sumptuous, 485
Spinach and Artichoke Tartlets, 162
Spinach and Feta Roll-Ups, 144
Spinach and Pine Nut Bundles, 178
Spinach and Water Chestnut Dip, Classic, 35
Spinach Polenta Crostini, 230
Spinach Tofu Dip, 10
Tomato and Spinach Salsa, 72
Warm Spinach Dip, 37
Spring Scallion and Tomato Shooter, 121
Springtime Dill Dip, 10
squash
Acorn Squash Sage Shooter, 119
Butternut Galette with Basil Drizzle, 173
Peppery Roasted Squash Pâté, 438
Squash-Spiked Chicken Liver Pâté, 462

strawberries
Jicama Strawberry Salsa, 95
Strawberries and Cream, 515
Strawberry and Rhubarb Salsa, 91
Strawberry Rhubarb Shooter, 111
Strawberry-Topped Brie, 390
Sugarcane with Marinated Beef, 352
Sugar-Coated Concord Grapes, 528
Sultanas, Curried Cashews with, 457
Summer Borscht, 106
Summer Tomato Salsa, 70
Suneeta's Cilantro Mint Chutney, 93
Super Simple Crostini, 221
Super Simple Polenta Crostini, 228
sushi, 153–54, 293
Sushi Pizza, 317
Sushi Rice–Stuffed Shrimp, 305
Sweet-and-Sour Cipollini, 425
Sweet-and-Sour Sauce, Basic, 547
sweet potatoes
Caramel-Glazed Sweet Potato Skewers, 328
Clam Tomato Chowder, 126
Crab and Sweet Potato Canapé, 308
Indian-Spiced Sweet Potato Chips, 214
Mini Sweet Potato Muffins with Maple Syrup Glaze, 520
Roasted Pepper and Sweet Potato Dip, 25
Spicy Sweet Potato Wedges with Maple Glaze, 415
Sweet Potato Cakes, 416
Sweet Potato Galette, 417
Sweet Potato Spread, 26
Sweet Scallop Appetizer, 318
Sweet Sesame Snap Squares, 455
Sweet Wontons, 526
Swiss Chard and Mozzarella, Grilled Pizza with, 251

T

tahini
Baba Ghanouj, 18
Cauliflower and Lentil Hummus Spiked with Cumin, 53
Chicken Kabobs with Tahini Sauce, 341

Easy Tahini Dip, 23
Hummus from Scratch, 51
Tahini-Spiked Beet Spread, 21
Walnut Hummus, 57
Zucchini Hummus, 49
tamarind
Cumin Mint Cooler, 98
Date and Tamarind Chutney, 94
tapenades, 45–46
Taramasalata, 60
Tartar Sauce, Easy, 266
Tartlet Pastry, 164
tartlet recipes, 160–69, 359
Thai Coconut Shooter, 124
Thai-Inspired Green Mango Salsa, 89
Thai Peanut Dip, 43
Thandai, 109
thyme (fresh)
Butter-Crusted Black Cod, 319
Butter-Crusted Oysters, 316
Cinnamon-Sugar Phyllo Bunches (v), 518
Salty Almonds with Thyme, 506
Smoked Brie, 388
Thyme-Scented Popcorn, 458
Thyme-Spiked Cheese Sticks, 395
Tinga, 466
Tipsy Tomato Shooter, 104
toasts, 238–41, 261, 401–2, 510
tofu
Baby Bok Choy and Tofu Bundles with Peanut Sauce, 157
Chile-Fried Tofu, 324
Indian-Spiced Tofu with Cucumber Raita, 325
Spinach Tofu Dip, 10
tomatillos, 71
Fresh Salsa Verde, 71
Panko-Crusted Tomatillos with Summer Tomato Salsa, 446
Tomatillo Vinaigrette, 540
tomatoes. *See also* tomatoes, cherry/grape; tomatoes, sun-dried; tomato sauces
Avocado Black Bean Salsa, 84
Barbecue Sauce, Basic, 553
Black Bean and Feta Shooter, 113
Bloody Mary Salsa, 73
Braised Tomato Bruschetta, 500
BTs on Lettuce, 59
Ceviche, Classic, 283
Chili con Queso, 495
Clam Tomato Chowder, 126

Eggplant, Tomato and Basil Rolls, 139
French-Style Grilled Cheese, 272
Fresh Tomato Salsa, 70
Fried Green Tomatoes, 445
Greek Salad Dip, 59
Green Gazpacho, 101
Green Tomato Salsa, 71
Grilled Pizza with Braised Leeks and Tomato, 252
Ground Beef and Chile-Laced Empanaditas, 185
Indian-Spiced Tomato Cooler, 98
Maple-Glazed Bacon and Tomato Lettuce Wraps, 156
Middle Eastern Salad Rolls, 136
Mini Tomato and Olive Tapenade Puff Pastry Tartlets, 168
Oregano-Spiked Pork Meatballs, 356
Panko-Crusted Tomato with Camembert Cheese, 398
Pepper Confetti Salsa, 84
Puff Pastry Tomato Tart, 358
Roasted Corn Salsa, 82
Roasted Tomato and Pumpkin Seed Dip, 22
Roasted Tomato Crostini, 226
Roasted Tomato Dip, 23
Salmorejo, 30
Sangrita, 99
Shrimp Bisque, 125
Shrimp Salsa, 96
Spiced Feta, 377
Spring Scallion and Tomato Shooter, 121
Summer Tomato Salsa, 70
Thai Coconut Shooter, 124
Tinga, 466
Tipsy Tomato Shooter, 104
Tomato and Spinach Salsa, 72
Tomato Avocado Shooter, 112
Tomato Balsamic "Jam", 72
Tomato Basil Polenta Gratin, 444
Tomato Gazpacho, 102
Tomato-Mozzarella Bruschetta, 232
Tomato–Ricotta Salata Bruschetta, 232
Two-Tomato Coulis, 544
tomatoes, cherry/grape
Anchovy-Spiked Leek and Tomato Galettes, 172
Anchoyade on Pita, 247

Asparagus Salsa, 79
Baked Goat Cheese, 381
Cheesy Avocado Dip, 28
Dill-Spiked Smoked Trout Spread (v), 297
Eggplant Caviar, 19
Greek-Style Eggplant Dip, 19
Indian-Spiced Shrimp Kabobs, 334
Marinated Calamari Antipasti, 312
Mini Grilled Cheese with Havarti, Fresh Basil and Tomato, 272
Oven-Roasted Cherry Tomato Sauce, 546
Quick Zucchini and Jerusalem Artichoke Crostini, 420
Roasted Cherry Tomato Vinaigrette, 541
Sauce Vierge, 544
Spanish-Style Pizza, 244
Tomato and Cheese Canapés, Perfect, 390
Tomato and Cheese Skewers, 327
Tomato Mozzarella Galettes, 174
Tomato Pizza, Not-Your-Average, 250
Tomato-Stuffed Bacon Rolls, 136
tomatoes, sun-dried
Chicken and Sun-Dried Tomato Croquettes, 347
Goat Cheese and Sun-Dried Tomato Crostini, 224
Mushroom Tomato Spread, 44
Prosciutto and Smoked Mozzarella Eggplant Rolls (v), 135
Roasted Red Pepper Coulis, 543
Santorini-Style Fava Spread, 496
Slow Cooker Eggplant Caviar, 499
Smoked Chicken–Stuffed Yellow Pepper, 479
Stuffed Mushroom Caps, 385
White Bean Bruschetta (v), 237
tomato sauces (as ingredient). See also salsa
Cocktail Meatballs, Classic, 470
Cocktail Sauce, 547
Eggplant Parmesan Brochettes, 331
Louis Sauce, 284
Margherita Pizza Pockets, 253

Uptown Ham and Cheese, 262
Tonnato, 64
Tortilla Chip–Crusted Chicken with Avocado Ancho Chile Dip, 477
tortillas
Black Bean Quesadillas, 441
Cheese Quesadilla, Classic, 152
Chicken and Black Bean Quesadillas, 476
Mini Braised Pork Tacos, 158
Red Bean Quesadillas, 442
Tropical Fruit Salsa, 92
Tropical Fruit Soup, 523
Truffle-Spiked Potato Croquettes, 409
Truffle Vinaigrette, 542
tuna
Arugula-Spiked Tuna Bruschetta, 236
Chile-Spiked Tuna Tartare, 280
Lemon and Soy-Scented Tuna Slices, 280
Pan Bagna, 257
Poppy Seed–Crusted Yellowfin Tuna, 282
Potted Tuna, 278
Seared Tuna on Brioche, 273
Spicy Soy-Marinated Tuna, 281
Spicy Tuna-Stuffed Eggs, 279
Tonnato, 64
Tuna and Artichoke Scoop, 63
Tuna and Roasted Red Pepper Dip, 62
Tuna Poke, 278
Tuna Sushi, Classic, 153
Tuna Tapenade, 46
Tuna Tartare with Toasted Pine Nuts, 281
White Asparagus with Tonnato, 403
turkey. See also chicken
Cubano, Elena Ruz, 260
Oven-Roasted Artichokes, 363
Roast Turkey Pinwheel "Logs", 273
Smoked Turkey and Asparagus Rolls, 132
Turkey Sliders with Chipotle Mayo, 267
Twisted Butterfly Shrimp, 304
Two-Tomato Coulis, 544
Tzatziki, 14

U

The Ultimate Mozzarella en Carozza, 263

Ultimate Nachos, 212
Uptown Ham and Cheese, 262

V

veal
    Country-Style Pork Terrine,
        502
    Country Terrine, 464
vegetables. *See also specific*
        vegetables
    Broccoli Raab Bruschetta, 234
    Crudités for Dipping, 31
    Grilled Vegetable Bruschetta,
        235
    Grilled Vegetable Skewers, 326
    Kimchi-Spiked Beef Crostini,
        221
    Navy Bean Salsa, 77
    Vegetable Samosas, 196
    Vegetable Tempura, 423
    Warm Mushroom Salsa, 82
Vegetarian Cabbage Rolls, 451
Vegetarian Vietnamese Fresh
        Rolls, 138
vinaigrettes, 540–42
vodka
    Martini-Marinated Salmon,
        290
    Vodka-Spiked Gravlax with
        Honey Mustard Sauce, 287
vol-au-vents, 170–71

W

walnuts
    Creamy Gorgonzola with
        Walnut Polenta Crostini, 228
    Muhummara, 24
    Walnut-Dusted Cheese Balls,
        372
    Walnut Hummus, 57
    Walnut-Laced Gorgonzola and
        Leek Roll-Ups, 147
    Walnut-Spiked Blue Cheese
        Bundles, 177
    White Bean Bruschetta (v), 237
    Zesty Cheddar Crisps, 207
Warm Anchovy Dip, 29
Warm Apple Sour Cream, 522
Warm Banana Salsa, 85
Warm Croissant, Brie and
        Caramelized Onion
        Sandwiches, 271
Warm Eggplant Salsa, 76
Warm Mushroom Salsa, 82

Warm Pineapple with
        Mascarpone Cheese and
        Basil, 397
Warm Prosciutto-Wrapped Dates,
        130
Warm Salami and Red Pepper
        Salsa, 96
Warm Spinach Dip, 37
Wasabi Aïoli, 537
water chestnuts
    Mango Water Chestnut Salsa, 88
    Spinach and Water Chestnut
        Dip, Classic, 35
watercress
    Creamy Watercress Dip, 9
    Egg and Watercress Rounds,
        259
watermelon
    Cucumber Watermelon Salsa, 90
    Feta-Spiked Watermelon Salsa
        with Chile, 92
    Fruit Skewers, 330
    Rum-Spiked Watermelon
        Shooter, 112
    Watermelon Cooler, 105
wieners. *See* sausage
wine
    Brown Sugar and Peach
        Sabayon, 527
    Butter-Crusted Black Cod, 319
    Champagne and Raspberry
        Dip, 68
    Dressy Fennel à la Grecque, 431
    Fondue Toasts, 238
    Lemon Sauce, 354
    Oregano-Spiked Pork
        Meatballs, 356
    Pepper-Wrapped Chorizo, 149
    Polenta Tamales, 443
    Pork Rillettes, 465
    Potted Salmon, 289
    Red Pepper Chive Shooter, 123
    Risotto Balls, 439
    Shrimp Bisque, 125
    Stewed Potatoes with Truffle,
        405
    Strawberry and Rhubarb Salsa,
        91
    Sweet Onion Shooter, 115
    Watermelon Cooler (v), 105
wonton wrappers
    Cheese and Peach Wontons,
        392
    Savory Fried Shrimp Wontons,
        203
    Steamed Pork Dumplings, 202

Sweet Wontons, 526
World's Greatest Applesauce, 524
wraps and rolls, 128–58

Y

yogurt. *See also* sour cream
    Almost-Indian Chicken
        Kabobs, 345
    Baba Ghanouj, 18
    Banana Lassi, 110
    Blueberry and Yogurt Dip, 67
    Chicken Kabobs with Tahini
        Sauce, 341
    Cilantro Lime Dip, 11
    Cucumber Avocado Shooter,
        105
    Feta and Yogurt Dip, 16
    Feta Cucumber Dip, 13
    Fig Yogurt Dip, 67
    Garlic Dipping Sauce, 469
    Green Goddess Dipping Sauce,
        9
    Indian-Spiced Tofu with
        Cucumber Raita, 325
    Mango Lassi, 110
    Roasted Carrot and Yogurt Dip,
        20
    Roasted Garlic Sour Cream
        Dip, 61
    Roasted Red Pepper Tzatziki,
        14
    Smoky Eggplant Dip with
        Yogurt, 17
    Spicy Carrot Cooler, 107
    Springtime Dill Dip, 10
    Summer Borscht, 106
    Tahini-Spiked Beet Spread, 21
    Tzatziki, 14
    Yogurt Flatbread, 217
    Yogurt Mint Chutney, 94

Z

Zesty Cheddar Crisps, 207
zucchini
    Crispy Zucchini Fingers, 419
    Grilled Vegetable Bruschetta,
        235
    Grilled Vegetable Skewers, 326
    Quick Zucchini and Jerusalem
        Artichoke Crostini, 420
    Roasted Zucchini Dip, 44
    Zucchini Fritters, 418
    Zucchini Hummus, 49
Zucchini Flowers, Fried, 424